The Dinosaur Filmography

THE DINOSAUR FILMOGRAPHY

Mark F. Berry

FOREWORD BY DONALD LESSEM

McFarland & Company, Inc., Publishers
Jefferson, North Carolina, and London

The present work is a reprint of the illustrated case bound edition of The Dinosaur Filmography, *first published in 2002 by McFarland.*

LIBRARY OF CONGRESS CATALOGUING-IN-PUBLICATION DATA

Berry, Mark F.
The dinosaur filmography /
Mark F. Berry ; foreword by Donald Lessem.
p.   cm.
Includes bibliographical references and index.

ISBN-13: 978-0-7864-2453-5
softcover : 50# alkaline paper ∞

1. Dinosaurs in motion pictures.
2. Motion pictures—Catalogs.   I. Title.
PN1995.9.D53B47   2005   791.43'662—dc21   2002007623

British Library cataloguing data are available

©2002 Mark F. Berry. All rights reserved

No part of this book may be reproduced or transmitted in any form or by any means, electronic or mechanical, including photocopying or recording, or by any information storage and retrieval system, without permission in writing from the publisher.

Front cover: Poster art for the British theatrical release
of the 1977 film *The Last Dinosaur*

Manufactured in the United States of America

McFarland & Company, Inc., Publishers
Box 611, Jefferson, North Carolina 28640
www.mcfarlandpub.com

To my family

ACKNOWLEDGMENTS

This volume would most certainly never have been possible without the gracious and amiable assistance of many people. I offer my utmost thanks:

To Donald "Dino Don" Lessem, for gracing my work with a wonderful foreword.

To Jim Aupperle, John Carl Buechler, Wah Ming Chang, Stephen Czerkas, Jim Danforth, Roger Dicken, Chris Endicott, Ernest D. Farino, Jeff Farley, Ray Harryhausen, Ralph Helfer, Peter Kleinow, Arnold Leibovit, Hal Miles, Alvin Rakoff, Phil Tippett, and Stan Winston for taking the time, through telephone interviews and written correspondence, to tell me of their dinosaur-making adventures.

Again to Jim Aupperle, Wah Ming Chang, Stephen Czerkas, Roger Dicken, Ernest D. Farino, Hal Miles, and Phil Tippett for contributing photographs and memorabilia which exponentially improved the quality of this volume's illustrations.

To Tim Cole for contributing rare production stills from *King Kong* and *The Son of Kong*.

To John Ballentine for providing screening prints of *The Lost Whirl* and *The Ghost of Slumber Mountain*, and kindly sharing material from his unmatched collection of Ray Harryhausen literature.

To Jim Rodkey, for providing screening prints of Willis O'Brien's early Edison Company short features.

To Hal Miles for sharing research and opening archives, and providing a screening print of the never-*ever* seen *Emilio and His Magical Bull*.

To Lisa Cook and Melissa "Mel" Gauthier at Tippett Studios, and Katie Wright and Lyn-Del Pedersen at Stan Winston Studios, for their tireless schedule-juggling, interview-scheduling efforts; and again to Tippett Studios for providing a screening print of *Prehistoric Beast*.

To Myrna De La Rosa for translating the Spanish-language dinomovies *Aventura al Centro de la Tierra*, *El Bello Durmiente*, and *La Isla de los Dinosaurios*. *Gracias* Myrna!

To Neil Pettigrew and Harris Lentz, III, for their insights as authors who have been there before me.

To Judy Harris for reading my little essay on *The Beast from 20,000 Fathoms*, and planting the seed of this book with words of encouragement.

To my nephew and "dinosaur buddy" Joshua for sitting with me through dozens of dinomovies good, bad, and ugly, offering a young perspective, having the *chutzpah* to get me a photo made with Ray Harryhausen at Archon 20, and being my friend.

To my brother John for his outstanding memorabilia photography and computer assistance, and watching Godzilla movies with me on Channel 5's "The Big Show" when we were kids.

To my father Ephraim for not only letting his 7-year-old son use his wind-up 8mm Revere, but uncomplainingly serving as cameraman while said 7 year old operated a sock-puppet dinosaur.

To my entire family for their inexhaustible love and support as this project grew and grew, taking more and more of my time away from them.

And to my mother Elsie, who in 1962 looked into a newborn baby's eyes, and resolutely refused to listen to the voices of doom, and gave me not only life, but a wonderful life.

CONTENTS

Acknowledgments vii

Foreword by Donald Lessem 1

Preface 3

THE FILMOGRAPHY 7

Between pages 294 and 295 are 16 color plates containing 22 photographs

*Appendix A: Dino-Cameos and Paleo-Plots —
Films with Dinosaurian Themes,
Plot Elements, or Isolated Dinosaur Scenes* 431

*Appendix B: Lost Worlds —
Dinosaur Films That Might Have Been or Might Yet Be* 435

*Appendix C: It Came from Japan —
A Chronology of the Quasi-Dinosaurs
from Toho Studios* 449

Bibliography 453

Index 463

"I personally feel that the definitive dinosaur movie has yet to be made"
— Ray Harryhausen

FOREWORD

by Donald Lessem

The Dinosaur Filmography is a work of serious scholarship. I almost hate to say so, because it may discourage dino-fans from seeking it out as the funny series of essays or handy, insightful guide to special effects that it is.

The author of this one-of-a-kind archive, Mark Berry, obviously watches far more dinosaur movies than can be healthy for any grown man. Of that we can all be envious. He's also a dogged researcher who interviews filmmakers and ferrets out reviews and hilarious interviews with eye-popping starlets from decades past. He's a special-effects maven who understands the nuances of Vaseline on lenses and other tricks of the movie masters. He's a fluid writer who can communicate technology and trivia in a manner that makes the former comprehensible and the latter compelling. And he's a lively, often hilarious critic and aficionado. We know it must have hurt him personally, but he freely admits that critics attacked Ray Harryhausen's delightful dino-dementia *The Valley of Gwangi* "with the vehemence of the Japanese army bombarding Godzilla."

This book is fun. For Berry, I suspect it was as much hard-earned fun as the dinosaur films profiled were for the obsessed special effects artisans who made the movies. For the rest of us, Berry's book and the films it honors and probes are a joy.

There was never a better marriage than B-movies and B-dinosaurs. Strangely, wondrously, the two are inextricably linked through our fascination with both. That fascination probably surpasses the inherent quality of the movies themselves.

Movies can be an art form. Dinosaurs were arguably nature's greatest creation. Dinosaur movies are neither art nor marvel. Yet they are enduring, endearing, engaging. No matter how furry the bikinis on the "actors," how iguana-like the dinosaurs, how non-scientific or downright nonsensical the plots, dinosaur movies enchant.

Why? I dunno. Certainly, it has something to do with the magic of both movies and dinosaurs. Movies, even bad ones, realize fantasies as no other art form does. So the first moviegoers would throng to see a simple cartoon of "Gertie" the dinosaur. So, decades later, another generation queued up in record numbers for *Jurassic Park*, and swore it was a film full of dinosaurs, when dinosaurs are on screen for only 17 minutes—tribute both to Spielberg's artistry and to the sheer wonder of newly developed computer graphic representations of dinosaurs.

The recent plethora of special-effects wonders, from the 17 minutes' worth in *Jurassic Park* to the wall-to-wall dinosaurs in *Jurassic Park III* (and God knows how many sequels to come), threatens to turn dinosaurs into just another Freddy Krueger clone, and the charm of clever special effects into hoary antiques.

But none of that high-priced, high-tech cheapening of the magic of dinosaurs changes the wacky charm of extinct special effects dinosaurs, all the clay-animated and stop-motion marvels detailed so carefully in this book.

Mark Berry has done us all a great service. Years from now, when old dinosaur movies are even more beloved, fans will be turning to Mark's book and laughing, marveling, learning what lies behind the lens of wonderful works of love, if not art—the movie dinosaurs.

"Dino Don" Lessem was a technical advisor to the Jurassic Park *film and ride and to Disney's* Dinosaur. *He has hosted and written documentaries for NOVA and the Discovery Channel and is the author of more than 20 books on dinosaurs for children and adults.*

PREFACE

*"You just can't beat a good dinosaur movie,
or even a bad one, for that matter"— Neil Pettigrew*

Filmmakers have been putting dinosaurs on the screen quite literally since the dawn of the cinema. The discovery of the amazing creatures in the 19th century lit a flame in the human imagination, and moving pictures provided a chance to reimagine the ancient animals in a new way, beyond what the written word, or an artist's rendering, or even a massive but stationary skeleton could provide.

I immensely enjoyed writing this book as it allowed me to combine three of my favorite things: writing, movies (the arena of special effects, in particular) and dinosaurs, for which I have never outgrown my fascination. There have been previous books on this subject, but they have been more in the order of surveys or overviews rather than in-depth references. There have also been wonderful, detailed articles and essays on particular films, but they are scattered in countless books and periodicals over many decades. I believed that an exhaustive reference on dinosaur cinema, combining in one source a great amount of previously published information with as much new research as I could accomplish, would be a useful and enjoyable volume. While writing, I have tried to critique the entire film — direction, acting, and so on — not just the dino effects. With a few exceptions, which are noted with "not viewed" (and consequently are not star rated — see the next paragraph), I have personally seen every film included in this book.

Each film's coverage opens with the title, followed by a quote from the film's dialogue and a star rating (from no stars at all for the worst to four stars for the best). Following the star rating is the year of release; country of release; name of the releasing company; a notation of "BW" (black and white) or "C" (color), and the running time in minutes. Credit and cast listings follow, and for some films a tag line from the ad campaign is provided. Last comes a plot summary and other descriptive text, which in the longest entries is divided into "commentary," "people and production," and "special effects." For minor films or films on which little information was available, not all of these divisions are present.

The criteria for inclusion in the book are fairly simple. The movie must show on screen one or more creatures represented as *prehistoric, reptilian,* and *nonhumanoid* (sorry, no Gill Men). Inaccurate portrayals such as magnified live reptiles are included, as long as the *intent* is to represent a real or fictional "dinosaur." These guidelines allow the inclusion of *One Million B. C.* and its offspring, as well as films featuring plesiosaurs (i.e., *Loch Ness*) and Dimetrodons (i.e., *Journey to the Center of the Earth*). I know that these latter two species are not dinosaurs, but *The Dinosaur, Dimetrodon, Pterosaur, and Sea-dwelling Mesozoic Reptiles Filmography* was too long for a book title. And about the Brontosaurus/Apatosaurus thing: We all know that Apatosaurus is now considered to be the correct name for this perennially popular species, but a large percentage of dinofilms were made back when it was still the good old "bronto." So, in the text, you will find many more references to Brontosaurus than to Apatosaurus.

Not eligible for this volume are films featuring only prehistoric *mammals*, disqualifying the woolly mammoths of *The Jungle* and the saber-toothed cat in *Sinbad and the Eye of the Tiger*. Likewise, movies including prehistoric "cavepeople" but lacking any primordial reptiles, such as *Creatures the World Forgot, Quest for Fire,* and *Clan of the Cave Bear*, are ineligible. Mythical creatures like the medieval dragon of *Dragonslayer* and the Aztec bird-god Quetzalcoatl, seen in *The Flying Serpent* and *Q*, are also outside the scope of this work. When a creature is clearly referred to as a "dinosaur" in the script, said creature earns inclusion even if he or she looks nothing like a real dinosaur; see *Reptilicus* as a prime example. Conversely, if the dialogue specifies that a creature is *not* of dinosaurian or prehistoric origin, that film is excluded. (I am frankly grateful that Matthew Broderick's character in the big-budget American version of *Godzilla* orally confirmed that the titular beast was not paleo-related, thus letting me off the hook as far as that picture is concerned.)

A word of explanation is in order regarding the decision to place a particular movie in the main body or in Appendix A: Dino-Cameos and Paleo-Plots. Consider *Robocop* and *Women of the Prehistoric Planet* as examples. *Robocop* includes a nifty and quite plausible stop-motion Tyrannosaurus, whereas *Prehistoric Planet* features one very short sequence of a "giant" lizard. The humble lizard finds his way into the main entries because the picture as a whole, despite having only one short and puny "dinosaur" scene, concerns the exploration of a "prehistoric" environment. *Robocop*, though its dino is much more impressive, is relegated to the back material because the overall film is utterly unrelated to any prehistoric or dinosaurian themes.

The common wisdom on evolution is that some evolutionary branches simply tailed off into nothing. So it is with dinosaur movies: Sometimes, despite large investments of work and dollars, a picture just doesn't make it to the screen. It is sometimes possible to find bits of information on "lost" films with a little digging in industry magazines or the biographies of people in the film industry. Appendix B: Lost Worlds is a sort of museum, displaying reconstructed skeletons of dinosaur movies that were never completed (or, if completed, were never released).

Much thought went into how to deal with the giant-monster/pseudo-dinosaur films from Toho Studios. With sporadic exceptions, Godzilla's connections to his prehistoric origins faded into nothingness after the first few films, and only rarely did a special guest monster appear which could even loosely be called a dinosaur. So with a heavy heart, I have reluctantly assigned Godzilla and all his cohorts to an appendix (Appendix C: It Came from Japan), chronologically listing all of Toho's Godzilla features with notations regarding their "Dinosaur Content." For a definitive examination of these titles and many other Japanese genre films, I enthusiastically recommend *Japanese Science Fiction, Fantasy, and Horror Films* by Stuart Galbraith IV, an exhaustive, affectionate, and tremendously entertaining volume.

As this book goes to press, the dinosaur film genre is approaching its first centennial, and the dinosaur movie shows no signs of any impending extinction. There will be lulls and booms, but new generations will come along, and humankind will not, I believe, ever cease to be fascinated with — and make movies about — these bizarre and wonderful beings of Earth's dim and distant past.

Mark F. Berry
Summer 2002

THE FILMOGRAPHY

Adam Raises Cain

not viewed 1919, USA. BW, Silent.

CREDITS: *Director/Animator* Tony Sarg.

A young boy and his playmates frolic on and around a dinosaur skeleton, using its long neck as a slide and so on, in this animated comedy short. The images are animated frame-by-frame as black silhouette figures against a light background. Puppeteer and animator Tony Sarg also featured a dinosaur in his later film *The First Circus*.

Adam's Rib

not viewed 1923, USA.
Famous Players—Lasky. BW/C, Silent.

CREDITS: *Director/Producer* Cecil B. DeMille.
CAST: Milton Sills, Theodore Kosloff, Elliott Dexter, Anna Q. Nilsson.

Critics have never been kind to this early effort from the legendary DeMille, which is essentially a soap opera of a society wife, her neglectful husband, her dutiful daughter, and a deposed king who woos both women. *Adam's Rib* is set in modern times but features an extended prehistoric flashback sequence filmed in a primitive two-color process, and another segment set in an exhibit hall full of dinosaur skeletons.

Adventures in Dinosaur City

"You gotta be pulling my tail ... that's your idea of a dinosaur story?"

* 1991, USA. Smart Egg Pictures. C, 88m.

CREDITS: *Director* Brett Thompson. *Producers* Luigi Cingolani, George Zecevic (executive), Lisa Morton (associate). *Screenplay* Wili Baronet and Lisa Morton. *Story* Wili Baronet. *Creatures Designed and Created by* John Criswell. *Visual Effects Supervisor* Chojii Kikugawa.
CAST: *Timmy* Omri Katz. *Mick* Shawn Hoffman. *Jamie* Tiffanie Poston. *Link* Pete Koch. *Missy* Megan Hughes. *Rex* (performance) Marc Martorana. *Tops* (performance) Tony Doyle.

Teenagers Timmy, Jamie, and Mick are anxious to watch the newest episode of their favorite cartoon TV show, "Dinosaurs." Unfortunately, they decide to watch it on the big monitor in Timmy's parents' interdimensional physics lab, and before you know it they are zapped into the show's fictional world. In this reality, the heroic Rex (a Tyrannosaurus), his partner Tops (a Protoceratops), and the diminutive Forry (a wisecracking

French poster for the "Ninja Turtles" knockoff *Adventures in Dinosaur City*, a misfire in any language.

Rhamphorynchus) lead the forces of good against the evil Allosaurus, Mr. Big, and his Neanderthal henchmen, "The Rockies." When Link (the head Rockie) swipes a vital fuse from Saur City's powerplant, Rex and his pals team up with the teenagers to vanquish Mr. Big and recover the item before Saur City has a total meltdown. They successfully infiltrate Big's tower headquarters, do away with him, grab the fuse and run (or fly, in Forry's case). With Saur City saved, Rex and Timmy say a tearful goodbye and the kids return to the everyday world.

COMMENTARY: In the early nineties, the *Teenage Mutant Ninja Turtles* franchise was raking in money by the ton and *Adventures in Dinosaur City* was one of the inevitable *Turtles* clones. Unfortunately, it bears the unmistakable signs of having been written by adults who only *think* they know what kids will find "hip." These dubious *Adventures* are a mélange of humanoid man-in-suit dino caricatures (very much in the mold of Jim Henson's *Dinosaurs* television show), *Flintstones*-inspired gadgets (the elevator is powered by bats holding onto ropes), slapstick Neanderthals right out of *Caveman*, and of course, many elements from the *Ninja Turtles*. The effort that went into the script is evidenced by lines like "what in the hot lava is goin' on here?" and "for roaring out loud!" The nightclub act is "Rock-el and her Million Bee Cees," the cavegirl/gangster moll does a bad Mae West impression, and much of the running time consists of silly pseudomartial-arts hand-to-hand combat (or "hand-to-claw" combat as the script would surely call it). The one bit showing some creativity is the brief film-within-a-film, directed by Jordan Reichek, of the fictional cartoon program which spawns the alternate world. Though all we get to see is the opening, it's a dead-on-target imitation of kids' television in the nineties, and it's too bad that the rest of the movie is so badly off-target. There are nice touches in Michael Stuart's production design and John Logan's art direction, but even their work owes much to previous influences. And will someone please explain, if "Mr. Big" is supposed to be an Allosaurus, why does he have a horn on his snout?

The Age of Mammals

**½ 1981, USA.
Charles Cahill & Associates. C, 10m.

CREDITS: *Directors* Doug Beswick and Mark Wolf. *Written by* Gail Morgan Hickman and Jim Aupperle. *Process Photography* Doug Beswick. *Animation Effects* Mark Wolf. *Models by* Tony McVey, John Holmes. *Technical Advisor* Gretchen Sibley.

It's the close of the Mesozoic Era, the "Age of Reptiles," and the reign of the dinosaurs is ending. A Brontosaurus munches on a plant, an Allosaurus dines on a carcass—but soon the mighty dinosaurs will disappear and the humble mammals, up to then represented only by small shrewlike creatures such as the Deltatherium, will inherit the earth. It is the dawn of the Cenozoic Era: the "Age of Mammals." The Eohippus, diminutive ancestor of the modern horse, is idly grazing when he is pounced upon by the giant predatory flightless bird, Diatryma. We see the largest land mammal ever known, the Baluchitherium, standing twice the height of a full-grown African elephant. Bizarre creatures like the shovel-snouted Platybelodon and the 12-foot armadillo predecessor, Glyptodon, walk the earth. The giant ground sloth, Megatherium, lets his guard down and falls prey to the saber-toothed cat, Smilodon. As the climate cools, the woolly mammoth is well-equipped to survive in the Ice Age, but soon the appearance of early Neanderthals heralds the coming of modern man. "Will man survive?" we are asked. "The choice is ours."

COMMENTARY: *The Age of Mammals* essentially picks up where Wah Chang's 1971 educational short, *Dinosaurs ... The Terrible Lizards*, leaves off. *Mammals* opens at the end of the Cretaceous period, providing a chance for a couple of brief dinosaur shots. Two cuts of a Brontosaurus kick things off, followed by three cuts of a very sinister-looking Allosaurus, but on balance the *Age of Mammals*' animation is a bit unambitious. In Chang's film many of the creatures strut freely around the frame, but *Mammals* has far less action. Most of the animals do not even walk, but are content to merely swish their tails, look around, and chew. Certainly the models themselves are beautifully detailed and meticulously constructed, and there are some lively moments including some dandy scenes of the Diatryma and Smilodon doing what carnivores do. The Smilodon in particular is given a great deal of character by the animator, and emerges as the film's most impressive beast. It's interesting to note that the "rippling fur" effect, just as in *King Kong*, is not at all detrimental to the scenes' effectiveness.

Tony McVey sculpted this artful Allosaurus for the opening sequence in *Age of Mammals*.

Conceding that the animals are not as dynamic as one might hope, *The Age of Mammals* is still great fun for animation fans and well worth seeking out. Along with Karel Zeman's *Cesta do praveku*, it's a rare chance to see some of the fantastic creatures of the Cenozoic Era brought to animated life.

PEOPLE AND PRODUCTION: *The Age of Mammals* was originally conceived as a "sequel" to Wah Chang's *Dinosaurs ... The Terrible Lizards*, according to coscripter Jim Aupperle. "Steve Czerkas and I started to develop that project with the idea that it would be a good way to break into stop-motion," Aupperle told the author. The planning began not long after Chang's educational short was released. As Aupperle recalled, "*Dinosaurs ... The Terrible Lizards* had come out and we thought ... since there was one already done, it would be a good way to follow it up." Czerkas built an animation puppet of a giant sloth and some test footage was shot, but then the project's momentum waned for a time.

Enter writer-producer Gail Morgan Hickman. "Gail and I decided to collaborate on it," said Aupperle. "We were both wanting to do a puppet film, and we contacted Cahill, the same producer that released Wah's film." A budget was agreed upon and a contract was signed. "Gail was primarily building the puppets and I was going to animate them," Aupperle noted. "We got as far as doing a Uintatherium ... Gail built a very nicely armatured little Arsinoitherium that I actually shot some footage on, and I also did a few shots of a Diatryma that he built." Hickman would soon leave the project for a more serious writing assignment, and Aupperle departed to begin work on *Planet of Dinosaurs*. "I remember even shooting the Diatryma on some of the same test setups we were doing for *Planet*," said Aupperle.

Cahill still wanted to continue, however, and so the project didn't die. "Marc Wolf then became involved ... he was primarily the mover behind it," Aupperle reported. Doug

Beswick, who had performed all of the animation for *Dinosaurs ... The Terrible Lizards*, also came aboard. "Doug was brought in to make sure that it could be done technically, as well as it could be," Aupperle continued. "So, Marc and Doug were the ones who really finished it up." All of the animation in the film is the work of Wolf and Beswick, but the script written by Aupperle and Hickman survived intact.

Allegro Non Troppo

"You might call it a film of magic, a ... Fantasia!"

***½ 1976, Italy. Specialty Films. C. 75m.

CREDITS: *Director* Bruno Bozzetto. *Producer* Bruno Bozzetto. *Subject and Scenario* Bruno Bozzetto, Guido Manuli, Maurizio Nichetti.
CAST: *Girl* Marialuisa Giovanni. *Orchestra Leader* Nestor Garay. *Presenter* Maurizio Micheli. *Designer* Maurizio Nichetti.

COMMENTARY: *Allegro Non Troppo* is at once a tribute to, a satire of, and a worthy successor to Walt Disney's *Fantasia*, all the while earning its own place on the short list of important animated feature films. Producer-director Bruno Bozzetto embraces the *Fantasia* connection with an amusing prologue wherein Bozzetto's fictional alter ego enthusiastically describes his idea to the audience, only to receive a phone call from Hollywood informing him that classical music and animation had earlier been married by someone named "Frisney, or Prisney," or something. This conceit leads to a series of live-action interludes which connect the animated segments. These zany, often slapstick bits will not be everyone's cup of tea, and are negligible interruptions in comparison to the innovative, often masterful animation. The six animated vignettes are kicked off by Debussy's *Prelude to the Afternoon of a Faun*, a tragicomic gem about a past-his-prime satyr trying anything and everything to entice one of the joyfully naked nymphs cavorting all around him. Next is Dvořák's *Slavonic Dance No. 7*, interpreted as a light-hearted commentary on the fad-following fickleness of modern man.

The third piece is what most concerns us here — a wry and insightful look at evolution set to Ravel's *Bolero*. In this lengthy segment, life is spawned from the dregs inside a Coke bottle dropped by a passing space ship. The strange creatures that subsequently evolve are recognizably prehistoric, yet noticeably different from those we know. Unlike the *Rite of Spring* sequence in *Fantasia*, which strove for and achieved a level of zoological accuracy, Bozzetto's "dinosaurs" are rather more fanciful in design. The evolution segment is a perfect interpretation of the music and is the centerpiece of *Allegro*, with a final shot that's a wow. After *Bolero*, the proceedings take a dark turn with *Valse Triste*, by Sibelius, underscoring the tragic plight of a solitary house cat yearning for half-remembered happier times now long since past. The images here are so affecting that the viewer may have difficulty putting them out of mind. Bozzetto wisely lightens the mood with the next piece, Vivaldi's sprightly *Concerto in C Minor*, detailing the efforts of a happy, busy bee and the disastrous effects caused by a pair of picnicking (human) lovers. The final segment employs Stravinsky's *Firebird* (which had been seriously considered for *Fantasia*) in a rather wild variation on the Garden of Eden story. This time, the serpent is unable to tempt Adam and Eve and so eats the apple himself, with unhappy results.

The lowbrow live action notwithstanding, *Allegro Non Troppo* is a resounding triumph with its own unforgettable dawn-of-life sequence. It showcases the boundless potential of animation, while proving that it is possible to revisit old territory with totally original results.

Along the Moonbeam Trail

not viewed 1920, USA. BW, Silent.

CREDITS: *Director/Producer* Herbert M. Dawley.

A group of youngsters travel to the moon in a magical aircraft and discover prehistoric animals, including a Trachodon, Tyrannosaurus, Stegosaurus, and a particularly aggressive pterodactyl. No prints of *Moonbeam Trail* are known to exist, but the stop-motion dinosaur footage apparently consisted entirely of Willis O'Brien animation snipped from *Ghost of Slumber Mountain*.

The Animal World

"The animal world — the world of which we know so little."

* ½ 1956, USA. Warner Bros. C, 82m.

CREDITS: *Director* Irwin Allen. *Producer* Irwin Allen. *Written by* Irwin Allen. *Narrators* Theodor Von Eltz, John Storm. *Supervising Animator* Willis O'Brien. *Animation* Ray Harryhausen. *Special Effects* Arthur Rhoades.

AD LINE: "Two billion years in the making!"

"Once upon a time, about two billion years ago," a voice says, "there lived ... no one. Nowhere." But then the first single-celled life appears in the oceans and slowly evolves. The amphibians invade the shores, but only the reptiles truly "conquer the land." The Age of Reptiles is marked by the reign of the dinosaurs, brought to life on screen with approximately nine minutes of stop-motion animation.

The dinos' story, as told here, begins in the Jurassic Period. A peacefully feeding Brontosaurus is forced to flee by the appearance of a hungry Allosaurus. The bronto lays an egg, and soon the deceptively tiny hatchling breaks out of its shell. A Stegosaurus, also enjoying a meal, is attacked by an agile Ceratosaurus and a fierce battle ensues. The stego makes a valiant stand but falls in the end. Before the meat-eater can enjoy his kill, another Ceratosaurus comes along to fight for the prize. Ironically, neither of the big predators is to win this contest as they both topple from a cliff while blinded by the passion of combat. Proceeding to the Cretaceous Period, near the end of the dinosaurs' rule, a Triceratops scrounges for withering vegetation when his mortal enemy the Tyrannosaurus appears. Their impending contest is interrupted, though, when the volcano erupts! The eruption, serving as a metaphor for the end of the dinosaurs' age, kills the Triceratops and the T. rex (as well as the Jurassic dinosaurs seen earlier).

With the dinosaurs finally gone, the lowly mammals' ascension is chronicled, with discussions of science versus the Bible and the relationship between man and animal. Flight evolves, and the skies are invaded by the insects and other creatures, including the prehistoric Rhamphorynchus and pterodactyl (represented by still photos). The wilds of Africa, animal oddities, man-animal competition, hunting and whaling, circuses and zoos, and the animals of the forest and desert round out the program, and we close on this cautionary note: "The reign of man over the animal world is perhaps really just beginning, and hopefully, this is not The End."

COMMENTARY: The fact that *The Animal World* is remembered today, when remembered at all, only for its impressive dinosaur sequence is not surprising, since the rest of the film wanders from merely bland to embarrassingly inane. The narration tries to inject cleverness, humor, and drama rather than just letting the inherent wonder of the animal kingdom speak for itself. If ever there was a film demanding to have its special effects judged independently of the whole, this is it, and the one-and-a-half star rating given this picture is in no way a reflection of the nifty dinosaur segment. In fact, the dinos single-handedly save *The Animal World* from a much lower grade.

It is a fact that documentaries, more than other pictures, tend to date badly. Even Disney's beautifully-photographed, award-winning "True-Life Adventures" often resorted to gimmicks, so the tone of *The Animal World* is fairly representative of that era. But even the hokiest moments in the Disney efforts can't compete with the sometimes unbearable narration of *Animal World*. "I wouldn't

The Animal World stop-motion puppets, like this egg-laying Brontosaurus, weren't always the best, but Ray Harryhausen brought them to blood-pumping life.

want to be quoted, but they say he modeled for the original outboard motor!" describes a crocodile speeding through a swamp. Maniacal mad-scientist laughter is heard as a trapdoor spider waits. A man wearing a barrel accompanies the assertion that "this would be the well-dressed man in a world without animals from which to get raw materials." The narration is strewn with cutesy humor ("the adventures of super sowbug"), unfunny puns ("the survival of the *fattest*"), too-grave seriousness ("arch enemy of the termite … the dreaded ant"), and even "funny" racial stereotypes ("It's no one but us squirrels, boss, tendin' tuh bizness"). The script even resorts to alarmism, warning that if birds ceased to eat bugs for one summer, "the atmosphere would be choked with trillions of flying creatures, bringing an end to all mankind." Admittedly, I did enjoy hearing the sound effects from *Them!* (1954) during the ant-termite battles.

Animal lovers, who seemingly would enjoy a nature documentary, would definitely not enjoy parts of *The Animal World*: not the sad scenes in the bullring, or the gunpowder-fired harpoons blasted into whales (a spray of red erupts from the blow hole of one dying giant), or the big-game hunters tracking down elephants even as the voice-over points out their threatened extinction. From a technical standpoint, too, the picture largely fails, doomed by its piecemeal construction. Footage was collected from dozens of libraries and archives rather than being shot specifically for this project, and though the narration tries to knit the sequences together, there are some jarringly awkward segues. Some fine nature photography is shown at times, but the great variance in color balance, grain, and camerawork gives a hopelessly choppy effect.

The dinosaur sequence, however, is great fun. Though it doesn't open the film as is sometimes reported (actually starting about 14 minutes in), it occurs near enough to the beginning to make most of *The Animal World* seem a huge letdown. The fact that the sequence was done completely as "tabletop" animation allowed for the full beauty of Technicolor to be maximized, and the resulting images are striking. "We did not have the problem of double printing where you have to combine people with animals," Ray Harryhausen explained. Though working with dinosaur puppets that were not up to the quality of those he would later use in *One Million Years B.C.* and *The Valley of Gwangi*, Harryhausen succeeded in creating his remarkably "animalistic" movement. If one forgets for a moment about technical analysis, and actually tries to envision what dinosaurs in these situations would really do in nature, it's not hard to imagine that they would behave exactly as Ray's creations do. They seem to react, and sidle, and thrust and parry, and *think*, just as real bears or wolves or leopards do in the real animal world. The tiniest details, down to the stegosaur's chewing motions, ring true. Harryhausen's talent and the beautiful Technicolor hues combine to create, as author Paul Mandell once put it, "a picture book come to life."

The mechanical dino torsos used for the closeup shots are a bit ungainly but are sufficiently well-made, and the narration of the dinosaur segment is actually some of the movie's best. It is thankfully straightforward and shtick-free, but is dated by references to now-obsolete paleontological theories. *The Animal World*'s dino-vignette is marred only by two moments. One is the very first shot of the sequence, where a model caveman with a sword is eaten by the Brontosaurus! The script excuses this inexplicable shot with the conceit, "Man had not yet been created, but if he had been..." The other misstep, so to speak, is the shot of the two lifeless model ceratosaurs falling off of the cliff. Nonetheless, these two glitches are easily forgiven during the enjoyment of the sequence. Though not as unknown as it once was, this brief but sensational saurian soap opera remains one of Ray Harryhausen's more obscure bits of work. It has never been released on video, and probably never will be. But seek it out, friends, it's worth it just to see Ray and Obie team up one last time for nine minutes of dinosaur heaven.

PEOPLE AND PRODUCTION: In 1951, producer-director Irwin Allen was honored with an Oscar for his ocean-life documentary *The Sea Around Us*, based on Rachel Carson's book. A few years later, Allen followed up that success with *The Animal World*, an even more ambitious effort chronicling the entire evolution of life. According to the Warner Bros. publicity department, "some 3 million feet of color film" was assembled and "integrated with the material filmed at the Burbank studio." Allen asserted that this was "the largest amount of film ever exposed for a single feature production."

For the dinosaur segment, Allen originally planned to use model dinosaurs placed into stationary dioramas. Later, he discussed with Ray Harryhausen the possibility of using some footage from the animator's never-completed 16mm project *Evolution*, but that idea was soon discarded. "There wasn't enough footage to begin with," Harryhausen explained, "and so [Allen] decided to get Willis O'Brien on the project." Allen was impressed with Obie's past body of work, and stated at the time that he hired him "as a tribute to a true genius."

Allen and company obviously realized even before *The Animal World* was released that the dinosaurs were its best selling point, because even though the dinos occupy less than ten of the film's 82 minutes, over 95 percent of the content of the studio pressbook was dinosaur-related. The prehistoric stars also adorned the cover of Dell's tie-in comic book. As Irwin Allen himself said of O'Brien and Harryhausen: "I was surrounded by geniuses, and they made me look good."

SPECIAL EFFECTS: Just as *The Animal World*'s advertising emphasized the dinosaurs, the names of Willis O'Brien and Ray Harryhausen were also trumpeted in press releases. In a publicity article titled "Man

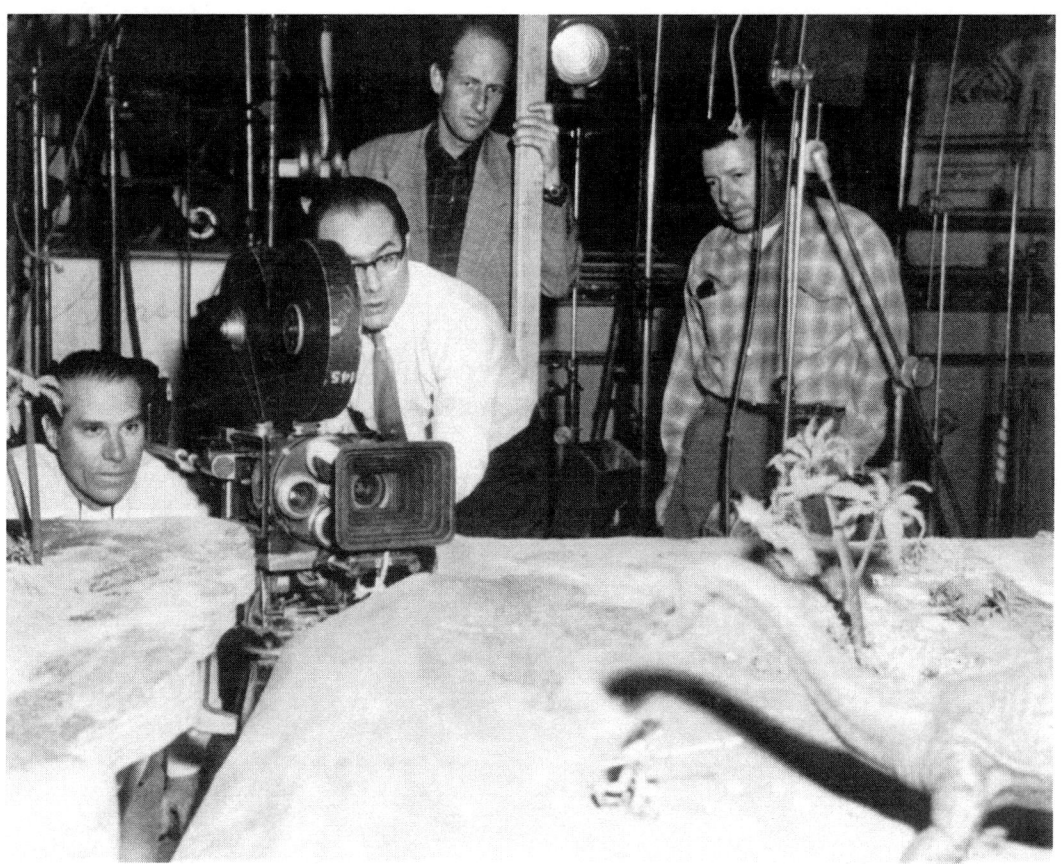

Writer-producer-director Irwin Allen (behind camera, with glasses) and animator Ray Harryhausen (in background, hand on pole) examine a stop-motion set-up for *The Animal World*.

Behind Monsters Makes Mighty Scenes," Harryhausen is described as "a youngish, balding man," with "one of the rarest jobs in the motion picture industry ... an animator in the field of stop-motion photography." The article also quoted Ray talking about his craft. "I often have to act the role of a dinosaur, or an ape, or a flying saucer," he pointed out, "to feel how to move the models in portraying a certain kind of scene."

The effects team for *The Animal World* consisted of O'Brien and Harryhausen (their only collaboration other than *Mighty Joe Young* and the never-filmed *Valley of the Mist*), as well as Arthur Rhoades and his staff at the Warner Bros. prop department. Obie is credited as "Supervising Animator," but Harryhausen did all of the actual animation himself over a period of six or seven weeks, cloistered in a secluded section of the studio. O'Brien designed the miniature set-ups as well as the dinosaur models themselves. He based his designs largely on the classic paintings of Charles R. Knight, whose renderings were the accepted norms for dino appearance until the 1960's. Rhoades and his team, namely Pasqual Manuelli and Harold Wilson, constructed the miniature sets and the dinosaur puppets, which were fabricated by using injected foam to fill the outer skin. This technique saved time compared to the traditional method of building up layers of "muscle" over the steel armature, but the final result was not as satisfactory. The tyrannosaur, allosaur, and one of the ceratosaurs were reportedly all the same model, "redressed" to play the different roles.

The prop department also made some

A quartet of very mixed dinosaurs — Stegosaurus, Triceratops, Brontosaurus, and Tyrannosaurus — try to flee from geological upheavals in the climax of *The Animal World* dino sequence.

larger-scale, mechanically actuated models to be intercut with the animated shots, a tactic later repeated in *Dinosaurus!* and TV's *Land of the Lost*. "We had some double-size ones for closeups, that worked by wires," Harryhausen explained. "Obie wasn't happy with them — neither was I — but Irwin Allen seemed to want to do that for closeups." Since there were no "Dynamation" style rear-projection shots needed to combine animated and live-action footage, Harryhausen was able on this one occasion to employ a time-saving technique. "We used two cameras to get twice the amount of footage for the same amount of time," he explained. The ploy worked well, too, and even after multiple viewings this author has been unable to definitively tell which animation appears twice. "It was done in such a way that you're not *supposed* to be aware of it!" Harryhausen pointed out with a smile. The animator even

paid homage to his unfinished *Evolution* by having a Ceratosaurus leap dramatically into frame, an action reprised from the *Evolution* test reel.

In its original form, *The Animal World* was gruesome at times, with real and animated scenes of gory predatory behavior. "The whole movie was too bloody," Harryhausen recalled. "He [Allen] had lions killing antelopes and buffaloes, and chewing on them while they were still kicking ... and so he said 'make the dinosaur sequence just as *bloody!*' So I had big slabs torn off the Stegosaurus, dripping with blood." However, after one advance screening, Allen changed his mind. "Those all had to be cut out after the first preview," Harryhausen explained.

Conflicting reports have appeared over the years regarding Harryhausen's own opinion of the *Animal World* animation. So, I asked him. "Well, it was just tabletop miniatures;

it wasn't anything outrageous," he said. "The models were too simplified — they didn't have a texture on them and they looked a little too simple — but some of the animation I think was quite good. It was the thing that got the best criticism." Even 14 years later, when recycled as a caveman's remembrances in *Trog*, it was *still* the thing that got the best criticism!

At the Earth's Core

"Oh, how very disappointing!"

* 1976, U.K. Amicus/American International Pictures. C, 90m.

CREDITS: *Director* Kevin Connor. *Producer* John Dark. *Screenplay* Milton Subotsky; based on the novel by Edgar Rice Burroughs. *Special Effects Supervisor* Ian Wingrove.
CAST: *David Innes* Doug McClure. *Dr. Abner Perry* Peter Cushing. *Dia* Caroline Munro. *Ra* Cy Grant. *Ghak* Godfrey James. *Jubal* Michael Crane. *Hoojah* Sean Lynch.

AD LINE: "Behind a barrier of molten lava, winged creatures ... like guardians of the gates of Hell!"

Somewhere in Wales during the 19th century, British scientist Dr. Abner Perry and American financier David Innes board a huge mechanical drilling vehicle known as the "Iron Mole," for its first test run. However, something goes terribly wrong and the duo emerges in an unknown, quasi-prehistoric subterranean world known as Pellucidar, home to a variety of ancient plants and strange, giant animals. Before long, David and Dr. Perry are captured by the ruthless Sagoths — stormtroopers of the evil, birdlike Mahars who rule Pellucidar. Along with many other prisoners captured from Pellucidar's scattered tribes of humans, they are taken to serve as slaves in the Mahar city. The workers are needed to man the massive, intricate machinery which controls the volcanic lava. David becomes romantically smitten with the beautiful Princess Dia, and he forms a friendship with Ra, a warrior who reveals to him the true extent of the Mahars' evil. Inspired by the teamwork of David and Ra, the formerly warring tribes of Pellucidar finally unite against the Mahar tyranny. With freedom secured for Pellucidar, Dr. Perry and David prepare to board the Mole and return to the surface, and Dia must decide whether to go with David or remain behind in the world she knows.

COMMENTARY: *At the Earth's Core* is not a dinosaur movie. It is included here only because it is so often thought of as such, and because it is so closely linked to the dino-movies *The Land That Time Forgot* and *The People That Time Forgot*. One actual Mesozoic species — Rhamphorynchus — is mentioned by name, but the scene where Peter Cushing identifies one of the cheap-looking Mahars as a Rhamphorynchus is the most ludicrous piece of celluloid paleontology since Claude Rains pegged a baby gecko as a Tyrannosaurus rex in 1960's *The Lost World*. The Mahars actually look more like the result of some genetic experiment that went monstrously wrong, as if someone crossed a cockatoo with *Gappa the Trifibian Monster*, but the suffering of the viewing audience is no worse than that of the cast and crew during filming. "One of the beasties — a flying Mahar, I believe it was called — clonked me on the head," Caroline Munro recalled in a *Famous Monsters* interview. "They flew it in on a wire, a Mahar suit with a very hot man inside it." The overall effects work in *At the Earth's Core* is the poorest of the AIP/Amicus Burroughs trilogy, and one model in particular has become quite infamous: the frog-lizard-monster (called a "mosop" in the story) which not only breathes fire from a visible metallic fuel nozzle in its craw, but also, when shot from its perch by an arrow, plummets to the ground and explodes!

Doug McClure, surprisingly good as Bowen Tyler in *The Land That Time Forgot* and its sequel, shows far less conviction here. Lovely Caroline Munro, though third-billed, actually gets very little screen time and even less to do. Making *Core* marginally bearable is Peter Cushing's humorous performance as

18 • *Aventura al Centro de la Tierra*

David Innes (Doug McClure) takes on the "Giant Saurus" while *At the Earth's Core*.

the slightly addled Dr. Perry. He's given some nice vinegary dialogue and he delivers it with a twinkle in the eye and tongue noticeably in cheek. It's a fun twist on the musty, stereotyped British scientists of so many films (including *The People That Time Forgot*). Despite Cushing's efforts, *Core* remains the weakest of all the "subterranean Lost World" films. *Journey to the Center of the Earth*, *Where Time Began*, even *The Last Dinosaur* are all more entertaining than this forgettable, cheap-looking dud.

Aventura al Centro de la Tierra

** 1964, Mexico. Producciones Sotomayor/Columbia. BW, 78m.

CREDITS: *Director* Alfredo B. Cravenna. *Producer* Jaime Sotomayor. *Written by* Jose Maria Fernandez Unsain.

CAST: Jose Elias Moreno, Javier Solis, Kitty de Hoyos.

When a young couple on a cave tour is attacked by a subterranean creature, one of the world's leading zoologists, Professor Diaz, assembles an elite investigative team: Laura Ponce, geologist; Jaime Rocha, big-game hunter; Dr. Peña, physician; Hilda, Diaz's shapely secretary; and assorted guides and bearers. Amazing discoveries come quickly. A hideous one-eyed monster attacks the party before being driven away by gunfire, and Laura's geologic talents enable her to realize that the cave is rich with diamonds.

Chivalrously (or chauvinistically) leaving the ladies behind, the men follow the cyclops' blood trail into an undiscovered grotto and cross a lava pool on a shaky rope bridge. They find the cyclops but when Rocha tranquilizes it, the falling creature impales itself on a stalagmite! Professor Diaz pronounces

As was usually true of American films, the poster art for Mexico's *Aventura al Centro de la Tierra* promised much more than the picture could deliver.

the "living fossil" (living until the stalagmite, anyway) to be the greatest find in the history of science, but later considers aborting the expedition when a vicious bat-man attacks from above. Rocha, having overheard Laura talking about the diamonds, schemes and murders to try and secure the riches for himself, but money can't help him when one of the bat-men strikes again. The creature kills Rocha and Laura, and swims away through a water-filled cave with the captive Hilda. While Dr. Peña (Hilda's boyfriend) pursues, the bat-man kindly offers a live rat and a freshly torn-in-half snake to the girl, but she doesn't seem hungry. Peña snatches Hilda away but the love-struck bat-man follows her back to the camp. The men use Hilda to lure the creature into a hail of bullets, but when the dust settles there's no trace of the prehistoric relic.

COMMENTARY: Like a lot of low-budget American monster movies, *Aventura al Centro de la Tierra* (*Adventure at the Center of the Earth*) was doomed to see its earnest approach, capable actors, and moody atmosphere ultimately done in by some very, very poor monsters.

The film begins with a lengthy on-screen text crawl discussing mankind's eternal attempts to decipher its own origins. From Aristotle to Darwin to today, we are told, man has realized that the most important moment in all history was the creation of the human being. Following this rather overblown intro, the story settles into a fairly standard "*Lost World/Journey to the Center of the Earth*" kind of tale, with shades of *The Black Scorpion* thrown in. It also has a "Beauty and the Beast" theme that obviously recalls many films from *The Creature from the Black Lagoon* to *King Kong*. Like *Black Lagoon*'s "Gill Man," the bat-man grabs pretty Hilda, dives into the water and swims off with her, and as in *Kong*, the misunderstood monster's fatal attraction for beauty lures him to a bullet-ridden demise. There's even a cheap version of the *Kong* "spider-pit sequence," when a man falls into an abyss and is instantly set upon by a huge arachnid.

The shadowy lighting and dramatic black-and-white photography by Raul Martinez Solares beautifully exploit the stark scenery inside Mexico's Cacahuamilpa Grottos, and the music by Raul Lavista is a considerable improvement over his score for *The Beast of Hollow Mountain*. The actors take the whole thing very seriously and give able performances. Director Alfredo B. Cravenna shows a knack for the genre and manages to squeeze a bit of life out of some very well-worn cinematic scare tactics. He also sprinkles in little bits that add to the foreboding feel, like one scene where three of the expedition's bearers silently and somberly place *escapularios* (small religious symbols made of cloth) around their necks. But the picture's strengths are largely shot down by the dreadful monsters. Neither the cyclopean monstrosity nor the hairy bat-man is remotely adequate, and despite the attempts at gruesomeness (a fair amount of ketchuppy-looking blood), the *monstruos* generate snickers instead of shivers.

The dinosaur scenes in *Aventura* are all lifted from other pictures. There is "The Fight" from *One Million B.C.*, the fin-backs and ceratosaurs from *Unknown Island*, and some crude puppet dinosaurs from *El Bello Durmiente*. Most of this footage appears as a film-within-a-film shown by the professor while briefing his team; the only "dinosaur" in the main story is one glimpse of the *Unknown Island* fin-back. Interestingly, *Aventura* contains several shots of the *Unknown Island* creatures which do not appear in the 1948 film, and must be outtakes or test scenes.

In the article "Mexi-Monster Meltdown" in *Monster! Illustrated* (#2), author Steve Fentone mentions that *Aventura* is one of his "perennial faves in all-out Meximonstermania." For the uninitiated, however, it will prove an extremely mixed bag.

Baby ... Secret of the Lost Legend

(a.k.a. *Dinosaur ... Secret of the Lost Legend*)

The mother Brontosaurus and her offspring swim off into the sunset in the sentimental last scene of *Baby*.

"I thought I really had something."

**½ 1985, USA. Disney/Buena Vista. C, 92m.

CREDITS: *Director* B. W. L. Norton. *Producer* Jonathan T. Taplin. *Written by* Clifford and Ellen Green. *Dinosaurs Created and Engineered by* Isidoro Raponi and Roland Tantin. *Special Effects Supervisor* Roland Tantin. *Miniature Consultant* Paul Huston. *Special Photographic Effects Supervisor* Philip Meador. *Special Effects Cinematography* Peter Anderson. *Matte Artist* Michael Lloyd.

CAST: *Susan Matthews-Loomis* Sean Young. *George Loomis* William Katt. *Dr. Eric Kiviat* Patrick McGoohan. *Nigel Jenkins* Julian Fellowes. *Cephu* Kyalo Mativo. *Kenge Obe* Hugh Quarshie. *Colonel Nsogbu* Olu Jacobs. *Sergeant Gambwe* Eddie Tagoe. *Dr. Pierre Dubois* Edward Hardwicke.

AD LINE: "The greatest adventure ever born!"

At a fossil dig in remote Africa, young paleontologist Susan Loomis and her husband George near the end of their six-month stay. One day, the dig's sinister leader, Dr. Eric Kiviat, and his assistant Nigel leave camp without explanation. With Kiviat away, Dr. Dubois of the Red Cross recruits Susan to help him investigate a food-poisoning outbreak at an isolated village, caused by the meat of an unknown animal. Joined by her husband and their pilot-guide, Kenge Obe, she follows a trail of clues from a dying village chief who whispers "Mokele-Mbembe" and scratches an eerily familiar shape in the soil, to the reported upriver location of the carcass where Kenge drops them off, to a peaceful encounter with a tribe called the Kaleri and their chief, Cephu. The scheming

Kiviat enlists the services of the brutal Colonel Nsogbu and his band of mercenaries, and races to catch up.

By a pristine lake, Susan and George are amazed to discover a family of living brontosaurs: adult male, adult female, and hatchling. The humans gain the animals' trust, especially that of "Baby," but Kiviat, Nigel, and the soldiers soon appear. They tranquilize the female and machine-gun the charging male in sheer panic, but Susan and George are saved from certain death by Cephu and the Kaleri. Kiviat soon recaptures the couple, however, and forces them to join his helicopter search for the hatchling. Susan and George make a daring escape and flee on foot with Baby, but the infant catches the scent of its captive mother and swims right into Kiviat's clutches. Just when all seems lost, Kenge Obe appears and informs Susan and George that he has spotted Kiviat's encampment from his airplane, and with the added help of Cephu and his people, the bronto-rescue is on. The freed mother goes on a minor rampage, killing Nigel along the way, but Kiviat tries to escape with Baby in a truck. Susan and George give chase and cause Kiviat to crash, allowing the huge and angry mama to finish him off. The seemingly lifeless Baby miraculously revives under its mother's ministrations, and Susan and George decide to let the Mokele-Mbembe remain "just another legend."

COMMENTARY: This should have been a great dinosaur movie. I wanted the filmmakers to take aim at all of the wonderful possibilities and hit nothing but bull's-eyes. Unfortunately, for every bull's-eye hit, there's a corresponding cow chip to be trodden upon. Why couldn't they stick with the old fashioned wonder-of-nature adventure elements that make the picture's first half so much fun? There was nothing wrong with allowing the indigenous African women to appear in their traditional, topless dress—it adds to the believability—but why did they have to put in the racist overtones, utterly out-of-place profanity, and casual, almost comic-relief violence? *Baby* repeatedly builds momentum, only to shoot itself right in its big bronto foot every time.

Unlike most "lost world" tales, *Baby* is grounded in reality, at least inasmuch as the Mokele-Mbembe is a "real" legend. (It must be said that the film also shares several plot points with a *Land of the Lost* episode entitled "Dopey.") Sean Young and William Katt are well-cast and immensely appealing as the young couple, and Patrick McGoohan is effectively (and thankfully) understated in the villain's role. A strong supporting cast includes the wonderful Kyalo Mativo as Cephu, and Julian Fellowes as the essentially decent but weak-willed Nigel.

The film's early reels are popcorn-munching fun, as Susan and George follow the trail of clues in what amounts to a well-paced detective yarn. Director B. W. L. Norton hits all the right notes during these scenes—the blurry photos stolen by Kiviat, Susan's intriguing conversation with Dr. DuBois, and particularly the great scene with the dying native chief—as the story crisply builds to the first sighting of the dinosaurs. All the while, Jerry Goldsmith's score heightens the action perfectly, with sprightly jungle-esque percussions giving way to full-blooded, symphonic crescendos when appropriate. The cinematography by the gifted John Alcott captures the primordial beauty of the Ivory Coast locations, which really look like places where a dinosaur might still live. *Baby* reaches its high point with the moment of discovery, as we see the massive brontosaurs browsing by a primeval lake. Everything works here—the dinosaurs are convincing and even majestic, Young and Katt don't overact, and the music is triumphant. In a way, it's a shame that *Baby* doesn't end right there.

The film can never really figure out what to do with the dinosaurs once they're found, continually turning what could and should be assets into liabilities. For instance, in one sequence Cephu and his men rescue Susan and George from Kiviat's mercenaries, using simple weapons to overcome the soldiers' high-caliber firepower. The notion of "primitive" tactics and pure cunning overcoming modern machines and technology is a neat idea, later explored during the Ewoks' battle against the Imperial forces in *Return of the Jedi*. But then, having established the theme, the script blithely trashes it by having Cephu pick up a stray machine gun, paste a goofy grin on his face, and proceed to mow people down left and right. Why? The story finally gets somewhat back on track during the finale, as the mother crashes through everything in her path to rescue her offspring. Though oddly reminiscent of *Gorgo*, it's satisfying to see Mama exact a little revenge on the idiot humans who gunned down her mate.

Most reviews of *Baby* savagely attack the special effects, usually failing to point out that the clunky scenes (and there are some) are sizably outnumbered by more successful shots. Overall, the dinosaur re-creations in *Baby* are good enough, and occasionally better than that. Effective moments include the aforementioned first sighting, the scenes of the mother being darted, and her vengeful rampage in the climax. The juvenile title character is subjected to a massive amount of screen time and many closeups, holding up remarkably well. Credit is due to Isidoro Raponi and his tireless crew, but no less so to the agile and skilled dino-performers who somehow overcame the cumbersome, confining suit to effect a passable imitation of a quadruped gait. With the exception of the too-large, catlike eyes, the dinos' design is understated and plausible, and their credibility problems owe more to the script than to the effects crew. The unforgivable scene of Baby crying big wet human tears over his fallen parent does more to undermine the creatures' believability than do any FX shortcomings. The film can also claim some outstanding miniature sets, especially the totally convincing "Dinosaur Lake" masterminded by ILM's Paul Huston.

Many of the problems with *Baby* can be traced to Disney's ill-advised attempts to prove that they weren't too "goody-goody" for 1980s audiences. Toward this end, they mixed in some cursing and automatic weapons, avoiding the "G" rating which was beginning to be seen as box-office anathema. In doing so they also seriously wounded what could have been a unique and wonderful dinosaur film, one which cried out for the traditional Disney treatment, or even better, a Eugène Lourié touch. The good things about *Baby* manage to keep it from totally losing its way, but can't hide all the maddening missteps.

PEOPLE AND PRODUCTION: *Baby* was the brainchild of screenwriters Clifford and Ellen Green, spawned by an interest in cryptozoology. They were particularly fascinated with the persistent legend of the "Mokele-Mbembe," a sauropodlike animal said to be living in the Congo basin. Producers Jonathan Taplin and Roger Spottiswoode, as well as Disney V.P. in Charge of Production Tom Wilhite, were all intrigued by the concept, and Disney soon had a *Baby* on the way. With only two films under his directorial belt, B. W. L. "Bill" Norton was tabbed to helm the picture, having received a glowing recommendation from no less than George Lucas himself.

Norton and Taplin personally went to Africa for location scouting. They visited Cameroon, Gabon and Kenya, but were finally won over by the unspoiled jungles and beautiful rivers of the Ivory Coast. The picturesque lake where several key scenes take place — dubbed "Dinosaur Lake" by the crew — was actually Lake Ingrakon near the country's capital of Abidjan. Director of photography John Alcott, an Oscar-winner for *Barry Lyndon*, seemed a perfect choice not only because of his talent but also due to his recent experience shooting *Greystoke* in the jungles of Cameroon. The too-optimistic initial plan called for all of the blue-screen and miniature photography to be done on the African locations, so as to achieve a consistent "look" in the lighting and appearance of the jungle backgrounds. It sounded good, but Paul Huston pointed out the impracticality of building and shooting miniatures on location and the work was finally done in

On location in Africa's Ivory Coast, director B. W. L. Norton sets up a shot with the star of *Baby*.

Mechanical FX maestro Isidoro "Izzy" Raponi takes a needed break atop the life-size Brontosaurus dubbed "Big Mama."

the controlled environs of a California studio.

The location shoot in Africa turned out to be far more difficult and demanding than anyone had foreseen. Trying to wrangle and maintain an assortment of temperamental mechanical dinosaurs, while staying on schedule in a jungle wilderness half a world away from studio support, was a bronto-sized headache. An endless stream of problems— almost-daily script changes, a revolving door of personnel, communication breakdowns, supply shortages, electrical power outages, various tropical fevers, the occasional poisonous green mamba — plagued the production. But Jonathan Taplin said he wouldn't have had it any other way. "It was definitely worth it," he summed up. "We couldn't have made *Baby* on a Hollywood lot."

SPECIAL EFFECTS: A number of special effects luminaries were consulted while deciding how to best realize the dinosaurian stars, including Disney veteran Harrison Ellenshaw, motion-control expert John Scheele, and stop-motion ace Jim Danforth. "I was involved in some early discussions," Danforth told the author, this despite the fact that the producers never for a moment considered using stop-motion and at the time had no idea *what* they wanted. Still, Danforth agreed to a meeting with a member of Tom Wilhite's staff. "I proposed that I do a series of design sketches and maquettes of 'Baby' and his parents, and leave it to them to figure out how to bring the characters to life," Danforth recalled. The staffer agreed and Danforth was busy working up a price for the job when "they called me to say that they had a Tim Burton disciple, Rick Heinrichs, who could do this and that they didn't need me."

Scheele, having recently worked on Disney's *Tron*, was himself destined to leave *Baby* after only three months, but along with his father, William (longtime director of the

Cleveland Museum of Natural History), did contribute to the dinosaurs' reality-based look. Based on the Scheeles' suggestions, dino-sculptor James Kagel amended his original design to make it a bit "cuter," and some artistic license was necessarily taken. The nostrils were moved from their actual top-of-the-head position to the more familiar end-of-snout location so that Baby could accomplish his required sniffing, and the feet were modeled after elephants rather than sauropods to make it easier for the dino-performers to walk. One big point of contention was the look of the eyes, and as the on-screen evidence shows, a successful design was never achieved.

With stop-motion and full animatronics ruled out, a consensus was reached — though with considerable reservations — to go with a dinosaur suit/cable-controlled hybrid. The man primarily charged with making the scheme work was mechanical and creature effects veteran Isidoro Raponi, longtime associate of creature-maker Carlo Rambaldi and alumnus of *Close Encounters of the Third Kind*, *E. T.*, and *Alien*. "We did a lot of research with the experts in dinosaurs — all the information about the length, the height, what kinds of food they were eating," Raponi said on TV's *Movie Magic*. Then, based on the information, "we decided what kind of dinosaur we wanted to build. The back and front legs were [operated by a] human inside; all the rest was cable-controlled or radio-controlled." Raponi's design for Baby's facial articulations provided up to two dozen cable-actuated movements, including the lips and mouth, eyes, eyelids and eyebrows, and nostrils. Controlled by as many as five operators, the complex mechanism endowed Baby with more than a dozen distinct facial expressions.

The suits consisted of a skeleton of fiberglass (chosen for its strength and light weight), urethane foam "muscles," a latex foam "inner skin," and an outer skin of pigmented rubber cement base. Almost $12,000 worth of latex alone went into making the dinosaurs. After manufacture at Disney in California, the dino components were shipped to the Ivory Coast to be assembled at one of the "dino-bases" on location. "The most difficult thing about *Baby* is the shape," Raponi pointed out in *American Cinematographer*. "The support for the animal is horizontal. Normally when I have made supports for creatures it has been vertical." Over 150 people auditioned as dino-performers, from whom Terri Girvin, Richard Aguirre, and Paula Crist were chosen. Crist had some helpful previous experience, having portrayed one of the simian stars in *Planet of the Apes*. The dino suits were carefully designed to strike a balance between looking authentic and not being excessively torturous on the human performer. Arm extensions were employed to make the front legs long enough, and backplates were custom-designed for each dino person to help with balance and hopefully reduce fatigue. Portraying a bronto was not a pleasant job — besides the muscle strain and claustrophobic isolation, the temperature inside the suit often soared to 140 degrees. "It was important that we got used to being on all fours, and that our muscles were well-toned for this particular type of activity," Paula Crist explained in *Cinefex*. "Every maneuver Baby made stressed different muscles in different ways." Due to the heat, discomfort, and effective blindness, stints inside the suit were limited to about 45 minutes.

There were seven specialized versions of Baby, ranging from the lightweight "running" suit to the heavily cabled, fully articulated model. Quarter-scale "miniature" adults were built to represent the mama and papa. They each measured about 15 feet in length and were given movement, like Baby, by a human performer inside. These were shot with high-speed cameras on quarter-scale sets, or blue-screened into background plates to give the illusion of enormity. There was also "Big Mama," a full-scale, 60-foot-long, minimally articulated version built for the scenes of the tranquilized female on the raft. (The sight during filming of a realistic, 60-foot "captured" dinosaur, floating along a real river in the heart of the Ivory Coast jungle, doubtless caused a few double takes.) Lastly, some full-scale sections of the adult animals were constructed for certain shots. These included a 12-foot head and neck for the mama, a 17-foot head and neck for the papa, and a 21-foot unisex tail, all articulated through a hydraulic/mechanical system designed by effects supervisor Roland "Ron" Tantin. A final touch was a "voice" for Baby created by Mark Mangini and George Budd using more than 20 different real animal sounds — including that of an "asthmatic cat."

With the headaches all behind them, Baby's creators were realistic when summing up their efforts. "If I had to do it over again," Raponi said, "I would build Baby in the same basic way — but I wouldn't do it at all unless there was enough time to refine everything and make adjustments." Director Norton also lamented the lack of precious time. "We learned as we went — but, unfortunately, we really had very little time for that."

Barney's Great Adventure

"I'm as real as your imagination!"

**½ 1998, USA. Polygram. C, 76m.

CREDITS: *Director* Steve Gomer. *Producers* Sheryl Leach, Dennis DeShazer; Jim Rowley (co-producer); Ben Myron (executive); Martha Chang (co-executive). *Story* Stephen White, Sheryl Leach, Dennis DeShazer. *Screenplay* Stephen White. *Visual Effects Supervisor* Max Anderson.
CAST: *Abby* Diana Rice. *Marcella* Kyla Pratt. *Cody* Trevor Morgan. *Grandma* Shirley Douglas. *Grandpa* George Hearn. *Barney* (voice) Bob West. *Barney* (body) David Joyner.

Young Abby, her mom and dad, her best friend, Marcella, and her big brother Cody pay a visit to her grandparents' farm. Abby and Marcella love their Barney doll and still believe in the power of imagination, but Cody thinks he's too grown up for such "kid stuff." But when the "real" Barney appears and shows Cody a Wishing Star, the boy wishes for an adventure unlike any before. His odyssey begins when the Wishing Star falls to earth and transforms into a magical egg. Trying to protect the egg, Barney and the three kids... Well, as they explain it to their grandparents: "We took that egg over to Miss Goldfinch, the bird lady, and her book said that it was a Dreammaker and that we needed to bring it back to the farm, only it took a ride on a truck, and then Barney helped us chase it but it rolled under a parade, so we went to a French restaurant, but at the circus the egg got tied to a balloon, so we made this log into an airplane..." (You get the picture.) Finally, a furry little troll named Twinkin hatches out, and helps Barney realize that his dream is sharing special times with the people he loves.

COMMENTARY: The favorite dinosaur of the 5-and-under contingent made his big-screen debut in this lively, colorful, gentle outing. Kids enjoyed it (my 2-year-old cousin's favorite part was the hot-air balloon rally), and, Barney jokes aside, it is surprisingly palatable for grown-ups. It keeps moving but isn't noisy, the three kid actors are likable, and the musical numbers are staged much "bigger" than those on the television show (Barney even gets to do a little scat singing!). Sidekicks B. J. and Baby Bop make a few unnecessary appearances, probably because the filmmakers figured that kids would be expecting to see them, but there are also a few tidbits thrown in for the adults. The script even takes a self-mocking jab at the Barney phenomenon. "Barney isn't just a little doll, he's very big!" Cody says, trying to convince his grandpa that the stuffed doll has come to life. "Oh, sure, he's big now, but you just wait," Gramps replies; "these fads come and go." Barney's Bullwinkle Moose-meets–Richard Simmons persona may grate on some folks, but kids love him, and adding a bit of gentleness and affection to a child's day is an accomplishment not without merit.

The Beast from 20,000 Fathoms

*"There is a monster, and
I think I can convince you!"*

***½ 1953, USA. Warner Bros. BW, 80m.

CREDITS: *Director* Eugène Lourié. *Producers* Hal Chester, Jack Dietz, Bernard W. Burton (associate). *Written by* Lou Morheim, Fred Freiberger; suggested by the *Saturday Evening Post* story by Ray Bradbury. *Technical Effects Created by* Ray Harryhausen. *Special Effects* Willis Cook.
CAST: *Prof. Thomas Nesbitt* Paul Christian. *Lee Hunter* Paula Raymond. *Prof. Thurgood Elson* Cecil Kellaway. *Col. John Evans* Kenneth Tobey. *Jacob Bowman* Jack Pennick. *Prof. George Ritchie* Ross Elliott.

AD LINE: "They couldn't believe their eyes! They couldn't escape the terror! And neither will *you*!"

At a remote Arctic outpost, Professor Thomas Nesbitt of the Atomic Energy Commission and military liaison Colonel John "Jack" Evans observe a huge nuclear test detonation which melts tons of ancient polar ice. Nesbitt and fellow scientist George Ritchie later catch a glimpse of a giant creature through the blowing snow, just before Ritchie is killed in an avalanche triggered by the weight of the beast. As the injured Nesbitt is evacuated to the States, the creature crosses the path of the fishing ketch *Fortune* out in the icy North Atlantic. The ruthless attack leaves only helmsman Jacob Bowman alive.

Back in New York, Nesbitt visits paleontologist Dr. Thurgood Elson in an effort to find someone who believes his story. Nesbitt proposes the theory that a prehistoric animal, frozen since the Mesozoic Era, could have been revived by the heat and energy of the atomic bomb. The notion intrigues Elson's attractive female assistant, Lee Hunter, but Elson dismisses the tale as pure fantasy. At Miss Hunter's urging, Nesbitt looks through sketches of all known prehistoric animals and picks out the one he saw. Hoping that Elson might be swayed if two independent observers identified the same creature, Nesbitt persuades *Fortune* survivor Jacob Bowman to accompany him to the university. When Bowman selects the same sketch—the fierce-looking four-legged carnivore "Rhedosaurus"—Elson convinces Col. Evans to investigate. A pattern of destruction is revealed, and Elson deduces that the beast is following the Arctic current southward towards its ancestral breeding grounds in the submerged Hudson River canyons. While the increasingly romantic Nesbitt and Miss Hunter wait topside, a delighted Elson spots the primordial survivor from a diving bell only to tragically become its next victim.

The rhedosaurus soon comes ashore and begins a panic-inducing rampage through New York City. The military's weapons inflict only minor wounds, and the slight injury they do cause reveals that the animal's blood carries a deadly, unknown disease. Nesbitt concludes that the only safe option is to use a radioactive isotope to destroy the contaminated tissues, and when the rhedosaurus is spotted within the tracks of a giant roller coaster at Manhattan Beach, the plan is initiated. From a vantage point aboard one of the coaster's cars, and knowing he has only one chance, crack marksman Corporal Stone coolly fires the deadly isotope grenade into the beast's existing wound.

COMMENTARY: The early moments of *The Beast from 20,000 Fathoms* are not promising. The overwrought narration laid over the documentary stock footage which opens the film foreshadows a typical 1950s B-monster flick (*King Dinosaur*, anyone?). However, to give up at this point would be a tragic mistake. Once the narrator shuts up and the movie gets rolling, *Beast* displays virtues totally unexpected given its truly humble pedigree.

It is unfortunately true that "monster movies" are often by-the-numbers pictures, directed in by-the-numbers fashion. But Eugène Lourié was not your average monster movie director, and his extensive background as a production designer and art director served him very well in his directorial efforts. If *Beast* looks like it costs more than its measly $200,000 — which it does — a huge chunk of the credit is due to Lourié. "In designing this film, I always had our limited budget in mind," Lourié wrote in *My Work in Films*, "but I was determined not to think 'small.'" *Beast* is rife with details — little bits of business that add texture and that are just not found in a typical low-budget monster opus: bits like the banter between the doomed lighthouse keepers, or the brief "leprechaun story" that Dr. Elson reads to Miss Hunter, or the empiricism debate between Elson and Nesbitt. Lourié's fundamental approach to fantastic subject matter resulted in films that were as credible as such tales can be. "In this kind of science fiction story," Lourié explained, "I felt only one fact was deliberately fictitious: the survival of a dinosaur after millions of years. From then on we had to develop the story in very realistic, everyday surroundings." This philosophy is evident in all of Lourié's dinosaur-themed films, and helps elevate all three to the upper levels of the dinomovie pack.

Adhering to this "realistic, everyday" approach, Lourié ingeniously uses the persistent, logic-based skepticism voiced by Dr. Elson and Colonel Evans to help sell the premise. When Elson mutters, almost to himself, "a Mesozoic animal alive today ... I could lose my job and my reputation listening to such nonsense," the audience is thinking the same thing. Colonel Evans, telling his Coast Guard chum about the creature, realizes how wild it sounds and warns, "if you laugh, I'll brain you." But then, finally, when Elson and Evans are at last convinced, so are we. This makes for a much more believable story than that offered in countless other creature features of the fifties, wherein everyone accepts the most outlandish of tales immediately and without question. (Perhaps the all-time best, or worst, example of this flaw is found in 1958's infamous *Attack of the 50 Foot Woman*, when the local deputy is first told about the reports of a gigantic human and responds, "A 30-foot giant? Ohh, no!") In *Beast*, the viewer is actually sold on the notion that, as the film's coming attraction trailer says, "it could happen!"

The performances are another strength, due equally to some excellent casting choices and Lourié's success in preventing the scenery-chewing which is so prevalent in other genre films of the period. The atypical cast is one of the better ensembles ever gathered for this type of film, with Paul Christian and Cecil Kellaway standing out. Christian's discernible accent and continental manner are refreshing changes from the generic all–American heroes of so many monster flicks, and Kellaway's turn as the grandfatherly Dr. Elson is one of the most entertaining supporting performances ever seen in a dinosaur film. In another movie, Elson might have been played by, say, Whit Bissell or John Hoyt, and either of those fine character actors would have done a solid, professional job. But Kellaway's twinkling eyes and gentle humor make one really care about the character, and that's practically unheard of in a B-monster movie. Kenneth Tobey is his dependable, assured self, and Paula Raymond has a quiet strength that is very appealing. The script, rather than serving up the usual hackneyed collection of cautionary scientists, blood-and-guts soldiers, and decorative females, instead offers recognizable and interesting characters with fairly well-drawn personalities. As Lourié put it, "by being believably real, the humans lend credibility to the beast." Equipped with its gifted director, skillful cast, and sober script, all *Beast* needed was a top-notch monster, and they had the right man to furnish one.

Beast marked Ray Harryhausen's first time in charge of the visual effects for a feature film, but his talent had already been honed by his own experimentation and his priceless experience on *Mighty Joe Young* (1949). Harryhausen knew that, on a Mutual Films budget, the time-consuming, labor-intensive techniques used so well by Willis O'Brien were out of the question. As Harryhausen explained to the author, "*Mighty Joe* got a reputation of being terribly expensive, for its day. We had three glass painting

Nice photographic study of Ray Harryhausen's fictional yet never implausible "Rhedosaurus" puppet, built by Ray himself.

artists, who were very expensive, and then you had to have a whole bunch of other people. So, I was trying to devise a simpler way of creating the illusion that these animated creatures were in the city." The evidence of his success is right up there on the screen. This modest little movie can boast a number of knockout set pieces, including the sinking of the fishing ketch, the lighthouse attack (the one scene which recalls Ray Bradbury's story), and the climactic showdown at the roller coaster. Harryhausen's rhedosaurus is a wonderful creation with a ruthlessly vicious look, and actually predates Godzilla as moviedom's first atom-spawned monster. (It's widely accepted, in fact, that *Godzilla* was at least partially inspired by *Beast*.) In what would become a Harryhausen trademark in years to come, the stop-motion creature is slickly and cleverly composited with the live footage. No other picture in the entire monster-infested decade of the 1950s, with the possible exception of Harryhausen's own later efforts, can top *Beast*'s special effects.

The Beast from 20,000 Fathoms is often applauded for its "dark" mood, and the careful use of lighting to heighten the sense of foreboding is found in all of Lourié's pictures. The two major animation sequences prior to the beast's arrival in New York demonstrate how important lighting truly is to the success of a miniature or special-effect scene. During the assault on the fishing boat, the "moonlight" is perfectly matched between the animation model and the oceanic background plate. Likewise, the lighthouse sequence is a masterpiece of silhouettes and shadows. All of Harryhausen's work is characterized by an uncanny talent for using light effectively (witness the ultra-creepy Medusa sequence in *Clash of the Titans*) and *Beast* is no exception. The atmospheric lighting is successfully extended to the live action, credit for which is due head cameraman Jack Russell, according to Lourié. "A no-nonsense technician," Lourié called Russell, "who created the moody realistic lighting throughout the picture." The lighting works hand in hand with the carefully paced, understated

Jacob Bowman (Jack Pennick) and Professor Nesbitt (Paul Christian) confer with Lee Hunter (Paula Raymond) and Professor Elson (Cecil Kellaway) at the museum. The full-size dino skeleton from *Bringing Up Baby* is in the background.

script and Harryhausen's artful animation to create the film's unique feel, and it is this feel more than any other factor which is responsible for *Beast*'s "classic" status. This unpretentious little picture is what every "monster movie" wants to be, but few are. It is straightforward yet with enhancing details, fast-paced yet not frenetically so, and takes the care to offer convincing human characters alongside its marvelous, melodramatic monster.

PEOPLE AND PRODUCTION: The posters and opening credits of *The Beast from 20,000 Fathoms* state that the film was "suggested by the *Saturday Evening Post* story by Ray Bradbury." However, the whole process of how the screenplay evolved, and just how Bradbury's short story fits into the picture, has been the subject of conflicting accounts and fading recollections. Although the exact history will probably never be deciphered, looking at all the evidence permits the construction of a tentative chronology.

In 1951, film producers Hal E. Chester and Jack Dietz operated a modest production company called Mutual Films, and had plans to produce three low-budget pictures for independent distribution. One of them — the only one which would ever be made — dealt with a prehistoric creature roused from eons of hibernation by an atomic blast. The story, which was at this time merely a rough outline, was called *The Monster from Beneath the Sea*.

That same year, in the June 23 issue of *The Saturday Evening Post*, there appeared a short story by noted science-fiction author Ray Bradbury. Titled "The Beast from 20,000 Fathoms," it told a poetic, even tragic tale of a dinosaurian survivor drawn to a remote lighthouse by the call of the foghorn. Mistaking the sound for the cry of another of its kind, it destroys the lighthouse in fury and disappointment, and returns to the sea. Accompanying the story was a striking illustration by James R. Bingham.

Exactly what happened from here on, and when, is unclear. In the "early spring" of 1952, Dietz and Chester contacted art director–production designer Eugène Lourié with an offer to direct their monster picture—Lourié's first directorial effort. In *My Work in Films* Lourié stated that, working with another writer, he "started to construct a story line showing live characters and action." They then "ran across" the story in the *Post*, and due to Bradbury's sizable following, they bought the rights to the story and added the lighthouse scenario to their screenplay. "Jack Dietz believed it would be advantageous to add his name to the main titles," Lourié explained.

However, Bradbury himself remembers it a bit differently. In Ted Newsom's article on Harryhausen's career in *Cinefantastique* magazine, Bradbury recalls being asked by Chester to read the *Monster from Beneath the Sea* script, with an eye toward possibly doing some rewriting. Once Bradbury read it and pointed out the similarities to his short story, the producers immediately took measures to acquire the rights (for a sum of $2,000). But obfuscating the history even more is the account reported by author Bill Warren in *Keep Watching the Skies!*, in which it was a screening of the finished film rather than a reading of the preliminary script that allowed Bradbury to note the resemblance.

As for Harryhausen, he is quick to admit that it is probably impossible to ever completely sort out what happened. In a *Filmfax* interview he said, "so many rumors have gotten out about it, I don't know which ones to believe." However, he did tell this author that the film's story could not have been inspired *entirely* by Bradbury's tale, since the early, fragmentary *Monster from Beneath the Sea* outline existed in embryonic form prior to the *Post* story's publication. "He [Dietz] already had a script when I came on the project," Harryhausen said. "It was just an outline when I read it; there was not even a concept of what the Beast looked like." Harryhausen also reiterated that the illustration in the *Post*, of the creature attacking the lighthouse, made a big impression on Jack Dietz, "and that's why Dietz wanted to buy the rights." At any rate, the producers trumpeted the *Post* connection when promoting the film, and the coming attractions trailer promised "The importance and impact of the *Saturday Evening Post* thriller that held millions spellbound!"

The screenplay's final form is a combined work. Certainly the original outline (possibly conceived by Chester) was fleshed out by director Lourié and his unnamed collaborator. The credited writers, Lou Morheim and Fred Freiberger, undoubtedly contributed as well; Lourié stated that they were asked to "polish the script and provide the dialogue." The movie retains the central image of Bradbury's story (minus the foghorn), and Harryhausen himself, mindful of the impact of *King Kong*'s "big finish," suggested the idea of the roller coaster climax. Though it's unlikely that it actually served as inspiration, an interesting *Beast* precursor was the 1942 Max Fleischer "Superman" cartoon, *The Arctic Giant*, in which an ancient frozen dinosaur thaws out and wreaks havoc on Metropolis!

Even though his is a supporting role, *Beast* benefits greatly from the presence of legendary monster fighter Kenneth Tobey. "I suppose they got me for *Beast from 20,000 Fathoms* because of *The Thing*," Tobey told Ted Newsom in *Filmfax*. "It starts out the same, up in the arctic. It was a very short shoot, compared to *The Thing* just a couple years earlier." Some of the naturalistic feel of the film can be credited to Tobey. "We've got

It is well-known that Ray Harryhausen's careful planning left very, very little of his animation work on the cutting room floor. What then to make of the five-second animation shot of the Rhedosaurus — seen nowhere in *Beast*— which turned up four years later in the preview trailer for *The Black Scorpion*?

a lot of dialogue up there in the arctic scenes where it's overlapping. That's my contribution. I think it helps the atmosphere, that's how you talk on stage." The actor has fond memories of the tightly knit *Beast* company, as he mentioned to Tom Weaver in a *Starlog* interview. "Paul Christian was the star and the girl was Paula Raymond, who became a friend of mine later," Tobey recalled. "[Eugène Lourié] was a designer of special effects and art direction and things like that, an extremely talented man. I also met Ray Harryhausen on *Beast*, and I'm very, very proud of that moment. He was extremely witty and very well-trained in his profession. I enjoyed that whole picture very much."

Made for $210,000, *Beast* was sold by producers Jack Dietz and Hal Chester to Warner Bros. for $450,000 — a move that they severely second-guessed when it grossed more than $5 million in its first run. Warners made only a few changes, inserting the brief stock-footage ballet sequence and replacing Michel Michelet's original music with a new, "bigger" score by David Buttolph. Even though Lourié at times referred to *Beast* as an "albatross" hanging about his neck, he wrote in his autobiography that directing the film "was a wonderful experience for me." He had mixed feelings about the finished product, but for the most part maintained a favorable view. "Overall, I felt that the picture did not fail us," he wrote. "The action moved forward, the story progressed, the tempo was never lost. Moreover, I think the picture had a specific tone of its own." In his book, Lourié related a brief story of taking the famous French film director Jean Renoir to a screening of *Beast*. "Renoir reacted just like the youngsters surrounding us," Lourié remembered. "'*Eh bien, mon vieux*,' he said. 'You surely had a wonderful time making this film.'"

SPECIAL EFFECTS: After being hired as director, Eugène Lourié had to select a technique to bring the *Beast* to life. His decision may have been swayed by his fond memories of some early animation films, including the work of the pioneering animator Ladislas Starevitch. "After a quick review of the different methods at our disposal, we decided that ... frame-by-frame animation was the most practical technique for us," Lourié stated. Hal Chester told Lourié about a young man who had worked with the legendary Willis O'Brien on *Mighty Joe Young*, and who could probably be hired for considerably less money. Lourié visited Ray Harryhausen's workshop and immediately decided that he was the right choice. "I felt that Ray would do a good job and be a valuable partner in our project," said Lourié. Willis Cook, veteran of such diverse projects as Fritz Lang's *The Blue Gardenia* (1953) and the famous stinker *Cat-Women of the Moon* (1953), was tabbed to handle the on-set "physical" effects.

Most of *Beast* was filmed within rented soundstages at the Motion Picture Center studios in Hollywood. The Arctic "snow set" took up all of the Center's largest stage. Keeping his promise to himself not to think small, Lourié wanted a full-size dinosaur skeleton to jazz up the museum set. So, his crew dusted off the papier-mâché bones created for RKO's *Bringing Up Baby* (1938) and he had his skeleton, at near-zero cost. "It took many days for my assistant and ingenious prop people to find which bones connected with each other," Lourié recalled. (No word on whether they found the elusive intercostal clavicle that caused Cary Grant so much grief.)

The entire live-action shoot took only twelve days. This included nine days of shooting at the Motion Picture Center, two nights at a Long Beach amusement park for the roller coaster sequence, and one day on the New York City street set at Paramount Studios. There was also a two-day trip to the real New York City to shoot background plates for the animation and a few location crowd scenes. Given the amount and complexity of the animation, Harryhausen's schedule was short as well — he had only "six or seven months" to complete the work.

Unlike most directors, especially first-timers, Lourié appreciated the special de-

The Beast from 20,000 Fathoms (actually a depth of *22.7 miles!*) invades an excellent miniature New York cityscape.

mands of incorporating animation with live action and designed his shots accordingly. "Only after choosing the New York locations could I decide how and where the beast would be placed in each shot," Lourié explained. "Sometimes while shooting I would make a quick thumbnail sketch to indicate where in the shot the beast had to be placed." Later, he would make photographic enlargements of shots into which he planned to add the creature, then trace the beast's proposed location. "These tracings went to Ray for his evaluation, and he often improved my ideas with his acrobatically clever animations," Lourié recalled.

Lourié and Harryhausen also worked together creating the climactic amusement park sequence. "After the principal photography was completed, I had some more miniatures to build and shoot," said Lourié.

"One of these was the roller coaster.... I worked with Ray, planning and shooting this sequence." The coaster miniature was precut, covered with rubber cement so as to burn nicely, and pulled apart with invisible wires. Harryhausen then choreographed his animation so that the rhedosaurus seemed to be tearing the structure to pieces. Interaction was further suggested by placing miniature chunks of coaster in the puppet's mouth.

The simplified split-screen effects technique which Harryhausen created for *Beast*, accomplished "in camera" and often needing no postproduction optical work, would be used by the animator for the rest of his career. Genre fans of the world would come to know this technique as "Dynamation." It worked something like this. The stop-motion animal is positioned in front of a rear projection screen and visually lined up with the desired area of the projected background image. A sheet of glass is placed between the animation setup and the camera, allowing both the surface on which the animal rests and a portion of the projected image to be matted out with black areas applied to the glass. Then the actual stop-motion photography is executed, with the jointed puppet and the rear-projected footage both advanced one frame at a time. Next, both the camera film and the rear-projected film are wound back, a negative matte is put in place to prevent double-exposure of the stop-motion element, and the unexposed areas of the scene are exposed in. The animated creature could even be made to appear "behind" objects like buildings or hills by simply matting out areas for the objects and then exposing them *after* the stop-motion elements. The method was ingeniously simple and, in Ray's hands, remarkably effective. "Dynamation," and its later incarnations, "Super-Dynamation" and "Dynarama," would serve the artisan well for nearly 30 more years of fantastical filmmaking.

Harryhausen created *Beast*'s animation effects using a special rear-screen process projector which had been built for another stop-motion fantasy a few years earlier. "That was part of the equipment on *Mighty Joe*," Harryhausen revealed, referring of course to RKO's *Mighty Joe Young*. "Harry Cunningham built four of them for *Mighty Joe*," Ray continued; "he was a specialist in that type of thing." When it came time to construct the rhedosaurus armature, Harryhausen didn't have to look far for help. His father, Fred, was a skilled machinist who had previously helped build sets and models for Ray's early 16mm fairy tales. "I designed the armature and he built it on the lathe — the joints," Ray recalled. "He also built the flying saucers for *Earth vs. the Flying Saucers*." All the build-up and texturing of the puppet was done by Harryhausen himself, a luxury he didn't have time for on many of his later pictures. "Sometimes I had to have the studio people do the sculpture, because it takes so much time to put all the detail on dinosaurs," he explained, "so I had to farm that type of thing out." The rhedosaurus fell victim to the monetary realities of low-budget filmmaking and suffered the same fate as many stop-motion armatures — it was cannibalized for parts. "I think parts of it went in the dragon for [*The 7th Voyage of*] *Sinbad*," said Harryhausen.

Every rhedosaurus shot in the film is stop-motion animation, with two exceptions — the brief shots of the beast's head as seen through the watery windows of the fishing ketch and the lighthouse, utilized a detailed hand puppet. Many people insist on believing that the name "rhedosaurus" was derived from its creator's initials, but Harryhausen told me that it was almost certainly just a coincidence. "Maybe it did, I don't know," he said. "But somebody else dreamt up the name; I didn't."

The creature's look was largely dictated by the demands of the script, and a conventional sauropod design was quickly ruled out. "We didn't want to make the beast a Brontosaurus," Harryhausen explained in a *Castle of Frankenstein* interview, "because it was too familiar a prehistoric animal and would instantly make the audience think of *The Lost World*." The standard, two-legged, allosaur/tyrannosaur design was also out of the question, due to the creature's aquatic proclivities. "I realized you had to have it so that it would be more like an amphibian," Harryhausen said, "so I gave it four legs, and the body took on a different structure than the known dinosaurs." The final design, incorporating a Tyrannosaurus-inspired head, a scaly, almost armored-looking body, and a sprawling reptilian stance, resulted in an original and effective movie villain.

The early 1950s saw Hollywood's brief fling with "3-D," and although there were no plans to shoot *Beast* in three-dimensions, Harryhausen did do some experimentation following the film's completion. The rhedosaurus model was, in fact, used for his 3-D tests. There was talk of using 3-D for Harryhausen's next project but the idea was abandoned, and fortunately so, according to Ray. "Although visually the test proved it could work with rear projection, for an animated picture it was very impractical," he said. He estimated that production of such a film could take "as much as three times" longer than that of a normal Dynamation film.

The Beast of Hollow Mountain

(a.k.a. *El Monstruo de la Montaña Hueca*)

"Why don't we start the stampede now and get it over with?"

**½ 1956, USA/Mexico. Nassour Studios/United Artists. C, 81m.

CREDITS: *Directors* Edward Nassour and Ismael Rodriguez. *Producers* William and Edward Nassour; coproduced with Peliculas Rodriguez-S. A. *Screenplay* Robert Hill. *Additional Dialogue* Jack DeWitt. *From an Idea by* Willis O'Brien. *Photographic Effects* Jack Rabin and Louis DeWitt.

CAST: *Jimmy Ryan* Guy Madison. *Sarita* Patricia Medina. *Felipe Sanchez* Carlos Rivas. *Enrique Rios* Edward Noriega. *Don Pedro* Julio Villarreal. *Panchito* Mario Navarro. *Pancho* Pascuel Garcia Pena. *Margarita* Lupe Carriles.

AD LINE: "One day after a million years it came out of hiding to ... kill! Kill! KILL!"

Deep within the wilds of Mexico looms the legendary Hollow Mountain. The locals say it harbors a fearsome beast "from the dawn of creation," which emerges from the surrounding swamps only during severe droughts. Near the mountain sprawls the Rancho Bonito cattle ranch, owned by American Jimmy Ryan and his Mexican partner and friend, Felipe Sanchez. Though some blame the cursed mountain, Jimmy suspects that their disappearing cattle are being rustled by his sinister rival, cattle baron Enrique Rios. The influential Rios is engaged to marry the lovely Sarita, daughter of the respected Don Pedro, even though her true feelings are for Jimmy. When Rios drives off Jimmy's ranch hands, he and Felipe are left with only 7-year-old Panchito and his widowed, oft-inebriated father Pancho to help run things. The romantic triangle also escalates when Sarita secretly urges Jimmy to leave, fearing that if her two suitors remain in conflict she will become either "a widow or the wife of a murderer." Jimmy considers Sarita's words and decides to sell the herd, split the profits with Felipe and move on. But suddenly little Panchito delivers alarming news: his "Pa-Pa" has gone off toward Hollow Mountain and has not come back. Jimmy and Felipe ride out in a desperate search, but find only a sombrero.

The day of the wedding arrives, but despite his apparent victory, the ever-scheming Rios is not content and plots to stampede Jimmy's herd. At the same time, Panchito sneaks off toward the swamps in search of his father, and Sarita rides off after him. Suddenly, the legendary Beast of Hollow Mountain appears and sets off a massive cattle stampede. The monster traps Sarita and Panchito in an old cabin, but Jimmy manages to get the woman and child out of harm's way. Jimmy chivalrously tries to help Rios as well, but the tiny cave in which they take shelter offers no protection for the doomed villain. After some townsfolk temporarily drive the beast away, Jimmy hits upon a plan. He lassos an overhanging branch and swings out over the swamp, using his own body as bait for the trap. The dinosaur, his tiny brain unable to register anything but the sight of prey, can't resist the temptation and wades haplessly into the deadly bog. Jimmy and Sarita embrace as the ancient creature sinks into its murky grave.

COMMENTARY: Some 13 years before dinosaurs and cowboys shared the screen in *The Valley of Gwangi*, Nassour Studios bought the rights to another Willis O'Brien story and gave moviegoers this very first "dino-western." Unlike *Gwangi*, however, which teemed with all sorts of prehistoric fauna, *Beast of Hollow Mountain*'s lone Allosaurus doesn't show up until the final reel. Up until then the film could be mistaken for a typical "B" western, and a mundane one at that.

In his entertaining survey of the dinosaur genre, *Hot-Blooded Dinosaur Movies*, author James Van Hise fondly reminisces about watching this movie on television, with no prior knowledge of the dinosaur in the climax. "As a kid I can still remember staying up to watch this on the late show and almost falling asleep until suddenly, there's a dinosaur!" he recalled. "No one can sleep through this monster's rampage." His story made me wish I could have also seen it with the surprise intact, but I already knew the dinosaur would appear as will most everyone who watches it from now on. Without the surprise of a prehistoric creature suddenly invading a seemingly routine oater, the movie itself is not especially memorable.

The situations and characters have all been seen in countless westerns going back to the silent era, and almost no B-western cliché is left unused. There is the prominent citizen who's actually the bad guy, a woman torn between the hero and the villain, a wild fistfight which turns over a number of produce stands, a cattle stampede, and a lot of dialogue like "start thinkin' with your head instead of your gun!" The acting ensemble is average at best. Guy Madison has a nice laid-back cowpoke persona and even does a fair approximation of John Wayne's trademark walk. Patricia Medina is adequate, Carlos Rivas is wooden, and Eduardo Noriega is astoundingly wooden for a villain. The film's strengths include the craggy, unspoiled shooting locations, as well as cinematographer Jorge Stahl's skillful use of them. A big weakness is Raul Lavista's generic and unremarkable music score, which pales in comparison to the sweeping *Gwangi* themes of Jerome Moross.

Even though the trumpeted "Regiscope process" was only advertising blather, there are some unusual animation effects. While the closeups of the beast were done through conventional stop-motion, the wide shots of the dinosaur walking and running were accomplished using a technique known as "replacement animation." In this process, multiple models are constructed, each in a slightly different pose. Instead of incrementally moving a jointed armature as in regular stop-motion, the entire figure is "replaced" with the next figure in the sequence for each frame. The technique can be very effective, and the *Hollow Mountain* replacement animation provides the best dinosaur shots in the film, but even in 1956 there was nothing groundbreaking about it. The method had in fact been George Pal's choice for his famous "Puppetoons" some fifteen years earlier.

While the replacement animation sequences are successful and enjoyable, the "armatured" stop-motion work doesn't come off as well. As Don Shay pointed out in *Cinefex*, "the effectiveness of the running scenes made the slipshod conventional stop-motion in the rest of the film look that much the worse by comparison." The movement is simply nowhere near as fluid or as dynamic as Obie or Ray Harryhausen would have undoubtedly provided. The long, perpetually wagging tongue certainly doesn't help, nor do the cheap prop dino feet used for some ill-advised insert shots. Unlike the titular stars of *The Beast from 20,000 Fathoms* or *The Valley of Gwangi*, the *Hollow Mountain* creature is neither featured prominently enough nor animated expertly enough to develop much character, though S. S. Wilson offers a differing opinion in *Puppets and People*. "Far less purposeful than the average monster, the Tyrannosaurus is rather refreshingly stupid," Wilson asserts. "It pursues first one person, then another, being easily distracted by shouts and gunfire, and it even responds to minor wounds, pausing in seeming consternation."

The animation–live-action composites are mostly inferior. There are exceptions, including one dazzler of a shot showing Jimmy and Enrique fleeing on horseback as the dinosaur gives chase, but by and large the rear-projected elements are grainy, pale, and even out of focus. The Beast's demise is admittedly original and probably more plausible than the fates of some other movie monsters, but wading into a mudhole and

A tiny, articulated stop-motion puppet doubles for villainous Enrique Rios (Edward Noriega) in the "bad guy's demise" scene from *The Beast of Hollow Mountain*.

sinking out of sight is just not terrifically *cinematic*. After the viewer endures the dull cowboy story for an hour, and is rewarded as the monster finally brings the movie to life, the climax seems anything but climactic.

Ultimately, *The Beast of Hollow Mountain* is memorable only for its peculiarities and "firsts." The sheer oddity of its structure — standard horse opera for an hour followed by a 20-minute dinosaur movie — makes it unique in genre history. It was the first stop-motion dino picture in Cinema-Scope, the first to employ replacement animation, and, other than Czech filmmaker Karel Zeman's *Cesta do praveku*, the first in color. Unfortunately, its distinctions are not enough to fully offset its limitations. The story is too familiar, the characters too dull, and the monster too late to raise *The Beast of Hollow Mountain* out of the middle of the dinosaur movie pack.

PEOPLE AND PRODUCTION: Willis O'Brien conceived and wrote stories for many films over his career, almost none of which ever reached fruition. In the mid–1950s, he penned *The Beast of Hollow Mountain*, a film treatment about a giant lizard and pair of competing ranchers. Details of O'Brien's original scenario (which underwent massive changes before filming) are revealed in Don Shay's exhaustive O'Brien career retrospective in *Cinefex* magazine. In Obie's story, cattleman Hank Oliver is found murdered and his rival, Jim Larkin, immediately becomes suspect number one. Larkin's wild-sounding stories of a giant reptile fall on deaf ears, and his swift and unjust punishment is prevented only by the arrival of stalwart Sheriff Dean Roberts and his Native American companion, John Longtooth. Roberts, Larkin, and Longtooth track down and trap the beast, but it escapes and ransacks the village before the sheriff finally gets the drop on the creature and saves the day.

Brothers William and Edward Nassour were intrigued by the story and bought the rights for a small sum. Edward reportedly gave a verbal promise to O'Brien that he would be engaged to work his stop-motion magic once production began, but when the time came, Nassour (who had an intense interest in special effects and stop-motion) rebuffed O'Brien and chose to oversee the animation personally. He brought aboard budget effects-makers Jack Rabin and Louis DeWitt to handle the optical work, leaving O'Brien's skimpy "from an idea by" as his only credit. The picture was filmed entirely in the mountainous regions of Mexico, near the villages of Cuernavaca and Tepoztlan. According to one press release, the fiesta seen in the film is an authentic, age-old Mahuatl ceremony, and "special permission was granted director Nassour for its filming." *Hollow Mountain* was a joint effort with the Mexican production company Peliculas Rodriguez-S.A. and Ismael Rodriguez is credited as co-director with Edward Nassour, but what contributions Rodriguez made to the picture are unknown.

SPECIAL EFFECTS: The words looked impressive, emblazoned not only on the movie's ads but even in the actual opening credits: "Introducing the New Nassour REGISCOPE Process—Animation in Depth." Sadly, any expectations these words may have raised in the unknowing viewer would be quickly dashed. By now most dinomovie buffs are aware that the Nassours' ballyhooed "Regiscope" process was a *Hollow* claim, but Edward Nassour went to some lengths to tout his breakthrough technique. He even "revealed" the secrets of Regiscope in a *New York Times* article. "The Regiscope machine predetermines every movement of any inanimate object to be used in the motion picture and records it on a tape," Nassour explained. "The 'actor' is then electronically controlled in all of its motion." It was pure hype, though some have suggested that Nassour actually attempted to develop and planned to use such a process and was simply unsuccessful in making it work. Whatever the whole story, "Regiscope" was destined to have no more actual substance than something like *Valley of the Dragons*' unabashedly fictional "Monstascope," existing only in that most astounding of all fantasy worlds: the imagination of a good publicist.

The grandiose claims attached to "Regiscope" were seemingly endless. "The greatest advance in animation-with-depth processes in the history of the motion picture industry," roared the press releases. It was described as a "process by which inanimate objects are made to move realistically and which producer-director Edward Nassour developed after 18 years of experimentation." There were also seeming attempts to persuade the audience that the creature was actually as big as it looked on screen. "The process is used to create and impart motion to a 14-foot-high prehistoric carnivorous animal," the publicity said. "It is animated through Regiscope as a living, breathing menace, one of the most awesome ever to be seen on the screen." The hype even stated that developing Regiscope required "the wizardry of electronics, the making of hundreds of puppets of animals and human beings, exposure of thousands of feet of film and the expenditure of several hundred thousand dollars," and that "Regiscope can control the motion of puppet-like figures and give them changes of expression down to $1/64$ of an inch." Finally, the publicity promised that *Hollow Mountain* was only the first Regiscope picture, and "will be followed by others from the Nassour Studios." The others, of course, never materialized.

While the fictional tales of the *Beast of Hollow Mountain* dino effects are well documented, the true story behind the film's animation is harder to pin down. One popular account says that the *Hollow Mountain* animation model began life as the puppet created by Marcel Delgado for Willis O'Brien's original *Gwangi* in the early forties, but there are problems with this scenario. "I think not," Jim Danforth told the author, "because I have seen, and held in my hand, the *Beast of Hollow Mountain* animation model. It's very large, it's larger than the *Gwangi* puppet would have been, and it's built in a different way." Ray Harryhausen likewise expressed doubts, pointing out to me that "the one in the picture certainly didn't look like the one Obie had." A possible answer is that the Nassour Studios acquired the *Gwangi* puppet, dismantled it, and used it as

A somewhat ill-designed full-size claw gropes after Jimmy (Guy Madison) and Enrique Rios (Edward Noriega) as they hide inside the ***Hollow Mountain***.

a pattern to construct their own model. "Obie sold it to them or gave it to them or something," Harryhausen stated, "and they tore it apart, and remade ... not a very good Allosaurus." Jim Danforth concurs. "They may have had the *Gwangi* armature, and probably did," Danforth said, "but I'd just be really, really surprised if that armature, parts of it even, was in *The Beast of Hollow Mountain*."

Uncertainty also surrounds the identity of the *Hollow Mountain* animators. Willis O'Brien certainly did no animation, despite Edward Nassour's reported promises. Nor did the credited effects artists, Jack Rabin and Louis DeWitt, though they did handle the compositing of the completed animation with the live action. There has even been speculation that Edward Nassour did it himself. However, stop-motion historian Hal Miles, based on personal conversations with William Nassour and Edward Nassour's son, Edward Jr., told this author that the principal animator was cinematographer Henry Sharp. "Sharp did most of the conventional stop-motion animation," Miles stated, pointing out that Sharp's credit on the original screening print was "Special Effects" before being changed to "Assistant to the Producer" on the release prints. "Edward Nassour did a few shots, but supervised everything in that he was the overall director-producer. Rabin and DeWitt did the optical work combining the animated and live elements, along with setting up the actual process stop-motion setups." Clips of the *Hollow Mountain* stop-motion turned up on television in the 1960s as stock dinosaur footage in the *very* short-lived time travel sitcom, *It's About Time*.

Compared to the conventional stop-motion, details regarding the film's "replacement" animation are not quite as elusive. It was the work of a talented sculptor named Henry Lyon, who personally constructed all of the replacement figures and executed the actual animation. "Edward felt that since Lyon had created the replacement figures he would be the best individual in lining them up during animation," Hal Miles explained. *Hollow Mountain* marked the first attempt to use replacement animation for a fantasy character in a live action film. Although the striding motion is beautiful, there are inherent limitations. "Henry Lyon used a system similar to [George] Pal's, where you made a separate figure for each position, which is not quite practical," Ray Harryhausen told me. The process can only be used for "repetitive cycles," Harryhausen pointed out, "and you have to make them very stylized so you can cut them out easily." In addition, a flickering effect is often noticeable, due to the difficulty in achieving identical paint jobs on every figure.

El Bello Durmiente

**½ 1952, Mexico. Producciones MB/Cinematográfica Valdés. BW, 76m.

CREDITS: *Director* Gilberto Martinez Solares. *Producers* Óscar J. Brooks, Felipe Mier, Germán Valdés. *Story and Adaptation* Juan Garcia, Gilberto Martinez Solares. *Production Design and Prehistoric Effects* Edward Fitzgerald.

CAST: Germán Valdés ("Tin-Tan"), Lilia del Valle, Wolf Rubinskis (Ruvinskis).

A team of archeologists discovers a 10,000-year-old caveman, perfectly preserved. No, not preserved ... alive! And still possessing memories of a time long ago...

Back in man's primitive era, there lived a timid fellow named Tricitan who would much rather woo the ladies than hunt down giant animals. One day he discovers a beautiful girl who has sprained her ankle. They really like each other, and when Tricitan croons a lilting love song—describing what a nice cave he'll provide, and so on—he wins her heart. But Tricitan has a rival for her affections, a brutish villain named Tracatá from a neighboring hostile tribe. When war looms, the God of the Water makes a suggestion. If Tricitan were to marry the daughter of the other clan's chief, war can be averted. Tricitan is reluctant, but when he realizes that the chief's daughter is actually the girl he loves, he tricks Tracatá into believing that the girl's rotund mother is the marriage candidate. The enraged Tracatá feigns friendship and slips Tricitan an herb to make him "sleep for ten thousand winters."

Tricitan awakens ten thousand winters later, surrounded by archeologists. He is amazed that the female in the group looks exactly like his lady love, and appalled when he finds that she's engaged to the dig's financier, Heinrich Wolf—who looks just like Tracatá! The lady scientist is fascinated and wants to study the specimen, while Wolf favors stuffing him as a display. As Tricitan tells the girl stories of their prehistoric courtship—"you and I stopped a war from happening," he says—she begins to have flashbacks. She even kisses her fiancé in the rubbing-of-noses style from eons ago. Finally, with the wedding imminent, the ancient and benevolent gods send an enchanted earthquake which halts the ceremony and rekindles the girl's subconscious memories, and she gives Tricitan a 20th-century kiss. "I've been missing out all this time!" a delighted Tricitan exclaims.

COMMENTARY: Part caveman-and-dino movie, part slapstick, part romantic fantasy, part musical—whatever genre you try to put this picture into, it won't entirely fit. The prehistoric segment has more bonks on the head than an all-night Stooge-a-thon, but things get less goofy and more romantic as the film progresses. *El Bello Durmiente* is an odd, flawed little curio that's hard to dislike.

Various elements of *El Bello Durmiente* (*The Beautiful Dreamer*) recall ideas and scenes from other films and television shows, most of which came along years *afterward*. The parallel-plot device with the same actors appearing in both "worlds" is of course remindful of *The Wizard of Oz*; the design of the caveman town is very much in the style of *The Flintstones*; and the whole sequence where the lady scientist cages, studies, and tries to "civilize" the unearthed Neanderthal is uncannily similar to *Trog*—though *Durmiente* actually handles the scenes more believably!

The movie that *El Bello Durmiente* most strongly resembles, at least during its prehistoric scenes, is *Caveman*. Nearly 30 years before Carl Gottlieb combined clownish cave dwellers, comic dinosaurs, and physical comedy into a goofy slapstick mix, Tin-Tan had already done it. One of main things Gottlieb wanted to do with *Caveman* was to transplant "cartoon" comedy into the live-action arena, which is exactly what *Durmiente* does. In *Caveman*, a big brute picks up a boulder to throw it, but forgets to let go and gets yanked out of frame by his own projectile. Here, the villain pounds the hero over the head with a huge club, incrementally driving him into the ground like a railroad spike. The inspiration for either scene could have come from any one of countless "Looney Tunes" shorts.

If *El Bello Durmiente* can hold its own with *Caveman* in the comedy department, the dinosaurs are no contest. *Caveman* had several of the greatest special effects animators of the era behind its dinos; *Durmiente* did not. But to be fair, the simple, fancifully designed hand-puppet and marionette dinosaurs created by Edward Fitzgerald (art director on *The Black Scorpion*) serve the story adequately. The Brontosaurus, Tyrannosaurus, Stegosaurus, and pterodactyl are cartoony dinos in a cartoony movie, and are not asked to be major characters as were the stop-motion comedians of *Caveman*. Despite their crude construction, it's hard not to smile when the bronto snatches away Tracatá's club during his backswing, or when the T. rex starts moving to a mambo beat during a big production number. The film in fact has some terrific Latin music by esteemed composer Manuel Esperon, including a jazzy number called "Mambo Prehistórico!"

Tin-Tan, whose real name was Germán Genaro Cipriano Gómez Valdés Castillo, was a gifted cinematic clown and a huge star in Mexico during the 1950s and 1960s. His physical, pratfall style of comedy could be compared to Jerry Lewis's, though it's not a perfect analogy. Myrna De La Rosa, a friend who kindly translated *El Bello Durmiente* and two other Spanish-language dino films for me, told me a bit about Tin-Tan. "In general, Tin-Tan was in *very* silly movies," she said. "But they're usually cute, and they're entertaining and people like them, and I don't think they make movies like that anymore."

The Birth of a Flivver

not viewed 1916, USA. Edison/ Conquest Pictures. BW, Silent.

CREDITS: *Director/Animator* Willis O'Brien.

A pair of savvy cavemen invent the wheel, but quickly give up on their goofy scheme when they are unable to persuade a mule-headed Brontosaurus to pull their wheeled cart. Chronologically the third of Obie's comedic stop-motion puppet shorts, following *The Dinosaur and the Missing Link* and the dinosaurless *Morpheus Mike*.

Brute Force

(a.k.a. *In Prehistoric Days*)

not viewed 1913, USA. Biograph. BW, Silent.

CREDITS: *Director* D. W. Griffith.
CAST: Robert Harron, Mae Marsh, Wilfred Lucas.

Live-action sequel, of sorts, to Griffith's earlier *Man's Genesis* (1912), apparently reusing some of the same footage. Creatures include a cosmetically-altered snake and alligator, and what is likely cinema's first full-size dinosaur mock-up: a towering horned meat-eater possibly meant as a Ceratosaurus. In his biography of Griffith, Richard Schickel capsulized the simple plot as follows: "Bobby Harron, the 'Weakhands' of the earlier [*Man's Genesis*], portrays the leader of a community struggling upward toward civilization and defending it against assault from neighbors still lost in darkness." Rating the film, Schickel called it "neither worse nor better than its thematic predecessor."

Carnosaur

"*It came out of a damn chicken egg!*"

* ½ 1993, USA. Concorde/ New Horizons. C, 83m.

CREDITS: *Director* Adam Simon. *Producers* Mike Elliott, Roger Corman (executive). *Written for the Screen by* Adam Simon. *Based on the Novel by* Harry Adam Knight. *Production Design* Aaron Osborne. *Special Make-Up and Creature Effects* John Buechler and Magical Media Industries, Inc. *Visual Effects Supervisor* Alan Lasky. *Sculptors* Michael F. Jones, Jeff Farley. *Mechanics* John Crawford. *Dinosaur Consultant* Don Glut.
CAST: *Dr. Jane Tiptree* Diane Ladd. *Doc* Raphael Sbarge. *Thrush* Jennifer Runyon. *Sheriff Fowler* Harrison Page. *Fallon* Ned Bellamy.

AD LINE: "Driven to extinction. Back for revenge."

Genetic scientist Dr. Jane Tiptree, "the woman who can think 50 unthinkable thoughts before breakfast," has withdrawn from public view to conduct sequestered research for the giant Eunice Corporation. Knowing Tiptree's history, one Mr. Fallon of the government's Advanced Research Projects Administration is getting nervous. But even he couldn't have imagined her achievement: the creation of genetically engineered dinosaurs.

Meanwhile, the folks around Climax, Nevada, near Tiptree's secret lab, are falling ill with strange flulike symptoms. At the neighboring Eunice-owned rock quarry, "Doc" the alcoholic night watchman discovers a trespasser and is surprised when it turns out to be an attractive blonde environmental activist. Doc is initially unimpressed by the girl calling herself "Thrush" and calls the local sheriff, but the lawman is preoccupied with a rash of gruesome killings. The culprit is one of Tiptree's dinosaurs—a vicious killer-clawed Deinonychus which has somehow escaped. Its victims will soon include the wayward teen daughter of the plant manager, the unfortunate Sheriff Fowler, and a pair of Eunice employees sent out to locate the creature. When Doc discovers the two bodies and the Eunice truck, he cleverly traces the mystery to Tiptree's lab. At gunpoint, Tiptree explains her plans to wipe out the disastrous human race with an engineered virus (a really nasty one — Tiptree's receptionist runs a fever of 113 degrees!) and clear the earth for her dinosaurs. While Fallon and other top officials huddle in an emergency bunker to discuss plans for repopulating the human race, Doc obtains a serum from Tiptree — who dies moments later giving birth to a dinosaur — and races to save Thrush. He's pursued back to the quarry by a T. rex, but uses the mechanical muscle of a skiploader to defeat the dinosaur. Just when Doc thinks help has arrived, it turns out to be the military "Code Blue" team ... and they remorselessly carry out their orders.

COMMENTARY: Maybe it was "reverse backlash" from the megasuccess and major studio glitz of *Jurassic Park*, or reverence for Roger Corman's reputation, or who knows what, but for some reason, a lot of critics have been inexplicably kind to the grungy, unexciting 83 minutes that are *Carnosaur*.

There are way too many things in *Carnosaur* that simply don't make sense. Corman of all people must know that a budget creature movie needs a straightforward plot, no-nonsense editing, and most of all, energy. *Carnosaur* has none of these, and is in fact one of the most convoluted dinoyarns ever filmed. Maybe it's just me, but a flood of questions presented themselves as I watched. How did the Deinonychus escape? If the dinos are hatching from chicken eggs, what's the deal with the huge eggs in the lab? And why does Tiptree need human hosts? Why do all those TVs show a rotating "Eunice" logo? Why are so many characters named after birds? And how in the world did Doc figure everything out and immediately appear at Tiptree's secret complex, based on one overheard radio message?

The *Carnosaur* cast is anchored by three-time Oscar nominee Diane Ladd, who does what she can with her ill-conceived role. Raphael Sbarge is adequate, and pretty Jennifer Runyon (memorable in a hilarious scene in *Ghostbusters*) has an attractive girl-next-door earthiness. But the characters they play are surely the gloomiest congregation of wet blankets ever to inhabit one movie. Tiptree looks too depressed and dispirited to project any villainy. Doc is supposed to be an "anti-hero" ("your basic funky dropout," as Sbarge put it), but just comes across as a hapless sad sack. Thrush is a little less jaded, but doesn't really seem to hold out any hope either. One wonders why any of them bother to get out of bed. Only Harrison Page's steadfast sheriff has any zest for living, that is until he and the Deinonychus simultaneously kill each other in the silliest mutual-murder scene since the climax of *Duel in the Sun*.

There is nothing wrong with a movie having a pessimistic, even fatalistic tone. There are great films — *Testament*, *The River's Edge*, and *Taxi Driver* to name three — that are relentlessly downbeat. But no matter how dark the story, the audience must have something or someone to give a fig about. As in the dismal *Alien 3*, the *Carnosaur* doom and gloom accomplish nothing other than to sap the picture of any energy it tries to muster. It's easy to see what the filmmakers were going for, especially in the climax — they were trying to take an old monster-movie cliché and turn it on its ear. In almost all fifties monsterpics, just when all would seem lost, the hero would discover some sort of hidden vulnerability and vanquish the threat at the last minute. *Carnosaur* sets up its audience to think that the same thing is going to happen here. Doc finds the viral serum, injects his girlfriend, kills the tyrannosaur ... everything's going to work out, right? Wrong! In come the biohazard-suited stormtroopers! They machine-gun Doc and Thrush with about 500 bullets, burn the place to the ground, dumbly destroy the only hope for mankind, and do indeed turn the old cliché on its ear. But what is the point? That the government is evil, stupid, or both? That mankind is silly? That genetic science will result in human women giving birth to tyrannosaurs? Whatever the intentions of *Carnosaur*'s makers, the irony, satire, or social comment just doesn't come through.

So we are left to consider the special effects that create the dinosaurs and the gruesome results of their attacks, and it must be said that both dino and "splatter" fans will be disappointed. A film requiring dinosaurs to be such major players was a very ambitious (maybe too ambitious) project to attempt on a Roger Corman budget, but John Buechler and crew accepted the challenge and pulled out every trick in the book. They used puppets of all sizes, miniature sets, forced perspective, new ways of building creatures, and new materials, all to try and fulfill the script's requirements with the funds available. And they managed to turn out some pretty impressive-looking dinosaurs. But to get great results with such meager resources, *everything* has to click. First, the dinosaurs have to look good. Then, it's up to the direction, lighting, photography, choreography, and editing to maximize the illusion, and this is where *Carnosaur* falls woefully short.

The full-scale, 16-foot-high T. rex is at its best as it pulls and struggles against the skiploader, lurching around the frame, and the puppeteers can breathe some life into it. It's at its worst when it's on screen by itself and its limitations of mobility are exposed. The more articulated, one-fifth scale counterpart is considerably livelier. Buechler's team was working against time, against budget, and against history, too—almost never has a full-size mechanical movie monster worked very well, even when backed by much bigger bankrolls. The *Carnosaur* T. rex had the potential to turn out better than most, but is continually betrayed by the unimaginative ways in which it is photographed.

The Deinonychus attacks lead to most of the gore effects which, though intended to be extremely grisly, are not much more convincing than the dinosaurs. Nothing seems to spill out no matter how big the wound, and all the innards look awfully stretchy. In one tired scene obviously inspired by the famous "chest-burster" in *Alien*, a goo-covered baby dinosaur pops through Diane Ladd's stomach wall. But the image has no shock value, instead seeming almost comical as Ladd tears her abdomen open with her fingernails to help the little critter out.

Interestingly, if *Carnosaur* had been intended as a simple and affectionate tribute to Corman's fondly remembered B-monster pictures of the fifties, the creature effects would have been fine just as they are. But instead the film wants to be taken very seriously. It wants to be thought-provoking and scientific and shocking and foreboding and all that, and its dinosaur sequences just aren't up to those kinds of demands. But for all the budget constraints, it is actually the disjointed, funereal story and the ineffectual photography and cutting that make the film such a disappointment. *Carnosaur* was supposed to stand out from the pack of "safe, PG-rated dinosaur stuff" that appeared in 1993; but despite all the blood-red mayhem, it ultimately bites off more than it can chew.

PEOPLE AND PRODUCTION: Roger Corman's low-budget entry into the genetically engineered dinosaurs market got its start three years earlier, when he discovered the novel *Carnosaur* during a book-signing tour. Corman secured the rights but production didn't commence until a somewhat bigger dino-picture began gearing up. In Marc Shapiro's article for *Starlog*'s "Dinosaur" special, producer Mike Elliott explained: "When [Corman] heard about *Jurassic Park* going into production, he felt that now was the time to shoot our movie, because he knew he could make the movie faster than anybody else and get it out there first." Effects creator John Buechler had a different slant: "I don't think it's so much a matter of getting it out first as the fact that there is suddenly a reason to do a dinosaur movie."

Adam Simon, veteran of several previ-

Teenage bad girl Janie (Norita Golanos) meets a bad end, getting her innards ingested by a John Buechler Deinonychus in the gory *Carnosaur*.

ous Corman-related projects, was tabbed to helm the movie, and one of his first decisions was to largely forget Harry Adam Knight's novel. Several treatments and drafts were also rejected, and the writing job finally fell to director Simon. "I knew going in that we could not blow people away with our dinosaurs the way *Jurassic Park* would," Simon explained. Consequently, the book's large variety of dinos was scaled down to a more manageable two, and less FX-heavy plot elements were introduced. The film had a comparatively luxurious production schedule as Corman pictures go. Simon had a whopping six months to complete his research and writing, and the effects team had ten weeks of pre-production time to create the scaly stars. Even the 18-day principal shooting schedule was lavish compared to many Corman pictures.

Carnosaur's "big name" was Diane Ladd (yes, mother of *Jurassic* star Laura Dern), joined by the laid-back Raphael Sbarge and Jennifer Runyon. Sbarge, who previously machine-gunned a T. rex in *My Science Project*, was delighted with the chance to work with Ladd. "She was able to bring a real sense of believability to the role," he stated, and perhaps realizing the limitations of the film's special effects, added "that was the biggest challenge we faced as actors: making all this seem real." Made for around $800,000, *Carnosaur* had a regional theatrical run but was largely a video release. Director Adam Simon kept a sense of humor about the project. "My theory is that if you don't want to be accused of ripping off one movie," he said, "you rip off 10."

SPECIAL EFFECTS: To create the dinos, Roger Corman turned to John Buechler and

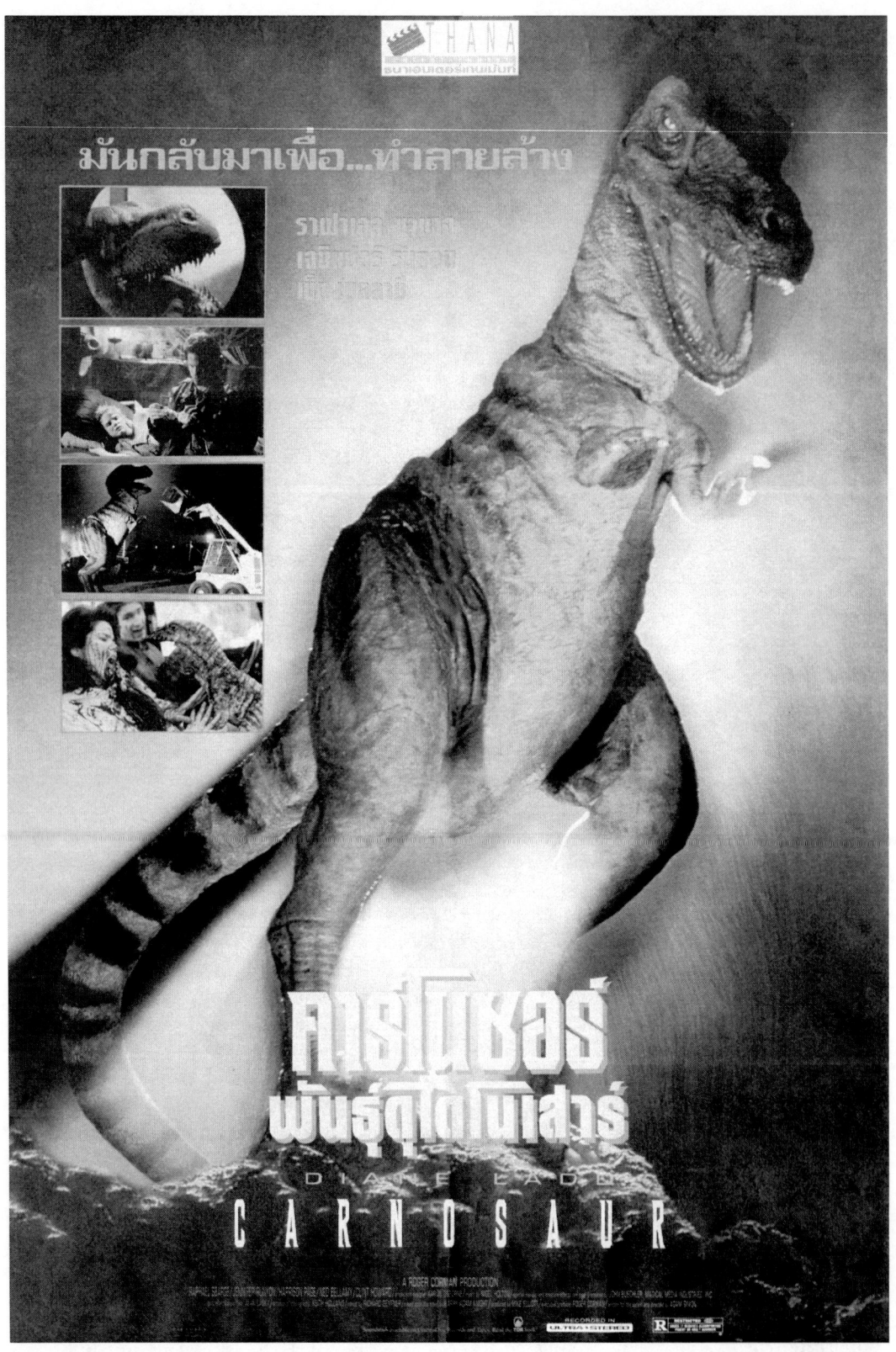

Filipino poster for *Carnosaur* features the one-fifth scale T. Rex in lieu of the less-agile full-size beast.

Magical Media Industries. "A lot of people have passed through [Roger Corman's] doors there, and many of them are Academy Award winners today," Buechler told this author. "I mean visual effects guys, make-up effects guys, and out of all those people, he called me in to do *Carnosaur*. I just felt very beholden to the guy." Corman dislikes stop-motion and optical effects due to the time lag between filming the shots and seeing the results, and so decreed that all of the dinosaurs would be "real-time" creations.

Buechler hired Mike Jones to sculpt the Deinonychus and Jeff Farley to sculpt the T. rex. "There were about 10 weeks of pre-production," Farley told the author. Working in oil-based clay, Farley spent two weeks on the sculpture. "All the while, John and Roger would give suggestions, and John would relay to me any changes and things like that." The final product basically had the upright stance of the old-style, 1950s T. rex, and was not quite what Farley had in mind. "Roger really wanted to keep it sort of 'B-movie' looking," Farley explained. "I mean I cheated it a little bit; I was able to get a little bit of a 'tilt' in there, but not as much as I wanted."

Farley's rex measured about three feet, or about one-fifth the size of the full-scale puppet. "That was created first," Farley revealed, "to use as a model for the building of the [never used] suit version as well the full-scale prop that was built by Kenneth J. Hall." The 3-foot creature was by far the more articulated creature. "John Buechler brought in John Crawford to supervise all the animatronics for the show," said Farley. "He took sort of a low-tech approach, using a cable-controlled 'waldo' system, as well as some radio control for the eye blinks and things like that." In FX lingo, a "waldo" is a device that, when moved by a puppeteer, generates simultaneous, corresponding movements in an animatronic puppet. With a waldo, complex creatures can be controlled by fewer operators, lessening the need for precise coordination among multiple puppeteers.

About seven of the ten weeks allocated for dinomaking was spent on the miniature T. rex, leaving only three weeks to construct the life-size, 16-foot-tall, 25-foot-long model. Sheets of a high-strength, lightweight polyurethane called L-200 were cut, shaped, and glued together to form the understructure, which was then covered with urethane foam skin. A scaly texture was added by manually searing the pattern into the foam with a hot tool. Due to the light weight, the movements of the huge rex could be produced by simple pneumatic actuators. "If we create [the full-size creature] with standard procedures, and sculpt it and mold it and cast it, it would weigh close to two and a half tons," Buechler said on *Movie Magic*. "The final creature that I delivered weighed 450 pounds."

The small and full-scale beasts were both used in the climactic battle with Doc's skiploader—a sequence which Buechler freely admits was "nearly shot for shot modeled on the finale of *Aliens*." In some shots, the 3-foot puppet was placed on a miniature set, complete with scale model Doc and skiploader. But the heavy use of the miniature set is symptomatic of the biggest problem with the *Carnosaur* effects—that the director and cinematographer were never on the same page with the FX people. "All of that stuff should've been shot on location, there with the people," Buechler explained. "But as it worked out, we didn't get to do that. We had to re-create in miniature that whole place. And shooting black backgrounds? It just made it so much cheaper-looking." Buechler and crew had expected to make extensive use of the "forced perspective" technique and designed the scale T. rex with that in mind, but it didn't happen. "Hardly any of the forced perspective material that we had planned was shot," Buechler said. "I think there's only two or three forced perspective shots in the whole movie." A pterodactyl puppet also went unused. "It was going to be a shot at the end of the movie, where all the dinosaurs are dead now," Buechler revealed. "So you know, everything's fine, the government has burned out all the bodies, and then the camera pulls back and you see this little pterodactyl. They never shot it. They never got around to shooting a lot of stuff that they had planned."

Carnosaur proved to be an exercise in exasperation for John Buechler. "It was really quite frustrating for me that a lot of time — very little money — but a lot of ingenuity was spent in trying to make very little look like a whole lot," he commented. "*Carnosaur* could have looked great, because they had some *amazing* locations, but I was just astounded by how little of it they captured on film." As has happened before with other films, the experience and advice of the effects personnel were, to say the least, not fully utilized. "Adam [Simon] is a good writer," Buechler emphasized. "The script was witty ... and it could've worked. But you can't write a passage like 'the dragon flies down and destroys the village' without the technical ability to make it happen." Buechler's views are borne out by the evidence of *Carnosaur II*— a film which used the exact same models and yet delivered far superior dinosaur sequences.

Carnosaur II

*"They got nukes here?
Nukes and dinosaurs?"*

****½ 1994, USA. Concorde/
New Horizons. C, 82m.**

CREDITS: *Director* Louis Morneau. *Producers* Mike Elliott, Roger Corman (executive), Mike Upton (associate). *Screenplay* Michael Palmer. *Production Designer* Robert de Vico. *Special Creature and Visual Effects* John Buechler and Magical Media Industries. *Special Miniature Effects* Anthony Doublin. CAST: *Jack Reed* John Savage. *Tom McQuade* Cliff DeYoung. *Ben Kahane* Don Stroud. *"Monk" Brody* Rick Dean. *Jesse Turner* Ryan Thomas Johnson. *Sarah Rawlins* Arabella Holzbog. *Ed Moses* Miguel A. Nunez, Jr. *Joanne Galloway* Neith Hunter.

AD LINE: "Back for another bite!"

When communication is suddenly lost with the top-secret government installation known as Yucca Mountain, a Department of Energy repair crew is sent in. The squad's eyepatch-wearing foreman, Ben Kahane, makes the unpopular announcement that this particular mission will be directed by Defense Department bureaucrat Maj. Tom McQuade. The motley crew — "Monk" Brody, Sarah Rawlins, Ed "Mo" Moses, and Jack Reed — chafes under McQuade's command, and when their 'copter lands they quickly realize that there is much more going on than they've been told. The mess hall is a bloodspattered shambles ("somebody didn't like the food I guess," Monk quips), and they find that a teen boy named Jesse is the only person alive. Ben is dragged off by an unseen predator down on isolated sublevel D, while up in the control room a voracious Deinonychus preys on Moses. Jesse leads the survivors to the outside while pilot Joanne Galloway warms up the chopper, but when a dinosaur appears in the cockpit both she and their means of escape are destroyed.

Back inside, McQuade spills the whole story. It seems that a biotech firm, "messing around with DNA," created living dinosaurs which proceeded to go on a killing spree. All the animals were destroyed, but a clutch of intact eggs was brought to Yucca Mountain for safe keeping. Compounding the problem, the installation is not just a simple mining facility but actually a storage dump for radioactive waste and decommissioned nuclear weapons ... and the containment system is failing. Young Jesse uses his computer skills to summon help and the group frantically scrambles toward the exit, but Sarah, Monk, and McQuade never make it. Jesse drags the injured Jack with him to the surface, but a slavering T. rex blocks the path to the rescue chopper. The boy somehow wrestles the dinosaur into an elevator shaft with a forklift, and escapes with Jack just moments ahead of the atomic holocaust.

COMMENTARY: A sequel to *Carnosaur* in only the broadest terms, *Carnosaur II* is unexpectedly fun. Though hardly a frame goes by that isn't derived from other pictures — one in particular — it's a solid and effective dino-thriller that towers above its morose predecessor.

The makers of *Carnosaur II* weren't shy about borrowing ideas from anyone and everyone, but the parallels with James Cameron's stylish *Aliens* (1986) are unavoidable and almost endless. Contact with an isolated outpost is lost. A tightly knit squad is sent in, accompanied by a smarmy outsider with a hidden agenda. They find a traumatized youngster who has somehow survived and who is "adopted" by one of the group. They realize they're in over their heads and are picked off one by one. They try to escape by air but a creature turns up in the aircraft, kills the female pilot, and causes a crash. One man who has been disliked turns out to be okay in the end, staying behind with a wounded comrade and killing several creatures in a suicidal explosion. The small band barricades themselves against the enemy, but soon have to worry about an impending atomic blast as well. Finally, a heroic human uses a forklift to defeat the biggest baddest monster, and the survivors barely outrun the nuclear fireball.

Yucca Mountain in *Carnosaur II* is asteroid LV-426 in *Aliens*, and the Huey helicopter is the Drop Ship. Jack Reed is Ripley, Jesse is Newt, and Major McQuade is Carter Burke with a little bit of Lieutenant Gorman mixed in. Monk is Private Hudson, Galloway is Private Ferro, and Ben Kahane is Sergeant Apone. Effects-maker John Buechler admitted that the finale of the original *Carnosaur* was based on *Aliens*, but the sequel turned out to be a case of "you ain't seen nothing yet." It would have been an appropriate nod to their principal source if the filmmakers had eschewed the Roman numeral and simply called this film *Carnosaurs*.

Aliens was the major inspiration, not the only one. Flashlights emit Spielbergian light beams that stab through blue-white mists, and Richard Wagner's "Ride of the Valkyries" blasts from the helicopter as in *Apocalypse Now*. Jesse incorporates a lot of Edward Furlong's character from *Terminator 2: Judgment Day* (James Cameron again) in addition to his "Newt" influences. There's even a nod to *Jurassic Park*, with the Deinonychus now endowed with an eerie, porpoiselike clicking vocalization like a *Jurassic* raptor. But if it's true that *Carnosaur II* is a copy, it's equally true that it's a good one. Well-paced and well-acted, crisply edited, directed with élan by Louis Morneau, and with a dozen times the energy of the murky original, the picture has a slickness that belies its limited resources. The Yucca Mountain sets look authentic, and only by the meagerness or omission of what should be the "money" FX shots does the budget show through. The helicopter crash is puny when it should be a wow (remember the Drop Ship crash in *Aliens*?) and the final atomic blast is represented only by bright light streaming through the rescue chopper's windows.

Michael Palmer's screenplay offers dialogue that's snappy and plausible, and the acting is worthy of an A-list picture. John Savage is strong and earnest, Cliff DeYoung is just as convincingly oily as was Paul Reiser in *Aliens*, and Arabella Holzbog has an appealing levelheadedness that recalls Mary Elizabeth Mastrantonio in *The Abyss*. Rick Dean makes the crude and rude Monk strangely likable, and Miguel A. Nunez, Jr., provides some light moments as the motor-mouthed Moses.

Unfortunately, *Carnosaur II* is still a low-budget, direct-to-video picture, and inevitably has some lesser moments. One of the goofiest comes during the first dinosaur attack. We don't see the dinos, but we do see almost everything else in the room flying through the air. Chairs, plates, people ... you name it and it's airborne. Either the creature is having a temper tantrum or else genetically engineered dinosaurs produce intense poltergeist activity. The finale is another disappointment. Yes, the whole movie parallels *Aliens*, but they had already copied the beast-versus-forklift climax in the first *Carnosaur*. Couldn't something other than a near-replay — albeit a much more effectively staged one — have been concocted? And why, if the whole mountain is about to go up in a nuclear blast that will "make Hiroshima look like a campfire," is it so confoundedly important for Jesse to run back and recover their piddly little detonator?

A few brow-knitting scenes aside, *Carnosaur II* delivers the dinomovie goods. The film successfully implies that dinosaurs are milling all about the installation as opposed to the two solitary beasts of the original, and the Deinonychus attack on Moses is far and away the best dinosaur sequence in any of the three *Carnosaur* entries. Smoothly mixing dynamic puppetry with a top-notch man-in-a-suit version, and optimizing the effectiveness through deft cutting, inventive angles and lighting effects, the result is an exciting and scary sequence. The first *Carnosaur* could have looked this good, but at least they got it right on the second try.

SPECIAL EFFECTS: This sequel was inevitable. As FX creator John Buechler put it, "*Carnosaur* was, for all of its technical failure, the most successful movie that Concorde/New Horizons ever made, so they *had* to make a sequel." After his frustrations on the original, one might have thought Buechler reluctant to return. "Well, no," he explained to the author. "I didn't have a bad experience with Roger [Corman]. He pretty well knew what went on ... and that's why he gave me more of a free rein in the second movie."

Reuse of the existing dinosaurs meant that much less preproduction time — and less money — was required. The fact that the dino scenes are so much better in *Carnosaur II* was not the result of improving the dinosaurs; in fact, their condition had deteriorated. "In *Carnosaur II* we used the same models," Buechler affirmed. "Now they were a year older and, I mean, foam latex has a shelf life, and mechanical parts don't move as accurately after a year." A few touch-ups, a bit of augmentation to the Deinonychus head, and they were ready to go again. "Basically it was a matter of wiping off the dust and trying to glue the cracks in the foam together," Buechler said.

The director this time was Louis Morneau, who would go on to make the handsome and misunderstood fifties-monster homage, *Bats*. "He had an aesthetic feel for things," Buechler commented. "He was an editor for many years ... he knows how shots go together." Not only the dinosaurs but almost everything looked better in *Carnosaur II*. "They shot a little bit longer, and the locations certainly were more grand," Buechler pointed out. "It was good use of good locations." For his part, Buechler was glad to finally see his creations perform like he knew they could. "They're the same dinosaurs," he reiterated. "They're just shot the way they were designed to be shot."

Carnosaur 3: Primal Species
(a.k.a. *Primal Species*)

"We're gonna need a few more resources."

* 1996, USA. Concorde/New Horizons. C, 81m.

CREDITS: *Director* Jonathan Winfrey. *Producer* Roger Corman. *Screenplay* Scott Sandin. *Make-Up and Creature Effects* Magical Media Industries, Inc. *Visual Effects* Anthony Doublin.

CAST: *Col. Rance Higgins* Scott Valentine. *Dr. Hodges* Janet Gunn. *Polchek* Rick Dean. *Sanders* Rodger Halston. *Gen. Mercer* Anthony Peck. *B. T. Coolidge* Terri J. Vaughn. *Ferguson* Billy Burnette. *Rossi* Morgan Englund. *Proudfoot* Justina Vail.

AD LINE: "Terror will never be extinct."

A vile terrorist gang gets a surprise when they ambush a military convoy — instead of uranium, the hijacked truck contains three intelligence-enhanced dinosaurs which proceed to rip them to shreds. Col. Rance Higgins and his elite four-person antiterrorist team are sent by General Mercer into the waterfront warehouse where the truck is stashed. Rance is also expecting uranium and has no idea dinosaurs are involved, but finds out fast when two team members, Ferguson and Coolidge, are killed by something that "looked like a lizard on steroids!"

Back at headquarters, Rance is introduced to attractive blonde dino-researcher Doctor Hodges, who explains that the creatures— two Velociraptors and a Tyrannosaurus— can outrun any living animal "except the cheetah." Rance and his two remaining men, Polchek and Sanders, supplemented by four Special Forces troops, are sent back in with orders to take the dinos alive.

They track the creatures to their lair aboard a cargo ship moored at the port. The soldiers take the ship to sea, hoping to use its refrigeration system to immobilize the reptiles. But the cagey Velociraptors easily pick off two of the soldiers, and Polchek runs afoul of the T. rex while trying to destroy her eggs. The gruesome carnage finally convinces Doctor Hodges to back down on her "take them alive" stipulation, and they decide to rig the ship with explosives and blow everything to pieces. The last two marines, Proudfoot and Rossi, are killed while placing the charges, leaving Rance and Doctor Hodges (who never gets a first name) to escape the T. rex, set off the explosions, and end the menace.

COMMENTARY: As much as *Carnosaur II* was an unexpected pleasure, *Carnosaur 3* is a complete misfire. Lacking a single frame of plausibility, C3 brings the *Carnosaur* "trilogy" to an abrupt and forgettable conclusion.

Nothing in *Carnosaur 3*—characters, situations, dialogue, or dinosaurs—is faintly credible. Scott Valentine sets the dismal pace with one of the most misguided performances in creature-feature history. He horrendously overplays his tough-soldier shtick, going through the entire movie with the corners of his mouth drawn painfully downward into a bizarre, human tragedy mask. Rick Dean, so enjoyable as Monk in *Carnosaur II*, can do nothing with the ridiculous lines he's given this time. Only Justina Vail as the defiant but doomed Proudfoot manages to attain any believability and the movie's best moments occur, of all places, during a scene where she arm-wrestles Polchek. Otherwise, all the characters are utter cartoons typified by Janet Gunn's stereotypical "Lady Scientist," complete with wire-rimmed spectacles and a frumpy pulled-back hairstyle.

C3 has an overall air of cheapness that rivals the humblest of Roger Corman's early quickies. Most of the first two-thirds takes place in a warehouse—about as generic and unexciting a setting as one could imagine. When the story takes to the sea it finally provides some visually interesting setups, even though the "let's blow the whole thing" resolution is by now a moldy cliché. Various other tired plot points recall *The Blob* (using cold as a weapon) and *Reptilicus* (having a "dead" creature regenerate itself).

The dinosaur scenes are largely disappointing, but for reasons having more to do with the behavior of the creatures than their appearance. Explained in the story as the result of the 'saurs having been given "traces of human DNA," their exhibitions of intelligence are, like so much of the picture, blasted through the boundaries of common sense. The dinosaur puppets and suits seem to have held up well and still look good, but the attacks are not staged or photographed with the flair of *Carnosaur II*. The finale is a bright spot—a taut and well-executed little sequence with the T. rex stubbornly butting her head against the cargo carrier within which Rance and Doctor Hodges have taken shelter.

Unfortunately, a few scattered clever moments and a decent finish cannot begin to rescue this slapdash sequel from ruin. So, with this disheartening festival of overacting and under-budgeting, we say goodbye to the down-and-up-and-down *Carnosaur* saga.

PEOPLE AND PRODUCTION: When Roger Corman decided to do one more *Carnosaur* film, FX creator John Buechler agreed to return for part three. "Well, when it got around to *Carnosaur 3*, Roger wanted to make another movie," Buechler recalled, "but it had a lot less money than the first or the second one." And no matter how ingenious you are, if the resources are limited enough, it's going to show. "The director

[Jonathan Winfrey] was a good guy," Buechler said. "He was pretty talented, but unfortunately he had absolutely nothing to work with." Whereas *Carnosaur II* had some surprisingly opulent sets, the third entry had to make do with "Roger's little stage," as Buechler put it. "It was a bunch of black spaces with a few flats ... then he got on to the ship for a day or so. He made it look like as much as he could." As of this writing, it appears *Carnosaur 3* will be the last of the series, and the reason goes back to the original, according to Buechler. "People were so disappointed by the lack of 'movie' in the first one," he pointed out. "So even though *Carnosaur II* was ten times the movie the first film was, it didn't make the sales. I would say that if *Carnosaur II* was the first movie, they'd still be making *Carnosaur* movies."

Cave Girl Island

(a.k.a. *Beach Babes 2: Cave Girl Island*)

"I'm all out of ideas."

1994, USA.
Torchlight Entertainment. C, 78m.

CREDITS: *Director* Ellen Cabot. *Producers* Karen L. Spencer, Scott Hamre (associate). *Screenplay* Mark Michelini.
CAST: *Xena* Sarah Bellomo. *Sola* Tina Hollimon. *Luna* Stephanie Hudson. *James T. Renford II* Lenny Rose.

Yet another direct-to-video "movie," this time from Charles Band's erotic "Torchlight" label, with a few stop-motion clips from *Planet of Dinosaurs*. The plot of this nudity-spiced idiocy involves three intergalactic bimbos who crash-land on a prehistoric island which isn't *really* a prehistoric island but is just made to look like one. It is lorded over by a loopy megalomaniac named Renford, who plans to turn it into "the biggest most popular brothel in all the world" and wants the girls as his star attractions. The ladies escape with the help of Renford's lovable hunchback (who actually provides a couple of good laughs), and fly off with their new human boyfriends. This unwatchable mess is notable — if that's the word — only for the presence of the gorgeous Ms. Bellomo, who as "Roxanne Blaze" made a brief splash in adult films with her pretty girl-next-door wholesomeness. Director "Ellen Cabot" is actually David DeCoteau, who helmed *Prehysteria 3* as "Julian Breen" and executive-produced *Galaxy of the Dinosaurs*. Fred Olen Ray shows up in the "Special Thanks" list during the end titles, and a credit is given for the "Wrap Party D. J." Enough said.

Caveman

"One Zillion, B.C. ... October 9th."
**½ 1981, USA. United Artists. C, 92m.

CREDITS: *Director* Carl Gottlieb. *Producers* Lawrence Turman, David Foster. *Writers* Rudy de Luca and Carl Gottlieb. *Special Visual Effects* Effects Associates, Inc. *Visual Effects Supervisor* David Allen. *Visual Effects Crew* Jim Aupperle, Randall William Cook, Spencer Gill, Pete Kleinow, David Stipes, Laine Liska. *Special Effects Supervisor* Roy Arbogast.
CAST: *Atouk* Ringo Starr. *Lana* Barbara Bach. *Lar* Dennis Quaid. *Tala* Shelley Long. *Tonda* John Matuszak. *Ock* Avery Schreiber. *Gog* Jack Gilford.

AD LINE: "Back when you had to beat it before you could eat it..."

It's a day like any other for a small tribe of prehistoric cavepeople, with big strong brutes like Tonda having their pick of the food and female companionship while scrawny guys like Atouk get nothing. When Atouk's best friend, Lar, is injured by an attacking "Big Horned Lizard" he is considered to be a burden ("pooka") and is thrown out, and when Atouk makes one too many plays for Tonda's girl, Lana, he gets the boot as well.

During their travels, Atouk and Lar begin to find and join with outcasts from other tribes. They first meet a pretty cavewoman named Tala and her father Gog, who is blind, and before long they have a whole

"Misfit Tribe"— people of various skin colors, physical types, and even sexual orientations. Surviving encounters with the Big Horned Lizard, a portly Tyrannosaurus, and a mother pterodactyl, the tribe grows and prospers, and during one historic night they discover fire, invent cooking, and create music (with Atouk on drums, natch). They even find a way to keep Tonda and his flunkies at bay, using fire ("haraka"). But one day, while Atouk and the men are out rescuing Lar from a snow monster, Tonda's gang invades the Misfit camp and abducts all the women! The Misfits inventively arm themselves with spears, axes, and catapults, and with Atouk riding the now-domesticated Big Horned Lizard into battle, Tonda is defeated. At last, Atouk seems to have everything he wanted — Tonda is vanquished, the tribes are united, and Lana is his. He climbs to the top of the highest rock to receive the accolades of his people, sweeps Lana into his arms ... and tosses her into a big pile of organic fertilizer. Having finally realized what a self-centered flake Lana really is, he joins Tala his true love, "and they lived happily ever after."

COMMENTARY: Maybe some subjects are just not good candidates for spoofs. Case in point: It's virtually impossible to lampoon a supermarket tabloid because the real thing is so outrageously, meteorically over the top to begin with. Perhaps this factor explains part of the problem with *Caveman*, a broad send-up of the cavepeople-and-dinosaurs genre. When the "serious" movies being targeted contain such sights as cavewomen with eyeliner and permed hair, or a 20-ton dinosaur being scolded by a buxom blonde in a Jurassic string bikini, well.... Conceding this limitation, there is still no doubt that a considerably funnier movie could have been made. As demonstrated so hilariously in the near-classic *Airplane!* (released a year before *Caveman*), the best spoofs result from taking the touchstones and clichés of the target film and multiplying them exponentially. Take a simple cliché, like the "hysterical-woman-who-must-be-slapped," turn it sideways, amplify it to its loony zenith, and you've got one of the many laugh-out-loud sight gags of *Airplane!* Yes, *Airplane!* had its scatological bits, but in *Caveman* it seems nearly every gag in the picture relates to armpits, bodily waste, or gastrointestinal distress. "Gag," indeed.

Caveman does seem to know something about the films it's spoofing. Various bits inspired directly by scenes from *One Million B.C.* include Atouk's expulsion from the tribe, Lar falling in a river and drifting far downstream, the fishing women, and the "savage table manners" scene. In *Caveman*, Tala tries to take advantage of circumstances in order to get rid of her romantic competitor, Lana, just as Ayak attempts to rid herself of Sanna in *When Dinosaurs Ruled the Earth*. But *Caveman* displays only a rudimentary grasp of visual comedy, time and again missing opportunities to draw laughs from its abundant source material. *Caveman*'s best use of a concept from the earlier films — intentional or not — is the "Misfits" theme. In both *One Million B.C.* and its remake, an aging and infirm member of the tribe falls and no attempt is made to assist him. If he's no longer physically able, he is thought to be of no use, and no value is assigned to his experience, wisdom, or intellect. *Caveman* follows up on this concept by having certain "Misfits" fit this pattern. Lar's injury, Gog's age and blindness, and Ta's diminutive stature have clearly caused them to be discarded by their peers. But rather than leaving them lying pitifully in a hole as in the previous films, *Caveman* rallies them together and allows them to prove that they are equal, even superior, to those who abandoned them.

The unquestionable highlights of *Caveman*, and by far the best and funniest reasons to watch the movie, are the dinosaurs. Although the live action is woefully short on imagination, the animated actors are considerably more inspired. The movie's prehistoric comedians include the goofy Big Horned Lizard who's always looking two ways at once, the Howling Lizard who vocalizes as a coyote, a rooster, or an owl depend-

*Tyrannosaur as comedian—*Caveman *cast the perennial dino villain in a new role as a big, hapless "Schlemielosaurus."*

ing on the time of day, and a rotund, seemingly somewhat aged Tyrannosaurus whose sly smirk suggests nothing so much as a scaly, 50-foot Bill Murray. The mama pterodactyl is played fairly straight—her groovy polka-dot color scheme notwithstanding—and is so expertly animated that she visibly seems to catch and ride the updrafts as she flies. These critters are not only top-notch stop-motion effects in the technical sense, but are also responsible for most of the biggest laughs.

The animators were given a somewhat loose leash and allowed to have some fun with the dino antics. The tyrannosaur's habit of wringing his hands as he anticipates a tasty caveman snack is one example, an idea that Randy Cook conceived while storyboarding the sequence. As Cook recalled, "the movie is so nuts, you could damn well make the monsters do anything you wanted," or at least *almost* anything, and the range of comedic expressions that the effects team coaxed out of their saurian stars surpasses even the comic capers of *The Son of Kong.* And like Carl Denham rescuing Little Kong from the quicksand, the dinosaur scenes in *Caveman* come along just often enough to save the film every time it starts to sink.

While the dinosaurs are excellent, the human cast is a mixed bag. Ringo Starr and Dennis Quaid are good, displaying a fine slapstick aptitude. Jack Gilford and Shelley Long are basically wasted, and Barbara Bach is, shall we say, no Victoria Vetri. Former pro footballer John Matuszak gives it all he's got, but I couldn't help imagining big Richard Moll, who can elicit bellylaughs with a single facial expression, being brought out from under his Abominable Snowman makeup to play Tonda instead. Lalo Schifrin's appropriately unusual and jaunty music is another plus—sort of like if Danny Elfman had scored *One Million Years B.C.*—and veteran cinematographer Alan Hume (*The Land That Time Forgot, The People That Time Forgot*) effectively captures the stony Mexican locations.

If *Caveman* was supposed to do for cavepeople-and-dinosaur movies what *Airplane!* did for airliner-in-distress movies, it just doesn't quite make it. Thanks mostly to the dinosaurs it remains a watchable, periodically funny send-up, and certainly deserves a pat on the back for trying something new and different with stop-motion animation. If only the flesh-and-blood characters had been a bit more *animated* themselves.

PEOPLE AND PRODUCTION: During *Caveman*'s genesis, director Carl Gottlieb and the producing duo of Larry Turman and David Foster were justifiably excited that they had a genuinely original project on their hands. "*Caveman* really is different," Gottlieb told author Scott Valentine in *Cinefex*. "That's because it is a comedy-prehistoric-effects picture. There have never been any." The notion had been spawned by a *Tonight Show* skit featuring, of all things, Buddy Hackett in a loincloth. Turman and Foster selected Gottlieb, who had written *Jaws* for the screen, to flesh out the basic idea and develop a screenplay.

Jim Danforth was the producers' first choice to handle the visual effects. He was reluctant to commit due to some reservations regarding the script, but eventually signed on. "I had Randy Cook come in," Danforth recalled, "and we brainstormed some funny sequences, and Randy drew them up." When United Artists officially green-lighted the picture, it seemed things would really get rolling, but the fictional trials and tribulations experienced by the story's characters paled beside the real-life struggles which *Caveman* would endure on its rocky road to completion. The production would have to survive multiple personnel changes in the areas of optical effects (Jim Aupperle out, Spencer Gill in), production design (Joe Alves out, Phil Jeffries in), storyboarding (Randy Cook out, Mike Ploog in), and eventually, visual effects (Jim Danforth out, David Allen in). There were also mechanical failures, missed communications, personality conflicts, and other assorted gnashings of teeth. Given the amount of turmoil which plagued *Caveman*, it is a testament to the talents of those involved that it turned out as well as it did.

SPECIAL EFFECTS: Even though Jim Danforth departed before the film's completion, the year of planning and design he put into *Caveman* greatly influenced the visual effects. For example, although the dinosaurs were always envisioned as comedic, it was Danforth's idea that they should also have a comical appearance. "They shouldn't just *do* funny," he urged Gottlieb, "they should *look* funny!" Danforth conceived the tyrannosaur as "kind of sleepy-eyed and snaggle-toothed ... an old, fat, degenerate Tyrannosaurus," as he put it, while the Horned Lizard's look was indirectly the result of a misunderstanding. Gottlieb had originally imagined the character as a conventional Triceratops and referred to it in the script as a "horned lizard." When Danforth read "horned lizard," that's what he designed: a lizard with a horn! Despite the mix-up, Gottlieb liked and approved the design — one of the few serendipitous moments of *Caveman*'s stormy production.

In addition to dino-designing, Danforth also directed many of the live-action scenes to which animation would later be added. In fact, all such scenes were directed (or codirected with Gottlieb) by Danforth or David Allen. Sequences helmed by Danforth include the first appearances of the Horned Lizard and the tyrannosaur, the ledge trail encounter, and the final battle with Atouk riding the Horned Lizard, to name a few. David Allen directed the pterodactyl scenes, the Horned Lizard "pumpkin trail" sequence, and others. The one stop-motion sequence that Danforth animated, involving the Tyrannosaurus chasing Atouk, Lar, and Tala back and forth while Gog wonders where the heck everybody went, was unfortunately not used in the final film.

The climactic battle is a great example of Danforth's unflagging efforts to push visual-effects boundaries. Atouk was originally going to ride a live water buffalo, but Danforth conceived a more inspired scenario in which our hero enters on the spiny back of the Big Horned Lizard. This sequence would traditionally have been done by cutting between closeups of the live actor on a full-size mechanical dino section, and long shots of the stop-motion puppet with a human puppet on its back. But the Danforth-devised "split-Ringo" shots, as they were called, placed the real Ringo Starr right

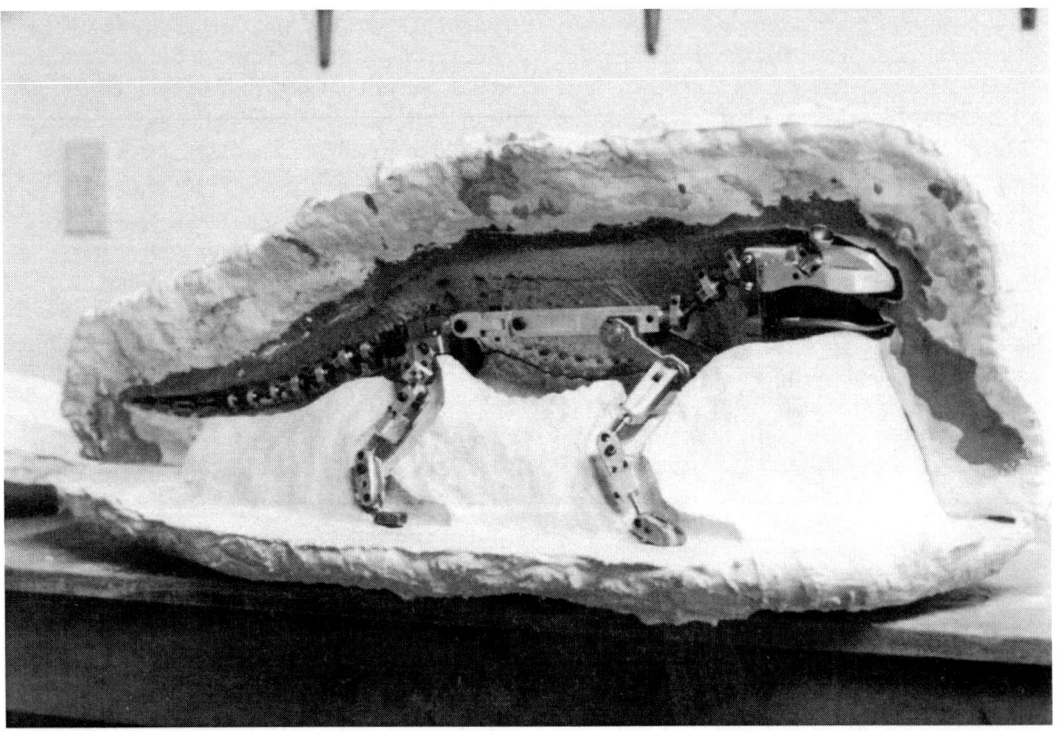

The jointed armature, or "skeleton," of the Big Horned Lizard animation puppet, shown inside its mold during construction.

atop the stop-motion lizard. This was done by filming Ringo on location at Los Organos, Mexico, "riding" Roy Arbogast's mechanical lizard back. Another background plate, with no Ringo, was also shot using the same camera angles. These were combined with a horizontal split screen to produce a somewhat bizarre-looking image of Ringo — from about the thighs up — seemingly floating in midair. The Lizard puppet was then animated in front of this rear-projected footage in a more or less standard "Dynamation" set-up. A half-puppet of Ringo (lower torso and legs only) was placed onto and animated with the lizard. Painstaking alignment of the stop-motion models with the real Ringo's rear-projected top half produced striking shots of an obviously live Ringo astride the fantastic beast. Conceived and designed by Danforth, these exacting shots were executed by David Allen.

Although most of the FX design was completed with Danforth at the helm, much of the animation remained undone at the time of his departure, and several ideas which existed only in his head never saw fruition. He wanted, for example, to provide a contrast between the lumbering T. rex and the Big Horned Lizard. "My idea was that the Tyrannosaurus was this big ponderous guy," he explained, "but that the Horned Lizard was the comedian — the *real* comedian — and he was going to be a very start-and-stop, more birdlike kind of lizard." But the scenes were not filmed until after Danforth left, and the creature's animation was ultimately handled in conventional style. "It just came out at what I call animation speed, you know, 'monster speed,'" Danforth observed. "That was my big disappointment, was the Horned Lizard."

Not all of Danforth's *Caveman* memories are unpleasant. "I got a kick out of the fact that I got to design the dinosaurs," he reflected. "And getting to direct on location, and direct Ringo Starr, and stuff like that was fun." But the behind-the-scenes machinations were another story. "I hated the politics ... I didn't like duking it out day after day after day." Many problems apparently stemmed from the fact that, aside from Danforth and his crew, almost no one on the picture had any experience with or appreciation of the unique considerations indigenous to an effects-heavy film, nor did they make any effort to avail themselves of the wealth of experience on the payroll. Finally, after a year of frustrations, Danforth left the production. "I said that's it, I'm outta here, time to go to England and work for Ray [Harryhausen, on *Clash of the Titans*], and that's what I did. But as I say, I did enjoy the creative aspects of it."

With Danforth's departure, David Allen was installed to oversee the completion of the visual effects. Allen, Peter Kleinow, Jim Aupperle and others had been brought aboard early on as the primary crew of Effects Associates, Inc.—a visual effects facility founded by Danforth specifically for *Caveman*. In his new capacity, Allen decided that his efforts could best be spent as a facilitator and problem solver, smoothing the way for the actual animation to be executed by Pete Kleinow and Randy Cook. Most of Allen's animation, primarily of the pterodactyl, was accomplished prior to Danforth's exit. "After I was put in charge, it seemed to me the best use of my time would be in knowing what the fellows doing the actual work would need so that their minds would be free and clear of distractions," Allen said in *Cinefex*.

Most of the stop-motion animation in *Caveman* is the work of Peter "Sneaky Pete" Kleinow and Randall William "Randy" Cook, a pair of veterans with long histories in the field. Cook had worked with David Allen on several projects, including *The Crater Lake Monster*, the offbeat entry *The Day Time Ended* (1980), and the even more offbeat *Q* (1982). In addition to animating, Cook also did the initial storyboarding of the

The wacky-eyed Big Horned Lizard (left) and the "fat, degenerate" Tyrannosaurus offer a glimpse of Jim Danforth's often overlooked sense of humor.

effects sequences and conceived much of the dinos' comic shtick, including the tyrannosaur's "oh, my head!" pantomime in his last shot. He also sculpted a Brachiosaurus and a Triceratops for some planned but scrapped "browsing shots," intended to invoke the feeling of dinosaurs being commonplace in Atouk's world.

Pete Kleinow's stop-motion experience dates all the way back to his "Gumby" days at Art Clokey's studio, where Jim Danforth also had his first animation job. In the sixties, he worked at Project Unlimited on such films as *7 Faces of Dr. Lao* and *The Power*, then rejoined Project cofounders Wah Chang and Gene Warren in the seventies to animate dinosaurs for TV's *Land of the Lost*. More recently, he animated Go-Motion sequences for *The Terminator* (1984) and *Terminator 2: Judgment Day* (1991). "I joined up with *Caveman* right from the beginning," he told the author, "and started building the sets and helping to get things ready." As things worked out, it was Kleinow who performed a large percentage of the *Caveman* animation. "Only because I work pretty fast," Kleinow continued. "Dave did some shots, and Randy did quite a few shots, but I certainly did the majority of the animation." Shots animated by Kleinow and Cook are in some cases cut together within a sequence, though such a practice is never desirable. "When the tyrannosaur is stoned — we've established that he ate the plant — I did all that, set it up and shot it," Kleinow explained. "Then Randy did the shot where he does the 'big eyes' and falls slowly over into space. We had to do this thing any way we could to get it done, but it's not good when the work of two animators is side by side — there's always going to be a discrepancy between styles."

Besides Danforth, Allen, Cook, and Kleinow, the FX roster included still more familiar names. The physical/mechanical effects were supervised by Roy Arbogast, veteran of such films as *The Thing* (1982), *Return of the Jedi* (1983), *Starman* (1984), and *Close Encounters of the Third Kind* (1977), for which he netted an Oscar nomination. Arbogast and his team created *Caveman*'s special props and sets, including the snow beast's ice cavern and the cooked pterodactyl egg. They also built full-size dino sections — a tyrannosaur foot and the Horned Lizard's tail and back — to intercut with the animation. Lastly, an uncredited member of the effects team was none other than *When Dinosaurs Ruled the Earth* alumnus Roger Dicken. He constructed the "Howling Lizard" over the unused Ceratosaurus armature made for *When Dinosaurs Ruled*. In addition, reportedly, one of the human puppets seen in *Caveman* was built over an armature originally used during *Mighty Joe Young*!

The Crater Lake Monster

"I can hardly wait to hear your explanation of this one!"

** 1977, USA. Crown International Pictures. C, 85m.

CREDITS: *Director* William R. Stromberg. *Producer* William R. Stromberg. *Original Story and Screenplay* William R. Stromberg and Richard Cardella. *Stop-Motion Supervisor* Dave Allen. *Special Mechanical Effects* Steve Neill. *Special Miniature Effects* Tom Scherman.

CAST: *Sheriff Steve Hanson* Richard Cardella. *Arnie Chabot* Glenn Roberts. *Mitch Kowalski* Mark Siegel. *Dr. Richard Calkins* Bob Hyman. *Dan Turner* Richard Garrison. *Susan Patterson* Kacey Cobb. *Ross Conway* Michael Hoover. *Paula Conway* Suzanne Lewis.

AD LINE: "A beast more frightening than your most terrifying nightmare!"

In a forgotten "Indian cavern," near a sleepy hamlet on the shores of Crater Lake (not the real National Park), paleo-researchers Dan and Susan discover some amazing cave paintings of a human in combat with a Plesiosaurus. That same fateful night, a fiery meteor plummets into the lake and begins to heat the surrounding waters.

Six months pass, and strange things begin to happen. A bird watcher sights a massive creature near the lake, but his report is not taken seriously by no-nonsense sheriff

Steve Hanson. The sheriff begins to pay more attention after a visiting senator rents a rowboat from bumbling bumpkins Mitch and Arnie, only to have his decapitated head wash ashore a few hours later. The monster continues his rampage, attacking (nonfatally) a traveling magician and his wife, while Doc, the town doctor, examines the senator's remains. Despite Doc's conclusion that the senator was killed by a huge, unknown animal, Steve remains unconvinced until he personally encounters and empties his revolver into the beast. Brought in to analyze the creature's tracks, Susan is seized by a transport of scientific rapture which enables her to uncannily deduce exactly what has happened: "A living Plesiosaurus, hatched from a dormant egg by some incredible freak accident!" A debate ensues regarding whether the prehistoric relic should be killed (Steve's vote), protected for its scientific value (Doc, Dan, and Susan's), or exploited for financial gain (Mitch and Arnie's). Just when the voices for keeping the animal alive seem to be winning out, it attacks again and seals its fate. At the base of the ski run, Steve jumps into a snow plow and jams the sharp grader blade into the thing's flesh. The monster claims Arnie as its last victim, and then expires from its wounds.

COMMENTARY: With his first feature film, William R. Stromberg set out to make an affectionate throwback to the fondly remembered B-monster pictures of the fifties. In some ways he succeeded, and it's fun to contemplate what *The Crater Lake Monster* might have looked like had it been made twenty years earlier — Kenneth Tobey as the sheriff, Mara Corday as Susan, Richard Denning as Dan and, most definitely, John Agar as Doc. Stromberg's tale gets off to a swell start, with ominous shots of the misty lake, the "scientific" exposition with the cave drawings (a neat idea), and the mysterious meteor. But then it all starts to slip away into a mire of too-bad acting, incredible dialogue, utterly needless subplots, and positively excruciating "comedy." It's just too much weight for even a good monster — and *Crater Lake* has a good monster — to carry.

Even the worst monsterpics of the 1950s generally stuck pretty much to the subject. They might be padded with ludicrous pseudoscientific jargon or hackneyed science-versus-military debates, but it all came back in some way to the monster. *Crater Lake* forgets this, and so we are forced to sit through a liquor store robbery–double murder, a dull car chase (it *is* the seventies, remember), and worst of all those lovable lugs, Mitch and Arnie. Their recurring appearances throughout the early reels are humorless and irritating, yet brief enough to be bearable. But at about the 50-minute mark comes an interminable passage of the dim-bulb duo, hastily shot, reportedly to replace a planned stop-motion sequence that was scrubbed at the last minute. It seems we've lost *The Crater Lake Monster* and tuned in a picture called *Mitch 'n' Arnie Get Drunk*, and the proceedings grind to a lifeless, thudding halt.

The acting is not just bad, but extremely bad, even *Planet of Dinosaurs* bad. Richard Cardella's barely adequate performance is the high point, with the rest going downhill from there. Not that the cast were given much to work with — the script is loaded with stiff dialogue and a lot of moments that make you go, "hey ... wait a minute!" Like when the senator becomes the monster's first meal, and his boat gets filled with blood despite the fact that he was in the water long before he was bitten. Or later, when Doc and Steve discuss the crisis. "I think for the moment we should keep this to ourselves," Doc says. "All right," Steve replies, "I'll start notifying everyone around the lake." Besides Mitch and Arnie's misadventures, the plot also meanders through various other superfluous side roads. In one rather distasteful bit, a lowlife hoodlum strolls into a liquor store and idly murders two people, complete with realistic pools of blood seeping from the victims. Such a scene doesn't belong in a supposedly fiftiesesque giant-monster movie.

As too often happens, the special effects turn out to be the only thing worth watching. The monster animation is consistently skillful, which is no surprise considering who the animators were, but somewhat unambitious. There is little interaction between monster and human, and most of what there is comes courtesy of Steve Neill's full-size prop head rather than any intricate Dynamation-style wizardry. There are exceptions, like the spiffy shot of the monster cringing away from the burning boat as the firelight flickers on its skin, but David Allen said it himself: "*The Crater Lake Monster* was not going to be a film to enlarge the vocabulary of special effects." Stop-motion enthusiasts will still find plenty to enjoy, and the fine detail of the model helps sell the illusion of great size, but the final battle is more letdown than showdown. Besides being derivative of *Dinosaurus!*, the confrontation is over almost before it starts. With the marvelously spooky locations and once-in-a-lifetime roster of stop-motion talent, there existed the chance to fashion a minor classic in the mold of *The Beast from 20,000 Fathoms* or *The Giant Behemoth*. The monster holds up his end, but to understand the problems with the rest of the film, one has to imagine *Beast* padded out with 30 minutes of Leo Gorcey and Huntz Hall.

PEOPLE AND PRODUCTION: In the mid–1970s, a period when most cinematic dinos were being portrayed by rod puppets or men in suits, producer-director William R. "Bill" Stromberg wanted to do a monster movie using the time-honored stop-motion process. Stromberg had earlier worked at Art Clokey's studio and Cascade of California, both of which had produced a lot of stop-motion work and groomed a number of top animators. Originally contemplating a "Bigfoot" tale, Stromberg changed the villain to a Plesiosaurus but kept the mountainous and wooded "Pacific Northwest" type of setting. Production soon commenced on an early incarnation of the film, financed by (and starring) Stromberg himself, but only when Crown International Pictures came on board did the project get rolling. Crown's funding came with some conditions, however. All of the completed footage was discarded, and the shoot essentially started over from scratch.

Huntington Lake in the High Sierras provided the filmmakers with a naturally atmospheric backdrop in which to place their primordial beast. "You couldn't have asked for a better moody situation," coscripter Richard Cardella recalled. The location shoot was plagued by some too-foggy days and unfortunately timed irrigation drainage, the latter producing a rapid drop in the lake's level and associated continuity headaches. An eclectic, largely unknown cast was signed, including Stromberg's longtime friend Cardella, ex–Playboy Bunny and Playboy jet stewardess Kacey Kathleen Cobb, and former Ringling Bros. Barnum and Bailey Circus clown Mark Siegel. But during postproduction, Stromberg's control of things began to dwindle as Crown International imposed more and more influence. Stromberg (very rightly) feels that the editing in particular suffers, with jarring transitions and unclear plot points throughout. Despite the delays and the inclusion of a decent amount of animation, the picture still came in at under $200,000. For some reason, the film's advertising art depicted a bipedal, Tyrannosaurus-like dinosaur totally different from the actual aquatic antagonist; but few people noticed, as the film failed to find box-office success.

SPECIAL EFFECTS: In one scene of *The Crater Lake Monster*, small-time magician Ross Conway tells his wife that there are "no manufactured illusions here." But he's wrong, there are plenty of manufactured illusions here, and they're definitely *not* the work of small-time magicians. Bill Stromberg was adamant from day one that the creature would be brought to life through stop-motion. "The only way really to give realism to the monster is with animation," Stromberg told S. S. Wilson in *Cinefantastique*. "The guys in suits just don't make it." Led by David Allen, in charge of the effects for the first time on a feature film, the team also included Randy Cook, Phil Tippett, Jim Danforth, and Jon Berg. The stop-motion footage is supplemented with shots of a full-scale, four-foot-long monster head created

The detailed Plesiosaurus puppet in *Crater Lake*, sculpted by David Allen and Phil Tippett.

by make-up artist Steve Neill.

Despite seven years having passed since his excellent work on *When Dinosaurs Ruled the Earth*, David Allen still hadn't had the opportunity to spearhead a film's special effects. So when *Crater Lake* came along he took it, awful script and all. "I don't remember thinking too much about the script one way or the other," Allen said, quoted in Marc Shapiro's *When Dinosaurs Ruled the Screen*. "All I knew was that here was my chance to key my first film and so I went for it." Besides doing animation, Allen also storyboarded the effects sequences and set up the "Dynamation" style composites (dubbed "Fantamation" in the film's advertising). Starting with a Jon Berg–constructed armature, the sculpting process was begun by Allen and completed by young Phil Tippett. "I was delighted that Phil was willing to finish it up with that much of it already done, but he did a real good job," Allen said in *Cinefantastique*. "He made it quite a bit thicker than I had imagined, and I think that worked to the advantage of it." Tippett likewise described the design as "kind of a 'beefy' plesiosaur," but with a small added touch. "I put a kind of vestigial fin on its back," Tippett explained, "but it was pretty much a generic thing." Phil actually had his own idea for the monster's look, but it failed to win approval. "I designed something for Bill [Stromberg] that he didn't like, that was more like an ichthyosaur," Tippett recalled, "but he wanted something more like a classic plesiosaur."

About half of the animation in the film was done by Allen, with the balance accom-

Actors react to the stop-motion star of *The Crater Lake Monster* in this "Fantamation" composite.

plished by the all-star team of Cook, Tippett, and Danforth. "I quickly realized I'd need some other people to come in and do some scenes," Allen told Doug Murray in *Space Trek* (no. 1). "Phil Tippett did a few shots, and Randy Cook did quite a few." For Tippett, *Crater Lake* came along just as his career was about to take off to a galaxy far, far away. "It was at the same time Jon Berg and I were doing the chess set for *Star Wars*," Tippett told the author. "You know, I'd go do a couple of shots for Dave, and come back and work on the chess set." Danforth's involvement in the animation of *Crater Lake* was more limited. "I don't know how many scenes I did ... three or four I suppose," he recalled. "I remember the one where [the monster] is sort of behind some bales of hay, and another one where the grader is charging for him." One shot that Danforth animated has become notable — even infamous within the circle of rabid stop-motion fans — by its absence. "Jim ... did this real nice scene in which the shadow of the snow plow blade crosses the creature's back," Allen remembered. "As near as I can figure, it was just tossed out without anybody giving it a second thought." When speaking with this author, Danforth didn't recall the shot in question. "I don't know what happened to that snow plow shot; it's a mystery to me," he said. "If they say it was great, I hope it was great, but I don't remember it." Watching the sequence, it does appear to be missing a shot or two.

On the subject of missing shots, there is also the case of the "Hoedown Sequence." During the film, the character Arnie speaks of an upcoming hoedown at which he plans to make a play for Dora the waitress. The soiree is never mentioned again, but it was originally to be the site of a major animation set piece. "A huge, fantastic sequence," as stop-motion historian Hal Miles told the author, wherein the monster would have attacked a massive barn filled with partygoers. Unfortunately, Bill Stromberg's contract with Crown International specified a final — and inflexible — delivery date, and the deadline arrived before the hoedown showdown was shot. To replace the lost running time, an additional, squirmingly lengthy episode of Mitch and Arnie in the woods was filmed. The hoedown scene, which according to Miles "probably would have been one of the more spectacular sequences in the movie," went unfilmed.

In spite of such budget-dictated frustrations, Phil Tippett seems to have pleasant memories of *The Crater Lake Monster*. "It was enjoyable collaborating with Jon Berg, who I'd known for years, and Dave Allen," Tippett said. "And it's always great to be able to help people and friends out on their first picture. I'd known Bill Stromberg for many many years, since I was a kid. Bill lived in San Diego County where I was growing up, and was the only person I had run into that was interested in doing any kind of stop-motion work." As for David Allen, he was able to look back on the film with a clear eye. "You add all these little things up [and] it falls just short of inviting comparison with some of the things you've seen from Ray and Jim," he observed. "The animation was all right; the background projection was shot very unsteadily." Various problems, Allen felt, were beyond his control, "so I took a particular credit on the film, something like ... stop-motion supervisor or something. Trying to disassociate myself from the overall results which I can't, and won't, take complete credit for."

Curious Pets of Our Ancestors

not viewed 1917, USA. Edison/ Conquest Pictures. BW, Silent.

CREDITS: *Director/Animator* Willis O'Brien.

A little-known entry in Willis O'Brien's series of slapstick shorts, and possibly the last one to feature prehistoric animals. *Curious Pets* is now apparently a "lost" film.

Demon Sword

(a.k.a. *Wizards of the Demon Sword*)

"*Foolproof plans are hard to come by, son!*"

** 1990, USA. American Independent Productions. C, 87m.

CREDITS: *Director* Fred Olen Ray. *Producers* Grant Austin Waldman, Fred Olen Ray (coproducer), Drew Waldman (associate). *Screenplay* Dan Golden, Ernest D. Farino. *Miniatures* Mark Williams Effects. *Special Effects Animation & Titles* Bret Mixon.

CAST: *Lord Khoura* Lyle Waggoner. *Ulric the Elder* Russ Tamblyn. *Thane* Blake Bahner. *Melina* Heidi Paine. *Damon* Dan Speaker. *Omar* Jay Richardson. *Selena* Dawn Wildsmith. *Slave Master* Lawrence Tierney. *Seer of Roebuck* Hoke Howell.

Beautiful young Melina, daughter of Ulric the Elder, is captured by the minions of evil Lord Khoura. Ulric is the Keeper of the magical Blade of Aktar: "the key to unleashing the most awesome and malevolent powers of darkness known since the dawn of mankind!" Luckily, Melina is immediately rescued by Thane of Hawksridge, a brash soldier of fortune who offers to help free her father from Ulric's dungeon. As the befuddled Khoura tries to decipher the Blade's secrets and his bickering lieutenants Selena and Omar ineptly struggle to recapture Melina, Thane and the girl search for the benevolent sorcerer known as the Seer of Roebuck. They wander aimlessly until Thane finally deigns to ask for directions: "Take the main road out of town to the Wasteland, hook a right at the Last Outpost of Humanity, you can't miss him." The wizened Seer reveals a horrible secret: the Blade's evil side can only be released by using the weapon to kill the Blade-keeper's first-born child ... Melina! Still the plucky girl presses on until she's nabbed by a bounty hunter and delivered to Khoura. Thane, however, having joined forces with another young warrior named Damon, infiltrates the castle and sets Ulric free. Easily besting Selena and Omar, Thane and Damon reach the captive Melina just in time. The desperate Khoura cold-bloodedly kills Damon, but Thane snatches the Blade of Aktar from Khoura's belt and plunges it into the diabolical despot.

COMMENTARY: Though released on video by the folks at Troma, Fred Olen Ray's *Demon Sword* is nothing like most of Troma's way-over-the-top output. It is instead a fairly routine tale of good versus medieval, loaded with dull spots and stretched with stock footage but buoyed by an overall lighthearted air and some enjoyable supporting characters.

Unlike some of Fred Olen Ray's films which attempt to maintain at least a certain measure of seriousness, *Demon Sword* is a lampoon all the way. From the intentionally stilted dialogue ("are you telling me I've wandered into his evil realm of corruption?") and the no-brainer jokes (a Quasimodolike thug says, "I had a hunch he'd say that"), to the casting of Lyle Waggoner as the evil Khoura (possibly named after Tom Baker's villainous magician in *The Golden Voyage of Sinbad*), it's obvious that Ray *meant* for us to laugh this time.

The comedy is lukewarm but some of the gags would have been funnier with a better delivery. Waggoner, when given one deliciously juicy bit of villainous dialogue, utterly drops the ball. "You will suffer the fires of eternal damnation for this," the bound Melina says defiantly. "My dear," Khoura replies, "I *am* eternal damnation." It's a great line which begged to be delivered with an unctuous leer — Waggoner projects it like an off-camera game-show announcer hawking Rice-a-Roni. Dawn Wildsmith, one of the best things about Ray's *The Phantom Empire*, again brings some life to the proceedings, but it's veteran character actors Lawrence Tierney and Hoke Howell who steal the show. Tierney has fun as a slave trader who is just not having a good day, and Howell's cackly-voiced performance as the Seer of Roebuck is great fun — sort of like if Yoda, from the *Star Wars* films, had been played by Walter Brennan.

Animator Bret Mixon contributes some nice rotoscope effects — lightning arcs, vanishing sorcerers — but as in *Phantom Empire* all of the dinos are from *Planet of Dinosaurs*. Only a few shots are used and they have absolutely nothing to do with the story. People walk by the creatures, make a comment or two, and go on their way. The preposterously massive weapons used in the sword-fight scenes make the duels look like walk-through rehearsals, and girl watchers will be disappointed in the minimal amount of skin. Coscripter Ernest Farino would revisit the quasi-medieval genre as director of *Planet of the Dino-Knights*, a much more entertaining yarn, but *Demon Sword* offers more talk than action and more snores than 'saurs.

PEOPLE AND PRODUCTION: Never one to waste an opportunity, Fred Olen Ray jumped at the chance for a weekend's use of some castle and dungeon sets constructed for Roger Corman's *Wizards of the Lost Kingdom II*. "I told [Grant] Waldman I thought we should move on this right away," the director recalled in *The New Poverty Row*. "We filmed for two days, using the leftover interior and exterior castle sets and costumes, and walked away with enough footage to cut thirty-five minutes of film."

The urgency caused by this short window of opportunity spawned what is surely one of the more unusual "collaborations" in screenwriting history. "I had known Fred for some time and he knew I wanted to get into writing and directing," Ernie Farino recalled to the author. "He said, 'What I need you to do, by *this weekend*, is write *only* the scenes in the castle — we don't have time to write the whole script yet.' So, it was an interesting challenge." Using only Ray's rough storyline, Farino wrote the castle-bound scenes while having to extrapolate the action of the intervening passages. "I had to sit down and sort of outline it, and then write scenes 1, 3, 9, 12, 15, 27, and 35 or whatever, and the end," Farino continued. "Then, figure out when — by the outline — they were going back inside the castle and dungeon and so on ... and then *imagine* when I got to scene 15, for instance, what *might* have transpired in the meantime!" Farino met his deadline and the castle segments were filmed on the Corman sets as planned. Fred Olen Ray then turned his attention to postproduction tasks on two other pictures, and not until months later did sufficient funding become available to complete *Demon Sword*. Of course by then Farino had moved on to other projects, and Dan Golden stepped in to write all the non-castle scenes. "It's a very bizarre story and I don't know how we managed to pull it off," Farino concluded, but noted that Ray seemed to be satisfied with the results. "It has its 'Fredlike charm' to it, that's for sure."

Dinosaur

"Who booked this trip, anyway?"
* * ½ 2000, USA.
Walt Disney Pictures. C, 83m.

CREDITS: *Directors* Ralph Zondag, Eric Leighton. *Producers* Pam Marsden, Baker Bloodworth (coproducer). *Screenplay* John Harrison and Robert Nelson Jacobs; based on an original screenplay by Walon Green. *Story* Thom Enriquez, John Harrison, Robert Nelson Jacobs, Ralph Zondag. *Visual Effects Supervisor* Neil Krepela, A.S.C. *Digital Effects Supervisor* Neil Eskuri.
VOICES: *Aladar* D. B. Sweeney. *Plio* Alfre Woodard. *Yar* Ossie Davis. *Zini* Max Casella. *Suri* Hayden Panettiere. *Kron* Samuel E. Wright. *Neera* Julianna Margulies. *Bruton* Peter Siragusa. *Baylene* Joan Plowright. *Eema* Della Reese.

AD LINE: "You have never seen anything like this."

The Late Cretaceous. An Iguanodon egg, spared during a Carnotaurus attack, begins an amazing odyssey which eventually sees it deposited into a colony of lemurs on an isolated island. A family group — patriarch Yar, daughter Plio, and youngsters Zini and Suri — adopts the baby as their own. They name him, "Aladar."

Aladar grows to adulthood, wanting only for the companionship of his own kind, until one night a gigantic meteor devastates the island. Aladar and his furry family reach the mainland and seek safety in the company of a huge, multispecies dinosaur herd, led by a battle-hardened Iguanodon named Kron. As Kron and his lieutenant, Bruton, drive the herd onward towards the fertile but far-off "nesting ground," Aladar and his lemur kin fall in with some of the older dinos struggling to keep up. Eema, a weary but wise Styracosaurus, and Baylene, the last Brachiosaurus, quickly take to the newcomer and caution him to stay away from Kron's sister Neera. A much-needed rest stop is cut short when the bloodied Bruton reports a Carnotaurus in the area, and Eema and Baylene simply can't go on. Aladar won't leave them behind, so the small band — along with Bruton, too injured to continue — takes shelter in a huge cave. When the carnotaurs attack, Bruton gives his life to save his new friends while they flee deeper into the tunnel. They reach an apparent dead end but the indomitable 70-ton Baylene breaks through the wall ... and into the nesting ground! But Eema realizes that their usual passageway is blocked by a rockfall, so Aladar heads back to show the herd the newly discovered route.

Kron has no patience with Aladar's meddling and Neera has to break up their ensuing fight, but a much bigger problem appears when a huge Carnotaurus blocks their escape. "Stand together!" Aladar cries, striding out *towards* the predator, and as the others join him one by one the carnotaur becomes completely flummoxed. Until, that is, he spots an easy target — the solitary Kron. Aladar and Neera manage to knock the carnivore off a cliff, though not before Kron is mortally wounded. Finally, the exhausted but united herd follows Aladar and his mate into their new home.

COMMENTARY: In so many ways, *Dinosaur* is a remarkable achievement. In other ways, it is hardly more substantial than one of Disney's quickly produced direct-to-video sequels. Walt Disney himself believed in making quality films and letting the box office take care of itself, but *Dinosaur* shows every sign of having been constructed on an assembly line of demographics and marketing statistics rather than being an attempt to make a terrific film.

The talking dinosaurs inevitably stir the most debate. Despite the filmmakers' arguments to the contrary, it *would* have been possible to tell a compelling animal story without English-speaking characters, and films exist to prove it. Leaving that aside, if they *had* to speak, would it not have been possible to give them some better lines and a more original story? It seems so odd to put in years of work to create these staggeringly realistic representations, only to sabotage all the efforts with a rubber-stamp plot and a sauropod-sized load of "comedy relief" as clever as a *Prehysteria* sequel. Maybe nobody pointed out that *talking* dinosaurs don't have to be *talky* dinosaurs.

The idea of talking animals can work and work wonderfully. The animatronic barnyard gang of *Babe* (1995) and the cel-animated rabbits of *Watership Down* (1978) both made for terrific films. There are reasons those movies are better than *Dinosaur*, and it all starts with the script. In *Watership*, everything is played straight and the intelligent story takes itself seriously. (I think the British accents help somehow, too.) There is comic relief—a Zero Mostel–voiced seagull named Kehaar assists the rabbits—but it is used judiciously as a light change of pace rather than a hammering, yammering succession of shtick. Was the amazing visual technology of *Dinosaur* really created just to show an Iguanodon "meet-cute," a sitcom lemur family, and (two) baby-wetting gags? Incredibly, *Dinosaur* might have had yet another comic character—the Brachiosaurus was originally conceived as a young male named Sorbus with a fear of heights, prompting him to walk around with his head constantly carried low.

Dinosaur may actually have worked better in cel animation than in CG—cartoony dialogue needs cartoony characters—but then again it's derivative enough of Don Bluth's *The Land Before Time* without adding another similarity. To consider a few parallels: A ragtag herd of mixed dinosaurs sets out across a desolate wasteland in search of a lush green oasis; they are led by an earnest, undaunted youngster with a heart of gold; the carnivores don't talk and the herbivores do; the different species must learn to work together to survive; and their Edenesque paradise is seemingly a well-enforced "no predators" zone. Supplementing the *Land Before Time* elements are plot points from many other sources. The "misfit dinosaurs" (a term often used by *Dinosaur*'s makers in interviews) are remindful of the "Misfit Tribe" in *Caveman*, attempting to show that cooperation is preferable to the prevailing philosophy of "only the strong survive." The Carnotaurus climax reprises the Allosaurus raid in *One Million Years B.C.*, as the courage of one inspires the previously passive others to make a stand. And of course the whole film is essentially a remake of Howard Hawks' *Red River* (1948), with Aladar as Montgomery Clift and Kron as John Wayne. (If only the funny sidekick in *Dinosaur* could've been voiced by Walter Brennan, as a toothless ol' Stygimoloch, maybe.)

So much for the bad news, now the good. There are moments and passages in *Dinosaur* that are nothing less than awesome, and they begin with the opening prologue: seven minutes of dino-paradise. The number of species, the sweeping vistas, the energy of the camera moves, the triumphant music all click, and the dinosaurs themselves look wonderful and so very alive. Their wrinkles and flesh folds, scars and colors, horns and frills, ponderous strides and sprinting gaits, and everything about them is absolutely right (until they start to ... you know). The attack of the malevolent-looking Carnotaurus, tinged a deliciously evil blood-red, is an instant adrenaline rush, and the sequence somehow gets even better when the Pteranodon plucks the egg from the river. The camera follows as the creature soars above valleys, cliffs, waterfalls, and sprawling herds of hundreds of dinosaurs. It looks for all the world as if someone put a Steadicam on a time-traveling helicopter and flew over some Mesozoic version of the Serengeti. But then the egg is dropped onto the island and the horrendously cute baby hatches, and urinates on a lemur ... and the grandeur factor takes a decided downturn. This is not to imply that *Dinosaur* would have been better as a plotless travelogue, just that it would have been nice if the story, so saturated with possibilities, could have simply maintained a bit of *dignity*.

Another phenomenal sequence comes along about a third of the way into the film. It is twilight, everything is at peace, a shooting star appears. But then another, and another, and soon hundreds of glowing streaks illuminate the sky. The animals sense something is very, very wrong. The ominous feel is gripping — it's a masterpiece of mood. Then the Big One, surrounded by a coma of roiling oranges and reds, approaches and hits, with overtones of an atomic blast amplifying the tragic atmosphere. The similar sequence in *T-Rex: Back to the Cretaceous* had the advantages of the large IMAX format and 3-D effects, yet this one chillingly tops it. The meteor impact is simultaneously beautiful and frightening, which raises the question of the scariness factor. *Dinosaur* earns its PG rating, and the night I saw it several small fry climbed into parents' laps for added security during the Carnotaurus attacks. There's nothing terrifying though, and no gory stuff; the predatory carnage is always obscured by dust, shot from very long distance, or not shown at all.

The voice cast is strong, though D. B. Sweeney's guy-next-door delivery makes for a pretty bland hero. In fairness to Sweeney — he proved in *The Book of Stars* (2000) that he can be terrific in a voice-over role — the character is *written* blandly and the intentionally "horsey" facial modifications given to Neera and Aladar (Alydar?) add to the generic feel. The heavies, Kron and Bruton, are voiced in stereotypically graveled tones by Samuel E. Wright and Peter Siragusa but at least have some pizzazz. In contrast to the plain-featured Aladar, these brutes are given so many ridges, knobs, and bumps on their noggins that they look downright Klingonesque. Ossie Davis has one of those character-rich voices that's made for animation, Alfre Woodard is fine as the steady Plio, and Hayden Panettiere invests little Suri with heart. Max Casella can't be blamed for Zini's excesses; he just played the role he was given. Joan Plowright brings a stateliness to the towering Baylene (the British accent factor again), and Della Reese plays Della Reese better than anybody. Actually, Eema is a fun character, and if she was the comic relief — the *only* comic relief — *Dinosaur* would be a considerably better film.

The story admittedly picks up steam towards the end, and it's no coincidence that the film gets better when the dialogue gets scarcer. The final showdown between the herd and the Carnotaurus is a satisfying climax, and Aladar's simple plea, "Stand *together!*" is Sweeney's finest moment. The shot of Aladar advancing alone, and then one after another of his comrades stepping into frame is a great bit of visual construction, and the carnotaur's confused, fidgety reaction is the most believable animal behavior in the film.

Technically, *Dinosaur* is beyond reproach. The dinosaurs are masterpieces, inhabiting majestic landscapes both green and barren; everyone on the modeling and animation teams is to be commended. Sound designer Christopher Boyes, a *Jurassic Park* alumnus whose incredible work on *Titanic* (1997) was a major (though unheralded) part of that film's impact, does another exemplary job. The score by James Newton Howard is generally very good and occasionally terrific,

The "good guys" of *Dinosaur* in a promo portrait — Eema the styracosaur, Baylene the brachiosaur, and Iguanodons Aladar and Neera.

though in places a bit too reminiscent of the music in Disney's remake of *Mighty Joe Young* (which itself recalled the music from *The Lion King*).

In one scene of *Barney's Great Adventure*, a skeptical boy says to Barn, "Look pal, real dinosaurs don't talk." It would have been interesting to see the result had *Dinosaur*'s makers listened to that lad — what a wondrous fountain of creativity that decision might have unleashed. *Dinosaur* is entertaining, sometimes extremely so. Dino aficionados won't be able to help but enjoy the sights on display, though most such folk I've talked with find the spectacular BBC special *Walking with Dinosaurs* more compelling. With a tighter, smarter, fresher script and without having all its edges rounded off by excessive handling, *Dinosaur* truly could have been the "ultimate dinosaur movie," instead of merely a visually impressive but otherwise familiar Disney flick. In *Walt Disney's Fantasia*, author John Culhane quotes Walt himself offering guidance to Wolfgang "Woolie" Reitherman, supervising animator on *Fantasia*'s dinosaur sequence. "Don't make them cute animal personalities," Walt urged. "Make them real!" Walt and Woolie, where were you when we needed you.

PEOPLE AND PRODUCTION: Preproduction on Willis O'Brien's original *Gwangi* began in 1941, and Ray Harryhausen finally filmed the reworked version, *The Valley of Gwangi*, in 1969. That's a long time, but only slightly longer than *Dinosaur* was in the works in one form or another. Like Aladar's egg, this *Dinosaur* went through quite a journey before it finally hatched.

While making *Robocop* (1987), Phil Tippett, producer Jon Davison, and director Paul Verhoeven discussed ideas for a dinosaur picture unlike any other. They envisioned it as a visual story with no dialogue — no narration, no "thought" voice-overs, no talking — and when pitching the project cited

Jean-Jacques Annaud's films such as *Quest for Fire* (1982) and *The Bear* (1989) as evidence that such a story could be successfully told. Writer Walon Green was brought aboard to pen the screenplay. "Walon wrote this very interesting script that I liked a lot," Tippett stated in *Cinefantastique*. "You can imagine the kind of thing Paul Verhoeven would be interested in. It was very visceral and prehistoric without any people or narration. We hoped to get our ideas across by using pantomime, music, sound effects and carefully constructing the scenes." But problems arose involving the budget and some large-scale changes that Disney insisted upon. "They wanted to turn the dinosaurs into Disney-esque animals," Tippett said, foreshadowing the eventual film.

By the early 1990s, Tippett had still not given up on *Dinosaurs* (the film's earlier plural title) and was thus reluctant to commit to a different dinosaur project he was being offered. "As it happened, that's when Steven Spielberg was trying to solicit my involvement in *Jurassic Park*," Tippett told the author. "So even while I was waiting for meetings on the Disney lot, I would be reading the unpublished galleys of the Michael Crichton manuscript." Finally, as Tippett put it, "Paul and Jon and I did not quite see eye to eye with what Disney wanted to do," and all three went their separate ways.

Left with the embryonic project, Disney execs gave Tom Smith (previously general manager of Industrial Light & Magic) a green light to research ways that it might be done economically. An investigation of European animation facilities found none of sufficient quality and capacity and Smith would soon be assigned to a different project, but before leaving he recommended that David Allen be put on the job. Disney followed the recommendation, according to Chris Endicott, Allen's longtime friend and associate. "For about six months Dave was heavily involved," said Endicott. Andrea Von Sholly sculpted a prototype of the lead character, which at that time was *not* going to be an Iguanodon, but some kind of ceratopsian — a Styracosaurus or Monoclonius or something." Allen knew there was no way to do an all stop-motion film on the budget being mentioned and began to consider alternatives. A stop-motion and rod-puppet combination was tentatively settled upon, with Will Vinton Studios to host the work. "They [Disney] felt that the facility was adequate for our needs," David Allen said in *Cinefantastique*. "They were trying to get us to use some of their animators, which might have worked out fine. At the time I wasn't too sold on the idea because they were so into the clay-only approach, but I think they have some wonderful animators." Again, though, *Jurassic Park* reared its massive head. "Disney kind of got cold feet," said Chris Endicott. "They said, 'Let's just wait until *Jurassic Park* comes out and see how that changes the landscape.' So they basically just let the picture go and that was that, until it got brought out again as a CG feature."

The astonishing success of *Jurassic* helped convince Disney to ramp up production on *Dinosaur*. In 1995, Ralph Zondag (previously involved with *The Land Before Time* and *We're Back: A Dinosaur's Story*) and Eric Leighton were hired as directors — Zondag to helm the story development and post-production phase, Leighton to direct the animation itself. A Herculean task awaited — animators had to be hired, software written and modified, background plates filmed on locations worldwide, characters designed, and the story finalized, a task that continued almost to the end of production. By the time the film was finished, a veritable swarm of scribes had put in their two cents worth. It is an oversimplification to say that the plans evolved from a totally dialogue-free story, to a "think-talk" story, to a talking story, but that was the basic chronology. Ralph Zondag feared that the think-talk idea would leave the viewer "somewhat disconnected from the characters," and Eric Leighton said of the no-dialogue scenario, "We actually *tried* to do that, but it's very difficult to tell a story that way." Some of the reasons cited for the final decision bordered on the bizarre. Leighton even said that, due to the success of *Babe*, "the fear was that people would think that we just didn't want to spend the money to make the lips move." The final choice was destined to generate a lot of commentary — not all positive — from critics, audiences, and the filmmakers themselves.

So the dinosaurs would talk; it was now left to determine what they would say. In *Starlog*'s official *Dinosaur* tie-in magazine, producer Pam Marsden discussed the effort to prevent the dialogue from getting too contemporary. "We wanted to keep it timeless and epic," Marsden said. "No one ever says, 'Hey, that's cool,' 'Cowabunga, dude,' or any of that hip stuff. So, from that perspective, we limited the language we could use." But she went on to mention that their self-imposed rules "became less constricted" as more humor found its way into the script. This relaxation may explain why, though there are no "cools" or "dudes," there are lines like "we're outta here!" and "that, children, is what's known as a *jerkasaurus*." An anonymous *Dinosaur* staffer revealed to this author that many of the film's artists and technicians were not pleased by the way things were unfolding. There seemed to be a general consensus that speaking dinosaurs might be a workable concept if properly done, but that the execution went woefully wrong. As instructions for new scenes and dialogue came down from above, winces, cringes, and cries of "say it isn't true!" were commonplace among the animators and tech staff. Though almost nobody liked the increasingly shtick-laden lines, everyone gave their all to make the best of what they were handed.

Discarding an early scheme to shoot the entire film with miniature settings, the decision was made to photograph live backgrounds in multiple locations and composite the CG characters into these Vistavision plates. The 18 months of location work utilized an innovative device dubbed "Dinocam," providing dynamic camera movements with computer precision on a dinosaurian scale. "The height of the dinosaurs in these shots was too high for most camera cranes and too low for most aerial camera setups," visual effects supervisor Neil Krepela explained. "But a cable-suspended motion control camera could get views from as low as a foot off the ground to as high as seventy feet in the air." Chosen locations included Venezuela, Australia, Western Samoa, three Hawaiian islands, the Mojave Desert, Florida, and even the Los Angeles County Arboretum. It would be up to the 48 animators and 350-person crew staffing Disney's brand new digital animation studio — "The Secret Lab" — to populate 1,300 shots with 30 species of prehistoric creatures.

SPECIAL EFFECTS: It seems odd to discuss the "special effects" in *Dinosaur*, since as one of its makers once said, the film itself is "one long special effect." As such, it presented a challenge in terms of pure digital workload that eclipsed *Jurassic Park*, or its sequel, or anything else done up to that time.

The dino designers always knew that a lot of "artistic license" would be taken, particularly with the leading characters, but much effort still went into learning everything possible about the real animals. Not only were Jack Horner and Don Lessem consulted — as they had been on *Jurassic Park*—but also a number of leading paleo-artists as well. The input of William Stout, Mark Hallett, Doug Henderson, Brian Franczak and others was synthesized with the visions of directors Leighton and Zondag, then finished by visual-development artist David Krentz. "It would be safe to say I completed the designs," Krentz told author Bill Warren. "There were many people who had a crack at it, but I was involved in the finalization, and actually designed a few from scratch." To assist in character recognition, the four principal Iguanodons were given distinctive traits. "So that's why we put a mountain on Kron's nose, and a loaf of bread on Bruton's face," Krentz explained.

It's comforting to learn that many of the digital animators retained an affection for "classic" techniques, the artists who mastered them, and the films which couldn't

The earnest Aladar, certainly no (Iguano)Don Juan, finally finds his love match in the rouge-cheeked Neera.

have been made without them. Neil Krepela wanted, as he put it, "to get back to that experience we all had when we first saw *King Kong*—Skull Island! Wow! I would love to go there." Krepela hoped to achieve a mythic, legendary quality. "Like many things that are mythological in the human sense, it takes on a feeling that's not quite what we know reality is," Krepela explained. "Of course, Ray Harryhausen was the master of this, taking myths and making them real." Thom Enriquez, *Dinosaur*'s director of story, is a huge *Kong* fan. "Back when I first saw the re-release of *King Kong*, there was no merchandising in those days," he stated in the *Dinosaur* official magazine. "I couldn't go back to see the movie again because it cost too much, so I just sat down with a piece of paper and tried to draw King Kong and the dinosaurs I had seen in the movie." Even Doug Henderson, who guided the "look" of the Cretaceous environments, reportedly drew inspiration from *Kong*'s evocative, glass-painted jungles.

About one third of *Dinosaur*'s animators came from the stop-motion community. "Neera" supervising animator Joel Fletcher has a particularly lengthy feature résumé, including *The Nightmare Before Christmas* (1993), *Dragonworld* (1994), and *Magic Island* (1995). Like others, he looked at film of modern large animals for clues, but also found inspiration in the dinosaur classics of Ray Harryhausen and Jim Danforth. "That was all just ingrained in my head since I was a little kid," he told author Kyle Counts. While appreciating CG's capabilities, Fletcher unabashedly pines for earlier times. "I do miss the hands-on part of stop-motion," he said. "In some ways, computers are kind of evil, because they make it so easy … if you make a mistake, you just redo it. Stop-motion has that energy and magic about it. Subliminally, you know someone's there, making that happen." Fletcher concedes the limitations of the old methods but points out that digital animation has its own drawbacks. "CGI gets too many hands in the mix," he asserted. "Whereas with stop-motion, there's just the one guy in that room, and he's in this Zen-like trance, doing his animation. And somehow that translates over. It has more power."

With the computing cycles and manpower available, it's hard to realize that some planned shots had to be scrubbed. One sequence had Aladar saving several compatriots from the jaws of an aquatic Mosasaurus, but the number of dinos, the intricate action and the added headaches caused by water sealed its fate. Another nixed sequence would have seen Aladar and Kron staging a fight on the edge of an active volcano. "We finally realized, 'We have to do fur, we can't be worrying about lava,'" Pam Marsden recalled. "Every day was about picking our battles."

If one looks closely enough, nearly 30 prehistoric species—not all dinosaurs—can be found in *Dinosaur*. The Iguanodon, Velociraptor, Carnotaurus, Brachiosaurus, and Styracosaurus are most prominently featured, but supporting and background species include Ankylosaurus and other ankylosaurs, Pachyrhinosaurus and other ceratopsians, Parasaurolophus and other hadrosaurs, Oviraptor, Struthiomimus, Stygimoloch, Pteranodon, Ichthyornis, Koolasuchus, and still more.

The Dinosaur and the Missing Link

**½ 1915, USA. Edison/Conquest Pictures. BW, Silent.

CREDITS: *Director/Animator* Willis O'Brien. *Producer* Herman Wobber.

Subtitled "A Prehistoric Tragedy." First and probably the best-known of O'Brien's short animated comedies, financed by Herman Wobber. As in all of Obie's slapstick one-reelers, all of the characters are represented by fairly crude stop-motion puppets, made by sculpting clay over a jointed wooden armature. The plot this time has the Duke, Stonejaw Steve, and Theophilus Ivoryhead competing for the love of Araminta Rockface, while "Wild Willie, the Missing Link" terrifies the populace. When Willie mistakes a brontosaur's whiplike tail for a tasty snake and gets knocked out by the perturbed dinosaur, Theophilus takes the credit and wins Araminta's heart with his bravery. This film was purchased for exhibition by the Edison Company and earned O'Brien his job there; the studio later re-released it as *The Dinosaur and the Baboon*. Obie's ability to inject life into a stop-motion simian can already be seen, even in the lowbrow antics of "Wild Willie."

Dinosaur Babes

"Knowledge is always a frightening thing to the savage mind."

* 1996, USA. Take 2 Productions. C, 93m.

CREDITS: *Director* Brett Piper. *Producers* George Barnes, William T. Threlkeld, Bill Mesce, Jr. (executive), Vic Hunter (associate). *Written by* Brett Piper.

CAST: *Zach* Rick Bureau. *Shifty* Mike Whitehead. *Bruno* Jeff Corniello. *Lona* Melissa Ann. *Leela* Kathi Trotter. *Monga* Iris Lynne. *Gretta* Kelly Lynn. *Mook* Dianne Thorne.

"Four million years ago, the first true humans and the last of the dinosaurs briefly coexisted," but it was not a harmonious situation. Three clueless cavemen named Zach, Shifty, and Bruno return from a hunt one day and find that almost everyone in their village has been massacred. A lone survivor tells of the raiders who abducted three of their women: Leela, Gretta, and Mook. Unbeknownst to the fellows, the girls have been taken by an all-female tribe led by the brutal Monga, and poor Mook has already been sacrificed to a Tyrannosaurus rex. Searching for their ladies, the guys stumble upon a wrecked spaceship and easily defeat the three mutant humans who suddenly attack them. Meanwhile, the beautiful Lona, from Monga's tribe, gets caught in an unauthorized tête-à-tête with the captive Leela and is cruelly punished—an act which will later motivate her to turn against Monga and side with Zach's faction. Zach and his pals evade a horned Centrosaurus and a vicious Carnotaurus and finally reach Monga's village. They lure the Centrosaurus into camp as a diversion and manage to liberate the girls, but Monga hunts down and captures all but Zach and Lona. Zach discovers an ancient ray gun inside the ruined spacecraft and uses it to rescue his friends, just as Leela is about to become the next sacrifice.

COMMENTARY: One would not expect a straight-to-video entry with a title like *Dinosaur Babes* to be a good movie, but one might hope that it would offer some mindless fun. *Dinosaur Babes* is neither good nor fun, but rather slow and schizophrenic. Sometimes it wants to be a spoof, giving its heroes names like "Shifty" and having them slip and fall on piles of dino dung. Other times it wants to be titillating, repeatedly undressing comely starlets Melissa Ann and Kathi Trotter. Still other times it seemingly wants to be taken seriously, and the whole subplot with the spaceship and the "genetically altered sub-humans" is played dead straight. *Dinosaur Babes* is also mean-spirited and misogynistic, taking every opportunity to have its lovely ladies beaten, hung upside down, or eaten alive by parasites. Interspersed among all this strangeness are a comparatively large number of dinosaur scenes, some of which are surprisingly good. The Brontosaurus, Stegosaurus, and Carnotaurus are stop-motion effects, the Tyrannosaurus and Lambeosaurus are live-action puppets, and the Centrosaurus is some of both. The animation style is a bit unusual and very lively, with a lot of "zip pans," but the backgrounds and miniature settings betray the low budget. The live-action puppets are better than expected, with handsome detailing and paleontologically correct design. It's just too bad that these often-impressive dinosaurs weren't put to better use than in service of this incomprehensible bore.

SPECIAL EFFECTS: The special effects are the work of the talented Brett Piper, who earlier had produced, directed, and created animation for the deliciously titled *A Nymphoid Barbarian in Dinosaur Hell*. Though he is the credited writer and director of *Dinosaur Babes*, and it was initially his project, he disavows the picture in its present form. Interviewed by Kevin G. Shinnick in *SPFX* (#5), Piper talked about the movie's troubled history. "I offered it to Troma first," Piper recalled. "I called them up, talked to Lloyd Kaufman and said, 'you know, I've got a house full of dinosaurs and you guys like movies with lots of babes, why don't we do a movie called *Dinosaur Babes*?'" But the Troma folks wanted to do a major rewrite, and "I said no," Piper explained.

The project eventually ended up with Take 2 Productions, and it was not a happy relationship. "I haven't even seen the thing," Piper said. "As soon as they had all the footage they needed, they yanked the thing out from under me and finished it themselves. They basically took the raw footage and made the movie, so the movie you see is simply not mine." On a lighter note, Piper also talked a bit about the dinosaurs. "I had them lying around the house," he said of the dino puppets. "The only one I made for the movie was the giant mutant T. rex head." *Dinosaur Babes* also required a derelict spacecraft. "Actually it's a vacuum cleaner," Piper revealed. "I walked into a used vacuum cleaner shop, picked one out of a junk pile, took it home and three hours later it was a space ship."

Dinosaur Island

"Are you sure you never hit your head when the plane crashed?"

**   1993, USA. Pacific Trust. C, 80m.

76 • *Dinosaur Island*

CREDITS: *Directors* Jim Wynorski, Fred Olen Ray. *Producers* Jim Wynorski, Fred Olen Ray, Mike Elliott (executive), Craig Nevius (associate). *Screenplay* Bob Sheridan and Christopher Wooden. *Story* Bob Sheridan. *Special Visual Effects* Hal Miles and Milestone Productions. *Live Action Dinosaurs* John Carl Buechler and Magical Media Industries.

CAST: *Capt. Jason Briggs* Ross Hagen. *Pvt. John Skeemer* Richard Gabai. *April* Antonia Dorian. *June* Michelle Bauer. *Pvt. Wilbur Turbowski* Peter Spellos. *Pvt. Wayne Kincaid* Tom Shell. *Sgt. Ben Healey* Steve Barkett. *May* Griffen Drew. *Queen Morganna* Toni Naples.

AD LINE: "Just like paradise, only better looking."

An army transport plane suddenly falls from the sky into a remote region of the Pacific. On board are Capt. Jason Briggs, his second in command, Sgt. Ben Healey, Buzz the pilot, and three hapless enlisted men: John Skeemer, Wayne "the Brain" Kincaid, and Wilbur "Turbo" Turbowski. They wash ashore on an uncharted island swarming with bikinied beach babes and hulking prehistoric monsters, and Buzz almost immediately becomes the first victim (of the monsters, not the babes). Queen Morganna distrusts the strangers, but one girl notices a smily-face tattoo on Skeemer's saggy bicep. "You bear the mark!" she says, identifying the GIs as gods who will destroy the huge T. rex — "The Great One" — that's the scourge of the island. Three of the girls, whom Skeemer names Miss April, Miss May, and Miss June, somehow "prepare the men for battle" by frolicking topless in the creek. The well-prepared fellows proceed to ineptly gun down a Triceratops, but lose Sergeant Healey and exhaust their ammo in the process.

Despite their help in ending the island's agricultural blight, Queen Morganna still doesn't like the guys' influence on her population. Hoping that Briggs can find a way to leave (and thus take his men with him), she reveals a cache of weapons left on the island during World War II. Now well-armed, Briggs, his men, and their girls set out in search of the Great One. They lure the beast into the open and unleash a hail of gunfire, but only when Turbo lands a grenade in its mouth does it finally succumb. Morganna finally gives her blessing to the young couples and even convinces Briggs to stay behind as her new king.

COMMENTARY: Cinematically speaking, 1993 could be called the Year of the Dinosaur. There were awe-inspiring dinos (*Jurassic Park*), bloodthirsty dinos (*Carnosaur*), big dinos for little kids (*We're Back*), and little dinos for bigger kids (*Prehysteria!*). We even had Dennis Hopper as a dino (*Super Mario Bros.*), so why not horny dinos too? So we ended up with *Dinosaur Island*, which brings a whole new meaning to the term "giant monsters on the loose."

Intended as a sort of homage to both *One Million Years B.C.* and, interestingly, *Mysterious Island* (1961), *Dinosaur Island* includes both hallmarks of Hammer's 1966 classic — marauding dinosaurs and feminine pulchritude — while owing much of its plot to the howlingly bad 1952 relic *Untamed Women*. *Island* and *Untamed* both have a planeload of soldiers marooned on an uncharted island populated by prehistoric monsters and an all-female tribe. Continuing the parallels, the island's queen is suspicious of the strangers, while her younger subjects are much more hospitable. *Dinosaur Island* even hints that the tribe is connected to the Druids, also the supposed ancestors of the *Untamed Women*. A final inspiration was the lowbrow military comedy *Stripes* (1981), and the three lovable-loser GIs seem to be directly patterned on the roles played by Bill Murray, Harold Ramis, and the late John Candy.

The cast is not nearly as bad as one might imagine. Ross Hagen manages to sound authoritative even when barking out lines like "let's snap to, we've got bigger fish to fry!" The three principal cavegirls — Antonia Dorian, Griffen Drew (also in *Dinosaur Valley Girls*), and the venerable Michelle Bauer — are beautiful, say their lines clearly, and seem to be enjoying the whole thing. Toni Naples plays it deadly serious as Mor-

Dinosaur Island **managed to wring some more mileage out of the ambitious full-scale T. rex built for** ***Carnosaur.***

ganna, and sexploitation star Becky Le-Beau — in a sly in-joke — has a bouncy cameo as the "Virgin Sacrifice." The actors playing the GIs seem to be doing intentional impressions of their *Stripes* counterparts, which is okay as long as you can pull it off. Tom Shell and Peter Spellos are fine as the egghead and the soft-hearted lug, but Richard Gabai, bless him, just can't deliver a punch line to save his life.

The outlandish plot keeps things moving briskly, leaving thankfully little time to ponder the nagging continuity questions. For example, the opening narration states that all three soldiers have the rank of private, so why does Captain Briggs twice call Kincaid "Lieutenant?" After June defeats Morganna in their ritual challenge, why is Morganna still the queen? And why do the cavegirls have "tribal" names for the Brontosaurus ("thunder beast"), Triceratops ("beast of armor"), and Tyrannosaurus (the "Great One"), but just call a pterodactyl a pterodactyl? The intentional laughs are discouragingly scarce but there are occasional gems, like when April first mentions the "Great One" and a puzzled Skeemer mumbles, "Jackie Gleason?" The movie could use more such moments, and a larger dose of dino-movie in-jokes would have made a nice alternative to lines like "you got a problem with your privates, Private?" and "don't you know where pterodactyl eggs come from?" With Roger Corman involved, one could have even hoped that *Dinosaur Island* might have done for dinomovies what the much funnier *Hollywood Boulevard* (1976) did for B-movies, making fun of their absurdities while simultaneously paying affectionate tribute to those indomitable souls who defy all odds to make them. If *Dinosaur Island 2* is ever filmed, let us hope Joe Dante directs.

Unlike the dino comedians in *Caveman*, the dinosaurs of *Dinosaur Island* are played completely straight. However, extensive use of the full-size T. rex from *Carnosaur* causes some of the dino scenes to be laughable after all. Helped by dim lighting and quick cutting, the big mock-up was passably effective in *Carnosaur* and especially *Carnosaur II*, but is here brought into the glaring sunlight and left on-screen for long stretches, and as the *Motion Picture Guide* accurately points out, "seems to intimidate our heroes mainly by threatening to fall on them." The slightly gory shot of a cave beauty having her arm chewed by the immobile rex was described by Brad Linaweaver in *Famous Monsters* magazine as "scary (with an eerie twilight glow)" and "symbolic of the appeal of this kind of movie." To this author, it just looks like the poor lass got her arm stuck in a video-store standee for the latest *Land Before Time* sequel.

The stop-motion dinos are better than the statuesque T. rex puppet but sadly get far less screen time. Despite their brief appearances, animator Hal Miles managed to infuse his creations with a surprising amount of character. The Triceratops sequence features a unique bit of action, as the wounded beast is forced to "carry" his left forelimb like a puppy with a gimpy paw. The too-short pterodactyl sequence also has a great moment, when the creature descends and menaces our heroes in a flapping, darting, and enjoyably familiar manner. "That's my *One Million Years B.C.*, 'homage-to-Ray' kind of shot," Miles told me. "The wing flap timing is actually directly from *One Million Years.*" Miles had an astonishing ten days, rather than the months that would be allotted on a big-budget picture, to set up and animate his dinosaurs, but anything the work lacks in fluidity it makes up for in Miles' obvious affection for stop-motion history.

Watching *Dinosaur Island*, the thought occurs that the various attempts over the years to combine dinosaurs and comedy have fallen close to and all around the bull's-eye, but have never scored a direct hit. *Dinosaurus!* offered a likably comic Neanderthal thrown into modern times, *Caveman* gave us fantastic and funny dinosaurs combined with bathroom jokes, and *Dinosaur Island* stirs a helping of bare breasts into the mix, but they've all been lacking in one way or another. Until that ultimate dino-comedy is cooked up, a goofy and good-natured snack like *Dinosaur Island* will have to do.

PEOPLE AND PRODUCTION: *Dinosaur Island* brought together a trio of B-movie heavyweights: Fred Olen Ray, Jim Wynorski, and the legendary Roger Corman. Ray had previously featured dinosaurs in *The Phantom Empire* and *Demon Sword*, but where both of those efforts used dino footage recycled from *Planet of Dinosaurs*, *Dinosaur Island* would have all-new effects. Ray once again called on *Phantom Empire* alumni Ross Hagen and Michelle Bauer, who are probably the two biggest names on the *Island* roster. "My friends hate me," Hagen jokingly told author Mark Altman in *Femme Fatales* magazine. "Most people have to go to work for a living." The decided lack of "star quality" is evidenced by the advertising, which tried to beef up Richard Gabai's recognition factor by pointing out that he was in *Assault of the Party Nerds*. (In such a case, would it not perhaps be better to say nothing at all?) A more familiar name rolls by during the end titles, under the heading "Special Thanks," but don't get the idea that Ray Harryhausen contributed to the movie in any fashion. "I guess they wanted it as an homage or something, I don't know," Harryhausen told the author. "I had no connection with the picture."

The screenplay is based on a story by Bob Sheridan (who also plays the ill-fated Buzz), but its tone underwent some changes between conception and production. Interviewed in *Famous Monsters of Filmland* (#202), Fred Olen Ray talked about the modifications. "The film originally started out as sort of a 1940s thing with World War II soldiers as opposed to modern day, but Roger thought modern day would be better. And they wanted it a little more comical than we originally anticipated." A fondly remembered comic book called *Star Spangled War Stories*,

Hal Miles animates the luckless Triceratops, doomed to serve as target practice for the soldiers on *Dinosaur Island*.

which featured WWII soldiers fighting prehistoric beasts in the South Pacific, also provided inspiration. The real intent of the picture never changed, however, and it was summed up by Ray: "Every time you wished Raquel Welch's or Martine Beswick's top would pop off and it didn't, well, now it does!"

Locations employed during the 10-day shoot included Leo Carillo State Beach, where the discovery of the underworld ocean in *Journey to the Center of the Earth* had been shot thirty-five years earlier. Three days were spent north of the San Fernando Valley at Vasquez Rocks, the "burial ground" and village shots were done at David Carradine's ranch, and that old B-movie standby Bronson Canyons filled in for the rest. A bonus awaited the filmmakers at Vasquez Rocks— some exotic prop foliage constructed for the big-screen version of *The Flintstones* was still in place, and a few establishing shots were captured before the *Flintstones* crew called a halt. One last day of "closed set" shooting for the frolicking-in-the-river sequence, and it was a wrap. The film, always intended to go straight to video, was shot on 16mm.

SPECIAL EFFECTS: Unlike many filmmakers through the years who have shunned stop-motion animation as "too expensive," Fred Olen Ray agreed to add stop-motion to *Dinosaur Island* because he was looking to *save* money. Effects artist Hal Miles had a previous association with Ray (on *The Alien Within*), and had some already-completed stop-motion puppets made for a planned educational short called *The Dinosaur Zoo*. "I approached Fred with the concept of doing *Dinosaur Island* with stop-motion dinosaurs," Miles said, "at which time he told me that Roger Corman wanted the T. rex that John Buechler had built for *Carnosaur* to be in this picture." Realizing there were still plenty of other dino scenes, Miles signed aboard.

Hal Miles' interest in special effects began as a youngster. "It seems like every effects artist has a movie that possessed them," Miles said, "and for me it was *Mighty Joe Young*. So I graduated from high school in 1978, and in December gathered my little films and puppets and whatnot, and flew to Los Angeles." He was hoping to land a job with Cascade Pictures of California, home at one time or another to a multitude of top FX creators. "Back then, the effects community was still a very small, closely knit group of people," Miles explained. "They were not only professionals, they were fans, so we all got along great." In the coming years, Miles would contribute mechanical, animatronic, and digital effects to more than fifty feature films, including *The Abyss* (1989), *Terminator 2* (1990), and *Body Snatchers* (1992).

Miles animated a total of 43 stop-

The nifty stop-motion tylosaur animated by Hal Miles, seen here head-butting Private Kinkaid (Tom Shell) in a digital composite, was inexplicably replaced in the release print by a nondescript hand-puppet dino.

motion shots for *Dinosaur Island*. Yes, 43 shots, and no, there aren't that many in the movie, due to some rather inexplicable decisions from above. Originally, the first dinosaur sequence (where "Buzz" meets his fate) was to have been a rather extravagant stop-motion set piece featuring an attacking Plesiosaurus. "I had a puppet already built for *The Dinosaur Zoo* which was more like a tylosaur," Miles explained, "which still fit into the scheme of it being an oceanic type of creature." Unlike the well-publicized brontosaur-attack climax for *One Million Years B.C.*, this time the work was actually done. Miles animated a full-blown 21-shot sequence with the tylosaur which he described as "the best work I had done on this picture." In a turn of events that is puzzling to say the least, the powers that be decided to replace the entire stop-motion sequence with another *Carnosaur* hand-me-down, and did so without informing Miles. "So, I'm at the cast-and-crew screening and I'm going, 'okay great, the first big sequence is coming up,' and then … it's this hand puppet," Miles lamented. "That was kind of disappointing." (This author was given the opportunity to see the tylosaur animation, and *Dinosaur Island* suffers for its having been eliminated.)

The excision of the tylosaur left the 10-shot Triceratops encounter as the movie's only sizable stop-motion sequence. But again, Miles was bound by decisions from above. "They left the sequence intact," Miles explained, "but I tried to talk them into making the cuts a little longer. In the shot where he actually falls over, he has to pick himself up so fast because the cut that they had already approved was just so fast." The remainder of the stop-motion consists of four Brontosaurus shots (two pairs of two), two shots which show one of the crop-destroying insects, and three pterodactyl shots. Miles had animated two additional pterosaur closeups — one of which had the creature preening itself like a bird — but they were replaced by yet another hand puppet. All of the animation is Miles' work but he is quick to credit the contributions of his assistant, Jim Davidson. "Jim was just fantastic, and a real dinosaur enthusiast also," Miles said. "His help was just priceless on this film."

In addition to the animation, Miles also handled the picture's "forced perspective" effects. In this time-honored technique, two subjects (often a miniature prop and a live actor) are photographed — one close to the camera, one far away. Since film is a two-dimensional medium, the human eye will perceive the two objects as vastly different in size rather than at different distances, and a small foreground miniature can be made to appear gigantic. Effective use of this technique requires careful attention to detail, and if the depth of field is insufficient to hold sharp focus on both subjects, the illusion is ruined. In *Dinosaur Island*, the first two forced-perspective shots show the group walking through the skeletal ribcage, and the dead Triceratops with the soldiers behind it. These shots were done with the same 16mm Arriflex camera being used to shoot the entire picture, and turned out fine. But then the shoot fell behind schedule and Miles lost the services of the principal camera. He had to do the remaining forced perspective shots, including the giant egg and the big stone idol, with "a bizarre 16mm camera that was made out of plastic, even the lens!"

Despite the inevitable low-budget-oriented frustrations, Miles has fond memories of *Dinosaur Island*. "All in all it was one of the most relaxed and fun shoots I've been on," he noted. "And what a great wrap party at David Carradine's!"

Dinosaur Valley Girls

"I've got a feeling weirdness isn't over yet."
** 1996, USA. Frontline Entertainment, Inc. C, 94m.

CREDITS: *Director* Donald F. Glut. *Producers* Kevin M. Glover, Daniel J. Mullen (executive), Melodee M. Spevack (associate). *Written by* Donald F. Glut. *Special Visual Effects* Thomas R. Dickens. *Creature Animatronics* Ken Walker.

Stop-Motion Cinematographer/Animator Thomas R. Dickens.

CAST: *Tony Markham* Jeff Rector. *Hea-Thor* Denise Ames. *Dr. Benjamin Michaels* William Marshall. *Ro-Kell* Karen Black. *Ur-So* Ed Fury. *Beeg-Mak* Harrison Ray. *Daphne Adrian* Griffen Drew.

Action-movie star Tony Markham is preparing to shoot *Feet of Fury IV*, but he's troubled. Fed up with his spoiled girlfriend, Daphne, and plagued by inexplicable visions of dinosaurs and a beautiful cavewoman, he visits paleontologist Dr. Benjamin Michaels. The scientist shows Tony a strange artifact, supposedly possessing the power to grant wishes, and Tony suddenly finds himself surrounded by stegosaurs and flying reptiles in a strange prehistoric milieu called "Dinosaur Valley." He is chased by a vicious Allosaurus and runs into a stunning woman — the same dino and girl seen in his dreams. The girl, Hea-Thor, is part of an all-female faction who split from their barbaric male counterparts. The younger tribeswomen are fascinated with Tony but their leader, Ro-Kell, carries a torch for the men's chief, Ur-So. Tony for a while allows himself to enjoy the ladies' "hospitality," but finally vows to be true to Hea-Thor. The cavemen, incited by Ur-So's hot-tempered lieutenant, Beeg-Mak, raid the female camp — unaware that Tony has schooled the girls in martial arts! Ur-So and Ro-Kell finally decide they have better things to do than fight, and when they make up, everyone does. After driving off the pesky Allosaurus and making a final jaunt back to the present-day museum, Tony returns to Dinosaur Valley. He finally makes a friend out of Beeg-Mak (by kicking him in the jaw), and lives happily ever after with Hea-Thor.

COMMENTARY: Making a lighthearted, sexy, dinosaurs-and-cavegirls comedy — a really good one, that is — is proving to be quite a challenge. *Dinosaur Island*, a fun but flawed little picture, got some things right. The dreadful *Dinosaur Babes* featured a few good dinosaur special effects and absolutely nothing else. Then in 1996 came *Dinosaur Valley Girls*, written and directed by Donald F. Glut. This one also gets some things right, but like *Dinosaur Island* — and *Caveman* too — it misses a lot of chances to be much better.

The film's title and the amusing pseudo-prehistoric variations of the typical "valley girl" names ("Buf-Fee," "Bam-Bee," "Mee-Shell," and so on) offer a promising start. But before long the plot and humor get awfully familiar — the magical artifact, the scatological gags, and the "modern" guy reacting to his alien surroundings with glib one-liners. "What am I doing?" Tony quips to his cell phone. "This is out of my calling circle!" The leaders' names are references to previous pictures; Ro-Kell is a tribute to the heroine of *One Million Years B.C.*, and Ur-So refers to the muscular hero, Ursus, played by Ed Fury in a couple of 1960s strongman flicks.

Part of the trouble with *Dinosaur Valley Girls* is that it never commits to a tone. It has too much flatulence and too many "Three Stooges" sound effects to be serious, and too much "straight" plot and dialogue to be likably goofy. Its naughty bits are surprisingly tame and the music-video dream sequence midway through the film (an ode to an Allosaurus called "Jurassic Punk") is the most jarring musical interruption in a prehistoric creature movie since the "Tivoli" segment in *Reptilicus*. Still, many of the individual gags work. I liked the dubbing of housecat and lion sounds over the obligatory "catfight" scene, and Tony's constant references to other movie stars and films (including *Jurassic Park*) are enjoyable.

The cast includes such surprising names as Karen Black and the venerable William Marshall, who has one of the greatest voices ever to boom from a soundtrack. Denise Ames is gorgeous, projecting much more intelligence than a typical B-movie ornament, and the several genre-related cameos include Forry Ackerman and author Bill Warren. The dinosaurs, likewise, are more than adequate. The Allosaurus is the star, realized through a combination of animatronics and stop-motion animation. The robotic puppet has impressive detail and intercuts unexpectedly smoothly with the animated version. All of the stop-motion dinos—Allosaurus, Camptosaurus, Pteranodon, Saltasaurus—recall those in *Dinosaur Island* and *Planet of the Dino-Knights*, in that they are obviously the work of talented artists who were given far too little time.

Faults and all, *Dinosaur Valley Girls* is a moderately engaging diversion for adult genre fans. It has flashes of directorial flair from first-timer Glut, a catchy score, pretty girls, intermittent laughs, and production values and effects that often defy the low budget. It's just that with such a great title and "Dinosaur Don" at the helm, one would hope the whole thing might be a bit more *fun*.

PEOPLE AND PRODUCTION: The project that would evolve into *Dinosaur Valley Girls* began when Don Glut's friend Kevin M. Glover was offered the chance to produce a number of erotic but frugally budgeted pictures for the Playboy Channel. Glover asked Glut about possibly writing and directing one of the films, and Glut soon had the idea to combine the saucy shenanigans with a dino theme. When Glut hit on his title both he and Glover knew it was ideal, but a possible problem arose with the discovery that Fred Olen Ray was trying to launch his own cavebabes-and-dinos picture, called *Dinosaur Girl*. "Two such similar titles would certainly cause confusion," Glut wrote in *Dinosaur Valley Girls: The Book*. "Though I'm not certain as to the reasons, Fred graciously offered to change his title." (Fred's picture was made as *Dinosaur Island*.) Though Glut's movie was definitely of the modern variety, he issued a mandate that every actor playing a caveperson had to watch the original *One Million B.C.* at least once.

Glut decided not to take the Playboy Channel deal, and the film's sexual content was toned down. "Originally the cavegirls were supposed to go topless throughout the entire film," Glut revealed, "but that idea proved to be a bust. The shift towards a tamer film was due to two factors. First, Glut and Glover wanted to "ensure that the nudity and other such aspects of the picture not cross over that imaginary line into the realms of raunchiness or sleaze," as Glut stated. Second, several of the actresses playing the Dinosaur Valley girls began to balk at doing the topless scenes they had contracted for. "Kevin and I began to worry seriously about ending up with an unreleasable product," Glut admitted, "a movie too tame for the so-called R-rated type market and too low budget to compete in the mainstream." But most of the ladies—even star cavebabe Denise Ames—eventually overcame their shyness.

Interiors were shot on the multipurpose "cave set" designed by production designer Jeffrey Luther. Locations included Pearblossom, California, as "Dinosaur Valley," the Raymond M. Alf Museum of Paleontology in Claremont, and dear old Bronson Canyon. *Dinosaur Valley Girls* began principal photography (on 16mm) on April 3, 1995, and wrapped on April 18—a Roger Corman–like 16-day shoot. As planned, the picture was edited into two versions: one for family viewing and one with the spicier bits included.

SPECIAL EFFECTS: The first effects artist unofficially connected to *Dinosaur Valley Girls* was Jim Danforth, who was on board for "several weeks" before reconsidering. "He told me that the people making this film would benefit more from his involvement in it than the other way around, which was absolutely true," Glut stated, "and that he was tired of just pushing puppets on other people's movies. I understood Jim's feelings perfectly." The next possibility was Tom Scherman. "Tom was a genius at creating convincing special effects on a budget and on time," Glut noted. Though he was ill, Scherman accepted an advisory position on the film, with sculptors Mike Jones (a veteran of *Carnosaur*) and Thomas Dickens to do the hands-on work. But Scherman's untimely passing and Jones' departure left Tom Dickens with a hairy job. "Though Tom had never held the reins on a project this involved before," Glut recalled, "he agreed to give it his best."

At the outset, Don Glut silently vowed to create all-new dinosaur effects and not resort to the use of any stock footage, and he stuck to it. Thomas Dickens, along with a small crew that included Joseph Grossberg, toiled away in studio space rented at David Allen Productions. They brought to life not only the featured Allosaurus, but also the armored sauropod Saltasaurus, Camptosaurus, the old favorite Stegosaurus, the flying Pteranodon, and the meat-eating Carnotaurus, beating Disney's *Dinosaur* as the movie debut of that species. A Pentaceratops, to have been ridden by a cavegirl, fell victim to the strict budget.

The dinos were designed with input from paleo-artist Gregory Paul, then sculpted by Dickens. Stop-motion animation was the main technique, supplemented with a one-fifth scale animatronic Allosaurus. The seven-foot-long mechanical creature had multiple articulations, actuated by servo motors and cable controls. All of the Allosaurus scenes— stop-motion and live-action — were directed by Dickens. As Glut summed up, "I was content knowing that, in Tom's hands, our dinosaurs and other Mesozoic animals would be among the most accurate yet to appear in a Hollywood motion picture."

Dinosaurs ... The Terrible Lizards

*** 1971, USA. Charles Cahill & Associates. C, 10m.

CREDITS: *Created and Produced by* Wah Chang. *Animation* Douglas Beswick. *Script* Aylsworth Kleihauer. *Technical Consultant* Dr. J. R. MacDonald.

As a titanic tyrannosaur looms, a voice tells us that "for almost 150 million years, dinosaurs were part of the world's life." A graphical timeline makes clear at what times the various forms of life—fishes, amphibians, reptiles, mammals, birds, and man— debuted upon the earth, and in the case of the dinosaurs, when they vanished. Some dinosaurs like the Brontosaurus were impossibly huge, standing as large as a house and weighing as much as 12 automobiles. Not all dinos were giants, though; the nimble Coelophysis was a small carnivore that relied on speed to survive. All manner of dinosaurs walked the land — lumbering, plated stegosaurs, an endless variety of parrot-beaked "horn-faces," strangely crested duckbills— but the most formidable of all was the Tyrannosaurus rex, whose "huge head was mostly mouth!" As the end of the Cretaceous period approached, some dinosaurs like the heavily armored Ankylosaurus still survived, and majestic flying reptiles like the Pteranodon continued to rule the skies. But finally the Mesozoic era came to an end, and "the last of the dinosaurs were gone about 70 million years ago."

COMMENTARY: *Dinosaurs ... The Terrible Lizards* is an unexpectedly polished-looking film, especially in light of the limited resources from which Wah Chang created it. The animation is skilled and the puppets are excellent, without exception. Chang managed to save some time and effort by fashioning more than one head which could be fitted onto the same body, thus converting a Triceratops into a Styracosaurus, then into a Monoclonius, then into a Chasmosaurus, and so on. This tactic helped allow him to parade a small smorgasbord of saurians across the screen, with no fewer than 13 different prehistoric species glimpsed or featured during the film's ten-minute run time.

Throughout the film, Chang adds little touches that are unusual for an "educational" film, and that reflect the care he always brought to his art. The Pteranodons, for instance, do not merely glide through a blank sky, but are instead shown in the background of a dramatic up-angle shot of a Lambeosaurus. When the T. rex and the Styracosaurus are distracted by the volcanic eruption, Chang doesn't just cut back and forth but offers some nifty composites of the stop-motion dinosaurs staring at the real volcano. Even the simplest shots demonstrate Chang's artistic eye.

The classic dino battle, pitting T. rex against Triceratops, as shown in *Dinosaurs ... The Terrible Lizards*.

Dinosaurs features some of Douglas Beswick's earliest work but reveals the skill he already had developed. His animation here is naturalistic yet always interesting, spiced with tiny bits of business that uncannily mimic real animals. From the ahead-of-its-time birdlike striding of the Coelophysis, to the remarkable realism of its chewing motions, Beswick's animation is lively, fluid, and eminently "dinosaurian."

The film is of course somewhat dated by its narration — the good old Brontosaurus is said to have spent its hours in the swamps "finding support for its huge body." But the voice-overs are not quite as stiff as one would expect and even offer a nice twist at the end, when the narrator asks some questions without giving the answers. The idea was to give school teachers a shortcut to initiating some classroom discussion, and I for one would have loved to have my fifth-grade science class kicked off by the question: "How do we know as much about dinosaurs as we do?"

PEOPLE AND PRODUCTION: Wah Chang already had a good bit of experience with short films before making *Dinosaurs ... The Terrible Lizards*, as his first short dates back to the 1930s. "I had gotten a leave of absence from high school to work on a string puppet film," he told the author. "It was a short that was a takeoff on Mae West, the Marx Brothers, and *King Kong*, all in one." Unfortunately this film, called *The Lost Island*, never saw completion, but many of Chang's later shorts did. "While at George Pal's studio, and also at John Sutherland's, we did a few Army and Navy training films," Chang recalled. "When I left Sutherland's, I did some

86 • *Dinosaurus!*

Wah Chang with the Tyrannosaurus animation model for *Dinosaurs ... The Terrible Lizards*, later to be recycled for television's *Land of the Lost*.

medical films—one on Caesarian section, one on oral surgery, one on polio." His great work for the special effects company Project Unlimited, which he cofounded with Gene Warren and Tim Baar, kept him busy through the late 1950s and much of the 1960s, and in the latter half of the decade he did design work for the television shows *The Outer Limits* and *Star Trek*. But by 1970 he was ready to tackle an ambitious educational film that he had in mind.

Dinosaurs ... The Terrible Lizards "was made for schools," as Chang explained. "They still use it, and it's been over 25 years." Given Chang's long association with stop-motion animation, he knew it was the only method to choose for his dinosaur film, and he found an ideal person to handle it. "I had Doug Beswick do the animation," Chang continued. "I produced the film, and made all the dinosaurs and sets, and [did the] photography and the sound effects." Chang put some of his dinosaurs back to work a couple of years later, when he rejoined his Project Unlimited partner, Gene Warren, to create effects for the TV program *Land of the Lost*.

"I used some of the dinosaurs from the school film," Chang noted. "I also made some additional dinosaurs, and some of them were live-action, just the upper body, for closeups."

On a closing, personal note, this author was 12 years old when *Land of the Lost* came on the air, and I still remember it vividly and very fondly. I credit it as one of the main reasons I fell in love with both dinosaurs and the art of stop-motion animation.

Dinosaurus!

"I never had so much fun in my life!"
*** 1960, USA. Universal. C, 84m.

CREDITS: *Director* Irvin S. Yeaworth, Jr. *Producers* Jack H. Harris, Irvin S. Yeaworth, Jr. *Screenplay* Dan E. Weisburd and Jean Yeaworth; from an original idea by Jack H. Harris. *Special Photographic Effects* Tim Baar, Wah Chang, Gene Warren.

CAST: *Bart Thompson* Ward Ramsey. *Chuck* Paul Lukather. *Betty Piper* Kristina Hanson. *Julio* Alan Roberts. *The Neanderthal* Gregg

Martell. *Mike Hacker* Fred Engelberg. *Dumpy* Wayne Tredway. *Chica* Luci Blain. *Mousy* Howard Dayton. *Jasper* Jack Younger.

AD LINE: "Alive! After 70 million years! Roaring! Walking! Destroying!"

A tiny Caribbean island nation, in an effort to lure "big boats" and much-needed tourist dollars, has hired Bart Thompson's construction company to enlarge their harbor. One day Bart's girlfriend, Betty Piper, goes for a dip and discovers a frozen Brontosaurus and Tyrannosaurus rex on the channel bottom. Dino-crazy Julio, young sidekick of Dumpy the bulldozer driver, is agog when the "critters" are winched up. But the sinister "Island Manager," Mike Hacker (Julio's legal guardian and a major thorn in Bart's side), discovers another prehistoric relic: a preserved Neanderthal man. "We are going to take him to the mainland and sell him for a fortune," Hacker tells his henchmen, Jasper and Mousy. But a strange storm somehow revives both dinosaurs and the caveman, and when Bart investigates with his right-hand man Chuck (who says "Roger!" a lot and is in love with Chica, Hacker's unwilling moll) they find only a trail of huge footprints. With the telephones out, they decide to shepherd the villagers up to the old fortress on the hill and try to hold out until the arrival of the morning mail boat.

While Chuck and Chica tend to the islanders, Bart, Betty and Dumpy head for the shortwave radio in Betty's parents' house — the very house where the Neanderthal and Julio have already met and become friends. Hacker and his goons show up, but the caveman gives Hacker a pie in the face and escapes with Julio on the back of the Brontosaurus. Bart and friends try to help, but it's up to the caveman to save Betty from the stalking Tyrannosaurus. He takes her to an abandoned mine tunnel, and while she fends off his romantic overtures, the two dinosaurs begin their inevitable battle. The caveman returns to the jungle and rescues Julio, but the tyrannosaur finishes off the bronto and pursues them back to the mine. Hacker (abandoned by his yellow-bellied goons) enters the mine through an overhead opening, only to be trapped with the others. Fortunately, Chica's father had taught her as a little girl how to "make bombs out of bottles and gasoline" (!), and thus armed, Bart drives the T. rex away. But the damage has been done, and the tunnel begins to collapse. The caveman somehow holds up the splintering timbers with the last of his ancient strength, giving Julio and Betty precious seconds to escape. Hacker isn't so lucky.

The survivors arrive at the old fortress, followed by the relentless Tyrannosaurus. In a desperate gambit, Bart leaps behind the controls of a huge construction crane. A fierce struggle ensues, until one telling blow from the massive metal arm sends the dinosaur toppling into the sea. Everyone cheers jubilantly, and the mail boat finally arrives.

COMMENTARY: A fearsome Tyrannosaurus Rex, loose on an isolated tropical island, bears down on a helpless tour vehicle and begins to tear it apart, as his glaring eye peers in the window at the terrified occupants inside. No, it's not *Jurassic Park*—this scene was first filmed some 33 years before *Jurassic*, for *Dinosaurus!* Often overlooked in discussions of yesteryear's dinocinema, few dinomovies ever made come any closer to successfully achieving their aims.

Unlike many pictures with loftier ambitions, *Dinosaurus!* never lets its reach exceed its grasp. It sets out to be a light, humorous, good-natured yarn about two dinosaurs, a caveman, and a young boy, and that's what it is. Producer Jack H. Harris specifically wanted his dinosaur picture to be kid-friendly, and he made it that way "by cutting down on the sex and violence," as he explained in a press release. "Overemphasizing these two elements has been the main cause of a decrease in popularity of movies about science fiction," Harris asserted, and whether he was right or wrong, his philosophy of wholesomeness paid off here.

Dinosaurus! bubbles with an old-fashioned, simplistic, Saturday-matinee kind of fun, and the picture works best if you don't ask a lot of needless questions (like, why did Bart climb from one skiff into the other before diving into the bay?). It has good guys, bad guys, a good dinosaur, a bad dinosaur, last-second escapes, a damsel in distress, selfless heroism, funny bits which are actually funny, and a nifty climax. Add a straightforward plot, clever special effects, and a likable cast, and you've got a treat for dino-crazy kids of all ages. Played straight, *Dinosaurus!* would be mediocre at best, but Jack H. Harris fortunately decided to start off the new decade by taking a comedic turn from the direction of most of the creature features of the 1950s. The comedy bits work well — thanks largely to a perfect bit of casting — making *Dinosaurus!* the funniest intentionally funny dinomovie since the 1934 oddity *Secret of the Loch*.

If one looks over the cast, there isn't a "name" to be found. The picture in fact represents the only lead role for Ward Ramsey, and virtually the entire cinematic career of Kristina Hanson, yet they are not bad at all. Ramsey shows enough granite-jawed, everyman-hero appeal to make you wonder why he didn't get more work, and Hanson is a real looker with a nice June Cleaver wholesomeness, yet still brazen enough to strip down to her sleek black swimsuit right in front of Bart. ("What in the world are ya doing now?" a flustered Bart sputters as Betty unbuttons her blouse.) Fred Engelberg makes an interesting heavy, though just exactly what accent he's supposed to have remains an utter mystery.

The engaging performers make the tiredest of film clichés tolerable, even the inevitable "bumbling henchmen." Hacker's two witless goons, played by Jack Younger and Howard Dayton, are the best pair of bumbling henchmen you're likely to find — Jasper, the Michael J. Pollard look-alike, and Mousy, who seems to have slithered straight off the set of *West Side Story*. Sarcastically commenting on Jasper's cleverness, Hacker says "your intelligence never ceases to amaze

Little Julio (Alan Roberts) teaches "Caveman" (Gregg Martell) about the quest for fire — 20th century style — in ***Dinosaurus!***

me; I didn't know you were an anthropologist," to which Jasper replies modestly, "aw, not a very good one, boss—I mean, I ain't been to church in years!" Young Alan Roberts' delivery is stiff at times, but he has some great lines. When Betty mentions that the bronto "doesn't look as mean as the other one," Julio calmly announces, "he's not mean, he's her-BEEV-orous!"

Then there is Gregg Martell's wonderful portrayal of the heroic, perplexed Neanderthal. As Julio says, he truly is "one terrific caveman!" Although the scene where he investigates a "modern home" is undeniably broad comedy, Martell refuses to overdo it. It is easy to imagine how another actor could have mugged his way through this bit and single-handedly sunk the movie in the process, but Martell plays it just right. With apologies to Mature, Richardson, Starr, and others, Martell's noble Neanderthal is the best caveman in movie history.

Like Martell's performance, the special effects in *Dinosaurus!* are also "just right." Even though the dinosaur animation is certainly a level (or two) below the polished, fluid artistry of the legendary animators, the energetic action serves the film well. The dino scenes' biggest drawback is the use of mechanically actuated models for the closeup shots. It's not that these live-action puppets are that bad—they are actually rather impressive—it's just that they don't match the look of their stop-motion counterparts and the contrast is distracting when the two are intercut. Although the *Dinosaurus!* animation has been savaged by some observers, it is legitimately comparable to the work in *Journey to the Beginning of Time* or *The Beast of Hollow Mountain*. In fact, the stop-motion "dino sinking in the mud" scene in *Dinosaurus!* is much better than the comparable shot in *Hollow Mountain*. All of the animation sequences seem well thought out, with the best wisely saved for last. The showdown between Bart and the T. rex is a socko set piece, with clever camerawork and snappy editing combining to get the most out of the serviceable animation. This sequence also originated a scenario which would turn up repeatedly in the years to come: the climactic battle between monster and man-made machine. For some examples see *The Crater Lake Monster*, *Aliens*, *Carnosaur*, and, rather unimaginatively, *Carnosaur II*.

Dinosaurus! (don't forget the exclamation point!) serves as a good reminder not to fall into the trap of taking movies—especially dinosaur movies—*too* seriously. Such films, after all, are supposed to be fun. Director Irvin Yeaworth has pointed out that American critics simply didn't "get" the picture. "The French 'New Wave' magazine *Cahiers du Cinéma* was the only one that reviewed *Dinosaurus!* the way *I meant it to be*," Yeaworth said. "One of the things that we thought *Dinosaurus!* should do was to appeal to the kids on one level and to the parents who were sitting there with 'em, expecting a kids' picture which they wouldn't enjoy, on *another* level. That's what we tried to do in *Dinosaurus!*" And you succeeded, Irvin. For all its far-fetchedness, hokey dialogue, and dino clichés, *Dinosaurus!* remains both fun and funny—a satisfying little movie about little boys and dinosaurs, and friendship and heroes.

PEOPLE AND PRODUCTION: Three years after finding Antarctic dinosaurs in *The Land Unknown*, Universal-International offered another dino tale, this time set in the Caribbean and filmed in living color. The picture began in the mind of producer Jack H. Harris, as he explained in Tom Weaver's *Interviews with B Science Fiction & Horror Movie Makers*. "The original idea was a dinosaur picture, but I didn't want to do a prehistoric film," Harris recalled. He consulted with writer Alfred "Alfie" Bester, who "brought up the touch of having them long-buried under the sea and blasted out by men building an island harbor." Next, noted sci-fi author Algis Budrys worked with Harris for a fortnight, "and we came up with all the characters and how they interplayed," Harris said. Dan E. Weisburd then penned his screenplay, which the Yeaworths polished into its final, lighthearted version. "I started in the middle and [Jean] started at the begin-

Thirty-five years after a Marcel Delgado Brontosaurus got caught in the mud in the silent version of *The Lost World*, it happened again in *Dinosaurus!*

ning and we did a rewrite, a final draft of the screenplay," explained Irvin Yeaworth, also in an interview with Tom Weaver. "Jean went through the whole thing and created all the comedy sequences." About the funny bits, Jack Harris said: "I was sort of on the fence about it, but it tickled me so much that I gave in."

The "island harbor" setting necessitated the finding of a suitable shooting location, and St. Croix filled the bill. "In the Virgin Islands Jack and I scouted St. Thomas and Charlotte Amalie," Yeaworth recalled, "but then we found some better deals on St. Croix." While on location, Yeaworth hired Bill Jersey to shoot a CinemaScope short about the making of *Dinosaurus!* The featurette, titled *Virgin Islands, U.S.A.*, was circulated by Universal "as sort of a sneaky commercial for *Dinosaurus!*" Yeaworth said.

As with *The Land Unknown*, Universal decided not to tax the *Dinosaurus!* budget (about $450,000) with any big star salaries. Still, it's quite possible that Steve McQueen would have played Bart were it not for some differences between the actor and producer Harris, stemming from their association on *The Blob* (1958). The reason Kristina Hanson was hired becomes abundantly clear when reading the studio's promotional literature, which is strewn with references to "the statuesque Swedish beauty's 37-23-35 bathing suit figure." Though the cast is mostly anonymous, a scan of the credits does reveal a few familiar names. Most notable is cinematographer Stanley Cortez, whose filmography runs the gamut from forgotten low-budget fare such as *Abbott and Costello meet Captain Kidd* (1952) and genre films like *The Angry Red Planet* (1959), to such all-time classics as *The Magnificent Ambersons* (1942) and *The Night of the Hunter* (1955). Look fast for a cameo by Jack H. Harris, as one of the tourists on the boat at the very end of the film.

All of the shots not captured in the Virgin Islands were filmed back in Hollywood, though not at Universal. "It was a better deal for us at California Studios," Yeaworth explained, "which had a large stage which was just perfect for us." In all, the live action took about five months to complete, with the effects work requiring considerably more time.

SPECIAL EFFECTS: After exploring and eliminating other possibilities, Jack H. Harris finally settled on stop-motion animation as the primary means for creating the movie's dinosaurs. "One guy wanted to take lizards and stick them in there, but I wouldn't hear of that," Harris said in Weaver's *Interviews*. "I met George Pal and he said I ought to talk to these guys," Harris recalled — "these guys" being Wah Chang, Gene Warren and Tim Baar of Project Unlimited. "They were excited and I was excited, so we got together."

Like Eugène Lourié with *The Beast from 20,000 Fathoms*, Irvin Yeaworth was very involved in the creation of the film's animation sequences. "I've always been a storyboard person," Yeaworth said, "so with Jack Senter, our art director, we sketched every single sequence that was related to the animation so that the guys knew exactly what we were going for." All through the FX shoot, the *Dinosaurus!* crew had available an unofficial but very esteemed advisor. "I was in contact with Warren and Chang and Baar and, of course, Willis O'Brien, who was very interesting," Yeaworth said. "We spent a lot of time with Obie, before we started shooting and then after." Yeaworth obviously enjoyed his time with the legendary trick man. "It was just *great* to have a chance to be with the man," he remembered. "He had a wonderful way of talking with *any*body as though they were buddies, colleagues." O'Brien had in fact helped convince Jack Harris to use the stop-motion technique.

The names Chang, Warren, and Baar are of course synonymous with Project Unlimited, and some genre references seem to make the assumption that the animation itself was accomplished by one or more of these men. However, except for a few scenes animated by Warren in Project's early days (such as the wonderful "Yawning Man" in 1958's *tom thumb*), the threesome generally left the hands-on animation to their capable staff. As far as the *Dinosaurus!* animation goes, "Tom Holland did some, Don Sahlin did some," Wah Chang told this author. The monster versus machine finale was a combined effort of Phil Kellison and Dave Pal. "Phil was not normally a Project Unlimited employee," Jim Danforth told me, "but he animated the steam shovel in the steam shovel–Tyrannosaurus fight. The tyrannosaur was animated by Dave Pal." *Dinosaurus!* was filmed a full year before Danforth joined Project Unlimited, "but I would drop by and visit Ralph [Rodine] because he was a friend of mine, and see what they were doing," he recalled.

Also contributing to the effects effort were *King Kong* veterans Marcel and Victor Delgado. "At that time, Victor Delgado did a lot of work on building the dinosaurs," Wah Chang said, "because we had two that were large mechanicals. Marcel Delgado did most of the sculpting, and his brother Victor did the mechanics." As was usually the case with Project Unlimited's work, Wah Chang supervised the effects photography. As it turned out, the *Dinosaurus!* special

Veteran puppet maker Marcel Delgado puts the finishing touches on the *Dinosaurus!* tyrannosaur.

A pair of Project Unlimited techs put the live action mechanical Brontosaurus through its paces.

effects cost more than the entire budget of Yeaworth's earlier hit, *The Blob*.

Although the human stars had considerable trouble finding acting jobs following *Dinosaurus!*, the film's dinosaurian actors did manage to land some TV work. The stop-motion Brontosaurus guest-starred on the *Twilight Zone* episode, "The Odyssey of Flight 33," about a jet airliner that travels back in time. The sequence was not recycled *Dinosaurus!* footage, but rather a couple of brief but new animation shots using the same stop-motion puppet. The mechanical Tyrannosaurus showed up (this time it *was* clips from *Dinosaurus!*) to menace Gilligan, the Skipper, and the rest of the castaways in a dream sequence from the *Gilligan's Island* episode "The Secret of Gilligan's Island." That dream sequence, in fact, is a funny spoof of the caveman-and-dinosaur genre (with a particular plot resemblance to *Teenage Caveman*), made some 13 years before the movie *Caveman* tried the same thing!

Doctor Mordrid

"Just tell me what kind of weirdness to expect and I'll handle it!"

★★½ 1992, USA. Full Moon/Paramount. C, 76m.

CREDITS: *Directors* Albert Band, Charles Band. *Producer* Charles Band. *Screenplay* C. Courtney Joyner; based on an original idea by Charles Band. *Visual Effects* David Allen Productions. *Animation* David Allen, Chris Endicott, Randall Cook. *Special Photographic Effects* Motion Opticals, Inc.

CAST: *Dr. Anton Mordrid* Jeffrey Combs. *Samantha Hunt* Yvette Nipar. *Kabal* Brian Thompson. *Tony Gaudio* Jay Acovone. *Adrian* Keith Coulouris. *Gunner* Ritch Brinkley. *Irene* Julie Michaels.

Age-old sorcerer Anton Mordrid keeps a silent vigil from his New York brownstone, until one day the disappearances of large quantities of alchemic elements signal that the moment has arrived. Mordrid visits the mystical Fourth Dimension, his original home, and confirms his fears: Kabal, evil alchemist and Mordrid's lifelong rival, has escaped and is preparing to unleash an apocalypse upon humanity. Mordrid's friend Gunner, the Fourth Dimension's lone sentinel, couldn't prevent Kabal's escape, but with the last of his magic he did succeed in keeping the hideous netherworld monsters known as the "Hellspawn" imprisoned ... for now.

As a showdown looms, both sorcerers enlist the help of mortals. Kabal finds a young couple — a pair of thrill-seeking outcasts — to do his earthly legwork. He uses the man, Adrian, as a simple flunky but needs the blood of the girl, Irene, to complete his sorcery. Mordrid befriends Samantha "Sam" Hunt, an advisor to the NYPD on occult matters. Hindered by interference from well-meaning Detective Tony Gaudio, Mordrid must reveal his true nature to gain Sam's trust. With her help, Mordrid (or at least, his spirit) escapes the police and races to the Cosmopolitan Museum, where resides the medieval "philosopher's stone" that Kabal requires as an alchemic mixing vessel. "You're too late," Kabal boasts, and on a whim he casts a life-restoring spell on the Museum's imposing Tyrannosaurus skeleton. But the overconfident Kabal is preoccupied with his attempts to release the Hellspawn, and is unprepared when a giant mastodon skeleton, reanimated by Mordrid, battles its way past the T. rex and gores the evildoer clean through. Though victorious, Mordrid has revealed too much to the mortals and his superior compels him to return to the other side. "You'll see me again," he tells Sam, and vanishes in a swirl of light.

COMMENTARY: Charles Band's Full Moon Entertainment turned out its share of bad movies during the early 1990s, and quite a few surprisingly good ones too. *Doctor Mordrid* is a good movie, within the context of its ambitions and resources. At its best, it breaks through its limitations and direct-to-video stigma, and even at its worst, it survives them.

A lot of little things add up to help *Mordrid* succeed. The Bands' direction is at its most imaginative, and for the most part the movie "looks" right. Mordrid's apartment is a beautifully appointed set, loaded with all sorts of nifty Dark Ages sorcery gadgets, and his pet raven, "Edgar Allan," is an appropriate touch. Combined with a nice cast, efficient script, and David Allen's special effects, the result is a "satisfying little film" as Leonard Maltin aptly put it.

In his Full Moon filmography for *Cinefantastique*, John Thonen took Jeffrey Combs to task for playing Mordrid "like a CPA taking an extension course magic class." That isn't how I see it. To me, Combs' understated and clearly thoughtful performance was just what the *Doctor* ordered. He plays the role in a Sherlock-Holmes-as-alchemist sort of way — serious, always thinking, but never lacking courage or humor when called for. As wise Eugène Lourié repeatedly reminded us, the more fantastic the story, the greater the necessity for "believably real" characters, and Combs makes Mordrid about as real as possible. Though convention dictates that the villain must be more flamboyant than the hero, Brian Thompson never takes Kabal over the top, and his growing irritation at Mordrid's pesky devotion to "good" is palpable and slightly humorous. Likeable Yvette Nipar makes a real person out of her obligatory love interest, and Ritch Brinkley is great fun as Gunner, the good ol' boy who guards the Fourth Dimension.

It is a common trap in films like this to try and justify the existence of supernatural beings by giving them a detailed and convoluted backstory, bogging things down in the process, but *Mordrid* happily avoids the temptation to overexplain its premise. Conceding that C. Courtney Joyner's screenplay leans heavily on coincidence, it thankfully tells us just what we need to know about Mordrid and Kabal and then gets on with matters.

The highlight of *Doctor Mordrid* is the mastodon-tyrannosaur showdown. Delightfully combining two of Ray Harryhausen's trademarks—dinosaurs and living skeletons—David Allen conjured up what author Neil Pettigrew called "a sequence that has long been the dream of many a stop-motion fan." Pettigrew is dead right; it's hard to imagine any Harryhausen aficionado who wouldn't enjoy this gem. Not only is it a visual feast which could belong in a far more prestigious film, it's also a sort of magical metaphor for the art of stop-motion animation. Like the rival alchemists in the script, animators wave their hands and fantastic, impossible creatures come to enchanted life.

Except for a few betraying moments, *Doctor Mordrid* looks like a much more opulent production than it actually is, and it could almost pass for a full-fledged theatrical release. Threatening to give "direct to video" a good name, *Mordrid* is an enjoyable, clever fantasy and one of Full Moon's finest.

PEOPLE AND PRODUCTION: Charles Band grew up around moviemaking. "Charlie was on all my sets, when I was directing movies in Europe," recalled Albert Band, veteran director and father of Charles. As a boy Charles even appeared on-screen in the Italian sword-and-sandal epic, *The Avenger* (1962), directed by his dad (credited as Alfredo Antonini). More recently the elder Band became heavily involved with his son's direct-to-video productions and even returned to the director's chair for certain films, including *Prehysteria*, *Prehysteria 2*, and *Doctor Mordrid*. Although both their names appear in the credits, "we didn't codirect *Doctor Mordrid*," Albert pointed out in *Cinefantastique*. "It wasn't like we were both on the set at the same time. We have the same vision for the picture, long discussions, lots of rehearsals together, and then he went on and did his shtick, and I would shoot, depending on his availability." Charles' brother Richard composed another of his many Full Moon scores for *Mordrid*, and Charles' son Alexander played the young boy marveling at the museum's T. rex skeleton.

It has been reported by multiple sources that *Doctor Mordrid* was inspired by Marvel Comics' *Dr. Strange*. In fact, John Thonen wrote in *Cinefantastique* that Charles Band "hatched this *Dr. Strange* clone idea, in conjunction with legendary Marvel Comics writer Jack Kirby, back in his Empire days" (referring to Band's pre–Full Moon company, Empire Pictures). For the title role, the filmmakers tabbed genre veteran Jeffrey Combs, alumnus of *Re-Animator* (1985), *From Beyond* (1986), and many others. "It's make-believe," Combs said, musing on the appeal of superpowered heroes like Anton Mordrid. "You know, when you were a kid and you used to put a towel around your neck and run around the back yard ... well, maybe you didn't. But I did."

Doctor Mordrid blatantly sets up a sequel, and Yvette Nipar (rhymes with "viper") said in a publicity interview that there would "probably be another one." Yet despite the obvious plans, no follow-up appeared.

SPECIAL EFFECTS: To handle the numerous special effects for *Doctor Mordrid*, Charles Band turned again to David Allen Productions. Whatever the overall merits of Full Moon's output, animation fans can at least be thankful for the few extra bits of Allen magic that Band's efforts provided.

Chris Endicott was one of David Allen's assistants at the time of *Doctor Mordrid*, and had a big influence on the film's signature animation sequence. "When the script arrived at the studio, it featured a T. rex skeleton fighting a Pteranodon skeleton," Endicott revealed to the author. "And I said to David, 'you know, with a Pteranodon, its wing is only one long finger.' Sure, the sorcerers are magic, but it was just going to look weird having this thing flying." Endicott remembered a striking Frank Frazetta painting of a mastodon with its huge tusks dominating the image, and offered a suggestion. "I asked David, 'what if we had the tyrannosaur fight a mastodon?' First of all, you never see them together in a movie because they're separated by tens of millions of years, and it'd just be kind of neat seeing this thing that's bipedal, fighting something that's got these two long tusks." Allen liked the idea and ran it by Charles Band, who gave an enthusiastic thumbs-up.

The animation puppets had an unusual genesis. Years before, David Allen had built a model display for an early incarnation of *The Primevals*, incorporating a commercially available Glenco Tyrannosaurus skeleton model. "He heavily modified it to come across as part of an alien museum display of prehistoric creatures," Endicott recalled. "I mentioned that I had this very same original kit as well as one of a mastodon, and David asked if I might bring them in." Unlikely as it sounds, "that tyrannosaur kit sort of became the starting-off point for the stop-motion puppet, and because the kit was so small, the puppet was small." The mastodon was from a different model company and proved too inaccurate to serve as more than a rough inspiration. "The guys at Doug Beswick's studio basically resculpted the mastodon from scratch, to scale with the T. rex," Endicott explained. Beswick, George Wong, and Yancey Calzada constructed the armatures, did all the build-up work and surface detailing, and delivered the puppet pair completely finished and ready to animate.

The majority of the animation was done by Allen himself, with Randy Cook and Chris Endicott contributing a couple of shots each. "David did about 95 percent of it," Endicott reported. "Randy did a couple of shots, one of which shows the T. Rex taking a running lunge at the mastodon only to be thrown to the floor. I did the first shots of the T. rex moving its head, and the shot over its shoulder where it's snapping down at the police." Besides the skeleton battle, four additional stop-motion cuts reveal the "Hellspawn" trying to break out of the Fourth Dimension. "There are some 'guest stars' in that scene," Endicott pointed out. "There are two puppets from *The Primevals*, the skull-headed guy is a *Subspecies* puppet modified by Mark Rappaport, and the werewolf from *The Howling* is in the background." The Fourth Dimensional world itself was a section of full-sized set, composited into a detailed miniature designed by Dennis Gordon.

Almost the entire museum sequence, not just the animation shots, involved movie magic. "When you see the movie, hopefully you believe that you are in some kind of a hall of fossils," David Allen said in a Full Moon featurette. "We don't have any, in fact, in the set." Other than the animation puppets themselves, there were only two small skeleton sections built. One was a T. rex foot, seen in the foreground early in the sequence. "That was about a half-scale foot," Allen revealed. "A pretty straightforward perspective effects shot, of the kind that have been done since the silent days." The other prop appeared in the tyrannosaur's skull-smashing "death" scene, which was handled differently than the rest of the fight. "Most of the scenes of the dinosaur skeletons are done through model animation," Allen explained. "This scene however, where it has to fall and shatter, seemed to me to be a little too difficult to animate convincingly." A special breakaway skull, cast from a fragile plaster called Gypsnow and attached to a short spine-and-ribcage section, was constructed by Rappaport and Joseph Grossberg. Several duplicates allowed for some trial-and-error during filming. "We shot multiple takes with a high-speed camera in front of a large transparency of the background," Endicott remembered, "trying to get one that looked good."

Mordrid's prehistoric skeleton sequence has achieved the status of many previous dinosaur scenes by becoming "stock footage." The animation turns up in an ultralow-budget Full Moon hodgepodge called *Planet Patrol*, incongruously worked into a yarn about four perfect-skinned teens who wear spandex and protect the galaxy. *Planet Patrol* was pasted together from two episodes of an unsold television series sandwiched around an edited version of Full Moon's *Kraa! The Sea Monster*, which also featured the evil-fighting youngsters.

Ein Ruckblic in die Urwelt
see under *Ruckblic*

El Bello Durmiente
see under *Bello*

Emilio and His Magical Bull

"Emilio ... his head is full of dragons."
★★½ 1975, USA.
Nassour Productions. C, 46m.

CREDITS: *Producers* William Nassour, Edward Nassour, Martin B. Cohen (coproducer) and Martin Nosseck (coproducer). *Screenplay* Paul Rader, Ted Perry, Martin B. Cohen, Martin Nosseck. *Chief Technician* Henry Lyon. *Art Director* John Datu Arensma. *Director of Photography* Henry Sharp, A.S.C.
VOICES: Thurl Ravenscroft, Ted Knight, Judy Howard, Sara Bernier, Dallas McKennon, Wendell Niles.

Emilio is a young Mexican farm boy who lives near the town of San Esteban. He is a dreamer, a believer in dragons and fantasies, and magic. Emilio's dad scoffs at his son's impractical notions, but decides to allow the lad to take their calf to sell in the faraway marketplace. Along the way, Emilio meets up with a smooth-talking gypsy and is persuaded to swap the cow for a baby bull. Called "The Star Bull," the animal is said to be endowed with magical powers. Emilio's papa is understandably furious but the youngster is fascinated by the whole magical story, and one night he dreams of a fantastic adventure in a strange prehistoric land. A vicious Allosaurus picks a fight with the Star Bull, as a pterodactyl and other primeval flying creatures look on. The dinosaur is no match for the Star Bull, and is defeated as Emilio's dream ends.

One day, the famous matador Señor Garza passes through San Esteban and immediately wants the magnificent bull for the ring. Emilio's father eagerly accepts Garza's offer, but that night Emilio goes to San Esteban and arranges a desperate, impossible deal with Señor Garza — if he can find an even greater animal, Garza will return the Star Bull. Emilio realizes that despite Garza's public image, he is not an honorable man. "He was drinking tequila and had a girl sitting on his lap!" he tells Miguel, boyfriend of his sister Melena. When the day of the bullfight arrives, the cocky Garza boldly sends the *banderilleros* and *picadores* away so that he can fight the Star Bull alone. The crowd initially cheers for Garza, but when they see the great heart of Emilio's bull, their allegiances change. Unable to break the will of the Star Bull, Garza cowardly dives out of the ring and Emilio and his friend are reunited.

COMMENTARY: To say that *Emilio and His Magical Bull* is a "seldom-seen" film would be a massive understatement. It was released to a few theaters in 1975, received a generally favorable response, and promptly vanished. It's a bit of a shame, too, because although the 45-minute fable has definite flaws, it's an interesting and occasionally inspired attempt at an art form that has too seldom been tackled.

Emilio and His Magical Bull is accomplished entirely through replacement animation photographed on miniature sets, the same basic technique used by the Rankin-Bass company in the 1960s to produce such beloved Christmas specials as *Rudolph the Red-Nosed Reindeer*. Some of the *Emilio* sets and settings are mundane, but a few, like the interior of the church in the opening se-

Two specimens from Emilio's prehistoric dream — a somewhat harpylike pterodactyl (top) and a mean Allosaurus, about to win second prize in a fight against the Star Bull.

quence, are beautifully appointed. The replacement figures themselves also vary in quality; some are greatly detailed while others show unmistakable signs of haste. The animation is generally pleasing, although as the film proceeds one subconsciously gets the feeling that everything is moving just a tad too slowly. This phenomenon is particularly troubling during the action sequences like the dinosaur battle, and the climactic bullfight is almost completely without energy. The filmmakers also had some problems with the very difficult task of synchronizing the mouth movements with the dialogue. The voice actors say their lines clearly but with little flair, and unfortunately this is especially true in the principal role of Emilio.

Ultimately, *Emilio* may be more watchable as a technical exercise than as a story. It's a fanciful yarn that wants to be a magical fable, but must settle for a measure of charm. Numerous changes were made to Willis O'Brien's story, to no great benefit, and the filmed version can't quite maintain the fairy-tale quality it tries for. Dinosaur lovers especially will be disappointed to find Obie's giant reptile demoted to a mere dream-sequence appearance, as well as by the fact that the nifty-looking pterodactyl which also appears never gets to do anything. It also seems strange that the romance between Miguel and Melena is left unfulfilled. One can *assume* that with Garza disgraced, Melena would realize that her true feelings are for Miguel, but a quick shot of the lovers strolling off arm in arm would have been nice. In fact, the whole story seems to just stop, rather than *finish*. *Emilio* is an admirable effort, but is likely to be more fascinating to animation aficionados and dino-movie buffs than to the children for which it was made.

PEOPLE AND PRODUCTION: *Emilio and His Magical Bull* began as a story outline called *Emilio and Guloso*, written in the mid–1940s by Willis O'Brien and his wife, Darlyne. The story's "monster" element was limited to a "giant lizard" which reportedly resided in the wilderness near Emilio's home. When Obie expanded the story and retitled it *El Toro Estrella* (The Star Bull), he added much more prehistoric content. In this tale, Emilio and a party of Indians venture into a time-lost valley where they encounter a flock of pterodactyls, a Triceratops, and a pair of battling allosaurs, one of which fights a losing battle with the Star Bull in the climax. The story finally evolved into a film project titled *Valley of the Mist*, which for a time promised to be Obie's grand follow-up to *Mighty Joe Young* before eventually falling through.

In 1950, producers Edward and William Nassour purchased the option on *Valley of the Mist*. But again the ill-fated project, now called *Ring Around Saturn*, dwindled and collapsed. The idea was reimagined by the Nassours a few years later as an all-animated featurette, with the title changed yet again to *Emilio and His Magical Bull*. Don Shay reported in *Cinefex* that Edward Nassour put about two years of work into *Emilio*, but production was again halted and the film lay unfinished. Finally, after two decades had passed, "producers Martin B. Cohen and Martin Nosseck stepped in with sufficient funds and enthusiasm to complete it," Shay stated. According to a review published at the time in *Box Office* magazine, *Emilio and His Magical Bull* premiered at the Picwood Theater in Westwood, California, on December 17, 1975.

SPECIAL EFFECTS: Possibly underestimating the massive task he was facing, Edward Nassour originally hoped to do all of the animation himself. As stop-motion historian Hal Miles told the author, "Edward was attempting to do the animation, but eventually had Henry Sharp and Henry Lyon, and a few amateurs, help out." Sharp and Lyon had worked with the Nassours before, having accomplished most of the stop-motion animation seen in *The Beast of Hollow Mountain*. The Allosaurus sequence in *Emilio* in fact utilizes the same replacement figures, long waggly tongue and all, which Henry Lyon constructed for *Hollow Mountain*. The effect is not as pleasing in *Emilio* as in *Hollow Mountain*, though, because "it's shot improperly," Hal Miles said. "The few shots in *Emilio* that look really smooth were actually done by Lyon and Sharp," Miles asserts. "The vast majority of the other shots were done by either Ed or the amateurs."

Evolution

"Man turns to solve the greatest mystery of all, the mystery of — Himself."

★★ 1923, USA. Red Seal Pictures/Inkwell Studios. BW, 41m., Silent.

CREDITS: *Director* Max Fleischer. *Scientific Supervision* Edward J. Foyles, of the American Museum of Natural History.

Evolution is an ambitious but unavoidably superficial documentary, now badly dated as well, attempting in 40 silent minutes to trace life's roots all the way back to the origin of the universe. Artwork and simple animation depict heavenly bodies condensing from whirling stardust, creating planets upon which volcanic activity proliferates. Vapor rises from the surface to form clouds, and torrential rains cool the fires. Single-celled life begins in the waters, evolving over millennia into the first backboned creatures. Gills become lungs, fins become legs and the "land-water" creatures appear, followed by the true land-dwellers, the reptiles. "The ages roll on and reptiles grow to monstrous size," illustrated at first by static sculptures of Tyrannosaurus, Allosaurus, Stegosaurus, and Brontosaurus. The dinosaurs then come briefly to life, courtesy of some Willis O'Brien animation taken from 1919's *The Ghost of Slumber Mountain*. Of the seventeen stop-motion cuts in *Slumber Mountain*, nine appear — some noticeably shortened — in *Evolution*.

The first animation shot portrays a Brontosaurus wading into a pool, followed by a feeding "Three-Horn Dinosaur" (Triceratops) and a brief Triceratops-Triceratops battle. After two more quick cuts of the horned dinosaur, the "Tyrant Giant Lizard" (Tyrannosaurus) enters, and the last three cuts reveal the ceratopsian unsuccessfully defending itself against the attacking tyrannosaur. Given the sorry condition of the surviving prints of *Slumber Mountain*, the *Evolution* sequence actually offers a clearer view of these particular shots than does the original film. After the dinosaurs come birds and mammals, the Ice Age, a discussion of maternal instinct, the primates, and finally the forms of early man. This last segment is notable today by its enthusiastic coverage of "Piltdown Man," a prehistoric hominid found in England's Piltdown quarries around 1915. At the time of this film's release Piltdown Man was still widely considered a monumental find, but it was later revealed to be an intentional fraud and became one of the most notorious hoaxes in the history of the natural sciences. The cave-dweller sequence concludes with "The Walking Ape-Man of Java," described as "the first known human being" but sounding like a great title for a 1950s B-monster flick.

In the 1920s, the documentary film and indeed the entire filmmaking craft was still in its infancy, but even in this context *Evolution* is poorly constructed. There is actually a "preliminary" dinosaur sequence, featuring paintings, models, and a cursory demonstration of skeletal reconstruction, before and separate from the main dinosaur sequence described above. Much of the information itself is now woefully out of date, and there is even a hint of exploitation in the form of some *National Geographic*–style nudity, all female of course. But despite its drawbacks, this creaky but thankfully straightforward relic is actually more watchable — the dinosaur sequences notwithstanding — than Irwin Allen's similar but painfully smug 1956 entry, *The Animal World*.

Fantasia

"His purpose was — in his own words — to express primitive life."

★★★½ 1940, USA. Disney/RKO. C, 120m.

CREDITS: *Directors* Samuel Armstrong (*Toccata and Fugue in D Minor, The Nutcracker Suite*); James Algar (*The Sorcerer's Apprentice*); Bill Roberts, Paul Satterfield (*Rite of Spring*); Hamilton Luske, Jim Handley, Ford Beebe (*The Pastoral Symphony*); T. Hee, Norm Ferguson

(*Dance of the Hours*); Wilfred Jackson (*Night on Bald Mountain/Ave Maria*). Production Supervision Ben Sharpsteen. Story Direction Joe Grant, Dick Huemer. Musical Direction Edward H. Plumb. Narrative Introductions Deems Taylor. With Leopold Stokowski and the Philadelphia Orchestra.

COMMENTARY: Overlooked and dismissed on its initial release and possibly a bit overanalyzed in years since, *Fantasia* stands as a watershed in animation history. To briefly recap, *Fantasia* represents Walt Disney at his most innovative, a wholly original concept whereby classical music (or "art music" as a college professor of mine preferred) was interpreted in film animation. Released right between a brutal Depression and an even more brutal world war, *Fantasia* probably couldn't have come along at a worse time in terms of its chances to be a popular success.

The seven musical vignettes run the gamut from frivolous to solemn, innocent to demonic, comic absurdity to gripping drama, although things do take a little while to get going. The first piece is J. S. Bach's *Toccata and Fugue in D Minor*, visualized as purely abstract shapes, colors and motions, and *Fantasia* doesn't hit its stride until the second chapter and Tchaikovsky's *Nutcracker Suite*. Animation any more purely *beautiful* than these glowing, jewel-toned flowers, crystalline winter scenes, and hummingbirdlike fairies has never been done. Next up is arguably the film's most famous segment, with Mickey Mouse enjoying his finest hour as the title character of Paul Dukas' *The Sorcerer's Apprentice*.

The fourth episode is Igor Stravinsky's *Rite of Spring*, often called simply "the dinosaur segment." Yes, it is "cartoon" animation, but in 1940 no one had seen anything like this. *King Kong* had offered marvelous dinosaurs but the *Fantasia* fauna was in bursting Technicolor, rendered in dramatic highlights and shadows that any of the great cinematographers would have been proud to achieve in live action. The sequence begins at the beginning, literally—a journey through space towards the just-formed earth. Decades before the space program, 1940s audiences witnessed immensely beautiful scenes of celestial phenomena—comets, galaxies, nebulae—that have such depth as to suggest a "3-D" effect. Prophetically, photographic images remarkably similar to these artists' renderings would one day be captured by the Hubble Space Telescope, named for the same Edwin P. Hubble who served as an expert consultant on the *Rite of Spring* segment.

On a young earth enveloped in a primordial, volcanic atmosphere of oranges and ochres, the conditions arise to bring forth life. Single-celled creatures emerge in the oceans, then jellyfish, invertebrates, bony fish, amphibians, and finally the great animals of the Mesozoic. Toothy mosasaurs and long-necked plesiosaurs rule the sea, overlooked by craggy cliffsides populated with nesting pterosaurs. Herds of brontosaurs graze, a feathered Archaeopteryx narrowly escapes a predator, baby ceratopsians and sauropods are watched over by parents, and a duckbilled Parasaurolophus, interestingly envisioned with a skin membrane connecting its crest and back, dines on plants. All live in fear of the mighty Tyrannosaurus rex—the embodiment of merciless nature—towering, unstoppable, with eyes and mouth that seem to glow blood-red. The fleet-footed animals can often escape, but a lumbering Stegosaurus has no choice but to stand and fight a hopeless battle. The stegosaur has perhaps the most dramatic death of any cinematic dinosaur, with a look in his eyes that indicates he knows he's done for. One terrific shot starts on the spiked tail as it writhes and collapses, then pans slowly along the massive body to the tiny head, just as the eyes close. For eons the dinosaurs dominate, but then the earth warms, and dries, and the searing sun exhausts the last of the great animals as they uselessly search for food. At last only their bones remain, buried under rust-colored strata for humans to find and wonder at millions of years later.

At the picture's midpoint, a jazzy, "impromptu" jam session and a slightly corny

The promotional artwork for *Fantasia* often highlighted the dinosaur sequence.

conversation with the "Sound Track" serve as a sort of intermission and lead into the next segment, Beethoven's *Pastoral Symphony*. Disney places this composition in a mythical vale of grass and flowers and waterfalls where fauns cavort, unicorns gallop, winged horses soar, "centaurettes" bathe (surprisingly "topless"), and natural phenomena are effectively personified by the gods and goddesses of Mt. Olympus. Next comes Amilcare Ponchielli's *Dance of the Hours*, a ballet presented in basically realistic terms—except that the human dancers are replaced by comedic ostriches, hippos, elephants, and alligators (all wearing ballet slippers!). After this sublime silliness, the raw power of the final vignette hits like a hammer. Moussorgsky's *Night on Bald Mountain* flawlessly segued into Franz Schubert's *Ave Maria* is truly, as Deems Taylor says, "a picture of the struggle between the profane and the sacred." With apologies to the magnificent dinosaurs, *this* is *Fantasia*'s artistic zenith. Chernobog, the god of darkness in Slavonic mythology, is as perfect a personification of evil as has ever been put on film. The nightmarish visions realized by Disney's artists meld with Moussorgsky's compelling music to create a macabre interlude that could well scare the popcorn out of some youngsters, and give their parents a few cold chills as well. Then the church bell tolls, each strike hitting Chernobog like a bullet, and *Ave Maria* floats over the land to herald the approach of dawn and the victory of lightness over dark.

So visually memorable are the images in *Fantasia* that they have seemingly inspired—consciously or otherwise—similar imagery in later films. Echoes of the slithery spirits in *Night on Bald Mountain* can be found in *Poltergeist* (1982) and even more

The terrifying tyrannosaur closes in on its plated prey in a spellbinding scene from *Fantasia*.

clearly in the climax of *Raiders of the Lost Ark* (1981), which also recalls Chernobog's column of flame shooting upward only to be sucked back in on itself. The scene of the brontosaurs lifting their heads one by one is reprised in *Jurassic Park*, when Doctor Grant imitates the call of the brachiosaurs. There are unmistakable reflections of the *Fantasia* tyrannosaur in the "Sharptooth" of *The Land Before Time*, and the mixed herd trudging wearily across the sunbaked landscape was re-envisioned by Disney—in computer animation—for *Dinosaur*.

In his indispensable work *Walt Disney's Fantasia*, author John Culhane wonderfully summarized the achievement of the *Rite of Spring* artists: "When the animators took the next step and visualized these creatures in motion, they transformed prehistoric monsters from creatures who had long been done with life to creatures who were once again alive." Considered separate from *Fantasia* as a whole, the 22 minutes of *Rite of Spring* constitute one of the best "dinosaur movies" ever filmed.

PEOPLE AND PRODUCTION: *Fantasia*, referred to throughout much of its development simply as the "Concert Feature," can trace its origins to the dawn of sound films and Disney's "Silly Symphony" animated shorts. In the late 1930s, Disney began production on a "special" short, *The Sorcerer's Apprentice*, with Leopold Stokowski conducting Paul Dukas' famous scherzo. As its costs climbed past the $100,000 mark, a strategy was sought by which this two-reeler could be profitably used. Quoted by John Culhane, Stokowski recalled the birth of the Concert Feature: "When it [*Apprentice*] was almost finished, Walt said to me: 'Why don't we make a bigger picture with all kinds of music?' and that led to *Fantasia*."

Animation started in January 1938 and the film was completed nearly three years later, a mere *two days* before its world premiere on November 13, 1940. Most film critics embraced Walt's bold innovation; music critics, though complimentary of the stereophonic "Fantasound" technology pioneered for the film, had decidedly mixed reactions. Very few patrons ever got the chance to experience Fantasound, as the demands of wartime curtailed the ability of theaters to obtain and install the additional sound horns and other equipment. The combined receipts from its limited and sporadic initial release and its first rerelease in 1946 failed to recoup the film's production costs. Finally in 1956, sporting a new magnetically recorded soundtrack that somewhat recreated the effect of Fantasound, *Fantasia* found an audience and became a moneymaker.

The *Rite of Spring* segment was directed by Bill Roberts and Paul Satterfield, with Roberts concentrating on the dinosaur sequences. The episode was spawned at a story conference in 1938 when Deems Taylor proposed using the Stravinsky composition. "This is marvelous!" Walt exclaimed, as quoted by Culhane. "It would be perfect for prehistoric animals ... there could be beauty in the settings." *Rite of Spring* was subdivided into eight parts—Trip Through Space, Volcanoes, Undersea Life and Growth, Pterodactyls, Family Life, Fight, Trek, and Earthquake—which continually tested the ingenuity of Disney's artists and technicians. The uncannily realistic lava was a creation of effects animator Josh Meador, who blew air bubbles up through a slurry of oatmeal, mud and coffee and filmed it at high speed to slow down the action. Special processing, film dyeing, and animated augmentations then produced the final images.

Disney's animators were often helped in visualizing their pen-and-ink creations through the use of props, models and puppets fabricated by the studio's special effects and model department. As a member of that department, future effects luminary Wah Chang helped bring three of Disney's classics to the screen. "They were in production on *Bambi*, *Pinocchio*, and *Fantasia*, all at the same time," Chang recalled to the author. "We did some things for *Fantasia* ... some floating ghosts which were sort of a special effects thing for *Night on Bald Mountain*, and some dancing snowflakes for *The Nutcracker*. I did a mannequin of a deer for *Bambi* that the artist could pose in different positions. And the most we did was on *Pinocchio*."

For the dinosaur sequence, Disney reportedly sought the input of such notables as Roy Chapman Andrews and Barnum Brown in quest of scientific authenticity. One of the first matchups considered when planning the big battle scene was a T. rex against a Triceratops, but an anonymous story man—who knew his dinosaurs—had another idea. "No," he said, apparently with much conviction, "we want to use the Stegosaurus because of this action of his tail with the four spikes." As usual, Walt knew just what he wanted for this sequence, and he wanted it to be "as though the studio had sent an expedition back to the earth 6,000,000 years ago." Let us not nitpick Walt's slight timeline error—his intent and vision were perfectly clear. A vintage quote from *Time* magazine speaks volumes about the *Fantasia* dinosaurs: "The New York Academy of Science asked for a private showing of *Rite of Spring*, because they thought its dinosaurs better science than whole museum loads of fossils and taxidermy."

Fig Leaves

not viewed 1926, USA.
Fox Film Corporation. BW/C, Silent.

CREDITS: *Director* Howard Hawks. *Producer* William Fox.
CAST: George O'Brien, Olive Borden, Phyllis Haver.

This 7-reel comedy looks at various time periods throughout history, and includes a large-scale Brontosaurus—with wheels. Like Cecil B. DeMille's *Adam's Rib* (1923), it features a sequence filmed using an early two-color system. Besides director

Hawks, another notable contributor was art director William Cameron Menzies (*Gone with the Wind, The Thief of Bagdad*, etc.).

The First Circus

**½ 1921, USA. BW/color tints, Silent.

CREDITS: *Producer* Herbert M. Dawley. *Animator* Tony Sarg.

This entry in the "Tony Sarg's Almanac" series of animated films shows the goings-on at the "Stonehenge Circus, 30009 Years Ago." Included are a pair of acrobats who use a sauropod dinosaur as a prop in their act, balancing on its head, landing on its tail, and walking a "tightrope" which is actually a very long snake stretched between the dino's head and tail. The inventive animator and puppeteer Sarg apparently used dimensional objects rather than flat cut-outs to create his silhouette animation, and the entertainment value of his expert work still holds up well.

The Flintstones

"*Have a yabba-dabba-doo time, a dabba-doo time...*"

*** 1994, USA. Universal/Amblin. C, 90m.

CREDITS: *Director* Brian Levant. *Producers* Bruce Cohen, William Hanna, Joseph Barbera, Kathleen Kennedy, David Kirschner, Gerald R. Molen (executive), Colin Wilson (coproducer). *Written by* Tom S. Parker and Jim Jennewein, and Steven E. De Souza. *Special Visual Effects* Industrial Light & Magic. *Visual Effects Supervisor* Mark Dippe. *Animatronic Creatures* Jim Henson's Creature Shop. *Supervisor for Jim Henson's Creature Shop* John Stephenson. *Special Effects Supervisor* Michael Lantieri.

CAST: *Fred Flintstone* John Goodman. *Barney Rubble* Rick Moranis. *Wilma Flintstone* Elizabeth Perkins. *Betty Rubble* Rosie O'Donnell. *Cliff Vandercave* Kyle MacLachlan. *Sharon Stone* Halle Berry. *Pearl Slaghoople* Elizabeth Taylor.

Fred Flintstone, that Stone-Age, blue-collar everyman, has a knack for getting in a jam. When he gives his best pal, Barney Rubble, some money to help Barn and his wife Betty adopt a son, Barney repays the kindness by swapping aptitude tests with his none-too-brilliant buddy. As a result, Fred is given a vice presidency at Slate and Co., unaware that the promotion is part of a devious embezzlement plot hatched by slimy executive Cliff Vandercave and his sultry secretary, Miss Stone. Despite perks like a swanky office complete with his own "Dictabird," Fred finds that executiveship has a downside when his first task turns out to be firing Barney! Fred and wife Wilma bask in luxury while Barney toils away at menial jobs, and it's not long before the Rubbles get fed up with Fred's posturing.

Things are no better for Fred at work, where he is duped into firing all the quarry workers to implement Vandercave's dubious automation system. Fred turns out to be a little smarter than Vandercave thought (not much, but a little) and uncovers the scheme, but it's Wilma who realizes that Fred's Dictabird will contain more than enough recorded conversations to convict Vandercave and exonerate Fred. When Miss Stone is won over by Fred's good-heartedness, Vandercave kidnaps Pebbles Flintstone and Bamm-Bamm Rubble and tries to swap the children for the incriminating Dictabird. "Give me the bird!" Vandercave cries, as a conveyor carries the kids toward the huge rock slicer. But with help from Barney and Miss Stone, Fred manages to save the tots and encase Vandercave in a slurry of crushed stone, sand, and water. Mr. Slate names the invention "concrete" (after his daughter, Concretia) and offers a legitimate promotion, but Fred decides he'd be happiest back at the controls of his trusty brontocrane.

COMMENTARY: The first thing on screen when *The Flintstones* starts is "Steven Spielrock Presents," and you know, if they have the *chutzpa* to do that, the picture is probably going to hit most of the right notes, and you're probably in for some fun. Well it does, and you are.

Director Brian Levant talks over a scene with Fred and Barney (Rick Moranis, John Goodman [right]). The Stone Age autos were actually electrically powered and fully driveable.

It's a pretty reliable Hollywood rule of thumb that any movie with as many writers as *The Flintstones*—*Variety* reported the number at 35—will most likely stink. This is an exception. The final script is a bit convoluted but ultimately proves a satisfactory vehicle for an outstanding cast. The filmmakers struck gold with every choice, from the obvious (who else but John Goodman could play Fred?) to the offbeat (Rosie O'Donnell sparkles as Betty despite a physical dissimilarity to the cartoon version). Kyle MacLachlan makes a nice oily bad guy, and what can you say about Elizabeth Taylor playing Pearl Slaghoople (an inspired idea from Kathleen Kennedy) except that it's the best bit of casting since David O. Selznick picked Vivian Leigh. Taylor's appearances as Pearl are priceless, due equally to the her skillfully comedic performance and the sharp and unexpected dialogue. "When I think of all the *sacrifices* your father made for you," Pearl laments. "Lambs, oxen ... your brother Jerry." Eat your heart out, Leslie Nielsen!

The entire ensemble does a great job of turning their cartoon predecessors into real characters. There's a nice "buddy" chemistry between Goodman and Rick Moranis, who thankfully doesn't go overboard trying to exactly duplicate the 'toon Barney as does Stephen Baldwin in the *Flintstones* prequel. We get a terrific non-human character, too—the wisecracking Dictabird, hilariously voiced by Harvey Korman.

Besides offering good laughs, *The Flintstones* is also a triumph of visual design. There are so many little jokes lurking in the backgrounds it takes a quick finger on the "pause" button to begin to catch them all. The prehistoric gags, a mainstay of the cartoon, are brought to life with joyous abandon. Some bits are obvious of course—the "Universal" logo at the film's opening reads "Univershell." But look again—that's not all. The globe behind the word has all the continents still connected as the ancient supercontinent of Pangaea.

Not surprisingly, some of the biggest grins come courtesy of the dinosaurs and other primordial species that serve as pets, transportation, and household appliances. One great critter follows another — the "pigasaurus" garbage disposal, the mastodon shower head, the pterodactyl airplane (pteroplane?), Fred's marvelous brontocrane, and of course Dino, (cave)man's best friend. Even the no-brainer gags are fun, like a playground called "Jurassic Park" or a "RocDonald's" restaurant, complete with sign reading "over 19 dozen sold."

A toast to director Brian Levant for not spoiling *The Flintstones* by "updating" it or "modernizing" it or doing any of those other things that have ruined a lot of film versions of old TV shows (can you say *Mission Impossible*?). Levant was emphatic that *The Flintstones* would be brought to the screen utterly faithfully, with no bad words and no cynical viewpoints. The famous opening and closing title sequences were recreated in live action almost frame for frame, and even Fred's "twinkle-toes" bowling was enacted by a very game John Goodman. *The Flintstones* is silly and lightweight and even a little corny, and it's also a boulder-sized good time.

PEOPLE AND PRODUCTION: By 1992, *The Flintstones* had been hanging around Amblin Entertainment in development purgatory for over three years, while a multitude of treatments and scripts failed to get a thumbs-up. Finally, television sitcom veteran and longtime *Flintstones* fanatic Brian Levant struck box-office gold (and caught Amblin's attention) with the comedy *Beethoven*, and his patient lobbying to helm the *Flintstones* was rewarded. With Levant aboard and Steven Spielberg's unswerving choice to play Fred — John Goodman — signed up as well, *The Flintstones* was finally under way. In addition to serving as executive producers, original *Flintstones* creators William Hanna and Joseph Barbera joined Jay Leno, Laraine Newman, and the original voice of Wilma, Jean Vander Pyl, in doing cameos in the film. For the role of Sharon Stone, Levant and producer Bruce Cohen wanted to cast ... Sharon Stone. Though the *Basic Instinct* star was reportedly "delighted" by the idea, previous commitments forced her to decline.

Still lacking a satisfactory script, Amblin elected to give Levant a shot. "I think they realized that, in me, they had someone who could restore the script to its roots and do a very faithful adaptation," Levant said in Jody Duncan's *The Flintstones: The Official Movie Book*. His solution was to fill a room with a gaggle of comedy writers and turn them loose. "We'd all talk it out and change things and throw things out," Levant recalled. "Spielberg was editing *Jurassic Park* at the time and he'd come in for a couple of hours every day to drop in ideas." Besides Spielberg, other *Jurassic* alumni on the *Flintstones* team included producer Colin Wilson, art director Jim Teegarden, special effects supervisor Michael Lantieri, visual effects supervisor Mark Dippe, and director of photography Dean Cundey, whose résumé had earned him a reputation as the master of "effects films."

The Flintstones obviously presented one of the biggest production design challenges in movie (pre)history. Virtually everything that appeared on-screen — from a paperweight to a bowling alley — had to be conceived and made from scratch. William Sandell, veteran of such films as *Robocop* and *Total Recall*, was hired as production designer, and along with a small army of art directors, set designers, and illustrators set about turning the filming locations at Vasquez Rocks and the real-life Cal Mat rock quarry into a Flintstonian world. As the "stone" houses were fabricated from foam and erected at Vasquez Rocks, an otherworldly vision of suburbia took shape. "Even those of us in the art department were stunned by it when we first saw it," Sandell commented. Prop master Russell Bobbitt and crew created almost 3,000 "stone age" props, while costume designer Rosanna Norton and her team made nearly 2,000 costume pieces — none of them shoes.

The Flintstones wrapped in mid–August 1993. It had been a pressure-packed and

The full-scale "Brontocrane" for *The Flintstones* was one of the largest puppets ever made by the Henson Creature Shop.

physically demanding shoot, but by all accounts an enjoyable one. A comparatively relaxed postproduction phase now lay ahead, since the film was not due for release until the summer of 1994. "Shooting this movie was the most fun I've ever had," Rick Moranis asserted. "It was a combination of great people, light and playful material ... and the fact that we were working for a company that was making billions of dollars on *Jurassic Park*, which meant that we were under no pressure at all."

SPECIAL EFFECTS: By the time *The Flintstones* was completed, Brian Levant had gained a great appreciation of the difficulties in translating cel animation action to the real world. "Just to do the bit where Fred slides down the tail of the dinosaur, flops into his car and takes off," Levant said in *Cinefantastique*, "took about 20 hours to do what takes three seconds in animation."

As with *Jurassic Park*, the prehistoric beasts of Bedrock would be a seamless mixing of CGI and live-action puppetry. With the accent on fun rather than frights, Jim Henson's Creature Shop was a natural choice to provide the puppet characters. But the Henson group was brought aboard fairly late and had to conceptualize, design, refine, and build over 20 creatures in only 12 weeks. During this developmental phase, creative supervisor Jamie Courtier continually faxed drawings from the Creature Shop in London to Amblin in California for Levant's examination. Once the final look was set, the creatures were sculpted as six-inch maquettes and then reproduced in full size.

Coming on the heels of *Jurassic Park*, *The Flintstones* allowed Industrial Light & Magic to apply their newly honed talents in a different sort of way. Mark Dippe, covisual effects supervisor on *Jurassic*, moved into the top spot this time. "When we first came on the show, we were only going to do a small number of 3-D computer generated shots, and the rest of our shots were going to be rod removals and composites," Dippe said in *Cinefex* (no. 58). Eventually the digital load would expand to over 70 total shots, more than 40 of them being CG characters. "This was my first time out as visual effects producer," ILM's Judith Weaver recalled, "and it was supposed to be my little training bra show with only nine shots—by the time it was over, it turned into a size DD."

The first big creature shot created was the TWA (Triassic World Airlines) pterodactyl airliner. This brief but complex fly-by utilized a full-size cabin set, with live people aboard, mounted on a motion base and photographed in front of a bluescreen. The CG 'dactyl was then animated to match the pitching of the cabin and the two elements were digitally composited. "The pterodactyl looks the most like a real dinosaur," digital artist Carolyn Rendu asserted, "and I'm convinced that it's because it was the first thing we tackled after *Jurassic*. It took a while to disassociate from that and get into a more humorous vein." Director Brian Levant originally wanted to keep the CGI to a minimum, emphasizing the "live" creatures in the interests of spontaneity, but the flexibility offered by digital animation steadily increased ILM's contributions.

The three most prominent critters in the film are Fred's dog, Dino, the brontocrane, and the acerbic Dictabird. Of these, only the Dictabird would be exclusively animatronic, with the other two realized through both digital and puppetized means. The Creature Shop's brontocrane, spearheaded by mechanical design supervisor Verner Gresty, was one of the largest puppets ever built by the Henson group. As with any creature, the bronto was first created as a full-size clay sculpture, although its great weight dictated a steel support instead of the usual wire frame. The sculpture was then used to make molds for a foam latex casting. "The full-size sculpt of the *Flintstones* Brontosaurus was more than 20 feet long, and there was over a ton of clay in it," Jamie Courtier explained in Matt Bacon's *No Strings Attached*. The head and neck were cable-controlled for up-and-down moves and hydraulically powered for sideways motions, while precision motors generated facial expressions.

For shots beyond the capabilities of the three full-scale mechanical sections—head and neck, back (with operator cabin), and tail—ILM provided a fully digital brontocrane. "The wide shots are wonderful because they show these gigantic beasts moving really slowly, dropping rocks and picking them up," Mark Dippe enthused. "Those are some of my favorite shots in the movie." Relying even more heavily on ILM's animation was the character of Dino. Although the dinosaurian dog was originally conceived as a man in a suit with a servo-articulated animatronic head, the frenetic gymnastics required of the character forced the filmmakers to go digital and use the puppet Dino head only for closeups. ILM also provided "Kitty," the Flintstones' pet saber-toothed cat. Though only sparingly seen, Kitty marked ILM's first success at creating realistic CG fur—a skill they would later polish to near perfection for the remake of *Mighty Joe Young*.

Special effects supervisor Michael Lantieri proved to be just as indispensable on *The Flintstones* as he'd been on *Jurassic Park*. The multiple duties of Lantieri and his team included construction of more than twenty "prehistoric" automobiles, building the quarry's gigantic "rock-slicer" machine, and as in *Jurassic*, designing physical gags to allow the CG creatures to seemingly affect real-world objects. Lantieri also worked closely with the Creature Shop crew, building sets and support equipment for the creatures and their operators. "This movie was kind of the flip side of *Jurassic*," Lantieri observed in Duncan's book. "Almost a chance to poke fun at the things we'd had to take so seriously on that film."

Besides the star beasts, both The Crea-

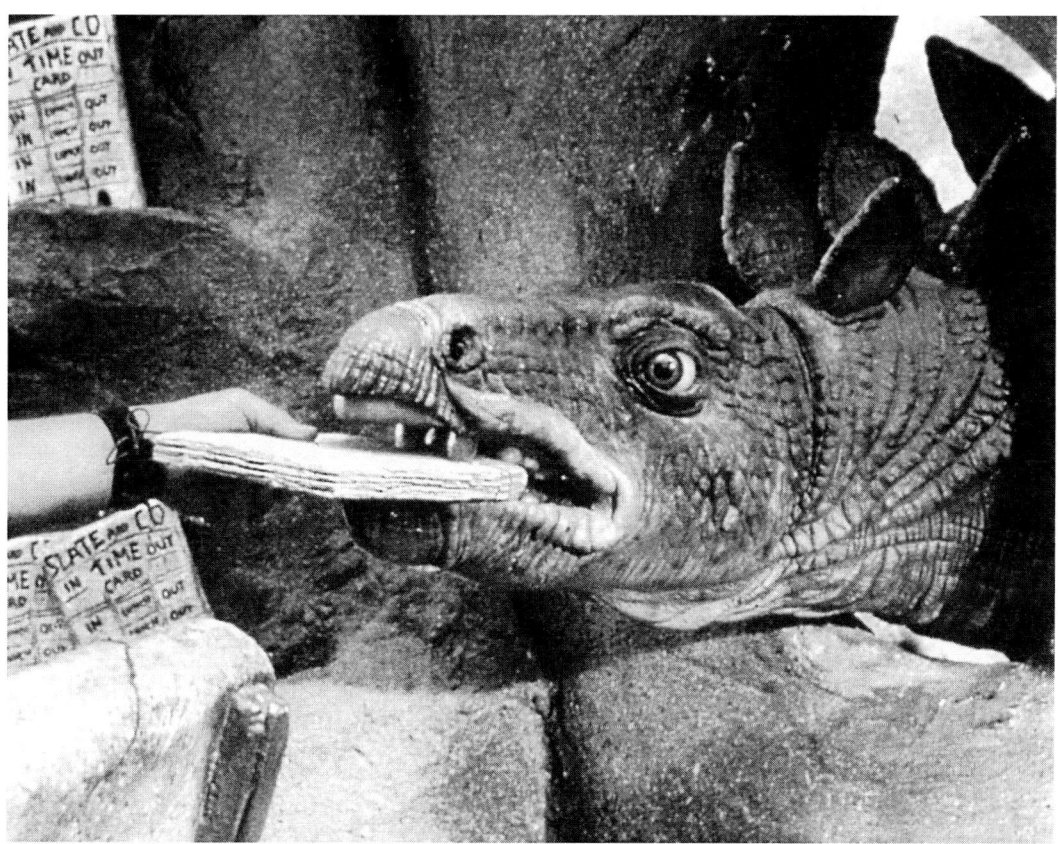

The Stegosaurus time clock was another meticulous Creature Shop creation, though seen only briefly on-screen.

ture Shop and ILM enriched the whole "Bedrock" ambience with numerous background and supporting critters. The Henson artists contributed a mastodon water faucet, a lobster lawn mower (which later doubled as a bowling pin setter), and a Stegosaurus time clock. ILM added a pair of whimsical-looking "Nessie" types of lake monsters and, in true cartoon fashion, a ring of tiny pterodactyls circling Fred's head after a sock in the jaw. The total effect of everyone's efforts resulted in a film that "far exceeded my expectations," Brian Levant said. "Everything that I've ever done or ever been interested in came together in this project."

The Flintstones in Viva Rock Vegas

"First cooked food, now this ... what'll they think of next?"
★ ½ 2000, USA.
Universal/Amblin. C, 91m.

CREDITS: *Director* Brian Levant. *Producers* Bruce Cohen; William Hanna, Joseph Barbera, Dennis E. Jones (executive), Bart Brown (co-producer). *Written by* Deborah Kaplan and Harry Elfont, and Jim Cash and Jack Epps, Jr. *Special Visual Effects and Creature Animation* Rhythm & Hues. *Visual Effects Supervisor* Douglas Hans Smith. *Creature Effects* Jim Henson's Creature Shop. *Creature Effects Supervisor* Jamie Courtier.
CAST: *Fred Flintstone* Mark Addy. *Barney Rubble* Stephen Baldwin. *Wilma Slaghoople* Kristen Johnston. *Betty O'Shale* Jane Krakow-

ski. *Chip Rockefeller* Thomas Gibson. *Gazoo/ Mick Jagged* Alan Cumming. *Pearl Slaghoople* Joan Collins. *Col. Slaghoople* Harvey Korman.

Before the Flintstones and Rubbles settled down as next-door neighbors, the two couples had to meet, fall in love and get married, and it all came together in the entertainment capital of the prehistoric world, Rock Vegas...

Wilma Slaghoople, heiress to a sizable fortune, is fed up with her upper-crust life and runs off to downtown Bedrock. In a fit of rebellion, she takes a waitressing job at the Bronto King alongside her new friend Betty O'Shale. Just-hired quarry workers Fred Flintstone and Barney Rubble take the girls on a date, and after some brief confusion regarding who's dating whom, love blossoms. But Chip Rockefeller, Wilma's shallow society suitor, is desperate to marry into the Slaghoople fortune in order to pay off a massive debt incurred while building his new Rock Vegas casino. The scheming Rockefeller invites Fred, Barney and the girls to the casino, where he sees to it that Fred wins big and then loses bigger. With Fred deep in debt, Rockefeller frames him for the theft of Wilma's pearl necklace and has the poor sap thrown in the clink with Barney. But unknown to Chip, a smug yet benevolent alien named Gazoo has befriended Fred and Barney as part of his mission to observe human mating rituals, and helps them escape. Sneaking back into the casino in showgirl drag, Barney makes up with Betty and Fred makes up with Wilma, leaving Chip to explain his lack of funds to a couple of rather bad-tempered fellows.

COMMENTARY: There was apparently enough source material in the animated series, and enough inspiration in self-professed *Flintstones* superfan Brian Levant, to produce one clever and fun movie. One, not two. Levant and crew grasp for ways to add freshness to *Viva Rock Vegas*—making it a "how they started" prequel, moving the action out of Bedrock—but the well was awfully dry. The cast is good if not quite up to the level of the original, led by Jane Krakowski's bubbly, youthful Betty. England's Mark Addy is a likable Fred, Stephen Baldwin tries too hard to exactly copy the cartoon Barney, and Kristen Johnston, a wonderful comedienne, is simply miscast as Wilma. Gazoo was never an inspired idea, in the animated series or in this movie, though Alan Cumming makes the most of his occasional good lines and provides a few laughs. Cumming is far less enjoyable as Mick Jagged in an exceedingly ill-advised subplot. Listen fast for Rosie O'Donnell, the first movie's Betty, as the voice of the octopus masseuse.

The trademark "Stone Age" gags, a major part of the earlier film's appeal, still provide moments but for the most part seem stale and forced, and the dinosaur content is meager. There is a glimpse of a neat roller coaster made of three brontosaurs, another swell pterodactyl airliner (a "BC-10"), and one shot of a fantastical 600-foot-long sauropod serving as an automobile bridge that's impressive in its sheer scope despite its whimsical nature. Unfortunately, there is also a gag involving a brontocrane with abdominal gas which, frankly, I'm surprised Brian Levant sanctioned. Amongst all the tedium are a few glimmers—Ann-Margrock ... I mean, Ann-Margret (voice only) belting out the picture's title song, a self-effacing *Jurassic Park* joke ("that's a dumb idea ... who's gonna *pay* to see *dinosaurs*?"), and some impeccable digital compositing of Gazoo with the other characters—but Levant and company would be well-advised to stop this "franchise" here before it truly hits rock bottom.

PEOPLE AND PRODUCTION: With *The Flintstones* grossing more than $350 million worldwide, the only thing surprising about the appearance of a sequel was that it took six years. Producer Bruce Cohen, one of several returnees from the earlier film, heartily endorsed the return of director Brian Levant. "Brian is 'Mr. Flintstone,' and knows more about the lore of Bedrock and the TV show than anyone alive today," Cohen asserted. When the cast was announced, eye-

Fred, Wilma, Betty, and Barney (Mark Addy, Kristen Johnston, Jane Krakowski, Stephen Baldwin) have all their wishes "granite" in *Viva Rock Vegas*.

brows raised at the notion of the very British Mark Addy portraying Fred Flintstone. "It's odd to be playing an American character," Addy admitted, "but to be playing an American icon is even scarier." Many of the same designers and artists from the earlier film were reassembled for the sequel, and production designer Christopher Burian-Mohr was happy to again work for Levant. "He wants to get everything on film," Burian-Mohr said. "We know if we make it, he'll shoot it." Filming of *Viva Rock Vegas* started in April 1999 on several of the same locations—Vasquez Rocks, the Cal Mat quarry, and so on—used in *The Flintstones*. The film was released in April 2000, possibly hoping to gain a small boost from the "prehistoric" hype surrounding Disney's *Dinosaur* which hit screens a couple of weeks later.

SPECIAL EFFECTS: The prehistoric puppets in *Viva Rock Vegas* were again the work of Jim Henson's Creature Shop, with Rhythm & Hues taking over for Industrial Light & Magic on the visual effects. Animal appliances new to the sequel included a juicer, a really bizarre vacuum cleaner, and an octopus masseuse who doubles as a croupier. There's also "puppy Dino," hatched from an egg Fred wins at a carnival. *Viva Rock Vegas* represented a sizable assignment for Rhythm & Hues. "On *The Flintstones* there were roughly 66 visual effects shots," said coproducer Bart Brown, "and on this one we have more than 200." Additional effects houses, such as Cinesite, Metrolight Studios, Perpetual Motion Pictures, and Threshold Digital Research Labs, were in fact hired to help complete the effort, and collaboration was sometimes necessary—the bronto roller coaster, for instance, was a Henson company design brought to life at Rhythm & Hues. The impossibly huge "Bronto Bridge" was a favorite shot of Brian Levant. "I really wanted to have a Bronto Bridge where Fred and Barney drive across the back of a 600-foot-long Brontosaurus," the director recalled. "This required quite an amalgamation of design and talents to make this a reality."

Flying Elephants

**½ 1927, USA. Hal Roach/Pathé. BW, 20m, Silent.

CREDITS: *Director* Fred Butler. *Producer* Hal Roach. *Supervising Director* F. Richard Jones. *Titles* H. M. Walker.
CAST: *Mighty Giant* Oliver Hardy. *Twinkle Star* Stan Laurel. *Blushing Rose* Viola Richard. *Saxophonus* James Finlayson.

If, as author Don Glut once suggested, Willis O'Brien's early Stone Age comedies are the forerunners of *The Flintstones*, then *Flying Elephants* is the forerunner of Carl Gottlieb's 1981 spoof, *Caveman*. Both films use the basic "caveman" clichés—big clubs, dim-witted brutes, scantily-clad women, marauding beasts—as fodder for silly slapstick. The two movies have some nearly identical gags, even though *Elephants* has almost as many good laughs in its 20 minutes as *Caveman* has in its hour and a half. In this prehistory saga (the only Laurel and Hardy two-reeler not set in present day), Ollie as the Mighty Giant and Stan as Twinkle Star compete for the affections of the king's beautiful daughter, Blushing Rose. Ollie pretty much sticks to his familiar persona, but Stan's character is an odd, very effeminate "merry swain" who flits about and tosses flowers like a skinny, goofy Cupid. The comely cavegirls, flaunting bare midriffs and lots of naked thigh in 1927, are led by the lovely young Viola Richard as that "goodly wench," Blushing Rose.

The film's strange title comes from a comment made by Ollie. "Beautiful weather—the elephants are flying south," he says, at which point we cut to a shot of three cartoon-animated elephants doing just that. The shooting locations in the desert country of Nevada give the proceedings a decidedly *One Million B.C.* look, but the dinosaur content is limited to a single shot of a conspicuously slow Triceratops frightening Twinkle Star out of a thicket. The creature (so white it must be a rare albino strain) was played by a man, or very possibly two men, in a hastily-fashioned suit. Several live animals, including a bear and a mountain goat, also make appearances, the latter destined to head-butt poor Ollie over a cliff and leave the curly-haired Stan as the romantic victor. Despite Fred Butler's name in the credits, Roach Studio historians maintain that Hal Roach actually handled the directing duties.

Galaxy of the Dinosaurs

"I'm not gonna run from you anymore, you cheap Godzilla ripoff!"

1992, USA. Suburban Tempe Company. C, 62m.

CREDITS: *Director* Lance Randas. *Producers* J. R. Bookwalter, David DeCoteau (executive). *Story* Thomas Brown. *Written by* John Killough. *Special Make-up* Bill Morrison.

CAST: *Capt. Kronik* James Black. *Morda* Christine Morrison. *Benj* Tom Hoover. *Prof. Geting* Bill Morrison. *Dr. Forband* Scott Emerman. *Graft/Gurtorious Gonimus* James L. Edwards. *Bob the Caveman* Joseph Daw.

AD LINE: "An utterly stupefying exercise in extreme madness, moronicness, and mutant alien monsters!"

"ALL NEW!" shriek the words on the *Galaxy of the Dinosaurs* video box, but *Galaxy* is actually one of several titles to reuse the excellent stop-motion from *Planet of Dinosaurs*. The animation is absurdly intercut with new shot-on-video footage that takes the word "amateurish" to new depths. Not only is the film-versus-video contrast jarring, the new scenes all take place in a dense woodland which rather fails to match the rockbound terrain in *Planet of Dinosaurs*. Maybe the extreme dissimilarity is meant as an intentional gag, but it's pointless to even discuss things like continuity or logic when dealing with something like *Galaxy of the Dinosaurs*. It is no exaggeration to say that it looks to have been conceived, written, photographed, and edited in the space of a day or two.

The plot of *Galaxy* is almost too idiotic to describe. Captain Kronik and a ragtag band of space travelers attempt to stop on Earth for a snack, but instead become stranded on the planet Gurgon (or so they think). They find to their dismay that the orb is overrun with killer dinosaurs, and as their numbers steadily decline, their every move is secretly watched by an unseen villain. The bad guy is revealed to be none other than galactic criminal (and Freddy Krueger lookalike) Gurtorious Gonimus, Kronik's arch enemy. Gonimus eventually falls victim to one of his own dinosaur creations, leaving Kronik and the lissome Morda to be the Adam and Eve of a new world ... or maybe not.

There aren't many things worse than a spoof without a single funny moment. Benj, the most obviously "comic" character, wears a Hawaiian shirt and whines about wanting a cheeseburger. "Bob the Caveman" shows up—apparently just having a caveman named "Bob" is supposed to be hilarious. The group gets stoned on hallucinogenic sprouts, some are preyed upon by dinosaurs, and a former crew member is unmasked as the villain. And that's pretty much it. The only flickers of life come at the very end: a revelation by Captain Kronik that puts a definite crimp in Morda's plans to repopulate the planet, and a moderately clever tribute to the "Statue of Liberty" shot from the original *Planet of the Apes*. *Galaxy of the Dinosaurs* ultimately has two distinctions: it proves that anyone with a camcorder, a free weekend, and J. R. Bookwalter's gumption has a chance to make a "movie" that will get nationwide video distribution, and it is the only dinosaur picture ever filmed in Mogadore, Ohio.

Gertie on Tour

not viewed c. 1917, USA. BW, Silent.

CREDITS: *Director/Producer* Winsor McCay. *Assistant animators* John McCay, John Fitzsimmons.

Sequel to Winsor McCay's popular cartoon *Gertie the Dinosaur*, presenting additional, similarly-themed antics of the cute Brontosaurus. This time McCay's backgrounds, and Gertie herself, were much more elaborately drawn than in the original film. Only a fragment of this sequel survives, showing Gertie being frightened by a tiny toad (she's accustomed to the giant prehistoric kind), playing with a train like a toy, and performing acrobatics for an audience of brontosaurs.

Gertie the Dinosaur

*** 1914, USA. BW, Silent.

CREDITS: *Director* Winsor McCay.
CAST: Winsor McCay, George McManus.

A pioneering animated film by cartoonist Winsor McCay, *Gertie the Dinosaur* (also known simply as *Gertie*) can legitimately be called the world's first true "dinosaur movie." Prehistoric creatures had appeared in previous pictures, but *Gertie* was the first time that a dinosaur served as a film's primary character. So groundbreaking was McCay's creation that the animation is still enjoyable for modern audiences.

Born in 1867, Winsor McCay began his professional career creating advertising illustrations and other promotional materials. Around the turn of the century, he went to work for the *Cincinnati Commercial Tribune*, and later toiled for other newspapers and periodicals including the *New York Herald*, *New York Telegram*, and *New York American*. He made his first experimental animated cartoon, using characters from his comic strip *Little Nemo in Slumberland*, in 1911, and soon followed it with *The Story of a Mosquito*. His next film, *Gertie the Dinosaur*, was an unmitigated success which thrilled viewers wherever it was exhibited.

Gertie describes the adventures of McCay's "wonderfully trained dinosaurus," as the ads stated. With assistance from John Fitzsimmons, who did the backgrounds, McCay created by hand approximately 10,000 separate drawings on rice paper. The project took McCay almost two years to complete, but when the drawings were registered, photographed, and projected, Gertie the impish Brontosaurus came to life. She peers out of a cave and hesitantly approaches the "camera," then proceeds to perform a variety of tricks on McCay's commands. She bows, raises her feet, eats a rock and a tree, catches a pumpkin in her mouth, and even meets some other prehistoric creatures. She tosses a woolly mammoth named "Jumbo" into the nearby lake (Jumbo takes revenge by squirting Gertie with a trunk-full of water), but the appearances of a fanciful flying lizard and dragonlike sea serpent are limited to quick cameos.

In his vaudeville act, McCay would stand to the side of the screen, cracking a whip and barking out the commands to his animated charge. Near the end, he would dart behind the screen at a moment coinciding with his appearance in the film as a live action figure, placed by Gertie herself onto her massive back. McCay later bookended the film with a live action framing sequence starring himself and fellow cartoonist George McManus, in which McManus bets McCay that he cannot "bring a dinosaur to life." As the success of *Gertie* and her generations of cinematic progeny attest, McCay wins his bet.

Gertie the Dinosaur

** c. 1915, USA. Bray Studios. BW, Silent.

CREDITS: *Director* J. R. Bray.

John Randolph "J. R." Bray's blatant copycat version of Winsor McCay's innovative cartoon, starring a similarly cute bronto. This knockoff *Gertie* had drawings more fully rendered than McCay's simple line art, but was not nearly as popular or successful. Bray, despite his penchant for making films based upon previous work (he also made *The Lost Whirl* in the late 1920s), was nonetheless a talented and notable contributor to early cinema. Other dinosaur-related cartoons from Bray included *A Stone Age Adventure* (1915) directed by L. M. Glackens, and *The First Flyer* (1918), a short educational cartoon about the pterodactyl and the origins of flight in the animal world.

The Ghost of Slumber Mountain

"I beheld grotesque reptiles and birds of the Prehistoric World."

The advertising art for *Slumber Mountain*, though striking, left Willis O'Brien's name conspicuously absent.

**½ 1919, USA. World Cinema Distributing Company, BW, 15m, silent.

As the 1920s approached and the Edison Studios began to falter, mirroring the dissolution of the Motion Picture Patents Company which for a time held a virtual monopoly on the budding film industry, Willis O'Brien prepared to move on from his slapstick cavepeople-and-dinosaur comedies to something bigger. He got his chance in 1918 when he met Herbert M. Dawley, a sculptor who, like O'Brien, was fascinated with putting prehistoric animals on film. Dawley put up $3,000 and Obie set to work on *The Ghost of Slumber Mountain*, based on his own scenario.

The film begins as two tykes ask their Uncle Jack to tell them a story, and "Unk" begins relating the tale of a camping trip with his pal Joe and dog Soxie to mysterious Slumber Mountain. "In the heart of the mountains," he says, "lies the stone covered grave and haunted cabin of a hermit known as 'Mad Dick.'" A voice leads Jack to that very cabin where he finds a strange telescope, and in a "rush of air like the whirr of an owl's wings," Mad Dick's spirit appears. (Rumors persist that Mad Dick is played by O'Brien himself.) At the ghost's behest, Jack looks through the magical scope and sees images of prehistory. A "Thunder Lizard, which must have been 100 feet long," browses for food. A flightless bird, Diatryma, grooms its feathers and dines on a snake. A pair of Triceratops briefly skirmish until an Allosaurus appears, kills one of the horned creatures, and comes after Jack. "His fevered breath was in my face, I could almost feel his fangs tearing my flesh...." Then the sun rises to reveal that it was all just a dream.

Before *Slumber Mountain*, Willis O'Brien had consulted with the eminent paleontologist Dr. Barnum Brown in preparation for some planned educational shorts with prehistoric themes. These featurettes were canceled with the downfall of the Edison Company, but O'Brien put his enhanced knowledge of paleoanatomy into his *Slumber Mountain* puppets. There are reports that Brown even helped script the film's dinosaur behaviors. The animation, all done by Obie, is a great leap forward from his caricatured comedies. Not only did he make the puppets much more accurate, he was already beginning to put in the little "bits of business" that would become a hallmark of his work. The Diatryma walks into frame, pauses, preens itself with its bulky bill and crouches its head down to scratch an ear, and it all looks uncannily like the actions of a real animal. The chewing motion of the Triceratops is so perfect it has never been surpassed, and the fight scene, though brief, foreshadows Obie's inspired battles in films yet to come.

Herbert Dawley's $3,000 investment was well-spent, as *Slumber Mountain* became a hit and grossed over $100,000. Obie's association with Dawley unfortunately turned sour when Dawley removed O'Brien's name from the credits and proceeded to claim that he had single-handedly designed, built, animated, and photographed the dinosaur sequences. Various sources report that *Slumber Mountain* was originally much longer than its surviving 15 minutes, and Dawley apparently used some of the excised footage in his 1920 release *Along the Moonbeam Trail* (now presumed a "lost" film).

The Ghost of Slumber Mountain is notable as more than just a stepping stone on Obie's progressive journey to *King Kong*; it is in fact the first movie to really begin to exploit the cinematic potential of dinosaurs.

The Giant Behemoth

(a.k.a. *Behemoth the Sea Monster* [U.K.])

"So, the old devil's done it again, has he?"

*** 1959, U.K. Allied Artists. BW, 80m.

CREDITS: Director Eugène Lourié. Producers David Diamond, Ted Lloyd (associate). Screenplay Eugène Lourié. Story Robert Abel and Allen Adler. *Special Effects Designed and Cre-*

ated by Jack Rabin, Irving Block, Louis DeWitt, Willis O'Brien, Pete Peterson.

CAST: *Steve Karnes* Gene Evans. *Prof. James Bickford* André Morell. *John* John Turner. *Jean Trevethan* Leigh Madison. *Prof. Sampson* Jack MacGowran. *Thomas Trevethan* Henry Vidon. *Submarine Officer* Maurice Kaufmann.

AD LINE: "Behemoth ... Invulnerable ... Untouchable ... The biggest thing since creation!"

At the Conference on Atomic Research in London, Californian marine biologist Steve Karnes lectures on the dangers of contaminations resulting from nuclear arms tests and atomic waste dumping. Karnes fears that a "biological chain reaction" may have already begun, but the only sympathetic voice in attendance is that of British nuclear physicist James Bickford. At that moment in a far-off Cornwall fishing village, fisherman Tom Trevethan is found by his daughter Jean and her friend John, covered with awful, radiation-like burns. With his last breath, he whispers "behemoth."

In London, Karnes hears a news report about the strange happenings and visits Professor Bickford. "There's rather more in it than the press reports, a man is dead," Bickford confides, and together they travel to Cornwall to investigate. Tests of the area show no radioactivity, but when Jean mentions her father's last word Karnes begins to suspect that a "strange marine animal" is responsible. Returning to London, Karnes and Bickford analyze sea-life samples gathered from all along the English coast. When a specimen is found contaminated with a strange glowing mass, Karnes tracks it to the waters off Plymouth and actually gets a brief glimpse of something in the distance. Karnes continues following the trail to the site of an unexplained sea disaster, where the steam ship *Valkyria* has been violently wrecked. Finally back in London, Karnes learns from Bickford that the mysterious glowing material removed from the fish contained cells "from the stomach wall of some unidentified species," proving Karnes' "behemoth theory" to be true.

Karnes and Bickford consult with the

Giant Behemoth poster from Australia, where it was known by its original, less redundant British title, *Behemoth the Sea Monster*.

eccentric paleontologist Dr. Sampson regarding a gigantic footprint found near Essex. Sampson identifies it as of "the old Paleosaurus family," and reveals two other facts: the Paleosaurus is strongly electric, "like an eel," and is likely heading for the fresh water of the Thames estuary. The behemoth slips past the London Port Authority's radar scans and capsizes a ferry loaded with men, women, and children. As the situation escalates to emergency proportions, Karnes and Bickford meet with the military to discuss strategy. Emphasizing that the radioactive animal must be destroyed in one piece, Bickford suggests introducing ten centigrams of pure radium into its body via a modified torpedo. But just then the behemoth comes ashore and decimates much of London. Before submerging again, Karnes and a young helmsman set out in a miniature submarine outfitted with special tracking gear, and thankfully make their one shot count. Karnes returns to shore amid congratulations, but he and Bickford soon hear a fateful radio bulletin from the States.

COMMENTARY: *The Giant Behemoth* is the least remembered and least revered of director Eugène Lourié's three dinosaur-themed films. With neither the genre-defining originality of *The Beast from 20,000 Fathoms* nor the Technicolor spectacle and warm-fuzzy plot of *Gorgo*, *Behemoth* often lies overlooked and forgotten. It is a fate it does not deserve.

Though hampered during production by limitations of all sorts, *The Giant Behemoth* possesses a variety of strengths which bludgeon its weaknesses into submission. It has a feeling, a rhythm, almost an elegance about it that sets it apart from all others of its kind. Coming near the end of the marvelous, monster-movie-mad 1950s, *Behemoth* represents—both chronologically and in practice—the end of that era. It was the last giant-monster-in-the-city movie in black and white, the last such production to utilize stop-motion, and the last film for which effects pioneer Willis O'Brien would oversee the animation of a prehistoric creature. Buoyed by Lourié's focused direction, the understated performances of a well-chosen cast, a taut, smart script, an unrelentingly foreboding mood, and some nifty special effects, *The Giant Behemoth* is perhaps the most underrated dinosaur film of all.

Yes, *Behemoth* has much in common with Lourié's *Beast from 20,000 Fathoms*—Lourié himself called it a "second edition of the *Beast*." Conceding the similarities, *Behemoth* stands as a different movie with a different and decidedly British personality. Films like *Behemoth* are often described as having a "documentary style," but what exactly does that mean? To me it simply means that the filmmakers attempt tell their story *as if it really happened*, despite the fantastic premise, and certainly nobody in the dinomovie field did this as well as Lourié. Even though the script was written hurriedly and under duress, the tense and efficient result shows few signs of haste. The story to a great degree takes on the feel of a good detective yarn, as Karnes and Bickford employ equal measures of forensics, technology, and Holmesian deductive reasoning to piece together the clues and solve the puzzle. Perhaps not until *The Andromeda Strain* eleven years later did a genre film so earnestly attempt to depict the methodical investigation of a scientific mystery.

Although certain characteristics of the monster itself had to be fictionalized, in every other aspect the screenplay sticks to real science. From Karnes' early reference to "Operation Crossroads" (the actual codename for the Bikini atomic tests) and the radiation detection methodology (ionization chamber, radioautograph), to the dissection of the flounder ("good old *Pleuronectes flesus*" as Karnes says) and the forging of the torpedo's radium warhead, detail after detail rings true. One might fear that such meticulousness would bog things down; on the contrary, it actually makes the tale more compelling. Comparing this approach to the typical bubblegum sci-babble of most 1950s monster movies, the difference is staggering. Grimly, the film's greatest scientific truth lies in its real-world warnings about the dangers of nuclear testing and waste dumping. In every other example of the atomic paranoia B-movies of the Cold War years, the nuclear threat is wholly personified by a fantastic, fictional element—the Monster—which is always vanquished in the end. *Behemoth* stands alone in its cautionary message about the very real damage that humankind has done, and can still do, to our planet.

The Giant Behemoth was blessed with surprising talent in key positions. The cinematography by Ken Hodges and the art direction by Harry White neatly complement Lourié's direction. Hodges (whose lead cameraman, Desmond Davis, would direct Ray Harryhausen's *Clash of the Titans* 22 years later) recalls the look of Universal's horror classics of the 1930s, effectively using light and shadow to heighten the feeling of dread. Consider the early scene in which a worried Jean Trevethan decides to investigate her father's whereabouts. She stands in the kitchen in the background of the shot, light streaming from behind her through the doorway, into the darkened foreground. Her distorted shadow stretches across the bare floor. At the same time, the wind whistles mournfully outside, and the unlatched door slaps against its frame. By the time the girl grabs her coat and exits, you wouldn't be surprised to find Bela Lugosi lying in wait. The considerable number of exterior location shots, many photographed in an authentic Cornwall fishing village, maintain this same mood. At almost no time during the film does the sun shine. Instead, a grey, glowering sky hangs over the proceedings in nearly every outdoor scene. Edwin Astley's score, slickly alternating between soft, haunting themes, military rhythms, and brassy, anxious motifs, adds still further to the menacing feel. As a final touch, the "radiation burn" make-up effects by Jimmy Evans are credibly understated, making them all the more gruesome.

The acting roster for *Behemoth* is another huge plus, led by the chemistry between the perfectly cast Gene Evans and Andre Morell. Evans is the American, big, burly and beaming, his broad smile a testament to his affable good nature and Yankee enthusiasm. His Steve Karnes plays perfectly off Morell's stolid Professor Bickford. Circumspect and cerebral, Bickford is the very archetype of English reserve and restraint, yet never comes across as arrogant or cold. The supporting actors are just as proficient. John Turner is so likable and charismatic that you find yourself wishing he had more screen time, and Jack MacGowran provides the film's few light moments as Doctor Sampson, the paleontologist who's a couple of bones short of a skeleton. As in *The Beast from 20,000 Fathoms*, even the smallest of parts — Tom Trevethan, Doctor Morris, the trawler skipper, the overconfident admiral — are very nicely done. Of all the players, only Leigh Madison fails to make an impression, and is merely adequate.

In a rare occurrence, the human characters are treated as real people with real problems rather than simply as mannequins to react to the monster. In one scene, John laments the decimation of the fishermen's livelihood and asks pleadingly, "how are these men supposed to feed their families?" Early in the ferry sequence, we see a little girl holding her doll, followed near the end by an image of the doll, floating alone in the Thames. And when Trevethan is killed, he is put to rest in a very realistic and somber funeral scene that is quite striking for this genre, where any loss of life caused by the monster is usually very impersonal and unfelt. The funeral service also provides the opportunity to smoothly inject the Biblical account of the behemoth (Job 40:15), adding one more layer of verisimilitude.

The animation of the behemoth is a testament to what creative, dedicated people can accomplish even under the most trying of circumstances. The walking cycle that Pete Peterson bestowed upon the "Paleosaurus" is arguably the most naturalistic ever done for a movie creature of its supposed size. A believable illusion of great mass is one of the most difficult qualities to achieve with the stop-motion technique, but Peterson, under the tutelage of the master, Willis O'Brien, does it brilliantly. (It is puzzling to this day why Lourié always voiced such unqualified disapproval of the *Behemoth* animation.) The animal's huge, heavy gait, complementing the zoologically plausible musculature of the puppet itself, imparts a wonderfully "weighty" look to the stride that has never been surpassed. Careful lighting, of both the creature and the miniature sets it inhabits, matches the style of the rest of the picture and nicely augments the beautiful ambulation.

One shot in particular stands out as one of the most atmospheric pieces of monster animation ever created. Fairly late in the film, as Bickford's crew desperately works to complete the radium torpedo, the behemoth approaches the sleeping city under the shadowy cloak of the night sky. Seen almost entirely in silhouette, its silvery skin just reflecting the scant rays of dusky light, the beast enters the frame and slowly approaches from the distant background to the foreground in one lengthy cut, destroying power lines in its path, and ever so gradually becoming more discernible. Peterson even added a camera move, tilting sharply up as if trying to keep the towering head of the approaching dinosaur in frame. It's a great scene with an undeniable edge-of-the-seat quality, and at over 50 seconds in length (that's over 1,200 frames!), it must rank as one of the longest uninterrupted stop-motion shots ever done. When one considers the scant amounts of time, money, and resources available to Peterson and O'Brien, the images they delivered are all the more impressive.

Having so much to like makes it easier to forgive the flaws, but there are flaws. The shortage of animation footage, and the resulting repetition of shots, is the film's biggest weakness, and it's doubly frustrating because the work which is there is so very good. There are also some scattered technical glitches. During the "car crush" shot for instance, the projected footage behind the car can be seen to repeatedly stop and start during the shot, due to the decrepit condition of the only available rear projector. The mechanical head-and-neck prop, featured during the ferry sequence and in assorted other brief scenes, was unfortunately damaged prior to filming and looks quite stiff and lifeless. The limited number of extras results in some rather small-scale panic scenes, although this is tempered somewhat by the claustrophobic nature of the narrow London streets. The rotating "hypno-wheel" effect, superimposed whenever the creature projects its radioactive waves, somehow works okay within the context of the film but seems a bit hokey if one stops and thinks about it. Lastly, the stop-motion "swimming" shots of the behemoth during the climax, though unique, are not entirely successful. But these small blemishes do no great damage. Some have lamented that a low-budget effort like *Behemoth* should turn out to be the great Willis O'Brien's swan song, but Obie could have done a lot worse than this dark, intelligent, ominous little gem.

PEOPLE AND PRODUCTION: In view of the surprising quality that Eugène Lourié had managed to give *The Beast from 20,000 Fathoms* (not to mention the fact that it was a box-office bonanza), it was perhaps inevitable that he was subsequently approached to helm other genre pictures. In his book *My Work in Films*, Lourié described the fallout from *Beast*'s success: "I was getting scripts and offers to direct some sci-fi pictures, all of them unbelievably bad," he stated. Then along came producer Dave Diamond, with a project that Lourié found more intriguing. Initially, the film's menace was envisioned as a growing mass of radiation, and had nothing to do with a dinosaur. "Once again I was caught by the reputation of *Beast*," Lourié wrote. "The English producers insisted that our story had to deal with a visible physical creature, a monster, and they let us understand that it should be a duplication of *The Beast from 20,000 Fathoms*."

Working with his friend Daniel Hyatt (actually Daniel James, who also cowrote *Gorgo* using the Hyatt pseudonym due to the writers' blacklist), Lourié produced a preliminary draft of the screenplay in about ten days. The director wrote this draft only to meet a previously agreed-upon timetable and satisfy the contract, and delivered it with the presumed understanding that it would be extensively rewritten prior to filming. "But the rewriting was never done," Lourié pointed out, "and so I had to shoot this second edition of the *Beast*."

The only American in the otherwise all–British cast was Gene Evans, best known for his western roles. Evans was reluctant to do *Behemoth*, but changed his mind when producer David Diamond mentioned that it would be an English shoot. "I was in England during the War, right up 'til the [Normandy] invasion," Evans told interviewer *extraordinaire* Tom Weaver. "I kind of thought I'd like to go back there when I had money in my pocket." The clincher was meeting Eugène Lourié. "I liked him immensely," Evans said. "He was a hell of an artist, he knew music, he was a set designer and just an all-around talented guy. *He* tried to make a good mystery picture out of this, and *I* think it was a pretty good picture."

Live-action photography for *Behemoth* was completed in 24 days, double the 12-day schedule of *The Beast from 20,000 Fathoms*. It took 20 days to shoot the outdoor live action in London and the interiors at National Studios–Elstree, including one particularly difficult scene. "I walked in, and there was this flounder I was supposed to dissect," Gene Evans recalled. "Oh, man, that poor fish hadn't seen water in God knows how long! He was slimy and he stunk *so bad* that *two* of the people working with me got sick." The other four days were spent on location near Cornwall, not the most comfortable locale. "I still remember the cold — *bitter* cold!" Evans said. "It was tough, tough, tough, a dreary, miserable place. *Beautiful* — but at the time of the year we were there, it was really dismal." Evans obviously found the English actors much more pleasant than the weather. "Oh, yeah, Andre [Morell] was a character, I liked him," Evans stated. "There were some other very good people working in that film, too. Like the little man who played the museum curator, Jack Mac-Gowran — he was a wonderful character man in England."

Since *Behemoth* was a combined effort involving a British studio, rules stipulated that there must be a British codirector on the project. A young director named Douglas Hickox was assigned. "He was a nice fella," Evans said of Hickox, "but he was in a lousy spot. Well, you know, *any*body would be: A guy [Lourié] comes in with a script he's prepared, and then he's got to work with this other guy. But 'Dougie' was a competent director." Lourié also complimented Hickox, telling Paul Mandell that "Doug was then very young and a very good assistant."

SPECIAL EFFECTS: With *The Giant Behemoth*, Eugène Lourié again needed someone capable of bringing a gargantuan, prehistoric relic to life on the screen. Ray Harryhausen was deep into production on *The 7th Voyage of Sinbad*, so Lourié turned to the team of Willis O'Brien and Pete Peterson. Lourié had met the duo a couple of years earlier during the making of *The Black Scorpion*, a film he

Closeup view of the well-designed "paleosaurus" stop-motion model, animated by Pete Peterson for ***The Giant Behemoth***.

The infamous "car crush" shot which, as the stories tell, does indeed appear three times in *The Giant Behemoth*.

was slated to direct. Differences between Lourié and *Scorpion*'s producers prompted his early departure but he knew that O'Brien and Peterson had created some outstanding animation effects on a small budget, which was just what he needed for *Behemoth*. While Obie and Pete were an ideal choice to do the animation, it was feared by some that they simply didn't have the physical resources to pull off some of the other scripted effects shots. So, Jack Rabin and his Studio Film Services were brought on board. Rabin and his partners, Louis DeWitt and Irving Block, would handle the optical work, the ferry sequence (Rabin had the necessary water tank), and some of the other larger-scale stuff. O'Brien and Peterson, now actually under subcontract, would take care of the animation. To Lourié's disappointment, he had no involvement in the postproduction-effects effort.

All of the animation was accomplished by Pete Peterson alone, and just as *Behemoth* is an overlooked film, Peterson is an equally underappreciated animator. About 10 years earlier, Peterson had contributed to *Mighty Joe Young* (billed as "Second Technician"), animating the shots of Joe on the back of the escape truck. Then in 1957 came the aforementioned monsterpic *The Black Scorpion*. Though not a great example of the genre, *Scorpion* is worth seeing just to enjoy Peterson's beautiful work. His scenes of the eight-legged predators and other oversized crawlies, scuttling about in their dark lair, are some of the downright *creepiest* stop-motion images ever filmed. By the time *Behemoth* came along, Peterson was so debilitated by multiple sclerosis that he had to animate while sitting down, and consequently the animation sets for *Behemoth* were constructed very low to the ground. In spite of his physical burden, the quality of Peterson's small but sparkling body of animation work can legitimately be compared with that of his legendary mentor.

Even though O'Brien was past 70 years of age when *Scorpion* and *Behemoth* were made and was no longer doing hands-on animation, he was far from being a mere bystander. For *The Giant Behemoth*, he constructed the behemoth stop-motion puppet, designed and set up matte shots to composite the behemoth with live-action plates, and worked with FX jack-of-all-trades Phil Kellison to build the mechanical head and neck prop. The finely detailed head-and-neck was, once upon a time, a wonderful creation. The neck arched, the mouth opened, the eyes moved, and the whole thing was covered in latex skin cast from real reptile skin. One of Obie's original design sketches, published by genre historian-archivist Bob Burns, reveals the neck armature consisted of segmented hinge joints (rather than ball-and-sockets), fitted with a series of disc-shaped "vertebrae" to support and give form to the outer covering. Sadly, it would never be captured on film in all its glory. The day of its big scene — the ferry sinking — the filmmakers had rented a variety of equipment, including lights, a water pump, and a special high-speed camera, and the behemoth was working beautifully. So beautifully in fact, that someone on the set ("a very impetuous technician," as Kellison put it) began playing with the controls, eventually breaking the levers. With the small budget already stretched to the limit, paying another day's rent on the special gear was out of the question. So, the mechanical beastie had to play his scenes in his now much more immobile state.

A very talented model and miniature maker, Phil Kellison had a long career in the effects game, and did a lot of nice work on *Behemoth*. Besides his contributions to the head-and-neck puppet, Kellison built the 30" model ferryboat, some miniature barges which were used to add detail to the water-tank set, and the finely detailed, crushable cranes that the creature destroys during its first big rampage. Interviewed in Paul Mandell's painstakingly researched article, "Of Beasts and Behemoths," Kellison discussed his experiences. "Obie needed some miniatures made, which is how I got on *Behemoth*," he recalled. "I volunteered to do them freelance." Kellison was delighted to have the opportunity to work with Willis O'Brien. "I was impressed by O'Brien, of course, and I put my heart and soul into the miniatures I made. They were working cranes, yet they were set up so they could be animated and collapse." Also an experienced effects cameraman, Kellison photographed the sinking of his own ferryboat in Jack Rabin's tank.

Kellison also told Mandell about some of the shortcuts employed to stretch the meager effects budget, like the scene where the behemoth is seen next to the Parliament buildings. "Anyone can look at that scene today and see the animated spotlight traveling over the convolutions of the buildings," Kellison said. "You think you're seeing it in dimension. Not so! They were absolutely flat photo cutouts!" Still, as Kellison observed, the final result was amazingly effective. "The way things were set up and lit, it really looked quite good."

Gorgo

"I came to let him go back to the sea where he belongs."

★★½ 1961, U.K. MGM. C, 76m.

CREDITS: *Director* Eugène Lourié. *Producers* Wilfred Eades; Frank King and Maurice King (executive). *Screenplay* John Loring and Daniel Hyatt. *Original Story* Eugène Lourié and Daniel Hyatt. *Special Photographic Effects* Tom Howard, F.R.P.S., B.S.C.

CAST: *Joe Ryan* Bill Travers. *Sam Slade* William Sylvester. *Sean* Vincent Winter. *McCartin* Christopher Rhodes. *Prof. Hendricks* Joseph O'Conor. *Prof. Flaherty* Bruce Seton. *Dorkin*

Martin Benson. *Radio Reporter* Maurice Kaufmann.

AD LINE: "Towering over the cities of the world, as millions flee in awesome terror!"

Partners Joe Ryan and Sam Slade scrape out a living salvaging valuables from shipwrecks, always dreaming of that one big score. While anchored off tiny Nara Island in the Irish Sea, a massive seaquake strikes the area and they are forced to go ashore for supplies. They befriend a young orphan named Sean who works for the harbormaster, Mr. McCartin, and discover that the boy's tasks include sorting and cleaning a fortune in Viking artifacts recovered by McCartin's divers from the surrounding waters. Joe and Sam naturally make their own exploratory dive, but instead of treasure they find a primordial sea creature, released from a suboceanic cavern by the recent upheavals. When McCartin's divers balk at swimming with a monster, Joe and Sam offer to dispose of the beast and save McCartin's lucrative setup — for a price — and manage to capture the creature alive.

As the news spreads, two University of Dublin paleontologists are dispatched "to claim the creature for Ireland," and suggest that a continuous sea water spray would keep the animal's skin moist. Joe and Sam heed the suggestion, but since they've already agreed to a lucrative exhibition deal with Dorkin's Circus in London, the scientists are promptly dismissed. Joe discovers that Sean has stowed away to try and free the creature, and when asked why, he says, "maybe to save your silly skins for you."

The tranquilized "Gorgo," so-named in reference to the mythological Gorgon, is trucked to its circus home at Battersea Park. Gorgo briefly breaks free and kills a worker, and Sam grows uneasy. "Somethin's gonna happen, I can feel it," he warns Joe, and sure enough, the paleontologists report a startling revelation: Gorgo is merely a baby. "Where there are offspring, there are generally parents," Professor Hendricks asserts. He is proven correct when a 200-foot-tall creature emerges from the sea and destroys Nara Island. The gigantic parent follows a trail left by the water runoff from the infant, and neither the navy, nor the army, nor the RAF can stop its approach toward the Thames estuary. While Joe struggles to get Sean to safety, "the entire electricity of all industrial London" is channeled into a barricade at Battersea Park. But the unstoppable amphibian smashes the wires like toys, and the reunited creatures retreat peacefully to the sea.

COMMENTARY: With this final entry in Eugène Lourié's dinosaur trilogy, the director attempted to offer moviegoers a departure from the parade of formulaic oversized-monster films that attacked theaters in the 1950s, even though many hallmarks of that formula are present. The mass hysteria, the city under siege, and the military's unlikely inability to stop the beast all found their way into the finished film despite Lourié's protests, but at least his basic premise remained intact. This time, mankind doesn't win; it is the monster who strolls away victorious. (The humans don't really win in *The Giant Behemoth* either, but that's another story.) Despite its many familiar elements, and the inclusion of elements in direct opposition to Lourié's fundamental philosophies, *Gorgo* remains an entertaining if uneven twist on the venerable giant-monster genre. But make no mistake: while Lourié's first two dinopics can legitimately be called science fiction, *Gorgo* is an all-out "monster movie," from head to scaly toe.

It is *Gorgo*'s theme of parental protectiveness which sets it apart from others of its kind. Not since *King Kong* went hunting for Ann Darrow, had a giant monster been given such a tangible motivation for a rampage. Much of *Gorgo* is familiar, with images recalling Lourié's earlier dino sagas scattered throughout the story. The orphan with a perceptive empathy for the beast is another curiously persistent plot element in the oversized-monster genre, showing up in such films as *Mighty Joe Young*, *Dinosaurus!*, *The Valley of Gwangi*, and *Dragonworld*, to name a few. While *Beast* and *Behemoth* were decidedly moody and measured, *Gorgo* is strewn with shouts, screams, explosions and panic; whether this is one of *Gorgo*'s weaknesses or strengths depends upon who's watching. What is not debatable is the fact that *Gorgo* strays further from Lourié's basic tenets of fantastic filmmaking than do any of his previous entries.

Unfortunately, Lourié's control of the various aspects of production declined from film to film. He had a considerable amount of autonomy during the creation of *The Beast from 20,000 Fathoms*, but his jurisdiction diminished somewhat on *The Giant Behemoth* and still more on *Gorgo*. Lourié always strove for credibility in the details, however incredible the premise, and in his black-and-white dinosaur sagas was able to provide logical reasons why the creatures couldn't or shouldn't be blown to bits. In *Gorgo*, credibility crumbles under an onslaught of tank shells, rockets, depth charges and four-million-volt electrical wires. "Nothing can stop this beast so far, nothing!" cries the roving reporter, "not even point-blank cannon fire!" It is the "Godzilla principle," pure and simple — the monster is arbitrarily indestructible and never mind why. Nothing resembling this scenario appeared in Lourié's original story. "I wanted the creature to confront human beings, but there were no scenes of the military shooting at it and not being able to destroy it," Lourié explained to author Paul Mandell. "That concept is really ridiculous — those big guns would definitely kill anything." Fortunately the guns don't kill the movie, either, although they do punch a considerable number of holes in it.

It should be understood that the majority of *Gorgo*'s problems are directly related to story tinkering dictated by the producers, expressly against Lourié's wishes. The military histrionics were added and the principal characters were extensively rewritten, and the humans who populate the finished film are about as unlikable a bunch as you're likely to encounter. Joe and Sam are so coldhearted and unapologetically mercenary that an unwary viewer could easily imagine that the pair are being set up as the film's heavies rather than the heroes. The paleontologists obviously consider Gorgo to be their property, and are too snippy and rude to draw sympathy either. Even young Sean, the only character with any selfless motives, is a bit irritating at times. Some critics accuse *The Valley of Gwangi* of having a similar problem, but at least the *Gwangi* characters had some good traits to go with their failings. By the final reel, Joe and Sam finally get around to caring about and rescuing Sean, but by then it's almost too late to sweeten the bad taste left by the first hour.

The cast is fine, but with such generic and unsavory characters to portray the actors fail to register as well as do their *Beast* and *Behemoth* counterparts. Bill Travers (looking uncannily like Steven Seagal) and William Sylvester both have a natural, easygoing acting style, and do the best they can to make Joe and Sam likable. An obvious supposition is that the humans are deliberately painted in unpleasant strokes so the viewer will side with the creatures. But unfortunately it's difficult to wholeheartedly root for the Gorgos either, in light of the multitudes of innocent bystanders that the parent squishes during her hike through town. The lack of anyone, human or reptilian, to truly empathize with is *Gorgo*'s biggest weakness. (This same factor is why some *King Kong* observers feel that the restoration of the excised scenes of violence actually hurts the picture, by diminishing sympathy for Kong.)

While the changes forced upon Lourié are irrevocably damaging, and must have been very hard for him to swallow, he kept his chin up and kept plugging. As he recalls in his book, "I was committed to direct, and while directing tried my best to bring some logic to the embarrassing developments of the new story." His efforts were buoyed by the talented corps of artists with which he had surrounded himself, and Lourié (unlike his producers) was savvy enough to let them show their stuff. One outstanding contribution is noticed immediately, as Angelo Lavagnino's grand and very atypical music score begins. Lavagnino melds the oversized, rousing, giant-monster themes required by the subject matter with the melancholy orchestral stylings of the early sixties. One might fear that the effect of such a mixture would be rather like dinosaurs attacking *A Summer Place*, but somehow Lavagnino makes it work. Veteran art director Elliott Scott, whose career spanned the eras of moviemaking from the mid–1950s up to his crowning Oscar nomination for *Who Framed Roger Rabbit?* in 1988, provides some excellent and meticulous set design, both miniature and full-size. Scott's work is always characterized by clever and convincing details, and his scale model "dinosaur pen" at Dorkin's circus is a minimasterpiece.

The optical effects in *Gorgo* are uneven, at times wildly so. There are some obvious, recurring matte problems, with several shots of strangely transparent rubble falling on the panicked throngs and other scenes which feature the telltale "fringing" that always gives away imperfect traveling mattes. On the other hand, the picture also contains some moments as spectacular as any in monster movie history. The moody sequence where baby Gorgo is driven away by the Nara Island locals is spooky and effective, and even more impressive are the shots of the adult approaching the brightly lit Picadilly Circus at night. With real crowds fleeing at the bottom of the frame and the creature destroying perfectly matched miniature structures at the top, the illusion is technically flawless and visually magnificent. The man-in-a-suit method automatically turns animation purists against the film, but in the long run

The juvenile and adult specimens of Gorgo were represented by the same dino-suits, filmed in differently scaled sets.

the rubber costume is adequate and does no great harm to the picture. The two-legged dino design necessitated by the choice also helps to set Gorgo apart from Lourié's other prehistoric protagonists.

Ultimately, just as Gorgo the creature survives, so does *Gorgo* the movie. It survives its irritating heroes, bomb-proof beast, and inconsistent special effects to stand as one of the better man-in-a-suit monsterpics out there. It is regrettable that Eugène Lourié was not allowed to film his tale as originally envisioned, but the picture survives because even in the face of wholesale changes he was still able to inject just enough of the "Lourié touch" to make the difference. "I tried to make it as spectacular as possible," Lourié stated, and for the most part he succeeded. Though certainly the least sober and most outlandish of the director's dino trio, *Gorgo* achieves a fairly happy medium. It's a colorful, energetic yarn which combines Lourié's gift for atmosphere with some no-holds-barred monster action, and for once lets the "monsters" win.

PEOPLE AND PRODUCTION: *Gorgo*'s lineage can be traced back to 1953 and a screening of his *Beast from 20,000 Fathoms*. "The strongest and most unexpected reaction came from my daughter, age six," Lourié wrote in *My Work in Films*. "She cried, 'you are bad, Daddy, bad, you killed the nice beast.'" So, when the King brothers offered Lourié the chance to return once again to dinosaur territory, he saw an opportunity to make amends. "I again took the tired dinosaur out of retirement and joyfully destroyed the city of London once more," Lourié recalled, "this time in color and with a wonderful display of spectacular photographic effects." He was determined to add some fresh touches to the familiar monster-in-the-city tale. "For this picture I invented some novel approaches to the saga of a dinosaur confronting the cruel, civilized world," Lourié continued. "In keeping the promise I had made to my daughter, the monsters were not killed but retreated majestically back to the deep sea."

In 1958, before *The Giant Behemoth* was even released, producers Frank and Maurice King approached Lourié and inquired about the possibility of making another *Beast/Behemoth* type picture. The King Brothers had been producing films since the early 1940s, but had never tackled anything in the sci-fi/fantasy genre. Mostly they made gritty crime stories like *Dillinger* (1945), *The Gangster* (1947), and *Gun Crazy* (1950), which didn't necessarily prepare them well for *Gorgo*. Lourié, remembering his daughter's admonitions and doubtless hoping for the chance to direct a film under less meager conditions than he had experienced during his first three efforts, signed on to the project. He was commissioned to write a screenplay, and again working with his *Behemoth* cowriter, Daniel James (credited as Daniel Hyatt), penned a story called *Kuru Island*.

The Kings had a tentative collaboration deal with some Japanese producers, and thus Lourié set his story on a remote Pacific atoll, telling a gentle tale of a peaceful native people who discover the baby creature after an undersea cataclysm. Rather than a cheesy London circus, the animal is exhibited at the Tokyo Zoo until being rescued by its parent. "Although the locale was to have been Japan, it had nothing to do with the *Godzilla* type of story construction," Lourié explained to Paul Mandell. "The creature was not supposed to destroy the town, and there were no stock shots planned of military intervention. That is so totally boring." However, after Lourié and James spent two months writing the screenplay, the Japan deal collapsed and the setting was moved to Europe. Frank King even proposed Paris as a location and envisioned the animal climbing the Eiffel Tower.

Worse than the change of locale were other alterations to come. The King Brothers, now determined to incorporate the military mayhem and "indestructible monster" angle, employed two new writers to begin "revising" the screenplay. Gone were the wonder and innocence of *Kuru Island*; they were replaced with avarice and materialism. With the movie in the can and Lourié now departed, the producers couldn't resist still more tampering. The picture was re-edited and even more military footage was added. Though the final film retains only the core of Lourié's original concept, he held on to the pleasant memories. "Despite my misgivings about the screenplay, I enjoyed working with the English technicians and Fred Young, the cameraman," Lourié recalled, "and also with actors Bill Travers, Bill Sylvester, and others. Also the short location shooting in Ireland was a very pleasant experience."

One occurrence during the Irish location stint is a telling illustration of Lourié's practical, reality-based filmmaking philosophy. "I was marooned with Freddy Young and all his crew in a lighthouse at the end of a jetty in the port of Dun Laoghaire near Dublin," Lourié wrote. "The storm was terrific.... The port authorities ordered us to stay put until the storm and tides subsided." Through the wind and spray, Lourié sighted a cargo ship fighting its way through the massive waves and realized that it was a scene right out of the script. "I thought it would be a good chance to catch the scene," Lourié explained, but Young felt that the danger to the expensive camera equipment was too great. "'No way,' was Freddy's reply," Lourié recalled. "Later on I had to shoot the scene with a miniature ship in a studio tank."

In the years to come, Lourié made no secret of his regrets regarding his legacy as the "director of dinosaurs." But as a closing thought, it is interesting to note that not once, in any of Lourié's three prehistoric-monster films, is the word "dinosaur" ever spoken.

SPECIAL EFFECTS: Having employed stop-motion animation for the title creatures of his first two dinosaur sagas, Eugène Lourié changed tactics for *Gorgo*. "You have to use certain means that are most appropriate for the visual effect you are trying to achieve," he told Paul Mandell. Lourié had also been disappointed by his lack of involvement in the animation of *The Giant Behemoth*, and felt that he would have a greater level of control using the suit technique (a false hope, as it turned out). As he explained in *My Work in Films*: "Instead of the frame-by-frame animation ... I opted for a stunt man wearing the rubber-casted skin of the dinosaur. I also decided that only one miniature beast would be used for both monsters, however different in size." To make these different sizes apparent and convincing, a number of tricks were used. "For scenes with the 'baby' monster, the action was staged on a miniature set scaled down relative to the monster's size," Lourié explained, "but scenes with the giant 'mother' beast were shot with much smaller miniatures sized proportionally to the beast's size." Blue-screen compositing was employed when necessary to show both animals in the same shot.

In an interview conducted shortly before his death, Lourié admitted to author Tom Weaver that while he "had a big pleasure in shooting the picture," he was not completely content with the final results achieved with the suit. "I was not so satisfied with Gorgo itself, because frame-by-frame animation makes the animal more alive than the stuntman in the rubber suit," Lourié concluded. When discussing *Gorgo*, he would often relate an amusing incident involving the bulky monster suit. The costumes (there were three in all) were so heavy and unwieldy that walking in them was difficult at best, and when it came time to shoot the creature wading up the Thames River the stunt performers could barely slog along through the knee-high water of the miniature set. One of the costumes was eventually cut off at the knee and the clumsy monster feet discarded. As Lourié told Mandell, "it was a strange sight to see a dragon-like Gorgo wading through the water in white socks and tennis shoes."

Despite his misgivings about the suited monster, Lourié had nothing but praise for Tom Howard and his team at MGM-London who tackled the massive workload of optical effects. "The film in fact contained a multitude of difficult trick shots made mostly in unusual haste," Lourié wrote, and he can be forgiven if he was just a bit too kind when

The full-scale baby Gorgo is motorcaded through the (nearly deserted) London streets.

he concluded that "amazingly, only very few had some technical flaws." Howard was probably Britain's leading optical-effects expert at the time of *Gorgo* with a long and glossy list of credits to his name, and he won an Academy Award for George Pal's *tom thumb* (1958).

The construction of the Gorgo suit itself, like many aspects of the film, proceeded in directions quite different than Lourié planned. He wanted to keep the suit as lightweight as possible, not only to allow the stuntman some freedom to "act" but also to prevent the suit from being too uncomfortable. However, the technicians hired by the King Brothers had other ideas, and the suit design continued to become more and more complicated. "The movements of the eyes, ears and tail were all activated by independent hydraulic systems," Lourié explained to Mandell. "A helmet-like contraption was strapped onto the man's head, and the studio blacksmiths were manufacturing these supports that looked like the armor of a medieval knight!" Performing in the suit became such hard labor that multiple monster actors were required, working in brief shifts.

A neat bit of sleight of hand is used during the scenes of Gorgo being hauled through London. A full-size head, tail and pair of paws were constructed, with the beast's midsection made of nothing more than plywood framing. A tarpaulin covered the frame, leaving just the plastic body parts visible, and the subterfuge works very well — it looks for all the world like a real sea monster being trucked through London. However, watching the scene closely reveals a decided lack of spectators along the streets. It seems that Frank King was sure that the appearance of the monster motorcade would attract multitudes of curious onlookers, and he could avoid the expense of hiring paid extras. As Lourié tried to warn him, it didn't work out that way. "This Sunday morning was very dismal," Lourié told Tom Weaver. "The scenes we got were of empty streets, and occasionally a few people going, 'what the hell is *that*?'"

Horror of the Blood Monsters

"Well, at least you haven't lost your sense of humor."

1970, USA.
Independent-International.
C & B/W with color tints, 85m.

CREDITS: *Director* Al Adamson. *Producers* Al Adamson, Ewing Brown (associate), Charles McMullen (executive), Zoe Phillips (executive). *Screenplay* Sue McNair. *Directors of Photography* William (Vilmos) Zsigmond and

William G. Troiano. *Special Effects* David L. Hewitt. *Effects Editor* Fred Badiyan.

CAST: *Dr. Rynning* John Carradine. *Col. Manning* Robert Dix. *Valerie* Vicki Volante. *Willy* Joey Benson. *Lian Malian* Jennifer Bishop. *Steve Bryce* Bruce Powers. *Bob Scott* Fred Meyers. *Linda* Britt Semand.

AD LINE: "You'll SCREAM yourself into a state of SHOCK when you see — Bat Demons! Claw Creatures! Snake Men! Human Vampires!"

A sudden epidemic of vampirism on Earth is traced to a distant planet, and a scientific team is dispatched in rocketship XB-13 in a desperate effort to find a solution. The crew consists of gruff scientist Dr. Rynning (rhymes with pining), Commander Steve Bryce, Willy, Bob, and Linda. A meteor strikes the ship, and while ground controller Colonel Manning and his comely assistant, Valerie, try to regain communications, the crew sets down on a nearby planet for repairs. Amazingly it happens to be the very planet which harbors the vampire men who are causing Earth's blood-drinking plague.

They immediately notice that the atmosphere is constantly changing color, from blue to yellow to green to red, due to the dreaded "chromatic radiation." Rynning stays in the ship while the other four explore a world filled with prehistoric reptiles, woolly mammoths, lobster men, bat men, and of course, the vampire men. When they find a buxom young lady named Malian (wearing a Catalina swimsuit), they hold her down and surgically implant an electronic language translator in her head. "Don't worry, we're merely rearranging her brain waves," Dr. Rynning says reassuringly. Back on Earth, Colonel Manning and Valerie take a break from their controller duties to have some electronically enhanced sexual intercourse, while on the planet Willy falls in love with Malian. Bob is killed by one of the Neanderthallike brutes, but with Malian's help the rest manage to make repairs and lift off for home.

COMMENTARY: "I always tried to make 'em different," Al Adamson once said in a *Fangoria* interview. They don't get much different-er than *Horror of the Blood Monsters*, which if nothing else proves that it is possible to knit together a movie, get it distributed, and have it shown on real screens, despite having virtually *nothing* to work with. This wacky curio may be the all-time low point for Al Adamson, Sam Sherman, and Independent-International Pictures, which is an accomplishment not to be taken lightly. It is surely the low point for cinematographer Vilmos Zsigmond, who would go on to lens such films as *Deliverance* and *Close Encounters of the Third Kind*. As genre author John Stanley wrote, it has "everything but the sinking kitsch."

Blood Monsters unspools a succession of utterly jaw-dropping scenes. The prologue which explains the vampire plague is narrated by someone ("Brother Theodore," according to some sources) doing a terrible but unmistakable Bela Lugosi impression, so deeply is Lugosi identified with vampires. The early scenes at "Earth Control" seem inspired by, of all things, the "Time Central" scenes in David L. Hewitt's *Journey to the Center of Time*. The spaceship shots are from *The Wizard of Mars* (the Hewitt connection again), the Brontosaurus is from *Unknown Island*, the lizard dinos and the elephant-as-mammoth are from *One Million B.C.* (footage then 30 years old!), and the various bizarre humanoids of the Spectrum planet are from an unknown, possibly unfinished Filipino horror picture.

The few scenes actually shot for this movie are no less astounding. The acting is nonexistent except for Carradine's; he gives Rynning a feisty irritability and a bit of humor. Goofiest of all are the inexplicable digressions into the boudoir, where Robert Dix and Vicki Volante hook themselves up to the "Electronic Sense Amplifier" (a foil-covered box with a lot of phallic-looking light bulbs) and proceed to make virtual whoopee — a sequence that truly must be seen to be appreciated.

Despite being one of the worst excuses for a motion picture ever to be foisted on the public, the thing was a triumph of hype and exploitation. The simple color tinting was touted as "Spectrum-X — A New Dimension in Terror," and the movie probably holds the all-time record for most alternative titles. *Horror of the Blood Monsters* seems to be its original moniker, but at various times it has gone by *Vampire Men of the Lost Planet, Space Mission to the Lost Planet, Horror Creatures of the Red Planet,* and at least three or four others. A fitting final word comes courtesy of none other than Fred Olen Ray, in his book *The New Poverty Row.* "It took me four attempts," Fred admitted, "to actually make it through the film."

House II: The Second Story

"*Promise you won't laugh ...*"
** 1987, USA.
New World Pictures. C, 87m.

CREDITS: *Director* Ethan Wiley. *Producers* Sean S. Cunningham, Andrew Z. Davis (associate). *Writer* Ethan Wiley. *Make-Up and Creature Effects Design* Chris Walas. *Visual Effects Supervisors* Hoyt Yeatman, Eric Brevig. *Matte Paintings and Stop-Motion Flying Creatures* Mark Sullivan. *Stop-Motion Design/Supervision* Phil Tippett. *Stop-Motion Animation* Randal Michael Dutra, III. *Model Construction* Tamia Marg. *Armatures* Jon Berg. *Mechanical Effects Coordinator* Peter Chesney.
CAST: *Jesse McLaughlin* Arye Gross. *Charlie* Jonathan Stark. *Gramps* Royal Dano. *John* Bill Maher. *Kate* Lar Park Lincoln. *Lana* Amy Yasbeck. *Bill Towner* John Ratzenberger. *The Virgin* Devin DeVasquez.

AD LINE: "It's an all new house with brand new owners."

When Jesse McLaughlin moves into the massive old mansion in which his parents were murdered, he begins investigating his ancestry and learns that his great-great-grandfather was an adventurer-explorer who discovered a priceless Aztec artifact: a solid crystal skull with supposedly magical powers. Jesse and his loony pal, Charlie, proceed to dig up the body and sure enough, there's the skull. Also there is Jesse's ancestor, withered and decayed but otherwise alive. "Call me Gramps!" the rotted old coot cackles amiably. During a Halloween party that night, the skull's powers open an interdimensional door in an upstairs bedroom. A Stone Age barbarian appears and steals the skull, then retreats into a lush, dinosaur-filled jungle. Jesse and Charlie brave the prehistoric perils and retrieve the skull, but gain two new pets in the process: a pterodactyl chick and a "caterpillar-dog" named Bippy. Again the skull is stolen, this time by a party of Aztec warriors. Luckily, Jesse and Charlie get some unexpected assistance with the arrival of Bill Towner, "Electrician and Adventurer," hired to assist with the house renovations. Jesse, Charlie and Bill venture through another gateway into an Aztec temple, rescue a beautiful virgin, and reclaim the skull. Gramps' old arch-enemy, Slim (also zombiefied), comes looking for revenge, but Jesse bests him in an Old West–style gunfight. Gramps finally reckons he's had enough of this world and passes away for good, leaving Jesse, Charlie, the virgin, Bippy and the pterodactyl to ride off into the sunset.

COMMENTARY: If you make a horror-comedy and your cleverest gag is the film's title, you know you're in trouble. And the biggest trouble with *House II: The Second Story* is that it can't really decide if it's a horror-comedy, a horror spoof (different than a horror-comedy), or something on the order of Sam Raimi's *Evil Dead* films, which almost constitute a genre of their own. Due to its inability to establish and maintain any sort of tone, *House II* wastes a number of individually good ideas and imaginative visuals.

The dinosaur content of *House II* comes about halfway through the film. Called "a dazzling fifteen-minute prehistoric sequence" by Neil Pettigrew in *The Stop-Motion Filmography,* the set piece features a Brontosaurus, an adult and baby pterodactyl, and a fanciful, fictional carnivorous beast, all placed in a marvelously atmospheric jungle. The creatures are brought to life entirely through stop-motion animation except the

A stop-motion Brontosaurus browses in the marvelously atmospheric primeval valley created for *House II*.

pterodactyl chick, which is sometimes stop-motion and sometimes a detailed hand puppet. Considering the names that scroll by during the credits, one would expect the FX to be excellent, and they are. The bronto is impressive and convincing but is only given a cameo; Pettigrew was quite right to lament that more was not done with it. The adult pterodactyl has more screen time, allowing us the chance to appreciate its graceful and believable animated flying motions. The juvenile is played more for comic effect but is just as expertly realized, in both its stop-motion and hand-puppet incarnations. Another nifty stop-motion creature is Slim's "zombie horse," and it's appropriate too—what else should a decaying, skeletal zombie ride but a decaying, skeletal horse?

As enjoyable as the dinosaurs and other stop-motion creatures are, *House II* has too many digressions and course changes to succeed as a complete film. In fact, a whole subplot with Lar Park Lincoln, Amy Yasbeck, and Bill Maher (as a record label exec!) is so disconnected from everything else that I omitted it from the above plot summary. The actors are mostly okay, though Ratzenberger's character is just another variation of the comic-handyman played by Bill Murray in *Caddyshack* or John Goodman in *Arachnophobia*. The best performance is easily Royal Dano's turn as the crotchety Gramps. Unrecognizable under his rotten-corpse makeup, the veteran Dano is great fun whether lamenting his decayed state ("I'm a 170-year-old fart!") or commenting on popular culture ("ya got all them channels and nothin' interestin' tuh watch!"), and he manages to draw several chuckles from the mediocre material.

The ingredients are here for a fun outing; the recipe just isn't right. Not scary enough to be horror, not funny enough to be comedy, and unwilling to go fearlessly over the top, *House II* only comes alive when Dano or the dinos are on screen.

SPECIAL EFFECTS: Other than some major-studio blockbusters, few films of the 1980s could claim a better roster of effects artists than those assembled for the low-budget *House II*. Chris Walas, Hoyt Yeatman, Eric Brevig, Mark Sullivan, Phil Tippett, Randy Dutra, Jon Berg, and Peter Chesney all contributed, just to name the most familiar. Unfortunately for stop-motion fans, the animation is used only for short "throwaway" bits rather than for fully-developed sequences. (Except for *Clash of the Titans*, *Caveman*, and perhaps *Honey, I Shrunk the Kids*, this frustrating practice held true throughout the 1980s.) Most of the hands-on stop-motion animation in *House II* was done by Mark Sullivan and Randy Dutra. Sullivan executed the brontosaur's brief appearance and the flying shots of the adult pterodactyl. Dutra animated a bizarre prehistoric predator (called the "Fish monster" by the effects crew), the zombie horse, and the baby pterodactyl's romp through the house. In some shots, the pterodactyl chick is played by a very lifelike Chris Walas hand puppet, and the superb animation models are the work of Tamia Marg and Jon Berg. With such talents gathered, it's too bad that they weren't given the chance to do even more.

La Isla de los Dinosaurios

1966, Mexico.
Cinematográfica Calderón.
BW, 76m.

CREDITS: *Director* Rafael Portillo. *Producer* Guillermo Calderon Stell. *Screenplay* Alfredo Salazar. *Special Effects* Antonio Muñoz.
CAST: Armando Silvestre, Alma Delia Fuentes, Manolo Fabregas, Elsa Cardenas, Jenaro Moreno.

Professor Portillo finds himself ridiculed by his colleagues, due to his theories that an undiscovered island of "plantas y animales prehistoricos" exists somewhere in the Atlantic. He invites three of his loyal assistants, Paul, Esther, and Laura, on an expedition. They accept, excited by the promise of discovering unknown species, but a violent storm forces their four-seater plane down on a tiny speck of land. Luckily, it must be the one they set out for, because their experiments show that it is still in its prehistoric state.

Unknown to the group, a tribe of humans is living a Stone Age existence on the other side of the island. Even as Laura and Esther discuss the science of the ecosystem, the tribe's leader, Molo, loses a fight and gets tossed out of his cave. Molo and Laura soon discover each other, and the primitive man is entranced by the beautiful stranger. Despite Laura's fear, the two slowly start to understand each other, and she tries to tell Molo that she wants to return to her friends. When Laura is accosted by the new chief, Molo fights him again — more successfully — and regains his position as leader. Laura attempts to let the lovestruck Molo down easy, telling him what a splash he'd make with the girls back home, but after helping each other survive encounters with massive reptiles and a vicious gorilla the couple begin to really fall in love. But still, when she sees a signal flare from the professor, Laura braves a volcanic upheaval to return to her fellow explorers. She wants Molo to come with her to civilization but knows that he is a part of his primitive world ... and she decides that it will be hers as well.

COMMENTARY: Even the most diligent dinomovie buffs may not be aware that there were actually two *One Million B.C.* remakes released in 1966. The more famous one was made by Hammer Films and starred Raquel Welch; this super-obscure counterpart was made in Mexico and starred Alma Delia Fuentes. Both have direct connections to original *One Million* producer-director Hal Roach. The Hammer remake credits Roach

The *One Million B.C.* lizardosaurs turned up not only in the film *La Isla de los Dinosaurios* but also in its advertising art.

as associate producer, while *La Isla* is a coproduction from Mexico's Cinematográfica Calderon and Hal Roach Studios, Hollywood.

La Isla de los Dinosaurios (*Island of the Dinosaurs*) begins with the standard "Lost World" premise, but once the quartet reaches the island it becomes Tumak and Loana revisited. Absolutely everything is straight out of *One Million*—bad table manners, the hero's banishment and eventual return, the girl's civilized teachings, and even details like the symbolic "dropping of spears" to signify subservience. Stir in the inevitable stock footage reptiles and *La Isla* plays like a shot-for-shot but vastly inferior copy.

Aventura al Centro de la Tierra, another mid-sixties Mexican production with *One Million* clips, has flashes of creativity and an unexpectedly capable cast. *La Isla* has neither. Amateur acting, lifeless direction, and mundane photography predominate, and the few special effects actually done for this film are quite terrible. There are only two creatures that are not stock footage — a rubber water serpent (or something) which is kept far from the camera, and an actor in a gorilla suit shabby enough to make Charlie Gemora spin in his mausoleum. The sound effects are ridiculous (two wooden clubs crashing together make a noise like a skillet hitting a hub cap), and when the oh-so-sixties organ solos swell during the "romantic" moments, you'll think someone put on an old Eddie Layton album.

Supplementing the extensive *One Million B.C.* shots, a useless subplot also recycles lizard footage from 1955's benchmark stinker, *King Dinosaur*. And just as the main story follows the *One Million* narrative, this little side trip echoes the corresponding *King Dinosaur* sequence. What a frightening moment for a filmmaker — to realize that using castoff effects shots, from the cheapest picture Bert I. Gordon *ever made*, actually *improves* your production values. Ouch!

Island of the Lost

"Watch out for anything strange."
* ½   1967, USA. Paramount. C, 91m.

CREDITS: *Director* John Florea. *Producers* John Florea, Ricou Browning, Tam Spiva (associate). *Screenplay* Richard Carlson. *Story* Ivan Tors and Richard Carlson. *In Charge of Animal Sequences* Ralph Helfer. *Underwater Sequences Directed by* Ricou Browning.
CAST: *Dr. Joshua MacRae* Richard Greene. *Stu MacRae* Luke Halpin. *Gabe Larsen* Mart Hulswit. *Tupuna* Jose De Vega. *Lizzie MacRae* Robin Mattson. *Judy Hawilani* Irene Tsu. *Sharon MacRae* Sheilah Wells.

AD LINE: "Stranded in an age that never was!"

The noted anthropologist Dr. Joshua MacRae sets sail aboard the *Quest* for a remote region of the South Seas, anxious to prove his theory that an unknown island chain exists "somewhere below the Tuamoto Archipelago." His crew consists of his college-age daughter Sharon, high-school-age son Stu, and grade-school-age daughter Liz. They are joined by anthropologists-in-training Judy Hawilani and Gabe Larsen (who also happens to be an all–American football player), and Drippy the seal. En route, a romance blooms between Gabe and Sharon ("you're a lot prettier than plankton," he tells her), and the ship follows a "magnetic disturbance" to an uncharted island. Unknown to the explorers, there is already one human there: a young man named Tupuna, of a lost Polynesian race, who has been marooned by his people as a test of strength and bravery.

MacRae and party find the island populated with bizarre prehistoric ancestors of modern animals. Liz and Judy discover Tupuna, feverish after an attack by a poisonous fin-backed reptile, but Judy saves his life with some medicinal berries. The two young people are instantly drawn to each other, but before the courtship can get serious, a typhoon hits the island and sinks the *Quest*. The plucky group constructs a new boat, but their spirits are dampened when they learn from Tupuna that they'll all likely be killed — Tupuna included — when his people return. MacRae's party has broken a tabu by being on the island, and Tupuna has broken a tabu by failing to kill the strangers. The gang launches their homemade craft even as a war canoe from Tupuna's tribe closes in, and Tupuna, choosing the lovely Judy over an execution squad, happily goes with them.

COMMENTARY: This near-forgotten TV movie is so predictable, routine, and utterly bland that it is impossible to say anything fervently derogatory — or complimentary — about it. Like Ivan Tors' popular television programs of the period, it is easygoing and family-friendly, with an attractive if unexceptional cast. Richard Greene is enjoyably hammy (perhaps he got some dinomovie tips from his ex-wife, *Beast of Hollow Mountain* alumnus Patricia Medina) and lovely Irene Tsu virtually reprises her role from *Women of the Prehistoric Planet*. But despite its good nature, *Island* is ultimately so lightweight and perfunctory as to be nearly nonexistent. It superficially follows the traditional "Lost World" storyline but forgets to include the two qualities which have made that form so enduring — there is little anticipatory buildup to the arrival on the island, and no effort to instill a sense of wonder once there. The "typhoon" effects are particularly chintzy, looking as if they were generated by a couple of window fans, and the dialogue is no better. When the gang discovers a mile-wide pool of glowing, bubbling lava, Gabe helpfully announces, "it's some kind of volcanic action!" Later, Josh marvels that "there are things on this island that we all thought were completely extinct!" As opposed to what? Partially extinct?

Some may question this film's classification as a "dinosaur movie," but based on

The made-for-TV *Island of the Lost* was released theatrically in several countries. This Mexican lobby card emphasizes the film's underwater action rather than its prehistoric elements.

the *One Million B.C.* precedent, *Island*'s sail-backed prehistoric reptiles must qualify. The dentally augmented dogs, finned-and-frilled alligators, and backfin-equipped ostriches now seem campily humorous but are certainly more interesting than the wooden humans, and simply having the *chutzpa* to put a "prehistoric" sail on an ostrich's back warrants a kudo. Despite its "Lost World" elements, the film that *Island of the Lost* most strongly recalls is 1960's *Swiss Family Robinson*. That particular Disney adventure is just as implausible, but its grand scope to a great extent made up for its credibility gaps—in other words, it was BIG. Unfortunately, *Island of the Lost* is unequivocally small, in every sense of the word.

PEOPLE AND PRODUCTION: The animal action in *Island of the Lost*, and there's quite a lot of it, was supervised by Ivan Tors' long-time collaborator, Ralph Helfer. The two had first teamed up in the 1960's to create an assortment of successful, animal-themed television shows and movies. "He was the producer, and I had this huge company full of animals, so we formed a partnership," Helfer told the author, "and together we did everything from *Daktari*, which was four years prime time, to *Gentle Ben*, which was a couple of years, and many many others." The duo also made theatrical films, such as *Zebra in the Kitchen* (1965) and *Clarence the Cross-Eyed Lion* (1965).

In addition to the quasi–Dimetrodons played by finned alligators, *Island of the Lost* is also swarming with "saber-toothed wolves" and carnivorous killer ostriches. The alligators are on screen only briefly (and look awfully drowsy), but in real life were formidable creatures some seven feet long. So, how do you get a 500-pound gator to sit still in the make-up chair? "Usually with alligators you can put something over their eyes, and they become very quiet," Helfer explained. "You drape a towel or anything over them and they're much easier to work." The "saber-toothed wolves" were of course dogs wearing prosthetic fangs. "We always used either the Siberian Huskies, or the Shepherds," said Helfer, the latter being the case here.

The ostriches, accessorized with the latest in back fins and beak crests, seem comical at first but actually make pretty fearsome villains. Not that ostriches are the most trainable of animal actors. "You know, when you look at an ostrich head, it is taken up mainly by the eyes and the beak and doesn't leave very much room for a brain," Helfer humorously pointed out. "You can pet them, you can feed them, they're fine, but as far as directing them, they're either going to go to their own kind — other ostriches — or to food." As with human actors, make-up appliances like back fins are applied to ostriches and other animals with a specialized adhesive called spirit gum. "When you get down to the skin, be it on a bird or a person, it'll adhere to it," explained Helfer, "however, it washes off, comes off very easily." Helfer's contributions to the animal sequences were not limited to merely supplying and handling the animals and designing their prehistoric make-up. "When you do that kind of stuff, especially in those days, you're totally involved," said Helfer. "You're involved in the camera, in the angles of the camera.... I did most of the second unit, involving any of the animal action or stunts."

Island of the Lost carried on a long tradition of using live animals equipped with make-up prosthetics to portray prehistoric life. Beginning with D. W. Griffith's *Brute Force* in 1913 and continuing through *The Secret of the Loch, One Million B.C., King Dinosaur, Journey to the Center of the Earth*, Irwin Allen's *The Lost World* and others, the technique remained in use for over half a century. Excepting deliberate spoofs like *Amazon Women on the Moon* and *Dinosaur Valley Girls, Island of the Lost* was apparently the last film to employ the live-lizard strategy.

Josh Kirby ... Time Warrior: The Human Pets

"I gave up trying to understand human behavior years ago."

** 1995, USA. Moonbeam/Paramount. C, 90m.

CREDITS: *Director* Frank Arnold. *Prologue Directed by* Ernest Farino. *Producers* Vlad Paunescu, Oana Paunescu, Charles Band (executive), Debra Dion (executive). *Screenplay* Ethan Reiff and Cyrus Voris, and Paul Callisi. *Creature Effects* Mark Rappaport. *Visual Effects* Alchemy FX. *Visual Effects Supervisor* Joseph Grossberg. *Stop-Motion Animation* Robert Maine. *Stop-Motion Photography* Joseph Grossberg, Chris Endicott. *Digital FX Supervisor* Randall William Cook.

CAST: *Joshua Kirby* Corbin Allred. *Azabeth Seige* Jennifer Burns. *Dr. Zoetrope* Derek Webster. *Irwin 1138* Barrie Ingham. *William of Dearborn* John DeMita. *Lord Henry* Spencer Rochfort. *Lady Jennifer* Sandra Guibord.

Chapter 2: With Azabeth Seige moments from execution, Josh, William and company infiltrate the castle and launch their attack. Azabeth frees herself, and the battle is on! Henry and William face each other astride their "dragons," but William's Triceratops knocks Henry's Tyrannosaurus off its feet and tips the balance in William's favor. Meanwhile, Doctor Zoetrope learns that Irwin 1138 is nearby and readies his Time Armor for an escape, but Prizm knocks him unconscious and returns the Nullifier component to Irwin. As the battle winds down, Henry makes a final lunge for William but topples off the castle wall to his demise. Having returned the barony once again to William's benevolent leadership, Irwin's only problem is that the Triceratops has eaten the Nullifier component. But he whips up a dino laxative and announces that this too shall pass.

Their next stop is A.D.70,379, where the adventurers find Earth populated with giant, rotund, nearsighted mutant humans, and Doctor Zoetrope rather pathetically entwined in the web of an oversized spider. Imprisoned as the "pets" of a humongous, bratty kid, Josh's troupe must convince their fellow captives—a cowboy, a musketeer, a World War I German flying ace, and a Nordic warrior—to cease their bickering and work together to escape. Irwin and friends manage to reach the Time Pod and depart with the captured Zoetrope, while the other four fly off in the German pilot's airplane. But Zoetrope brainwashes Prizm into swiping the Nullifier components and escapes into the Time Stream with the magical creature in tow...

COMMENTARY: Chapter 2 of the *Josh Kirby* anthology is just as much fun as Chapter 1, for about 40 minutes. That's when the *Planet of the Dino-Knights* story actually concludes and the *Human Pets* begins. Up until then, all the things that made *Dino-Knights* click are still in place—snappy humor, on-target performances, and an intelligent tone that's never condescending. The dinosaur action culminates in the joust between the rival brothers aboard their saurian mounts, and though one cannot help but wish that the sequence was more opulently produced, it remains a unique bit of action that puts a fresh spin on the traditional Tyrannosaurus-Triceratops battle.

Unfortunately, when Ernest Farino's medieval adventure concludes, the mostly dreadful *Human Pets* installment takes over. Here, the overplayed, spoofy quality I had feared prior to watching Chapter 1—only to be happily surprised back then—comes thuddingly into reality. All the new characters are horrendous caricatures, and the funniest moment involves Azabeth cutting up a gargantuan pair of jockey shorts to make a rope. There are still a few clever bits, but overall the proceedings just get sillier and sillier until the Time Pod finally flies off with Zoetrope strapped to the top like Imogene Coca in *National Lampoon's Vacation*.

After *The Human Pets*, the *Josh Kirby* series again takes a turn for the better with the whimsical *Trapped on Toyworld*, and the story holds up serviceably through the last three chapters: *Eggs from 70 Million B.C.*, *Journey to the Magic Cavern*, and *Last Battle for the Universe*. However, Josh's adventures never again rise to the overall quality of the engaging story of the *Dino-Knights*.

Josh Kirby ... Time Warrior: Planet of the Dino-Knights

"Your primitive 20th-century reasoning ... is inescapable."

**½ 1995, USA. Moonbeam/Paramount. C, 89m.

CREDITS: *Director* Ernest Farino. *Prologue Directed by* Frank Arnold. *Producers* Vlad Paunescu, Oana Paunesu, Charles Band (executive), Debra Dion (executive). *Screenplay* Ethan Reiff and Cyrus Voris, and Paul Callisi. *Creature Effects* Mark Rappaport. *Visual Effects* Alchemy FX. *Visual Effects Supervisor* Joseph Grossberg. *Stop-Motion Animation* Robert Maine. *Stop-Motion Photography* Joseph Grossberg, Chris Endicott. *Digital FX Supervisor* Randall William Cook.

CAST: *Joshua Kirby* Corbin Allred. *Azabeth Seige* Jennifer Burns. *Dr. Zoetrope* Derek Webster. *Irwin 1138* Barrie Ingham. *William of Dearborn* John DeMita. *Lord Henry* Spencer Rochfort. *Lady Jennifer* Sandra Guibord.

Chapter 1: On an ordinary day in 1994, ordinary ninth-grader Josh Kirby is swept into an epic struggle between good and evil. Two brilliant scientists from the 25th century, the benevolent Irwin 1138 and the maniacal Doctor Zoetrope, are racing each other for possession of the Nullifier—an alien device capable of controlling time itself. Unable to destroy it, Irwin disassembled the thing and scattered its components to disparate times and places. Now Zoetrope, using his "Time Armor," is trying to track down and reassemble the Nullifier. With Josh along for the ride, Irwin and his magical sidekick, Prizm, follow Zoetrope to medieval England, but it's an England populated with dinosaurs as a result of Zoetrope's meddling with time. Josh and Irwin, joined by a warrior girl named Azabeth Seige, are caught up in a struggle between William of Dearborn and his brother Henry. The unscrupulous Henry has used his "Royal Dragon"— actually a T. rex — as a weapon of terror to unseat William and install himself as baron of the region. With Joshua's help, William evens up the odds by taming a dragon (Triceratops) of his own, and prepares to lead a daring raid on the castle. Time is against them, however. Henry has sentenced Azabeth to death, and Zoetrope, having installed himself as Henry's "Grand Wizard," is closing in on the Nullifier...

COMMENTARY: What a nice surprise *Planet of the Dino-Knights* turned out to be. Anticipating a mediocre sci-fi serial spoof like *The Adventures of Captain Zoom*, I was elated to be proven wrong. The funny and unexpectedly intelligent tale of the *Dino-Knights* has a wry, almost British sensibility, and a core concept oddly akin to *The Hitchhiker's Guide to the Galaxy*.

The opening is slow going, as characters are introduced (including Josh's widowed father — what is Moonbeam's obsession with single parents?) and the premise laid out. But when we meet Irwin 1138 — "the *second*-most brilliant man of the 25th century"— in his trouble-prone time machine, things quickly pick up. The dialogue, which I expected would be deliberately campy in a '30s "Flash Gordon" kind of way, is instead quirky and sharp, especially as delivered by the perfectly cast Barrie Ingham. "Time Armor is cooler than a Time Pod," Josh says, comparing Zoetrope's and Irwin's modes of time travel. "Do you think I don't *know* that?" Irwin snaps back, understandably sensitive to the fact that Zoetrope's intelligence exceeds his "by 8.6 cerebral grams." Also standing out from a solid cast is Spencer Rochfort, who plays Lord Henry with a humorous mixture of irritability, sarcasm, boredom and, after a well-aimed knee from Azabeth, intense pain. Besides, it's really hard to dislike a guy who, following a particularly lame joke from his court jester, feeds the unfortunate fellow to a Tyrannosaurus.

The dinosaur scenes were obviously choreographed, filmed and composited with haste but still offer some unique images. The T. rex puppet is nicely appointed with a spiked headpiece and reins for its armored rider, briefly evoking images of James Gurney's *Dinotopia*. The Triceratops has an exaggerated, slightly comical look which could be an artistic decision or just the result of having to make the puppet quickly, but either way he's likeable. The dino sequences, done with stop-motion and a few live action inserts, are merely serviceable, but the designs of the technological props are amusing without being corny. I especially liked Irwin's minivan-styled Time Pod and Zoetrope's "exo-skeleton," which resembles a cross between the ED-209 of *Robocop* and Robby the Robot.

With clever twists, a quasi-authentic medieval atmosphere, striking Romanian locations, a smattering of English drollery, a nifty Richard Band theme, and a bit more of an "edge" than most Moonbeam products, *Planet of the Dino-Knights* survives its budget and spins an entertaining yarn. Director Ernest D. Farino even worked in some subtle *Lawrence of Arabia* references (to the point that he became known on set as "Lawrence of Romania"). The fine work by Farino and all involved makes the *Dino-Knights* segment — which concludes in Chapter 2 — easily the best of the *Josh Kirby* tales.

PEOPLE AND PRODUCTION: The *Josh Kirby ... Time Warrior* series was an ambitious project for Moonbeam Entertainment. Ernest Farino — whose ample genre-related résumé includes spearheading the Ray Harryhausen *FXRH* fanzine, stop-motion armature work on *Caveman*, a writing credit on *Demon Sword*, and directorial duties on seven episodes of the "new" *Land of the Lost*— was selected as a director. "The concept was that this would be a continuing six-

Ernest Farino (center, in dark shirt) prepares to direct John DeMita (astride a cart covered with "dinosaur" skin) on location in Romania, during live-action filming for the *Josh Kirby* dino-jousting sequence.

part series—the first direct-to-video miniseries," Farino explained. "The idea was to release one video every two weeks or something, and everybody thought that was quite a clever approach." But before long, things began to go awry. "I was assigned the second episode, *Planet of the Dino-Knights*, and it turned out to be a really terrific episode to do," Farino recalled. "In Romania we discovered that while they had problems with things like spaceships and time machines, because of the availability of materials, medieval England was right up their alley." The film company had access to huge wardrobes, swords and other "medieval" props, and some excellent castle sets built for *Nostradamus* (1994). "The other director was an Australian named Frank Arnold, and the plan was that we would alternate," Farino continued. "When he was shooting episode one I'd be prepping episode two, and I'd shoot episode two while he was prepping episode three, and so on."

With the first four episodes completed, the tinkering began. "It was flattering, on the one hand," Farino told me. "They decided that *Dino-Knights* was a better movie, as such, and also it had dinosaurs and was a costume drama, and it would be stronger in this miniseries approach to go out with that one first." Inevitably, this tactic created some sizable continuity problems. "They couldn't just flip episodes one and two because they had to introduce Josh Kirby, set up the premise, introduce Irwin and Zoetrope, et cetera," Farino pointed out. "So they had to spend the first half of what was *now* episode one with Josh's introduction and then go to *Dino-Knights*, but now they've run out of movie running time so they have to continue *Dino-Knights* to episode two, and it becomes this real jumble." The resulting pastiche has characters meeting for the first time who act as if they already know each other well, and Josh commenting on the "Codes of Kang" in episode one although Azabeth doesn't mention them until episode two! "The ultimate irony is that they all came out at once," Farino lamented, "and so the whole idea that was the original impetus for the series was forgotten."

SPECIAL EFFECTS: Due to a combination of factors, *Planet of the Dino-Knights* did not feature Moonbeam's usual visual FX provider, David Allen Productions. "We had just come back from *The Primevals*," D.A.P.'s Chris Endicott explained. "Full Moon was kind of in transition, and David was busy doing other things. I was asked by [visual effects supervisor] Joe Grossberg if I wanted to help him work on the dinosaur sequence." The animation set-up was located at but not under the auspices of Allen's studio. "We were basically just using the space," said Endicott, "and later we moved to another location." Robert Maine animated the figures in front of a blue screen. "It was done very quickly," Endicott recalled. "Blue screen is so easy to light, and Rob is an incredibly fast animator. At times, he would do two or three shots a day."

Though the dino sequences serve the picture adequately, they are not what Ernie Farino had envisioned. "About two weeks after I returned from Romania, I got a call from Clark Henderson, a friend I'd worked with over the years," Farino began. "Fries Entertainment was making *Screamers* up in Canada and needed a visual effects supervisor. So, I went to Montreal." Meanwhile, the company which had taken over control of the *Josh Kirby* films "just wanted to get it *done*," Chris Endicott said. "They said, 'How can you finish this picture in the fewest number of stop-motion shots?' and we came up with an idea how we could do it. But it's not anywhere near what Ernie intended, and I know it bothers him." Especially since Farino had successfully overseen the editing of *Dino-Knights* while still in Canada. "I stayed in touch by phone and fax with the editor throughout postproduction," Farino emphasized. "She would periodically send me videotapes, and each time I'd look at the tape and make all my directorial notes ... all the normal interaction a director and editor have, even though it was long distance."

After four months in Montreal, Farino returned to Full Moon. "I walked in and said, 'So, what's happening with the animation?' And they said, 'It's done.' I said, 'What do you mean it's *done*?' And they said, 'It's done — you want to see it?' It was all done and I never even knew it had begun." Since his rich stop-motion background had been key to his initial hiring, Farino was understandably taken aback. "I think, by and large, they pulled it off fine," Farino said. "I don't mean to suggest that the animation was a failure or anything because I wasn't involved. It's just that there are some things that could have been in there, and maybe I could have answered questions or helped them solve problems quicker because I'd already thought it through. And unlike 99 percent of directors, I had this whole body of experience actually doing that kind of work." Farino, though surprised and disappointed at the time (he had even hoped to animate a shot or two himself) looks back on the mix-up pragmatically. "I'm sure it was just one of those things where you don't see the forest for the trees, and you're focused on the problem that's in front of you," he concluded. "I think it was simply an assumption that I'm off in Montreal working on some other movie, and therefore we've got to roll up our sleeves and get the job done, and that's that. I'm sure it was something as simple as that."

Many things didn't go as planned on the *Josh Kirby* films. The stop-motion Tyrannosaurus built for (yet barely seen in) *Prehysteria* was outfitted with a new head to portray the "Royal Dragon," but plans to also turn the *Prehysteria* chasmosaur into the *Josh Kirby* Triceratops fell through and a new puppet had to be made from scratch. The animation figures which represent the human dino riders were also built specifically for *Dino-Knights* — by Jim Danforth. "At one point, the stop-motion was going to be done by Danforth," Chris Endicott revealed. "While waiting to work out a deal with these guys, he started making the puppets ... so the two figures that are on top of the dinosaurs were made by Jim."

Journey to the Beginning of Time

(a.k.a. *Cesta do praveku* [*Voyage to Prehistory*])

"A trip any scientist would give his eye teeth to make!"

*** 1955/1966, Czechoslovakia/USA. C, 83m.

CREDITS: *Director* Karel Zeman. *Producer (U.S.)* William Cayton. *Screenplay* Karel Zeman and William Cayton. *Additional Dialogue (U.S.)* Fred Ladd. *Production Design* Ivo Mrdzek, Zdenek Rozkopal, Karel Zeman. *Trick Camera* Antonín Horak.
CAST: *Doc (Petr)* James Lucas (Josef Lukas). *Jo-Jo (Jirka)* Victor Betral (Vladimir Bejval). *Ben (Jenda)* Charles Goldsmith (Zdenek Hustak). *Tony (Tonik)* Peter Herrman (Petr Herrman). *"Cesta do praveku" Narrator* Bedřich Šetena.

AD LINE: "Four boys living the excitement every boy dreams about!"

On a "warm, hazy day in May," four young friends named Doc, Jo-Jo, Ben, and Tony stroll across the Queensborough Bridge bound for the American Museum of Natural History. On their way to Brontosaur Hall they pass a Haida Indian war canoe, complete with wooden figures of the boatmen. "Look at that medicine man!" Jo-Jo exclaims. "It's as though he's trying to hypnotize us from out of the past!" Forgetting Jo-Jo's comment, the boys enjoy their dinosaur tour while science-minded Doc takes notes in his special diary. Later on they go rowing on Central Park's lake, and when a strange cave beckons, they steer the boat inside.

Inexplicable things begin to happen once they exit the cave. The terrain changes, the weather turns icy, and on the riverbank they see a living woolly mammoth! Doc's theory, that the river is somehow carrying them back into time, proves true as they witness more and more visions from earth's past. They visit a caveman's dwelling, see a battle between two woolly rhinos, watch a saber-toothed cat stalk its prey, and narrowly escape the powerful carnivorous bird, Phororhacos. Braving storms, catching fish, chasing away crocodiles, the lads eventually reach the Mesozoic era: the time of dinosaurs. Giant Pteranodons soar overhead, horned styracosaurs and plated stegosaurs roam the land, and a Trachodon (then thought to be a hadrosaur) bathes in the shallows. A massive Brontosaurus swims by their boat, and the stegosaur wages a life-or-death struggle against a predatory Ceratosaurus. From the Mesozoic they drift into the even deeper past of the Paleozoic, with foot-long dragonflies and primitive amphibians such as the froglike Eryops. They finally enter the lifeless Precambrian era and arrive at the Beginning: the sea, where all life began.

Suddenly, the boys realize they're back at the museum, next to the Haida canoe. It was all just a dream ... except, why does Doc's diary look like it's been through a Paleozoic swamp?

COMMENTARY: *Cesta do praveku*, later to become *Journey to the Beginning of Time*, may be Karel Zeman's most straightforward, least stylistic film. Though it does contain examples of his unconventional mixing and matching of cinematic illusions, the narrative is exceedingly simple. Four dino-crazy boys magically go back in time, have adventures with dinosaurs and other prehistoric animals, and return to the present. There is little of the comedic, satiric, and "magical" qualities which typify most of Zeman's work. This is not necessarily a criticism, however, because the film still emerges as a one-of-a-kind dinosaur movie.

The one thing that sets *Journey* apart is its methodical (some would say too methodical) and very "educational" approach. Every

This American poster, like all of the advertising for *Journey to the Beginning of Time*, deliberately downplayed Karel Zeman and the picture's Czech origins.

change of terrain, every new plant or animal is greeted by a short informational spiel from Doc, who earned his nickname "because he wants to be a scientist." This structure may not make for dynamic action, but it seems to hold audience attention by generating a perpetual curiosity about what might be around the next bend. Paleo-savvy youngsters may have some fun pointing out certain "facts," like Brontosaurus being "biggest of the dinosaurs" or T. rex living in the Jurassic, which fail to fit the current body of knowledge. However, the film also foreshadows a dino theory that didn't become popular until thirty years later, when Doc points out evidence that "makes you wonder if lizards aren't related to birds!"

Even if the somewhat clinical storytelling leaves you cold, it's impossible not to enjoy Zeman's prehistoric menagerie. The early reels offer some overdue exposure for the interesting mammals of the Pleistocene epoch, usually overshadowed by the dinosaurs' popularity. It's a pleasure to see a woolly mammoth that is not played by a disgruntled, fur-coated elephant. Other treats include the terrific contest between the woolly rhinos, a bizarre six-horned Uintatherium, and an obscure elephant ancestor called Deinotherium more ancient than the mammoth. Arguably the best effects sequence in the film is Doc's harrowing encounter with the man-sized, meat-eating Phororhacos. The grotesque, flightless bird glances around, locks its predator's eyes on Doc (you can almost hear his silent "gulp!"), and sprints toward him. The bird's animated running cycle is spot-on, and the alternating cuts of Doc and his pursuer tearing through the shoulder-high grass are flawlessly matched.

No dinomovie in history has ever packed so many saurs into a mere 17 minutes of screen time. A highlight is the well thought-out (and bloody!) battle between the Stegosaurus and Ceratosaurus. Like all of Zeman's stop-motion, the action is enjoyable and theatrical if not as technically polished as that of the famous American animators, and some of the best animal scenes are not stop-motion at all, but live-action puppets. The crocodile swarm is very convincing and the puppetized Trachodon — in design, fabrication, and performance — is a marvelous bit of work. Zeman also impresses with his noncreature FX shots, such as the expansive, seamless composite of the boys rowing into the face of a wonderfully malevolent-looking thunderstorm. It's a disappointment that Zeman chose not to include an ape; considering the grand history of stop-motion simians, it would have been interesting to see what touches the Czech master would have come up with. Also odd is the lack of a Tyrannosaurus, especially after all the praise and superlatives Doc showers on the museum's T. rex skeleton.

As *Journey* nears its end, a fundamental flaw of the going-back-in-time storyline emerges: Once the age of dinosaurs is left behind, what's left? The first act sets up the scenario and whets our appetite, the second act is a dino lover's smorgasbord of giant brontosaurs and dive-bombing pterosaurs and battling stegosaurs, then the third act comes along with a two-foot tadpole and a buzzy dragonfly. These effects are proficient but simply cannot match the spectacle of the dinosaurs. By the time we get all the way back to the Precambrian, an era devoid of any life, the film is pretty much devoid of life as well. Things finally turn downright bizarre as the boys' arrival at "the beginning" is interpreted through kaleidoscopic lights, a reading from Genesis set to a dissonant music track, and some flowery musings from the previously analytical Doc: "a thousand volcanoes, gushing red from the furnace of creation!"

If the opening is slow and the finale lackluster, however, the marvelous middle is a jam-packed treat for both dinosaur and animation fans. With its no-frills plot and museum-tour flavor, *Journey to the Beginning of Time* won't be everyone's cup of tea, but it has two things that are fundamental to the genre: great dinosaurs, and wide-eyed kids to marvel at them.

PEOPLE AND PRODUCTION: So unique is

This stop-motion animated woolly mammoth is the first prehistoric creature encountered on the boys' *Journey to the Beginning of Time*.

Karel Zeman's body of cinematic work that it's impossible to categorize. The documentary featurette, *The Magic World of Karel Zeman*, perhaps sums things up as well as they can be. "Karel Zeman is not only a wizard," a voice says, "he is one of the brotherhood of poets, eternally young, with a heart of flame."

Zeman was born in Czechoslovakia in 1910 and made his first film, *A Christmas Dream*, in 1944. His previous employment had involved the construction of models and puppets for storefront displays, and this experience would serve him well in his filmmaking endeavors. In a film career lasting nearly four decades, he transported delighted audiences into his magic worlds where objects and drawings and dinosaurs come to life, and anything is possible.

Zeman's early works included a series of short puppet films featuring "Mr. Prokouk," a resilient, recognizable everyman whose daily tribulations satirized the social conditions in Czechoslovakia during the immediate postwar years. In 1949, Zeman created *Inspiration*, one of the most unique and remarkable animated films ever made. Here he painstakingly animated actual glass figures, bringing to life a fantastical world existing entirely within a single raindrop. In 1955, at a little studio in Gottwaldov, Zeman tackled his first feature-length production, *Cesta do praveku*. Although its American incarnation, *Journey to the Beginning of Time*, wouldn't find its way to U.S. theaters until the mid–1960s, its original release predates *The Beast of Hollow Mountain* and makes it the very first stop-motion dinosaur movie in color.

In 1966, producer William Cayton, known for his involvement with boxing-themed films, moved from the pugilistic to the prehistoric when he made a few alterations to *Cesta do praveku*, dubbed it in English, and released it under its new title. (The film's first stateside appearance was apparently a 1960 television showing, with its running time broken up into a series of short episodes.) Four boys resembling those in Zeman's film were employed for a new prologue and epilogue, directed by Fred Ladd and set in the American Museum of Natural History. The prologue introduces the mystical element of the Haida medicine man, while the epilogue offers the "did-it-really-happen?" conclusion. An interesting detail in the new opening is the attempt to explain the odd hats worn by the original Czech actors. While strolling across the Queensborough Bridge, "we passed a little man selling crazy carnival hats," Doc explains in voice-over, "and we were just feeling crazy enough to buy some!"

As usual, the official "pressbook" for *Journey to the Beginning of Time* didn't let anything—like facts—get in the way of good ad copy. One article described how William Cayton had "recently become an expert in prehistoric life, by virtue of the extensive research necessary" to make the film, and the producer more than once comes off sounding somewhat immodest. "I could take any event in the Earth's history, or in the Earth's future for that matter, and recreate it," Cayton announced, leaving us to ponder the cosmological dynamics of "re-creating" the *future*. The entire pressbook gives the impression that Cayton oversaw every aspect of production, including the animation, though it does credit Karel Zeman for directing the picture "from a screenplay by Cayton and himself." There is no mention of the film's Czech origin, or of the fact that most of it was shot over a decade earlier. It even tries to convince audiences that the young actors, whose real names were Anglicized for the American release, really were schoolboys from Queens!

SPECIAL EFFECTS: According to a press release, the animals in *Journey to the Beginning of Time* were created by "the magic of true-to-life stop-motion." Though stop-motion animation is the most prominent method, Zeman also employed small-scale live-action puppets, full-scale dino sections and, apparently, cel animation. *Cesta do praveku* marked the first time that Zeman mixed animation effects into an otherwise live-action film, and perhaps not since Obie's *The Lost World* thirty years earlier had so many animated puppets appeared in one movie.

During the middle portion of the film, Zeman parades an amazing number of extinct (and nonextinct) animals across the screen. Species brought to life through stop-motion animation include the woolly mammoth, woolly rhinoceros, flamingo, Deinotherium, Uintatherium, Phororhacos, Pteranodon, Styracosaurus (eating), Stegosaurus, and Ceratosaurus. Real-time puppets or puppet sections are used for the crocodiles, Trachodon, Brontosaurus (in the water), giant "tadpole," and the Eryops. In some scenes, it is difficult to discern exactly what technique Zeman used. The walking shots of the mammoth and the Styracosaurus, for example, look as if they could be flat "cut-out" animation (carefully illuminated and photographed), while the brontosaur's appearance on land is apparently a puppetized head and neck carefully married to a painting of the body and legs. Still other shots of the gazelles, saber-toothed cat, and giraffes have the appearance of traditional cel ("cartoon") animation.

With so much animation and puppetry to be done, it seems reasonable that Zeman may have enlisted one or more assistants, but none are credited on American prints of the film. Animators who worked on Zeman's *The Fabulous World of Jules Verne* (1958) and some of his later features included Arnost Kupcik, Jindřich Liska, and František Kremar, but whether any of these artists participated in *Cesta do praveku* is unknown to this author.

A battle between a fearless Stegosaurus and a hungry Ceratosaurus highlights the stop-motion dinosaur action in *Journey to the Beginning of Time*.

Curiously, the aforementioned featurette, *The Magic World of Karel Zeman*, goes to great pains to reveal how "forced perspective" was used to realize the shots of the boys investigating the dead Stegosaurus. The actors are shown walking on a distant scaffold, hidden behind and aligned with a glass-painted stego in the foreground. The documentary camera tracks back and to the side, revealing the secret, then tracks back to its original position and re-establishes the illusion. It's a fascinating insight ... except that the actual shots were not done like that at all! The real scenes were in fact filmed on and around a full-size mock-up of the dead dino. Forced perspective is a powerful tool but it does have limitations, and many of the shots in the "dead stego" sequence are beyond its capabilities. So, the behind-the-scenes vignette must have been created merely to demonstrate the technique. It could also have much to do with Karel Zeman and his magician's soul — revealing, yet not revealing, the secrets of his conjuring.

Journey to the Center of the Earth

"Oliver, this is sheer fantasy!"

*** 1959, USA. 20th Century–Fox. C, 129m.

CREDITS: *Director* Henry Levin. *Producer* Charles Brackett. *Screenplay* Walter Reisch and Charles Brackett; based on the novel by Jules Verne. *Special Photographic Effects* L. B. Abbott, James B. Gordon, Emil Kosa, Jr. *Prop Miniature Foreman* Herb Cheek.

CAST: *Prof. Oliver Lindenbrook* James Mason. *Alec McEwen* Pat Boone. *Carla Goetaborg* Arlene Dahl. *Jenny* Diane Baker. *Count Saknussemm* Thayer David. *Hans* Peter Ronson.

Edinburgh, 1880. Recently knighted geology professor Oliver Lindenbrook and his star pupil, Alec McEwen (his niece Jenny's fiancé), discover a long-hidden clue and embark on an expedition to retrace the journey of famed subterranean explorer Arne Saknussemm. They travel to Iceland, aware that unethical Swedish vulcanologist Doctor Goetaborg is trying to beat them to their goal, but never expecting to find him murdered. "He was against us, someone was even more against him," Lindenbrook observes, and that "someone" is Arne's evil descendant, Count Saknussemm. Lindenbrook hires a strapping Icelander named Hans as a porter, while Goetaborg's widow, Carla, uses a bit of blackmail to come along as well.

The group descends, and Saknussemm covertly follows. They persevere through hurtling boulders and violent earthquakes, but McEwen becomes separated from the group and is briefly captured by Saknussemm before Lindenbrook comes to the rescue. The count is tried and convicted by an impromptu tribunal, but is grudgingly allowed to join the expedition. The travelers fight past prehistoric Dimetrodons to launch their makeshift raft on a subterranean ocean, and finally reach the far shore. Saknussemm sates his appetite with Hans' pet duck, Gertrude, and the big Icelander is set on revenge until a rockslide does the job for him. The explorers' intrepidity is finally rewarded with a momentous discovery: the ruins of Atlantis. Arne Saknussemm's skeleton lies nearby, his fleshless finger pointing the way to a volcanic chimney and a way to the surface. A boulder blocks the passage, but the group takes cover in an ancient altar stone and prepares to blast it clear. A giant primordial chameleon appears as their fuse burns, only to be buried under a river of lava released by the explosion. The eruption carries the altar stone upward at breakneck speed, but the four adventurers somehow survive the wild ascent and return to a heroic welcome in Edinburgh.

COMMENTARY: Strictly speaking, *Journey to the Center of the Earth* shouldn't be in a volume on dinosaur films. But so many movies (and toy manufacturers) mix the sailbacked Dimetrodon of the Permian Period with the Dinosauria of the much-later Mesozoic Era, it's hard to exclude them. Besides, *Journey* fits the dinomovie mold in so many ways. When people say "they don't make movies like that anymore," this is the kind of movie they're talking about. This old-fashioned picture's emphasis on characters, and wholesomeness, and pure adventure for adventure's sake, is now practically extinct.

This tale delightfully recreates the feel of Jules Verne's era — or at least how we *want* that era to be — where the good guys (Pat Boone and James Mason) are good, the bad guy (Thayer David) is bad, and that's that. Boone makes a perfectly adequate Alec, wisely not even attempting more than a hint of a Scottish accent, but it's Mason and David who shine. Of all the villains in all the films discussed in this volume, the soulless Count Saknussemm is the most villainous. With a countenance that "menacing" doesn't begin to describe and a near-perfect performance, David plays Saknussemm as if he takes no delight in being evil; he simply sees no logical reasons to behave otherwise. He makes a marvelous entrance courtesy of Bernard Herrmann's evocative music and some effective chiaroscuro lighting, and has most of the best lines. "I don't sleep," he hisses distastefully. "I hate those little slices of death." James Mason is equally flawless, effortlessly commanding attention whenever he's on screen and making Lindenbrook eminently likable despite his abrasiveness. The high quality of the performances, direction, and script is only heightened by Herrmann's soaring score, raising the moments of discovery on magical notes as easily as it amplifies the perilous passages with sonorous woodwinds.

As others have said, *Journey* is the *one* movie to make live lizards really "work" as prehistoric creatures. This is due to the masterful technical details, the flow of the sequence within the story, and the fact that

Lindenbrook identifies them not as dinosaurs but as Dimetrodons, an ancient species — noticeably smaller than depicted here — which can be credibly impersonated by augmented iguanas. The beasts' devouring of their fallen comrade is a nicely merciless touch, and the photographic effects combining the reptiles and actors are of virtuoso quality. I defy the most eagle-eyed nitpicker to spot one glitch in the composite of the men in the surf looking at the creature on the beach, or the shot of the explorers dragging their raft past the feeding pack. The old-fashioned optical mattes in the Dimetrodon sequence are as flawless as any state-of-the-art digital composite.

The epilogue, showing the adventurers back in Edinburgh, makes a satisfying conclusion to an enjoyable picture. Lindenbrook's magnanimous speech, Alec's wedding-day mishap, and Carla's reeling in of her irascible but hopelessly hooked beau leave you with a glad feeling and a smile, which is about the best thing a movie can do.

PEOPLE AND PRODUCTION: *Journey to the Center of the Earth* persevered through several false starts and was finally made by 20th Century–Fox, with a screenplay by Charles Brackett and Walter Reisch (Oscar winners for 1953's *Titanic*). In *Keep Watching the Skies!*, Bill Warren noted that *Journey* was generally true to Jules Verne's book, with some puzzling exceptions. "Oddly ... two of the most visually-interesting concepts were deleted," he pointed out. "In the novel, they saw a giant man driving a herd of mastodons in a jungle, and prehistoric monsters battled around the raft as it rode across the underground sea." Directing was Henry Levin, a Fox veteran who would bring a similar sort of rose colored, quasi-authentic "period" feel to *The Wonderful World of the Brothers Grimm* in 1962. Shooting locations included Iceland, Edinburgh, and New Mexico's Carlsbad Caverns, where all filming was done at night so as not to interfere with the normal daytime tourist traffic.

The casting process was not always smooth. For reasons unknown, Alexander Scourby was replaced as Count Saknussemm by Thayer David, while Boone had to be talked into taking the job at all. He saw himself as a singer first and foremost, well-suited only to Bing Crosby–like film roles. According to author William Schoell, Boone acquiesced only after the producers agreed to a song or two. Boone's reservations steadily abated, and when it was all over he was pleased to have been a part of it. "But I can't take credit for it," he said. "I was not the visionary. I had to be dragged into it — but I'm happy I was."

Another casting headache confronted animal handler Ralph Helfer. "I had been hired to supply the lead animal star, identified in the script as an eider duck named Gertrude," Helfer wrote in *The Beauty of the Beasts*. A lengthy permit process precluded the importation of a real eider, so Helfer performed a clever make-up job on four tame, solid white ducks from his pond. Gertrude and her three stand-ins looked great, but their quacking repeatedly spoiled the soundtrack. Not to be defeated, he phoned his wife to bring four of their "Muscovy mix" to the shooting location. These ducks underwent the same cleansing and painting process and soon looked just as good as the first Gertrudes, with one improvement. "Muscovy ducks are quackless!" Helfer explained. "Although these ducks are usually multicolored, ours had bred with our 'Gertrude ducks,' and the result had been pure-white, quackless ducks."

SPECIAL EFFECTS: Being a Fox production, *Journey*'s effects were overseen by the studio's venerable master, L. B. Abbott. "Putting a popular Jules Verne classic on the screen was a difficult but rewarding task," he wrote in *Special Effects — Wire, Tape and Rubber Band Style*. Given the reputation of reptiles as actors, the Dimetrodon attack was not surprisingly one of the most difficult sequences. The chosen lizards were rhinoceros iguanas, with an overall nose-to-tail length of up to four feet. Herb Cheek's prop miniature shop fabricated some organic-looking dorsal sails from wire and foam rubber, with cloth strips at the base to

Count Saknussemm (Thayer David, right) and Prof. Lindenbrook (James Mason) interact with a giant Dimetrodon, courtesy of a bluescreen composite.

camouflage the attachment joint. An artistic paint job further blended the seams. Two dozen iguanas were made over, each outfitted with its own custom-sized back fin.

The make-up, though, was the easy part. "When we started working with these animals we discovered a terribly disappointing fact," Abbott recalled. "They moved at only two speeds, dead stopped (and I mean like a statue!) and high gear." With advice from the reptile handlers, a strategy was finally found which sporadically yielded bits of usable footage. A movie light would be trained on the iguana, and when it began to warm up and show signs of movement the lamp was quickly doused and the cameras started. "Occasionally, our actor would make two or three slow steps, but most of the time it would fly away," noted Abbott. "This caused the consumption of a great deal more film than we had anticipated originally."

In *Filmfax*, Pat Boone remembered shooting the live action for the Dimetrodon sequence. "They were like small dogs in actual size," Boone said of the iguanas. "What they did was put a guy on a ladder with a long pole with a rag on the end of it ... and we had to cringe and pull back and brace ourselves against this guy on a ladder with a rag on the end of a pole. We felt like idiots." The reptiles and actors were composited together using bluescreen techniques. To put a person in the foreground with a monster in the back, the person was photographed in front of a large bluescreen and composited with the background footage of the animal and miniature set. To put a reptile in the foreground and an actor in the back, the reptile was shot in front of a smaller bluescreen and comped with the background plate of the actor.

The "chameleon monster" in the climax was played by a two-foot tegu lizard, given a color-changing ability by the FX crew. "We did this by cooling the lizard to 40 degrees, at which point it became immobile," L. B. Abbott reported. "Then we could shoot some footage of it in its original color, repaint it, shoot it in the new color, and dissolve from the first to the second." Helped in no small measure by the excellent work of Abbott and his team, *Journey* was a financial winner for Fox. "Many people in the industry felt that an expensive fantasy done in period would be a sure loser at the boxoffice," Abbott concluded. "*Journey to the Center of the Earth* proved them wrong."

Journey to the Center of the Earth

"Well, they're just going to have to break tradition, aren't they?"

** 1999, USA. Hallmark Entertainment. C, 139m (home video version).

CREDITS: *Director* George Miller. *Producers* George Miller, Connie Collins, David Picker (executive), Robert Halmi, Jr. (executive). *Teleplay* Thomas Baum. *Visual Effects Production* Photon Visual Effects. *VFX Designer* Dale Duguid. *VFX Supervisors* Ian Johnson, Randy Vellacott. *Sauroid Prosthetics* Jason Baird.
CAST: *Prof. Theodore Lytton* Treat Williams. *Jonas Lytton* Jeremy London. *Alice Hastings* Tushka Bergen. *McNiff* Hugh Keays-Byrne. *Ralna* Petra Yared. *Casper Hastings* Bryan Brown. *Helen* Tessa Wells.

Boston, 1875. Geology professor Theodore Lytton is hired by the well-to-do Alice Hastings to go to New Zealand and find her missing husband, Casper. Theodore's nephew Jonas goes along, to the displeasure of his fiancée Helen. In New Zealand they are met by an imposing Scotsman named McNiff, whose local knowledge makes him a welcome addition, and by the insistent Alice also, a not-so-welcome addition — until Theodore begins to fall in love with her. They descend through the volcanic Mount Ruapehu and emerge in a strange world inhabited by dinosaurs and flying reptiles. Alice is abducted by a race of intelligent dinosaur-humans called Sauroids, while an indigenous human tribe drags the men off to an Aztec like village. The village is home to a beautiful girl, Ralna, whom Jonas had earlier glimpsed, and to Casper Hastings, enjoying a near godlike status with the simple natives. Casper leads a mission to rescue Alice, then reveals an amazing discovery: a miraculously medicinal plant called *zho-tan* with which he plans to make his fortune back home. As they prepare to return to the surface, McNiff announces that he's enjoying the local girls' hospitality and wishes to remain. The group's numbers are further diminished during the ascent — Casper falls prey to the Sauroids, and Ralna is cut off from the others by a cave-in. The remaining three stumble upon the Saknussemm Vortex — a whirling column of water which feeds the lake above — and ride it to the surface. Back in Massachusetts, Alice and Theodore get engaged, but Jonas leaves Helen and returns to the subterranean world to find Ralna.

COMMENTARY: Whatever its faults or virtues, this cable-TV adaptation is no closer to Jules Verne's *Journey to the Center of the Earth* than the 1961 quickie *Valley of the Dragons* is to his *Off on a Comet*. The title is the same, a geologist leads a party into the earth's interior, and there the similarities end.

According to a USA Network press release, "the story had to be updated so that modern viewers could relate to it." Here, "updated" refers to the attitudes toward women and certain character traits, rather than to any alteration of the time setting. But why, when *Journey*, or *The Lost World*, or any "classic" adventure novel is updated, is the basic motivation always changed from man's pure desire to explore, into something monetary or material? Professor Lytton only agrees to go because the wealthy Alice can pay handsomely, and Casper only leaves his idolatrous (and apparently sex-filled) existence because he thinks the *zho-tan* will make him rich upon his return.

Accepting the modernization of the story, this version does have a few good things. The early scenes include some well-photographed and apparently authentic Maori ceremonies, and the cast is able. Jeremy London is natural, and burly Hugh Keays-Byrne — with a *snake* tattooed *on his nose* — is enormously engaging. The sets and special effects vary in quality, from unconvincing (the soundstage cavern interiors) to excellent (a knockout shot of a mighty pterodactyl swarm). Don't look for the flying reptiles in the videocassette version, though, because when this TV two-parter was edited down to videocassette length the pterosaur attack was an inexplicable casualty. The fictional "Raptosaurus" is an uninspired, briefly-seen, computer-generated foe, while the Sauroids are played by actors in full-body suits. The costumes are fairly high-tech creations, with eyes that are particularly lifelike, but the overall face design is not too different from that of *The Hideous Sun Demon* (1959).

The network hype for *Journey* stated that "forty years after the original [1959 film], the cast still believes that the public will once again fall in love with the secret world below." But the James Mason version will likely be remembered long after this "epic" retelling has been relegated to the video store bargain bin.

SPECIAL EFFECTS: "The special effects are the stars of the film," actor Treat Williams asserted in a studio promo. A variety of traditional and digital techniques were employed to create the dinosaurs, Sauroids, and even the exotic landscapes. In one striking shot, a real geologic formation called the "Twelve Apostles," on the Australian coast, was spectacularly redressed through a mixture of computer graphics and matte painting techniques. Most of the effects scenes were devised by director George Miller, according to an article in *Sci-Fi Entertainment Magazine*. "I read the script, and the pictures just started popping into my mind," Miller stated.

For actress Tushka Bergen, *Journey* was her first experience playing opposite a special-effects creature which would not even be there until postproduction. "Sometimes, it would feel real silly," she said, referring to the sequence with the computer-generated Raptosaurus. "We're supposed to be reacting to a dinosaur and it was one of the set guys holding a stick with a paper head on it." The Sauroid suits and associated prosthetics were, as usual for such things, highly uncomfortable for the performers, who could only stand to keep the headpiece on for about 20 minutes at a time.

Journey to the Center of Time

(a.k.a. *Time Warp*)

"*Just what do you hope to accomplish by all this, if I may ask?*"

* 1967, USA. American General Pictures. C, 82m.

CREDITS: *Director* David L. Hewitt. *Producers* Ray Dorn, David L. Hewitt, J. Max Thornton (associate), and Dennis Hibshman (associate). *Screenplay* David Prentiss. *Special Visual Effects* Modern Film Effects.

CAST: *Mr. Stanton, Jr.* Scott Brady. *Dr. Karen White* Gigi Perreau. *Dr. Mark Manning* Anthony Eisley. *Dr. "Doc" Gordon* Abraham Sofaer. *Vina* Poupee Gamin. *Mr. Denning* Austin Green. *Dave* Andy Davis. *Susan* Tracy Olsen.

AD LINE: "RUN from the valley of monsters in the year one million B.C.!"

Things are not going well at the Institute for Temporal Research. Their corporate sponsor, Stanton Industries, has been taken over by the narrow-minded son of the recently deceased CEO who had been funding their studies. The younger Stanton and his associate Mr. Denning meet with three scientists: project leader Dr. "Doc" Gordon, Dr. Karen White, and Dr. Mark Manning. Stanton gives the trio only 24 hours to produce results or be shut down. Desperate for success, the reckless Manning "opens the photon cycling all the way" and the Time Lab (with Stanton aboard) is thrown forward 5,000 years into the midst of an apocalyptic global war. Coincidentally, a colonization starship from another galaxy has also become trapped in the conflict. The aliens' benevolent leader, Dr. Vina, tells the scientists they must return with a warning of mankind's fate, but they nearly collide with themselves on the way back. Stanton ignorantly causes a power surge which sends them zooming right through the present into the world of a million years ago, and their laser ruby is shattered while trying to fend off a dinosaur. Doc Gordon fatally falls from a cavern ledge while trying to obtain a replacement ruby, and the shifty Stanton departs in the Time Lab before Mark and Karen can stop him. Stanton dies in a time-stream collision, and when the lab reappears in the prehistoric world, Mark and Karen make a last futile effort to return to the present. They are ultimately caught in some sort of parallel universe, wondering if they are to be "the Adam and Eve of a brave new world."

COMMENTARY: Time travel stories are among the most popular of all science fiction subgenres, but are also among the trickiest. Such tales are narrative minefields, fraught with pitfalls at every step. Done well, one is rewarded with a thought-provoking, crowd-pleasing film like *The Time Machine* (1960), *Time After Time* (1979), or *Star Trek IV: The Voyage Home* (1986). Done under the limitations of American General Pictures, and one gets *Journey to the Center of Time*.

To be fair, *Journey* is far from the worst sci-fi quickie of the sixties. Mindless bombs like *Women of the Prehistoric Planet* had no ambitions other than the hope of a quick and modest profit. Like most of David L. Hewitt's pictures, *Journey* aspires to be something more — it simply hasn't the means. A big problem this time is the script, which is saturated with a disastrously high dose of pseudoscientific jargon. It often seems as if the entire film is nothing but technobabble, and long-winded technobabble at that. Doc Gordon can't just say "stabilize image," he has to say "stand by to activate image stabilization switch!" By the time the *Journey* ends, so have all attempts to make any sense of it.

Even with milk-money budgets, Hewitt often landed surprisingly capable actors. Scott Brady's natural delivery makes Stanton into a credible creep, and Anthony Eisley is a better actor than he was ever given credit for. Gigi Perreau has little to do but look pretty (very pretty, actually), and although it's always a bit sad to see once-respected actors toiling in D-grade pictures, Abraham Sofaer's wonderful voice still sounds exactly like a kindly scientist should. The milk-and-cookies duo of Dave and Susan, played by Andy Davis and Tracy Olsen, make it seem as though Wally Cleaver and his prom date have landed jobs at mission control, and gaunt Austin Green is strangely amusing as Mr. Denning. He seems to have no purpose whatsoever, but there he is anyway, hovering around, kibitzing, breathing down the necks of poor Dave and Susan and generally acting like an irritating in-law.

The evidence of *Journey*'s meager budget is everywhere, despite Hewitt's efforts to hide it. The "time travel" montages are just shots of the four lead actors superimposed over stock footage. To minimize construction time and cost, the alien starship and Central Control sets consist only of the principal props placed in front of black backdrops, and the scenes of the aggressor forces storming the starship are so pitiful as to be sad. The dinosaur sequence is just as skimpy, consisting of an exceedingly tame-looking pet lizard roaring at Gigi Perreau and a few black-and-white stock shots seen on the lab's viewscreen. For all its ambitions, *Journey to the Center of Time* is far too talky, illogical, and cheap to generate interest, and is frankly a chore to watch. There are the scattered clever moments which Hewitt's films always seem to have, but they are lost inside a story that's as ridiculous as it is tiresome.

PEOPLE AND PRODUCTION: In 1964, David L. Hewitt teamed with Ib Melchior on a not-bad little sci-fi picture called *The Time Travelers*, originally based on a script by Hewitt. Melchior directed the picture, and Hewitt (ingeniously employing variations of stage magicians' illusions) provided the special effects. Three years later Hewitt would himself direct a quasi-remake, grandiosely titled *Journey to the Center of Time*. The strongest connection between the two films is a scene originally written for the earlier entry, wherein the scientists petition their corporate benefactors for continued funding. Hewitt got the okay from Melchior and *Time Travelers* producer Bill Redlin to use the scene as *Journey*'s opening act. Much of the dialogue concerning the "TV-like eye" which can see "reflections of activity and

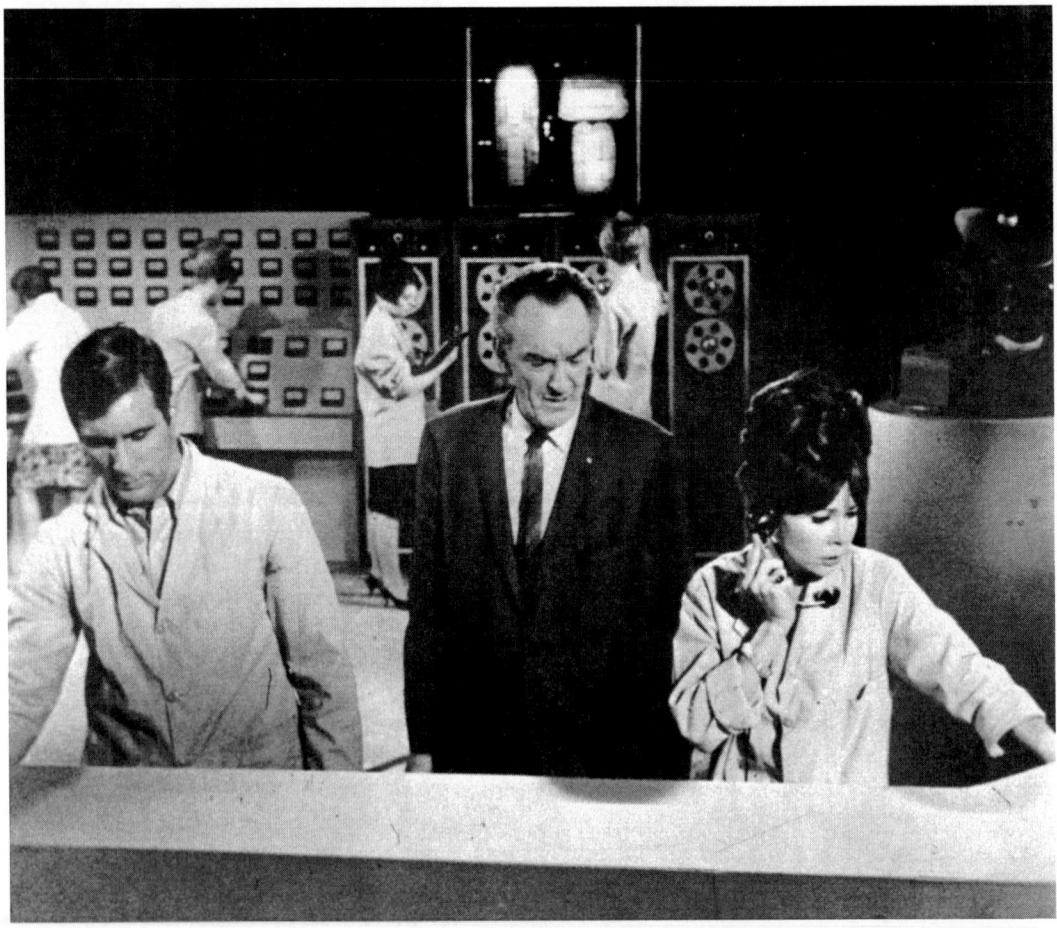

Nosy Mr. Denning (Austin Green) maddeningly comments on every action by perky mission controllers Dave and Susan (Andy Davis, Tracy Olsen) in *Journey to the Center of Time*.

things from some time before," is taken almost word for word from the *Time Travelers* script.

With a budget of about $100,000, *Journey* was reportedly the most expensive film released in the short history of American General Pictures, and Hewitt managed to assemble a solid B-movie cast. Anthony Eisley was only a few years removed from the popular *Hawaiian Eye* television series, and Scott Brady was almost a "name." Gigi Perreau was a former child star who began her career at age 18 months, and character actor Abraham Sofaer was a respected veteran of such films as *Stairway to Heaven* (1946) and *The Naked Jungle* (1953). In addition to directing—and more importantly, he surely felt—Hewitt would also handle the special effects. The shooting schedule was ten days.

Working on an American General picture was always memorable. In Tom Weaver's *Interviews with B Science Fiction and Horror Movie Makers*, Anthony Eisley talked about *Journey*. "There's only one explanation for that whole thing," Eisley said, "and that is that they spent $1.95 on the entire picture, and shot it in a studio the size of your den! But under the circumstances I think everybody did the best they could." Despite the ultrashoestring nature of AGP's films, Eisley had only praise for David Hewitt. "We always had a lot of fun," Eisley said of working with Hewitt. "If anybody would give this guy enough money to put what he wants on the screen, I think he could make quite a good picture."

SPECIAL EFFECTS: Several factors contributed to Hewitt's decision to "remake" *The Time Travelers*. "The money became available quickly and the fastest way to get a script together was to imitate his AIP film," Fred Olen Ray explained in *The New Poverty Row*. "This way he could instigate the wide range of effects he loved to create and make a picture based on one of his own stories." Considering the circumstances, Hewitt managed to get a surprisingly large quantity of effects on the screen. "*Journey* was Hewitt's first attempt at using the blue screen traveling matte technique," Ray stated, "which allowed actors to walk in front of his static matted view screens." Hewitt also stretched the effects budget by reusing some material from earlier films. There is a bit of footage from *One Million B.C.*, although most of the lizard shots are in color and seem to have been filmed just for this picture. The futuristic spaceport set seen in the Time Lab's view screen is from *The Time Travelers*, and for some reason we even get one fleeting shot of the "bat-rat-spider" from Ib Melchior's *The Angry Red Planet* (1959).

Journey to the Centre of the Earth

not viewed 1909, France. BW, Silent.

CREDITS: *Director* Segundo De Chomon.

Inaugural filming of Jules Verne's novel apparently contained some dinosaur scenes, but is now thought to be a lost film. Somewhat in the mold of Georges Méliès, the Spanish-born De Chomon was a cinema pioneer who made a number of early "fantastic films," including *Le Scarabée d'or* (*The Golden Beetle*, 1907) and *Voyage à la Planète Jupiter* (1908).

Jungle Manhunt

"When it comes to fool things, he's in a class by himself."

½ 1951, USA-Columbia. BW, 65m.

CREDITS: *Director* Lew Landers. *Producer* Sam Katzman. *Written for the Screen by* Samuel Newman.
CAST: *Jungle Jim* Johnny Weissmuller. *Ann Lawrence* Sheila Ryan. *Bob Miller* Bob Waterfield. *Bono* Rick Vallin. *Dr. Mitchell Heller* Lyle Talbot.

AD LINE: "See Johnny, a pal, and a glamor gal rout THE RAVAGING SKELETON MEN!"

There's trouble in Jungle Jim's neighborhood. A tribe of "bad natives," led by a renegade white man and escorted by the spectral "skeleton men," are abducting the able-bodied men from all the peaceful villages. Meanwhile, freelance photographer Ann Lawrence arrives in the jungle in search of fighter pilot–star quarterback Bob Miller, missing since World War II. When the Caucasian ringleader shoots Jim's native friend Bono in the right buttock, the pals get riled and team up with Ann and Tamba the chimp to investigate. Jim and company witness a raid on the Zengali village, but suddenly Bob Miller appears and turns away the attackers with exploding coconuts. Jim's group returns with Miller to "his village," a happy hamlet to which he has introduced modern advances like clotheslines and sidewalks.

The ex-quarterback joins Jim's team and they venture into the forbidding "Monagichi Land." Passing some uninterested prehistoric reptiles, they reach the headquarters of the bad natives and their white leader, Dr. Mitchell Heller, I.C. (Industrial Chemist). The evil Heller has found a way to use "what we call magma ... a hot solution of liquids and gasses" to make flawless synthetic diamonds. The captured natives serve as slave labor to mine the magma rock, but its deleterious radiation forces Heller to continually replenish his work force as the men die off. Heller threatens Ann, suggesting that she not "exchange the glow of beauty for the glow of

156 • *Jungle Manhunt*

Quarterback Bob Miller and photographer Ann Lawrence (Bob Waterfield, Sheila Ryan) critique the alligator-lizard battle from *One Million B.C.*, in a comic-book-style photograph digest of *Jungle Manhunt* published in the French magazine *Photo Adventures*.

anachronistic. The dialogue has Rick Vallin uttering lines like "many moons now, war drums beat," and "Jungle Jim, our friend, fight bad natives, drive away skeleton men." The skeleton men are supposedly used by Heller to terrify his superstitious victims into helplessness, but the problem is that most people won't find three studio extras doing silly walks while wearing dime-store Halloween costumes to be very terrifying. The picture's big comic moment has Jim swimming underwater and pulling on Tamba's fishing line, prompting the poor ape to think he has a bite and do a bunch of backflips. The mismatch between the new footage and the numerous stock shots (including a battle between an octopus and a shark — in an African river?) is staggering. The rear projection shots are clumsier than those in the cheapest Monogram Studios western, and all the raids on the "different" villages are the same footage of the same people fleeing the same huts burning with the same flames, with Lyle Talbot's pith helmet peeking over the same darned bush.

It's natural to compare *Jungle Manhunt* to the other Weissmuller film with *One Million B.C.* footage: *Tarzan's Desert Mystery*. Both have a similar type of female lead — a spunky, big-city gal who finds herself totally out of her element — but the results are total opposites. Nancy Kelly in *Desert Mystery* had a well-written, humorous role and played it wonderfully; Sheila Ryan gets a stale, completely phony character and can do nothing to salvage the situation. All the acting is abysmal, lethargically led by L.A. Rams quarterback Waterfield (the "famed gridiron star making his screen debut," as the publicity stated). The "lost world" elements have even

radioactivity," but Jim escapes with the girl and dynamites the river channel above the mine. As water floods Heller's lab, Bono leads the laborers to safety. Heller flees, but Jim pursues him to a cliff edge and the portly villain topples over the side. With Heller dead and the natives liberated (not to mention irradiated), the lovestruck Ann tosses her camera and announces she's staying in the jungle with Bob.

COMMENTARY: *Jungle Manhunt* is an archetype of everything that's bad about no-budget, assembly-line series entries. The filmmakers show contempt for their audience at every turn, apparently assuming that they could put literally anything on the screen and still make a few dollars.

Not a frame of *Jungle Manhunt* makes sense. The "African" tribes are obviously not African — they actually look like Hollywood-stereotyped Native Americans or Polynesians or maybe a cross between the two, making the scenes simultaneously insulting and less to do with the story than in *Desert Mystery*, and Lyle Talbot's sci-babble explanation of how he makes fake diamonds out of lava rock, cold water, and table sugar set a gibberish standard that wouldn't be topped until Jeff Morrow's "mu-meson" speech in *The Giant Claw* (1957).

Jungle Manhunt is the kind of twaddle that gives B-movies a bad name. It's nothing but superficial trappings and cardboard cutouts, apathetically regurgitated without a glimmer of creativity. Leslie Halliwell's *The Filmgoer's Companion* says of the Jungle Jim series: "It started ineptly and quickly became ridiculous." True of the series, true of this installment.

SPECIAL EFFECTS: Although the only "dinosaur" scene in *Jungle Manhunt* is the infamous fight from *One Million B.C.*, an all-new dinosaur sequence was actually filmed for this picture. Ellis Burman, maker of the dinosaur suits seen in *Unknown Island* three years earlier, fashioned an allosaur/tyrannosaur type of costume which was worn by a stuntman for a man-against-dino fight scene with Weissmuller. Author Don Glut published a photo of the suit, hanging on a rack in Burman's workshop, in his wonderful *Dinosaur Scrapbook*, and many reports state that some shots from this sequence are present in the *Jungle Manhunt* preview trailer. This reviewer has been unsuccessful in locating a print of the trailer for confirmation.

Cutting the battle from the release print must have been an eleventh-hour decision, because the film's advertising art is dominated by illustrations of the dinosaur—looking almost exactly like Burman's suit in the aforementioned photo. "His latest opponent is a dinosaur!" Columbia's press release promised. "The only weapon Johnny uses on the out-sized monster is a smallish hunting knife, but when he gets through with it, the dinosaur is as dead as the fabled dodo!" The ad copy had already lost credibility, though, by describing the *One Million B.C.* stock-footage combatants as a "Trachodon ... 40 feet tall and 100 feet long," and a "towering finned-back Stegosaurus, even larger!"

Jurassic Park

"Attractions so astounding, that they'll capture the imagination of the entire planet."

***½ 1993, USA-Universal/Amblin. C, 127m.

CREDITS: *Director* Steven Spielberg. *Producers* Kathleen Kennedy, Gerald R. Molen, Lata Ryan (associate), Colin Wilson (associate). *Screenplay* Michael Crichton and David Koepp; based on the novel by Michael Crichton. *Full-Motion Dinosaurs* Dennis Muren, A.S.C. *Live-Action Dinosaurs* Stan Winston. *Dinosaur Supervisor* Phil Tippett. *Special Dinosaur Effects* Michael Lantieri. *Co-Visual Effects Supervisor* Mark A. Z. Dippe.

CAST: *Dr. Alan Grant* Sam Neill. *Dr. Ellie Sattler* Laura Dern. *Dr. Ian Malcolm* Jeff Goldblum. *John Hammond* Sir Richard Attenborough. *Robert Muldoon* Bob Peck. *Donald Gennaro* Martin Ferraro. *Dennis Nedry* Wayne Knight. *Alexis "Lex" Murphy* Ariana Richards. *Tim Murphy* Joseph Mazzello. *Ray Arnold* Samuel L. Jackson. *Dr. Henry Wu* B. D. Wong.

AD LINE: "An adventure 65 million years in the making!"

At a dinosaur dig somewhere in the Badlands of Montana, paleontologist Alan Grant and his colleague (and significant other), paleobotanist Ellie Sattler, are hard at work excavating a Velociraptor skeleton when they are paid an unexpected visit by billionaire philanthropist John Hammond. The genial Hammond invites doctors Grant and Sattler to his private Costa Rican island for the weekend, for the purpose of inspecting—and hopefully endorsing—his new "biological preserve." When they arrive, joined by lawyer Donald Gennaro and mathematician Ian Malcolm, they discover to their astonishment that Hammond's wildlife park features living dinosaurs, cloned from DNA recovered from ancient insects preserved in amber. Accompanied by Hammond's two young grandchildren Lex and Tim, the group prepares to experience the first-ever tour of Jurassic Park.

Unbeknownst to the expectant group, Hammond's computer programmer, Dennis

Nedry, has been bribed by a rival genetics company into stealing some dinosaur embryos, and his treachery helps set into motion a series of events which ultimately leads to the escape of the park's dinosaurian denizens. A terrifying attack by a Tyrannosaurus rex leaves Malcolm injured, Gennaro dead, and Doctor Grant and the kids lost in the wilds of the park. Nedry, meanwhile, sees his scheme disintegrate before becoming the helpless prey of a venomous Dilophosaurus. After a peaceful, wondrous encounter with a massive brachiosaur, Grant and the courageous youngsters manage to make their way back to the visitors center. Ellie, with Jurassic Park game warden Robert Muldoon riding shotgun, succeeds in restoring power to the park's systems, but Muldoon fatally underestimates the cunning of the pack-hunting "raptors." Left in the supposed safety of the visitors center by Grant, the children are horrified to realize that a pair of raptors have found their way into the building. Keeping their wits, the kids escape the huge kitchen through which the raptors have stalked them, and young Lex's computer know-how enables the group to restore communications and call for the rescue helicopter. Finally, with the raptors inexorably closing in and the humans hopelessly trapped in the central rotunda, the ancient predatory instincts of the tyrannosaur suddenly and ironically provide the group with a fleeting avenue of deliverance. Safely aboard the 'copter, the survivors are left to reflect on John Hammond's grand but tragic vision.

COMMENTARY: "I guarantee that you will believe that the dinosaurs are real," Steven Spielberg boldly said just before the release of *Jurassic Park*. It's hard to imagine a riskier promise for a dinomovie director to make, but as the film's astonishing popularity attests, it was one he was able to keep. *Jurassic Park* defined a new plateau not only for dinosaur movies but for the entire field of special and visual effects, while resoundingly reaffirming the indefatigable popularity of dinosaurs.

Spielberg has probably not received due credit for his direction of *Jurassic Park*, and has even been accused of rehashing his own earlier efforts. All great directors have themes, symbols, and imagery that become their hallmarks, yet John Ford has seldom been chastised for "rehashing" his use of Monument Valley. So if the raptor-cage prologue is actually a re-envisioning of the opening of *Jaws*, that's okay, because it's just as gripping this time around. Spielberg has mentioned that his affection for *King Kong* is "one of the reasons he wanted to make *Jurassic Park*," and on a pure adventure-film level *Jurassic* is often equal to its classic predecessor. For instance, one of the many masterful elements of *Kong* is its pacing, with every armrest-grabbing, breath-holding sequence counterbalanced by a lower-octane interlude, perfectly timed to allow the audience to regroup and get ready for the next adrenaline rush. The same is emphatically true of *Jurassic Park*.

Spielberg effectively borrows from not only his own *oeuvre* but also from earlier dinosaur adventures — enough to pay homage to the genre's history without becoming a ham-handed self-parody (like 1998's dreadful big-budget *Godzilla*). There's a *Kong* reference, naturally, and a banner that repeats the title of a Jim Danforth dino favorite, but there are also images that recall *The Valley of Gwangi*, *The Beast from 20,000 Fathoms*, *Dinosaurus!*, and even *Hatari!*, when the T. rex runs alongside and head-butts the speeding jeep. (We'll see more of the *Hatari!* factor in the *Jurassic* sequel.) Spielberg has a seemingly infallible knack for using lighting and timing and point of view to tap into an audience's basic senses, and milk every drop of excitement a scene has to offer.

The director realized from the beginning that the dinosaurs had to be the stars, but at the same time the audience *had* to identify with and root for the people. He counted on the skills of his actors to achieve this, and they didn't let him down. Jeff Goldblum is the ideal Ian Malcolm, and the same is true for Richard Attenborough as Ham-

Stan Winston's amazing T. rex gets in the face of Dr. Grant and Lex Murphy (Sam Neill, Ariana Richards) during the mesmerizing "Main Road Sequence."

mond — in fact, not enough has been said about the excellence of Attenborough's performance. Sam Neill is an extremely engaging actor, and Laura Dern surprised some folks by how easily she shifted gears to play an action-adventure heroine. The only thing wrong with Samuel L. Jackson's appearance is that he's not on-screen enough; ditto for the hawk-eyed Bob Peck as Muldoon. Ariana Richards and Joseph Mazzello are terrific in physically demanding roles, succeeding at the difficult task of portraying brave, intelligent children without becoming unnaturally and irritatingly precocious.

Then, there's Wayne Knight as Nedry, the picture's most damaging misstep. The problem is not the casting of Knight — he seems a great choice — but it's puzzling and a bit disappointing that the filmmakers fell into the clichéd trap of making the villain into a buffoon. It is truly, as Roger Ebert wrote, "as if one of the Three Stooges wandered into the story." Why not make him a sly, cunning, formidable sneak, and play up his cleverness with a slick, James Bondian sequence of him defeating security? Instead, he's made to squint and bumble, and we're asked to believe that the guy who set up the park's entire security protocol wouldn't recognize a Dilophosaurus as a dangerous animal.

Enough Nedry nitpicking; on to the dinosaurs. Maybe paleontologist Robert Bakker said it best: "The dinosaurs just knocked my socks off." The *Jurassic Park* dinos do not merely come after you, they spring from bushes and leap through ceilings and peer through windows and chase down jeeps and *breathe right down your neck*. The main villains, the T. rex and Velociraptors, are an inspired combination. It is quite unthinkable that *Jurassic Park* could have been made without the tyrant lizard king, and the cunning raptors are its perfect complement, being everything that the rex is not. Without broaching the issue of whether "more real" equals "better" (I for one cannot state that the *Jurassic* raptors are "better" than Ray Harryhausen's *One Million Years B.C.* allosaur), it must be conceded that these cinematic saurians were the closest we'd ever come to seeing living, breathing dinosaurs before our eyes.

Jurassic stirred some controversy by its very realism. Was it right to make a film that young kids would so desperately want to see and then make it too scary and intense for them? In the first place, kids are generally more savvy than grownups realize, though *Jurassic* certainly should be off limits for some youngsters. All in all the filmmakers probably did the best job possible of toning down Michael Crichton's gruesome prose without sacrificing the stomping and chomping a good dinomovie requires. In fact, we can thank Phil Tippett for one of the picture's most famous moments. Originally, the hapless Gennaro was to be bitten and then immediately lifted out of frame, and it was Tippett who emphatically told Steven Spielberg and Kathleen Kennedy, "we should see the guy just getting eaten, getting shaken, you know? You've gotta have a dinosaur eat a man in your movie!"

For all the terrific predators, the scenes of the gentler dinosaurs are just as grand. The Gallimimus stampede is brilliantly constructed to kick-start the adrenal glands. The Triceratops sequence is a minimasterpiece, and when the massive, magnificent Brachiosaurus first filled the screen, I was thinking *exactly* what Doctor Grant was saying: "It's ... it's a *dinosaur*." The brachiosaur's appearance, followed by the expansive "vista" shot of the herds gathering by the lake, all backed by John Williams' sweeping score ... they don't call it "movie magic" for nothing.

It isn't just the "money" scenes that made *Jurassic* a box-office phenomenon and a home video bestseller, it's everything. It's all the neat little details that just ring true, like the "Mr. DNA" cartoon that painlessly explains the scientific premise and which is, of course, just how a real "Jurassic Park" would do it. (It's also how George Pal did it in 1950's groundbreaking *Destination Moon*, using a Woody Woodpecker cartoon made especially for the film to explain the princi-

Tim, Alan, and Lex (Joseph Mazzello, Sam Neill, Ariana Richards) enjoy a peaceful interlude with a mammoth Brachiosaurus, a moment of wonder and awe sadly missing from the *Jurassic* sequel.

ples of rocketry.) It is the nuances of the dinosaurs, the brachiosaurs singing like whales, and the raptor's primitive confusion after slamming into Lex's reflection. It's the way the computer-generated dinosaurs have such palpable weight, the way their environment reacts so believably to their actions, and even the scenes that have no dinosaurs at all. Stan Winston, effects master and lifelong dino fan, once pointed out an overlooked fact. "The fallacy about this film was that the only things that made it work were the dinosaurs," he said. "Yes, the 14 minutes of dinosaurs are unlike anything you've seen before, but it's important to remember that we're talking about a film that runs over two hours. You're involved with it because of the way Steven Spielberg put it together." He put it together so well, in fact, that we don't merely enjoy, we almost *believe*.

PEOPLE AND PRODUCTION: One thing that nearly everybody — including author Michael Crichton — says about the novel *Jurassic Park* is that it seemed destined to be a movie. "When I was writing the novel, I was conscious of movies because that's where people's ideas about dinosaurs come from," Crichton asserted. "As I was working on it, I was thinking, 'For whoever reads this, movies will be their source of thinking, rather than the science and the ideas I'm drawing on.' On the other hand, there was this hope on my part. I knew the book would make a wonderful movie, and I couldn't help thinking, 'Wouldn't it be nice if...'" Almost as soon as Crichton finished the book, the wheels which would see his "if" become reality began turning.

A number of studios dangled top directors as bait and entered the competition to make *Jurassic*. Four of the finalists who emerged were 20th Century–Fox with Joe Dante, Warner Bros. with Tim Burton, Tri-Star with Richard Donner, and Universal with Steven Spielberg. But Crichton didn't want to merely auction off the book to the highest bidder. "There was a higher offer than Universal/Amblin, a much higher offer," he stated, but he believed that Spielberg had the best chance of actually getting the film *made*. For his part, Spielberg had been flirting with a desire to return to some of the genre territory of his earlier films like *Jaws* and *Close Encounters of the Third Kind*, and one *Fangoria* writer cheekily stated that he would also be attempting to "reanimate some old dinosaur bones—and his post–*Hook* career."

Producer Kathleen Kennedy clearly realized that *Jurassic*, for all its potential, was not a guaranteed success story. "There was always an element of fear on our part from the moment we decided to make this film," she told author Marc Shapiro. "Our major concern was the dinosaurs and how we wanted them to come across on screen. So on that level, we were constantly asking ourselves, 'Can this work?'" One factor that would determine if it could work was the effectiveness with which Crichton's novel could be turned into a filmable, affordable screenplay. Crichton himself began the task, distilling his book down to movie-sized proportions, after which Malia Scotch Marmo wrote a complete draft. For various reasons, Steven Spielberg felt that her take on the story was "a miss," and David Koepp was brought in. While writing what would eventually become the filmed version, Koepp sought the input of his predecessor. "Malia was very helpful," Koepp said in the book *The Making of Jurassic Park*. "If the situation had been reversed, I don't know that I would have been the same," he admitted. As with any hotly anticipated film, information began circulating long before many details were even set. One "preview" article reported that "audiences will get glimpses of a total of 12 different species," including such characters as the Triassic Herrerasaurus and the unusual carnivore, Baryonyx. Ultimately, the film's dino roster was reduced to seven.

Since one cannot make a dinosaur movie without dinosaurs (*Sound of Horror* notwithstanding), an early priority was selecting the artists who would populate the park with its prehistoric stars. Phil Tippett recalled to this author the first day he was contacted. "Kathy Kennedy calls up and says, 'Wouldn't you like to have a lot of fun working on a dinosaur picture?' And, at about that point in my career I knew that the *last* thing movies were, was fun when you were working on them. But, I said, 'yeah, sure, okay.'" It didn't take long for Tippett and his colleagues to conclude that Steven Spielberg was the right director for this movie. "I didn't realize how together he is on every aspect of filmmaking," Tippett commented. "He sees things nobody else sees." Michael Lantieri concurred. "He clearly wanted to take the idea of a dinosaur film to lengths it had not been taken to before," Lantieri said, "or he would not make the movie."

Spielberg has discussed his philosophy of choosing "really good actors" instead of mega-stars when it came to casting *Jurassic Park*, and Sam Neill acknowledged a fondness for prehistoric creatures. "I must admit that just the idea of being in a dinosaur movie, period, did have a certain appeal," he stated. Neill and Jeff Goldblum had some genre experience, but a big, FX-filled summer blockbuster was definitely *terra incognita* for Laura Dern. "Let's face it," she told Marc Shapiro, "*Jurassic Park* is not *Rambling Rose*. It's a dinosaur movie, and that alone makes it completely different." She mentioned that it was Nicolas Cage who helped convince her to take the plunge. "He stopped me in mid-sentence and said, 'Are you crazy? You not only get to be in a dinosaur movie, but the *ultimate* dinosaur movie, and you're asking if I think you should do it? Take it!'" Though Spielberg maintained that he largely got his first choices, other names did pop up: Richard Dreyfuss, Kurt Russell, and Harrison Ford as Grant, Daryl Hannah and Robin Wright as Ellie, Sean Connery as Hammond, even Kevin Costner as Malcolm. James Earl Jones, considered for the Park's "tour guide" voice-overs eventually done by Richard Kiley, ended up hosting the film's *Making of* video documentary.

Though Dern enthusiastically stated

that *Jurassic* was a great experience, that doesn't mean that she and fellow female cast member Ariana Richards didn't endure some icky moments. Dern well remembered having to search through a pile of dino droppings. "I don't know what they were made of, and I didn't ask," the actress recalled. "But Michael Lantieri definitely made them look real. There was stuff in those droppings that was truly terrifying." Miss Richards' sizable genre-film résumé may have somewhat prepared the young actress for her share of unpleasantries. "I got sneezed on," she said with a smile. "It was made of this clear, yellowish goo that they put in a big tank and added a little bit of spinach to. The stuff was shot out of the tank with a big blast of air. The scene took four takes, and it was really disgusting." Not as disgusting but surely much more uncomfortable was another physically challenging sequence: the "Main Road" attack. "We filmed the scene for about two weeks and we were covered in mud and rain was pouring down on us," Miss Richards recalled. "There also was a huge fan that blew cold air on us. That was the hardest part of all."

Not all of the production's harsh environmental elements were the work of the FX department. Just as the location shoot in Hawaii was about to wrap, hurricane Iniki made a dramatic turn worthy of a plot twist in a cheesy movie and slammed into the island. Iniki made Ariana Richards' 13th birthday a memorable one. "Yeah, that was a pretty scary thing," she recalled. "I think the worst part was after the hurricane, when we went out to look at everything, because it was so devastated." But the nervous hours were no doubt ameliorated by the camaraderie of the entire company. Coconspirators Sam Neill and Jeff Goldblum were even known to perpetrate a few practical jokes as they returned to the hotel after a day's shoot. "We were covered in blood and dirt, and Jeff had one leg all ripped up and in a splint," Neill devilishly revealed. "As we approached a big party of tourists ... we would start to argue about 100 meters away from the group. The argument would get more physical the closer we got, until I would start kicking him in his bad leg, and cursing him at the same time. This had a miraculous effect on the tourists."

Though the FX personnel often get the attention, there were other people equally vital to the "look" of the film, like cinematographer Dean Cundey. Having shot effects-heavy pictures before, he knew many of the concerns and pitfalls. "Getting mechanical creatures to look real is always a challenge," Cundey stated. "No matter how good the creatures are, if they're lit very flat and shown in static shots, you have a chance to look and examine and discover why it doesn't look quite right." His work on a groundbreaking Robert Zemeckis film was also a great teacher when it came to shooting things that weren't there. "My experience photographing *Who Framed Roger Rabbit?* was valuable from that standpoint," Cundey continued. "You develop a sense of what it would be like adding a two-dimensional image into film at a later time. How you can help it to look real with lighting and camera position."

One of the first people to officially join the *Jurassic* company was production designer Rick Carter. His three-year stint included designing "the overall look of the world" and acting as liaison between Spielberg (still finishing *Hook*) and the *Jurassic* FX team. "The development of the script went hand in hand with the production design, because both had to key off each other," Carter explained. "We had to break it down into things that were doable without stripping it so badly that you didn't have a movie — because you have to deliver on the epic level." To add an "epic" finishing touch to *Jurassic Park*, Spielberg again tabbed his favorite score composer, John Williams. "John and I [hadn't] made a movie like this together since *Jaws*," Spielberg stated on the soundtrack's liner notes. "It was a lot of fun for us to revisit a genre that we got such a kick out of 18 years ago."

Steven Spielberg, while always finding

Dennis Muren sights over a model Brachiosaurus in preparation for filming background plates for *Jurassic Park*. The white sphere assists the digital artists in matching the location lighting.

complimentary things to say about the dino-movies of yesteryear, made it clear that *Jurassic Park* would be a different kind of animal. "This isn't *Gorgo*, this isn't *Godzilla*," he said in the *Making of Jurassic Park* documentary. "This isn't *The Beast from 20,000 Fathoms*, this isn't *Dinosaurus!* and this isn't *The Lost World*." Not too surprisingly, however, he later sounded uncannily like another famous dinosaur film director. "The audience has to believe in order to take the journey," he said. "And I think an audience *will* buy into the most far-fetched fantasy, if it's done seriously and with a lot of credibility." Somewhere, I'll bet Eugène Lourié is saying "*Je suis de votre avis, mon ami*" ... and smiling.

SPECIAL EFFECTS: In a decade when the term "dream team" became an overused phrase, *Jurassic Park* could legitimately claim the "dream team" of special effects wizards in Stan Winston, Phil Tippett, Dennis Muren, and Michael Lantieri. "We looked at all the creature people," associate producer Lata Ryan said just prior to the film's release. "The Henson group, Rob Bottin, Kevin Yagher, KNB, Industrial Light & Magic. We searched high and low." But the fearsome foursome seemed destined to come together.

Stan Winston (*The Terminator, Aliens, Terminator 2: Judgment Day*) was excited by the possibilities of *Jurassic* from day one. "Every one of us who does the kind of work that I do, and that all the artists and technicians in my studio do, are huge dinosaur fans," Winston told this author. "And we wanted this to be the most *legitimate* dinosaur movie ever made." Winston's team drew on reference material from people like paleontologist Robert Bakker and paleo-artist Gregory Paul, as well as the film's credited advisors, Jack Horner and Don Lessem. "The script is pretty close to reality," Lessem asserted. "Spielberg wanted this to be as accurate as possible, and always took our suggestions into consideration. In many instances, he changed things on the spot to conform to what was scientifically true." Still, the only thing known with certainty about dinosaurs is the skeletal structure. "So, the designs," Winston concluded, "although they are paleontologically correct, are truly designs from Stan Winston Studio of what we felt a dinosaur was, based on all of the factual information that we could gather. It's a matter of looking at it and going, 'You know what? It feels right. It looks right.' And it's right because it *feels real*."

Winston and his team had done beautiful work in many earlier films, but for *Jurassic*, they surpassed themselves. The first Winston creation filmed was the ailing Triceratops, which was actually packed off to Kauai and shot on location. "The Triceratops had nine people coordinating every minor and subtle movement to bring it to life," Winston said back in 1993. "It's a perfect performance." For the stealthy Velociraptors, Winston's crew used a variety of techniques including a '90's take on the venerable man-in-a-suit method. There was also a "walking rig"—a suit, complete from the torso down—to allow the audience to see the raptor's feet touching the ground, a completely mechanical full-scale puppet, and a precisely detailed head and neck incorporating a counterweighted system (like a Steadicam camera mount) which resulted in uncannily fluid movements. A similar strategy was used for many of the Dilophosaurus shots.

The Winston group's *pièce de résistance* was the titanic T. rex. "Obviously, it was all a challenge, but the biggest challenge was the biggest dinosaur," Winston told me. "You know, in all of the books we've talked about it being 40 feet from the tip of its nose to the tip of its tail; the reality is it was like around 37 feet. But it was a big mother." Even with the technology available, making such a massive mechanism behave like a natural animal was incredibly challenging. "It was full size, and weighed *tons*, and had to move and be organic," Winston continued. When it swallowed that poor goat, it was "full-size, live-action goat eating," as Winston put it. "What we had to do was use all of the technology that people had used previously ... but then go beyond that and bring our kind of organic life, and attention to detail, and performance to these characters so that they would in no way look *robotic*." Special effects buffs have read the technical details of the flight-simulator-inspired motion base and the "waldo" telemetry control system, but it isn't the hardware that brought the rex to life. "Again," Winston reiterated, "it was back to performance." Although ILM's cutting-edge computer imagery garnered the lion's share of the media and popular attention, almost *two thirds* of the dino footage in *Jurassic Park* is actually of Stan Winston's animatronic actors.

Phil Tippett (*Star Wars, Robocop, Starship Troopers*) was one of the first FX artists contacted regarding *Jurassic Park*, and his contribution turned out to have enormous impact on the dinosaurs. "Their performance, their lifestyle, their movement, was greatly enhanced by the knowledge and understanding of Phil Tippett," Stan Winston emphatically told me. Unlike Winston, though, Tippett was not immediately enthralled by the project. He and Paul Verho even were still trying to get their dinosaur picture for Disney going, and besides, Steven Spielberg had voiced his hopes of doing *all* of *Jurassic*'s dinosaur scenes with full-size, physical creatures. "It really wasn't my forte," Tippett recalled to the author. "I said, 'if that doesn't work out, give me a call back. I'd like to work on it, but, giant robotic dinosaurs—I don't want 'em to fall on me.'" Luckily, producer Kathleen Kennedy did call Phil back. "What Kathy hired me to do was bridge that gap between cinema and natural history, and as it worked out for me, I'd done all of my homework previously, since I was a kid," Tippett enthused. "When I was working on *Prehistoric Beast*, every Thursday all the paleontologists at UC–Berkeley would come by my house or I'd go over to their labs, and we'd go out and drink beer, and have hamburgers, and talk about dinosaurs."

The escaped T. rex eyes young Lex Murphy (Ariana Richards) in an all-time classic shot from *Jurassic Park*.

When it became clear that the technology did not yet exist for building a full-scale, head-to-toe, *walking* tyrannosaur, Tippett came on board. He thought he would be creating a variety of full-body dinosaur scenes — to complement Winston's on-set performers — using his specialty and a staple of the dino-genre since the silent days: stop-motion animation. Specifically, he and his animators would use "Go-motion," a stop-motion derivative developed and honed at ILM and used with great results in films such as *Dragonslayer*. With Go-motion, a computer records an animator's manipulations of the puppet and then uses a model mover to repeat them during filming. This allows the puppet to move while the shutter is open and greatly diminishes stop-motion's characteristic "strobe" effect. Another intriguing idea was mentioned by Dennis Muren. "We did some tests in which we added blur to regular stop-motion using one of our morphing programs," Muren said in *Cinefex*. Though the tests were "very promising," all of the model animation plans were about to become history.

Dennis Muren (*E.T.*, *Terminator 2*, *The Abyss*) had taken a year off following his work on *The Abyss* to "learn everything I could about computers," as he put it. Beginning with the "Glass Man" in *Young Sherlock Holmes*, and progressing through the morphing effects in *Willow*, the pseudopod in *The Abyss*, and the T-1000 in *Terminator 2*, the ILM computer graphics group had been steadily building to the point that would make possible the digital dinosaurs of *Jurassic Park*. But as preproduction ramped up, nobody — including Muren — knew just what they could and couldn't do. "I spearheaded a CG test for *Death Becomes Her* for the scene where Meryl Streep has her head on backwards—and the skin on that looked pretty good," Muren recalled. "Maybe we were ready to try something bigger."

Early on, ILM's planned contributions were limited to digital "rod removals," compositing chores and, possibly, a CGI dinosaur stampede. "The initial path that we were going down was to build a lot of the stuff as Go-motion puppets and do the sequences that way," Phil Tippett stated. "There was one big stampede sequence that was designed primarily in long shot, that ILM was going to handle." But some surreptitious experimentation by ILM's Steve "Spaz" Williams began to show the technology's power. "Throughout the course of their development process, as ILM was developing their dinosaurs, they just kept pushing their camera in closer and closer and closer," Tippett said, "and the thing held up, and it looked incredibly interesting." So interesting in fact, that Spielberg made the gambler's decision to axe the Go-motion and commit totally to CGI for the animated scenes. "Dennis had kept me abreast of the evolution of this stuff, and by the time they got to their final test I could certainly see the writing on the wall," Tippett continued. "It was certainly a very devastating point in my life, in that it was very clear to me that the revolution had hit, and that these techniques we'd been using all these years had really seen their day." But the unique talents of traditional animators still had something to offer. "At that time, the computer graphics guys had pretty much done, like, flying logos and things for commercials, and they hadn't done any real behavioral animation," Tippett pointed out. "And the only folks that had, were stop-motion animators."

The need to bring hands-on animators into the virtual world resulted in the development of the Dinosaur Input Device, or DID. "During *Terminator 2* I had discussed with Phil an idea for building such a device," Dennis Muren recalled. "*Jurassic Park* presented the ideal opportunity to finally do it." Put simply, the four DIDs—two raptors and two tyrannosaurs—were stop-motion armatures interfaced with computers through encoders placed at all the pivot points. As Tippett revealed, the plan was for his unit to "deal with stop-motion through these input devices that Craig Hayes and Brian Knep and Rick Sayre developed. Tom St. Amand was very involved with the construction [of the armatures], and Rick and Brian were involved with the development of the software." The DIDs were used to animate a total of 15 shots for the "Main Road" and "Kitchen/Raptor" sequences.

Tippett's multiple responsibilities as the "dinosaur guru guy"—his term—left the actual animation duties to veterans Tom St. Amand and Randy Dutra. "There are very few CG animators," Dennis Muren observed in 1993, "but there are lots of great stop-motion animators. Between Phil and Tom and Randy, we had a [stop-motion] team that we knew could deliver." Once the main DID animation was recorded, the "secondary animation" was added by Tippett Studios' Adam Valdez. "I would animate the fingers, toes, and mouth ... the DID armatures had only a spine, neck, tail, legs and arms," Valdez explained in *Cinefex*. "With this system, we had the best of both worlds—we could get the energy and impact of a stop-motion shot, but we could also continue working on it after the first pass."

Few people have more appreciation for the art of stop-motion than Dennis Muren, but he also recognized that CGI has its own strengths. "One of the advantages of CGI is that shots can go on for a while," Muren commented in *Fangoria*. "It gave us an opportunity to understand the characters. We could handle shots like those in a wildlife documentary, and that helps sustain the believability of these animals." The final test was the viewing public—and their efforts passed with honors. "The ultimate experience of what we've done is that the audience is unaware of the technology and just gets into the spirit of what we've created."

Michael Lantieri (*Death Becomes Her, Hook, The Flintstones*) is sometimes the overlooked member of the dream team, but his

Phil Tippett alongside one of the Velociraptor DIDs — the "Dinosaur Input Device" which helped bring traditional animators into the digital age.

challenges in conceiving and supervising *Jurassic*'s multitude of physical effects were no less daunting than those of his colleagues. "They assembled a design team," he told *Cinefantastique*. "Stan, myself, Dennis, and Phil, with Rick Carter in the center to liaison between us. My primary responsibilities were the live-action effects … and interfacing between Stan and the visuals at ILM." One big challenge was the sheer weight of Winston's T. rex. "Just moving any of these things takes time," Lantieri emphasized. "Sometimes we had to open up the stage floor and anchor them into bedrock, because you're moving this weight around that could tear itself off the floor."

The entire *Jurassic Park* production company, including the FX team, had to work closely together and back each other up. Steven Spielberg's eleventh-hour decision to add a T. rex curtain call to the finale stretched the artists' intrepidity to the limit, and the sequence is a prime example of the coordination required. Spielberg's direction, the actors' performances, Phil Tippett's choreography, ILM's computer animation, Dean Cundey's cinematography, and Lantieri's floor effects all had to mesh perfectly. As Phil Tippett told me: "The timing beats on the rotunda sequence were very critical because there was one 8-perf camera and one 4-perf backup camera, and we had this one skeleton of the Tyrannosaurus that Michael Lantieri had rigged to blow up, and if we didn't get it right then it was all screwed." Obviously, rehearsals were many and meticulous. "I had a two-by-four with a big T. rex head target," Tippett continued. "We choreographed and rehearsed the '1, 2, 3, 4, BAH!' And we got it on the first take which, you know, we *had* to."

On-set safety was another major concern. "Every morning we had to say, 'We have a three-ton creature that is capable of maybe blowing a hose and falling on people," Lantieri said. "So every shot was meticulously storyboarded and we stuck very close to the boards." The presence of the formidable T. rex had some tangible benefits, as Stan Winston reminded me. "Any really great actor will let you know that fifty percent of acting is reacting," he said. "An actor will give a better performance if he is acting against another actor who is also giving a good performance, because it gives him something strong to react *to*." And his groundbreaking animatronic characters did just that. "The fact is, when those kids were in that car and that T. rex is coming down and smashing its way into it, that T. rex *really is* coming down and *is* smashing its way into it, and there's a danger factor there." Young Ariana Richards concurred, and often talked in interviews about "getting squashed" under the Plexiglas sunroof. "That was so frightening because the T. rex looked so real—it actually left teeth marks in the car because the mechanical head was really biting it," Richards told interviewer Tim Green. "That was the only moment that was really terrifying." Laura Dern also emphasized the value of having "real" dinosaurs. "We were all quite fortunate that the dinosaurs, in most scenes, were physically on the set with us," she said in *Fangoria*. "That made the whole process more honest."

All through the film's preproduction and production, the design team constantly brainstormed ideas, inventing new bits of business and discarding others. One concept for the Main Road sequence ultimately went unused because it was, as Phil Tippett told me, "just a little too weird." In the film, the T. rex attacks the "underbelly" of the tour vehicle. "We came up with, 'what would a tyrannosaur do?'" Tippett explained. "This Tyrannosaurus, if it's trying to get its prey out, would metaphorically think that the truck was an Ankylosaurus and the children were its heart, so it would whack it, turn it over on its back, and try to eviscerate it." From that point, though, the sequence departs from the original scenario. "We shot some scenes where it actually started to drag the car back to its lair," Tippett revealed, "and it ended up actually kind of being a little bit too creepy."

Jurassic was blessed with one asset that

films of its genre have historically been starved of: time. "Certainly we had a great deal of preproduction time to solve a number of issues," Tippett emphasized. "John Bell the art director and illustrator, and Dennis Muren and I would spend a great deal of time up in my studio, looking over Steven's storyboards, then going back and making alterations or suggestions, and we'd pass them back and forth and back and forth for three or four months." From these efforts, Tippett's studio "fleshed out" the storyboards with what were called "animatics." As Tippett elaborated, "the animatics were shot with stop-motion animation, with completely choreographed stop-motion puppets. They laid out the big action sequences: the raptor-kitchen and the main road attack, where we worked out and blocked a lot of the timing issues." Animated by Randy Dutra, Tom St. Amand, and Kim Blanchette, the animatics had great value from an artistic-creative standpoint, but had other benefits as well. "They really were the basis by which we were able to gain some speed on the set," Tippett pointed out, "and thereby save some money to do more special effects."

The four FX supervisors were only the senior members of a small army of artists and technicians, most of whom had a healthy appreciation of what had gone before. In creating the most believable dinosaur vocalizations ever heard in a movie, sound designer Gary Rydstrom used the same technique that Murray Spivack had employed for *King Kong* six decades earlier—he started with nature. "The first thing we did was record a lot of raw material from living animals," Rydstrom said in *The Making of Jurassic Park*, "and then piece them together in interesting ways." Sometimes, however, the attention paid to previous works was for the purpose of *avoiding* certain things. "I felt that the old ways of doing things had become a bit caricatured," co-visual effects supervisor Mark Dippe stated. "There are films with fantastic stop-motion, for instance, but it is always recognizable as stop-motion. I thought we could take advantage of new CG techniques and give the filmmaker a new kind of freedom."

The *Jurassic Park* dinosaurs are amazing not because of technology, but because of the talents of the human artists who brought them to life. One only has to look at other animatronic dinosaurs like those in the 1992 filming of Arthur Conan Doyle's *The Lost World*, or other CGI dinosaurs like those in the 1998 version of Conan Doyle's tale, to appreciate how superior *Jurassic* really is. The stunning effects work nabbed three Academy Awards: Winston, Muren, Tippett and Lantieri won for best visual effects, Gary Summers, Gary Rydstrom, Shawn Murphy, and Ron Judkins won for best sound, and Gary Rydstrom (again) and Richard Hymns won for sound effects editing. The effects also won the praise of dinosaur movie patriarch Ray Harryhausen. "Oh, yes! I enjoyed it," Ray told me. "I thought it was very entertaining, and it was remarkable what the computer could do. A wonderful job."

For all its photorealism and high-tech gloss, *Jurassic* shares a connection with the classic dinosaur films of yesteryear. "What you've got to remember," Michael Crichton asserted, "is that as a dinosaur movie, *Jurassic Park* comes from a tradition of all the other dinosaur movies we've ever seen." When I spoke with Stan Winston, he really brought Crichton's point home:

> The technology for *Jurassic* was really the technology used in *King Kong*—meaning that what they could do live, they did live. In *King Kong*, all they were capable of doing full size was the big head of Kong, and a hand that Fay Wray was in. We were able to create the entire dinosaurs, full size, and give them performance. In *King Kong*, what they couldn't do live, they did with animation—stop-motion animation. In *Jurassic Park*, what we couldn't do live, we did with animation—computer-generated animation. In today's world we have been able to take those technologies, put them together as they have been done in the past in classic movies, and do it in a way that is beyond what anybody had ever seen.

Lastly, Phil Tippett, who saw his entire artistic world changed by *Jurassic Park*, had this to say: "It was just one of those, you know, *metamorphosing* experiences, where the body dies and you're reborn! I mean, as horrific as it was for me, ultimately it panned out to be a lot of fun, and in many ways restored my faith in humanity."

Jurassic Park II see The Lost World: Jurassic Park

Jurassic Park III

"You mean there are two islands with dinosaurs on them?"

*** 2001, USA. Universal/Amblin. C, 91m.

CREDITS: *Director* Joe Johnston. *Producers* Kathleen Kennedy, Larry Franco, Steven Spielberg (executive), David Womark (associate), Cheryl A. Tkach (associate). *Written by* Peter Buchman and Alexander Payne and Jim Taylor; based on characters created by Michael Crichton. *Visual Effects Supervisor* Jim Mitchell. *Live Action Dinosaurs* Stan Winston. *Animation Supervisor* Dan Taylor. *Special Effects Consultant* Michael Lantieri.
CAST: *Dr. Alan Grant* Sam Neill. *Paul Kirby* William H. Macy. *Amanda Kirby* Téa Leoni. *Billy Brennan* Alessandro Nivola. *Eric Kirby* Trevor Morgan. *Udesky* Michael Jeter. *Cooper* John Diehl. *Nash* Bruce A. Young. *Dr. Ellie Sattler* Laura Dern.

It's the best of times and worst of times for Alan Grant. Amid his exciting fossil discoveries regarding Velociraptor intelligence, the living dinosaurs on Isla Sorna are deflating interest in traditional paleontology. So, when millionaire adventurer Paul Kirby and wife Amanda offer a dig-saving donation if the wary Grant and his protégé Billy Brennan will be their "guides" for an Isla Sorna flyover, they can't refuse.

Grant's suspicions that he's been lied to are soon confirmed. The Kirbys are actually divorced, are *not* wealthy, and their well-armed companions — Udesky, Nash, and Cooper — are there to serve as a three-man counter-dino force. The decent but desperate Kirbys are searching for their son Eric, who disappeared while parasailing with Amanda's thrillseeking beau. But within minutes of the rescue party's arrival, a gargantuan Spinosaurus kills Cooper and Nash, wrecks the plane, and demonstrates his might in a battle against none other than Tyrannosaurus rex.

The survivors set out for the coast and soon discover the remains of Amanda's boyfriend Ben — still wearing his parachute — adjacent to a clutch of Velociraptor eggs (two of which Billy secretly swipes). Entering, then quickly fleeing the raptor-infested cloning lab, the humans scramble for protection within a galloping hadrosaur herd. Back in the jungle the raptors kill Udesky, and only the still-alive Eric Kirby saves Grant from the same fate, but the family reunion is interrupted when the Spinosaurus breaches a containment fence and pursues the group to the edge of a great gorge. A boat moored on the river far below could provide transport to the coast, but Grant chillingly realizes that they have unknowingly entered a colossal "birdcage" just as a Pteranodon grabs Eric as food for its hungry chicks. Wearing Ben's repacked parachute, Billy daringly rescues the boy only to find himself chosen as the winged predators' substitute meal.

The group, minus Billy, sails downriver and emerges from the jungle to the sight of a magnificent brachiosaur herd on the sunlit riverbank. But the respite is shattered by the warble of Kirby's cell phone, previously swallowed by the spinosaur along with one of its human meals. Amanda gamely retrieves the dung-covered phone and Alan dials up Ellie Sattler, but he only has time to shout "Ellie! The river! Site B!" before the attacking Spinosaurus sinks the boat. Grant ignites the spilled, floating gasoline with a flare pistol and repels the predator, but the humans' ordeal continues back on land when they are trapped by the Velociraptors ... who want their eggs back. Amanda obliges and the creatures peacefully depart, hastened by Grant's imitation raptor-calls. The bedraggled bunch is at last met by Ellie Sattler and a veritable armada of Navy boats and helicopters, one of which bears the peck-marked but surviving Billy.

COMMENTARY: When I learned that Joe Johnston would be directing *Jurassic Park III*, my hopes for the film climbed significantly. Johnston had been an award-winning special effects artist before turning director, and had his *Jumanji* experience with computer-generated beasts, but what intrigued me most was the affection for classic movies so clearly demonstrated in his unfairly overlooked paean to Golden Age adventure, *The Rocketeer*. When *JP III* was finally released my optimism was, for the most part, rewarded.

Jurassic Park III is full of enjoyable homages to and reworkings of scenes from fondly-remembered genre films of years past. In tried-and-true monster-movie fashion, the super Spinosaurus (more on him later) is kept from full view at first, heightening anticipation for a clearer look. More specific nods — some surely intentional, others maybe not — include Eric "Carl Denham" Kirby's anti-dino gas bombs, the boy being carried off by a pterosaur as in *The Valley of Gwangi*, the Pteranodon chicks right out of *One Million Years B.C.*, and Grant's use of a flare pistol against a water-borne dinosaur — just like Jock Mahoney in *The Land Unknown*! Even the T. rex-versus-steam shovel sequence in *Dinosaurus!* is brought to mind when Paul Kirby takes refuge atop a derelict crane, but it probably is too much of a stretch to interpret the "Kirby" name as being inspired by James Franciscus' *Gwangi* character.

One sequence which is unquestionably an intentional tribute to earlier days is the T. rex-versus-Spinosaurus fight. "It's an homage to the Ray Harryhausen films, you know," Joe Johnston proudly admitted. "You always saw dinosaurs fight, and you always saw it in full frame. Most of them were wide shots, and you saw them up there wrestling with each other, and I wanted to recreate that in a modern version." He did an excellent job.

The only possible quibbles with the dino-duel are its brevity — I wanted it to go on for a while — and the fact that some dino-fans may rebel at seeing their beloved T. rex go down. Bigger is not necessarily better but the fin-backed (!) Spinosaurus is a delicious addition to the Isla Sorna roster, featured in two distinctly different but equally exciting sequences. The attack on the airplane is an adrenaline-charged gem of a set piece, gruesomely highlighted by the Spino's almost nonchalant administration of the *coup de grâce* to the unlucky Mr. Nash. The spinosaur's later destruction of the boat is more atmospheric (the firelight effects and aquatic milieu recall Jim Danforth's plesiosaur sequence in *When Dinosaurs Ruled the Earth*) and yet utterly believable. Spinosaurus and the related Baryonyx, with their crocodilian snouts and specialized teeth, are generally presumed to have been piscivorous (fish-eaters), so it makes sense that such animals would be at home in the water. This scene also brings to the screen, in amended form, Michael Crichton's terrific T. rex/river sequence planned for but axed from the original film.

The Spinosaurus is clearly the star of *JP III* but other species also have moments, especially the long-awaited Pteranodons. The sequence in the "birdcage" high above the gorge is not only the best sequence in part *III* but one of the best episodes in the *JP* series. Fog is an old standby of scary movies but it's seldom been used any better than when the humans get split up, unable to see each other at opposite ends of the decrepit bridge, and then the Pteranodon comes grotesquely *walking* out of the mist. "These creatures are beautiful in flight," Joe Johnston said, "but on all fours, if you can call it that, they're really quite hideous." It's an inspired idea from Johnston, providing what will surely become one of the franchise's touchstone images. It is interesting to note that, as the pterosaur carries Eric away, the ILM animators have pretty much equalled — but still not surpassed — Ray Harryhausen's remarkable "weighed down" illusion in *The Valley of Gwangi*.

Back fins are back in, style that is, with the sailbacked Spinosaurus at the top of the Isla Sorna food chain.

The Velociraptors, with redesigned skulls, bolder markings, and quills on their heads, are still terrific villains when properly used, as in the cloning lab sequence. The abandoned lab is a top-notch bit of set design and the dead, embryonic dinosaurs, suspended in vats of greenish fluid and looking like some sort of pitifully failed experiments, lend a creepy air of Frankenstein-like monstrousness to the segment. Other raptor scenes, such as their retrieval of the purloined eggs, are less effective and almost push the "intelligence" theme too far. Dinosaurs making cameo and supporting appearances include such returnees as Brachiosaurus, Stegosaurus, Parasaurolophus, and Compsognathus, along with newcomers like Corythosaurus, Ankylosaurus, and Ceratosaurus. Though none of them appear in full-blown sequences these guest dinos effectively give the feeling that Isla Sorna really is a "Lost World," and the red-hued, steely-eyed Ceratosaurus is a particularly cool-looking predator I hope to see more of in the future.

While the previously mentioned dinomovie homages come off very successfully and add to the matinee-adventure fun, there are a few moments that simply feel too familiar. The entire setup is in fact largely a replay of the first *Jurassic*, with Paul Kirby instead of John Hammond financially luring a reluctant Grant out of Montana. The Spinosaurus/airplane encounter, well-crafted as it is, is noticeably similar to the T. rex/jeep sequence in *Jurassic*, and the "gotcha!" scene where Amanda comes face to face with her decomposed boyfriend is a bit too "*Indiana Jones.*" Like *The Lost World*, this installment also skimps on the awe-and-wonder moments—the brief look at the brachiosaurs and stegosaurs on the riverbank is about all we get. I so much wanted a ground-level shot of the impossibly huge "alpha male" Brachiosaurus, looking up and craning his great neck around to watch the airplane pass overhead.

Jurassic Park III, though lacking the expansive, "epic" quality of the first and even the second films, is an extremely well-made and eminently enjoyable addition to the *Jurassic* saga and the dinosaur genre. Among its improvements over *The Lost World* are a thankfully simpler plot, fewer implausible twists, and more fully developed characters—relatively speaking of course. (An interesting phenomenon around the time of *JP III*'s release was the number of quotes, from the filmmakers themselves, which almost accidentally admitted to "problems" with *The Lost World*.) Writers Jim Taylor and Alexander Payne infused some fresh blood into the franchise, even working in a thread of the satiric humor that sparked their earlier *Election*. The cast is strong; Sam Neill settles nicely into his Alan Grant role and Laura Dern is engaging in her few scenes. Michael Jeter is on-target as the not-such-a-bad-guy Udesky, and dinomovie veteran Trevor Morgan (previously in *Barney's Great Adventure!*) also plays it just right. Téa Leoni (terrific in the underrated *Deep Impact*) and William Macy are very appealing, making passably real people out of their admittedly stock characters. Don Davis provides some effective, unobtrusive new music, although it seems somehow right that new arrangements of John Williams' original themes seem to accompany all the "big" moments.

It's difficult to imagine that any dinosaur film will ever equal the pure, wide-eyed delight of that first viewing of the original *Jurassic Park*, but *III* is a fast-paced and fan-friendly dino tale that proves there is still plenty of hot-blooded life in the *Jurassic* franchise. It's a full-throttle yet surprisingly old-fashioned adventure, crafted by a group of filmmakers who clearly love Obie and Ray and their fantastic offspring ... *almost* as much as we do.

PEOPLE AND PRODUCTION: Any doubt that there would be a second sequel to *Jurassic Park* evaporated when *The Lost World: Jurassic Park* grossed a record-smashing $92 million in its opening *weekend*. This time there was no Michael Crichton novel upon which to base the screenplay, though some of Crichton's characters returned and the author did reportedly sit in on a few preliminary development meetings. Early, discarded storylines included a second return of Jeff Goldblum as Ian Malcolm, a dinosaur attack on the Costa Rican mainland, and a "plane load of teenagers" crashing on the island. The final script is credited to Peter Buchman, Alexander Payne, and Jim Taylor but several others—including *Jurassic Park/Lost World* scribe David Koepp—made contributions along the way.

The constantly "in-flux" script was one of several issues that caused periodic though

Paul and Amanda Kirby (William Macy, Téa Leoni) recoil in horror as a giant Pteranodon approaches out of the fog.

minor controversies during the *JP III* production. Reports of disgruntled actors, on-set mishaps and other sundry punch-ups appeared on websites and in gossip columns, but most seem to have been routine road bumps amplified by the media. In the end everyone put a positive spin on things — which is of course expected — but the actors genuinely seem to have enjoyed themselves. Téa Leoni was particularly enthusiastic. "Hands down I'm having more fun that I've ever had on a movie," she beamed. "I am *so* open to *Jurassic Park IV* that I made a phone call somewhere in the middle of filming and said ... don't kill me, okay?" William Macy, whose off-hand mid-production comments ("$100 million ship without a rudder," etc.) made the papers and caused a few ripples, also pointed to the bright side. "I just had a daughter, and the idea of being able to do a *Jurassic Park*, which I *know* she will see, just was irresistible." The irrepressible Macy also mentioned the perks of shooting the physically demanding airplane attack sequence. "The good news was that almost all of us, sooner or later, ended up on top of Téa Leoni."

Steven Spielberg made it clear from the start that the *JP III* dinos would have a new director. When Joe Johnston, who had pitched himself as a possible candidate to helm *The Lost World*, got the call, his challenge was to make part *III* "feel like it was *Jurassic Park*" yet still be undeniably *his* film. The director prepared for the job by accompanying paleontologist Jack Horner to a real dinosaur dig, and his efforts behind the camera earned high marks from all involved. In particular, animatronic ace Stan Winston found the former effects wizard to be the ideal man for the job. "He had an edge on a lot of other directors," Winston said in Marc Shapiro's *Fangoria* article. "He knows the [effects] shorthand, he knows how things work."

A huge decision for any dinosaur film is the choice of creatures to feature, and for the second film in a row the wishes of the dino-loving public were heeded. Popular opinion ensured that the Stegosaurus turned up in *The Lost World*; now it would be the Pteranodons' turn. "I think the audience for a long time has been hoping that we would bring [in] flying dinosaurs," producer Kathleen Kennedy commented. When the filmmakers decided they wanted to out-tyrant the Tyrannosaurus, they consulted with Horner and selected the little-known but *very* large Spinosaurus. "A lot of dinosaurs have a very similar silhouette to the T. rex," Joe Johnston pointed out. "We wanted the audience to instantly recognize this as something else." Johnston also wanted a more "primordial" look for the Isla Sorna jungles, according to production designer Ed Verreaux. "Rather than it being all lush and green and shiny and pretty, what we're going to try to do is to make it look a little bit more old, a little bit more rotten, a little bit more swampy." Verreaux, along with greensman Danny Ondrejko and Michael Lantieri's crew, turned Universal's cavernous Stage 12 into just such a place. To augment the studio work the production went on location to the Hawaiian islands of Kauai and Oahu, as well as several venues around southern California. "Falls Lake" on the Universal backlot was painstakingly redressed — twice — to host the Pteranodon aviary and Spino-in-the-water sequences.

Principal photography kicked off on August 30, 2000, and finished just under five months later on January 20, 2001. But even before the new picture hit theaters, the buzz about the next chapter had begun. "Steven has a *great* idea for number four," Joe Johnston said with a gleam. "Whoever directs it is going to have his hands full!"

SPECIAL EFFECTS: For the third time in as many films, the dinosaurs were realized through the coordinated efforts of Stan Winston Studio and Industrial Light & Magic. The Winston crew — including John Rosengrant, "Crash" McCreery, Joey Orosco, and of course Stan — stayed largely intact through all three films. The ILM team had a less familiar look although visual effects supervisor Jim Mitchell, stepping into Dennis Muren's formidable shoes, and animation supervisor Dan Taylor are veterans of both previous *Jurassics*. Also returning (though curiously buried way down in the credits) was physical effects expert Michael Lantieri.

Another constant throughout the *JP* franchise has been scientific advisor Jack Horner, who in fact was brought in at an even earlier stage for part *III*. "For the first time, I actually got to come up with some of the animals and some of the storyline," Horner stated in a Universal featurette, and his input was a huge factor in choosing Spinosaurus as the new super-predator. Since the only substantial Spinosaurus fossil material was destroyed by World War II bombing raids, the movie Spino had to be designed from fragmentary references and records. "Stan [Winston] and his sculptors came up with a pretty good, original rendition of the Spinosaurus," Horner said, "and then I added my comments." Horner also made major contributions to the Pteranodon scenes, according to animation supervisor Dan Taylor. "We know in talking to Jack and some of the paleontologists here at Berkeley, that they were mainly gliders," Taylor recalled. "The nearest existing animal today that we could compare it to would probably be the albatross — a very stiff-winged bird that rides the currents."

The often-mentioned statistic that *JP III* had twice as many CG shots as *Jurassic* and *Lost World* combined did not mean a lightened workload for Stan Winston Studio. "It was 13 months from design to finish," Winston said in the British cine-mag *Empire*. "We built the T. rex, a couple of hydraulic raptors, male and female, we did raptor men in suits, raptor walking and running legs for close-ups, raptors' insert heads, a Pteranodon which was a combination of a man in a suit and animatronics, and we did five baby Pteranodon puppets," all in addition to the

The animatronic Spinosaur's powerful three-fingered "hands," here being touched up by a pair of FX technicians, put the T. rex's spindly limbs to shame.

mammoth Spinosaurus. Though no human actors have appeared in all three films, the venerable T. rex has. "Dusted off and completely re-skinned" as the JP III pressbook put it, the rex's third appearance lasts only until it comes up against the overwhelming Spinosaurus. And according to Winston, life imitated art when the robotic Spino wrenched the head off of its aged rival. "There is just literally no contest between the machines," he asserted, "much less the real animals." The tale of the tape concurs, with the rex at 9 tons and 300 horsepower versus the Spino's 13 tons and 1000 horses. "I will never, ever build an animal bigger than the Spinosaurus," Winston declared. "I will leave the business before that happens."

Spearheading the Winston Studio's efforts was effects supervisor John Rosengrant, who employed different versions of the 'saurs on a shot-by-shot basis. "When figuring out how it's going to be done, different methods come about," Rosengrant said in a filmed interview. "Walking legs, for example with the raptors, which I actually wear. We go through each sequence and sort of figure out if we can make these legs move this way, where it's human power ... or this should be a total hydraulic puppet because you're going to see it from the knees up." Though the Winston crew has broken new technological ground with each film, the basic means of controlling the robotic characters—the "telemetry device"—works so well that it has remained essentially unchanged. "It's a machine that resembles the shape of the dinosaur, where you have a head and you can twist and turn it and make the [dinosaur's] head twist and turn," Rosengrant explained. "On the Spinosaurus, [the puppeteers] are actually strapped into it, so that they move it around and what they do is translated to the dinosaur." The Tyrannosaurus and Spinosaurus required six puppeteers each; the raptor needed "only" four. The live-action Pteranodon babies were actually rod puppets, activated by a small army of puppeteers concealed beneath the nest set. Stan Winston is quick to give credit to his team. "I walk into that studio every day and say, 'Wow, that's really cool! Do some more of that and I'll put my name on it!'"

The Winston dinos again worked together — more closely than ever, in fact — with the Computer-Generated Imagery of Industrial Light and Magic. ILM provided over 400 visual effects shots (about 170 featuring dinosaurs) compared to less than 60 for *Jurassic Park*. "In this film … we had a chance to have our computer-generated dinosaurs interact with Stan Winston's animatronic dinosaurs," Dan Taylor noted. "In the other films we'd cut from ours to a cutaway of his … in this one we can actually make physical contact." ILM's visual effects supervisor Jim Mitchell offered a specific example. "In the fight sequence, we have Stan's T. rex lunging forward," he explained, "and we see the computer-generated Spinosaurus come from behind and actually bite into its neck." Such innovations afforded Joe Johnston the freedom to envision shots and sequences without fear of technological limitations. "I remember on more than one occasion asking Jimmy Mitchell, 'Can you do this?'" the director recalled in *Fangoria*. "He would say, 'Well, we've never done it before, but I think we can.'"

As impossible as it seemed to moviegoers that digital dinosaurs could get any more realistic than those in *The Lost World*, the ILM people were sure they could. New software tools included a simulator for creating skin movement over the underlying musculature, and a technique ILM calls "ambient occlusion" which produced a perfect match of the dappled, filtered light patterns (supposedly caused by the leafy forest canopy) visible on the animatronic creatures. The ILM team also had much more leeway to manipulate — or even replace — the live-action background plates, and several shots of the "Pteranodon canyon" featured entirely computer-generated landscapes. But however high-tech the tools, animation still depends on the talent of human animators. *Jurassic Park III* employed seven lead animators — including noted stop-motion veteran Tom St. Amand — and some 25 animators, not to mention dozens of computer graphics artists, compositors, and other specialists.

Michael Lantieri once again worked together with the Winston crew to create the mechanical and interactive effects, and the initial Spinosaurus attack was one of their most daunting tasks. The sequence required no less than four full-scale fuselage props, each designed to do something different. One would roll, one was gimbal-mounted to a specially-built "tree," and two were designed to crush themselves (actually via hydraulic rams) in concert with both the CG Spinosaurus and a life-sized live-action spino foot built by the Winston team. "I meet with the animators and we look at the creatures … and decide *really* what would be possible for them to do," Lantieri summed up, "then design interactive effects that work on set."

Lantieri, Mitchell, Taylor, and Winston are part of a 21st century FX community that seemingly has no limits. "There used to be a time where there were things that were possible and things that were impossible," Joe Johnston said. "And now, as long as you can convey to the artist or group of artists what it is you want, pretty much anything is possible." If the filmmakers will utilize this magic in service of ideas, stories, and imaginations rather than mere whiz-bang spectacle, movie fans have some great times ahead.

King Dinosaur

"Nobody's gonna believe this!"
½ 1955, USA. Lippert Pictures. BW, 63m.

CREDITS: *Director* Bert I. Gordon. *Producers* Bert I. Gordon, Al Zimbalist, Ralph Helfer (associate), John Bushelman (assistant), Al Zimbalist (executive). *Screenplay* Tom Gries;

based on an original story "Beast from Outer Space" by Bert I. Gordon and Al Zimbalist. *Special Photographic Effects* Howard A. Anderson Co. *Animal Supervision* Ralph Helfer.

CAST: *Dr. Ralph Martin* Bill Bryant. *Dr. Patricia Bennett* Wanda Curtis. *Dr. Dick Gordon* Douglas Henderson. *Dr. Nora Pierce* Patti Gallagher. *Narrator* Marvin Miller.

AD LINE: "You'll be SHOCKED! You'll be STUNNED! You'll be THRILLED!"

March 18 is a day like any other, until a new planet, christened "Planet Nova," suddenly appears and settles into orbit about the Sun. A huge rocket is readied and its crew assigned: zoogeographer Richard "Dick" Gordon, mineralogist Nora Pierce, medical doctor Ralph Martin, and chemist Patricia "Pat" Bennett. The ship carries all manner of equipment, including a portable nuclear power plant which can if necessary be converted into an atomic bomb! After several months, the foursome reaches Planet Nova. "Is it as lovely as it seems?" Pat muses. "Yes, if it's habitable," Ralph replies. Nora mentions that she really would like to visit the strange island sighted in the middle of a nearby lake. "Let the next people pay it a visit," Pat whines. "Let's get back to the ship and get out of here before something awful happens to all of us!" As night approaches, they realize that they have somehow become utterly lost. "Is this the way we came?" Ralph asks. "I'm not sure," Dick mumbles. Pat and Ralph go for a walk, but Ralph is seriously injured when he trips over a root and falls on top of an alligator.

Dick and Nora set out to locate the rocket and retrieve some supplies, while Pat tends to the injured Ralph. "You've been unconscious for a day and a half," Pat tells him. "Oh, I don't remember," Ralph replies. Dick and Nora soon return from their successful foray, bearing not only provisions but also a cute little "honey bear" (?) which they've named Joe. Nora finally gets her wish and sails with Dick and Little Joe to the island, where the "King Dinosaur" suddenly appears before them. "A Tyrannosaurus rex from Earth's prehistoric age!" marvels Dick, as he drags Nora into a cave. The king tries to squeeze in after them, but another giant lizard appears and a fight breaks out. Dick sends up a flare, bringing Pat and the miraculously recuperated Ralph scrambling to the rescue with portable A-bomb in hand. The king wins the fight and resumes trying to wedge his prickly dome into the cave, but another reptilian challenger arrives and another fight starts. "Oh, it's horrible!" Pat shrieks, handing Ralph a rifle. "Here, shoot it." Dick and Nora manage to escape during the latest tussle, but even though everyone is now safe and free to leave, they decide (apparently out of pure spite) to detonate their nuke and hideously contaminate the pristine environment. Dick admires the mushroom cloud for a moment, and they prepare to blast off.

COMMENTARY: *King Dinosaur* is a strong contender for the title of Worst Dinosaur Movie of All Time. In fact, if one eliminates films in which the dinos are merely supporting players, such as *Untamed Women* and *Robot Monster*, and subamateur "camcorder movies" like *Galaxy of the Dinosaurs* and *Saurians*, then the crown rests indisputably on the king's scaly noggin. The 63 minutes of *King Dinosaur* overflow with the hallmarks of a historically, monumentally bad movie: torturous dialogue, wretched acting, astounding continuity lapses, preposterous plot developments, endless stretches of filler, and effects which are anything but special. From the stock footage prologue to the stock footage finale, *King Dinosaur* represents the very nadir of the dinomovie genre.

Absurdities flow from the screen like porridge lava from a soundstage volcano as *King Dinosaur* unfolds, with one ludicrous moment following another. A few examples: The opening "building the rocket" montage shows tests performed on a *propeller-driven bomber*. The narrator introduces Doctor Martin and tells us that he has the "experience of treating most diseases and fatalities that overtake men." (Treating *fatalities*?) Judging by the sound effects, the rocket

Ralph (Bill Bryant) and Pat (Wanda Curtis) cower from an oversize alien reptile in a publicity paste-up shot for *King Dinosaur*.

explodes five times before it gets off the pad. After landing, Pat reports that "40 percent of the bacteria was completely unfamiliar," but seconds later Ralph yanks off his helmet and chirps, "Dick! Nora! The atmosphere checks out all right!" When they first spot the island, Dick remarks, "it looks like it's covered with heavy jungle growth," but when they visit it two days later, it "looks pretty barren!" The looniness even extends to the film's credits, which contain entries both for "Research" and "Technical Advisor."

Like everything else, the special effects in *King Dinosaur* are astonishing in their inadequacy. The rocket shots in the early reels are merely V-2 file footage, sometimes crudely superimposed over starfields or landscapes. The establishing shot of the rocket at rest on the planet's surface appears to be a cutout of a photo of the rocket, stuck to a still photo of the shooting location. To show the crew climbing down from the ship, the actors actually climbed down a stepladder, blocked from the camera's view by a miniature rocket fin in the foreground (at last, a flash of resourcefulness). The few optical effects are awful, consisting mostly of crude stationary mattes used to combine the actors with the "giant" animals, and the appearance of an oversized insect which menaces Ralph and Pat. Not surprisingly, in these primitive opticals the big bug glows like a Klieg light during some shots and becomes downright transparent during others. The effects in Bert I. Gordon's later pictures, inept as they were, would at least be an improvement over these embarrassing first efforts.

King Dinosaur does contain stock shots from *One Million B.C.*, but use of these scenes is limited to a few "nondinosaur" clips such as the mammoth and the giant armadillo, and one quick lizard shot. For most of the dinosaur action, animal handler Ralph Helfer orchestrated some original footage. They're still just lizards, but they're all-new lizards. Perhaps accepting the fact that modern reptiles will not look like dinosaurs no matter what you add to them (or perhaps just to save time and money), the filmmakers omitted the back fins and neck frills and just let the animals be themselves. Except, that is, for the jaw-dropping first appearance of the shaggy, scraggy, wattled iguana who plays the title role. The sight of this homely, humble little critter, marionetted up onto his hind legs by monofilament wires in an effort to make him "tower" like a T. rex, is one of the genuinely ridiculous moments in all of dinocinema. It's right at home in *King Dinosaur*, the most genuinely ridiculous dinosaur movie of them all.

PEOPLE AND PRODUCTION: Four years after giving the world *Lost Continent* (a near-classic by comparison), Lippert Pictures released one of Bert I. Gordon's earliest directorial efforts, *King Dinosaur*. Produced on a microscopic budget with meager resources and little time, it was probably inevitable that the picture would turn out as it did.

One notable member of the tiny production company was animal trainer Ralph Helfer. In addition to supervising Planet Nova's menagerie of wildlife, Helfer also served as associate producer for the ultralow-budget project. "It was such a small situation, you know," Helfer reminisced. "There were only a handful of us, and we all helped in getting that production done." Some sources claim that *King Dinosaur* was shot in as little as three days, but Helfer said the schedule wasn't *quite* that short. "No, we were up in Big Bear [California] for probably, under a week, just filming in the mountains up there, and I remember we shot at Bronson [Canyon], which is here in Los Angeles. I would say, somewhere around two weeks we shot it."

While pointing out the massive shortcomings of films like *King Dinosaur*, it's easy to forget that people (some, anyway) did put forth honest efforts under very limiting circumstances. "It brings back a lot of memories," Helfer told me, reflecting on *King Dinosaur* and other shoestring projects of his early years. "I mean, we all worked very hard

The conquerors of Planet Nova (from left: Patti Gallagher, Doug Henderson, Wanda Curtis, Bill Bryant) and their economy-sized A-bomb, clumsily pasted alongside a tongue-flicking lizardosaur.

on those films, and brought them to fruition, and got them out there on the screen, and that was quite a thrill in those days. We did a lot of stunts and P.R., I remember, with Wanda Curtis and Doug Henderson. Doug was great, he was a good friend as well as a good actor, and we had a lot of good fun with those productions." About Bert I. Gordon, Helfer said, "Bert was a nice guy. He was young, he was trying to break into the movie industry coming up with these small productions ... and I mean, we worked okay together."

Bert I. Gordon would go on from *King Dinosaur* to helm a succession of budgetarily challenged genre films in the '50s, '60s, and '70s. In keeping with his initials, Gordon often featured giantism as a principal theme, in films like *The Amazing Colossal Man* (1957), *Beginning of the End* (1957), *The Spider* (1958), *War of the Colossal Beast* (1958), *Village of the Giants* (1965), and *Food of the Gods* (1976).

SPECIAL EFFECTS: All of the live animals appearing in *King Dinosaur* (excluding those in the stock shots) were provided and supervised by Ralph Helfer, whose humane "Affection Training" approach would one day revolutionize the use of animals in films. Over the next four decades, Helfer's amazing animal stars enlivened such films as *The Lion* (1962), *The Island of Dr. Moreau* (1977), *Savage Harvest* (1981), and many others. *King Dinosaur*, though, dates from his beginnings in the business with his first company, Nature's Haven. "*King Dinosaur* was one of the first," Helfer said. "We had a huge python ... and I remember the 'giant' iguana lizard." Helfer is quick to point out that cold-blooded reptiles do not make the most dynamic actors. "What you have to do is work with their natural behaviors," he explained. "There are things that we can do that they would do naturally ... but you can't put anything artificial or commercial within the reptile." Besides the snakes and lizards, Helfer also furnished "Little Joe the honey bear," the film's intended comic relief. "Yeah, that was a kinkajou," Helfer recalled. "They're great on camera, they're a lot of fun and they're easy to manage." The short schedule presented no problems as far as acquiring the animals—they were already part of Helfer's menagerie. "Yeah, we had the iguanas and we had the python and various things we needed, so we didn't have to go outside and bring them in at all," Helfer continued. "Sometimes, when you had an animal, they would build a script around *it* rather than the other way around!"

Two years after *King Dinosaur*, Gordon and Helfer worked together again on *The Cyclops* (1957). Helfer provided a large python and oversaw the filming of a serpentine wrestling sequence, resulting in one of the most unique film credits ever seen: "Snake Fight Supervision." *Cyclops* features some "giant" lizards, too, so why isn't it included in this book? Because, as Russ (James Craig) explains to Marty (Lon Chaney, Jr.): "Those were not prehistoric creatures we saw—they're animals of our time, only grown to enormous size." So there.

In 1981, Bert I. Gordon reminisced about his first quarter-century in the film biz and his feelings toward special effects. "Back there, in the days of *King Dinosaur* and *The Cyclops*, my principal motivation and where I was at personally was making a film," Gordon told interviewer Kevin R. Danzey in *Amazing Cinema*. "Every aspect of it totally fascinated me—the camera, the story, the effects.... It took a number of years before the technical became secondary for me. In looking back, I would like to have had that happen earlier in my career, because to me, the technical in those days was as important as the story and the people, and it shouldn't be."

King Kong

"I'm going out and make the greatest picture in the world—something nobody's ever seen or heard of!"

**** 1933, USA. RKO Radio Pictures. BW, 100m.

CREDITS: *Directors* Merian C. Cooper, Ernest B. Schoedsack. *Producers* Merian C. Cooper, Ernest B. Schoedsack, David O. Selznick (executive). *Screenplay* James Creelman and Ruth Rose. *From an Idea Conceived by* Merian C. Cooper and Edgar Wallace. *Chief Technician* Willis H. O'Brien. *Art Technicians* Mario Larrinaga, Byron L. Crabbe. *Technical Staff* E. B. Gibson, Marcel Delgado, Fred Reese, Orville Goldner, Carroll Shepphird. *Sound Effects* Murray Spivack. *Settings by* Carroll Clark, Al Herman.

CAST: *Ann Darrow* Fay Wray. *Carl Denham* Robert Armstrong. *John Driscoll* Bruce Cabot. *Capt. Englehorn* Frank Reicher. *Charles Weston* Sam Hardy. *Native Chief* Noble Johnson. *Witch King* Steve Clemento. *Second Mate* James Flavin. *Charley* Victor Wong.

As the Great Depression grips New York City, the moviegoing public hungers for escapism. Film director Carl Denham, known for his exotic jungle adventures, has decided to give in to popular demand and include a "pretty face" in his new production, but his danger-seeking reputation makes it difficult to find an actress. On the New York streets he spots an attractive but downtrodden young woman named Ann Darrow, and over a hot meal she accepts his offer. Between screen tests on board Captain Englehorn's steamer, S.S. *Venture*, Ann finds time to fall in love with the ship's handsome first mate, Jack Driscoll. The *Venture* finally nears an unexplored island, "way west of Sumatra," where the natives are said to worship an all-powerful god known as "Kong."

The island and its unmistakable "mountain that looks like a skull" loom out of the fog. Denham, Driscoll, Ann, Englehorn and a dozen crewmen go ashore and witness a primitive ritual, enacted in the shadow of an ancient, gated wall. The native chief soon spots the visitors and becomes fascinated with the fair-skinned, blonde-haired Ann—"A gift for Kong," he says. The movie company judiciously retreats, but that night a party of islanders silently snatches Ann right off the ship. Driscoll and Denham give chase only to find her bound to a sacrificial altar, and they can only watch in horror as Kong appears. Not a myth but a living, gargantuan gorilla, he is smitten with the beauty and carries her into the jungle. Driscoll, Denham and a party of sailors try to follow, but their numbers are steadily thinned by the island's prehistoric fauna. They manage to subdue a charging Stegosaurus with Denham's gas bombs, but a belligerent Brontosaurus kills several men. Kong places Ann atop a dead tree and cleverly doubles back, catching his pursuers helplessly clinging to a log bridge over a deep ravine. The ape ruthlessly shakes the sailors off the log, then returns to Ann just in time to save her from a bloodthirsty Tyrannosaurus. Of the rescue party only Driscoll and Denham remain, and with the bridge gone Denham can go no further. Driscoll claws and scrambles and somehow trails Kong to his lair inside Skull Mountain, watching in awe as the ape vanquishes a serpentine Elasmosaurus and a massive pterodactyl. While Kong battles the flying reptile, Driscoll sneaks Ann away, and with roles now reversed Kong chases the couple all the way back to the Great Wall. Kong bursts through the gate and rampages through the village until finally being brought down by Denham's gas grenades. Suddenly the showman is seized by an idea—to bring Kong back alive!

On opening night, a beaming Denham introduces Ann, then Driscoll, and then the curtain rises to reveal "The Eighth Wonder of the World" shackled and chained. The flashing of the reporters' cameras enrages Kong and he rips free, cutting a swath of destruction through New York City as he searches for Ann. Destroying anything in his path—buildings, bystanders, an elevated train—he finally spots his prize through a hotel window and pulls her from the room. He instinctively heads for the highest point and crowds are soon looking up at the amazing sight of Kong, still holding Ann, atop the Empire State Building. But Driscoll has one last idea—armed airplanes—and as the machine guns riddle Kong's body he places Ann gently on the ledge, takes a final look, and falls to the street below.

COMMENTARY: While researching this book, I was honored to speak with a variety of outstanding film craftsmen, and I usually began the conversations by asking: "What first sparked your interest in 'fantastic' films?" One answer kept turning up. Jim Danforth: "In terms of special effects, I would say *King Kong*." Roger Dicken: "There was a little flea pit cinema in Portsmouth that would show the old movies ... and my first introduction to animation and monsters was *King Kong*." Jim Aupperle: "One of the earliest things must have been *King Kong*, and I just became really fascinated with wondering how these things were done!" Phil Tippett: "I had been, ever since I was a little kid, a big fan of dinosaur pictures, and one of my *big* inspirations was *King Kong*." Stan Winston: "*King Kong* is one of the *classic* movies and, for all people who are in this business, one of our favorites." And of course, Ray Harryhausen told me what he's told others: "I haven't been the same since!"

The chance to talk dinosaurs and fantasy films with Harryhausen—the "Son of Kong" as longtime friend Forrest J Ackerman once dubbed him—was a highlight of my research, yet as of that date I had never seen *King Kong* in a theater. Not surprisingly, the topic soon turned to that film which made such a remarkable impression on the 13-year-old Ray. "You *must* see it on the big screen," he told me. "Most people today see it on the little idiot box, and *it's not the same picture*." I knew he was right but I didn't realize how right until two months later, when a theater fairly close by decided to bring *Kong* back alive for a one-week run. Joined by my father, who at age 76 had never seen the film, I would get my chance.

A suite of Max Steiner's *Kong* score was playing while we found our seats, and as the lights went down and the familiar RKO logo appeared, Ray's enthusiastic words continued in my head. "You've got to see it on a theater screen ... you know, you look up at it and it's *awesome.*" The audience that night spanned the generations, and only after the film started did I realize that some of the younger ones were there not to experience a film classic, but to watch what they surely perceived as a hokey, old-timey movie far too naive for their modern sensibilities. However, I don't think they got quite what they bargained for.

The film started and I was struck as always by the ingenious economy of the script. "Is this the moving picture ship?" Weston asks. "Yeah, you goin' on this crazy voyage?" the dock worker replies. What other movie in history ever milked so much exposition out of 13 words? Already we know almost everything we need to know and are ready to dive into the story. Like the muscular title character, the narrative is all sinew and no fat. But as the early scenes unfolded the dialogue began to elicit snickers from some of the kids. The chuckling continued periodically throughout Denham's discovery of Ann Darrow and into the first part of the sea voyage, but things were about to change.

Even after a dozen viewings of my 60th Anniversary Edition home video, I saw things in the theater that night I had never seen before. I had never realized that Kong delicately uses a finger to unwind the rope winch on the sacrificial altar in order to release Ann. I had never seen the river in the lower left corner of the wide establishing shot of Kong's mountain overlook, an important bit of foreshadowing in light of how Jack and Ann finally escape. Even more striking than specific details is the sheer grandeur of the spectacle seen as it was meant to be. The opening of the towering gate doors, the famous fight with the Tyrannosaurus, Kong's final act of defiance atop the Empire State Building—just three of the countless scenes that are so magically magnified on the theater screen.

King Kong is a superbly told story, structured essentially in three acts. Act one encompasses the New York sequence and the sea voyage up until the *Venture* enters the fog bank, act two begins with the sighting of the island, and act three is the New York City finale. As we neared the end of act one, the condescension from the younger audience members began to dwindle. A few snickers greeted Ann Darrow's shipboard screen test, but they were the last. As the *Venture* emerged from the fog and Skull Mountain loomed, slouching bodies straightened up and leaned forward, whispered commentary gave way to breath holding, and giggles turned into *oohs* and *ahhs*. Even these streetwise 1990s kids, accustomed to knockout computer-generated visuals in everything from movies to fungicide commercials, fell under Kong's spell. By the time Merian C. Cooper's tragic hero ended his unwilling visit to civilization, everyone in the theater was mesmerized. After all these years, Coop, you still *got 'em.*

So much of the movie's power is anticipatory. The foreshadowing starts early, like when Ann mentions that Iggy the little monkey "likes me better than he likes anybody on board." If it's true that Kong's first appearance is among the film's least technically accomplished FX shots, it's just as true that it doesn't really matter because the audience is so enveloped by the storytelling. Max Steiner's music adds immeasurably to this feeling, allowing the audience to "see" Kong approaching musically before seeing him visually. "I think of a film as though it were music," Ernest Schoedsack once said. "It must have a beginning, a middle and an end, and should build up to climaxes, then allow some rest, then build again."

Though somewhat dated, the script is far less stilted than the vast majority of its contemporaries (for proof see the Oscar-winning "Best Picture" of 1931, *Cimarron*), and one reason it holds up so well is its strong real-world origin. It's a known fact that Carl Denham, in many ways, *is* Merian Cooper. Like Denham, Cooper had sailed the seas to exotic, unheard-of locales, and with partner Ernest Schoedsack did "make moving pictures in jungles and places," and was chastised for the lack of "love interest" in his films. *Kong* is also peppered with little factual details that combine to help make the incredible, credible. Englehorn mentions that the natives' tongue "sounds something like the language the Nias Islanders speak" (Nias is 125 kilometers west of Sumatra), and Ann laments the closing of New York's movie studios (the result of the industry's mass exodus to the temperate climes of California). I have a particular fondness for Driscoll's comment about having been "up at Angkor once," since my parents actually visited and photographed the Angkor Wat ruins in the late 1950s, when my father was assistant army attaché with the U.S. embassy in Vientiane, Laos.

Though *King Kong* can never be called a "dinosaur movie," the dinosaurs are an indispensable element. "Something, to my mind, that utterly *ruined* the remake was that there were no dinosaurs," Forry Ackerman once said. "To me, that was sort of like telling the Frank Sinatra story and not having him sing one note." As in *The Lost World: Jurassic Park* more than six decades later, the dinosaur action is led off by a Stegosaurus sequence. The stego scene is a mirror of the film's effects as a whole, with a wide variety of techniques ingeniously combined to produce the very best possible result. The animal appears in the distance, barely seen through a glass-painted jungle more atmospheric than any real one could ever be. Then the saurian is suddenly closer, and then it attacks and only Denham's gas bomb halts its charge. It staggers and turns and falls like a real animal and the men start walking toward it, and suddenly one realizes that the camera is following them—*tracking in* toward both the actors and the animation element, all in one cut! It's a great shot in a great sequence, and the idea of the "dead" animal suddenly reviving for one final thrust has since become a genre cliché. The only possible negative is the naturalism of Willis O'Brien's animation, so convincing that it almost makes the creature's brutal death uncomfortable to watch.

Every animation shot in *Kong* is a triumph, from the small throwaway bits like the prehistoric vulture pecking at the fallen tyrannosaur to the major set pieces like the Brontosaurus rampage. The bronto's behavior may put off some folks (who prefer to ignore the fact that any large herbivores like elephants or cape buffalo can be deadly if provoked) but he remains the best movie bronto ever, especially since most subsequent films have maddeningly relegated these beautiful behemoths to cameos and walk-throughs. Then there is the Tyrannosaurus. For *The Stop-Motion Filmography*, author Neil Pettigrew asked eight animation professionals to list their ten favorite stop-motion sequences. Five of the eight artists put the Kong-tyrannosaur battle on their lists, and four of them—David Allen, Steve Archer, Douglas Beswick, and Phil Tippett—ranked it number one. O'Brien's boxing experience served him well here, resulting in the greatest (and ultimately, grisliest) fight between two stop-motion beasts ever put on film.

The scenes of the Elasmosaurus in the cavern are dramatic evidence of O'Brien's attention to detail, and the pterodactyl sequence is equally effective. If there could be a quibble with these vignettes it's that Kong's three prehistoric opponents are progressively easier to defeat, a pattern counter to the relentless building of mood that distinguishes the picture as a whole. Obie's animation of Kong himself stands as the pinnacle of the art form—not technically, perhaps, but rather in terms of making a jointed puppet into a living, feeling *character*. This is stunningly demonstrated as the biplanes riddle Kong with bullets. He looks at the plane, then at his wounds, and his confusion is palpable. His natural enemies had

Marcel Delgado's titanic T. rex comes palpably alive amid the oppressive primordial jungles of Kong's island. (Note Fay Wray's artificial "stand-in" atop the tree.)

to bring tooth or claw in contact with him to inflict injury, but the planes ... One can "see" Kong thinking, "What's happening? They're not even touching me, yet they're killing me." Kong — the movie and the character — is truly O'Brien's masterwork.

King Kong represents one of those rare moments in any creative arena, when the planets aligned and the deities smiled and everything fell into place. Everyone was right where they had to be at the time they had to be there. Of course, there was Cooper and Schoedsack and O'Brien, but also so many more. The painstaking detail of Marcel Delgado's animation puppets has seldom if ever been topped. Max Steiner's perfect score defined a new plateau for film music. Ruth Rose's screenplay completely fulfilled Cooper's vision. Murray Spivack pioneered sound recording and effects techniques that became standards for decades. Mario Larringa and Byron Crabbe created primordial milieus from paint and glass that were at once believably real and fantastically unreal. Then there are the human actors, sometimes overlooked in praising the film's technical virtuosity. Robert Armstrong's magnetic Denham, Bruce Cabot's unassuming but determined Driscoll, Fay Wray's strong and vulnerable, innocent and sexy Ann, and an on-target supporting cast manage to strike every right note.

As the lights came up in the theater that night, I noticed a boy of about eight who had been sitting with his parents in the row right behind me. He stood, took a deep breath and exclaimed, "That's the best black-and-white movie I ever saw!" The enthusiasm in his voice more than counteracted any unintended qualification present in his words. It all goes to prove that a great film will always be great, and *Kong* ... is still King.

The appeal of *King Kong* can never be fully described in words, although people have been trying for many decades. *Kong* has been analyzed, dissected, and interpreted to absurd lengths (despite Cooper's insistence that it "was escapist entertainment pure and simple"), yet the whole is definitely greater than the sum of the parts. I believe Ray Harryhausen, whose wondrous career was so definitively shaped by *King Kong*, comes as close as possible to summarizing the secret of *Kong*'s success. As he told me:

> I think, [the secret was] the structure of the whole story. It was a perfect structure, a combination of sound effects, photographic effects, and music — Max Steiner's music was a *big* percentage of its success — and all these things impressed one. Where they took you by the hand from the Depression days and the mundane world, and brought you on an adventure that was so outrageous, you couldn't believe you were seeing what you were seeing! And yet it was just so convincing. I didn't know how it was done, but I knew it wasn't a man in a suit, and I knew the dinosaurs were not lizards with rubber fins glued on their backs. And so it had many different facets to make one impressed, particularly anyone with imagination.

That's it ... *imagination*. *King Kong* is nothing less than a triumph of imagination, of artistry and vision, technical skill and teamwork, perseverance and attention to detail. And you were so right, Ray; it *must* be seen on the big screen — the ultimate testimony to the magic of the movies.

PEOPLE AND PRODUCTION: Within the span of three short years, four things happened that together gave birth to *King Kong*. One: Merian C. Cooper — fighter pilot, aviation pioneer, adventurer, filmmaker — conceived an original idea for an unprecedented adventure movie, the seeds of which may have been planted by Paul B. Du Chaillu's book *Explorations and Adventures in Equatorial Africa*, or by friend Douglas Burden's tales of his journeys to Komodo Island. Two: RKO's David O. Selznick put Cooper in charge of evaluating present and future film projects at the struggling studio. Three: Visual effects innovator Willis O'Brien shot some test footage of prehistoric creatures for a proposed film called *Creation*. Cooper was unimpressed by the film's concept but was so excited by O'Brien's fantastic imagery that he abandoned his initial scheme — transporting an African gorilla to Komodo Island to battle one of the isle's massive "dragon" lizards — in favor of O'Brien's wizardry. Four: Ernest "Monte" Schoedsack, Cooper's collaborator on the "natural dramas" *Grass* (1925) and *Chang* (1927), grew frustrated over the constant delays while preparing to direct *The Lives of a Bengal Lancer* and decided to leave Paramount for RKO. "Coop" now had his concept crystallized, was in a position to promote it, had the technical means to realize it, and had his partner again at his side.

In a letter to Selznick dated December 15, 1931, Cooper described his "Giant Terror Gorilla, and the kind of scenes in which he should be used." He assured Selznick that such scenes *could* be created, "using an animated figure against a projection background, all played against a Dunning [traveling matte] foreground, with closeup work of full sized head mask, and hands and feet." Though Selznick once stated that "one of the biggest gambles I took at RKO was to squeeze money out of the budgets of other pictures for [*Kong*]," he believed in Cooper's talents. The RKO "money men," however, insisted upon a test reel. RKO Production 601 would be known at various stages as *The Beast*, *The Eighth Wonder*, *Kong*, and finally *King Kong*.

A well-known bit of *Kong* lore is Merian Cooper's coy statement to Fay Wray that she'd have "the tallest, darkest leading man in Hollywood." In her engrossing autobiography (wonderfully titled *On the Other Hand*), she tells the complete tale. "Merian Cooper asked me to go to his new offices at RKO," Wray recalled. "He showed me large drawings for a film he was planning; sketches of jungle scenes that were exotically beautiful and then, an astonishing one: the figure of a giant ape climbing up the side of the newly completed Empire State Building." Cooper then dropped the teasing line. "Even while my thoughts were flying toward the hope that Cooper might be waiting for Cary [Grant]'s arrival just as I was, Cooper went on to point at the giant ape and say, again, 'The tallest, darkest leading man in Hollywood.'" (In Wray's essay "How Fay Met Kong, or the Scream that Shook the World," she names Clark Gable in association with this anecdote.) Intrigued by the prospect of working with Cooper, Wray signed on. "For a while he had thought of Jean Harlow but recently had decided they could put a blond wig on me," she stated. "I received $10,000 ... for ten actual working weeks, which stretched out over a period of ten months." Rounding out the principal trio were Robert Armstrong and, in his first big role, Etienne Pelissier de Bujac, better known as Bruce Cabot.

Cooper and Schoedsack codirected the film, each handling particular types of scenes. Fay Wray reported that Cooper "directed all the scenes that were considered technical and tied to the animation that was prepared by O'Brien," while Schoedsack "did the 'people' scenes—on the ship, the arrival on Skull Island, the scenes before the Great Wall." Wray and her costars vividly remembered Coop and Monte. "Cooper and Schoedsack [both] gave me absolute freedom to make my own choices, and never made me feel that I was being directed," Wray pointed out. "There were often scenes that were done in one take." Robert Armstrong recalled shooting the test reel, and Cooper telling him to imagine he was seeing a 50-foot ape. Armstrong's reply: "I told him, 'I've been in this business a good many years, Mr. Cooper, but you tell me how I'm supposed to react to a 50-foot ape!'"

One famous scene in a picture loaded with them is the "undressing" sequence, one of the casualties when the film was censored for its 1938 rerelease. Schoedsack's recollections of the scene were published in the special *King Kong* issue of *Closeup* (no. 3). "The strip scene was done by Obie himself on his own, as a gag," he stated. "He contributed a lot of ideas for bits of business and the clothes tearing scene was all his." In a filmed interview, Fay Wray explained the illusion. "I had cut sections of my own skirt out, and then they were stitched back," she explained. "It was just like petals from a flower you might say, and just two or three of those, but it did give the *impression* that people have had, that he was removing clothes."

The undressing sequence, like the entire movie, is enhanced by Max Steiner's groundbreaking music score. Yet again it was Cooper who carried the torch, reportedly even offering to fund the effort after the RKO brass instructed Steiner to simply recycle some existing tracks for *Kong*. It was Steiner's suggestion that the early scenes, in the doldrums of Depression-weary New York, should play without music, and only after the *Venture* arrives at the fantastic island should the music begin. "*King Kong* was made for music," Steiner reflected. "It was the kind of film that allowed you to do anything and everything from weird chords and dissonances to pretty melodies."

The evolution of the *Kong* screenplay is not a cut-and-dried issue. Most accounts tell how popular British author Edgar Wallace was assigned to the project only to die of pneumonia almost immediately thereafter. "Actually, Edgar Wallace didn't write any of *Kong*, not one bloody word," Cooper stated, quoted in the indispensable volume *The Making of King Kong*. "I'd promised him credit and so I gave it to him." Most other accounts more or less agree with Cooper's, including letters that Wallace himself wrote to his wife during his short Hollywood tenure, but Mark Bezanson's essay "Edgar Wallace and Kong" (written for and published in *The Girl in the Hairy Paw*) offers a different view. Citing a 110-page document which "appears to be Wallace's personal draft," Bezanson asserted that "Wallace imagined and articulated on paper much of the narrative structure, many of the details of action and considerable amounts of the tone of this enduring film classic." He does, however, go on to state that "there is no question that the final draft of the screenplay was the work of Ruth Rose ... who had never seen Wallace's script."

Ruth Rose clearly based Carl Denham on Merian Cooper and, to a lesser extent, Jack Driscoll on her husband, Ernest Schoedsack, but she always denied connections between Ann Darrow and herself. Intentional or not, there are many similarities: Ann and Rose were both at one point out-of-luck actresses, both sailed on adventurous journeys to exotic destinations, and both met their husbands-to-be while on these journeys— Ann aboard the fictional S.S. *Venture*; Ruth aboard the real S.S. *Arcturus* as official historian of a New York Zoology Society expedition to the Galapagos Islands. The last in a succession of writers that included Wallace, RKO's Dudley Nichols and James Creelman, Rose managed to capture the "simple, fairy-tale quality" Cooper desired. "Monte and Creelman and I wrote some," Cooper said, "but Ruth did ninety percent of it."

A movie like *King Kong* is of course a trivia hound's paradise. Many of the tidbits are common knowledge, like Cooper and Schoedsack doing cameos as the biplane crew, or the fact that the great wall went up in flames in the "burning of Atlanta" in *Gone with the Wind*. Other trivia is not quite as well known — that the native huts were from King Vidor's *Bird of Paradise* (1932), or that sets from Cecil B. DeMille's *The King of Kings* (1927) were redressed to serve as the native village and the wall, or that the same sets were later reused again in the serial *The Return of Chandu*. Shots of the massive crowds gathering to attend Kong's opening night in New York were actually taken at the premiere of Charlie Chaplin's *City Lights*. Legendary Native American athlete Jim Thorpe portrays one of the native dancers, and Sandra Shaw — the actress casually dropped to the pavement by Kong — was Gary Cooper's one-time wife. Fay Wray's screams were often reused by RKO, including for Helen Mack in *The Son of Kong*. For the *truly* trivial, look on a shelf in RKO's *Genius at Work* (1947) for a number of *Kong* and *Son of Kong* props, or look in the background during *Christopher Strong* (1933) and you'll see a life preserver labeled "S.S. Venture." And speaking of life preservers, Fay Wray was reportedly approached to portray the 101-year-old Rose in *Titanic* (1997).

The cost of *King Kong* was given as $650,000, though Cooper stated that "we brought that picture in for only 430,000 ... but those bookkeepers tacked on the cost of *Creation* and a lot of so-called 'overhead.'" Either way, it was money well spent. *Kong* debuted March 2, 1933, playing ten shows a day at *both* of New York's largest theaters: Radio City Music Hall and the New Roxy. In the abyss of the Depression, the picture brought in almost $90,000 in its first four days at these two houses. It opened at Grauman's Chinese in Hollywood on March 24 and saw full national release on April 10. It is fortunate for fantasy-film lovers that it played Grauman's when it did, because that's where it was first seen by young Ray Harryhausen. As Ray told me (displaying his too often overlooked sense of humor): "I could have been influenced by Edward G. Robinson in *Little Caesar*, and probably be a Godfather today!" The film was re-released to great success in 1938, 1942, and 1952 — the '52 release is in fact credited as a major spark in kindling the giant-monster craze of that decade.

Inevitably, *Kong* was followed in less than a year by a sequel, and over the decades to come by innumerable copies, offshoots, spoofs, a notorious remake, and even a sequel to the remake. *Kong*'s success, both financially and artistically, made it a natural inspiration for others wanting to make films in the same vein. But none could ever equal the original that began as one man's vision. "Merian Cooper was a fascinating combination of high imagination, an implicitly rebellious nature, a political conservative, an intellect, an adventurer, and a visionary," Fay

Robert Armstrong, Bruce Cabot (right) and company act out the bronto-versus-raft sequence aboard a soundstage-bound raft mock-up. The brontosaur's image will later replace the large process screen visible in the background.

Wray wrote in her autobiography. "He had the exuberance of a young boy whose dreams of adventure are forever in the forefront of his mind."

SPECIAL EFFECTS: Innovation is commonplace in the world of movie special effects. If a method doesn't exist to do what you need, invent one. But perhaps never in cinema history has a film so exhaustively employed *every bit* of available technology, technique, and ingenuity as did *King Kong*. Processes old and new were refined, modified, combined, and pushed to the very edge of their potential. Somehow, Willis O'Brien and a remarkable team of technical artists tricked and cajoled and bludgeoned 1933 technology into producing the wondrous visuals that are still enjoyed today.

In 1931, O'Brien was six years removed from *The Lost World* and stinging over the cancellation of *Creation*, when Merian Cooper told him of the plans for *Kong*. Obie immediately commissioned Marcel Delgado, the talented sculptor who had fabricated *Lost World*'s dinosaur menagerie, to make the necessary stop-motion figures. Since the 1925 film, Delgado had refined his methods to produce much more realistic creatures. Each puppet had a jointed steel armature over which Delgado placed "muscles" of latex rubber, resulting in naturalistic flexing and bulging during animation. The remainder of the basic shape was built up with cotton.

The extra pains taken by Delgado are nicely explained by S. S. Wilson in *Puppets and People*. "Some puppet makers cast the skin in thin latex sheets from finely detailed clay models and apply the skin to the built-up armature; but for his nonfurred puppets, Delgado carried the build-up process right on through to the end, sculpting his skins in liquid latex. As a result of his effort, Delgado's creations, particularly those in *King Kong*, can withstand prolonged scrutiny in unblinking close-ups." Among Delgado's creatures on display in *Kong* are a Stegosaurus, Brontosaurus, Tyrannosaurus rex, Elasmosaurus, and pterodactyl, as well as a Teratornis (the primitive vulturelike scavenger). Delgado also made a mechanical brontosaur head, neck and back for the raft attack sequence, where the water precluded the use of stop-motion. "There's one thing the youngsters say to me that I like," Delgado said years after *Kong*. "They say, 'your animals look alive!'"

No test footage from Obie's *Creation* appears in *Kong*, but some of the puppets built for the aborted film were used. The Triceratops, Arsinoitherium, and Styracosaurus made for *Creation* were actually filmed for *Kong*, only to eventually be cut for reasons of running time and pacing. The presence on the near side of the chasm of the Arsinoitherium—a bizarre two-horned mammal of the Oligocene Epoch—was originally what had the sailors trapped on the log, but the sequence is so exciting the viewer never has time to wonder why the men do not retreat before being shaken off. The mammal was later replaced with the Styracosaurus, but it too was cut and had to wait for *The Son of Kong* to make its on-screen appearance.

The most famous of the "never-seen" *Kong* footage is the so-called "spider-pit sequence," which followed the fate of the sailors at the bottom of the gorge. It was apparently seen only by one test audience, because Cooper noticed how the sequence interrupted the story's propulsive pace and removed it from the film. It was by all accounts a horrific tableau, with nightmarish "giant insects," and "insects with octopus arms," and "giant lizards" creeping out of the shadows to feed on the injured men. All that remains of this lost sequence are some drawings, a still or two, and the weird stop-motion reptile that climbs up to menace Driscoll as he hides in the shallow cave. An entire episode of Kong fighting a group of Triceratops was also snipped from the jungle chase.

Augmenting the stop-motion creatures were a variety of full-scale constructs, including a head-and-shoulder bust, hand, and foot of Kong, as well as a pair of pterodactyl feet to grasp Fay Wray. In her book, Wray recalled how she spent some of her longest hours not in the grasp of a giant animal but in the top of a studio tree. "A battle scene between Kong and a Tyrannosaurus had been prepared by Willis O'Brien for rear projection onto a huge screen," she recalled. "I was placed in a tree alongside the screen.... From my position, all I could see was large blurry shadowy movements on the screen. It was like having the worst seat in the house, too close to define what the shadows were." The actress was understandably exhausted by the uninterrupted twenty-two-hour session. "But I kept moving," she affirmed, "kept reacting as though I really could see the fearsome creatures, and would scream when Cooper said, 'Scream! Scream for your life, Fay!'"

Besides O'Brien and Delgado, *King Kong* was blessed with a bounty of additional talent. Obie's primary animation assistant was E. B. "Buzz" Gibson, a former studio grip with no previous animation experience. He had an aptitude for the job, however, and animated several shots in *Kong* as well as—by multiple accounts—a great percentage of the stop-motion in *The Son of Kong*. Orville Goldner was a specialist in miniatures who in years to come would spark an interest in stop-motion in a young artist named Wah Chang ("Goldner was the one who got me started doing animation," Chang told me), and ultimately coauthor the definitive book *The Making of King Kong*. Carroll Shepphird was instrumental in the meticulous pre-designing of effects set-ups, and mechanical

Test shot for the Kong-versus-pterodactyl sequence. Note visible upper edge of painted backdrop.

whiz Fred Reese was a key contributor to the engineering of the full-scale Kong bust and other mechanized "gimmicks." Vernon L. Walker was a cameraman who worked on *The Lost World* at First National before becoming head of the camera effects department at RKO. Walker's crew included Clifford Stine, who went on to spearhead the outstanding optical effects in most of the fondly remembered Universal sci-fi films of the 1950s, and Linwood Dunn, later to have one of the longest and most illustrious careers in the history of visual effects.

The better-than-real jungles created for *Kong* were largely the work of Mario Larrinaga and Byron L. Crabbe. Enhancing the detailed miniatures and live plants, Larrinaga and Crabbe painted jungle backgrounds on multiple panes of glass, which when carefully aligned and photographed produced the illusion of almost infinite depth. Not only did this technique result in artistically ominous and primordial-looking environments, the multi-plane set-up also facilitated the addition of animated elements through the use of miniature rear projection—a tremendously valuable innovation that allowed pre-filmed live action to be inserted into a miniature set. (Marcel Delgado would later lament the fact that producers never again made such an effort to create believable miniature settings for animation.) A pair of ancient traveling matte methods—the Dunning process and the Williams process—were employed for composite scenes not suited to rear projection. The "log rolling" scene is a skillful Dunning shot; the elevated train sequence is an excellent example of the Williams.

The formidable task of creating sounds for Kong and his reptilian rivals was handed to RKO's Murray Spivack. Sound movies were still very new and Spivack had no choice but to invent his own ways of doing things. He knew the title character needed a vocalization that was unusual but still believable. "I went to the Selig Zoo and got all the roars I needed," he said in the documentary *It Was Beauty Killed the Beast*. "I then slowed these down to half speed and played the tiger growl backwards against the lion roar forwards, and it gave me sort of an *uncanny* roar." Spivack used his own voice and a megaphone to create Kong's "love grunts," as he called them. As for the dinosaurs, "The only enlightenment I got was that presumably most of them were reptiles," he explained. "So of course that put me into sort of the 'hiss' level, and I couldn't quite visualize a huge animal ten feet tall coming out on the screen and going 'S-s-s-s-s!' So I had to concoct noises for these animals."

Despite the fact that *King Kong* came along relatively early in Willis O'Brien's long career it would remain his unquestioned masterpiece, and he seemed to sense this even as it was happening. "*King Kong* represents the goal of more than twenty years," he said just after the picture's release. "For that long a time — and that is a long time in motion pictures — I have delved into bygone periods, studied the life of animals long before the descent of man, preparing myself for the day when someone would dare to reproduce on the screen the giant beasts that once ruled the world. Without knowing it, I was waiting for *King Kong*." Obie didn't just pull out every trick in the book, he wrote a new book. The outstanding piece of character animation represented by Kong is legendary, but the quality of the dinosaur animation shouldn't be overlooked. For the lengthy shot of Denham and Driscoll examining the dying Stegosaurus, he had the actors walk on a treadmill while a tracking shot of Marcel Delgado's magnificent puppet was projected behind them. The pterodactyl attack, once called by Obie the most difficult sequence in the film, took seven weeks to animate. The stumpy gait of the stegosaur, the massive striding of the brontosaur, the nimble footwork of the T. rex — all helped tremendously by Delgado's meticulous models — remain some of the best dinosaur stop-motion ever done. Just as Phil Tippett would do sixty years later for *Jurassic Park*, Obie and company studied the movements of elephants for ideas to make their animated animals more naturalistic.

Almost as fascinating as the true story behind *Kong*'s FX is the misinformation that has circulated over the years. In 1933, *Time* reported that the great ape was in reality a 50-foot-tall automaton, 36 feet around the chest, with ten-inch teeth and foot-long ears, and requiring "six operators" and "85 motors" to make him perform. (Some of these dimensions correlate with the actual details of the full-size head, which may somewhat explain the origin of such reports.) The same year, *Modern Mechanix and Inventions* published a two-page spread "revealing" how various scenes were done. Some bits were correct — the basic facts about the stop-motion dinosaurs, for instance — but most of it was pure fiction. A drawing illustrated how the shots of Kong scaling the Empire State Building utilized an ape-suited stuntman crawling up a slightly inclined mock-up building. The pages also described a preposterously convoluted and utterly nonexistent process, "known as 'animating,'" whereby sequential still photos of Fay Wray were meticulously cut out, trimmed to shape, and placed one at a time in the ape's hand. Maybe the most remarkable yarn is an AP wire story from the late 1960s. "King Kong is alive, well and happy as a security guard for a Chicago insurance company," the writer stated. Yes, the article tells us, Kong was portrayed by Carmen Nigro, a 5'6" stuntman who went by the "professional" name Ken Roady but was "known for 25 years as the Hollywood Apeman." Nigro disclosed several little-known details: that "Fay Wray was an animated doll," that he also played the gorillas in *Tarzan and His Mate* and *Mighty Joe Young*, that he learned to simulate simians while on safari with Frank

Buck, and that he wore "fur-covered ballet slippers with rubber suction pads on the bottom" in order to stay atop that building.

One would think that the phenomenal success of *King Kong* would have allowed Willis O'Brien to pick and choose from a torrent of offers. But it didn't happen. Winning an Oscar for *Mighty Joe Young* in 1949 was the only other real high point of Obie's career, and even that award generated no work. Ray Harryhausen, who called working alongside O'Brien on *Mighty Joe* "the great thrill of my life," told me a bit about Obie's frustrations. "Nobody wanted to know about animation, even though Obie won the Academy Award," Harryhausen lamented. "He tried to develop so many things, and nothing happened. People just weren't interested — Merian Cooper was the only one that was … *King Kong* was the peak of his career." In a particularly eloquent moment, Forry Ackerman had this to say about Obie's most legendary character: "He has an appeal beyond Gorgo, and Godzilla, and the other gigantic monsters, because somehow or other Willis O'Brien managed to insert a *soul* into that little creature."

King Kong Escapes

"It's still not the original."

* * 1967, Japan/USA-Toho Company, Ltd./Rankin-Bass. C, 96m.

CREDITS: *Director* Ishiro Honda. *Producers* Tomoyuki Tanaka, Arthur Rankin, Jr. *Screenplay* William J. Keenan, Kaoru Mabuchi. *Special Effects Director* Eiji Tsuburaya.
CAST: *Cmdr. Carl Nelson* Rhodes Reason. *Lt. Susan Watson* Linda Miller. *Lt. Cmdr. Jiro Nomura* Akira Takarada. *Doctor Who* Eisei Amamoto. *Madame X* Mie Hama.

There's trouble afoot when criminal genius Doctor Who and mysterious spy Madame X team up to get their hands on "Element X," a substance powerful enough to give its owner "nuclear domination of the entire *universe*." Doctor Who's robot double of the great ape King Kong proves to be an inadequate Element X miner, so Who decides to abduct the real Kong from Mondo (?) Island. At that moment, however, a trio of United Nations representatives — Cmdr. Carl Nelson, Lt. Cmdr. Jiro Nomura, and Lt. Susan Watson — are already exploring Kong's domain. Kong takes a liking to the lovely Susan and gallantly kills a Tyrannosaurus-like dinosaur and a giant sea reptile which threaten her, but Doctor Who soon arrives and captures both the ape and the U.N. trio. But when King Kong inevitably escapes and the good-hearted Madame X frees Nelson and his crew, Who reactivates Mecha-Kong and the race to Japan is on. In downtown Tokyo, Mecha-Kong grabs Susan and climbs a nearby radio tower with the real Kong in hot pursuit. The flesh-and-blood Kong wins the ensuing battle, saves Susan, pulverizes Doctor Who's ship and Doctor Who with it, thumps his chest in triumph, and starts his long trip home.

COMMENTARY: *King Kong Escapes* is a Godzillaless but fairly entertaining yarn, boasting a dinosaur that is the most "realistic" — relatively speaking — of any Toho saurian. The T. rex–like, man-in-a-suit dino that does battle with Toho's version of Kong doesn't look much like a real dinosaur of course, but it doesn't have missiles for fingers, or a buzz saw in its stomach, or three heads, and it's no more ridiculous-looking than the tyrannosaurs in *The Land Unknown* or *The Last Dinosaur*. The creature isn't called by name in the film, but was dubbed the "Gorosaurus" when the same suit showed up in *Destroy All Monsters*.

The movie is based on the animated series "King Kong," which aired on ABC during the late 1960s. It is not intended as a sequel to Toho's *King Kong vs. Godzilla*, but instead borrows quite heavily from RKO's classic. Kong becomes infatuated with a human female, saves her from a carnivorous dinosaur, sets her in a tree for safety, saves her from a snake-necked water monster, gets gassed by his captor, and climbs up a tall monument in the film's climax. The wide shot of the robot Kong falling from the tower seems a deliberate homage to the similar scene in the earlier film, and there are even a few lines that could be interpreted as intentional references to the 1933 entry. A reporter asks Nelson if Kong is to be taken to New York. "No," Nelson replies, "it would be, to say the least, *difficult* to care for him here in New York!"

If the convoluted plot doesn't lose you, *King Kong Escapes* can be fun. It takes itself more seriously than do many of the later "Godzilla" entries, and Kong actually comes off looking marginally less goofy than he did when battling Godzilla a few years earlier. Toho's stalwart effects master, Eiji Tsuburaya, provides some nifty miniature work, and the fight scenes are not bad as man-in-suit battles go. Maybe the most amazing thing about *King Kong Escapes* is that — karate-chopping tyrannosaur and all — it still offers more entertainment value than the infamous 1976 version could ever hope for.

King of the Kongo

**   1929, USA. Mascot Pictures.
BW, 213m.

CREDITS: *Director* Richard Thorpe. *Producer* Nat Levine. *Written by* Harry Sinclair Drago, Wyndham Gittens.
CAST: *Diana Martin* Jacqueline Logan. *Larry Trent* Walter Miller. *Chief of Secret Service* Richard Tucker. *Macklin* Boris Karloff. *Jack Drake* Larry Steers.

"They swear there's a — well, a dinosaurus — or some sort of monster animal in the Court of the Smiling Gods," warns second-banana villain Jack Drake in *King of the Kongo*, an early 10-chapter jungle-adventure serial. Drake works for the nefarious ivory trader, "Scarface" Macklin, who is constantly trying to outwit the good-guy duo of Secret Service agent Larry Trent and adventurer Diana Martin. Trent is searching for his brother and fellow agent, Tom Trent, while Diana hopes to find her long-missing father. Throw in a mysterious, ruined temple in deepest Africa (though it looks more like Southeast Asia), a cache of priceless jewels, the native "Wahili warriors," and the killer gorilla of the title (played by strongman/stuntman Joe Bonomo), and the result is an action-filled chapterplay which dates badly but was surely satisfying in its day.

King of the Kongo bridged the gap between the silent and sound eras, featuring silent passages, with intertitles, mixed with rudimentary sound sequences. (The sound recordings are now lost, rendering the film rather hard to follow in its surviving state.) Reportedly made for only $40,000, *Kongo* has some virtues which can still be seen today, including the glowering visage of Boris Karloff in an early role as the ruthless "Scarface" Macklin, and a nice performance by Jacqueline Logan as the intrepid Diana (she even did many of her own stunts!). The aforementioned "dinosaurus" is played by a live lizard with glued-on prosthetics but is photographed on a surprisingly detailed and impressive miniature "temple" set. The cinematography by future nine-time Oscar nominee Ernest Laszlo has a lot of atypical touches and camera angles for a 1929 production, and there are a couple of unexpected revelations in the final chapter.

The chapter titles are as follows: 1 "Into the Unknown." 2 "Terrors of the Jungle." 3 "The Temple of Beasts." 4 "Gorilla Warfare." 5 "Danger in the Dark." 6 "The Fight at Lion's Pit." 7 "Fatal Moment." 8 "Sentenced to Death." 9 "Desperate Chances." 10 "Jungle Justice."

King Solomon's Treasure

"Of course, no one in the club believed a damn word of the story."

*½   1978, Canada. Canafox. C, 86m.

CREDITS: *Director* Alvin Rakoff. *Producers* Alvin Rakoff, Susan A. Lewis, Harry Alan Towers (executive). *Screenplay* Colin Turner and Allan Prior; based on Rider Haggard's *Allan Quartermain*.

The "dinosaur" seen at left in this Finnish theatrical poster looks like one of the live, dressed-up reptiles from the 1960 version of *The Lost World*, much more than it resembles either of the puppet dinosaurs in *King Solomon's Treasure*.

CAST: *Sir Henry Curtis* David McCallum. *Allan Quartermain* John Colicos. *Captain Good, R.N.* Patrick Macnee. *Queen Nypeptha* Britt Ekland. *Alphonse* Yvon Dufour. *Umpslopogas* Ken Gampu. *Oldest Club Member* Wilfrid Hyde-White. *Stetopatris* John Quentin.

AD LINE: "The story of a fantastic journey into the heart of Africa a century ago."

England's greatest white hunter and adventure-seeker, Allan Quartermain, returns from Africa bearing a remarkable Phoenician medallion. Accompanied by two close friends, Sir Henry Curtis and Captain Good (variously known as "Goody"), and joined en route by his African guide Umpslopogas, Quartermain sets out to find the ancient empire of King Solomon. The group stops to spend the night at Reverend McKenzie's mission, but the next morning are forced to rescue McKenzie's young daughter Flossie from a creature of apparently prehistoric origin. McKenzie's French chef, Alphonse, joins the safari and they press on, undeterred by quicksand, a giant snake, a swarm of six-foot crabs, or even the unexpected appearance of a massive sauropod dinosaur ("an Apatosaurus or a Brontosaurus or a Diplodocus," Sir Henry says).

The explorers are intercepted by an ancient Phoenician ship and escorted to the Lost City, where the beautiful Queen Nypeptha takes an immediate liking to the boyish Sir Henry. Sensing him to be an honorable sort, she produces a map and asks him to take King Solomon's treasure away from her city, lest it tempt her people to violence. But just as the treasure is found, the city's greedy high priest makes a play for the gold and the nearby volcano begins to erupt. In the confusion, the valiant Umpslopogas takes an arrow meant for Quartermain and the high priest murders Queen Nypeptha, but her half-brother Stetopatris vows to rebuild their great city as its new king.

COMMENTARY: The imaginative writings of H. Rider Haggard have been translated to the screen with considerable success in films like *She* in 1935 and *King Solomon's Mines* in 1937. More recent adaptations, however, have been very lackluster productions, and *King Solomon's Treasure* is a tepid, negligible little picture. It does have the distinction of being the only Haggard adaptation ever to have dinosaurs added to the story, but the characters seem strangely unsurprised at discovering the prehistoric survivors.

The only traces of treasure in *Treasure* are amongst the cast. It's quite wonderful to see John Colicos, so often cast as a villain, getting a chance to play the hero. The inimitable Wilfrid Hyde-White injects his twinkly-eyed charm into a brief prologue and epilogue which frame the story, and Macnee and McCallum both have an easygoing way that is always engaging. Ekland is unfortunately stiff as the queen, but Yvon Dufour manages to make his comic French chef surprisingly palatable. There is, in fact, a lot of "comedy relief" in the picture, including culinary debates between Alphonse and Goody and clichéd antics like a chimp swigging a bottle of wine. (My favorite bit is when Sir Henry tries to rouse the Brontosaurus with a jaunty "Tallyho!") The very lighthearted tone, however, makes the sudden burst of sustained, rather gruesome (though not gory) violence in the final reel seem even more distasteful and out of place. There are some beautiful South African locations, but the mundane cinematography makes little use of them.

The special effects are uniformly poor. The giant crabs are laughable, even worse than those in Roger Corman's *Attack of the Crab Monsters*, and the oversized rubber snake is no better. The first dinosaur glimpsed (and I do mean glimpsed, the scene is so dark) seems to be some sort of frilled ceratopsian, but it's impossible to be sure. Based on what can be made out from its head and one leg, it was a simple hand or rod puppet. The other dino is a sauropod which is just as lifeless, consisting of a minimally articulated body in the background and a full-size prop tail draped in the foreground. The tail is needed for the scene where the explorers tie a rope to it and use the beast to haul their gear up a mountainside—a concept dinomovie fans will remember from *The People That Time Forgot*. And just like the Stegosaurus in *People*, the bronto "walks" with such nonexistent leg movement that comparisons to parade floats are inevitable. The optical effects are miserable, and the mattework during the crab sequence must be some of the worst ever done. When John Colicos fires his gun while blue-screened in front of a jungle background, the billowing smoke causes such a bizarre pattern of fluctuations and shimmers in the image that it seems Quartermain has been caught by a Star Trek transporter beam.

King Solomon's Treasure is a near-forgotten effort, a fate it truthfully deserves, and looks like it cost even less than its reported budget of $1.2 million. Yet it does have an affable sense of fun, and is really no less endurable than the subsequent Haggard adaptations *King Solomon's Mines* (1985) and *Allan Quartermain and the Lost City of Gold* (1987), even though they featured bigger budgets and the on-screen pairing of Richard Chamberlain and Sharon Stone. *Treasure* has a few diverting moments, and where else can you hear David McCallum imitate a brontosaurian mating call?

PEOPLE AND PRODUCTION: It would be fair to say that *King Solomon's Treasure* was not a project born of a burning artistic vision. "It was made for the worst of motives," director Alvin Rakoff stated in a letter to the author. The executive producer was Harry Alan Towers, not a man known to lavish large sums of money on a film, and veteran director Rakoff was given little to work with. "The budget was small if not impossible," Rakoff recalled. "It was a low point in my career and I needed the work." The principal actors, including Macnee, McCallum, and Ekland, were signed for only four weeks, with doubles used for any subsequent pick-up shots.

The Phoenician city set was built near Johannesburg, South Africa, and most of the exteriors were shot on location in Swaziland. The blue-screen work was done back at Bray Studios in England. With little else to depend on, Rakoff praised the work of his art director. "My main support was a designer named James Weatherup," Rakoff remembered. "James literally managed to build castles out of polystyrene, if not straw." But the headaches were endless. "An inexperienced Canadian crew, in South Africa, with one or two Brits, little or no money, a script I was forced to rewrite almost daily, a camera that had not been pretested and resulted in a massive number of shots being out of focus and subsequently junked ... et cetera, et cetera, et cetera. I would love to do it all again," Rakoff wryly summed up, "as a behind-the-scenes comedy."

SPECIAL EFFECTS: The credits contain no mention of who did the special effects, "because no one was in charge," as Rakoff explained. Veteran creature creator Roger Dicken was briefly involved with the project, but not for long. "I started work on creating some models for the film," Dicken told the author. "There were going to be some giant crabs in it, and a big lizard thing, but I had aggravation with the production company and didn't do the film." And the situation never did stabilize. "As far as I can remember we had several dinosaur experts," Rakoff recalled, "a revolving door of dinosaur men who changed from week to week; and then later, from day to day." With no effects supervisor on the job, Rakoff had no guidance in setting up the shots. "I never knew the size or scale of the monsters, or the exact position of the supposed beasts," he pointed out. "Guesswork, and the realization that King Kong also varied in size, carried us through the day." *Treasure* wasn't completely devoid of technical talent, though. "The model maker was Bill Warrington," Rakoff revealed, "but I don't think he finished the film." Dedicated FX buffs may remember Warrington from his excellent work on such films as *Enemy from Space* (1957), *A Night to Remember* (1958), and *The Guns of Navarone* (1961), for which he won an Academy Award.

The Land Before Time

"It was a journey ... toward life."

*** 1988, USA. Universal. C, 69m.

CREDITS: *Director* Don Bluth. *Producers* Don Bluth, Gary Goldman, John Pomeroy, Steven Spielberg, George Lucas, Kathleen Kennedy, Frank Marshall (executive). *Screenplay* Stu Krieger. *Story* Judy Freudberg and Tony Geiss.
VOICES: *Littlefoot* Gabriel Damon. *Littlefoot's mother* Helen Shaver. *Cera* Candy Hutson. *Ducky* Judith Barsi. *Petrie* Will Ryan. *Rooter/Narrator* Pat Hingle. *Daddy Topps* Burke Byrnes. *Grandfather* Bill Erwin.

AD LINE: "A new adventure is born."

In a long-ago prehistoric time, nearing the end of the age of the dinosaurs, the supply of "green food" needed to sustain the herbivores begins to dwindle. One mixed herd sets off for the legendary Great Valley, "a land still lush, and green." The longnecks have welcomed their newest arrival, a hatchling called Littlefoot, just in time for the journey. But an attack by the scourge of the leaf-eaters — the dreaded Sharptooth — leaves Littlefoot's mother mortally wounded. When a violent "earth shake" opens great gorges in the earth, Littlefoot is separated from his grandparents and must try to find the Great Valley by himself.

Soon joined by a feisty young threehorn named Cera, Littlefoot starts out. They begin to meet up with other young dinosaurs — Ducky the guileless bigmouth, Petrie the befuddled flier, Spike the gentle spiketail — which have also been cut off from their families. Truly, "there had never been such a herd before." With Littlefoot leading, the brave quintet marches on in search of the Great Valley, each day following the path of the "bright circle" across the sky. As days pass and their hopes fade, only Littlefoot's optimism and determination keep them going. Finally Cera has had enough and heads off on her own, but after narrow escapes from a treacherous tar pit and a fiery volcano, she contritely rejoins Littlefoot. Tired of Sharptooth's repeated attacks, the group decides to get rid of the predator once and for all. Using Ducky as bait, they topple a boulder onto Sharptooth's head and send him plummeting into a bottomless lake. With the last of their strength, the friends climb one final hill and behold the Great Valley. Families are reunited, Littlefoot finds his grandparents, and the peaceful herds begin their new life.

COMMENTARY: Animated films are often automatically categorized as "children's movies," and it's true that many of them, including *The Land Before Time*, are aimed primarily at youngsters. But the best of them have qualities which can be appreciated and enjoyed by kids and adults. Animation — great animation, that is — possesses some otherworldly quality with the power to captivate young and old alike.

The opening sequence of *The Land Before Time* is a small masterpiece. Bizarre primordial sea creatures cavort in an underwater ballet, moving to the strains of James Horner's outstanding music score and briefly recalling the grandeur of *Fantasia*. The prologue is so full of promise that it's a bit disappointing to find that only rarely does the film again reach such visual heights. This is largely due to the story itself, which dictates that much of the action must take place in a barren environment. Desolate vistas can have their own beauty, but having so much of the action transpire in such stark surroundings seems to put a built-in limitation on one of animation's greatest strengths: the portrayal of life. On the other hand, the rainy skies and craggy backdrops do create a real sense of foreboding, and the sustained dark mood makes it seem as if the plucky little band truly earns their happy ending.

A lot of *The Land Before Time* is, in fact, rather grim, and the scene of Littlefoot's mother succumbing to her wounds is likely to elicit some moist eyes among the youngsters (and some grownups as well, who may have *Bambi* flashbacks). Don Bluth doesn't let things stay *too* somber for *too* long, though; he follows the death scene with a wonderful lighthearted segment involving some baby fliers and a sought-after cherry.

Littlefoot the "longneck" (Brontosaurus) is soon to be separated from his enormous kin in Don Bluth's *The Land Before Time*.

The villainous tyrannosaur is ferocious enough to have caused a bad dream or two, but Bluth wisely shows discretion during the fatal attack on Littlefoot's mother and cleverly reveals the action only as a shadow play on a nearby rock face.

The primary "moral" of the story is, obviously, the value and necessity of working together as a group, despite all differences. "Three-horns *never* play with longnecks," Cera says early on, parroting her father's words. Later Littlefoot asks his mother "why," and receives the answer, "Because we're different!" But Littlefoot (fortunately) can't quite see what that has to do with friendship, and goes ahead and befriends the other species anyway. It isn't a subtle message, but it is a worthy one. The narrative weaves a nice mix of nature and mysticism, even intertwining the two. Littlefoot hears his mother's words as he looks into a tiny pool of water, and is symbolically guided to the Great Valley by an apparition of her which appears in the clouds.

The five main characters are an effective mix. Littlefoot the Brontosaurus is the levelheaded one, managing to lead the others in spite of all his insecurities. Cera the Triceratops is the cynic, and a bit loud-mouthed too, like a dinosaurian Lucy Van Pelt to Littlefoot's Charlie Brown. Ducky the hadrosaur is the ingenue, taking everything at face value and desperately seeking acceptance. Petrie the pterodactyl is the clown, with his broken English and faltering attempts at flight. Spike the Stegosaurus doesn't talk, merely observing and commenting with telling facial expressions. A nice supporting character is a swinelike reptile called "ol' Rooter," who dispenses to the grieving Littlefoot some timely philosophy on the "Circle of Life" (paging *The Lion King*). The voice actors are all excellent and the creatures have a thankfully restrained dose of anthropomorphism. Veteran character actor Pat Hingle plays the wise and gentle Rooter and also narrates the film, even though the promotional literature concurrent with its release names Fred Gwynne as the narrator.

With *The Land Before Time* Don Bluth

Spike the stegosaur, Petrie the pterosaur, Ducky the hadrosaur, and Littlefoot the sauropod. Cera the ceratopsian is absent from this photograph.

made a valiant attempt to revisit the animated classics of the past, and there are moments here and there when he succeeded. But even if Bluth's dino tale cannot quite match the magical artistry of a *Snow White*—either in its animation or its storytelling—it is an admirable effort and one of the better animated features of its era.

PEOPLE AND PRODUCTION: Producer-director Don Bluth has had a lifelong affection for animation. He joined Walt Disney Productions in 1955, and became a layout artist for Filmation Studios 13 years later. In 1971, he rejoined Disney for eight more years, contributing to films such as *The Rescuers* and *Pete's Dragon*. While at Disney, Bluth began work on an animated featurette in concert with Gary Goldman and John Pomeroy. Their film, *Banjo, the Woodpile Cat*, would go on to win numerous awards and honors. In 1982, Bluth produced and directed his first feature-length film, *The Secret of Nimh*, and teamed with (executive producer) Steven Spielberg on *An American Tail*.

With his next project, Bluth brought opulent animation and dinosaurs back together for the first time since *Fantasia* in 1940. *The Land Before Time* took nearly three years to make, and aspired to equal the revered, luxurious animation of Disney's early classics. The dinosaurs took shape only after endless visits to natural history museums, examination of fossils and dinosaur reconstructions, and studies of classic dinosaur art. Additionally, modern animals such as giraffes and elephants were observed and filmed, providing clues for the dinosaurs' movements.

No less painstaking was the design of the primordial landscapes. "The artists had to create a believable environment in which there was almost no foliage," a studio press release explained. "The creative license of animation allowed for colors that could enhance the beauty and dramatic impact."

The picture features "more than 600 background paintings" and "29 optical scenes which represent the highest state of the art for an animated film." In all, about one million drawings and 100,000 hand-painted animation cels were required to complete *The Land Before Time*.

As an interesting footnote, the *New York Post* reported in 1997 that, spurred by the box-office success of *The Lost World: Jurassic Park*, there was serious talk of turning *The Land Before Time* into a full-blown Broadway musical. "The time has come for dinosaurs on Broadway," producer Irving Welzer said.

The Land Before Time II: The Great Valley Adventure

"Aw, it wasn't much fun anyway."
** 1994, USA. Universal Cartoon Studios. C, 72m.

CREDITS: *Director* Roy Allen Smith. *Producers* Roy Allen Smith, Zahra Dowlatabadi (coproducer). *Screenplay* Dev Ross, John Loy, John Ludin.

VOICES: *Littlefoot* Scott McAfee. *Cera* Candace Hutson. *Ducky* Heather Hogan. *Petrie/Ozzie* Jeff Bennett. *Strut/Spike/Chomper* Rob Paulsen. *Grandpa* Kenneth Mars. *Grandma* Linda Gary. *Narrator* John Ingle.

Life is good for the peaceful dinosaur herds in the Great Valley. One day, though, Littlefoot, Cera, Ducky, Petrie, and Spike get scolded by their parents for playing near the dangerous Sinking Sand. Cera decides that they must do something to stop the grownups from treating them like hatchlings, and the opportunity arises when they see a shifty Struthiomimus pair stealing an egg from Ducky's family nest. The five youngsters follow the thieves—"Ozzie" and "Strut"—out of the Great Valley into the little-known outworld called the "Mysterious Beyond." They retrieve the wrong egg but decide to try and raise whatever hatches out. Undeterred by the fact that the hatchling is a baby Sharptooth, Littlefoot names the tyke "Chomper" and figures maybe he can teach him to eat green food. When Chomper's meat-eating instincts begin to emerge, Littlefoot accepts that a Sharptooth cannot grow up with a bunch of leaf-eaters. Suddenly a pair of full-grown Sharpteeth appear in the Great Valley, but it turns out that all they're after is their lost baby—yes, Chomper—and the reunited threesome helpfully drive off the egg-stealers before leaving peacefully.

COMMENTARY: If the above plot synopsis suggests that this tale is a bit less compelling than the original *Land Before Time*, the suggestion is accurate. Without the guiding hand of Don Bluth or the golden touch of George Lucas and Steven Spielberg, the first of what would turn into a whole herd of direct-to-video sequels is a mediocre effort in all areas. Though the animation is better than youngsters get on Saturday morning television, it is well below the classically inspired work in Bluth's film. The story is thin in some ways and convoluted in others, and totally does away with the spiritual angles that enriched the original. The characteristics of the five young heroes are maintained, but in broad, carbon-copy strokes that add nothing new. The voice actors are all adequate, though only Candace Hutson as Cera returns from the original cast.

The Struthiomimus duo which serve as the primary villains are played as goofy comic bad guys, with British accents that make them sound like the title characters of TV's *Pinky and the Brain*. While the single-minded, bloodthirsty Sharptooth of *The Land Before Time* provided a true sense of danger, "Ozzie" and "Strut" are just bumbling clowns. There is no sense that Littlefoot and party are in any peril, so there is no adventure in their "escapes." Then there are the eminently forgettable songs, obviously added because Disney's money-making animated features always include some sprightly musical numbers. With forced rhymes and ungainly tempos, these may be the most unsingalong-able tunes in kiddie movie history. *The Great Valley Adventure* is still better than a lot of other children's entertainment out there, and youngsters liked it enough that six more sequels (as of this writing) were spawned. It's colorful, and has dinosaurs, and features "kids" who get to do fun things, and urges its young viewers not to be in too big a hurry to grow up. Not a bad message, that.

The Land Before Time III: The Time of the Great Giving

"I do not feel good about this ... oh, no, I do not."

** 1995, USA. Universal Cartoon Studios. C, 70m.

CREDITS: *Director* Roy Allen Smith. *Producers* Roy Allen Smith, Zahra Dowlatabadi. *Screenplay* Dev Ross.

VOICES: *Littlefoot* Scott McAfee. *Cera* Candace Hutson. *Ducky* Heather Hogan. *Petrie/Mutt* Jeff Bennett. *Spike* Rob Paulsen. *Hyp* Whitby Hertford. *Nod* Scott Menville. *Narrator/Cera's father* John Ingle.

Littlefoot and friends are happy in the Great Valley, bothered only by the harassment of three bullies named Hyp (a Hypsilophodon), Nod (a Nodosaurus), and Mutt (a Muttaburrasaurus). But when a volcanic eruption blocks the Thundering Falls, the valley's water supply is cut off. Littlefoot's grandpa insists that everyone must work together to survive the crisis, but bickering soon breaks out. Fed up with the adults' sniping, the five pals head off to locate an alternative water supply. They stray into the Mysterious Beyond and fortuitously discover what happened to the Thundering Falls, but before they can return with the news a lightning strike starts a huge fire. Hyp and his sidekicks impulsively dash off to find their own water, Littlefoot's bunch follows, and the adults finally show up as well. When Cera's father sees how Hyp's dad berates his son, he realizes how badly he has been treating Cera. A pack of Velociraptors appears just as everyone makes up, but the day is saved when Littlefoot's brigade unblocks the Thundering Falls. The torrent replenishes the water supply, puts out the fire, and vanquishes the raptors. Hyp and his buddies befriend the little dinos, and all the herds work together to find the remaining green food left untouched by the fire.

COMMENTARY: *The Time of the Great Giving* brings nothing new to the *Land Before Time* series. It bears all the marks of a hurried, assembly-line, direct-to-video sequel: stock plot devices, bland animation, and little imagination. The principal new characters are three "teenage" bullies the likes of which have been seen countless times before. There's the leader of the trio who abuses his sidekicks almost as much as he does his victims, the sycophantic yes-man, and the dim-witted lug who has to be prodded to say "uhh, yeah!" Most viewers are likely to agree with Cera when she says, "they're beginning to get on my nerves!" At least the songs, led by the snappy, fifties-tinged "When You're Big," are a bit better than those in the previous installment. The animation quality is pretty much the same; the fire and smoke effects come off as very cheap-looking, but there are a few fairly successful attempts to convey the atmosphere of the drying valley. Overall, *The Time of the Great Giving* is a watchable, kid-friendly, but completely routine series entry.

The Land Before Time IV: Journey Through the Mists

"Life in the Great Valley remained the same."

** 1996, USA. Universal Cartoon Studios. C, 73m.

CREDITS: *Director* Roy Allen Smith. *Producers* Roy Allen Smith, Zahra Dowlatabadi. *Screenplay* Dev Ross.

VOICES: *Littlefoot* Scott McAfee. *Cera* Candace Hutson. *Ducky* Heather Hogan. *Petrie/Ichy* Jeff Bennett. *Spike* Rob Paulsen. *Ali* Juliana Hansen. *Old One* Carol Bruce. *Archie* Charles Durning. *Dil* Tress MacNeille.

One day, a migrating herd of longnecks arrives for a layover in the Great Valley. But as Littlefoot's grandparents prepare to greet them, Grandpa falls ill. The leader of the newcomers, known only as the "Old One," tells of a medicinal plant called the nightflower which might help him. The nightflowers grow only in a dank, oppressive region called the "Land of the Mists," but naturally Littlefoot wants to go anyway. He befriends Ali, a young longneck from the visiting herd, and persuades her to show him the way to the nightflowers. Cera, Ducky, Petrie, and Spike are a bit miffed at being left out, but quickly come to the rescue when Littlefoot gets trapped in a cave-in and Ali returns to seek help. The determined group is repeatedly menaced by a toothy, nearsighted crocodile named Dil and her partner in predation, a wisecracking Ichthyornis named Ichy. But with the help of Archie the kindly Archelon and Tickles the mouse, they escape the villains and return successfully with the sought-after flowers. The medicine does its job, and Grandpa is up and around in time to watch Littlefoot and Ali say their bittersweet goodbyes.

COMMENTARY: With *Journey Through the Mists*, the *Land Before Time* series plods on through very familiar territory, neither much better nor much worse than the previous two. On the plus side, the songs are a little better, though one might have expected 10-time Oscar nominee Leslie Bricusse to have made them more than just a little better. The best of the three is "Who Needs Ya," a give-and-take duet of comic put-downs between Ichy and Dil. Like the Struthiomimus duo in *The Great Valley Adventure*, the villains are played as bumbling comedians. This again precludes any sort of real menace, but at least Ichy and Dil are slightly funnier than Ozzie and Strut. The straightforward storyline is an improvement over the meandering plots of the previous two chapters, but is plagued by slow patches. The quality of the animation seems to have dropped yet another half-notch — at times it's so lazy that the animals' walking motions look wrong — and the only visual highlight is the brief sequence of the blooming, luminescent nightflowers. *Journey through the Mists* maintains the themes of cooperation and loyalty, but is content to simply rehash them rather than building upon them.

The Land Before Time V: The Mysterious Island

"I've gotta admit it ... this was a great idea!"
★★½   1997, USA. Universal Cartoon Studios. C, 73m.

CREDITS: *Director* Charles Grosvenor. *Producers* Charles Grosvenor, Rocky Solotoff (associate). *Screenplay* John Loy.
VOICES: *Littlefoot* Brandon La Croix. *Cera* Anndi McAfee. *Ducky* Aria Noelle Curzon. *Petrie/Mr. Clubtail* Jeff Glen Bennett. *Spike* Rob Paulsen. *Grandpa* Kenneth Mars. *Chomper* Cannon Young. *Elsie* Christina Pickles.

Another peaceful day in the Great Valley is shattered by a horde of "swarming leaf-gobblers" (locustlike insects), which leave every plant in the valley stripped bare. Reluctantly, the decision is made to leave the Great Valley in search of a new food supply. As spirits sag and tempers flare, Littlefoot and friends set out to find enough green food for everyone so all the herds can stay together and be friends again. Traveling far, they reach the "Big Water" (ocean) and cross a narrow land bridge to a vegetation-covered island, but an earth shake destroys the bridge just as they arrive. They are happy to find their old friend Chomper the baby Sharptooth, but aren't so happy to find his folks lurking nearby. Other dangers also await, including a "Striped Sharptooth," a hungry pterodactyl, and a "Swimming Sharptooth" (shark) that almost gets them, until a friendly Elasmosaurus named Elsie gives them a ride to safety. Back on the mainland, the grownups have discovered an oasis of lush plant life but are despondent over having lost the young ones. Just then, Elsie swims up with all five kids safely riding atop her back, and everyone agrees there is plenty to eat until the Great Valley is green once again.

COMMENTARY: For any parents who take the time to watch the *Land Before Time* videos with their children, it's a good bet that they will find *The Mysterious Island* to be an unexpected and welcome improvement in the series. It's funnier, and has better songs, and looks sharper than any since the original.

The comedic bits have more wit than any of the previous three entries, including one clever gag that uses subtitles to translate Chomper's parents' growls for the audience. When dad sees his son gathering green food (actually for his herbivore pals), he shakes his head and grumbles pensively, "Sometimes I worry about that boy." We even get a takeoff on the old Life cereal "Mikey" commercial, and a *One Million Years B.C.* homage with Ducky standing in for Raquel Welch! The songs, this time by Michele Brourman and Amanda McBroom, are a nice mix and are easily the best of the series. There's the melodic ballad "Always There," the big band styled "Big Water," and finally the Caribbean-flavored "Friends for Dinner," which is a sharp and witty look at the perils of having a carnivore as a dinner host. The "swimming Sharptooth" is the first truly menacing villain since the initial film, and the decidedly British Elsie, wonderfully voiced by Christina Pickles, is a fresh new character. "If you're going to be seasick," she tells her passengers, "let Aunt Elsie know ... so she can duck." The animation has a markedly different "look" than the preceding chapters, and is more dynamic and imaginatively staged. The story is a bit skimpy and the middle section is slow, but *The Mysterious Island* remains an enjoyable, better-than-average animated tale.

The Land Before Time VI: The Secret of Saurus Rock

"Grandpa longneck! Are you filling these children's heads with nonsense?"

* ½ 1998, USA. Universal Cartoon Studios. C, 76m.

CREDITS: *Director* Charles Grosvenor. *Producer* Charles Grosvenor. *Screenplay* Libby Hinson and John Loy.

VOICES: *Littlefoot* Thomas Dekker. *Cera* Anndi McAfee. *Ducky* Aria Curzon. *Petrie/Spike* Jeff Glen Bennett. *Doc* Kris Kristofferson. *Grandpa* Kenneth Mars.

One night, Grandpa longneck entertains the young 'uns with a story around the campfire (or lava fissure, in this case). He spins the tale of the "Lone Dinosaur," a mysterious longneck who sauntered into town, whipped the meanest Sharptooth ever known, and left just as suddenly as he came. The legend goes on to say that a great earth shake caused the rise of a massive rock formation in the shape of the Lone Dinosaur, and if anything ever happens to "Saurus Rock" as it's called, bad fortune will befall everyone. A few days go by, and a visiting longneck appears. He calls himself "Doc," but could he be the Lone Dinosaur? Littlefoot thinks so and begins to idolize the quiet stranger. When a rash of rotten luck hits the Great Valley, the grownups blame it on Doc's appearance, but Littlefoot is sure it's because he and his friends accidentally damaged Saurus Rock. Littlefoot needs the tooth of a Sharptooth to put things right and tries some dentistry on an apparently deceased beast, but when the monster revives Grandpa longneck shows up just in time. Gramps and Doc team up to defeat the Sharptooth, and as Doc saunters off into the sunset, Littlefoot realizes that his grandpa is really his hero.

COMMENTARY: *The Secret of Saurus Rock* is a definite departure from the style of the previous installments, but different doesn't necessarily mean better. This episode is notable only for the offbeat voice casting of Kris Kristofferson as the laconic Doc, and for one above average song. It's a bit much to see Littlefoot and his dino pals in full country-western mode (complete with a "yee-HAW!" or two), but it is fun to hear Kristofferson, his voice as gravelly as a fossil bed, explaining that he just has to mosey along because his "footsteps were planted on the wanderin' trail." The highlight of the show is the song "Bad Luck," a lively number by Michele Brourman and Amanda McBroom that even lets the mute Spike finally join in with some doo-wop background vocals! Otherwise, *Saurus Rock* is a sizable step backward from the enjoyable *Mysterious Island*, and a sign that the durable series may be facing extinction.

The Land Before Time VII: The Stone of Cold Fire

"I know it doesn't make much sense, but I saw what I saw."

** 2000, USA. Universal Cartoon Studios. C, 74m

CREDITS: *Director* Charles Grosvenor. *Producers* Charles Grosvenor, Daniel J. Wiley (associate). *Screenplay* Len Uhley.

VOICES: *Littlefoot* Thomas Dekker. *Cera* Anndi McAfee. *Ducky* Aria Noelle Curzon. *Petrie* Jeff Glen Bennett. *Spike* Rob Paulsen. *Grandpa* Kenneth Mars. *Rainbowface (male)* Charles Kimbrough. *Rainbowface (female)* Patti Deutsch. *Uncle Pterano* Michael York.

These are strange days in the Great Valley. Littlefoot sees a blue meteor soar overhead, a pair of mysterious "rainbow face" dinosaurs who "talk in riddles" keep hanging around, and Petrie's long-lost Uncle Pterano suddenly shows up with a pair of shady-looking sidekicks named Rinkus and Sierra. The youngsters love the charming Pterano but the grownups know the truth — he was ostracized years earlier for unthinkingly leading a group of dinosaurs into a deadly ambush of sickle-clawed Sharpteeth. When Ducky overhears Pterano's scheme to acquire the blue meteor — reputed to be a "Stone of Cold Fire" with great powers — she is taken hostage as the three fliers set out for the Stone's resting place atop Three-Horn Peak. Littlefoot and pals pursue with the rainbow faces secretly watching over them, guardian-angel style. Little Ducky almost coaxes Pterano's long-suppressed goodness to the surface, but both groups are dismayed to find that the stone possesses no magical powers after all. When an earth shake causes Ducky to fall from a ledge, Pterano saves her and makes amends for his infamous act of cowardice. The ever-curious Littlefoot senses that something is very different about the enigmatic rainbow faces, and what they reveal before departing the Great Valley fires his curiosity for a lifetime of wondering and discovering.

COMMENTARY: The *LBT* franchise crosses into *The Twilight Zone* with this seventh installment which, as these go, is about average. The animation and design are a little better, the songs a little worse, and the first two thirds is all talk, talk, talk. There are stylish flourishes, like Pterano theatrically brandishing his wings à la Bela Lugosi with his cape. Then there are tired retreads, like Rinkus' comic British accent which sounds exactly like "Strut" in *The Great Valley Adventure*. The little dinos riding the stone raft up the volcanic tube is straight from 1959's *Journey to the Center of the Earth*, and Littlefoot's heretical curiosity about what lies beyond recalls Robert Vaughn in *Teenage Caveman*. There is one great bit parents will enjoy — a self-effacing reference to the effects of Ducky's annoyingly repetitive speech patterns. Pterano's henchman Sierra, forced to carry the little chatterbox, finally snaps. "I've been puttin' up with that whiny little voice since we took off!" he laments. "No-no-no ... Yep-yep-yep ... It's drivin' me nuts-Nuts-NUTS!" Michael York (yes, *the* Michael York) is effective as Pterano, and it's great to hear the unique pipes of Patti Deutsch once again. Otherwise, *The Stone of Cold Fire* is strictly by-the-book stuff, laden with obligatory and heavy-handed life lessons: "We must be accountable for our actions" (good), "It's important to wonder about that which we don't understand" (good), and "There's good in everyone" (somewhat debatable).

The Land Before Time VIII: The Big Freeze

"Every sleepy-time it is the same thing!"

*½ 2001, USA. Universal Cartoon Studios. C, 75m.

CREDITS: *Director* Charles Grosvenor. *Producers* Charles Grosvenor; Daniel J. Wiley (associate). *Screenplay* John Loy.

VOICES: *Ducky* Aria Noelle Curzon. *Spike* Rob Paulsen. *Littlefoot* Thomas Dekker. *Cera* Anndi McAfee. *Petrie* Jeff Bennett. *Grandpa* Kenneth Mars. *Mr. Thicknose* Robert Guillaume.

Mr. Thicknose, a Pachyrhinosaurus reputed to be the oldest and wisest denizen of the Great Valley, tries to school Littlefoot's brigade, but his meandering orations hold little interest for the would-be pupils. Ducky is miffed at Spike's uncouth habits, and Spike is preoccupied with the herd of spiketails visiting the Great Valley, but everyone's attention soon turns to a sudden onslaught of winter weather. Most enjoy the snow, for a while, but Ducky and her mom worry that they are losing Spike to the spiketails. Soon everybody grows fearful of the worsening snowstorm, and when it is discovered that Mr. Thicknose knew of the blizzard's approach, the grownups seem to think he should have done something about it (?) and ostracize him from the group. Meanwhile, the wandering spiketails set out in search of food and Spike decides to go with them. Ducky, unwilling to let her brother go, follows along with Littlefoot, Cera, Petrie, and Mr. Thicknose right behind. After helping the children survive a massive avalanche and a sharptooth attack, Mr. Thicknose discovers a hot spring which has formed an oasis of warmth and nourishment. Following Thicknose's suggestion, Cera uses her ear-splitting voice to trigger a second avalanche and clear the passageway into the Great Valley, and Thicknose, now a hero, leads the dinosaurs to the hot springs where they can ride out the winter. Finally, Spike's love for Ducky and his adoptive mom — and his nose for food — lead him to the oasis as well.

COMMENTARY: As this seemingly unending series reaches its eighth installment, it becomes increasingly and depressingly clear just how little imagination it has. Though somewhat masked behind solid production values and an undeniable sheen of professionalism, all of the sequels have for the most part simply rehashed the same four or five plot devices. Strangers come to the Great Valley and upset the status quo; a natural phenomenon — often disastrous — renders the Valley temporarily uninhabitable; the youngsters venture into the Mysterious Beyond (still mysterious? after all their excursions into it?) on some important quest, right under the noses of the less-than-diligent adults; a meat-eating "sharptooth" makes one or two woefully inept attempts to snack on the brave tykes; and the adults grumble and gripe until being taught a lesson by the returning, triumphant kids. *The Big Freeze* actually has *all* of these elements, which may explain why the whole thing seems so dreadfully tired.

The three inevitable songs, again by Michele Brourman and Amanda McBroom, are okay, though parents may lament that "The Mad Song" contains step-by-step instructions for throwing a temper tantrum. Admittedly, the voice actors have been with the series long enough to become quite good in their roles, and the animation this time is some of the most elaborate and attractive in any of the sequels. Many children will enjoy *The Big Freeze*, and parents could certainly do worse in choosing for their youngsters, but it's a sad fact that commercialism has long since overshadowed inspiration in the *Land Before Time* series.

The Land That Time Forgot

"Our time together, gentlemen, promises to be extremely interesting."

**½ 1975, U.K.-Amicus/American International Pictures. C, 90m.

CREDITS: *Director* Kevin Connor. *Producers* John Dark, Max J. Rosenberg, Milton Subotsky, Robert H. Greenberg (executive), John Peverall (associate). *Screenplay* James Cawthorn and Michael Moorcock; based upon the novel by Edgar Rice Burroughs. *Dinosaur Sequences* Roger Dicken. *Special Effects Supervisor* Derek Meddings.

CAST: *Bowen Tyler* Doug McClure. *Capt. Von Schoenvorts* John McEnery. *Lisa Clayton* Susan Penhaligon. *Mr. Bradley* Keith Barron. *Dietz* Anthony Ainley. *Ahm* Bobby Parr. *Olson* Declan Mulholland.

AD LINE: "You will never forget The Land That Time Forgot!"

In 1916, as World War I rages in Europe, the German submarine U-33 torpedoes a British supply ship. The only survivors are American shipbuilder Bowen Tyler, British biologist Lisa Clayton, and British naval officer Mr. Bradley with a handful of his men. Adrift with no hope of rescue, the group makes a desperate play when the sub surfaces nearby. Much to the dismay of the U-boat's commander, Captain Von Schoenvorts, and his ruthless second in command, Dietz, Tyler and the small band successfully gain control of the sub. They head west to try and reach a neutral American port, little realizing that a bit of compass tampering has them actually sailing south. With their fuel almost exhausted, they spot a huge, uncharted, ice-bound land mass, and Captain Von Schoenvorts is certain they have rediscovered the lost continent of Caprona.

They find Caprona to be a lost world of lush vegetation and prehistoric animals. Pterosaurs circle overhead, a Diplodocus grazes nearby, and a vicious Mosasaurus snatches an unfortunate sailor right off the deck. As Von Schoenvorts, Bradley, Tyler and Lisa debate what wine to serve with Plesiosaurus, they agree that the far-off war is meaningless in Caprona. Further inland they discover tribes of primitive humans, and a friendly caveman named Ahm accompanies them back to camp. From their guest they learn that there are petroleum deposits in the area, and the mixed British and German group makes plans to refine the oil and refuel the sub. Meanwhile they continue to encounter more dinosaurs, including Allosaurus and Styracosaurus, and witness a battle between a Triceratops and a Ceratosaurus. But just as their refining chores are almost complete, they are attacked by a savage tribe. Lisa is captured, and Ahm is carried off by a massive pterodactyl. Tyler rescues Lisa, but when an outbreak of volcanic eruptions threatens the sub, Dietz gets panicky and insists upon leaving. Von Schoenvorts and Bradley refuse, but Dietz takes command at gunpoint and orders the sub under way. It's all in vain, though, as the heat overcomes the crew and destroys the U-boat. Resigned to remaining in Caprona, Tyler and Lisa exchange vows and face their uncertain future together.

COMMENTARY: In the years since its release, *The Land That Time Forgot* has acquired a reputation as a bad film, but it is not a bad film. It is, in fact, an engaging, dinosaur-filled adventure yarn, flawed but consistently fun. There seem to be two reasons that the picture is so unduly criticized. First, it does have moments that *are* bad, but bad moments exist in a lot of good movies. Second, it is often unfairly "lumped in" with the subsequent *At the Earth's Core* and *The People That Time Forgot*, both of which are decidedly lesser efforts. With the pieces that were in place, *Land* could have been glorious, but must ultimately settle for slightly above average.

Doug McClure's acting and Roger Dicken's dinosaurs often seem to share the critics' wrath. More on McClure later; but first the dinos. To begin with, the dinosaurs that stalk *The Land That Time Forgot* have two virtues that even their harshest detractors cannot deny. First, they're plentiful, and before the picture ends we see a pterodactyl, Mosasaurus, Plesiosaurus, Diplodocus, Allosaurus, Ceratosaurus, Triceratops, Styracosaurus, and Polacanthus—a whopping nine species. Second, they are thankfully based on real dinosaurs rather than being whatsit-sauruses like those that populate *At the Earth's Core* and the last two thirds of *The People That Time Forgot*.

The dino simulations themselves run hot and cold. The meat-eaters such as Allosaurus and Ceratosaurus are the least successful. Though nicely detailed, their motion is restricted and awkward and their heads seem to "bob about" unnaturally on their bodies. The horned herbivores like Triceratops and Styracosaurus come off much better. They have a believably bulky, stumpy-legged heft, and their gaits are far more credible than those of the carnivores. The two most lifeless dinos in the film are, not surprisingly, the full-size creations. The sailor-eating mosasaur head and the unflappable pterodactyl (neither done by Dicken) suffer from the same starched rigidity that almost always doomed attempts to build giant, life-size monsters. These big mockups look passable in still photos, but when they try to move it seems that rigor mortis has set in. Dicken's puppets, on the other hand, are always energetic if not always perfect.

Like the dinosaurs, Doug McClure's performance is not as bad as advertised either. He plays Bowen Tyler just like Burroughs wrote him — gregarious, physical, and stalwart. McClure and the entire cast play it straight, never winking at the camera, and the results are more than adequate. John McEnery and Anthony Ainley are surprisingly credible as Von Schoenvorts and Dietz (though McEnery's German accent was reportedly dubbed by actor Anton Diffring). Keith Barron exudes English resolve as the stiff-upper-lipped Bradley, and the lovely Susan Penhaligon makes the level-headed Lisa elegantly believable. The actors benefit from a sober, efficient screenplay by James Cawthorn and Michael Moorcock, which stays fairly true to the Burroughs novel. Rather than tossing off the voyage to Caprona as some necessary evil that must be endured until we get to the dinosaurs, the script uses the film's first 30 minutes to establish and flesh out the characters. (This portion of the story bears more than a passing resemblance to the real-life fate of the *Lusitania*.) On the negative side, Burroughs' complex concepts of Capronan evolution do not translate easily to the screen, and the whole notion of the "secret of Caprona" is never satisfactorily explained.

The picture is reminiscent of the stylish British genre films of the fifties in its lack of histrionics and no-nonsense tone. Nobody overacts or overreacts, and when the first dinosaurs are spotted nobody overdoes the awestruck expressions. The script doesn't hit you on the head with the revelation that Von Schoenvorts is not a "bad guy" but an honorable man; you simply realize it as the story progresses. There are even bits of droll humor, like when Dietz brags about Von Schoenvorts' skill in sinking a British warship. "He's not very good against lifeboats, though, is he?" the tubby Olson dryly replies.

The look of Caprona is generally impressive, due in considerable part to production designer Maurice Carter. The continent is rife with lush greenery, murky pools, panoramic landscapes, ominous mists, and mysterious glows, all enhanced by Douglas Gamley's full-blooded music score. Tiny details, such as Von Schoenvorts pausing to wipe the periscope's eyepiece, or a bleached dinosaur skull lying by the tar pit, add to the verisimilitude. The fine location photography by Alan Hume saves *Land* from the studio-bound aura which plagues many similar pictures such as *Unknown Island* and *Lost Continent*. Like the dinosaur effects, Derek Meddings' miniature and physical effects vary in quality, lamentable one moment but commendable the next. Meddings also orchestrated the obligatory eruption sequence, incorporating some actual volcano footage with simulated scenes. The eruption is geologically absurd but visually exciting, as real chunks of flaming debris seem to rain down perilously close to the actors.

Like the 1960 remake of *The Lost World*, *The Land That Time Forgot* must be called something of a missed opportunity. *Land* is more enjoyable and grown-up than Irwin Allen's rather goofy opus, but either film could have been elevated to the dinomovie penthouse had their makers simply utilized two resources that both productions were blessed with. First, they had imaginative adventure tales written by revered and beloved authors upon which to base their stories. Second, they had available the services of special effects artists with a true love and knowledge of dinosaurs. Sadly, in neither case were these men allowed to work their magic as they would have liked. Willis O'Brien, of course, had virtually nothing to do with Allen's lizard-infested *Lost World*, and here Roger Dicken was given only a fraction of the time which should have been allotted for such a formidable FX challenge. *The Land That Time Forgot* remains a surprisingly literate and generally absorbing tale, and is easily the best of the three mid-seventies Burroughs adaptations. No matter the critics, Dicken's dinos and Doug's derring-do provide just enough momentum to ride out the bumps of the frustratingly low budget, and keep *Land* above water.

PEOPLE AND PRODUCTION: "It took ten years to finally put this picture together. We're going to stick to the flavor of Edgar Rice Burroughs, as far as the portrayal, and the way that the book is written. My grandfather would have been very pleased and elated that one of his best science fiction works is being filmed right now." So said Edgar Rice Burroughs' grandson Danton Burroughs during the making of *The Land That Time Forgot*. Whether he still felt the same way upon seeing the completed picture is unknown, because after such a long wait to get the project going, far too little time was spent on the actual production.

Before principal photography began, there were some debates regarding the casting of the lead role. Producer Max Rosenberg wanted and actually signed Stuart Whitman, but AIP co-founder Samuel Z. Arkoff held out for Doug McClure. In the promotional featurette, *The Master of Adventure,* director Kevin Connor explained McClure's qualifications: "He's the Edgar Rice Burroughs idea of a hero. He's always cool, he always plays it straight, doesn't do anything dirty, never has any sex, he's a good lad." For the lone female role, they chose charming 24-year-old Susan Penhaligon, known to producer John Dark from *The Last Chapter* (1973). In spite of the restricted budget — a given when AIP was involved — the project could still boast some impressive behind-the-scenes talent. Production designer Maurice Carter's résumé included Oscar nominations for his art direction of *Becket* (1964) and *Anne of a Thousand Days* (1969), special effects supervisor Derek Meddings would later nab a Special Achievement Oscar for *Superman* (1978), and dinosaur maker Roger Dicken had of course been nominated with Jim Danforth for *When Dinosaurs Ruled the Earth.*

Land was profitable enough to spawn a pair of thrown-together follow-ups from AIP over the next two years. The cartoony *At the Earth's Core* appeared first, followed by *The People That Time Forgot*, a direct sequel to *Land*. All three starred Doug McClure, were directed by Kevin Connor, and were based on stories by Edgar Rice Burroughs. The trio became an unofficial quartet in 1978 when Columbia released *Warlords of Atlantis.* Though not from AIP and not based on Burroughs' work, it was nonetheless another Connor-directing, McClure-starring "lost continent–giant monsters" adventure. However, the *Warlords* creatures (created by Roger Dicken after sitting out *Core* and *People*) were in no way dinosaurish, eliminating it from inclusion in this volume.

SPECIAL EFFECTS: Just a few short years after *Dinosaurs Ruled the Earth*, Roger Dicken returned to prehistoric territory when he landed the dino-making job for *The Land That Time Forgot*. Dicken was immediately informed that stop-motion was not an option. He sold Milton Subotsky on the idea of "puppetized dinosaurs" with an impromptu hand-puppet show, done while kneeling behind an easy chair in Subotsky's office. "Then," as Dicken remembers, "the madness started. It was literally a very few weeks to create it all."

Working in his studio, Dicken set about designing and constructing his menagerie.

Bowen Tyler (Doug McClure) tries to close the hatch against an aggressive Plesiosaurus, as Olson (Declan Mulholland) struggles with his aim.

The puppets were "about the size of a big dog," as Dicken told the author, with metal skeletons, polyurethane foam bodies, and latex skin. The ceratopsians' horns were cast in fiberglass resin, which gave a nice splintering effect when one of the styracosaurs got his frill blown to bits by the submarine's gun. "We put a charge in that beastie, to do that," Dicken recalled. With time the most precious commodity during dino construction, Dicken saved it whenever possible. For instance, the spiky-backed Polacanthus briefly seen feeding on plants was only "half a dinosaur," Dicken revealed. "There's no point in making two sides if you're just going to have a quick shot." The creatures could drool courtesy of a "dribble tube" which controlled the saliva, and blink their eyes when a cord was pulled.

The dinosaurs were operated by Dicken himself with additional help as required, and getting the four-legged beasts to walk was a challenge. Dicken would insert one arm up into the head and use his other arm to operate one front leg, while two additional operators would work the other legs. The feet were equipped with threaded holes so that puppeteering rods could be bolted on. "We would have to get into a swinging motion of 'one-two-three-four' to get these things to trundle across the set," Dicken explained.

The film's two attempts at full-size monsters were not Dicken's doing. "I did not make the giant pterodactyl — that was a constant thorn in my side — or the huge head that was used in a closeup on the submarine," Dicken pointed out. In *The House of Hammer* (no. 14), special effects supervisor

A Roger Dicken rod-puppet Allosaurus rampages on a German lobby card for *The Land That Time Forgot*.

Derek Meddings told author John Brosnan about the big aquatic beast. "That head and its mechanism was built at Shepperton," Meddings said. "We did the shot several times and each time it got harder to raise the thing because of all the water it had absorbed—it got so heavy we had to put a block and tackle on it and pull it up very gently." The pterodactyl was hopelessly stiff and lifeless, but must be called an ambitious failure. Constructed at full scale with a massive 32-foot wingspan, the creature was suspended by piano wires from a rotating crane and photographed on location at Maidenhead gravel pit. Attention to camera angles and judicious editing prevented the crane from appearing on film, as the huge model swung around the central support like a carnival ride.

Roger Dicken sums up his work on *Land* realistically. "They're not perfect dinosaurs by any stretch of the imagination," he admits, but the variety of species and detailing of the puppets that he achieved in such a ridiculously short time frame remain impressive. Nobody would have wished harder for a top-line, lavish production than Dicken. "We needed miniature trees made, to give scale and all that," he lamented. "No miniature trees or hanging vines, I'd have liked all that sort of stuff, but, of course, I couldn't get it—I grew up with *King Kong*, after all!" Dicken is also quick to distance himself from the next film in AIP's Burroughs cycle. "Whatever the failings of [the *Land* dinosaurs], I am happy to say that I had nothing to do with the horrendous exploding creatures produced for *At the Earth's Core*," he stated with a smile. "At least with a puppet monster, you can project yourself through it."

It is noteworthy that the film's dino

effects got generally good reviews at the time of the picture's release in Great Britain; the bad buzz is a fairly recent (and American?) phenomenon. In the February 1975 issue of the British Film Institute's *Monthly Film Bulletin*, reviewer Jonathan Rosenbaum stated that "the show unquestionably belongs to the technicians who worked on the visuals," and that the film "can chiefly be regarded as a credit to its craftsmen." Likewise, in *Films & Filming* of May 1975, David McGillivray found the monsters to be "especially interesting." No details had been released on how the beasts were operated, so McGillivray was left to postulate. "The method is obviously cheap but nevertheless effective enough to give Ray Harryhausen a jolt," he contended, "but however it was achieved, the illusion — helped along by some judicious editing — is a clever one."

The Land Unknown

"What could be worse than that thing that attacked us?"

**½ 1957, USA. Universal-International. BW, 78m.

CREDITS: *Director* Virgil Vogel. *Producer* William Alland. *Writer* Laszlo Gorog; adaptation by William N. Robson. *Story* Charles Palmer. *Special Photography* Clifford Stine, R. O. Binger. *Optical Effects* Roswell A. Hoffman. *Special Effects Created by* Fred Knoth, Orien Ernest, Jack Kevan.

CAST: *Cmdr. Alan Roberts* Jock Mahoney. *Margaret Hathaway* Shawn Smith. *Lt. Jack Carmen* William Reynolds. *Dr. Carl Hunter* Henry Brandon. *Steve Miller* Phil Harvey. *Capt. Burnham* Douglas R. Kennedy.

AD LINE: "Not since the dawn of creation ... a sight like this!"

A navy task force arrives at Antarctica to investigate the mysterious "warm-water oasis" previously reported by the Byrd expedition. A helicopter is dispatched inland carrying Cmdr. Alan Roberts, Lt. Jack Carmen, mechanic Steve Miller, and reporter Maggie Hathaway. Suddenly enveloped by a massive cloud bank, the 'copter collides with a pterodactyl and plunges 3,000 feet below sea level before finally touching down in a steamy, haze-covered valley. Lacking the parts to repair their craft, the group decides to do some exploring.

Miller discovers a dead pterosaur (likely the one that hit the 'copter), but everything else in the valley is menacingly alive. The explorers watch a pair of giant reptiles in mortal combat, and become trapped by a terrifying Tyrannosaurus. The T. rex is suddenly frightened away by a weird wailing sound, and the mystery deepens when they find evidence of another human in the valley. Catching Maggie alone, the wild-looking stranger — actually Dr. Carl Hunter, sole survivor of an ill-fated 1945 expedition — forcibly takes her to his hidden cave. Ten years of the huge beasts and nine-month-long nights have seemingly turned Hunter into a beast himself, and he's even learned to control the dinosaurs by blowing through a conch shell (the strange noise they heard). When Maggie's companions find Hunter, he offers to furnish a spare part for their helicopter in exchange for the woman. Alan refuses the deal and takes Maggie back, but she later makes a selfless decision and slips away to join Hunter. The crazed Steve tries to beat Hunter into submission until Alan intervenes, asserting that "we're not going to dig our way out of here through human flesh!" Alan's compassion rekindles Hunter's dormant humanity, and he agrees to provide the needed parts. The men fix the helicopter just in time to escape the approaching Tyrannosaurus and fly to the rescue of Maggie and Hunter, about to fall victim to a giant Elasmosaurus. Alan hoists Maggie and Hunter into the hovering 'copter and dispatches the elasmosaur with a magnesium flare. The group returns to the flagship, arriving just before weather conditions would have forced the fleet to leave without them. Alan proposes to Maggie and suggests a honeymoon at the South Pole. "Well, it's *one* way of keeping warm."

COMMENTARY: *The Land Unknown* is the

only example of the man-in-suit, mechanical-mock-up, and live-lizard methods of dinosaur creation being combined in one film. Sadly, the suited creature suffers from poor design, the mechanical beastie is ruinously stiff, and lizards—despite decades of attempts to convince us otherwise—simply do not make good dinosaurs (even when referred to in the preview trailer as "the great Stegosauri!"). Yet even shackled with these misguided monsters, *The Land Unknown* never bores and only occasionally degenerates into camp. Just as great FX are sometimes not enough to rescue an otherwise rotten movie, a picture with other strengths can sometimes survive some mighty goofy dinosaurs.

Before the refugees from the Museum of Unnatural History lumber and swim into the film, *The Land Unknown* displays some good qualities. The opening reel has the so-called "documentary style" employed by so many genre films of the 1950s, and as fans know, this quasi-authoritative approach usually turned out more silly than serious. But *Land Unknown* does it better than most, incorporating some actual footage from the 1947 Byrd expedition while wisely omitting the self-important, bombastic narration that usually accompanied these sequences. Many details during the early scenes ring true, including various geographical names (Mt. Erebus, Ross Sea), helicopter jargon (collective control, push-pull tube), and even radio procedure (for once, they don't say "over and out"). On arrival in the valley, the documentarylike tenor gives way to some serviceable monster-movie melodrama and lets the unexpectedly appealing cast have some fun.

By the time Universal-International stopped fantasizing about big stars and actually hired some actors, *The Land Unknown* was inhabited by the cast unknown. But William Reynolds, Shawn Smith and Henry Brandon all give effective performances. Reynolds was a natural actor with a guy-next-door likability, Smith lends Maggie a convincing tenacity, and Brandon projects a wonderfully feral appearance, wisely sinking his teeth into the part rather than the scenery. Jock Mahoney was never a polished actor but found a good match for his talents in Commander Roberts, a pragmatic, no-nonsense scientist ideally suited to Mahoney's rather wooden screen persona. The script inevitably leans toward the stiff and preachy but is better than expected, especially in its happy omission of the irritating "comic relief" character so often deemed a necessity. The writers did give Maggie the unimaginative habit of swooning into a dead faint every time danger approaches, but the tensions and conflicts that break out within the group are handled in passably plausible fashion.

The film's best quality is the dank, primordial milieu in which it unfolds. Art director Alexander Golitzen, assisted by Richard H. Riedel, transformed Universal's largest process stage into a steamy and suffocating miniworld, perfect for incubating bizarre prehistoric creatures but causing pampered humans to weaken and lose hope, as their clothes and other man-made things disintegrate around them. The meticulously painted backdrops don't look totally "real" but are effectively unreal, and the skillful use of light and shadow by cinematographer Ellis W. Carter demonstrates how black-and-white can be an asset. In one well-constructed sequence, Carter dramatically alters the illumination—and the mood—inside the helicopter as it descends into the lost world. Joseph Gershenson's music, employing a simple two-note motif, adds to the atmosphere.

If Dino De Laurentiis had studied *The Land Unknown* before remaking *King Kong*, he could have learned that spending a fortune on a cumbersome mechanical monster often doesn't pay off. The Tyrannosaurus and Elasmosaurus were expensive, "high-tech" beasties, actually impressive in a certain way, but never remotely believable as living animals. The T. rex is a zoologist's nightmare. With glassy eyes, an upright stance and a humped back worthy of Lon

The giant but rather creaky Elasmosaurus bears down on plucky Maggie Hathaway (Shawn Smith) in *The Land Unknown*.

Chaney's stand-in, it is simply too comical to take seriously. Its arms seem frozen, the robotic-looking jaw opens wider than a rattlesnake's, and it walks like ... well, like there's a man inside. Its only saving grace is its single-minded, walnut-brained behavior—it just *knows* there are some tasty morsels in that helicopter and it's going to get them or get dissected trying. Cinematically, the Elasmosaurus is slightly better. Its mechanically smooth movements seem more appropriate for a water-borne animal, and the constant wetness of its skin lends an organic quality.

Virgil Vogel may seem a big step down from Jack Arnold, but his direction of *The Land Unknown* is solid from start to finish. He keeps things moving, holds the melodrama to a tolerable level, and even comes up with a few truly striking moments, like the creepy shot of the carnivorous plant snaking to life behind the unsuspecting Maggie. Vogel's efforts, the game cast, and a talented behind-the-scenes ensemble work together and save *The Land Unknown* from being killed by its own disappointingly dreadful dinosaurs.

PEOPLE AND PRODUCTION: During the mid–1950s, Universal-International turned out a steady stream of mostly quite good science fiction films. When it announced its Lost World picture, it roared that it would be a big-budget spectacular with big names (Cary Grant and Veronica Lake were mentioned), color and CinemaScope, and would be directed by the studio's top genre director, Jack Arnold. When all was said and done, well, it *was* in CinemaScope. It also retained producer William Alland, referred to in press releases as "U-I's expert in the field of science-fiction films." Alland produced many of the studio's sci-fi and monster entries during the period, including *It Came from Outer Space* (1953), *The Creature from the Black Lagoon* (1954), *Tarantula* (1955), and *This Island Earth* (1955), but his heart was not in *Land Unknown*. The directing job fell to former editor Virgil Vogel, who told interviewer Tom Weaver how he inherited the picture. "Universal sent me to the Astoria Studios in New York," Vogel recalled, "where I spent three or four weeks going through footage of the Byrd expedition, looking for stock footage we could use." As the "big" production steadily shrunk, "Jack [Arnold] kind of lost interest in it," Vogel said. Since he had no seniority on Universal's directorial team—his only previous experience being U-I's *The Mole People*—and was familiar with the project, he got the job.

Universal was blessed during this era with exceptional behind-the-scenes talent, in the exact areas most crucial to fantastic films. These artists are a major factor in the success—both at the time of release and today—of U-I's sci-fi/horror cycle. The stylish art direction of Alexander Golitzen, the often-masterful effects photography of Clifford Stine, and the optical magic of Roswell A. Hoffman enlivened many a movie fan's evening. Golitzen, Stine, and Hoffman reached their zenith with *The Incredible Shrinking Man* (1957), one of the most visually striking science fiction films ever made. *Tarantula* is another Stine showcase, for which he pushed the limits of the traveling matte process to achieve some of the most convincing illusions ever created with that technique.

When *The Land Unknown* was still planned as an epic, it was going to be shot on the Universal backlot. "They had a big place called Fall's Lake, which was surrounded by big rock cliffs, that they were going to use," Vogel told Weaver. But the budget withered, the plans changed, and it was moved indoors to the process stage. The cavernous stage housed a 300- by 100-foot pool which was dressed up as the prehistoric river, and great quantities of dry ice (heated by baby-bottle warmers!) filled the massive set with a thick haze. To add depth, the stage was surrounded by a painted backdrop called a cyclorama. "That's a big piece of canvas, about 75 feet tall and about 300 feet long," Vogel explained, which "hung all around the edge of the stage." Helped by the talents of Golitzen, et al., the simulated landscape would prove quite adequate. In *Cheap Tricks and Class Acts*, author J. J. Johnson calls the environment "easily the most surreal (and in a sense, gothic) setting of any fifties monster movie."

The actors finally signed for *The Land Unknown* were certainly not stars of the magnitude promised by the early ballyhoo, but the promotional department did their best. Jock Mahoney was trumpeted as "the first full-fledged movie stunt man to become a motion picture star," which is a reasonably defensible statement, but Shawn Smith was called an "acting discovery" despite having 25-plus films under her belt. Mahoney's presence had one definite fringe benefit: he could (and did) do all of his own stuntwork, including a high leap from the helicopter into the soundstage river. The athletic Mahoney even saved a life during production, swimming to and pulling out a fellow stuntman who had gotten in trouble in the water.

SPECIAL EFFECTS: "It is a distinct tribute to the genius of movie magicians that these towering prehistoric monsters have been manufactured to move with a fantastic realism which makes them completely lifelike and believable at all times." Such was the deadly-serious claim of U-I's publicity department, boasting about the dinosaur stars of *The Land Unknown*. The film's two principal dinos were ambitious, complicated, and comparatively expensive, but ultimately disappointing. Fred Knoth, who years before had supervised the miniature work for *One Million B.C.*, was in charge of making the dinosaurs, and the ungainly creatures eventually ate a big chunk of the budget. According to J. J. Johnson, Knoth oversaw the project, with the construction chores "spear-

The navy 'copter — actually a very good scale model of the real one — takes off just ahead of the attacking T. rex.

headed" by Jack Kevan (*The Creature from the Black Lagoon*) and Orien Ernest. Despite the dinosaurs' unconvincing nature, the studio's promotional people were undeterred. "The results were so remarkable that U-I has requested a patent on the fabulous monsters," the film's pressbook claimed, "and will not explain the method of operation other than to state that they involve a consolidation of chemistry, electronics, hydraulics, and human assistance."

The Tyrannosaurus and Elasmosaurus were the star dinos. (The Elasmosaurus is never called such in the movie, but is identified in the preview trailer and the studio's promotional material.) According to U-I, "it required almost three years and an estimated $60,000 worth of experimentation to produce these animals and make them operate with complete lifelike fluidity." The unique-looking Tyrannosaurus, a man in a suit, towered a whopping 12 feet tall. The suit performer had only to walk — all of the facial articulations were hydraulically controlled. "It was a heavy piece of equipment," Virgil Vogel explained. "Everything was hydraulic — the eyelids, the mouth and so on." An off-camera operator could open the mouth, blink the eyes and flare the nostrils, all from a remote panel. The hydraulic tubing ran from the controls to the dino head through a hole in the end of the tail. The T. rex survives the film but must have eventually met a bad end, because its decapitated head later turned up in the TV series *The Munsters* as "Spot," the pet dragon who lived under the staircase.

The water-borne Elasmosaurus, measuring a sprawling 15 feet wide, was even more complex than the T. rex. "They spent

A young studio visitor makes a close study of the unique-looking tyrannosaur suit constructed for ***The Land Unknown***.

a fortune on that," Vogel recalled; "it was a magnificent monster." The huge creation traveled on railroad tracks mounted to the bottom of the big pool, and like the rex was hydraulically actuated. Its operator (reportedly Fred Knoth) could articulate the trunk, neck, mouth, and flippers, although the neck and flippers are the only sections that move noticeably on screen. Locomotion was provided by an off-screen crew, pulling the beast along on its underwater rails.

The third man-made creature was the pterodactyl; as Vogel put it, it was "one of the cheapest things we had". As opposed to the unsuccessful but complex elasmosaur and T. rex, the pterodactyl was merely a static model on a string, relegated to a pair of fly-bys and a shot of it lying dead on the ground. The remainder of the "dinosaurs" were portrayed by those tried and true performers, live lizards—extremely BIG live lizards in this case. "Those were real monitor lizards, about eight or nine feet long," Vogel recalled. "They were handled by a guy by the name of Jimmy Dannaldson, who was probably one of the best animal trainers alive at that time." Their reptilian fight scene is particularly barbaric-looking—one hopes that the apparent savagery was achieved entirely through Dannaldson's expertise and cinematic illusion, and nothing more unpleasant.

When all was said and done, Virgil Vogel was basically satisfied with the film's effects sequences. "I thought that *The Land Unknown* had lots of good special effects,

The Last Dinosaur

"Here's to a successful bore!"

** 1977, Japan/USA. Rankin/Bass Productions/Tsuburaya Productions. C, 94m.

CREDITS: *Directors* Alex Grasshoff and Tom Kotani. *Producers* Arthur Rankin, Jr., Jules Bass, Benni Korzen, Masaki Iizuka, Kinshiro Ohkubo, Kazuyoshi Kasai (associate). *Tsuburaya Productions Producer* Noboru Tsuburaya. *Screenplay* William Overgard. *Special Effects* Kazuo Sagawa.

CAST: *Masten Thrust* Richard Boone. *Chuck Wade* Steven Keats. *Francesca Banks* Joan Van Ark. *Bunta* Luther Rackley. *Dr. Kawamoto* Tetsu Nakamura.

Masten Thrust, legendary big game hunter and the world's richest man, has run out of challenges and is struggling to adapt to an increasingly ecology-conscious world. His old juices start to flow, however, when one of his oil prospecting crews finds evidence of a living Tyrannosaurus in a mysterious Arctic oasis. Thrust assembles an expedition consisting of himself, his friend Dr. Kawamoto, Chuck Wade (the only survivor of the previous encounter), a Maasai tracker named Bunta, and daring reporter-photographer Francesca "Frankie" Banks. Using a manned drilling machine called the "Polar-Borer," the small band sets out beneath the Arctic Sea.

Within hours of arriving in the temperate valley, the explorers come face to face with a variety of prehistoric life—pterosaurs, a (previously unclassified) horned dinosaur, a tribe of Neanderthal-like humans, and the Tyrannosaurus rex. Thrust is obviously drooling at the prospect of taking the rex as the ultimate trophy, but has promised Kawamoto that "the animal will not be hunted." As time passes, things start to go sour. The mischievous T. rex swipes the Polar-Borer and steps on Doctor Kawamoto, the primitive tribe grows more aggressive, and Frankie finds herself falling in love with both Masten *and* Chuck! Thrust cites Kawamoto's death as an excuse to kill the tyrannosaur, but the ease with which the T. rex defeats an upstart Triceratops proves that he won't be an easy victim. Most of Thrust's hunting strategies involve the use of boulders—he uses one to drag the dinosaur down a hill and another as a catapult-fired projectile—but the assaults do little more than irritate the behemoth. Chuck luckily stumbles upon the Polar-Borer, but Bunta becomes the dinosaur's next victim and Thrust's obsession with killing it grows even stronger. Ignoring Frankie's pleas, Thrust sends her away with Chuck and resumes his battle against his dinosaurian Moby Dick.

COMMENTARY: *The Last Dinosaur* very much follows the basic "Lost World" plot structure, a well-used formula which still offers the opportunity for distinctive twists. This picture definitely *has* some distinctive twists, but they are sadly counteracted at every turn by a variety of frustrating weaknesses.

Last Dinosaur positively reeks of the polyester seventies with its bell-bottoms, long hair, and eyeglasses the size of picture windows. Rankin/Bass Productions had mined *King Kong* for their earlier USA-Japan collaboration, *King Kong Escapes*; here they seem to have borrowed heavily from *The Land Unknown*. The "polar oasis" setting, female reporter, and mother ship standing vigil are all right out of the 1957 entry—even the star tyrannosaurs look similar. Resembling the T. rex in *The Land Unknown* is, of course, not a good thing, and here lies the biggest problem. Not only the title Tyrannosaurus but all the film's dinosaurs are unforgivably inept. For one thing, they're too big. Way too big. There's nothing wrong in playing with scale to serve a creative purpose but these critters are preposterously huge, from the charging horned dino to the nearly Godzilla-sized T. rex. And speaking of Godzilla, this author is certain that on more than

The Last Dinosaur pushes the Polar-Borer into his lair, proving that certain body moves and positions render man-in-a-suit dinosaurs even more obvious.

one occasion the Big G's trademark roar can be heard on the soundtrack.

Though the Tyrannosaurus wasn't given any glowing dorsal plates or radioactive breath, the FX crew from Tsuburaya Enterprises seems to have spent little effort to make rex or his fellow saurs remotely believable. The nondescript ceratopsian is not based on any known species, and the barely glimpsed pterosaurs are far too bulky. The Triceratops is probably the least ridiculous dino even though it looks to have been operated by two men inside, like a vaudeville horse. If the dinosaurs are visually woeful, they are behaviorially a bit better. The tyrannosaur's slow-witted confusion at Frankie's between-the-legs escape is a neat touch, and a quick throwaway scene shows him catching a fish—a little "wildlife documentary" moment most movies wouldn't bother with. And it's hard not to cheer the outright *chutzpa* of the sequence where the big guy dumbly watches the vine-tethered boulder roll past, unaware that it is tied to his tail, only to have it yank him comically off his feet a few seconds later. It's one of the most audacious man-versus-dino shots of all time.

Clunky creatures aside, there is much to enjoy in *The Last Dinosaur*. Unlike the generic humans who often inhabit these films, Masten Thrust (is that a great name or what?) and his cohorts are decidedly different. The character dynamics are truly interesting, with not merely a love *interest* but a bona fide love triangle. Frankie, well played by Joan Van Ark, is credibly attracted to both Chuck and Masten for totally different reasons, setting up an occurrence that's far too rare in genre films: a character has to *make a choice*. Richard Boone anchors the picture with a curiously off-center performance that consistently keeps the audience guessing. He never delivers a line with quite the cadence

The T. rex is down, but rallies to win this fight against a fearless Triceratops in *The Last Dinosaur*.

or inflection anticipated, and the result is either fascinating or disconcerting, depending on the viewer.

The Last Dinosaur is a classic "good news, bad news" routine. It has an effective score by Maury Laws, but a campy title song (performed by jazz vocalist Nancy Wilson). There is some primordial-looking location photography, but it rests awkwardly alongside the studio-bound effects sequences. In some shots the optical composites are excellent, in others they are jarringly crude. For every clever moment there's one to make the viewer shake his or her head incredulously, like when the catapulted boulder sinks into and laughably rebounds from the beast's latex cranium. Even the title represents a good idea the filmmakers just couldn't quite pull off. The "Last Dinosaur" refers of course not only to the single surviving T. rex but also to Thrust himself—his Great White Hunter–male superiority sensibilities making him a "dinosaur" in a changing society. It's a parallel which could have been subtly effective but turns out obvious and heavy-handed.

According to author Stuart Galbraith, *The Last Dinosaur* was "scheduled to open theatrically in New York City, but was pulled at the last minute and instead made its U.S. debut as a TV movie for ABC." A wise move, that, because as bad as the dino suits look on television, it's chilling to envision them blasted onto a giant theater screen. Still, no other film discussed in this volume flirts so closely with both ends of the quality spectrum. With better dino FX and a few script tweaks, the picture could have risen into the genre's upper levels; without Richard Boone and the well-developed characters, it would have sunk near the bottom. *The Last Dinosaur* is a strange animal—almost great, yet at times not even good.

The "Legend of Dinosaurs"

(a.k.a. *Legend of Dinosaur and Monster Bird*)

"Now, listen! You do this ... you've got to do a better job!"

1983, Japan (1977).
Toei Company, Ltd. C, 90m.

CREDITS: *Director* Junji Kurata. *Producer* Keiichi Hashimoto. *Screenplay* Masaru Igami, Isao Matsumoto, Ichiro Otsu. *Special Effects* Fuminori Ohashi.
CAST: *Ashizawa* Tsunehiko Watase. *Akiko* Nobiko Sawa. *Akira* Shotako Hayashi. *Junko* Tomoko Kiyoshima. *Masashira* Fuyukichi Maki.

In the dense forest near Mt. Fuji, a solitary hiker falls into a strange ice cave and sees a 6-foot prehistoric egg beginning to hatch. News of her discovery reaches a greedy geologist named Ashizawa, whose "father found a stone egg once," and he hurries to investigate. Coincidentally, his on-again, off-again girlfriend, Akiko, is also in the area to photograph the big festival at nearby Lake Sai. Their reunion is interrupted though, when a series of strange occurrences begins. A man and woman are killed on a pedal boat, a lakeside stage is ripped apart by unseen forces during a concert by "Beau Yatani and his Happy Country Music Show," and Akiko's best friend, Junko, eerily vanishes from a rowboat while Akiko is scuba-diving beneath.

Ashizawa is sure that a dinosaur is responsible (he's wrong; it's actually a Plesiosaurus), but his scientist pal reminds him that "if a dinosaur appears, we'll also have magnitude-five earthquakes." Akiko is determined to go diving again, but Ashizawa belts her across the face and insists on going himself. Meanwhile, a pair of monster hunters suddenly decide that "if there's a dinosaur, it wouldn't be very strange if there was also a pterodactyl," and so, they go searching for one. When they actually find one (hatched from the egg in the ice cave) it kills them. After Ashizawa's show of concern for his girl, ironically it is Akiko who ends up rescuing *him* from the water. The lovers travel through an underwater passage and emerge at the exact spot in the forest where the monsters have decided to fight. A gargantuan battle ensues (between the monsters, not the lovers), but a massive earthquake interrupts the struggle. Fires rage, the ground shakes, the wind howls, the monsters lurch about, and the man drags the woman through the trees. The earth finally rips open and swallows the behemoths, and almost Akiko too, but Ashizawa manages to hang on.

COMMENTARY: *The "Legend of Dinosaurs"* may be the most monotonous, unimaginative, utterly uninteresting dinosaur movie ever thrown together. With neither the outrageous, slightly guilty pleasures of Toho's goofier giant-monster efforts (though goofy it certainly is), or the more intelligent appeal of a good dinosaur fantasy, *Legend* is a wholly forgettable entry. In a cruel tease, the opening sequence in the ice cave is quite striking and promising, with some unusual camera angles and staging, and is the only scene in the film that features appropriate music. After this scene, it's downhill all the way.

The village mayor explains part of the problem when he laments, "we don't have any budget!" But that cannot be used as an excuse for *Legend*'s total lack of creativity, effort, and common sense. Continuity is completely absent. Plot elements are introduced and then forgotten, the absurd, choppy story bounces around even more spasmodically than the ridiculous pterosaur marionette, and the "hero" is a mercenary, girlfriend-slapping jackass. Situations are clumsily copied from many previous films, with Steven Spielberg's classic *Jaws* especially victimized. No hoary monster-movie cliché is left out, and the dinosaurs are nothing short of embarrassing. The Plesiosaurus mock-ups—both the small-scale puppet and full-size head-and-neck prop—resemble a living creature to the same degree that a scarecrow resembles a human being. Incred-

Even in still photographs, the rock-hard stiffness of the *"Legend of Dinosaurs"* plesiosaur is clearly visible.

ibly, the pterodactyl is even worse. The crude, rigid model is constantly either plowing through the treetops with one wing low like a bomber with three engines out, or literally and visibly dangling on its string. Defying impossible odds, it looks even more ludicrous than the infamous pop-eyed buzzard of 1957's *The Giant Claw*.

Since the only version of *The "Legend of Dinosaurs"* readily available is dubbed in English, I don't know what the original Japanese dialogue was like. But as dubbed, the characters utter bizarre lines that vault beyond "unintentionally funny" into the realm of sheer incredulity. In one scene, a character played by an American actor bursts in and tells the mayor, "It's big news! Nessie's in Lake Sai now!" Pardon me, did you say ... Nessie? As in the *Loch Ness Monster*? Finally, just when you think the end is mercifully approaching, along comes the excruciating "climax" during which our heroic lovers dangle over a bottomless pit for what is, I swear, at least three hours.

At first glance, *The "Legend of Dinosaurs"* seems intriguing. After all the kiddie-cartoony plot elements that took over the Toho Studios monster movies during the 1970s, you would think it would be quite interesting to see a Japanese studio take a crack at a straightforward, paleontology-themed dinosaur picture. In this case, you would be *disastrously* wrong.

Loch Ness

"It's down there ... it's out there. I know it is."
***   1996, U.K. PolyGram/
Working Title. 100m.

CREDITS: *Director* John Henderson. *Producers* Tim Bevan, Eric Fellner, Stephen Ujlaki, Debra Hayward (associate), Nicky Kentish Barnes (coproducer), Judith Hunt (coproducer). *Written by* John Fusco. *Creature Effects* Jim Henson's Creature Shop. *Special Visual Effects* Peerless Camera Company. *Visual Effects Supervisor* Kent Houston.

CAST: *Dr. Jonathan Dempsey* Ted Danson. *Laura MacFeteridge* Joely Richardson. *Water Bailiff* Ian Holm. *Adrian Foote* James Frain. *Isabel MacFeteridge* Kirsty Graham. *Dr. Robert Mercer* Harris Yulin. *Gordon Shoals* Keith Allen. *Andy McClain* Nick Brimble.

AD LINE: "For 1500 years one legend remains undiscovered, undisturbed ... until now."

Jonathan Dempsey is a once-respected American scientist who has ruined his reputation with a well-publicized and unsuccessful search for Sasquatch. He is thus none too happy when his boss, Doctor Mercer, sends him to Loch Ness to take over for Doctor Abernathy, who has died in a mysterious accident. The already-irritated Dempsey can't stomach the fanatical Nessie hunters in his hotel and migrates to the quieter Moffat Arms, a small inn owned by beautiful local lass Laura MacFeteridge. Although it's off-season, Dempsey finds an ally in Laura's young daughter Isabel and is allowed to stay. Dempsey and his eager research assistant, Adrian Foote, obtain a boat from Laura's frustrated suitor, Andy McClain, but they soon run afoul of the patriarchal water bailiff—the fiercely protective "keeper of the loch." Despite the bailiff's disdain and some fervent resistance by the tourism-dependent locals, the scientists complete their high-tech sweeps and Dempsey pronounces the Nessie legend dead.

On his last night at the loch, Dempsey learns two things: that he's becoming very attracted to the lovely Laura, and that she believes her daughter Isabel possesses a sort of sixth sense called "St. Columba's Gift." Dempsey is reluctantly packing to leave when Doctor Abernathy's camera turns up with a roll of exposed film inside, and what Dempsey sees on the photos prompts him to grab Adrian and rush back onto the loch. McClain's boat is destroyed in a violent collision—possibly with a large animal—but when the burly Scot beats the tar out of Dempsey it has much more to do with Laura than the boat. Isabel gives the bruised Dempsey a handmade get-well card with a sketch of the "water kelpie," and he is astounded by the resemblance between the girl's drawing and Abernathy's photo. Isabel and Dempsey strike a friendly bargain, and in a hidden grotto deep beneath Castle Urquhart the awe-struck Dempsey sees a legend come alive. But when he ignores Isabel's warning and starts taking flash photos, the serenity—and the child's trust—are shattered. When the ecstatic Doctor Mercer sees Dempsey's photos, he schedules a media event at London's Natural History Museum, and Dempsey must decide whether to become the most famous scientist on earth or regain the love of Laura and Isabel.

COMMENTARY: At one point in *Loch Ness*, Ted Danson and 9-year-old Kirsty Graham discuss Nessie. "I have to see it before I can believe it," Danson's world-weary character says. "No, Mr. Dempsey," the child replies, "you have to believe it before you can see it." This line is a bellwether of the entire film; if you like it (as I do) you'll enjoy the movie (which I did); if you're tempted to make fun of it, you won't.

Loch Ness is an unapologetically old-fashioned, sentimental, romantic fable. Its central idea of an utterly beaten man being uplifted by the influence of a magical place, the love of a woman, and the faith of a child, is almost—dare I say it?—Capraesque. The film is in fact so counter to the jaded, coarse pictures dominating the box office in the 1990's that its makers didn't even release it theatrically in the United States. Admittedly, there is nothing brand new here. The picture is a deliberate throwback to a more innocent time, and its plot twists, characters, and themes have all been seen before. But as *Loch Ness* proves, even if you know where you'll end up, the getting there can still be a treat.

Ted Danson, near perfect as Dempsey,

leads a wonderful cast. Danson gives a strikingly unselfconscious performance, allowing himself to look disheveled and grungy in most scenes, and doesn't even hide his thinning hair as a more vain actor surely would have. Joely Richardson is positively luminous, and it's a shame such a lovely and captivating actress hasn't been seen more on American screens. James Frain is immensely likable as the boyishly enthusiastic Adrian — he even gets to do a boffo Colin Clive impression! — and newcomer Kirsty Graham gives a touching, nuanced performance. The youngster is aided by some dialogue which, in a truly rare cinematic occurrence, is not overly precocious or sitcom-cute but actually sounds like something a real nine year old might say.

John Fusco's script and John Henderson's direction work together as each part of the story connects to another. Unlike films such as *The Lost World: Jurassic Park*, which is strewn with arbitrary and irrational plot points, all the little bits of *Loch Ness* fit neatly together. The "jealous suitor" may be a stock character, but it makes sense that McClain will eventually beat up Dempsey, which precipitates Isabel's get-well card, which Dempsey connects to Abernathy's photo, which foreshadows what will happen when Dempsey takes his flash picture, and so on. It all falls into place with a satisfying tidiness, showing that Fusco and Henderson didn't introduce elements just to forget them when convenient. Look on top of Dempsey's automobile in the final shot, near the edge of the frame, and you'll see a red bicycle. Dempsey remembered his part of the bargain he struck with Isabel ... because the filmmakers remembered.

Loch Ness inevitably has some blemishes. One big one is Gordon Shoals, a "local color" character who adds nothing to the film and uncomfortably recalls the "Mad Scotsman of Killikranky Castle" in Larry Buchanan's rather dreadful *The Loch Ness Horror*, but his two appearances are mercifully brief. The script also struggles with the water bailiff. Well-played by Ian Holm, the wizened bailiff is presented as a hard but sternly honest man, and no matter how badly he wanted to protect his beloved loch it just doesn't figure that he would condone the barbaric and underhanded tactics used against Dempsey.

Loch Ness has also been chastised for its scarcity of creature shots; but the judiciously used effects seem appropriate to the story, and when the time comes Nessie does deliver the goods. As in *Jurassic Park*, animatronics and computer-generated imagery (CGI) were combined to realize the beastie, and on a smaller scale *Loch Ness* melds the techniques just as skillfully. Nessie looks marvelously prehistoric, showing great zoological credibility but with a hint of the "magical" as well. Even though we know the creature is there, and we will get to see it, the moment of discovery still manages a surprise (which I have left intact by omitting it from the above plot summary) guaranteed to bring a smile.

Two more *Loch Ness* contributors demand mention. It could be argued that a cinematographer could hardly go wrong given the beauty of the Scottish Highlands, but Clive Tickner successfully captures the feeling as well as the scenery. *Loch Ness* marked the first time since *The Private Life of Sherlock Holmes* in 1970 that the storied loch had served as a filming location, and Tickner's work makes it doubly lamentable that the picture was immediately banished to the tiny TV screen. Lastly, the Celtic-flavored music score is by turns haunting, tragic, defiant, and triumphant, and is arguably Trevor Jones' best to date. It is certainly one of the best and most effective scores among the films discussed in this volume.

Loch Ness is not a masterpiece, and maybe it isn't even great. But what it tries for it gets right, and one only has to look at

Opposite: The slightly mystical Isabel McFeteridge (Kirsty Graham) and Bruce the dog are featured on the British poster art for *Loch Ness*.

Magic in the Water to see how many things can go wrong in a film of this kind. In one scene, Laura states what would happen if a prehistoric survivor was actually found, and her fear of "10,000 nature lovers queuing for a McNessie burger" and "the kelpie performing tricks for a few sardines" is all too believable. The film's most telling point is the realization that it would be just as disastrous to definitively *prove* the legend as to disprove it. Some things should remain in the realm of mystery and myth, and of the magical question, "What if?"

PEOPLE AND PRODUCTION: Given the popularity of Loch Ness lore, it's surprising that the monster has so seldom been explored in film. The 1934 British curio *The Secret of the Loch* suffered through the indignity of having an iguana portraying the monster, but was buoyed by a droll and witty script and the no-holds-barred performance of Seymour Hicks. *What a Whopper!* (1961) used the monster legend only as a comic device. In 1983, the aforementioned cheapie, *The Loch Ness Horror*, was unleashed, a festival of fakery—fake accents, fake-looking monster, even a mock Loch—which entertains not in spite of its ineptitude but only because of it. Then in 1996, writer John Fusco's tale, rooted in his genuine affection for the Scottish Highlands area and its people, finally made it to the screen.

Over the years, other potential Loch Ness monster films have fallen by the wayside. In the mid–1970s, Hammer Films' Michael Carreras attempted to launch a $7 million epic called *Nessie*. Unfortunately, despite the grandiose plans—7 mil would have been a truly monstrous budget for Hammer—and a possible collaboration with Toho Studios (!), this intriguing project was never filmed. Still more intriguing is the thought of a "Nessie" picture from the duo of Charles Schneer and Ray Harryhausen. Schneer mentioned the idea during an interview at the National Film Theatre in London, published in *FXRH* magazine. "We have often talked about it as a theme for a picture," Schneer said, "but we've never really got much further than that ... we've seen scripts submitted to us about the Loch Ness monster." And producer Ivan Tors, known for animal-related films and television shows, also had a Nessie project in the works in the seventies. The jacket notes for his book *My Life in the Wild* stated: "Mr. Tors's current adventure is the making of the definitive movie about the Loch Ness monster for Metro-Goldwyn-Mayer."

John Fusco's *Loch Ness* story was born during childhood. He spent hours raptly listening to the tales told by his Scottish grandmother, Isabel, for whom he would name a key character in his screenplay. "My grandmother is from Coatbridge and my mother is from Glasgow so I grew up with stories about the old country and the water beastie," Fusco said in a studio press release. "My grandmother believed in it so I did too. Anyone who called my grandmother a liar would have had a hard time!" Stephen Ujlaki optioned the script in 1990, and the following year a deal was inked with the English production company Working Title. "A fairy tale for adults," an enthusiastic Ujlaki said of the script, "with something of the Brigadoon about it."

Loch Ness would be John Henderson's debut as a feature film director, though he was a veteran of countless television productions. Henderson attests that Ted Danson and Joely Richardson (daughter of Vanessa Redgrave) were his first and only choices for the lead roles. He liked Danson because he felt that "the audience would care about him," and was impressed by the versatility Richardson showed by playing an American in *I'll Do Anything*. The principal cast was completed by veteran character actor Ian Holm, energetic James Frain, and unknown Kirsty Graham, who was chosen from over a thousand girls at open audition. "She has an uncanny talent for filling the screen whenever she appears," Henderson commented.

With script, director, cast, and budget (reported by *Cinefantastique* as $10 million) in place, filming commenced in September

1994. The first two weeks were spent at Inverness at the northern end of the loch. Many scenes, including the shots of Dempsey and Adrian aboard the *Rose Valley*, were actually photographed on Loch Ness. The company then moved about 90 miles north for two weeks in the small village of Diabaig, on the shores of Loch Torridon. Set dressers, carpenters, and greensmen gave the town a mild makeover, and a picturesque holiday cottage became the "Moffat Arms." Eilean Donan Castle, on the shore of Loch Duich, stood in for the famed Castle Urquhart. Finally, it was on to Pinewood Studios for eight weeks of shooting the Moffat Arms interiors, as well as the live-action footage for the pivotal "discovery" sequence in the subterranean cavern set.

SPECIAL EFFECTS: The special effects bringing Nessie to life were the combined, coordinated effort of Jim Henson's Creature Shop and Peerless Camera Company. The Creature Shop, now a bustling enterprise with locations in England and California, unofficially began during the production of the groundbreaking, all-puppet film *The Dark Crystal* in 1982. In the years since, the company has created mesmerizing creatures for *Babe*, the live-action *101 Dalmatians*, *Labyrinth*, *The Flintstones* and countless other films. Also having grown tremendously since its humble beginnings in the mid seventies, Peerless Camera Company had blossomed into a state-of-the-art facility with multiple capabilities, including optical and digital compositing, motion control, and CGI. Its numerous film credits include *Twelve Monkeys*, *Aliens*, *The Adventures of Baron Munchausen*, and another collaboration with the Henson company, *The Muppets' Christmas Carol*.

Loch Ness gave the Creature Shop artists their first opportunity to use the facility's new real-time computer graphics setup. Using this system, the monster's actions could be performed "live" on the cavern set with the composited image instantly viewable on a video monitor. For the first time, a CG creature could be "directed" simultaneously with the human actors. In Matt Bacon's *No Strings Attached*, CGI modeling supervisor Karen Halliwell elaborated on the technique. "The real-time system worked very well," Halliwell said. "The director didn't have fixed ideas of what he wanted, so we could try different moves until we found one he was happy with." The "rough animated templates" resulting from the on-set performance were then forwarded to Peerless Camera Company for final rendering and detailing. "It was decided to use the Creature Shop monster for closeups, and Peerless would provide computer graphics for the wider shots," visual effects supervisor Kent Houston explained. "As it turned out, the rapid advances in technology allowed computer graphics to be used for some closeup work as well."

The "Creature Shop monster" Houston mentioned was the Henson company's other major contribution to *Loch Ness*: a massive animatronic Nessie. "We built the head and neck as a full-scale animatronic on a big X-Y rig in a tank on the set," Creature Shop project supervisor Verner Gresty explained. Gresty's previous experience in bringing to life the giant "brontocrane" for *The Flintstones* was no doubt good preparation for overseeing the life-size Nessie, and he brought in artists from London's Natural History Museum to assure a paleo-correct plesiosaur. The head-and-neck rig, measuring over 15 feet altogether, was actuated by a hand-pumped hydraulic system which gave the performers a degree of precision and delicacy remarkable for such a massive creature. The cables, hoses, and operator console were concealed in the dark periphery of the grotto set. The kelpie's face was articulated using the Henson Performance Control System, which allows preprogrammed combinations of movements to be initiated with a single control. This pioneering system reduces the number of puppeteers required to operate a complex creature, and frees the performers to concentrate on nuances of character rather than complicated technical manipulations.

The Loch Ness Horror

"I think this 'monster' stuff is really gettin' to ya!"

* 1982, USA. Omni-Leisure International. C, 89m.

CREDITS: *Director* Larry Buchanan. *Producers* Larry Buchanan, Jane Buchanan (executive), Irv Berwick (associate). *Screenplay* Larry Buchanan, Lynn Shubert. *Special Effects* Image Engineering. *"Nessie" Created by* Tom Valentine, Peter Chesney.

CAST: *Dr. George Sanderson* Sandy Kenyon. *Kathleen* Miki McKenzie. *Spencer Dean* Barry Buchanan. *Jack Stuart* Doc Livingston. *Prof. Pratt* Stuart Lancaster. *Col. Laughton* Preston Hanson. *Brad* Eric Scott. *Fran* Karey Louis-Scott.

AD LINE: "There *is* something in these waters! And it *is* alive!"

It is to be a hectic three days around Loch Ness. Trouble starts when two inept monster-hunters, Red and Shorty, stumble on Nessie's lair and swipe her only egg. Shorty gets eaten but Red returns the egg to his boss, Professor Pratt, a former college teacher embittered by his students' preoccupation with carnality. Visiting American researcher Spencer Dean and Scottish biologist George Sanderson consult with crusty old local Nessie expert Jack Stuart regarding where best to look for the beastie, but instead of Nessie, Dean's sonar finds an intact World War II German bomber at the bottom of the loch. The next day, as Dean woos Stuart's granddaughter Kathleen, Sanderson lectures a group of touring college students on his theory that the creature is a Plesiosaurus. Two of the collegians, Brad and Fran, have their romantic tryst interrupted by the "Mad Scotsman of Killikranky Island," and Brad draws the ire of Nessie when he kills the old geezer. Kathleen is meanwhile taken hostage by the crazed Pratt, but she escapes with the egg when the prof becomes Nessie's next victim. While all this is happening, Colonel Laughton of Special Services shows up spouting a cock-and-bull explanation for the presence of the German bomber, but old Jack reveals the truth: Laughton is trying to protect his lifelong friend, the newly knighted Sir Donald Gregory, whose undeserved war-hero reputation would be ruined if the bomber is examined (don't ask). Laughton's aide sends local diver and demolition expert Alex Nicholson down to destroy the bomber, but he clumsily blows up the beastie and himself in the attempt. Realizing that Nessie is dead, Dean and Kathleen gaze at each other and return the egg to the loch to keep the legend alive.

COMMENTARY: "They call her-r-r a monster-r-r," ol' Jack Stuart says, R's rolling off his tongue with a bogus brogue as thick as a bowl of tattie-an'-neeps. After enduring *The Loch Ness Horror* the viewer may call her something too, though it's doubtful "monster" would be the choice. Nobody can accuse writer-director Larry Buchanan of skimping on plot twists. *Horror* has enough angles, detours, extraneous subplots and peripheral characters to rival a mid-seventies Toho entry: a vengeful professor with obligatory bumbling henchmen, a sunken Nazi bomber full of mines, an American expatriate explosives expert, a troupe of sex-obsessed college students, a romance, a military cover-up, and a deranged, battle-axe-wielding old Scotsman who talks to Nessie. All of which adds up to a hopeless, convoluted mess.

From beginning to end *The Loch Ness Horror* uncorks a ceaseless barrage of anachronisms. First comes Jack Stuart's magic telescope. In the 1940 prologue, as Jack watches the bomber approaching, the scope somehow provides a view from *directly above* the airplane. Then later when Kathleen looks through it, the amazing spyglass has already aimed itself precisely at the head of Alex Nicholson, half a mile away in a moving boat. Sanderson identifies the German plane as a "PBY," which is not a bad guess except that the PBY was used only by the Allies. Pratt heatedly explains to Red that the egg is far too fragile for automobile travel, then proceeds to haul it away in a VW bus. And while sneaking up on Pratt, the 30-foot plesiosaur momentarily hides behind a tree about 10 inches in diameter.

The only thing that makes *Horror* watchable, other than chuckling at its incongruities, is an overall air of good-naturedness. Not one character has an iota of credibility, and the attempted Scottish accents are … an adjective eludes me. But the actors, particularly Sandy Kenyon, all seem to be having a jolly time. Barry Buchanan recalls Patrick Wayne both physically and in his, er, *laid-back* delivery, and adorable Miki McKenzie makes what is apparently her only film appearance as the pretty granddaughter (in the movies all granddaughters are pretty — it's a rule). The dialogue is generally inept but does have moments, especially when poking fun at the young couple's cultural differences. Kathleen: "Is it true, Mr. Dean, that Americans go to the picture house more than once a month, and spend a lot o' time looking at magazines of naked women?" Dean: "Yes."

Then there's "Nessie" herself. The fact is that Peter Chesney, Tom Valentine and the FX crew managed to deliver a mechanical creature — head and neck only, of course — that is much more smoothly articulated than most low-budget, full-size movie monsters. Its mouth movements, the way its head fluidly tilts not only forward and back but also side to side, and its very alive eyes, are all impressively organic. It's a fine piece of engineering — the problem is in the conceptual design. Those alive-looking eyes are also big, innocent and

Much like *The Crater Lake Monster*, the beast depicted in the poster for *The Loch Ness Horror* bore no resemblance to the creature in the film.

friendly-looking, and when you add a pair of cartoony, antennalike horns and a toothy, happy grin, you have a Nessie far more suited to a children's TV show than to a so-called *Horror* movie.

The Loch Ness Horror is not a typical Larry Buchanan film. It's more family-friendly, has a more lighthearted tone, and shows none of the quasi-exploitative edginess that defined his most interesting movies. In getting away from his strengths,

Buchanan ended up with a very weak film which works on no level, and captures absolutely none of the mysterious, veiled "Loch Ness" aura that had inspired him to make it.

PEOPLE AND PRODUCTION: Larry Buchanan has a long history of B-movie creations to his credit, including sexploitation fare like *Under Age* (1964), retitled Roger Corman remakes like *Zontar, the Thing from Venus* (1966), campy near classics like *Mars Needs Women* (1966), art-house darlings like *Strawberries Need Rain* (1970), and even a prehistoric creature saga, *It's Alive!* (1968), which tells the story of a psychotic recluse who feeds unlucky passers-by to a Cretaceous gill-man called a "masasaurus."

In Buchanan's book *It Came from Hunger!* (subtitled *Tales of a Cinema Schlockmeister*) he devotes only a few paragraphs to *The Loch Ness Horror*, but does discuss how the project came about. "By 1982 I thought it was time for a family picture — that is, a film of, by, with, and for the Buchanan clan," he wrote. Buchanan and his wife, Jane, had visited Scotland and had been captivated by the mystical atmosphere. "The natives warmed their hands by the wood fires," Buchanan recalled, "hypnotizing us with their fanciful yarns of the monster in the loch." The couple decided to film their own version of the Nessie legend, and to make it a distinctly family affair. Larry wrote and directed, Jane executive produced, son Barry starred, daughter Dee played a small role (as Alex Nicholson's wife) and was the script supervisor, son Randy edited, and son Jeff was the "best boy."

Going on location to Scotland was a financial impossibility but Buchanan had "the perfect stand-in" in mind, and humorously asserted in a *Filmfax* article that "Lake Tahoe looks more like Loch Ness than Loch Ness does." Buchanan tabbed longtime friend Sandy Kenyon to play the scientist, and "a real Scottish lass, Miki McKenzie," essayed the naive Kathleen. Whatever the

The animatronic Nessie built for *The Loch Ness Horror*, as it appeared a few years later playing Jack the Ripper in *Amazon Women on the Moon*.

merits of the picture, and despite what he termed "some close calls with the underwater work," Buchanan has happy memories of the "very special" weeks that he and his family spent making The Loch Ness Horror.

SPECIAL EFFECTS: "Nessie" architect Peter Chesney and his company, Image Engineering, would rise from this *Horror* to a lofty position in the FX world, with major credits on such films as *Honey, I Shrunk the Kids* (1989), *The Hudsucker Proxy* (1994), *Waterworld* (1995), and *Men in Black* (1997). Likewise, Tom Valentine went on to *Lifeforce* (1985), *Deep Impact* (1998), and *Mission to Mars* (2000), among others. But for *Horror*, the effects crew had very little to work with. Their version of Nessie, remote-controlled from off-camera, consisted only of the head and neck and a small section of humped back. For scenes requiring her to "walk" on land, she was outfitted with a set of custom wheels.

Since even the most expensive mechanical monsters are often troublesome, it's not surprising that this budget beastie sometimes balked. "The umbilical cord leading to Nessie could order her to breathe smoke, roll her eyes, surface, submerge, or emit a savage scream," Larry Buchanan recalled. "Sometimes the signals got mixed up." This Nessie did have staying power, though, resurfacing four years later in the all-star comedy olio *Amazon Women on the Moon*. Sporting a top hat and cloak, Nessie turns up during a send-up of the "In Search Of" types of TV shows (titled "Bulls—or Not") which investigates the question: Was Jack the Ripper actually the Loch Ness Monster?

Lost Continent

"Not good, but at least not a total failure."
** 1951, USA. Lippert Pictures.
BW/tint, 83m.

CREDITS: *Director* Samuel Newfield. *Producer* Sigmund Neufeld. *Screenplay* Richard Landau. *Story* Carroll Young. *Opticals* Ray Mercer, A.S.C. *Special Effects* Augie Lohman.

CAST: *Maj. Joe Nolan* Cesar Romero. *Lt. Daniel Wilson* Chick Chandler. *Dr. Michael Rostov* John Hoyt. *Dr. Robert Phillips* Hugh Beaumont. *Dr. Stanley Briggs* Whit Bissell. *Sgt. Willie Tatlow* Sid Melton. *Native Woman* Acquanetta. *Marla Stevens* Hillary Brooke.

AD LINE: "Thrills of the atomic-powered future! Adventures of the prehistoric past!"

Three brilliant scientists, Doctor Phillips, Doctor Briggs, and Russian emigrant Doctor Rostov, are frantic when their experimental atomic-powered rocket malfunctions and goes careening off the radar screen toward the waters of the South Pacific. The air force dispatches Maj. Joe Nolan, his acerbic sidekick, Lt. Dan Wilson, and acrophobic mechanic Sgt. Willie Tatlow to fly the docs on a top-secret search mission. Joe quickly grows suspicious of Rostov, partly due to his coldly analytical outlook but mostly just because he's Russian. Suddenly the plane drops from the sky and crash-lands on an uncharted island, home to a nearly deserted native village. The one remaining woman explains that her fellow islanders were frightened away by a flame-spewing "fire bird," which landed on top of the "sacred mountain" in the distance. "It must be the rocket!" Rostov deduces.

The men clamber interminably up the craggy mountainside. "It seems like we been climbin' for days," Dan all-too-accurately observes. The exertion proves too much for the frail Briggs, who falls to his death despite Rostov's valiant efforts. The remaining five finally reach the top only to find everything bathed in a green glow. "Like a nightclub, only they forgot to bring on the dames," quips Willie. Their instruments indicate massive uranium deposits, but Willie is more alarmed by a huge Brontosaurus footprint ("Not even my top sergeant had feet that big!") and is downright terrified when a living specimen momentarily chases Phillips up a tree. The next day Rostov and Phillips wander off and become trapped by a male Triceratops, but the appearance of a rival male allows them to escape. Observing Rostov's loyalty to Phillips, Nolan realizes he's had the

Who fabricated this Triceratops and the other *Lost Continent* dinosaurs, and who animated them, will likely never be discovered.

Russian pegged all wrong. The group finally gets a break when Dan shoots a pterodactyl and they stumble on the rocket while tracking it down. Willie and Dan exhaust their ammo trying to draw a trio of pesky dinosaurs away from the missile, unfortunately leaving Willie defenseless against a murderous Triceratops. The survivors climb down the mountain, speeding up considerably when Rostov realizes that "the whole mountain is blowing up under us!" The geothermic energy and radioactive uranium make a violent combination, and the Lost Continent is destroyed forever.

COMMENTARY: *Lost Continent* occupies a singular niche in dinomovie history. Its release came toward the end of a really lean period for fantasy cinema in general, and dinosaur films in particular. This was an era when most filmmakers, if they wanted dinosaurs at all, would usually just unspool a few *One Million B.C.* clips. Incredibly, *Lost Continent* is the *only* dinomovie to utilize stop-motion in the entire 20-year span from *The Son of Kong* in 1933 to when the genre was given new life by Ray Harryhausen's *Beast from 20,000 Fathoms*. Unfortunately, this entry is hopelessly hamstrung by a parade of hackneyed characters and situations. The dialogue elicits snickers during the "serious" moments, while the "comic relief" is leadenly unfunny. The pacing is glacierlike, with the party taking almost 50 minutes — mostly meaningless padding — to reach the plateau. The science is indescribably ludicrous, and the stop-motion work is frankly among the worst ever seen in a feature film. Yet the picture is surprisingly watchable, mostly for two

A B-movie cast for the ages — Whit Bissell, Hugh Beaumont, Chick Chandler, Cesar Romero (who seems to be looking at the assistant director), John Hoyt and Sid Melton (standing) are shaken up by a plane crash near the *Lost Continent*.

reasons: a delicious cast of B-movie and television favorites; and some curious story elements, the motivation for which warrants some consideration.

A likeable cast can go far in making a bland screenplay digestible. How can you really dislike a movie with Cesar "Batman" Romero, John "When Worlds Collide" Hoyt, Hugh "Leave it to Beaver" Beaumont, Whit "I Was a Teenage Werewolf" Bissell, and Sid "Green Acres" Melton? However absurd the dialogue, the actors manage to deliver it with a straight face and even a bit of conviction. Hillary "Invaders from Mars" Brooke and "Jungle Woman" Acquanetta have few lines and very little screen time, and Acquanetta does not assist the men down from the plateau as reported in some synopses.

Despite the scant female presence, the opening reel has an odd penchant for sexual innuendo. Joe is busily wooing Marla, and things are just getting interesting when the air police show up to grab him for the mission. "What time is it, Sergeant?" Joe asks. "Two-thirty, sir," the sarge replies. "You'd have looked a whole lot better to me at three," a frustrated Joe laments. When Danny learns that the commanding officer wants to see him, he tries to figure what kind of trouble he might be in. "That dame said she voted last year," he mumbles on his way out the door. These suggestive asides add one more puzzling angle to a script already loaded with unconventional elements.

Lost Continent came along at a time when America's involvement in the Korean conflict and other forces were causing the patriotic, post–World War II victory glow to dwindle, and all through the film runs an unmistakable thread of contempt for the military. It isn't that strange to hear Willie carping about orders — griping enlisted men are a cinema fixture — but it is unusual to hear Danny reflect on his wartime experiences with such venom. "They slap a gun in one hand, a knife in the other, and in two seconds you're a South Pacific commando — what a *picnic*," he fumes. "You got liberated," Joe reminds him. "Yeah, I got liberated," Dan spits back, "*look* where it *got* me." This antiestablishment theme even extends to other branches of authority. Willie grumbles that carrying the scientists is "as bad as flyin' a bunch of congressmen," ridiculing both academia and the government in one sentence.

More noteworthy than the antiauthority attitude is the relationship between Nolan and Rostov. In 1951, the infamous House Committee on Un-American Activities was at the height of its power, and the Hollywood community was a frequent target. The so-called "Hollywood Ten" (the first ten motion picture personalities to be subpoenaed) were only the first of many screenwriters, directors, producers, and others to be placed on the "blacklist," and numerous careers were ruined. In *Lost Continent*, Nolan can be seen as a personification of this Cold War paranoia. He vehemently distrusts Rostov merely because he's Russian, sees conspiracies everywhere, and imagines hidden motives for every action. Finally, he realizes Rostov is trustworthy and his suspicions were unfounded. "I don't know why," Nolan confesses, "but for a while I had you figured for playing on the wrong team." "I'm a Russian," Rostov replies with a sigh; "I'm used to it." Is it too much of a stretch to imagine that the writers were condemning the fallacies and misguided jingoism of the Communist witch hunts, quietly slipping their editorial into the script of an innocuous little "B" dinosaur movie?

Whatever the political overtones of *Lost Continent*, as entertainment it has serious flaws. Almost any fifties sci-fi flick will spout faulty science but this may have set some sort of record, mostly with its torrent of spurious remarks about the mysterious power of (fanfare, please) *uranium*. First, the radioactivity causes (a) Willie's watch, (b) the plane's electrical circuits, and (c) the plane's "magnetic controls" to conk out. Rostov later explains (with a straight face) that when the atomic rocket ran out of fuel, "it was inevitably drawn to these fields," as if a runaway car with no gas would be inevitably drawn to a Texaco station. Finally, when Nolan begins to worry about the possible health risks of so much radiation, Rostov reassures him. "We're safe enough," the doc explains, "but if the uranium in those fields were *refined*, we'd have been dead hours ago." Whew, that's a relief.

The great thing about the animation work in *Lost Continent* is that it's there at all. Three cheers for the intrepid FX artists (whoever and wherever they are) who rolled up their sleeves and tried their hands at creating some stop-motion magic. As they discovered, it's not an easy art to master. The bronto scoots awkwardly along without lifting its feet, the ceratopsians move with an unnatural start-and-stop cadence, and all of the puppets are amateurishly designed. On the plus side, the film does offer the first Triceratops versus Triceratops battle since 1919's *The Ghost of Slumber Mountain*, and a surprisingly grisly one it is, with blood pouring from the mouth of the loser as it takes a horn through the chest. The balance of the effects are generally as mediocre as the animation, and one major optical gaffe is present. In the admittedly inventive, straight-down shot showing Whit Bissell falling away from the camera into the cloud layer below, a quick lap dissolve is used to complete his disappearance. Unfortunately John Hoyt was also in frame, and as Bissell enters the fog, Hoyt simply vanishes from the rock ledge! The rocket scenes make extensive use of stock footage from Lippert's *Rocketship XM* (1950), but the physical effects are not bad. The climactic quake-eruption is unspectacular but serviceable — again, kudos for not using *One Million* leftovers.

Ultimately, *Lost Continent* is notable

only for bravely bringing stop-motion back to the dinosaur film after a two-decade absence, and for the atypical attitudes manifested in its script. Burdened with endless, boring filler and worn-out situations, *Lost Continent* is likely to be of interest only to dinosaur lovers, stop-motion completists, and possibly Cold War historians.

PEOPLE AND PRODUCTION: Robert L. Lippert must have had a soft spot for dinosaurs. There were plans to include prehistoric creatures in his *Rocketship XM* (via *One Million B.C.* stock footage, according to FX artist-author Robert Skotak in *Filmfax*). That idea was scrapped, but only a year later the Mesozoic era did meet the space age in *Lost Continent*. Screenwriter Richard Landau (*The Creeping Unknown*), working from a story by Carroll Young (*Tarzan's Desert Mystery*), fashioned a tale combining a typical "Lost World" scenario, the burgeoning technology of rocketry and space flight, and the era's fascination with and fear of the atom. The indefatigable Sam Newfield, who helmed what may be the worst gorilla picture ever made in *White Pongo*, was tabbed to direct.

A talented writer can conceive a spectacular image, and create it in the reader's mind with the stroke of a pen. But it then falls to the effects artists, art directors and the like to get it on film, often with meager resources. Interviewed by Anthony Timpone in *Fangoria*, actor John Hoyt talked about *Lost Continent*'s infamous rock-climbing scenes. "We climbed this papier-mâché mountain for weeks trying to get the dinosaurs," he recalled. "That's the way they did things then. If you needed a forest, they built trees and everything was done in the studio."

The black-and-white *Rocketship XM* effectively used a reddish tint to suggest the devastated, radioactive Martian landscape, so it must have seemed logical to assume that if red could convey a stark wasteland, green could connote the lushness of a dense jungle. Logical maybe, but wrong. In fact, the green tinting has little effect of any kind, once you get used to it. The color does not make the soundstage jungles seem any more natural, nor does it distract the viewer from the imperfections of the dinosaur effects, which some have suggested was its true purpose.

The mountain's climactic explosion effectively put the clamps on any thoughts of a sequel, yet there is a film which is sometimes considered a follow-up. Called *The Jungle* (1952), it's a strange little item starring Cesar Romero, Rod Cameron, and Marie Windsor, set and actually photographed in India. *The Jungle* is a routine and somewhat tedious romance until the final reel, when a herd of living woolly mammoths (elephants with toupees) stampede across the screen! Other than Romero's presence, the prehistoric animal element, and the fact that it was from Lippert Pictures, it has no connection to *Lost Continent*.

SPECIAL EFFECTS: Little is known about the stop-motion animation in *Lost Continent*, beyond that which can be discerned by watching the film. The animated dinosaurs were all photographed on miniature sets, and the scattered shots that attempt to combine the puppets and live actors utilize simple rear projection. There are no Willis O'Brien–style glass shots, no traveling mattes, no miniature front projection, and since Ray Harryhausen wouldn't invent the technique for another two years, no "Dynamation." The special effects are credited to Augie Lohman, known for his real-time monsters and other "floor effects." While he undoubtedly supervised the film's effects, and may even have overseen the animation work, virtually all experts and historians agree that it is highly unlikely (though not impossible) that he personally executed the animation. The identity of the animator, as well as the maker of the models, seems to be lost to history.

August J. "Augie" Lohman was a reliable and prolific special effects artist throughout the 1950s, '60s, and '70s. Often working on low-budget productions, the imaginative Lohman took pride in his craft and created many memorable and convincing effects. Lohman's believable 11-foot fiberglass mollusk for 1957's *The Monster That Challenged*

Near the center of the jam-packed poster for *Panther Girl of the Kongo* lurks a Triceratops (inset) unmistakably from *Lost Continent*, but no footage is used in the film itself.

vegetable had malfunctioned just prior to its scheduled filming.

One of the few FX references to discuss *Lost Continent* at any length is *The Saga of Special Effects*, by Ron Fry and Pamela Fourzon. The authors are generally complimentary of the efforts, calling the mock-up mountainside "a masterpiece of construction, fashioned of materials strong enough to support the weight of [the] actors climbing its face," and pointing out that it "was even mounted on rollers to provide a greater variety of camera angles and set-ups." Discussing one effective shot of the actors leaping over an ever-widening chasm, Fry and Fourzon reported that the scene utilized "two massive segments of island ... mounted on mobile platforms, and then wrenched apart by crewmen to depict the earth cracking wide open."

A window of opportunity existed to make the *Lost Continent* dinosaurs much, much better. Ray Harryhausen was between *Mighty Joe Young* and *The Beast from 20,000 Fathoms* and thus available, but it was not to be. "I read about it and showed the producer some of my material, but nothing came of it," Harryhausen told me. "Somebody else did it." The *Lost Continent* dinos would later do their stock-footage duty (alongside the familiar *One Million B.C.* lizards) in the renowned stinker *Robot Monster*. One of the Triceratops models also shows up in the promotional art for the 1955 serial *Panther Girl of the Kongo*, but sadly does not appear on screen.

the World — requiring five operators and containing three miles of wiring — was one of the best cinematic terrors of the fifties. Lohman's work can also be enjoyed in such films as *Moby Dick* (1956), *Captain Sindbad* (1963), and *Soylent Green* (1973), and his effects for the 1960 disaster film *The Last Voyage* were Oscar-nominated. Robert Skotak has reported that Lohman actually built a complex carnivorous plant for *Lost Continent*, only to have its scenes snipped from the screenplay at the eleventh hour — actually a lucky break for Lohman since the vicious

Lost on Adventure Island

* 1985, USA. MVC Video. C.

CREDITS: *Director* Yancy Hendrieth. *Special Visual and Mechanical Effects Designed and Created by* L. B. Carvelo, Keith Finkelstein, David Dane. *Visual Effects and Animation Supervisor* Keith Finkelstein. *Special Effects Technician/Matte Painter/Miniature Set Construction* David Dane.

Here is a truly bizarre curiosity. *Lost on Adventure Island* (a.k.a. *King Dong*) is a cheap pornographic feature which, astonishingly, contains several original and surprisingly accomplished stop-motion animation sequences. A woman (X-movie starlet Crystal Holland) and her male companion are shipwrecked on a lost island. They spend the next eventful hour evading dinosaurs and befriending a giant ape when not engaged in other far less interesting pastimes. This author will leave evaluation of the "live-action" elements to others, and report solely on the visual effects.

The dino action begins with an attack by a beach-dwelling Plesiosaurus. It's a fairly sizable sequence with a well-made animation puppet, though the creature's sculpting lacks the intricate detail of its cousins in *When Dinosaurs Ruled the Earth* and *The Crater Lake Monster*. After escaping the flippered predator, the humans rescue a normal-sized (man-in-a-suit) gorilla from a trap, earning the gratitude of the ape's gargantuan (stop-motion) parent. This sequence also features an extremely fake-looking full-size hand. The stop-motion simian is a deliberate and somewhat successful copy of the original *King Kong*, and it's interesting to note that the animator's fingers produce the same "rippling fur" effect seen in the 1933 classic.

The film's final dinosaur set piece has our human hero menaced by a Tyrannosaurus type meat-eater, only to escape when the junior ape uses a rope to pull him up a cliff face. The carnivorous dinosaur is another nice puppet, but the animation of its bipedal gait never looks quite right. The remainder of the film's stop-motion involves the monster ape, concluding with a shot of the good-natured primate introducing the closing credits and winking at the camera.

The *Adventure Island* effects crew obviously had an affection for and knowledge of classic special effects techniques. The film contains a relatively plentiful 38 stop-motion cuts, about a third of which take the trouble to combine the animated creature with a live-action element. The composites are created through a variety of simple, stationary mattes and rear-projection "Dynamation"-style set-ups. One shot of the plesiosaur sequence appears to utilize miniature front projection, and there are even a couple of matte painting shots!

The animation in *Lost on Adventure Island* is not particularly dynamic or ambitious, but it is quite remarkable considering the kind of film it was made for. To rate the *Adventure Island* stop-motion work by comparison to more mainstream pictures, it is considerably better than the animation in *Lost Continent* and almost as good as that in *Dinosaurus!* — in other words, not too bad at all. Maybe someday a dinosaur-loving, financially strapped filmmaker, in need of some practically never-before-seen dinosaur stock footage, will yet deliver these innocent stop-motion creatures into a good old-fashioned B-movie where they belong.

The Lost Whirl

"Only men with brains understand my masterpiece, but I'll tell it to you anyway."

** 1928, USA. Bray Studios. BW, 22m, silent.

CREDITS: *Director* Glen Lambert. *Producer* J. R. Bray. *Animation* J. L. Roop.
CAST: Jack Cooper, "Bill" Irving, Andy Clyde, Molly McKay.

Not long after Winsor McCay released his popular animated short *Gertie the Dinosaur*, producer J. R. Bray jumped in with a competently made but unabashed knockoff, even going so far as to call his film *Gertie* as well. When *The Lost World* hit theaters in the mid-1920s, Bray obviously knew he didn't have the resources to attempt a copycat version of First National's million-dollar production and so settled for this two-reel send-up. Not really a parody, *The Lost Whirl* is a fairly typical silent comedy, full of sight gags and a particularly heavy dose of puns. The entire film ultimately turns out to be a set-up for one visual punch line at the very end.

A dejected author, unable to interest anyone in his story, prepares to jump off the pier and end it all when a bystander (who happens to be a producer) intervenes. "My company is looking for a good scenario," the producer says, and the tale unfolds on-screen as it is related by the author. One day, the king of a "mysterious cult" on the remote Isle of Moss impulsively feeds his queen to the Tyrannosaurus type of dinosaur worshiped by the group. Figuring Hollywood is the best place to find beautiful women, the king sends two henchmen to fetch a new queen. They skulk around the California beaches wearing fake beards which — as the script humorously points out — make them look like the "Smith Brothers" of cough drop fame, and finally spot pretty Molly ("the Postmaster's daughter ... the reason so many males arrived daily"). They grab her and sail back to the isle, unaware that her loyal beau is also aboard. Before Molly can be readied for marriage, her sweetheart sneaks her away and a great chase ensues. The carnivorous dinosaur pursues the lovers until a Brontosaurus intervenes, and the couple make a break for it during the saurian spat. They complete their escape as the bronto wins (!) the fight and traps the king and his court in their cave—The End. Back at the pier, the producer mulls over the story. "Tell me mister author," the producer says, "did you write that story all by yourself?" "Yes," the author proudly replies, sitting on the pier's railing. "I and I alone am responsible for it." (If you can't predict what happens at this point, I won't spoil it for you.)

Both of the dinosaurs in *The Lost Whirl* are realized with stop-motion animation. The puppets are quite ordinary and the animation is comparable in quality to that in Willis O'Brien's *The Dinosaur and the Missing Link* more than ten years earlier. The animator, J. L. Roop, is historically noteworthy — his name appears on several marker slates visible in the recently discovered stop-motion outtakes from *The Lost World*, though it is not known if any of his animation was used in the final film. Roop keeps things pretty simple in *The Lost Whirl* but does attempt a few tricks. He has his T. rex catch a bone tossed by its keeper, employs a tiny human puppet for a comic scene of the meat-eater picking up a man and tossing him through the air, and even uses a face shot of a live monitor lizard to represent a closeup of the brontosaur's head! An interesting curio, *The Lost Whirl* is ultimately notable only for Roop's *Lost World* connections and because, just this once, a Brontosaurus gets to vanquish a T. rex.

The Lost World

"Who can say what might be living in that jungle — as vast as all Europe?"
*** 1925, USA. First National Pictures. BW, silent.

CREDITS: *Director* Harry O. Hoyt. *Additional Direction* William Dowlan. *Producer* Earl Hudson. *Scenario and Editorial Direction* Marion Fairfax; from the novel by Sir Arthur Conan Doyle. *Research and Technical Director* Willis H. O'Brien. *Chief Technician* Fred W. Jackman. *Special Effects Technicians* Marcel Delgado, Ralph Hammeras, Hans Koenekamp, Vernon L. Walker. *Director of Settings and Architecture* Milton Menasco. *Ape Man Make-up* Cecil Holland. *By Arrangement with* Watterson R. Rothacker.

CAST: *Paula White* Bessie Love. *Edward E. Malone* Lloyd Hughes. *Sir John Roxton* Lewis Stone. *Prof. George Challenger* Wallace Beery. *Prof. Summerlee* Arthur Hoyt. *Mrs. Challenger* Margaret McWade. *Austin, Challenger's butler* Finch Smiles. *Zambo* Jules Cowles. *Ape Man*

Bull Montana. *Colin McArdle* George Bunny. *Major Hibbard* Charles Wellsley.

AD LINE: "Seven years to bring it to you — seven years of hard work — but now this strange and sensational story *lives* before you! You forfeit your right to see the greatest entertainment the brains of man have ever achieved if you miss *The Lost World*."

London reporter Edward Malone, yearning to impress his feckless fiancée, requests a dangerous assignment and is sent to cover a lecture by the volatile Professor Challenger. Tired of verbally defending his assertion that a "Lost World" exists on a remote Amazonian plateau, Challenger assembles a new expedition: Professor Summerlee, Challenger's leading detractor; Paula White, dutiful daughter of plateau discoverer Maple White; Sir John Roxton, a hunter-adventurer harboring an unrequited love for Paula; and Ed Malone, whose employers agree to finance the trip as a "rescue mission" for Maple White.

As the group reaches the base of the plateau, a flyover by a giant pterodactyl quickly validates Challenger's story. The five explorers climb an adjacent pinnacle and cross to the plateau on a fallen tree, leaving Challenger's butler, Austin, jack-of-all-trades Zambo, and their pet monkey, Jocko, at base camp. A curious Brontosaurus knocks down their bridge and strands them on the plateau, surrounded by an endless variety of dinosaurs and a brutish ape-man. A busy Allosaurus — "vicious pest of the ancient world" — kills a brave but outmatched hadrosaur, threatens a gallant mother Triceratops, and takes a bullet in the snout from Roxton's rifle. The allosaur finally gets ripped open by a horned Monoclonius, which is in turn doomed to be killed by a Tyrannosaurus. The next day Roxton discovers Maple White's remains in a cave, but on a happier note also finds that one end of the passage overlooks their base camp. "Have Miss Paula call Jocko," Austin shouts up to Roxton. "He'll climb anything to get to her!" After waiting out a violent volcanic eruption and resulting dinosaur stampede, Jocko dutifully scampers up the cliff with a lifeline in tow. The party descends and are hiking toward civilization when they pass a live Brontosaurus mired in a mud bog, having been forced by a predator over the edge of the plateau. With the help of the men of the Brazilian Geodetic Survey, plans are made to bring the beast to London.

Challenger begins his triumphant announcement when word comes of an accident. The cable snapped ... the cage dropped ... and the bronto is loose in the English capital! The frightened creature tears down monuments, wrecks buildings, panics thousands of bystanders and finally tries to cross London Bridge, but its weight is too great and the huge beast is dumped into the river. Challenger can do nothing but watch his prize escape; nor can Roxton, as his beloved Paula rides away in Malone's arms.

COMMENTARY: In addition to all of its well-documented "firsts" — first feature-length dinosaur movie, first combination shots of stop-motion creatures and live people, first film to feature the plot points which would later become clichés — *The Lost World* has one more remarkable distinction: it is the only dino picture ever made to actually generate thoughts in its audience, however fleeting, that maybe, somehow, the dinosaurs were *real*.

So many elements of *The Lost World* were copied over and over — the remote locale where dinosaurs still live, the volcano seemingly awakened by the strangers' arrival, the giant beast brought to civilization only to escape — that it gave its name to the entire subgenre. But its vast numbers of dinosaurs, especially the multiple examples of the same species, would never be equaled in any stop-motion dinomovie. We see multiple brontosaurs, a pack of allosaurs feeding on a carcass, a family group of Triceratops, and of course the incredible stampede shots, all of which sell the notion of a true dinosaur environment much more effectively than does the "one of this, one of that" situation usually seen. Way back in 1925, these dinosaurs were allowed to be *dinosaurs* in all their carnivorous glory, and this ancient film is still the grisliest stop-motion dinosaur picture ever made. The pterodactyl tears strips of meat from its kill, the allosaur's bullet wound gushes blood, the Monoclonius eviscerates the allosaur leaving a wad of entrails hanging from its horn, and the Tyrannosaurus almost bites off the ceratopsian's leg ... then starts eating him alive!

If the dino action is actually more true to life, the human characters are less so. The cast is good, but the art of movie acting was still in its infancy and the exaggerated expressions and mannerisms cannot help but seem quaint nowadays. Whenever Challenger is deep in thought, for example, Wallace Beery's voluminous eyebrows dart madly about as if trying to escape from his forehead. Beery's wild, unkempt look is a little overdone but his unflagging energy keeps things afloat during the movie's slower patches. Some have called Lewis Stone a bit overage for Roxton, but he gives the most natural performance in the film and his advanced years make his loss of young Paula even more poignant. (The comment of the bystander—"That's John Roxton ... *sportsman*"—is also a nice touch.) Bessie Love is appealing though she seems rather delicate for such an arduous ordeal, and the choice of Lloyd Hughes as Malone apparently cast the die for nearly every Malone to come. Something should be said about Bull Montana's turn as the ape man; not that his performance is that spectacular, but just enduring such obviously torturous make-up is worth a pat on the back.

Chronologically situated between *The Ghost of Slumber Mountain* and *King Kong*, the *Lost World* animation shows signs of both. Some scenes, like the Allosaurus-Trachodon fight are no better than the animation in *Ghost*, while others like the Monoclonius-Allosaurus encounter are practically the equal of the *Kong* stop-motion. (Some revelations from recently discovered footage also shed light on the wide disparity in animation quality, as we'll later see.) But if the animation is not technically flawless, its pure energy is extraordinary. Such bold, uninhibited behaviors Willis O'Brien gave his carnivores—leaping onto the backs of their prey, jumping in the air to snatch a pterosaur, trying to bring down huge sauropods even as they both run from the volcanic inferno ... this is how dinosaurs *should* be. Like Obie's animation, Marcel Delgado's models show that he was also learning by doing. Many of the bipedal dinosaur puppets have noticeable shortcomings, especially in their limbs, while the beautiful Monoclonius (originally intended as an Agathaumus, a species no longer considered valid) can hold its own with any ceratopsian puppet ever made.

Eight years before *Kong*, O'Brien was already bringing his creatures to life with tiny but wonderful flourishes. The brontosaur reacting to the sound of the tree falling, the mother Triceratops nudging her baby behind her at the first scent of danger, the allosaur's glowing eyes looming in the forest—all these little bits anticipate the greater things to come. In fact, a lot of the creative choices in *The Lost World* foretell those in *King Kong*. In *Kong*, Carl Denham mutters something about chains and tools and the story cuts straight to Kong on Broadway; in *Lost World*, Major Hibbard mentions a raft and the coming rains, and we cut to the bronto in London. In each case, the choice to leave out the potentially draggy transportation details—probably made for financial and logistic reasons rather than creative ones—actually helps the story's flow. It's a stretch to draw any connections between Kong and Bull Montana's ape man ... or is it? Both have the same reaction to finding their human adversaries trying to escape down a rope.

While *The Lost World* can be appreciated, analyzed, and still enjoyed today, what it was like for 1925 audiences can only be imagined. Absolutely nothing like it had ever been seen. Not only was the world much bigger—big enough to make a "lost world" seem a real possibility—but audiences were nowhere near as technology-savvy as they are now. The familiar "flickery" quality of early films (partially caused by the slower projection speed of only 16 frames per second) surely made the stop-motion "strobing" effect much less noticeable, as it rather matched the "strobing" of the entire film. It is not unreasonable to presume that seeing Obie's dinos in 1925 must have been something like 1993's audiences seeing *Jurassic Park* for the first time — only more so. Except for one primitive traveling matte shot in the London finale, the composites are simple stationary mattes; but they were impressive in their day and still hold up remarkably well.

Enjoyable now more as historical document than as motion picture entertainment in the traditional sense, *The Lost World* was a truly incredible achievement and in some ways is still as good as any filmed version of Conan Doyle's story. It stands as a testimony to the uncanny appeal of dinosaurs, both by its success upon release and by the fact that it remains one of the few films of the silent era still widely discussed today. It is truly the granddaddy of all dinosaur films to come.

PEOPLE AND PRODUCTION: Although this first full-blooded dinosaur film could never have been made without Willis O'Brien, the initial mover was Watterson R. Rothacker, up until then known as a producer of advertising films. Rothacker was greatly impressed with Obie's dinosaur scenes in *The Ghost of Slumber Mountain*, and even in his early comedy shorts. Rothacker hired the animator, and before long the two men were enthusiastically conceptualizing a feature film version of Sir Arthur Conan Doyle's adventure novel, *The Lost World*. In cooperation with First National Pictures, Inc., the extensive preparatory work for the unprecedented project was soon under way.

At least two years was spent on preproduction, a staggering length of time for the silent era. Among the impressive sets were a mock-up of a London street one eighth of a mile long, and a multitude of miniature jungle settings for the dinosaurs to inhabit. The lead cameraman was Arthur Edeson, who in the following years would shoot three of the most venerated horror films ever made: *Frankenstein* (1931), *The Old Dark House* (1932), and *The Invisible Man* (1933). The cast was headed by Wallace Beery, who earlier sampled the prehistoric genre as the villain in *The Three Ages*. Popular Bessie Love was brought in as the "love" interest — adding a woman to the party is a departure from Conan Doyle found in every film version of *The Lost World* to date. Make-up artist Cecil Holland turned a burly Italian-American actor named Luigi Montagna — better known as Bull Montana — into a fearsome ape man for the second time, the first being five years earlier for *Go and Get it*. Harry O. Hoyt was tabbed as director, but a complete second unit helmed by William Dowling was also formed in midproduction to help speed things along.

Despite threats of a lawsuit by Herbert M. Dawley, O'Brien's former employer who weakly tried to claim that Obie had copied his techniques, *The Lost World* was completed and opened in February 1925. Soaring reviews and brisk box office validated the picture's then-outrageous million-dollar cost. In an oft-told and apparently true bit of *Lost World* trivia, the film became in 1926 the very first picture ever shown to entertain airline passengers — the inaugural "in-flight movie."

Many decades after *The Lost World* ended its newsworthy theatrical run, an intensive effort to restore the film became a remarkable tale of cinematic paleontology. When released, *The Lost World* had a running time most reliably reported at 104 minutes. It was pulled from release four years later and licensed to Kodascope Libraries, where it was edited for nontheatrical distribution down to barely half of its original length. This chopping completely removed Malone's manipulative fiancée Gladys Hungerford (Alma Bennett), and the half–Portuguese girl, Marquette (Virginia Brown Faire), seen playing a guitar at a riverside waypoint. Also gone were numerous bits which added to the characters' personas,

244 • *The Lost World* (1925)

In this publicity shot, the *Lost World* human actors have been rather crudely added to a still photograph from the Allosaurus-Trachodon battle.

including a running gag based on Summerlee's fanatical fascination with beetles. The unkindest cuts of all for stop-motion fans were those which removed a sizable amount of dinosaur animation.

From 1930 onward, the scratched and deteriorating Kodascope prints were the only form in which the film could be seen. Then in the early 1990s, Lumivision released on videocassette and laserdisc the best reconstruction of *The Lost World* possible at that time. The Lumivision edition was produced by Scott MacQueen, who subsequently penned two fascinating articles for *Cinefex* detailing this filmic detective story. "The good news was that the motion picture collection at George Eastman House had swooped down in 1949 and grabbed the Kodascope 35mm nitrate dupe negatives just as the failing 16mm division was about to junk them," MacQueen wrote. "A complete 16mm master print and, later, 35mm fine-grain masters of three reels were made before the nitrate decomposed. This material allowed our laserdisc version ... to look vastly superior to any copy of the film seen since 1925 — but it was still only half the show."

Soon after the Lumivision release, however, more discoveries came to light. An 800-foot reel of animation outtakes, mostly of unseen sequences, was found by Petrified Films in their stock footage accumulation; some fragmentary 35mm material was located in the Library of Congress; and most spectacularly, a preservation negative — itself incomplete — was discovered in the Czech national film archive. "Fortunately, the Czech copy complements the truncated Kodascope version in such a way that the two prints essentially interleave," MacQueen revealed. "Ninety-five percent of the narrative and ninety percent of the full screen footage should be accounted for in the reconstruction." The only disappointment is that, as of this writing, the George Eastman House has neither released nor discussed releasing its restoration on home video or otherwise.

There's still more. A matter of months before the writing of this book was completed, came word of a new reconstruction from noted film restorer David Shepard and Serge Bromberg, unrelated to the Eastman House efforts. In an interview published online in the *Dinosaur Interplanetary Gazette* "e-zine," Shepard discussed the project. "The question was whether or not we could obtain equivalents to the various film elements used by Eastman House," he began. "We quickly had those and, I believe, more." Not surprisingly, the restoration utilized footage from many sources. "A 35mm print with Czech titles; four 16mm tinted Kodascope abridgments; two prints of a one-reel version made as a classroom film by Encyclopædia Britannica, which had eight unique shots; a 1925 trailer; a demonstration reel apparently prepared for a 1925 meeting of the Society of Motion Picture Engineers; and a 1927 interview film with Sir Arthur Conan Doyle." Unlike the Eastman restoration, this version was to be released on VHS and DVD in April 2001. The new print even includes a badly scratched but still-delightful snippet of the original film's final scene: the swimming Brontosaurus watching a passing ship as he paddles toward his South American homeland.

SPECIAL EFFECTS: In the early 1920s, special effects pioneer Ralph Hammeras took a job working for Earl Hudson at First National Pictures. He felt that the full-time position offered more security than did the independent effects company he owned and managed, but that wasn't his only motivation. "Another reason I signed the contract was because Mr. Hudson told me that he had a man by the name of Willis O'Brien who did the most unusual things, like making prehistoric animals come to life on the screen," Hammeras wrote to author Don Shay. "He said he thought that we would make a good combination in working on a picture he was going to make called *The Lost World*."

O'Brien had advanced from his initial cartoony shorts of clay cavepeople and comic

Test set-up for a carnivore-ceratopsian tussle in *The Lost World*. The top of the painted backdrop and foreground edge of the miniature set are visible in this photograph.

dinos to the realistically modeled dinosaurs of *The Ghost of Slumber Mountain*, and was now ready for the next step: the world's first feature-length "dinosaur movie." A technical triumph in itself, *The Lost World* was also another waypoint on Obie's climb toward the mastery of his craft represented by *King Kong*. First National's involvement was serendipitous, bringing together the core of the *Lost World* FX team: O'Brien and Hammeras, Fred W. Jackman, Hans Koenekamp, and Vernon L. Walker. Jackman was a multiskilled "trick man" (as effects artists were called at that time), already in place as head of First National's effects department. So talented was effects cameraman Koenekamp that when Jackman was later put in charge of photographic effects on *Noah's Ark* (1929), he specifically requested Koenekamp's par-

ticipation. Vernon L. Walker would go on from First National to RKO, making key contributions to *King Kong* and heading that studio's camera effects department until his death in 1948. With the animation and photographic effects in these good hands, all *The Lost World* needed was somebody to make half a hundred dinosaurs.

Marcel Delgado was earning 18 bucks a week as a grocery clerk and taking night classes at the Otis Art Institute when he met Willis O'Brien, a story he later recalled to author George Turner. "One night he asked me, 'would you like to work in motion pictures?' I told him, no, I wanted to be an artist and didn't want to lose any time at it." O'Brien was persistent, though, and persuaded the young man to visit the studio lot. "Obie met me and took me to this little studio," Delgado continued. "There was a phone, some cameras, pictures all over ... 'How do you like your studio?' he asked me. It was a 21 year old boy's dream! So I signed up and worked for the next couple of years building dinosaurs for *The Lost World*." Improving on the earlier wooden and wire-armatured puppets, Delgado made the *Lost World* dinosaurs using steel armatures, built up with bath sponge and covered with rubber skin. He based his models on the dinosaur art of preeminent paleo-artist Charles R. Knight, whose paintings were showcased in New York's American Museum of Natural History.

Prefiguring the astonishing level of detail in *Kong*, O'Brien was already adding subtle touches to his work. Clear varnish was used as simulated saliva, while dark chocolate made very satisfactory blood when shot in black and white. The animation was filmed on a 75 by 100 foot shooting stage appointed with miniature trees, plants, boulders, and the like, all carefully sized to match the scale of Delgado's saurians. "We built our miniatures on tables or platforms about three feet above the floor," Ralph Hammeras explained. "This was done so that O'Brien would be in a comfortable position when he was working. The miniature sets also had to be built shallow in depth, so that O'Brien could reach into the set without disturbing any of the foliage while animating."

Simple stationary mattes allowed the actors and dinosaurs to appear in the same shots—the first time such a sight had been presented. Though not as striking as the complex composites of *Kong*, there are still some eye-grabbing images. Particularly impressive is the faultless composite of the explorers (in the background) examining the bog-bound Brontosaurus (in the foreground). The stampede sequence has earned a place of honor in animation lore, and why not? Never again would so many stop-motion dinosaurs cavort in a single shot. For the monster-in-the-city climax, Obie and crew used every method they could find, again foreshadowing his later *Kong* efforts.

The sequence features the stop-motion bronto, a full-scale foot, and a massive life-sized tail. In one of the many scenes snipped from the film, a full-sized mechanical head and neck poked through a window and quickly broke up a card game. The finale's "money" shot of the beast lumbering down a London street as thousands flee its path was accomplished through a primitive traveling matte process, and although close scrutiny reveals some flaws, it is completely satisfactory within the flow of the film.

For years it was assumed that O'Brien himself performed all of the *Lost World* animation (with the possible exception of a few stampede shots) but the discovery of the aforementioned "lost" footage has cast doubt on this. The very thing that caused many of these shots to be "outtakes" was the fact that the animator had been accidentally photographed for a single frame, and Obie "is not among the gentlemen caught inadvertently by the lens," Scott MacQueen wrote. "Moreover, the production slates identify the sequence animators by name." One interesting name that shows up is "Roop," a somewhat unusual surname that surely must refer to J. L. Roop, the credited animator for Bray Studios' 1928 parody *The Lost Whirl*. The rediscovered, never-before-seen animation footage is a buried treasure for dinosaur and special-effects aficionados. The scenes, included as a special supplement on the home-video release of the Shepard-Bromberg reconstruction, include a Stegosaurus-Allosaurus battle, a whole family of brontosaurs browsing at a water hole, additional cuts of the allosaur-pterosaur encounter, and more great stuff.

Willis O'Brien's creations have impressed countless people in a hundred different ways, so it seems fitting to close with a few appreciations. On the television series *Movie Magic*, renowned paleontologist Dr. Robert Bakker marveled at the prophetic behaviors that Obie animated. "At that time, if you went to a museum you would see Brontosaurus restored as a very slow animal, stupid animal, living alone, stuck in the swamps," Bakker said. "Willis O'Brien has brontosaurs in a *herd*, moving over dry land and spreading dust, and defending their young against meat-eating allosaurs—it's a wonderful tableau." In a BBC documentary, Ray Harryhausen summed up his view of O'Brien's driving vision. "No one had ever seen a dinosaur on the screen, only in still paintings, in a museum, or skeletons," Ray said. "And that, I believe, fascinated Willis O'Brien most—the idea of trying to put on the screen things that you *can't possibly* photograph." But this author's favorite description of Obie comes from Ralph Hammeras: "An ingenious man, and a fabricator of the imagination."

The Lost World

"Fakes, they'll say. ... Fakes!"

* ½   1960, USA. 20th Century–Fox. C, 98m.

CREDITS: *Director* Irwin Allen. *Producer* Irwin Allen. *Screenplay* Charles Bennett and Irwin Allen; based on the novel by Sir Arthur Conan Doyle. *Special Photographic Effects* L. B. Abbott, James B. Gordon, Emil Kosa, Jr. *Effects Technician* Willis O'Brien.

CAST: *Lord John Roxton* Michael Rennie. *Jennifer Holmes* Jill St. John. *Ed Malone* David Hedison. *Professor Challenger* Claude Rains. *Gomez* Fernando Lamas. *Professor Summerlee* Richard Haydn. *David Holmes* Ray Stricklyn. *Costa* Jay Novello. *Native Girl* Vitina Marcus. *Burton White* Ian Wolfe.

AD LINE: "Here is the most amazing of all possible worlds! Your mind won't believe what your eyes tell you! This is not 150,000,000 years ago! This is today!"

London's "indomitable zoological professor" George Edward Challenger returns from an Amazon expedition reporting an astounding discovery: prehistoric dinosaurs still thriving on a remote jungle plateau. "Were they *big* dinosaurs?" sneers his colleague, Professor Summerlee. "I do not deal in *small* dinosaurs," Challenger replies. A new excursion is mounted consisting of Challenger, Summerlee, noted adventurer Lord John Roxton and reporter Ed Malone, whose employer is financing the trip. They rendezvous with their helicopter pilot, Gomez, and his sycophantic sidekick, Costa, at a small Amazonian trading post, and find Jennifer and David Holmes (the daughter and son of Malone's boss) also waiting there. This complicates matters, since Jennifer and Roxton are ex-flames and Malone is just beginning to fall for her. Their helicopter is wrecked by an unseen animal during their very first night on the plateau, and the next day they sight what the natives call *curupuri*—living dinosaurs. Tensions between Malone and Roxton erupt into a fight, but the scuffle halts when Roxton discovers the diary of plateau pioneer Burton White. The journal reveals that White's party was supposed to have been guided by Roxton, who for self-serving reasons never showed up.

The following morning a shot from an unknown gunman grazes Summerlee, but that's the least of their worries when Malone and Jennifer (and her poodle) return to camp and find that their comrades have been captured by the plateau natives. They are soon trapped as well, but a beautiful native girl, earlier befriended by David, helps them escape to the cave home of Burton White. The blind old man directs them to the Cave of Fire—the only passage off the plateau—where they discover a fortune in diamonds, a clutch of dinosaur eggs, and a man-made dam holding back a lava pool. Suddenly Gomez announces his intent to kill Roxton in retribution for the death of his brother, who died with the abandoned White expedition, and admits that it was his earlier attempt on Roxton's life which wounded Summerlee. Malone tackles Gomez and a stray gunshot awakens a giant reptile, but when Roxton saves Gomez from the beast—which eats Costa instead—Gomez pronounces them even and sacrifices himself to release the lava onto the monster. Volcanic blasts annihilate the Lost World as the survivors reach the jungle floor, and they prepare to return to London with a fortune in diamonds and a baby Tyrannosaurus.

COMMENTARY: Much like *The Son of Kong*, discussions of Irwin Allen's version of *The Lost World* usually dwell on what might have been and what the film is not, rather than what it is. It is not a crowning moment for Willis O'Brien, it is not a faithful adaptation of Sir Arthur Conan Doyle's novel, and it is not a worthy remake of the pioneering silent film. So, just what is it? It's a juvenile, coarse, and unsatisfying "adventure," which despite some handsome production values ultimately offers no adventure at all.

Though its ending is truer to the original story than was that of the '25 film, Allen's *Lost World* otherwise strays drastically from Conan Doyle's tale. The changes are uniformly for the worse, many of them the direct result of ham-fisted attempts to make a line-by-line copy of Fox's *Journey to the Center of the Earth*. *Journey* was based on a classic adventure novel; it cast a venerable English actor as the expedition leader; it took a woman along despite the vehement objections of others; it featured a "cute" animal sidekick; it included the discovery of a legendary locale (Atlantis in *Journey*; El Dorado here); and it employed live reptiles as its prehistoric menace. Instead of mechanically aping these details, the filmmakers should have noticed the more intangible things that actually made *Journey* work. Like keeping the cast down to a manageable number, and never forgetting that James Mason was the hub upon which everything turned. Here Claude Rains is only fourth-billed, and for the film's second half is reduced to being just another member of a too-large ensemble that's a far cry from Conan Doyle's tightly knit foursome.

Claude Rains was 72 at the time of *The Lost World* but still makes a commanding Challenger until being done in by the screenplay and Allen's cartoonish direction. Fernando Lamas brings dignity to Gomez and David Hedison is an adequate Malone, but Michael Rennie is astoundingly drowsy as Roxton and Jill St. John has no hope of doing anything with the ill-conceived Jennifer. The sloppy script calls Jennifer "as brave as a lioness" and then has her to panic, scream, and fall down every time danger strikes. Summerlee, painfully overplayed by Richard Haydn, bickers tiresomely with Challenger, Roxton seems simultaneously smug and bored, the sniveling Costa is an insulting ethnic stereotype, and David is surely the most superfluous character in genre film history. From the heavily padded exposition to the gecko-as-tyrannosaur finale, *The Lost World* is crass, garish, and heavy-handed.

It's a familiar tale to fans of Willis O'Brien how disappointed he was to learn that the color *Lost World* remake, about which he had been so excited, was to feature "gagged-up lizards" (O'Brien's term) instead of stop-motion. But even disregarding such "if only" indulgences and examining the effects on their own merit, they are still sadly inadequate. This is not a criticism of L. B. Abbott and his associates—their work is as professional as always; it simply comes back to the fact that modern lizards look nothing like dinosaurs. Abbott asserted that the reptiles "naturally move the way monsters should," but of course the problem is not that lizards can't make serviceable *monsters*, it's that they can't make good *dinosaurs*. The scaly actors are well-photographed, though, and skillfully matted into the live action.

Not content with mere back fins, the lizard dressers glued horns, plates, barbels, and even a floppy rubber neck frill on the critters; but the more prosthetics they added, the goofier the animals looked. The frill, for example, makes its wearer look rather like some sort of ancient idol one might find inside a pyramid. We hear sound effects of great trees falling every time one of the behemoths trudges through the forest, as if large animals never use the same trail twice. The specter of possible animal abuse always hangs over scenes like the big dino battle, which is not only distasteful but also a blatant copy of the famous fight in *One Million B.C.* On a better note, the physical and optical effects are generally excellent. The lava pit and the Cave of Fire are convincing, and other than the "giant" spider (which glows a neon green) the mattework is proficient. Paul

Tie-in comic book version of the 1960 *The Lost World*. Other dinomovies in Dell's popular "Movie Classics" series included *The Land Unknown, Dinosaurus!* and *The Animal World*.

Sawtell and Bert Shefter deliver a superior music score, especially during the beautiful shots of real Amazonian scenery describing the journey to the plateau, and the art direction by Duncan Cramer and Walter M. Simonds is imaginative if sometimes gaudy.

In the film's closing moments, Challenger finds a dinosaur egg, and unlike most cinematic dino eggs which are portrayed as five or six feet long, this egg is fairly accurate in both size and shape. After all, they were bound to get *something* right.

PEOPLE AND PRODUCTION: The success of 1959's *Journey to the Center of the Earth* not only cleared the way for *The Lost World*, it actually spawned it. In his book, *Special Effects — Wire, Tape and Rubber Band Style*, Fox effects maestro L. B. Abbott talked about the origin of the project, which for him began during a meeting at the Fox production office. "I realized that the leader of the group was a gentleman named Irwin Allen," Abbott wrote. "He held an option on a property called *The Lost World*." Allen's option was going to expire in less than three hours, and Abbott's boss Sid Rogell had to decide on the spot whether to green-light the project. "Mr. Rogell turned to me and asked, 'Bill, can we make this picture?' I said 'Yes,'" Abbott recalled. "In 1960 we made the film."

Writer Charles Bennett had been an Irwin Allen favorite for years, so it was no surprise that he was tabbed to screenwrite *Lost World*. Interviewed by Tom Weaver in *Starlog*, Bennett talked about the film: "He [Allen] liked the idea of prehistoric monsters and things like that, so he asked me to write the script," Bennett said, also recalling his personal meeting with the novel's author years earlier. "I was playing Dr. Watson in *Sherlock Holmes and the Speckled Band* at a theater in Paris," he remembered. "I was only 24 at the time, and Conan Doyle was in front. He came 'round after the performance and said that I was the finest Watson he had ever seen."

Bennett, whose first dino screenplay was 1934's *The Secret of the Loch*, defended his decision to eliminate the silent version's dinosaur-in-London finale. "We didn't do that because the Conan Doyle novel doesn't end that way," he pointed out. "Our ending was the escape of the people from the 'lost world.'" The Jennifer Holmes character was intended not only to add the requisite love interest but also to provide an odd sort of "name" recognition, because according to a rather incredible press release, Irwin Allen believed that "audiences will be looking for a character named Holmes," simply because the story was written by Conan Doyle!

David Hedison was at the time under contract to 20th Century–Fox, but wasn't in love with *The Lost World*. "It was one of those pictures that the studio wanted me to do, and I felt I had to do, and I didn't want to go on suspension — all that sort of thing," Hedison explained in a television interview. "I didn't like the script, I didn't believe in the script, and I'd get on the set and I'd see Jill St. John in pink tights holding a poodle." He was more complimentary toward the FX, saying "all of the monster stuff and the dinosaurs, all that worked very very well." Casting the musically inclined Fernando Lamas offered a fringe benefit publicity wise, and the studio actually released a 45 rpm record as a *Lost World* tie-in.

SPECIAL EFFECTS: The main reason for Irwin Allen's refusal to consider stop-motion animation dated back to the dinosaur sequence in *The Animal World*. Though impressed with the quality of Ray Harryhausen's work, he had been very frustrated by the time-intensive nature of animation. "The process was just agonizing," Allen recalled, "getting back the footage in little pieces over weeks and weeks." Besides, *Journey to the Center of the Earth* had used live lizards and had been a hit, so why get off a winner? That was the thinking, anyway.

Willis O'Brien, age 74, was thrilled to taste the possibility of one more top-of-the-line production, only to be utterly dismayed at Allen's decision. "They claim that the live technique looks smoother, that animation is jerky," O'Brien would later say. "They felt it would take too long to animate. I don't agree

Many test shots were taken of the elaborately made-up reptilian actors. This unfortunate crocodilian is adorned with at least a dozen "dinosaurian" accouterments.

with them. It takes quite a crew with these reptiles." Ray Harryhausen, though not on the project, was also taken aback by the lizards. "Of course [I was disappointed], and so was Obie," Harryhausen said in *Filmfax*. "He was flabbergasted that they would go that way, but it was cheaper, and I don't think it was as good." Unable to change Allen's mind, O'Brien's contributions were minimal and many sources report that he actually did almost no work on the film. "He didn't, no; they just used his name," Harryhausen told this author. "He *wanted* to, you know — when we made *The Animal World* together for Irwin Allen, Obie was constantly telling him, 'why don't you remake *The Lost World* in animation?' He thought at first [Allen] was going to go ahead but … they did it the 'easy' way by gluing fins on alligators. They didn't look like dinosaurs, they just looked like something out of *Flash Gordon*." Obie did create many storyboards (for the hoped-for animation sequences, not the lizards), and may have designed some of the CinemaScope split-screen setups, but that's it.

A true legend of special effects, L. B. "Bill" Abbott steadily rose through the 20th Century–Fox ranks from assistant cameraman to operative cameraman, then to director of photography, and then to head of the special effects camera department in 1943. He assumed overall leadership of the department in 1957 and retained that position until his retirement from full-time moviemaking in 1970. He periodically returned to work for the next several years whenever his unique services were needed, and finally retired with four Academy Awards on his mantle. *The Lost World* began a recurring association between Abbott and Irwin Allen. "I personally feel that a great many of us in the industry owe Mr. Allen a sincere 'thank you,'" Abbott would later state, "for all the employment his tireless organizational efforts provided for us."

With the lizard decision made, Abbott set out to do the best job he could. Recalling the difficulties encountered with the rhinoceros iguanas used in *Journey to the Center of the Earth*, Abbott called in animal handler Jim Dannaldson for some reptilian guidance. Dannaldson had overseen the massive monitor lizards of *The Land Unknown* three years earlier, and brought in two of the behemoths (named "Selangor" and "Pahang") for *The Lost World*. The big dino fight pitted one of the six-foot-long monitors, outfitted with a ceratopsianlike neck frill, against a caiman alligator wearing the obligatory back fin. An iguana with horns added over his eyes made a brief appearance, a smaller species of monitor portrayed the lava monster, and a gecko lizard represented the baby Tyrannosaurus. The lizard scenes utilized a selection of generic animal roars, but a typical bit of studio hyperbole claimed that "there were 13 sound editors working on the voices of the animals who roamed the earth in 150,000,000 B.C.!"

Many of the dinosaur scenes were photographed on a "miniature" jungle set measuring 40 feet wide and 20 feet deep. Art director Walter Simonds outfitted the set with a variety of odd-looking greenery, including grapevines turned upside down to give an exotic touch. Overcranking the camera is a common strategy used when filming miniatures to create an illusion of size and mass, but filming at three times normal speed requires intense lighting. Multiple arc lamps did the trick but also heated the studio to the point that the jungle set actually began to steam, and Abbott reported that "the lizards, whose native habitat is in areas that reach 120 degrees F., seemed to enjoy the heat and acted very well." He didn't always find the scaly actors so cooperative though, recounting one incident where he had to frantically hold off a suddenly cranky monitor until pal Jim Dannaldson came to the rescue.

The dino jungle wasn't the picture's only impressive miniature set; the imposing lava pool in the Cave of Fire was another ingenious creation. "The pool itself was a product of Herb Cheek, head of the prop miniature department," Abbott stated. "He built a miniature set raised six feet above the stage floor with a cliff section matching the full-size cliff set." The pool was equipped with transparent cooking dishes mounted in its floor, beneath which were thousand-watt lamps to provide a glowing effect. The lava was actually "driller's mud," a lubricant used in the oil well business but also a trusted tool of many a trick man, and the final effect was augmented with charcoal dust, lighter fluid, and Sterno pellets. The climactic explosion "was borrowed from some earlier picture — I forget which," Abbott wrote. "It was matted above a painting of the plateau done by Emil Kosa, Jr., in his usual brilliant style."

The film's promotional literature makes repeated mention of a pterosaur sequence, which supposedly occurs right before the discovery of the native girl. "The explorers are attacked by a flying dinosaur, a pterodactyl," the official synopsis stated. "The bird-like creature has leathery, 20-foot long wings, and it is finally driven off with rifle fire." But it's nowhere to be seen in the actual film — the live reptiles are the only prehistoric beasties on-screen. Stock footage of these lizards would turn up in many of Irwin Allen's television series in the years to come, including *Lost in Space, The Time Tunnel* and *Voyage to the Bottom of the Sea*. Surprisingly, brief clips of the Irwinosauruses can also be glimpsed in *When Dinosaurs Ruled the Earth*.

The Lost World

"It's nothing remarkable — we've all seen igneous extrusions before."

**½ 1992, Canada/U.K. Harmony Gold/Silvio Berlusconi. C, 97m.

CREDITS: *Director* Timothy Bond. *Producers* Frank Agrama, Daniele Lorenzano, Norman Siderow, Harry Alan Towers (executive). *Screenplay* Peter Welbeck (Harry Alan Towers). *Special Effects Created by* Image Quest, Ltd. *Effects Director of Photography/Supervisor* Peter Parks. *Animatronic Supervisor* Richard Gregory.

CAST: *Prof. Challenger* John Rhys-Davies. *Prof. Summerlee* David Warner. *Edward Malone* Eric McCormack. *Malu* Nathania Stanford. *Jim Darren* Peter Mercer. *Jenny Nielson* Tamara Gorski. *Chief Palala* Fidelis Cheza.

AD LINE: "They were searching for something fantastic ... what they found was unbelievable."

Bombastic professor George Edward Challenger has gained possession of a sketchbook from a deceased American explorer, and is so intrigued that he plans a new expedition into untamed central Africa. Accompanied by his staunch rival, Professor Summerlee, Canadian reporter Edward Malone, wildlife photographer Jenny Nielson, and Malone's young pal Jim, and joined en route by a resourceful young woman named Malu, Challenger reaches the plateau. The immediate sighting of an Anatosaurus pair proves Challenger's claims, and Summerlee duly apologizes for the doubts he expressed. In an eventful first day, Summerlee falls into a pterodactyl nest, Malone becomes attracted to both Jenny and Malu, and Jim spots an aborigine painted like a human skeleton. Returning from a harrowing encounter with a slender-snouted meat-eater, Malone, Malu and Jim find their companions gone and a trail of blood leading into the jungle.

At the skeleton tribe's village, the captives are adorned with leafy garlands in preparation for sacrifice to a Tyrannosaurus, but Jim creates a diversion and the prisoners—including some plateau natives—are rescued. One of the freed natives is Palala, chief of a peaceful tribe who welcomes the explorers as guests. Malu learns that the two tribes were once united, until the aggressive skeleton tribe began to worship the "evil ones"—the carnivorous dinosaurs—instead of the herbivorous "good ones" venerated by Palala's people. With the help of the chief's daughter Imana, Summerlee discovers that the strange leaf garlands contain a medicinal compound required by the meat-eating dinosaurs. "We were the chocolate," as Summerlee explains, "and these plants were the medicine." With Malu having killed the rabble-rousing witch doctor who incited the tribal split, the two factions reunite. But Palala will only reveal the way home in exchange for the party's vow that they will return if needed again. At the base of the plateau Challenger is accosted by his treacherous translator, Gomez, who blames the scientist for his brother's death, but the scoundrel is no match for Challenger. Back in London, the Institute's skeptics are as loud as ever until Jim walks in ... with a live baby pterodactyl.

COMMENTARY: This iteration of *The Lost World*, the first since Irwin Allen's in 1960, is in a few ways terrific and in other ways is hardly better than the Allen version. Considering that it is based on the seminal dinosaur novel and is a remake of the prototypical dinosaur movie, there are astoundingly few dinosaurs to be seen.

As Challenger, John Rhys-Davies leads a superior cast. So memorable and likable in small roles in the *Indiana Jones* films, Rhys-Davies brings Conan Doyle's bellicose professor to life with a flawless balance of pomposity and good humor, volatility and reason. His energy and charisma extract more from the script than it really has to give, especially during the humorous passages. David Warner is equally good, never turning Summerlee into the caricature he has often become, and his verbal jousts with Challenger are smartly written. Eric McCormack is an engaging Malone (he actually resembles the 1925 Malone, Lloyd Hughes), Nathania Stanford endows her obligatory "native girl" with dignity, and Darren Peter Mercer is perhaps the least irritating tagalong kid ever seen in one of these movies. With such casting success, it's interesting to wonder who may have played Lord Roxton had the character not been written out.

After the encounter with the Anatosaurus (now properly called Edmontosaurus) Ed Malone comments, "the Anatosauri were not at all intimidating." Sadly, they're not at all impressive either, especially for a "first sighting" scene which should be a wow. Instead of awe and wonder, we get a comic shot of a dinosaur licking Jenny's camera lens. The quality and quantity of the film's puppet dinos are such easy targets for criticism, but it must be said—one sequence in the 1925 *Lost World* has more and better dinosaurs than this picture and its sequel combined.

Most of the dinosaurs look fine, or at least the isolated parts which we see look fine, but their fragmented construction prevents any sort of dynamic action. "Percy," the baby pterodactyl, is a complete miss, inadequate in both design and performance. It is too cute, never seems alive, and the cel animation used to show it flying away in the film's final shot is laughable. The nighttime scene of Malone, Malu and Jim being menaced by the unidentifiable carnivore is neatly set up, and a life-saving trick involving melon juice is a clever twist, but again the creature's faults minimize the effectiveness. Summerlee's altercation with the adult pterodactyl is the best dino sequence; most of the beast is shown, and it looks plausible and is energetically puppeteered.

The story is initially faithful to Conan Doyle's novel only to steadily drift away. The main plot threads of the film's second half—the divided tribes, "good ones," "evil ones"—are nowhere near Conan Doyle, though Summerlee's solving of the sick-dinosaurs mystery does have a satisfactorily Holmesian feel to it. The script disappointingly embraces that "herbivore–good guy, carnivore–bad guy" philosophy seen in *Dinosaurus!*, *The Land Before Time*, and *Dinosaur*, then adds insult to injury by not knowing when to end. The making of the pact to return, the defeat of Gomez at the base of the plateau, Challenger's vindication at the institute, and the group's hearty toast "to the Lost World!" all seem like "last scenes" before the real last scene—the release of Percy from the zoo—finally arrives. Better to dwell on the picture's strengths: a true spirit of adventure mixed with a sense of humor, an excellent music score, and a fine cast with great camaraderie, especially John Rhys-Davies—maybe the best G. E. Challenger we'll ever see.

PEOPLE AND PRODUCTION: A Canadian-British coproduction, *The Lost World* was

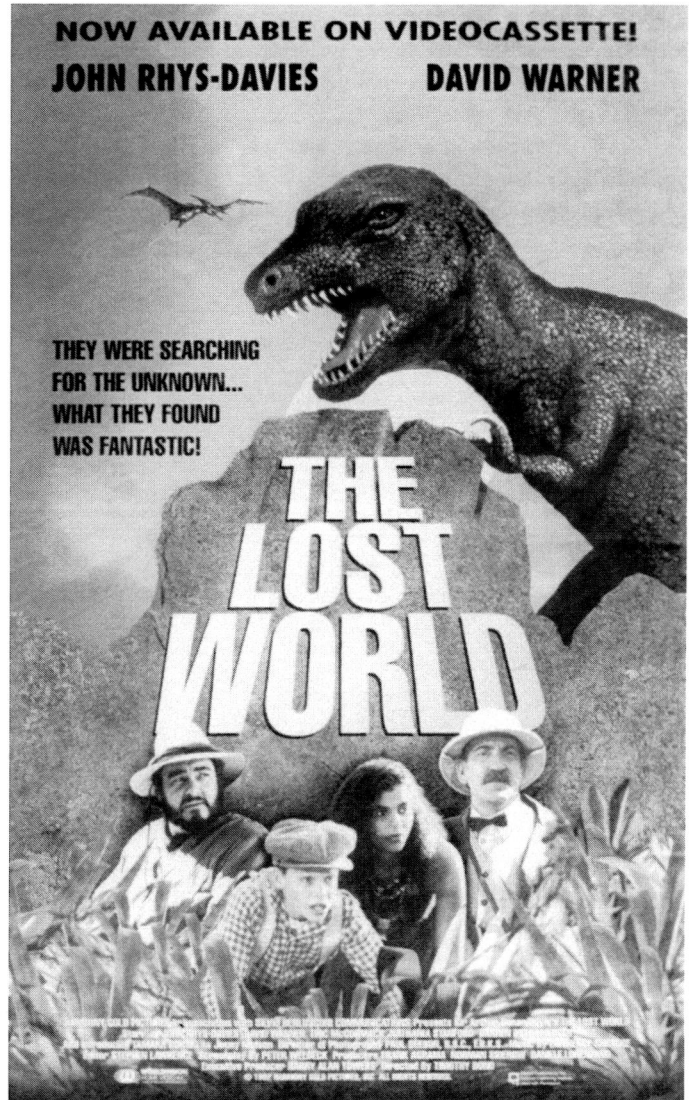

Video store poster for 1992's version of *The Lost World* offers a better view of a better-looking dinosaur than does the film itself.

filmed concurrently with its sequel, *Return to the Lost World*. Location photography took place in Zimbabwe, prompting the story's change of locale from South America to Africa. Both films were directed by Timothy Bond, veteran of numerous television shows, and were written for the screen by Harry Alan Towers under the pseudonym Peter Welbeck. The special effects were handled by Image Quest, Ltd., a British firm founded by Peter Parks. Noted for their innovations in combining microscopic photography with large-format cinema, Parks and Image Quest have contributed impressively to such IMAX films as *On the Wing* (1986), *The Secret of Life on Earth* (1993), and *Cosmic Voyage* (1996). Their cutting-edge work on these high-profile projects makes the meagerness of the *Lost World* effects all the more puzzling; it must be assumed that the effects budget was horrendously small.

The Lost World
(a.k.a. *Sir Arthur Conan Doyle's The Lost World*)

"Now you insist on continuing in this folly!"

* 1998, Canada. Fries Film Group/Trimark. C, 98m.

CREDITS: *Director* Bob Keen. *Producers* Danny Rossner, Murray Shostak, Barry Barnholtz, Omar Kaczmarczyk (executive), Irene Carter (associate). *Script* Leopold St. Pierre and Jean Lafleur; based on the book by Sir Arthur Conan Doyle. *Special Make-up Effects Designers* Twins F/X II. *Digital Visual Effects* Image Animation and Big Bang Animation.

CAST: *Prof. Challenger* Patrick Bergin. *Amanda White* Jayne Heitmeyer. *Arthur Malone* Julian Casey. *John Roxton* David Nerman. *Prof. Summerlee* Michael Sinelnikoff. *Djena* Gregoriane Minot Payeur. *Azbek/Myar* Russell Yuen.

In the year 1934, famed scientist Maple White and his guide, Azbek, are killed atop a remote Mongolian plateau, but Professor George Edward Challenger agrees with White's theory that prehistoric life exists there. When showman Oscar Perreault offers to finance an expedition — with an additional $100,000 for anyone who brings back a live dinosaur — Challenger jumps at the chance to prove his assertions. Joining Challenger are his chief rival, Professor Summerlee, Maple White's daughter Amanda, hunter John Roxton, and reporter–amateur balloonist Arthur Malone.

By plane, train, halftrack, and balloon they travel, joined along the way by Mongolian guides Djena and Myar (sister and brother of the late Azbek). Challenger's claims are confirmed when a flock of pterodactyls is spotted, but unfortunately the pesky beasts proceed to kill Myar and rip open the balloon's helium envelope. The group survives a crash-landing and takes shelter in a primitive man-made stone structure, but Roxton reveals his true colors when he draws a gun and flaunts a baby Centrosaurus with which he plans to claim the $100,000 bounty. His scheme goes disastrously awry when he falls into the lair of a subterranean predator. Other than the blossoming romance between Malone and Djena, things go steadily downhill from there. Summerlee is drugged by a Neanderthal's blowgun and becomes a T. rex meal, and Roxton — yes, back again — clumsily blows himself up in an attempt to maroon the others. While trying to make a parachute out of balloon fabric for a desperate escape attempt, the survivors are attacked by a pack of turkey-sized predators. The T. rex also returns and kills Djena, but the grief-stricken Malone takes revenge by blowing the rex to bits using a natural methane vent. The blast's force knocks Challenger and Amanda off the cliff, and they parachute to freedom.

COMMENTARY: This negligible reworking of Sir Arthur Conan Doyle's story is largely a disaster. Plodding, depressing, and at times purely silly, the film's only noteworthy accomplishment is its displacement of Irwin Allen's 1960 "epic" as the worst *Lost World* ever.

Every cinematic version of *The Lost World* has rewritten Conan Doyle in various ways, but the choices here are dumbfounding. We are left to ponder how a lush jungle thrives in the high elevations of Mongolia, and why the hostile, dinosaur-worshipping tribe lives not on the plateau with the dinos, but down at the bottom. And what in the world have they done to poor John Roxton, besides making him an American? He cruelly torments Djena, lusts after Amanda, defies Challenger's authority, warns Summerlee "you better not hold us up, old man," and tries to murder the lot of them. By comparison, *Unknown Island*'s Capt. Tarnowski was an eagle scout.

There is nothing wrong with taking 45 minutes to reach the plateau as long as the journey scenes serve a useful purpose. Here they do not. The entire film, both before and after arrival in the Lost World, is stunningly slow. (Whatever their flaws, at least the '92 and '99 versions have some *energy*.) Great chunks of screen time are eaten up by shots of the actors trudging through the snow down below and through the trees up on top.

Patrick Bergin is an odd choice for Challenger, but shows signs he could have handled the role just fine in a better picture. David Nerman goes overboard as the corrupted Roxton, puffing maniacally on his stogie, bulging his eyes out and cackling like a hammy hyena. Julian Casey makes for a unique and interesting Malone, but Jayne Heitmeyer and Michael Sinelnikoff have very little to do. The Mongolian girl, Djena, played by unknown Gregoriane Minot Payeur, is an original character full of possibilities that are never explored.

The fact that Bob Keen was an FX creator before turning director makes the scarcity of dinos puzzling (many of the dino appearances are just three-second throwaways) but star Patrick Bergin provided some telling info in a *Fangoria* article. "Bob did a great job," Bergin asserted. "When you're doing a low-budget movie, your CGI is limited. Bob really sold the effects, though I do feel we relied too much on the monsters rather than the characters." The captured baby dino looks good, but the pterodactyl attack is meager compared to the ones in the following year's *Lost World* and *Journey to the Center of the Earth*. The "little raptors" are plainly inspired by the "compys" of *The Lost World: Jurassic Park*, and are likewise realized through a combination of CGI and live-action puppetry. The puppet versions are fine, but the CG raptors (and the T. rex as well, erroneously given three-fingered forelimbs) are not pleasing. Their movement is too quick and springy, the momentums are not natural, and there is little sense of mass when the big guy ambles by. One shot in particular has a bouncy, "tiptoeing" gait that is strikingly similar to the early test scene of *Jurassic Park*'s CG tyrannosaur, shown in the *Making of* documentary.

There are very few good moments. During Summerlee's hallucinatory death scene, the tyrannosaur creepily morphs into a living skeleton—echoing the professor's earlier lament that he "only knows them as bones." A briefly mentioned idea, that dinosaurs would have continued to change had they really survived until modern times, is logical and intriguing but is realized only through a half-seen cameo featuring an armored Brontosaurus. The shooting locations, in Quebec and British Columbia's Pacific Rim National Park, are attractive if unspectacular, and the music score is only average. Maybe the worst thing about this gory, dreary picture is that every time another second-rate made-for-video *Lost World* is made, the chances dwindle that we shall ever see the all-out big-screen treatment that Conan Doyle's enduring novel still cries out for.

The Lost World

(a.k.a. *Sir Arthur Conan Doyle's The Lost World*)

"Where these beasts are, is not a place where you want to go."

** 1999, Canada/Australia. New Line/Telescene/Village Roadshow Pictures. C, 93m.

CREDITS: *Director* Richard Franklin. *Producer* Darryl Sheen. *Executive producers* Leslie Belzberg, John Landis, Jeffrey M. Hayes, Greg Coote, Robin Spry, Bruce Moccia, Paul Painter. *Written by* Jim Henshaw and Peter Mohan; based on a story by Sir Arthur Conan Doyle. *Visual Effects* Photon VFX, Hybride Technologies. *Miniature Design and Fabrication* Pro FX, The Model Smiths.

CAST: *Prof. Challenger* Peter McCauley. *Marguerite Krux* Rachel Blakely. *John Malone* William de Vry. *Lord John Roxton* William

Snow. *Veronica* Jennifer O'Dell. *Prof. Summerlee* Michael Sinelnikoff. *Assai* Laura Vazquez.

Inspired equally by a journal of a dead explorer and by a burning desire to prove to his derisive colleagues his claims of a time-lost Amazonian plateau, Professor George Edward Challenger itches to return to the trackless South American jungles. When a mysterious woman named Marguerite Krux (pronounced "crew") offers to finance the expedition, Challenger assembles reporter John Malone, adventurer Lord John Roxton, the skeptical Professor Summerlee and the dauntless Marguerite, and the expedition is launched.

Venturing inland by canoe and on foot, the explorers sight the plateau and ascend in a hydrogen balloon. Moments after their less than perfect landing, Malone is rescued from an aggressively carnivorous plant by a beautiful blonde woman. The stranger, Veronica, came to the plateau as a child with her British parents who have been missing for ten years. She has survived by her wits and with the help of her friend Assai, daughter of the chief of the nearby Zanga tribe. While Marguerite, Malone, and Summerlee head for the Zanga village (hoping to make friends), Roxton, Challenger, and Veronica set out in search of a pterodactyl egg as proof of the Lost World's existence. Secretly, though, Marguerite makes a self-serving bargain with the Zanga chief, promising to deliver Veronica as his bride if he will reveal a safe passage down from the plateau. Fate seems to be on Marguerite's side when the dreaded ape-men capture Assai and leave Veronica incapacitated, but Malone rescues the Zanga princess and her return puts a stop to the nuptials. The explorers' departure is halted by a violent earthquake — blocking their subterranean exit route — and by another attack from the ape-men. Thinking quickly, lovebirds Malone and Veronica lead a Tyrannosaurus rex into the ape-men's midst and the diversion allows everyone to retreat to the now friendly Zanga encampment. "We'll find a way home," Challenger tells Summerlee, "and until then, we've got the greatest grounds for research a scientist could ever dream of — a whole Lost World."

COMMENTARY: This *Lost World* remake, the third in the space of seven years, is a made-for-television entry designed to kick off a syndicated weekly series. In several ways this effort particularly resembles Irwin Allen's 1960 version — not good news. The early sequence of Challenger being jeered by his colleagues is *very* similar to Allen's picture, with some nearly identical dialogue. We also have a woman financially forcing her way into the expedition against the men's chauvinistic wishes (a plot device which has became a cliché in itself), and an attempted escape through a volcanic cavern.

Conan Doyle's story is left in the dust after the first half-hour, and the subsequent proceedings owe more to previous dino-movies than to Conan Doyle. The prologue recalls the opening scene of *Jurassic Park*, the pterodactyl sequence borrows from *One Million Years B.C.*, Veronica's escape between the tyrannosaur's legs echoes *The Last Dinosaur*, there are shades of *When Dinosaurs Ruled the Earth* in the tribal celebrations and dances, a rampaging beast provides a timely diversion as in *The Mighty Gorga*, and a briefly seen foot-long caterpillar looks just like a baby *Mothra*!

Finding a gorgeous girl in a navel-baring outfit was seemingly a "lost world" prerequisite during the decade — Nathania Stanford in the '92 *Lost World*, Petra Yared in the '99 *Journey to the Center of the Earth*, and here Jennifer O'Dell as the Tarzanesque Veronica. O'Dell seems awfully "California" for the role but she's good in one of the film's best scenes, which pokes fun at the very clichés it's employing. When the party first encounters Veronica, Summerlee chides Challenger for his attempts at communication. "This isn't Edgar Rice Burroughs!" Summerlee blusters. "You don't expect her to understand English, do you? Why don't you try grunting?" The tactic seems to work, until Summerlee realizes the girl is grunting the "Ode to Joy" by Beethoven! "If you don't like it, I know a little Chopin," she deadpans.

Though the whole thing has the unmistakable air of a TV movie, the acting roster is respectable. Australia's Peter McCauley is a well-chosen Challenger, William Snow — another Aussie — makes Roxton a likable rogue, and Michael Sinelnikoff's portrayal of Summerlee recalls Cecil Kellaway's turn in *The Beast from 20,000 Fathoms*. Interestingly, Sinelnikoff had previously portrayed the same character in the otherwise unrelated '98 version of *The Lost World*, but is given much better dialogue this time around.

The creature scenes are not plentiful. The only two major sequences are the pterodactyl attack (when Roxton steals the egg) and the T. rex chase, which is a fun bit of business. The sauropods as usual are limited to a few brief cameos. The dinosaur effects — a combination of puppetry and digital imagery — are only occasionally impressive. The skin textures lack detail, and the movement just doesn't look quite "right." There is an attempt to show the pterodactyl struggling with its added load when it picks up Roxton, but the effect is not as successful as that achieved by Ray Harryhausen in *The Valley of Gwangi*. There is one neat shot in the T. rex sequence with a slick background-to-foreground focus shift, and overall the effects are the best of the decade's three *Lost World* incarnations.

It is strangely comforting to see that all the great dinomovie clichés ... that is, *hallmarks*, were still alive at the threshold of the 21st century. This *Lost World* is lightweight and forgettable but does have an excellent music score by Garry McDonald and Lawrence Stone, some gorgeous Australian locations, and a really cool if unlikely treehouse condo right out of *The Swiss Family Robinson*. It's not Conan Doyle but it does offer some tongue-in-cheek fun, and is at least an improvement from the previous year's *Lost World* debacle.

PEOPLE AND PRODUCTION: The enduring qualities of Sir Arthur Conan Doyle's seminal novel were not lost on producer Jeffrey M. Hayes. "This is a project that involves dinosaurs, natives, the Amazon, ape-men, headhunters, diamond caves, a lost world," said Hayes, one of the show's *seven* executive producers. "It's a production designer's dream and a producer's dream as well!" He was also enthusiastic (perhaps just a bit too much) about the dinosaurs. "As far as the effects are concerned, we utilized the most cutting edge techniques to make our dinosaurs as real and as believable as those in *Jurassic Park*," Hayes asserted.

Director Richard Franklin was quick to admit that his film took liberties with the original novel. "When Conan Doyle wrote it, it was a story about a bunch of men who go up the Amazon," Franklin said in a filmed interview. "We've changed the story — indeed every film version from the 1926 [sic] version on has added women to the story." He also mentioned one other major departure. "In our version of it, of course, they don't come back, because we're hoping it will become an ongoing series!"

SPECIAL EFFECTS: The visual effects were provided by Australia's Photon VFX (which also contributed dinosaur FX to the 1999 TV movie *Journey to the Center of the Earth*), and Quebec's Hybride Technologies. The miniature and puppet work was a collaboration between two Australian effects houses: Pro FX and the Model Smiths.

On the Model Smiths' Internet site, David Tremont published an in-depth article on creating the ambitious T. rex chase sequence. As often happens, time and money concerns ultimately dictated the FX strategy. The solution finally settled upon "was to use a mixture of a costume puppet (worn up to the waist) and animatronics for face and tail movements," Tremont reported, "with some digital tricks to add more facial expressions, chest breathing and breath vapour along with other muscle movements." Tremont volunteered to personally puppeteer the rex. "My enthusiasm overpowered my common sense," he recalled. Only Tremont's lower half was actually inside the suit — his upper half protruded from the creature's back. A

The sexy but self-sufficient Veronica (Jennifer O'Dell) forges an uneasy truce with a race of half-dinosaur, half-humanoid beings in television's 1999 reimagining of *The Lost World*.

blue shirt, hood, and pair of gloves turned him into a sort of human blue screen and allowed him to be digitally removed from the shots during final compositing.

The rex suit consisted of a "fiberglass and alloy armature," supporting skins made of foam latex. "The puppet had to look as little like a man in a suit as possible," Tremont pointed out, "so foot extensions were used to give the animal a much more real look."

But the extensions meant that Tremont could not actually walk or maintain his balance in the suit, so an overhead track and flying rig provided support. "This rig was set so I could be lifted up and down and pulled forward," Tremont continued, "so during the shots the guys would pull the rig along and I had no choice but to go along for the ride and try and keep up with the pace."

Tremont provided the gross body and leg movements, and operated the head and jaws using a control rod protruding from the back of the creature's neck. Finer motions, such as eyeblinks and squints, flaring nostrils, and snarling lips were radio controlled. "With all the shots done, it was on to the 2D compositing and manipulation, to put the T. rex into all the scenes," explained Tremont. "A lot of it was removing rods and cables (and me) and other things like moving the tail higher or bending the legs a little more." As compositing progressed, one drawback of the flying rig was revealed. "Being in a harness took a lot of my weight away," Tremont noted, "so in a couple of shots the T. rex had a floating feel about it." Like many previous FX artists, Tremont lamented the lack of one precious commodity. "Compromises had to be made to get it done on time, which can be a disappointment because we all know that we could do better if we had a little more time to work," he summed up. "We are aware of these limitations when we take on the jobs, and have to come up with ways of achieving good results within these constraints."

The Lost World

"It's like opening a window ... on the beginning of time."

*** 2001, U.K. BBC/A&E Network. C, 150m.

CREDITS: *Director* Stuart Orme. *Producers* Christopher Hall; Tim Haines (co-producer), Kate Harwood (executive), Jane Tranter (executive), Delia Fine (executive, for A&E). *Written by* Tony Mulholland and Adrian Hodges; based on the novel by Sir Arthur Conan Doyle. *Animatronics & Apes* Jez Harris, Richard Gregory. *Visual Effects* FrameStore. *Visual Effects Supervisor* William Bartlett. *Animation Supervisor* Virgil Manning. *Special Effects* Paul Verrall.

CAST: *Prof. George Challenger* Bob Hoskins. *Prof. Leo Summerlee* James Fox. *Lord John Roxton* Tom Ward. *Edward Malone* Matthew Rhys. *Agnes Cluny* Elaine Cassidy. *Reverend Theo Kerr* Peter Falk. *Chief* Nathaniel Lees. *Achille* Tamati Te Nohotu. *Maree* Nicole Whippy. *Gladys* Joanna Page.

London, 1912. Controversial paleontologist George Challenger yearns to explore a mysterious Amazonian plateau, described in the journals of a 17th century missionary known as Padre Mendoz. Before long, Challenger and three companions—noted hunter Lord John Roxton, reporter Edward Malone (hoping to impress his flighty girlfriend, Gladys), and Challenger's foil Professor Leo Summerlee—are bound for Brazil. At a jungle mission founded by Reverend Theo Kerr, the staunchly anti–Darwinist reverend and his niece, Agnes Cluny, join the party. Kerr's hidden motives surface after everyone else has crossed a log bridge from a narrow pinnacle onto the plateau, and the emotional Kerr shockingly dislodges the log. "This place belongs to the Devil," he cries, marooning the five. "It is no part of God's kingdom!"

The Lost World is found to be rife with spectacular and dangerous prehistoric fauna. A young Hypsilophodon and a giant Iguanodon pose no threat, but the party must flee a Pteranodon rookery when the huge, winged creatures become agitated. Agnes and Malone encounter the plateau's top predator, Allosaurus, escaping death only when the dinosaur falls into a camouflaged pit dug by an unknown Indian tribe. The multilingual Agnes enlists the Indians' help in rescuing the professors from a colony of savage ape-men, also saving the chief's son Achille in the process.

At the Indian village, Challenger is surprised to be "recognized" by the tribal chief as the divine reincarnation of Padre Mendoz. Except for Achille, who resists Challenger's ban on killing the captured ape-people, the natives welcome the visitors. Challenger studies the Diplodocus, Agnes and Malone become romantic, Roxton woos the chief's daughter Maree, and Summerlee devises schemes for escaping the plateau, but the peace is shattered when the caged apemen slather themselves with dung and begin a strange collective howling. Challenger too late deduces what they're up to—*calling* a pair of allosaurs into their enemies' village—and the resulting carnage leaves the chief dead and the explorers running from the enraged Achille. Roxton is wounded but holds the Indians at bay, allowing the others to escape through a cave unblocked by Summerlee's homemade explosives. But waiting in the jungle below is Reverend Kerr, near madness. Having long ago visited the Lost World, he could never reconcile his view of Creation with the living evolutionary evidence, and is determined to keep the plateau hidden. He draws a pistol and grapples with Summerlee, a shot is fired, and Kerr falls. The group waits for Roxton as long as possible, then heads for home.

In London, Malone is secretly pleased to find Gladys engaged as it frees him to marry Agnes. At the Natural History Museum a beaming Challenger proves his claims by unveiling a living Pteranodon, but Malone and Summerlee observe the ensuing pandemonium—and think back to the bloodshed on the plateau—and suddenly realize that revealing the Lost World will condemn it. Challenger agrees, reluctantly, and proclaims the whole business a hoax. And the Pteranodon? Merely "an Amazonian vulture, cleverly made up."

COMMENTARY: Previous filmings of Sir Arthur Conan Doyle's *The Lost World* have had varying degrees of British participation, but leave it to the venerable BBC to finally make a proper job of it. This handsome production blends a smart script, exceptional cast, and some superb dinosaurs into what is, on balance, the best cinematic interpretation to date of Conan Doyle's enduring tale.

This *Lost World*—the fourth film in ten years and the sixth overall—often looks to the 1925 version for inspiration. Scenes reimagined from the silent classic include the early sighting of the pterosaur, climbing the pinnacle and felling the tree, Malone's apeman encounter during a treetop reconnoiter, and the nocturnal attack of the Allosaurus, though this last segment fails to include the eerie glowing eyes seen in the original movie. For the sixth time in six films a woman has been added to Conan Doyle's all-male party, but this example seems the least forced and most successful of the lot. Much credit is due Elaine Cassidy's naturalistic performance but screenwriters Adrian Hodges and Tony Mulholland have also pulled off a difficult feat, tweaking and amending the novel in ways that actually improve it as a film.

The new plot twists are plausible and intriguing and the new characters, especially Agnes and Reverend Kerr, have a surprising resonance. What a pleasure to suddenly realize that the human characters in a dinosaur movie have become "real" and you actually care about what happens to them! The writers even mix a bit of allusion into certain names. The fiercely devout missionary is called Theo, a prefix denoting God, while Summerlee's first name becomes Leo, i.e. "The Lion," both the animal and the character being symbolic of Great Britain itself.

The superior teleplay provides great opportunities for the actors, and they don't disappoint. Matching Miss Cassidy's excellence are Bob Hoskins' energetic yet rational Challenger, Tom Ward's youthful, dashing Roxton, Matthew Rhys' unsure but willing Malone, and Peter Falk's tortured Kerr. There must be something about Summerlee that prods actors into a broad, overly theatrical style, and James Fox falls somewhat into this trap, but his performance steadily improves throughout the film. Nathaniel Lees as the tribal chief makes an impression in a supporting role, likewise Joanna Page with her humorous turn as the excruciatingly fickle Gladys. This production is in fact a fine example of how to include bits of humor in this sort of tale without resorting to the dreaded "comedy relief" character. Besides the actors, credit is due production designer Rob Harris, director of photography David Odd, director Stuart Orme, and the beautiful New Zealand locations for giving the picture such an opulent feel; it truly has the look of a theatrical release.

In terms of being unimpeachably convincing, the dinosaur effects in *The Lost World* can be matched, or perhaps just *barely* topped, only by those in the *Jurassic Park* films. The creatures of the plateau are hugely impressive in appearance, movement, and behavior, and the major set pieces are supplemented by a sizable helping of atmospheric cameos. Dino-sound designer Terry Brown supplies an organic variety of chirps, screams, and roars, and the compositing of the dinosaurs with the location landscapes is as flawless as the animals' design. At last, a movie Iguanodon that really looks like an Iguanodon! The discovery of the pterosaur rookery (a fantastic episode from Conan Doyle's novel, filmed here for the first time) is pure joy, as the imposing swarm of Pteranodons takes wing to drive away the pesky humans. The gigantic Diplodocus is beautiful if too-briefly seen, and the animation of the baby pterosaur darting around the London museum is astonishing. The allosaur assault on the Indian village is another thrilling if quite violent set piece, but the best dino sequence is the mid-film appearance of the lone Allosaurus and its pursuit of Agnes and Malone through the jungle. The creature's chilling entrance, the dynamic tracking shots of the sleek and muscular predator, the incredible animation of its huge mass and relentless stride, flawless editing, great music, and simply the adrenaline-stoked *pace* of the entire pursuit, make for not only this picture's finest segment but one of the top dinosaur sequences ever filmed — period.

Best of all, *The Lost World* never forgets the awe-and-wonder factor — those "wow" moments which are all too scarce in the otherwise amazing *Jurassic Park* trilogy. Its 150-minute running time never seems overlong, and the believable flesh-and-blood characters build and maintain interest both before and between the dinosaurs' appearances. The story's thoughtful explorations of human qualities both noble and abhorrent — curiosity and inflexibility, acceptance and prejudice, compassion and cruelty — stay true to the spirit of Conan Doyle even when straying from his narrative details.

PEOPLE AND PRODUCTION: As preproduction for *The Lost World* ramped up, the filmmakers were determined to avoid the soundstage and instead find natural locations which would fulfill Conan Doyle's visions of the primeval Amazonian milieu. The most obvious choice was Brazil itself, but the real Amazon presented problems. "Not only do we need a rain forest jungle, but we also need the magical place that is the plateau," producer Christopher Hall explained. "My assessment of Brazil is there is an awful lot of river, and there is an awful lot of jungle, but to get anything more than that we would have to travel a great, great many miles." South Africa and Queensland, Australia were promising contenders, but in New Zealand they found a venue that "absolutely tells the story." The temperate climate was another big plus, providing the tropical conditions necessary without unpleasant extremes. "The sun is shining, it's very lush, but it is possible to work here," Hall summed up. "We're not horribly humid, and we're not being eaten and bitten, and everyone's having a *relatively* nice time."

The moderate temperatures were no doubt appreciated by Malcolm Shields and his cohorts, who portrayed the primitive ape-men. The intricate make-up required to turn human actors into the hairy "missing links" of the script was uncomfortable enough without having to perform in hot weather. "You do get used to it," Shields said of the make-up. "We sit here for [an] hour and a half, two hours, having all the various other touches done, blending in the eyes, making sure we can breathe properly and that kind of thing, and then seeing the transformation happen." Then follows a 30-minute warm-up period before donning the fur-covered "muscle suit." Shields handled the ape-man choreography, portrayed a lead ape-man himself and hand-selected the rest of the principal performers. "The two I brought up from the U.K., Paul Joseph and Jane Howie, had dance backgrounds and martial arts backgrounds, and very physical theatre backgrounds," Shields pointed out. "Then I came over to New Zealand, and I was looking for two other what we call 'hero apes' who were going to be in the full prosthetic as well, and found Mason West and Julia Walshaw. So these were people that I *needed* to get."

The Lost World premiered on BBC1 in two parts, shown on Christmas Day and Boxing Day (December 26), 2001.

SPECIAL EFFECTS: *Lost World* co-producer Tim Haines was the series producer for the BBC's mega-popular television documentary, *Walking with Dinosaurs,* and he isn't the only contributor common to the two productions. Both shows feature computer-generated animation from the British FX company FrameStore (which is also providing 1700 FX shots for Hallmark's *Dinotopia* mini-series), as well as animatronic dinosaurs created by Crawley Creatures & Associates. "There is still a role for animatronics, particularly in the big close-ups," Haines said, explaining why the mechanical and digital techniques were both used. "The computer can fool the eye making a dinosaur run through a puddle and splashing but if you want a close-up of him dipping his nose into water and moving it back and forth, a computer-generated nose wouldn't look right."

The Crawley Creatures project supervisors on *The Lost World* were Jez Harris and Richard Gregory, both *Walking* alumni. Gregory, previously on the FX team for the 1992 version of *The Lost World,* discussed the animatronics in a BBC featurette. "When we worked on the series *Walking with Dinosaurs* ... we were always filming in such remote places, we couldn't take a lot of mechanical equipment with us," he noted. "So we redesigned the dinosaur heads so they were lightweight, so we could actually carry them to, literally, the tops of mountains to operate." A special support rig, worn by Gregory, was designed to bear the weight of the head and leave the puppeteer free to operate the articulations, "so it becomes a huge hand puppet." For the villainous Allosaurus, not just the head but also a front arm, lower leg, and tail were built for interaction with the actors and physical sets. "We work very closely with FrameStore, who are creating the computer-generated dinosaurs," Gregory explained. "Because we work closely, we actually work and create similar sculpts ... so between the two of us, we can marry together the two sets of pieces— the virtual dinosaurs and the mechanical dinosaurs—and by clever intercutting of the shots, often you can't tell which are which."

The cost of the digital dinosaurs was held in check by doing the work on "off-the-shelf" computers, a strategy made possible by the fact that television requires much lower image resolution than film. Like so many before them, the FrameStore animators found nature the best guide, visiting safari parks to study the motion dynamics of elephants and other large animals. FrameStore founder Mike Milne, talking about the CG animation techniques initially established for *Walking with Dinosaurs,* was quick to acknowledge the field's pioneers. "In a sense, we were standing on Industrial Light & Magic's shoulders," Milne said, quoted by author Joe Fordham. "They had led the way, and we adapted that so that we could deal with large quantities of animation relatively quickly." *Lost World* animation supervisor Virgil Manning, who also served as senior computer animator on the *Walking with Dinosaurs* followup *The Ballad of Big Al,* summed up FrameStore's post–*Walking* advances: "Changes we have introduced have led to better muscle movement in the dinosaurs and we have used higher resolution texture maps.... The main change that viewers should notice, though, is the bolder animation."

The Lost World: Jurassic Park

"Hang on to something!"

**½ 1997, USA. Universal/Amblin. C, 129m.

CREDITS: *Director* Steven Spielberg. *Producers* Gerald R. Molen and Colin Wilson, Kathleen Kennedy (executive), Bonnie Curtis (associate). *Screenplay* David Koepp; based on the novel *The Lost World* by Michael Crichton. *Full-Motion Dinosaurs* Dennis Muren, A.S.C. *Live Action Dinosaurs* Stan Winston. *Special Dinosaur Effects* Michael Lantieri. *Dinosaur Supervisor* Randal M. Dutra.

CAST: *Dr. Ian Malcolm* Jeff Goldblum. *Dr. Sarah Harding* Julianne Moore. *Roland Tembo* Pete Postlethwaite. *Peter Ludlow* Arliss Howard. *John Hammond* Sir Richard Attenborough. *Nick Van Owen* Vince Vaughn. *Kelly Malcolm* Vanessa Lee Chester. *Dieter Stark* Peter Stormare. *Ajay Sidhu* Harvey Jason. *Eddie Carr* Richard Schiff. *Dr. Robert Burke* Thomas F. Duffy.

AD LINE: "Something has survived."

Ian Malcolm, his reputation in tatters due to his "wild stories" of the events on Isla Nublar, is summoned to the bedside of the ailing John Hammond. There is another island, Hammond explains, where an entire "lost world" has been flourishing in the intervening four years. Hammond has managed to keep it a secret, but when a wealthy, vacationing British couple happens upon the island, their daughter is injured and Ingen's money-grubbing board of directors takes control. Hoping to rally public opinion to his side, Hammond asks Malcolm to join a four-person documentary crew. Malcolm balks, until he realizes that paleontologist Sarah Harding—his girlfriend—is already on the island.

Accompanying Malcolm and Sarah are equipment specialist Eddie Carr, videographer Nick Van Owen, and Malcolm's (stowaway) daughter Kelly. They've barely had time to set up their high-tech lab–dormitory trailers before Hammond's nephew Peter Ludlow arrives with a much bigger contingent, including big-game hunter *extraordinaire* Roland Tembo and paleontologist Robert Burke. Ludlow's party proceeds to capture a variety of dinosaurs for exhibition at "Jurassic Park San Diego," and Tembo has a second agenda: to hunt and bring down a full-grown Tyrannosaurus rex. Nick turns Ludlow's captive dinosaurs loose for a destructive romp through the Ingen compound and, in a case of compassion overcoming common sense, brings an injured baby T. rex to the trailer for medical treatment. The parent tyrannosaurs, not perceiving the benevolent intentions, destroy the trailers and make a meal of Eddie. With both groups' equipment ruined, they have no choice but to join forces and make a treacherous hike across the island to the abandoned communications center. Burke is killed by a Tyrannosaurus, and Tembo loses both of his companions—his assistant, Dieter Stark, is felled by a pack of tiny Compsognathus, and his tracker and friend, Ajay, can't escape a Velociraptor ambush. Nick manages to send a distress call, but Ian, Sarah, and Kelly have to outwit several raptors to reach the helicopter. As the 'copter leaves the island, Sarah looks down and sees the tranquilized male T. rex—and the infant—being readied for shipment.

Something goes wrong during the tyrannosaur's voyage, and the pilotless ship crashes into the San Diego dock. The enraged T. rex emerges and goes on a rampage through the streets, but Ian and Sarah use its baby as bait to lure the creature back to the barge. Ludlow is also there, still hoping to salvage his project, but instead becomes the first prey of the juvenile T. rex. At last, with CNN covering every moment, the reunited dinosaurs are taken back to the Lost World.

COMMENTARY: "Boy, do I hate being right all the time," Ian Malcolm says in *Jurassic Park*. But in this sequel, his wisdom finally falters. He tells Ludlow that "taking dinosaurs off this island is the worst idea in the long, sad history of bad ideas," but he's wrong—it was a fantastically good idea. Because if they had never taken the Tyrannosaurus back to unsuspecting San Diego,

The *Lost World* tyrannosaur clan — father, mother, and baby — posing for a family portrait.

this sequel would have to rank as an unmitigated misfire. *The Lost World* has a variety of puzzling flaws and relies solely upon its dinosaurs to keep things going, but they do come through — especially the T. rex. In the climax of *Jurassic Park*, the heroic tyrannosaur only had to save Grant, Ellie, and the kids. This time, the titanic T. rex upstages the mundane story and single-handedly — bless those little two-fingered arms — saves the whole movie.

There is virtually nothing negative that

one can say about the dinosaur scenes, but from a narrative standpoint the film is rather a mess. Some of Ray Harryhausen's pictures have been criticized as being merely frameworks upon which to hang the visual effects, but not one of them contains plot points as forced and thoughtless as does *The Lost World*. We need a kid on the island? Kelly stows away. We need to maroon Malcolm and party there? The boat captain won't stay and the radios (for some reason) won't work. We need an excuse to use the "high hide?" Kelly says "I wanna go somewhere *high!*" And so it goes.

A common thread running through many of these illogical scenes is Kelly Malcolm, who is never believable from her first appearance to her unlikely gymnastic heroics. (It was Roger Ebert who pointed out "the ancient principle that every gymnast in a movie sooner or later encounters a bar.") Incredibly, she is not even allowed her moment of wide-eyed, awestruck wonder at seeing the dinosaurs for the first time. In 1993, screenwriter David Koepp said of *Jurassic Park*: "We didn't want it to seem like [Lex and Tim] were there just to have kids in the movie." He succeeded back then; maybe he should have remembered that statement this time.

The film has moments that spit in the face of common sense so emphatically as to be unignorable. Accepting that dinosaurs have been cloned back to life is easy compared to believing that a man as capable as Roland would have a schmoe like Dieter as his lieutenant, or that a cold executive like Ludlow (a hideously stereotyped character) would go into a potentially corporation-saving video conference half-smashed, or that a scientist who's "worked around predators" for years would traipse across a dinosaur-infested wilderness wearing a blood-soaked jacket. We're not supposed to wonder why not one of those dozen other people who *didn't* have headphones on could hear Dieter calling. And don't ask what dismembered the ship's crew inside that cramped steering house, given that the only dinosaur on board was an 18-foot-tall, seven-ton tyrannosaur.

The whole "hunters and gatherers" idea, which started as a tiny notation scribbled by Spielberg on a production sketch and eventually became the guiding philosophy of the entire narrative, is a problem in itself. It must have seemed a good idea in the beginning, but it simply doesn't work as well as the filmmakers surely hoped. The mercenary-soulless-corporate faction versus the noble-humanistic-underdog faction is a plot device that's been cranked out too often, including for Jan De Bont's adrenaline-drenched but brainless 1996 popcorn flick, *Twister* (co-written by Michael Crichton and executive produced by Spielberg).

The actors had the deck stacked against them with such unreal actions to perform and cookie-cutter characters to portray, but they sometimes managed to make something out of very little. The highlight is definitely Pete Postlethwaite as Roland Tembo, "the last of the philosopher-hunters," as he described his role. Tembo, though unavoidably reminiscent of Richard Boone's Masten Thrust in *The Last Dinosaur*, is David Koepp's best creation. Julianne Moore, who like Laura Dern in *Jurassic* was known for work in "smaller," character-driven films, is a fine actress and does what she can. Richard Schiff is effective as the kind-hearted Eddie, Jeff Goldblum shines on the sporadic occasions when he's given good dialogue, and Thomas Duffy has some fun playing a paleontologist who's obviously inspired by Dr. Robert Bakker. (But why not just have the entertaining Bakker play himself?) The problems surrounding the character of Malcolm's daughter are in no way a reflection on Vanessa Lee Chester; she was doomed by the script before she ever stepped on set. One other actress deserves mention — Camilla Belle, who plays Cathy Bowman in the film's opening vignette. Asked to react not to a single lumbering behemoth but a swarming pack of quick-moving, ratlike predators all around her — which were of course not there — the youngster does a remarkable job of selling the effect.

Miss Belle's skillful pantomime is one

element of many — including an ironic cry of "Cathy darling, *lunch is ready!*" from the girl's mom — that make the "teaser" such a dynamite sequence. The film's dinosaur scenes are uniformly as strong as the story is weak, and it's apparent that much more thought, imagination, and effort went into the dino sequences than into the plot. As we near the island, John Williams' music gets better, we see the fog shrouding the coastline, and we feel a tingle that things are about to pick up. And they sort of do, but only when the dinos come on screen.

The first big dinosaur set piece is the Stegosaurus herd, and it's a wow. The digital artists had made definite advancements since *Jurassic* and showed their stuff by having one of the outlandish-looking beasts amble lazily across the frame, right in front of the camera, offering the chance to appreciate the phenomenally organic detail. The sequence also recalls the stego scene in *King Kong*, in which the animal grazes harmlessly in the background until suddenly someone yells "he's gonna charge!" and all hell breaks loose. The same basic structure is used here, and it still works. After the stegos pass, Ian asks his stunned cohorts what they expected to see and sets up an amusing dinomovie in-joke: "Animals," Nick replies, "maybe ... big iguanas."

The next big set piece is the "roundup," a sequence inspired by the animal-capture scenes in the 1962 John Wayne adventure *Hatari!* It's a dino spectacle with all sorts of species — Parasaurolophus, Gallimimus, Pachycephalosaurus — galloping across a dusty plain and looking unimpeachably convincing. We also see an impossibly huge Mamenchisaurus (owner of the longest neck of all time) and even get to ride between the legs of one of the behemoths in a crowd-pleasing shot. It's disappointing and a bit puzzling, though, that the giant sauropods are limited to this one brief walk-through, since the sheer size of the really massive species is such a big part of the human fascination with dinosaurs. The capture of the Parasaurolophus harks back to Harry-hausen's spectacular roping of the title character in *The Valley of Gwangi*, while the entire roundup sequence points out an entertaining capability of computer animation. The mechanics of an animal's movement completely change when shifting from a walk to a run, and this change is *extremely* difficult to accomplish in stop-motion. It has been done — the baby dino in *When Dinosaurs Ruled the Earth* and the Ornithomimus in *Gwangi* are two examples — but stop-motion dinosaurs usually do not run so much as they "walk fast." The dino roundup, and the Gallimimus stampede in *Jurassic*, give us the chance to see dinosaurs really stretching it out and running free.

Nick's rescue of the baby T. rex leads to the major set piece of the film's middle section: the T. rex-versus-the-trailer. The baby rex is another astonishing animatronic creation, and Janusz Kaminski's cinematography is at its most inventive during these scenes. Kaminski, in fact, does such a good job of putting the viewer into the situation that acrophobics may not want to watch. The bit with Sarah on the glass, enhanced by the nerve-jangling, glass-cracking sound effects, is definite white-knuckle stuff. The whole trailer sequence shows off the detail, articulation, and "performances" of the animatronic tyrannosaurs, and their live on-set destruction of Eddie's vehicle is another triumph for Stan Winston Studio. The Velociraptors likewise remain delicious villains with their sinister countenance and eerie vocalizations, and the lengthy raptor sequence in the abandoned village is cleverly designed to raise goosebumps. All that junk scattered about the compound provides so many possible raptor hiding places that you feel a constant urge to look behind you. But, of course, as soon as you do, then something *else* is behind you. It creates a spiraling sense of anxiety — torturous in real life but great fun in a theater seat.

The Lost World is bookended by its two best parts: the ghoulish grabber of a prologue, and the knockout tyrannosaurian finale. The San Diego sequence pays affectionate tribute to decades of rampaging movie-saurs from the 1925 *Lost World* and the radioactive beasts and behemoths of the fifties, to *Gorgo* (also a parent searching for its captive infant) in the sixties. There's a *Godzilla* gag with the running Japanese businessmen (one of whom supposedly says in Japanese, "I left Tokyo to get away from all this!"), and the "S.S. *Venture*" is obviously a nod to Capt. Englehorn's boat in *King Kong*. And look for the shot where the T. rex scratches his ear in homage to Willis O'Brien's *Kong* tyrannosaur, just as Ray Harryhausen's "Gwangi" had also done. The design team pulled out all the stops for a quarter-hour of newfangled, old-fashioned, monster-matinee glee.

The final act is so much fun that, on first viewing, this moviegoer left the theater with a big smile and a good feeling. But eventually the flaws begin to nag. The dark photography that was supposed to be "moody" turns out murky, the attempts at comedy relief (Ludlow getting tipsy, and so on) are inexplicable, and there are holes in the story big enough to drive a Mamenchisaurus through. When I asked Ray Harryhausen, who enjoyed *Jurassic Park*, to compare the sequel to the original, he said: "Oh, it was even more interesting, technically." Notice that last, carefully added word: *technically*.

As the magnificent stegosaur herd goes by, Jeff Goldblum's character says, "Yeah, 'ooh, ahh,' that's how it always starts ... but then later there's running and screaming." That line sums up the two basic elements of a dinosaur film: "ooh, ahh" and "running and screaming." *Jurassic Park* had these elements well-balanced. The T. rex and Velociraptors were complemented by the stately brachiosaurs and the strangely vulnerable Triceratops, with the Gallimimus stampede pitched nicely in the middle. *The Lost World* is so determined to be "darker" and "harder-edged" that the running and screaming almost overwhelms the oohs and ahhs. The magic of dinosaurs—that unique and undefinable aura of wonder that sets them apart from even the most incredible creatures of fiction—is captured just often enough to make *The Lost World* enjoyable, even as it reminds us that it could have been so much more.

PEOPLE AND PRODUCTION: If it's true that the novel *Jurassic Park* was destined to become a movie, it's equally true that *Jurassic Park* the movie was destined to spawn a sequel. Even before publication of Michael Crichton's follow-up book, which he titled *The Lost World* as a nod to Sir Arthur Conan Doyle's classic tale, work had already begun on the second film.

Screenwriter David Koepp had strayed somewhat from Crichton's narrative when translating *Jurassic Park* to the screen and did the same with *Lost World*, only more so. "I wanted to take the best stuff from the book, of course, while adding things of my own," Koepp said in Jody Duncan's *The Making of The Lost World*. The film version's biggest detour transports the T. rex to the mainland and sets it loose in a major city, a finale that had been on Spielberg's mind for some time. As executive producer Kathleen Kennedy recalled, "finally [Steven] got to the point where he said, 'you know, I just *really* think that this is what we need for the movie. I think it's what the audience really wants to see.'" This new third act was appropriately true to the story's namesake—the 1925 film version also added a monster-in-the-city climax to Conan Doyle's novel.

The Lost World also mined Crichton's original *Jurassic Park* novel for some material which hadn't been used in the first film. "There were two scenes in particular that Steven and I were both sorry to see go," Crichton said in a 1993 *Fangoria* article. "One was the Tyrannosaurus rex attacking the boat in the water ... the other is the scene under the waterfall, with the T. rex's head coming through it." Although the boat sequence still wasn't used, the waterfall episode was. Also resurrected from the first book was the young girl's encounter with the Compsognathus pack. "It was a terrific scene in the book that just didn't fit the story we were telling in the first movie," Koepp explained. "But it provided a wonderful opening for this movie."

For every scene added another had to be chopped, and the biggest victims were the flying reptiles. At one time or another, two major Pteranodon appearances were on the books. One sequence had Ian's party escaping some hungry raptors by deploying hang-gliders from their backpacks and flying off a cliff, only to be set upon by an equally rapacious pterosaur. The other, which was actually the climax until being replaced by the San Diego scenario, involved a Pteranodon attacking the rescue helicopter which has just picked up the survivors from the communications building. Despite intense lobbying from producers Colin Wilson and Gerald Molen, production designer Rick Carter, and assistant art director Dave Lowery (calling themselves the "Royal Pterodactyl Preservation Society"), the fliers were destined to be relegated to a mere cameo in the film's final shot.

Since *Lost World* took place on a different island than *Jurassic*, different-looking locations were needed. A scouting trip to New Zealand found some amazing environments, but as production proceeded the plans changed from a sizable main-unit shoot there to a limited second-unit junket, and finally to no New Zealand at all. "It's great to talk about exotic locations," said location manager Peter Tobyansen, "but, at some point, you have to face the practical issues." Rick Carter thought that the ancient redwood forests of northern California would make an effective and far more logistically feasible substitute, and Tobyansen concurred. The Hawaiian island of Kauai, a major location for *Jurassic Park*, was briefly employed again for the compy attack prologue and assorted establishing shots, and scenes of the good guys releasing the caged dinosaurs were shot at the Los Angeles County Arboretum.

When casting the sequel, Spielberg knew he wanted Jeff Goldblum back. Reportedly, almost nothing was done until he signed, and Goldblum (who has fond memories of seeing *King Kong vs. Godzilla* at age 11) was happy to return. Other actors were chosen as the screenplay evolved, and according to Jody Duncan, Spielberg asked David Koepp to specifically tailor the Sarah Harding role for Julianne Moore. As with Carole Landis in *One Million B.C.*, physical fitness was a factor in Moore's casting. "It was truly the most physically demanding film I've ever done," Moore said. "You show up, you think well, today I'm in a harness, today I'm really muddy, or today I'm in a waterfall or whatever, and you *do* it." Sir Richard Attenborough was coaxed back for an extended cameo, as were Ariana Richards and Joseph Mazzello for much smaller ones. The featured youngster this time — a Koepp-created hybrid of two kids from Crichton's book — would be played by Vanessa Lee Chester, who echoed the sentiments of most kids when she learned the part was hers. "All I could think," she later recalled, "was, 'Whoa! *Dinosaurs!*'"

A lot of the *Jurassic* department heads returned for *The Lost World*, but not all. Two notable absentees were cinematographer Dean Cundey and "Dinosaur Supervisor" Phil Tippett. "I offered the film to Dean first," Spielberg said in *American Cinematographer*, "because I would certainly never pull a sequel away from a great cameraman." But Cundey was getting ready to direct a picture of his own. "After Dean told me he was unavailable, I went straight to Janusz [Kaminski]," Spielberg continued. "He tells a cinematography story on top of the writer's or director's story." As for Tippett, he did say that *Jurassic* had "cured [him] of dinosaurs" for a while, but that wasn't the only reason he passed up *The Lost World*. "I had other things going on — we were developing *Starship Troopers*," Tippett explained to the author. "What's interesting is opening up new ground, because nobody else is an expert in it. If you're coming in on the heels of an incredibly successful picture then you have to deal with the 'franchise' contingent, which generally is not making up new, really cool stuff, it's just doing a lot more of the same thing. So it's just not as fun."

Dr. Harding (Julianne Moore) meets Stan Winston's remarkable baby Stegosaurus, kicking off one of the best sequences in *The Lost World: Jurassic Park*.

Jurassic Park and its sequel may be two of the most "high-tech" films ever made, but that didn't keep Spielberg from drawing inspiration from earlier, more modest pictures. "When Michael told me that the basis for his new book was going to be a ... human incursion into a real prehistoric land, I got very excited," the director said in *Premiere*. "As a popcorn muncher when I was a kid, I always loved those kinds of movies—*King Kong*, even some of the B's, like *Dinosaurus!* and the Jock Mahoney film called *The Land Unknown*." For the San Diego climax, Spielberg referenced "a lot of the 1950s monster movies, like *The Beast from 20,000 Fathoms*, *Gorgo*, and all those other 'chase, crush and devour' films."

The Lost World wrapped principal photography just before Christmas 1996, five days ahead of schedule. But if it doesn't represent Spielberg's creativity at its height—and it doesn't—there is a reason, one that the director mused on in Peter Biskind's *Premiere* article. "I'll tell you how *Schindler's List* changed me as a filmmaker, how I beat myself up in the making of *The Lost World*," Spielberg said. "I found myself in the middle of the sequel to *Jurassic Park*, growing more and more impatient with myself with respect to the kinds of films I really like to make. And often feeling that I have stuck myself in Doc Brown's DeLorean and gone back in time four and a half years, and that I was just serving the audience a banquet, but I wasn't serving myself anything challenging."

SPECIAL EFFECTS: Going into *Jurassic Park*, Dennis Muren was worried that it

Sarah Harding (Julianne Moore) dangles precariously over a salivating Velociraptor in an edge-of-the-seat moment from *The Lost World: Jurassic Park*.

would not be possible to deliver dinosaurs as believable and impressive as a 1993 audience would expect. Preparing for *The Lost World* Muren was worried again, for a different reason. "I knew we didn't have the same element of surprise and novelty working for us this time," Muren stated in Duncan's *Making of*. "And I knew that people might not have as big a reaction to the CG in this show as they'd had to *Jurassic Park*." But Muren, and all of the *Lost World* effects artists, were determined to try.

For a brief time, Stan Winston and his team had a more fundamental concern: Would the sequel have any animatronics at all? "Lots of people suggested that *The Lost World* should be all CG," noted Michael Lantieri, whose responsibilities connected him intimately with both the Winston and Muren groups. "But we realized that the mix brings something to the life of the creatures that we don't think can be gotten just mechanically or just digitally." In retrospect, it seems unlikely that there was any real chance of Winston's characters being ousted — remember, Steven Spielberg had originally hoped to use physical creatures for *all* of the *Jurassic Park* dinosaurs.

It was certain that the memorable dino villains from *Jurassic* — the T. rex and Velociraptors — would return, but the balance of the roster still had to be chosen. The first definite addition was the Stegosaurus. The absence of the popular stego from *Jurassic* had spawned thousands of letters to Spielberg and Universal, and even Winston Studios' Mark "Crash" McCreery had been disappointed. "It's such an outrageous, weird-looking creature," McCreery said in 1993. "Well, maybe next time." Of the seven species seen in *Jurassic Park*, all but the Brachiosaurus and Dilophosaurus returned.

New dinosaurs were selected based on input from both the digital and animatronic FX teams, and from Jack Horner, again on board as paleontology advisor. The bizarrely-crested Parasaurolophus, seen in the first film during a couple of brief but impressive herd shots at the watering hole, was given a bigger role, and the brachiosaur's design was used as the starting point for the gigantic Mamenchisaurus. A predator referred to as a "super-raptor" was considered, but Spielberg felt it was "too much out of horror movie" and wisely stuck with real creatures such as Pachycephalosaurus and Pteranodon.

There's also the tiny but vicious Compsognathus—"like chickens from hell," as Peter Biskind aptly put it—but the little guys do provide a chance to nitpick the movie's paleontology if one is so inclined. Burke identifies them onscreen as "Compsognathus triassicus," but there's no such species. There is a dinosaur called Procompsognathus triassicus which, as Burke says, was "found by [Eberhard] Fraas in Bavaria," and there is the Jurassic species Compsognathus longipes. Other than the similar names the two species are unrelated, and since the creature's design incorporates characteristics of both, it's unclear just what they're supposed to be.

The Lost World had a bigger CGI workload than *Jurassic*, but most of the digital animation team from the first film had moved on. "Just finding the number of people we would need and the kind of talent we would need was a big deal," Dennis Muren recalled. With Phil Tippett also gone, stop-motion veteran and *Jurassic* alumnus Randy Dutra was charged with ensuring that the new animators maintained the naturalistic movements and behaviors so evident in the 1993 hit. "The danger with computer animation is that anyone who can access animation software can make anything move," Dutra said in *Cinefex*. "But the question is, does it move with any understanding or knowledge?" Determined to instill as much animalism as possible into the dinos, Dutra put together a zoological "highlight reel" as a starting reference. "There were specific behaviors I wanted to see in these dinosaur performances, so I assembled this video," he explained. "It was something I would be able to run for the animators, so they could get to the meat of the job right away." The stop-motion–CG hybrid Dinosaur Input Device (DID), created for and used to great effect in *Jurassic Park*, was no longer required. "No, by then ILM had their whole thing down, their whole process down," Phil Tippett told me, "and they didn't need to do that."

In addition to offering Spielberg the freedom to design more dynamic camera moves and complex compositions, Muren also wanted to heighten the tiny, naturalistic details. Augmenting Randy Dutra's animal video, ILM artists went to sundry wildlife parks and reserves to study and photograph additional large mammals and reptiles. "We were trying to actually have the muscles and flesh and fat pockets under the animal's flesh move, as you would see on the side of an elephant that was walking by you," visual-effects producer Ned Gorman said. Armed with all the information they could gather, the computer animators brought the beasts to life. "Once the [CG] model is made, the animator will then be able to animate the character, one frame at a time," Dennis Muren explained. "Then once the animator is done with it the shot will go to the technical director, who will sort of 'make it look real.' They'll apply a skin to it, and combine it with the background."

Paralleling the CGI innovations, animatronic advances promised to allow even more dynamic interaction between the on-set dinosaurs and the live actors. A case in point is Eddie Carr's memorable demise—a scene requiring Stan Winston's crew to work closely with stunt coordinator Gary Hymes. "There are literally two CG shots in that entire sequence," Winston emphasized. "There's one CG shot where you see the two dinosaurs come out of the woods. Then the entire sequence of eating the car, tearing the windshield off, tearing the seats out, ripping the door off, and ripping the guy out of the car, is all real, all live. Not one CG shot. Then, the shot where we actually rip him apart is of course two CG rexes and a CG actor." The shots of Dr. Burke being snatched through the waterfall and of Peter Ludlow being dragged off the stairs in the ship's hold were also done by the Winston T. rex, live on set.

No fewer than three of the new Winston Studio characters were dinosaur babies: a Stegosaurus, a Triceratops, and a Tyrannosaurus rex. The 8-foot-long, 400-pound baby stego was shipped to the redwood forest and shot on location. By contrast, the massive adult stego was 26 feet long and some 16 feet tall. (Though the adult was also brought to the forest location, logistics and safety concerns eventually and unfortunately relegated the giant creature to a brief, caged appearance later in the film.) The juvenile Triceratops, constructed to near completion for *Jurassic Park* before being scrubbed, was finished and finally made it to the screen. Since the animal would be seen only in a cage, its complex mechanical understructure was removed and replaced by a human operator on all fours, incongruously recalling the titular star of *Baby ... Secret of the Lost Legend*. But the juvenile T. rex was an animatronic tour de force. Three incarnations were made: a lightweight, minimally articulated model for long shots, a fully detailed partial puppet for insert shots, and an amazing, untethered, battery-powered animal. "We had a totally self-contained animatronic and robotic T. rex, that could be carried around by Jeff or Julianne or Vince and had complete body motion," Winston enthused. "No cables, no bundles of wires, nothing."

As in *Jurassic*, the human performers were happily surprised to so often have their saurian costars right there with them. "It was such a beautiful animal," Julianne Moore said of the baby Stegosaurus. "I mean, there she was—completely present and alive!" Moore was equally impressed, in a different way, with the tyrannosaurs. "They were really scary," the actress recalled. "One of the mechanical heads got a little close to the trailer and actually hit it. I screamed bloody murder!" Besides making their performances easier, it's apparent that the actors purely enjoyed having "live" dinosaurs around. As Vince Vaughn put it, "To have this real dinosaur, that's moving and reacting and biting at you, that you get to play with, is just a lot of fun!"

Spielberg's drastic, midstream alteration of the movie's third act necessitated some scrambling on the part of the FX personnel. "The change in the ending was a big deal for us, but it was one I was all in favor of," noted Dennis Muren. "I really liked the idea of bringing the T. rex to the city." One reason he "really liked" it undoubtedly dates to his very young days. "The earliest memory I have of seeing any sort of dinosaur was *The Beast from 20,000 Fathoms*," Muren recalled on TV's *Movie Magic*. "I think I was about seven, and I remember hiding behind the seat in the movie theater in downtown Los Angeles, and sort of sticking my head up, and then having to cower down again." It doesn't take much of a stretch to find homages to Ray Harryhausen's *Beast* throughout the climactic rampage of Muren's T. rex.

It's tempting to assume that, with *Jurassic Park* behind them, a lot of the effects work for the sequel was already done, but that's not how it worked. For instance, the two full-size tyrannosaurs needed for *Lost World* did reuse the "skeletons" from the main T. rex and the insert head built for the first film. So, deep down they were the same dinosaurs, "but of course refurbished and actually brought up to another level," Stan Winston told me. "Every movie is R & D for the next movie. So, the T. rex in *Jurassic Park* was completely rebuilt, redesigned mechanically using much of what we had developed on *Jurassic*, and taken to the next level so that it could be faster and react more violently and at the same time with more finesse." And the eternally energetic creature creator promised even greater things to come. "We're now going into *Jurassic Park III*, and we are beyond anything we have done in *Lost World* or *Jurassic Park* ... we're out–Jurassic-ing *Jurassic*."

Magic in the Water

"It's just that it makes no rational sense!"
** 1995, USA/Canada. TriStar Pictures/Triumph Films. C, 100m.

CREDITS: *Director* Rick Stevenson. *Producers* William Stevenson, Matthew O'Connor, Karen Murphy (executive) and Tony Allard (executive), Christian Loubek (associate). *Screenplay* Rick Stevenson and Icel Dobell Massey. *Story* Ninian Dunnett and Rick Stevenson, and Icel Dobell Massey. *Visual Effects* Fantasy II. *Visual*

Effects Supervisor Gene Warren, Jr. *Go-Motion Animator* Peter Kleinow. *Orky Created by* Make-Up Effects Unlimited. *Creature Design* Errol Clyde Klotz and Rick Stevenson. *Creature Effects Supervision* Bart J. Mixon.

CAST: *Jack Black* Mark Harmon. *Joshua Black* Joshua Jackson. *Ashley Black* Sarah Wayne. *Dr. Wanda Bell* Harley Jane Kozak. *Uncle Kipper* Frank Sotonoma Salsedo. *Hiro* Willie Nark-Orn. *Joe Pickled Trout* Ben Cardinal. *Mack Miller* Morris Panych.

AD LINE: "In a small town on a peaceful lake a mythical creature is about to come to life."

Divorced dad Jack Black is too busy to spend time with his kids, teenage Joshua and pre-teen Ashley, but agrees to take them on a vacation to a picturesque town in northern British Columbia. The town, Glenorky, is the reputed home of an ancient, Nessie-like lake monster called Orky. Young Ashley is quick to believe, but her vacation soon turns sour when it becomes clear that her dad would rather answer his cell phone than race his daughter to the beach. One night though, Jack has a close encounter with Orky, and thereafter begins to rediscover his lost childhood (and act really strange). When he meets attractive local psychologist Dr. Wanda Bell, he learns that her therapy group is full of other men suffering from the "Orky Complex." Ashley worries about her dad, but finally learns what's going on from an eccentric Indian elder known as Uncle Kipper. He explains that Orky is sick, and his sickness is manifested in Dr. Bell's patients. The creature is suffering because local baddie Mack Miller is polluting the water with toxic waste, but when Josh and Ash get in over their heads trying to stop the illegal dumping, it's up to Orky to save them. His heroic act seems to be his last, however, as he succumbs to the poisoning. But with a leap of faith from Ash — and maybe a little mystical help from Uncle Kipper — Orky may yet return.

COMMENTARY: The featured creature of *Magic in the Water* is another of those borderline, quasi-dinosaurish beasties which, like the "Loch Ness Monster" of *7 Faces of Dr. Lao* is included in this compilation for the sake of completeness. Nowhere is the animal referred to in paleontological terms, but he has a clearly Plesiosaurus-based design. But any way you look at Orky, the film is disappointing. *Magic* seems to be an earnest attempt on the part of Rick Stevenson to craft a fun-for-all-ages "magical" fable, but there are just too many missteps. The kids are scripted as irritating brats (in the beginning anyway), the bad guy is an utter cartoon, and the Japanese scientists in an undeveloped subplot are extremely stereotyped. There are too many detours and slow spots, and the whole metaphorical angle about Orky and the psychology patients may be a bit abstract for the youngest viewers. The story recalls pieces of everything from *E.T.* and *Prancer* to, of all things, the TV movie *Return to Mayberry*, and just can't hold the right note.

The best part of *Magic* is on dry land: newcomer Sarah Wayne. Despite being handed a character who is downright obnoxious in the early going, Wayne perseveres and delivers a convincing performance. I also enjoyed Frank Salsedo's dignified turn in what could have been another condescending "wise old Indian" role. A few "magical" moments do turn up here and there, like the throwaway scene of the two boys "catching" fish as the animals jump right into their boat, and the cloudwatching scene with Jack seemingly reshaping the clouds at will. The special effects bringing Orky to life are rather meager. The Go-motion swimming shots are nicely done but disappointingly scarce, and when he peeks in at the kids there is a close-up of an adequately lifelike mechanical eye. We finally get a better look at Orky out of water, but even then it's only his head, neck, and a bit of flank, and he's so "sick" by this point that he doesn't have to do much.

Lurking somewhere just beyond this movie's grasp was a satisfying, whimsical fable, but the filmmakers just couldn't quite extract it from all of the muddled peripherals. So, instead of *Magic in the Water*, we are left with watered-down magic.

SPECIAL EFFECTS: Stop-motion veteran

The fanciful imagery of the *Magic in the Water* poster, showing Ashley Black (Sarah Wayne) sitting atop Orky's head, is unfortunately more imaginative than the on-screen tale.

Peter Kleinow animated the Go-motion shots of Orky at Gene Warren, Jr.'s, Fantasy II, a company which he helped to form. "The shots where the monster is swimming through the water — all those shots are stop-motion," Kleinow told the author. "The model was actually quite large; I'd say about three feet long. Michael Joyce, a good mechanic and model builder who worked with us at Fantasy II for several years, built the armature." Kleinow animated the creature in traditional stop-motion fashion, but using a Go-motion model mover to move the puppet very slightly during each exposure and thus produce a naturalistic motion blur. "It was all run by Go-motion, as far as the *trajectory*," Kleinow continued. "We programmed it to go through the gross movements, then I animated it as it went along. I think it worked out fairly well." Illuminating the scenes to appear as though they were actually filmed in a turbid lake was not an attempt to hide any shortcomings of the model, but rather to add a bit of mystery to the images. "We tried not to go overboard with it, but to keep it as it would look in murky water," Kleinow explained. "I think it came out looking pretty good; I don't think very many people would think of it as stop-motion."

The Mighty Gorga

"Are you sure you know what you're letting yourself in for?"

* ½ 1969, USA. American General Pictures. C, 86m.

CREDITS: *Director* David L. Hewitt. *Producers* Robert H. O'Neil and David L. Hewitt. *Screenplay* David Prentiss, Jean Hewitt. *Titles and Effects* Modern Film Effects.

CAST: *Mark Remington* Anthony Eisley. *April Adams* Megan Timothy. *Dan Morgan* Scott Brady. *"Tunga Jack" Adams* Kent Taylor. *George* Lee Parrish. *Witch Doctor/Mort* Bruce Kimble. *Kabula* Sheldon Lee. *Arnold Shye* Gary Kent.

AD LINE: "The Greatest Horror Monster Alive!"

In desperate need of a blockbuster attraction, small-time circus owner Mark Remington heads for Africa in search of a legendary giant ape. On arrival (we know it's Africa from the bongo drums on the soundtrack) he proceeds to the compound of wild animal dealer "Tunga Jack" Adams, only to find that Jack's daughter April and her right-hand man, George, have been running the compound ever since her father's mysterious disappearance. Like Mark she has financial woes, with shifty competitor Dan Morgan constantly scheming to gain control of her operation. April and Mark decide to take George and head off on safari, in search of Tunga Jack, the giant ape, and a fabled lost treasure to boot, unaware that the avaricious Morgan is following them.

Even as the explorers trek into "the interior," the witch doctor of the Lost Tribe is informed of their approach by jungle drums. He summons the towering ape known as "Mighty Gorga," worshiped as a god and protector, to dispatch the interlopers. Meanwhile, Mark and April leave George behind at "base camp" and finally reach the plateau. Gorga surprisingly comes to their rescue when they encounter a vicious Tyrannosaurus, but they let their guard down and get captured by a party of "Indians" (?) from the Lost Tribe. "When I stumble a few million miles from the wrong time zone, I tend to get a little confused," Mark explains. April is thrilled to find Tunga Jack living in the native village, and not only that, he knows of a volcanic passageway down from the plateau. When Gorga (having a majestically bad hair day) attacks the village, the explorers use the diversion to escape. Inside the cave they find a cache of priceless jewels and a dragonlike saurian, but successfully reach base camp as the plateau explodes. Just then the crazed Morgan appears and shoots George dead, and is about to do the same to Mark when Gorga (having somehow transported his bulky frame down the mountain) puts the squeeze on the villain. Mark is so grateful that he decides to let the magnificent ape remain free.

COMMENTARY: One might think that a film featuring the shoddiest movie dinosaur ever seen, *and* a gorilla suit *worse* than the ones in *King Kong vs. Godzilla* and *Konga*, would either be a nonstop laugh riot or absolutely intolerable. *The Mighty Gorga*, though unintentionally funny at times, is neither. David L. Hewitt made some of the flat-out cheapest pictures of the sixties and they couldn't help but look it, but his affection for the material always resulted in movies that were somehow a bit more entertaining than they had a right to be.

Trying on a microscopic budget to fashion a remake/tribute/knockoff of the most beloved and opulently produced "giant monster" film ever made seems a no-win scenario, but Hewitt tried anyway. In keeping with *Kong* he knew there should be some dinosaurs, but all he could come up with was a stock-footage, stop-motion *dragon* and a hapless, homemade Tyrannosaurus prop that will forever protect all other cheap movie dinos from the title "worst ever." Stiffer than the string-puppet pterosaur in *The "Legend of Dinosaurs,"* less believable than *Unknown Island*'s rubbersauruses, sillier-looking than *Reptilicus*, this tyrann-eyesore takes the (cheese) cake. With "articulation" consisting only of some lower jaw movement caused by shaking it up and down, the accursed thing defies both description and explanation.

As bad as the dinosaur is, the Gorga suit is nearly its match. With its immovable, googly-eyed visage and Larry Fine-meets-Phyllis Diller hairdo, it too must be seen to be appreciated. Needless to say, the fight between the two is fairly hilarious—the picture's worst and funniest moment. On a couple of occasions, April echoes the thoughts of the film's audience and becomes an on-screen FX critic, incredulously asking "what was that ... that THING!?" after the tyrannosaur attack, and remarking "I can't believe this thing's real!" while examining Gorga. On the bright side, these comments do provide the film's two most believable lines.

The optical effects in *Gorga* are no better than the creature simulations, though Hewitt deserves an E for effort. He combines his dragon-osaurus with his live actors via static mattes (instead of merely cutting back and forth), and even employs some rudimentary front projection to place Gorga into a shot with Mark and April. Unfortunately, the effect achieved is not unlike watching someone in a gorilla suit standing in front of a home movie screen. Not only is the projected image exceedingly grainy and washed-out, the actors do not appear to be looking even vaguely in the direction of the ape. Saving money any and every way possible, Hewitt even employed the practice of "showing" something merely by mentioning it. "What kind of trees are those?" April asks in awe. "Not trees at all," Mark replies, "they're giant mushrooms!" And since the scene never cuts away to show us what they're supposedly looking at, how can we argue?

At least the cast has traces of quality. Whatever you say about Anthony Eisley, don't ever say he loafed through a

The truly astonishing Tyrannosaurus prop from *The Mighty Gorga*, in all its dime-store glory.

role. In even the shabbiest pictures, Eisley seemingly took his job seriously and never allowed his performance to degenerate into either camp or apathy. Scott Brady was a reliable heavy, and Megan Timothy ... well, she's got a nice Britishy accent and some *major* false eyelashes. The most entertaining portrayal in *Gorga* is undoubtedly Bruce Kimble's of the witch doctor. Wearing "Indian" make-up unworthy of Republic's cheapest Z-western and clutching a scepter which appears to be a prop skull on a broomstick, Kimble (who also portrays Mort the Clown) struggles heroically — and visibly — to keep from laughing while slow-ly in-ton-ing his ceremonial entreaties to the titular ape.

The screenplay by Jean Hewitt and David Prentiss is long on clichés and very short on making sense. Tunga Jack claims that his bodyguard "doesn't let me out of his sight," then 30 seconds later decides to "sneak out and see *if* I can *find* him." At other times it sounds like *Abbott and Costello Meet Gorga*, particularly during one indescribable exchange between Mark and George regarding April and a certain water buffalo. But give the writers credit for audaciousness. In *Kong*, the natives simply staked out Fay Wray and ran for cover, but here the witch doctor actually admonishes Gorga that he won't get any more maidens until he kills the unwelcome explorers — a loopy twist on the "no-dessert-until-you-eat-your-vegetables" ploy.

In addition to the obvious ideas taken straight from *Kong*— Tunga Jack even learned about Gorga from a dying native in a canoe — *Gorga* also apes *The Son of Kong* (heroine bandages finger of friendly gorilla), the silent *Lost World* (heroine goes on expedition to find lost father), the 1960 *Lost World* (a path down from the plateau through a volcanic tube, complete with lost treasure), and even *Lost Continent* (rock climbing, and more rock climbing). There are in fact so many elements from other dinomovies that it's tempting to judge *Gorga* as a goofy but affectionate homage to the genre rather than merely a crass rip-off of same. *The Mighty Gorga* is, of course, not a good movie, but it is entertainingly bad. And it's not a smug, condescending kind of bad-movie enjoyment either, but an earnest, good-natured kind.

PEOPLE AND PRODUCTION: *The Mighty Gorga* was the final production in the short, shoestring life of American General Pictures, and what better way to go out than with a *Kong*-inspired giant ape tale? But like all AGP efforts, *Gorga* was cobbled together from astonishingly meager resources.

David L. Hewitt made the gorilla suit himself, and according to more than one report personally donned it to play the title role. The suit wasn't really a suit, but rather a head-and-coat ensemble that only went down to waist level — hence the lack of full-length shots of Gorga. In his book *The New Poverty Row*, Fred Olen Ray reported that the headpiece was made of solid foam rubber, sufficiently hollowed out to fit over Hewitt's noggin. "For the body," Ray stated, "he took a coat and sewed fake fur on it," then finished it off with "a homemade rubber chest." The suit reappeared as part of a Chamber of Horrors exhibit in Al Adamson's *Dracula vs. Frankenstein* (1972), proving that nothing goes to waste in the world of no-budget cinema.

With a real trip to Africa laughably out of the question, Jungleland and Africa USA served as stand-ins, and Hewitt padded his running time with a few last-minute location shots. The scenes of Anthony Eisley at "The Gardens" were simply shots of the actor meandering around a zoo. A quick flight to San Diego provided the airliner footage, with cameraman Gary Graver filming furiously until a stewardess came along and called a halt. "Dave's a hell of a good guy, and a talented guy," Eisley told interviewer Tom Weaver, "but I don't think anything he's ever tried to do ever translated on film 'cause he's never had the wherewithal to do it."

For a long while, Hewitt had visions of refashioning *The Mighty Gorga* into something a bit more substantial, but they never materialized. Fred Olen Ray stated that "the

Poster art for David L. Hewitt's hopeless but affectionate *King Kong* salute, *The Mighty Gorga*.

old dinosaurs were to be replaced with quality stop-motion animated ones and the remaining cast members, of which only Eisley remains now, were to come back as older characters via a new *Lost Horizon* storyline." And Jim Danforth told the author that Hewitt and an associate were "basically redoing all the effects scenes for *The Mighty Gorga*, so that Dave could reissue it as a complete, live-action/stop-motion, Ray Harryhausen kind of movie." Reportedly, Hewitt even hoped to include a sequence in 3-D.

SPECIAL EFFECTS: The first thought that comes to mind when watching the brief stop-motion sequence in *The Mighty Gorga* is, "it must be from another movie." First, the animation puppet itself was obviously designed to represent a mythological, medieval dragon, not a prehistoric animal. Second, an American General Pictures budget would certainly not support any time-consuming stop-motion work. The dragon/dinosaur of Gorga's world was actually created and animated nearly ten years earlier by the FX company Project Unlimited.

The story begins during the muscleman-movie craze of the early 1960s, when Project was contracted to do some effects inserts for an Italian-made epic known as *Goliath and the Dragon*. "We made a big dragon," Project's Wah Chang told the author. "We made the head and sent it to Italy, and we made a smaller stop-motion dragon, and did the animation here. It was cut in with the big head that had the actors with it. I never did see the movie." Comparison of the stop-motion sequences from *Goliath* and *Gorga* clearly shows that it is the same animation model on the same miniature cave set. However, the same exact shots do not appear in both films, so the *Gorga* footage is apparently made up of outtakes or test shots.

The *Goliath* animation was accomplished by none other than Jim Danforth and Victor Delgado (brother of Marcel "*King Kong*" Delgado), using a dragon puppet sculpted by Wah Chang. "Victor and I basically split up the animation," Danforth explained. "Victor had had more experience doing professional monster stuff than I had, because he'd done a little bit on *Mighty Joe Young*. So he was working days, and then because I didn't have any social or family responsibilities ... I animated at night." They animated different shots rather than attempting to continue each other's work, which would have been highly impractical. "So I probably did half of it and Victor did half of it," Danforth reckoned. The dragon looks decidedly on the thin side in *Gorga*, due to the fact that *Goliath* was a widescreen film and the anamorphic stock footage was not unsqueezed. "He looked good skinny," Hewitt contended.

Hewitt boldly attempted a couple of front-projection composites for the scenes where Anthony Eisley and Megan Timothy first encounter Gorga. Fred Olen Ray described the effort in *The New Poverty Row*:

> He bought a roll of Scotch-lite material and attached it to a four-by-eight-foot piece of plywood, which was then propped up in the front lobby of AGP's small offices on Lankersheim Boulevard in North Hollywood. Unable to afford the necessary interlocked projector-camera system needed for such a shot, cinematographer Austin McKinney cut the shutter blades down on an old 35mm projector and shot the scene five times, finally achieving one take that did not have the flickering effect associated with an out-of-sync process shot.

If Hewitt's résumé as a director is minor, his body of work in the field of special effects is much glossier and includes such A-list entries as *Willow* (1988), *Honey, I Shrunk the Kids* (1989), and *Terminator 2: Judgment Day* (1991).

The Mighty Kong

"There's more than one way to get a gorilla off the Empire State Building!"

* 1998, USA. Lana Film Company/Warner Bros. C, 72m.

282 • The Mighty Kong

The punchless, generic T. rex of *Mighty Kong* can't compete with its animated relatives in *Fantasia* or *The Land Before Time*, let alone the '33 *Kong*.

CREDITS: *Director* Art Scott. *Producers* Lyn Henderson, Denis De Vallance, Koichi Motohashi (executive), George W. Drysdale (executive), Bob Meister (associate). *Screenplay* William J. Keenan.
VOICES: *Carl "C. B." Denham* Dudley Moore. *Ann Darrow* Jodi Benson. *Jack Driscoll* Randy Hamilton. *Roscoe* William Sage III. *Ricky* Jason Gray-Stanford. *Captain* Richard Newman.

An animated *King Kong* is an intriguing idea. The ominous mood of the 1933 favorite, translated through the endless possibilities of the animation medium, could make for a great movie. This is not it. *The Mighty Kong* is a strictly commercial and utterly negligible endeavor, cranked out to ride the popularity of animated features and the "Kong" name to a quick profit. The animation, farmed out to various houses in China and South Korea, is worse than the cheapest *Land Before Time* sequel. *Mighty* follows the plot of RKO's original, albeit in the most superficial, one-dimensional terms imaginable, and not counting the new "happy" ending and the "waterfall shower" scene taken straight from the 1976 remake. The humor is mostly lame, but peppered with a few cute bits. "I've got my eye on a thousand-acre spread for him in south Jersey," Denham says. "He can't survive in *Jersey*!" Ann replies, "*Nobody* can!"

While the '33 *Kong* has not one wasted frame, this knockoff needs a dozen pointless filler scenes just to attain its meager 72-minute length. The sea voyage is padded with a ragamuffin cabin boy, his lovable monkey sidekick, Denham's bumbling assistant, and a pseudo–Polynesian production number. Yes, *The Mighty Kong* is a *musical*, with songs by the Academy Award–winning duo of Richard M. and Robert B. Sherman. Their work here is uninspired, but it cannot be denied that Jodi "*The Little Mermaid*" Benson can flat-out *sing*.

In place of the artistry of Marcel Delgado and Willis O'Brien, *The Mighty Kong* offers a few throwaway dinosaur cameos unworthy of the animation in a breakfast cereal commercial. A pterosaur flies by, a green-backed Triceratops chases Driscoll, and Kong battles a Tyrannosaurus rex. This Kong–T. rex fight doesn't quite equal Obie's version, however—the dinosaur roars and charges, Kong throws him off and belts him, and the saurian falls dead, all in 17 seconds. The New York sequence is equally butchered—Kong plays the clown while using a lamp post as a golf club and when a blimp pilot spots the massive ape on top of the building, he helpfully announces "That's him!" Finally, after Dudley Moore (?) delivers a modified version of the famous last line, Kong opens his eyes and flushes the point of the entire story down the drain. I know it's a kids' movie, but a good kids' movie must first and foremost be a good movie.

Monster

(a.k.a. *Monstroid*; *It Came from the Lake*; *The Beast from Beyond*; *The Toxic Horror*; *The Toxic Monster*)

"*It's the old 'monster-in-the-lake' bit again!*"

1978, USA. Academy International. C, 77m.

CREDITS: *Director* Kenneth Hartford. *Producers* Kenneth Hartford, Kenneth J. Fisher (associate). *Story* Kenneth Hartford. *Screenplay* Kenneth Hartford, Walter Roeber Schmidt, Herbert L. Strock, Garland Scott. *Special Effects* Ken Hartford, Steve Czerkas, Marc Wolf.
CAST: *Bill Travis* Jim Mitchum. *Pete* Tony (Anthony) Eisley. *Al Barnes* Phil Carey. *The Priest* John Carradine. *Andrea Anderson* Andrea Hartford. *Glen Anderson* Glen Hartford. *Patty Clark* Connie Moore.

AD LINE: "This film is a reenactment of four days of terror that rocked the small village of Chimayo, Colombia."

Al Barnes, boss of the Durado cement company, dispatches ace troubleshooter Bill Travis to a small Colombian town to investigate reports of a monster disrupting local plant operations. Upon arrival, Travis is accosted by snoopy reporter Patty Clark who wants to know what the heck he's going to do about the pollution being pumped into the nearby lake. That night, the girlfriend of company bigwig Pete goes skinny-dipping in the toxin-infested water, only to have a grunting beast slog out of the lake and maul her to death. Plant supervisor Sam suggests that she was killed by a shark, but his teen daughter Andrea finds the theory implausible ("A *shark*? In the *lake*?!") and teams up with her brother Glen to try and photograph the real culprit. The photos convince Sam, Bill and Pete of the monster's existence, and as the local priest prays for divine intervention, a scheme is hatched to blow up the reptile by dragging a dynamite-stuffed sheep across the lake with a helicopter. The beast takes the bait but Pete has a sudden clumsy fit and fumbles the control box into the water. While the local constable holds the monster at bay with a rowboat paddle, Bill retrieves the detonator and blows the mossy menace to kingdom come. Everyone cheers, and would have lived happily ever after, too, if not for the two dozen more monster eggs hidden across the lake.

COMMENTARY: Whether the eponymous Monster is a "dinosaur" or not is extremely iffy, but no less a genre presence than Tom Weaver has classified it as such. He called it "the screen's first mustached dinosaur" in his "Cinematosaurs" article for *Starlog*'s 1993 dinosaur issue, and this author is not about to argue. Whatever the creature is—it looks like a hybrid of dinosaur, caterpillar, and catfish—the film is a ludicrous, coarse catastrophe, made even more absurd by its claim (stated twice!) to be "based on actual events."

The acting roster features several stal-

The titular *Monster* (looking more plausible than at any other moment in the film) is challenged by a constable armed with a boat paddle.

wart veterans, none of whom can hide their misery. Phil Carey is given nothing to do but molest his secretary and spew out gratuitous profanity. The wonderful John Carradine, so often and sadly wasted in rotten movies during his final years, barely shows up. Even the dependable Anthony Eisley can muster little enthusiasm this time, and the film's best performance is turned in by "Takai" the german shepherd. (Despite their inclusion in various movie guides, neither Cesar Romero nor Keenan Wynn is in this picture—a fact for which they were surely grateful.) The story is incomprehensible, with some bad dialogue for the ages. When young Glen asks, "You don't believe me, do you?" Bill replies, "Son, it's kind of hard to believe stories about sharks and monsters and elephants in lakes." Er, what was that about *elephants*? A subplot about a woman being branded a witch by the superstitious locals is worse than useless—it seems like it belongs in some *other* really rotten movie.

Lacking a single redeeming quality, *Monster* is a bottom-of-the-barrel disgrace. Toward the end of the film, obnoxious reporter Patty Clark looks right into the camera and says: "What you have just witnessed is not a movie of the week. ... It is stranger than fiction, which the truth always is." I guess so—no fiction writer could imagine a film this awful.

PEOPLE AND PRODUCTION: It's a rare movie that is so very bad that you can't find someone, somewhere with something nice to say about it. *Monster* is one such rarity. Anthony Eisley, who could usually find some sort of silver lining in even his darkest cinematic clouds, couldn't do it for this one. "That was a disaster," Eisley told Tom Weaver. "Most people going in felt that they could get a few bucks out of it and forget it, and that nobody would ever see it. Of course the only flaw in that theory was that apparently [Hartford] did get it finished to some extent and some people have seen it — but you can only hope there aren't that many!" Veteran director Herbert L. Strock, who despite what the credits say actually directed the film, is no happier. "Actors came out of the sewers," Strock said, also to Weaver. "We didn't have the time to teach them to act, we had a cameraman who had his own ideas, we had no one on the crew we could rely on. We shot this miserable mess for almost a month." Special effects creator Stephen Czerkas, who did some super work for *Planet of Dinosaurs*, also prefers not to remember *Monster*. "What can I tell you? I was young, I needed the money," Czerkas stated in a letter to the author. "It was a really silly project where I had to make the monster look like a promotional sketch that the producer sold the project on. Terrible design." To call *Monster* "low-budget" or "shoestring" would be a gross understatement. "Incredibly cheap production," Czerkas recalled. "I think I still have the check for two thousand dollars (my total effects budget) which bounced higher than any of the props I made." Ironically, the closing credits state that the film was made in association with an entity called "Major Financial Investments."

Monster from a Prehistoric Planet

(a.k.a. *Gappa the Trifibian Monster*)

"Don't be stupid, there's no fish like that!"

 * 1967, Japan. Nikkatsu Corporation. C, 90m.

CREDITS: *Director* Haruyasu Noguchi. *Producer* Hideo Koi. *Screenplay* Iwao Yamazaki, Ryuzo Nakaishi; based on a story by Akira Watanabe. *English Dialogue* William Ross. *Director, Special Effects Unit* Akira Watanabe.
CAST: *Hiroshi* Tamio Kawaji. *Yoko* Itoko Koyanagi. *Saburo* Kokan Katsura.

This film sneaks into this volume only because of its utterly misleading title, and because the characters are always talking (in the English version) about seeing an animal "actually hatch from a dinosaur egg" and things like that. So it's included for the sake of completeness, even though author Stuart Galbraith is exactly right in stating that the monster is "a standard Japanese whatzit, and not a dinosaur." The plot, as many have noted, is straight out of Eugène Lourié's *Gorgo*. A baby "prehistoric reptile" hatches on a lost South Pacific isle (despite the title, there are no outer-space story elements) and is brought back to Japan to serve as the star attraction of a greedy entrepreneur's theme park. Unfortunately, the animal "can communicate with others of its species," a talent which enables his ticked-off parents to track him down. The only "giant monster" entry from Nikkatsu studios, *Monster from a Prehistoric Planet* has little to set it apart from others of its kind. The monsters don't look that bad on the ground, but become rather ludicrous when they take to the air with their teeny-weeny wings. There's lots of destruction, but the models and miniatures are not even as good as Toho's weakest efforts. As in *Gorgo*, there is a young boy who tries to tell the idiot adults to set the baby free, and a happy ending where the offspring rejoins his or her folks, but the film is so humdrum that only the most stalwart "suit-mation" fans are likely to stick around until the family reunion.

Monsters of the Past

 *½ 1923, USA. Pathé. BW, Silent.

This episode of the "Pathé Review" series of short films features sculptress Virginia May, who may or may not have done the rudimentary stop-motion animation. One scene shows May "sculpting" a clay Tyrannosaurus by filming her tearing a finished sculpture apart and running the footage backwards! The animated scenes feature a Brontosaurus and a rather fanciful T. rex–Triceratops fight.

My Science Project

"No Outer Limits I ever seen had this stuff."
* 1985, USA. Touchstone Films.
C, 95m.

CREDITS: *Director* Jonathan R. Betuel. *Producers* Jonathan Taplin, E. Darrell Hallenbeck (associate). *Written by* Jonathan R. Betuel. *Visual Effects Supervisor* John Scheele. *Special Mechanical Effects Supervisor* Michael Lantieri. *Photographic Effects Supervisor* Philip Meador. *Tyrannosaurus Rex Built and Animated by* Doug Beswick Productions, Inc. *Tyrannosaurus Rex Sequence Consultant* Rick Baker.
CAST: *Michael Harlan* John Stockwell. *Ellie Sawyer* Danielle Von Zerneck. *Vince Latello* Fisher Stevens. *Sherman* Raphael Sbarge. *Detective Nulty* Richard Masur. *Lew Harlan* Barry Corbin. *Bob Roberts* Dennis Hopper.

Mike Harlan, an intelligent, car-obsessed, underachieving high school senior, is told by his teacher Bob Roberts that he must turn in a science project if he wants to graduate. Newly dumped by his shallow girlfriend, Mike agrees to a date with pretty but slightly nerdy yearbook reporter Ellie Sawyer. He takes her to a nearby decommissioned air force base in search of some "Gizmo" he can pass off as a science project, and has no idea that what he finds is actually an alien artifact from a UFO crash in 1957. Strange things begin happening, especially after Mike takes it to the school lab and Bob hooks it up to a 110-volt outlet. In a swirl of purple, the Gizmo generates a time/space vortex over the school, and warps Bob — a sixties relic who pines for the flower power days of his youth — into another dimension. Mike and his fast-talking pal, Vinnie, shut down the Gizmo by dynamiting an electrical tower, but only until Sherman the school geek ignores Ellie's warnings and powers it up again. Detective Nulty thinks Mike has something to do with the blown-up power lines, but when the weirdness starts again Mike and Vinnie flee the police station and rush to the school to save Ellie. Taking Sherman along, they wander through halls and classrooms populated by people and creatures from the past and future, finally coming face to face with a Tyrannosaurus rex. Fighting past the dinosaur to the lab, Mike rescues Ellie and shuts down the Gizmo for good. A giddy Bob soon appears, ranting about what a groovy time tour of the sixties he's been on, and tells Mike he has an "A" on his science project.

COMMENTARY: *My Science Project* has a well-made prologue, set in 1957, revealing how the time-altering "Gizmo" came to be stashed in a military scrap yard. The tornadolike "vortex" swirling over the high school is a neat visual effect. The Tyrannosaurus is one of the most believable-looking nonstop-motion movie dinosaurs to come along until *Jurassic Park* rewrote the rules in 1993. And those are the only three good things about *My Science Project*.

"Fantasy's rules say you've got to be absolutely meticulous about setting up reality," Jonathan Betuel asserted in *Cinefex*, "so that the audience is *with* you when things go awry in the second act." The director's statement is largely true but frankly puzzling when applied to *Project*, because there is not one character in the film who is believable for one second, and without plausible characters there can be no "absolutely meticulous" reality. Every role is written as a pure cliché and many of the actors compound the sin by hideously overacting. Raphael Sbarge's comedy-skit nerd is excruciating, and Fisher Stevens' Brooklynite-Italiano-wiseacre-Lothario shtick almost causes physical pain. Dennis Hopper gives it a try to no avail (although the Gizmo's powers for dimensional travel may explain how he ended up King of Dinohatten in *Super Mario Bros.*), and the usually engaging Barry Corbin is stuck in a nothing role as Mike's dad. Betuel for some reason had the talented Richard Masur doing a bad Clint Eastwood impersonation as Nulty, a character that Corbin could have had some fun with. The script kills twenty minutes with the sequence of the

Disney FX artists at work sculpting the huge life-size T. rex mock-up for *My Science Project*.

kids dynamiting the power lines—then Sherman plugs the Gizmo back in and the entire episode becomes utterly meaningless. Anyway, couldn't Mike have simply found the utility panel and thrown the main breaker ... but never mind.

The T. rex sequence is the highlight, or rather the only light, of the movie. Well-designed and effectively photographed, the set piece is marred only by its brevity and, like the rest of the picture, the torturous dialogue ("Suck lead, lizz-arrrd!"). Doug Beswick, stepping away from the stop-motion arena, delivers a nifty rod- and cable-actuated Tyrannosaurus that does everything asked of it and looks darn good doing it. Its movement is limited but credible, and an excellent miniature set provides a palpable sense of size. It's typical of the film's lack of wit, however, that the goofy kids just happen to have a grenade launcher, and must, of course, kill the dinosaur. The movie itself was long since deceased.

PEOPLE AND PRODUCTION: Director Jonathan Betuel burst onto the Hollywood radar with his screenplay for *The Last Starfighter* (1984), a fun and effective sci-fi/fantasy which was one of the first films to make extensive use of computer graphics. Jonathan Taplin, producer of *Baby ... Secret of the Lost Legend*, green-lighted Betuel's *Project* script only a year later, despite two attached stipulations: Betuel would direct, and the film would include a fairly sizable dinosaur sequence. "If someone at a studio was telling me 'Why the dinosaur?,' it was a pretty good indication they didn't share the fantasy," Betuel said in Stephen Rebello's *Cinefex* article. "Studios have a nasty habit of offering you a lot of money to detach yourself from your script." A scheduled ten weeks of principal photography began in August 1984. Several locations were used, including a real, abandoned high school gymnasium for the T. rex sequence's establish-

A technician at Doug Beswick's studio gives the rod-puppet Tyrannosaurus of *My Science Project* a last-minute touch-up before shooting.

ing shots and cutaways. The first unit shoot wrapped, on time and under budget, on November 4. The full-scale dying/dead tyrannosaur had been built by the Disney studio effects crew and shot as part of the first-unit work, while the meticulous scenes of the articulated puppet dino, farmed out to Douglas Beswick and his team, were still awaited.

SPECIAL EFFECTS: The *Project* visual effects were overseen by John Scheele, like Jonathan Taplin a *Baby* alumnus. The headaches of *Baby* were still fresh in his mind as Scheele designed the full-size, fallen T. rex, complete with plenty of gooey entrails blown out by the grenade. "Let's say the guts were a little in-joke," Scheele said in *Cinefex*. "We inserted chewed-up sections from the Baby miniature into this beast's stomach." One of the life-size tail mechanisms from *Baby* was also re-used but the hydraulically powered T. rex arm, which took some artistic liberties with the fossil record, was made just for *Project*.

Phil Tippett and Jon Berg were coming off their spectacular work on *Dragonslayer* (1981) and were the obvious choice to provide the tyrannosaur action, but Tippett was tied up with *The Ewok Adventure* (1984). Make-up magician Rick Baker, on board as a "special advisor and creature consultant," enthusiastically endorsed Doug Beswick for the job. "I just looked at it as a chance to show people what I could do," Beswick recalled. "Phil, Jon and Rick have done wonderful work, so I can't blame anyone for wanting to go to them first." Beswick, of course, had plenty of dinosaur experience—

the educational short *Dinosaurs ... The Terrible Lizards* and *Planet of Dinosaurs*—it just wasn't *well-known* experience. With Baker in his consulting role, Beswick put together a talented team with all the skills needed to realize the sequence. "It's a pretty ambitious undertaking on everybody's part to try and have a full rod puppet really walk around," Beswick said.

It became apparent right away that the look of the full-size T. rex would need to be changed when designing the puppet, and everyone agreed that making the one-eighth scale tyrannosaur look *good* was more vital than slavishly matching the design of its large counterpart. The eyes were made more sharklike, and "we also gave it detail like making the teeth look really gunked up with tartar and food debris," Beswick added. A skeletal armature was fabricated from "aluminum and plumbing pipe," and mechanical whiz Ted Rae fashioned a "breathing mechanism" to be installed in its chest cavity. When sculpting the dinosaur, Tom Hester tried to keep it as paleo-correct as possible within the existing limitations. The finished creature had 35 control cables and needed eight operators when all of its articulations—including eye blinks, furrowing brows, pulsating throat, and a very organic tail swish—were simultaneously required. "Doug's mechanics," as Ted Rae put it, "are like beautiful Swiss clockwork."

Overspeed filming tests were done at 48 and 60 frames per second to find the most realistic effect, and the sequence was photographed by veteran Disney cameraman Peter Anderson. Copious amounts of fog provided atmosphere while hiding support struts and control cables, and the live actors were added to certain shots using bluescreen techniques. Unfortunately, lighting mismatches between the scenes in the real gymnasium — shot weeks earlier with none of the dinosaur crew present — and the miniature effects stage necessitated a good deal of reshooting, which in turn necessitated a hasty repair job on the battle-scarred puppet.

The dinosaur sequence ultimately cost nearly a half-million dollars, and Scheele seemed generally happy with the results. The rod puppet's walking ability "was never perfect," Scheele said, "but since it was for no more than half a step in any one cut, it never really had to be." Stop-motion veteran Beswick seemed satisfied as well. "I think it's something everybody's going to be really impressed with," he said. "It does have a different look than stop-motion." With all the limitations—including having two weeks suddenly chopped from their FX schedule—Baker, Beswick and company attempted to get as much on the screen as possible. Look fast and you'll even see a pterodactyl, hand-animated by Gary Trousdale, glide past at the beginning of the sequence. "We had the pleasure of pulling the original *Fantasia* artwork and referring to it for this element," Scheele stated. "One of the advantages of working at Disney is that you can access this priceless material."

Mystery of Life

not viewed 1931, USA.
Universal. BW, 62m.

CREDITS: *Director* George Cochrane. *Host* Clarence Darrow.

I had hoped to be able to locate a print of this all-but-forgotten evolution documentary and thus give it full inclusion in this volume, but was unsuccessful. In fact, there seems to be very little even known about this film. *Mystery of Life* apparently covered ground similar to that of Irwin Allen's *The Animal World* a quarter-century later, and like Allen's film it used stop-motion animation to illustrate the Age of Dinosaurs. Where Irwin Allen commissioned Willis O'Brien and Ray Harryhausen to create an all-new dino animation sequence for *Animal World*, it was some of Obie's old "stock footage" from *The Ghost of Slumber Mountain* that pulled the duty in *Mystery of Life*. (See the still on the next page.)

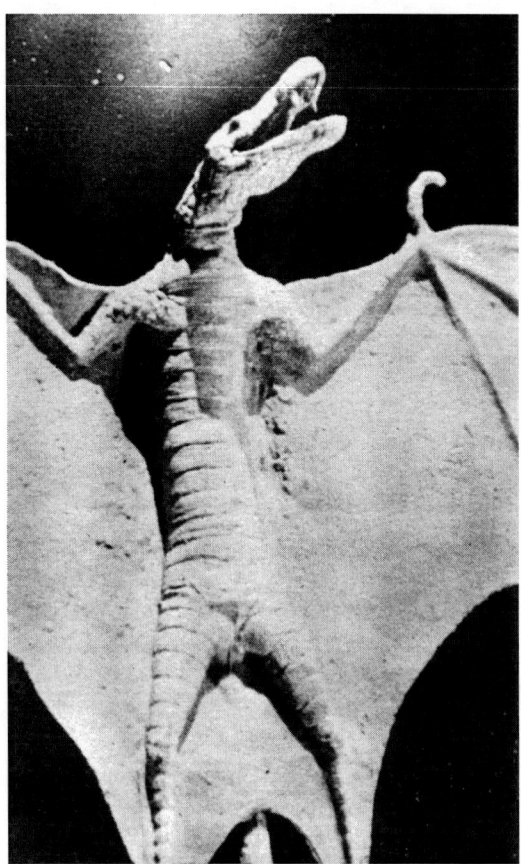

A pterosaur — possibly meant as a Rhamphorynchus — seems to be uttering a cry in one of the few known stills from the near-forgotten *Mystery of Life*.

A Nymphoid Barbarian in Dinosaur Hell

(a.k.a. *Dark Fortress*)

"I've become a barbarian— but not just any kind of barbarian!"

*½   1990, USA. Chapter V Enterprises/R.I.P./Troma. C, 81m.

CREDITS: *Director* Brett Piper. *Producers* Alex Pirnie and Brett Piper. *Written by* Brett Piper. *Special Effects* Cheap Tricks Unlimited, Mark Frizell.
CAST: *Lea* Linda Corwin. *Marn* Paul Guzzi.

AD LINE: "The prehistoric and the prepubescent, together at last!"

In a postnuclear, apocalyptic world, where radiation has "turned our pets and livestock into gargantuan, horrifying creatures," a plucky woman called Lea somehow scrapes by. Despite the scarcity of unmutated men, she does find one clean-cut fellow named Marn, but their romance is threatened by a wasteland full of monsters. Some are dinosaurish mutations of everyday critters like beetles, dogs, bats, and alligators. Others are more humanoid, most notably a 7-foot warrior and his platoon of flunkies who look like ape-reptile hybrids. Lea and Marn are separated but each encounters a good Samaritan — Lea is rescued by a disfigured hermit who wears a mask to hide his hideous countenance, and Marn is assisted by an old man who collects relics from before the holocaust. The giant warrior fails time after time in his attempts to possess Lea and is finally eaten by a pair of hungry moat monsters, leaving Lea and Marn to trek onward.

COMMENTARY: Despite its title and the fact that it was released by Troma, *Nymphoid Barbarian* is not a spoof, or a gorefest, or a sexploitation flick. So, what is it? It is an assortment of quite good, traditional stop-motion set pieces interspersed throughout a procession of live-action scenes so boring as to be stupor-inducing. Yet as odd as it sounds, Linda Corwin gives a good performance. There is very little dialogue and her line readings are as flat as everyone else's, but from a physical standpoint she's impressive. She projects a convincingly feral, animalistic persona, seemingly always coiled to strike, and tackles several athletically challenging scenes that would have a "name" actress whining for a stunt double. Alex Pirnie's ineffective villain constantly reminded me of the "Guaddi" in 1950's *Prehistoric Women*, but one mustn't be too hard on a film in which the bad guy's henchmen are billed in the credits as "Featured Reptilian Goons" and "Secondary Reptilian Goons."

The stop-motion sequences offer joyfully old-fashioned fun, and the designs of the mutated animal-dinos are imaginative and bizarrely plausible. Only the "alligatorsaurus" (as Neil Pettigrew dubbed it) looks something like a "real" prehistoric creature, and if the film did not have "Dinosaur" in its title it probably would have not been included in this volume. The picture plays like a microbudgeted, unscripted knockoff of Ray Harryhausen's mythology-based adventures, but with no quest, no goal, no story arc whatsoever. At the beginning of the movie Lea and Marn are trying to survive a desolate world of monsters and barbarians, and at the end, they pretty much still are.

SPECIAL EFFECTS: "I've done two films where I really had no serious problems," writer-director-animator Brett Piper said in *SPFX* (#5). "One is out there under the title *A Nymphoid Barbarian in Dinosaur Hell*." The title was not Piper's—the film was originally called *Dark Fortress* and was, as Piper said, "a semi-medieval fantasy that got turned into a post-nuke thing." Unlike *Dinosaur Babes* which was completely reworked without Piper's input, *Nymphoid Barbarian* is essentially his film. "Troma bought it finished, changed the title and only added the prologue."

As always, Piper brought an old-school intrepidity to the *Nymphoid* effects. "Some of the special effects were in-camera matte shots," he told Kevin G. Shinnick. "The [puppets] were relatively tiny, I'd say about ten inches long. About the size of a dinosaur toy you'd buy in the store. The ones I've been making lately have been around twenty inches long." Piper is quick to assert that "There are no dinosaurs" in *Dinosaur Hell*, but also attests to an overall satisfaction with the film. "It isn't a classic," he reflected, "but I was surprised in re-

Fanciful *Nymphoid Barbarian* poster, depicting a woman who looks nothing like Linda Corwin and a dinosaur that looks nothing like any creature in the film.

watching it that most of what I was trying to get on film pretty much got there." If Piper's stop-motion bat-creature in *Nymphoid* seems more inspired by the Harpies in *Jack the Giant Killer* (1962) than those in 1963's *Jason and the Argonauts* (which it does), there is a reason. "When *Jack the Giant Killer* came out, I was 9 years old and I got to go see it in the theater and it made a huge impact on me," he recalled. "The funny thing is, when you're a kid it looks great."

On the Comet

"When I was a young officer, I was witness to some extraordinary happenings."

*** 1970, Czechoslovakia. Barrandov Studios. C, 77m.

CREDITS: *Director* Karel Zeman. *Writers* Karel Zeman, Jan Prochazka; based on Jules Verne's *Off on a Comet* (a.k.a. *Hector Servadac*). *Sets* J. Petru. *Cinematography* Rudolf Stahl. *Special Effects* Karel Zeman, F. Pickhart.
CAST: *Angelika* Magda Vasaryova. *Lt. Servadac* Emil Horvath. *Col. Picard* Frantisek Filipovsky. *Spanish Consul* Cestmir Randa. *Ester* Jirina Jiraskova. *Silberman* Vladimir Mensik. *Ben* Karel Effa.

Around 1888, in the French colony of Algeria, several lives are about to be intertwined by an astronomical upheaval. One day while surveying, Lieutenant Servadac of the French Army falls into the sea and is rescued by the beauteous Angelika, even as she swims away from the scheming Spanish consul who had kidnapped her. The consul is conspiring with a local sheik to overthrow the French forces, under the command of the befuddled Colonel Picard. Suddenly all plans are thrown askew by the appearance of a huge heavenly body in the sky. Servadac's reassurances that "it's probably just another planet heading for us at fantastic speed," aren't very reassuring.

The gravity of the passing comet rips away a huge chunk of the earth, carrying the local residents with it. While the colonel consults his sealed orders regarding "Situations of Incomprehensive Character," a massive herd of dinosaurs ("prehistorical cattle," as he calls them) marches on the fort. The animals are fortuitously driven off by the clanging of a wagonload of cooking pots, prompting the colonel to replace all his cannons with saucepans. With the end of the world seemingly at hand, the French, Spanish, and Middle Eastern adversaries put aside their quarrels and become friends. But just then, Angelika's brothers arrive to "rescue" her, ignoring her protests that she no longer needs rescuing. Servadac boards the consul's ship and pursues, passing a massive sea serpent and a prehistoric island along the way. He finally catches up with Angelika at the British-held Gibraltar and returns with her to the fort. The lovers are soon married, but the small society's harmonious existence is shattered when the group realizes that they're returning to Earth, and all their violently ethnocentric tendencies come flooding back.

COMMENTARY: Karel Zeman's *On the Comet* (*Na Kometě*) has three things in common with Edward Bernds' 1961 entry, *Valley of the Dragons*. Both are based on the same Jules Verne novel; neither of them bears more than the faintest resemblance to that novel; and both feature prehistoric animals though none appear in Verne's tale. In every other aspect, the two films are light-years apart. Where Bernds' formulaic quickie relied on stock footage for both its dinosaurs and storyline, Zeman's effort, though not ranking with his very best work, reveals his truly unique gift for visual artistry and fanciful style.

Zeman did not use stop-motion in the same manner as the great American animators. He employed it merely as one of many techniques on his varied palette of cinematic trickery, without necessarily worrying about duplicating nature. Zeman enjoyed playing with colors and styles, props and gadgets, and combinations of artistic media. His visual compositions seem almost experimental at times, and it is fitting that the only other filmmaker to whom Zeman might legitimately be compared is the turn-of-the-century pioneer Georges Méliès. Zeman freely melded all manner of elements—stop-motion, cel animation, puppets, models and miniatures, matte shots, woodcuts, paintings—to create fantastic imagery in a style that is his alone. At his best, as in 1961's *Baron Prasil* (a.k.a. *Baron Munchausen*), Zeman's storytelling equals his extraordinary visuals, and grand entertainment is the result. *On the Comet* doesn't quite hold together as a story, but still succeeds as a feast for the eyes built around some disjointed but individually clever sequences.

A stop-motion Dimetrodon pauses to watch Servadac's approaching ship during the all-too-brief "prehistoric island" sequence in *On the Comet*.

Humor is a Zeman staple, and the *Comet* comedy is decidedly on the zany side. (It is not surprising that Zeman and Monty Python alumnus Terry Gilliam have both filmed versions of the flamboyant "Baron Munchausen" tales.) When the planetary collision occurs and a military band is thrown skyward, the cymbal player never misses a beat and the whole ensemble resumes as soon as they crash back to earth. Taking stock of their predicament, the colonel blusters that they "are without orders, have a minimum number of troops, and (worst of all, seemingly) our supply of oatmeal is ruined!" And the scene of a motley crew of sailors, trying to drive off a sea serpent by adorning themselves with kitchen utensils and dancing maniacally around the deck, is just plain hysterical. Much of the funny business is in service of the film's satirical message, which isn't subtle and isn't supposed to be. Through slapstick symbolism (the colonel is a clueless, bumbling buffoon) and verbal irony ("we helped spread our *civilization*," the narrator states as a soldier's cigar sets fire to a native dwelling), the anticolonialism, antimilitarism sentiments are made blatantly clear.

The stop-motion dinosaur scenes are immense fun to watch, though they have virtually no connection to the rest of the film. One striking quality of the dinosaurs' march on the fort is the sheer number of models simultaneously on-screen. Not since Willis O'Brien's silent version of *The Lost World* some 45 years earlier were so many stop-motion dinosaurs animated in one scene. It's a bit frustrating that the puppets are so dimly illuminated that they appear almost as silhouettes in many shots, but it fits with the psychedelically overcast skies that hover over Zeman's landscapes. It's a dynamite sequence for dinosaur and animation buffs, as the throng of behemoths trudge toward the fort accompanied by appropriately "big" music. There are some simple but seamless composite shots combining the cavalry soldiers with the dinosaurs, and we even get a bit of "monster-on-the-loose" action when one of the towering meat-eaters chases the locals into the village bazaar. A few shots of live-action hand puppets are interspersed among the stop-motion, but their appearance is not jarring or detrimental.

The second dino sequence is the lesser of the two, but is still a minor gem. The briefly seen antediluvian island is terrifically atmospheric, with trackless jungles that look like they really could harbor a dinosaur. A handsome Dimetrodon—the only stop-motion "fin-back" ever animated for a feature film—ambles over to the shore and stares out at the passing ship. A pterodactyl soars through the primeval underbrush in a maddeningly short but beautiful scene, and a nicely detailed Styracosaurus bellows a greeting in another throwaway shot. Finally, the "transmutation of the species" is comically shown as a primitive fish (walking upright on its tail fins!) evolves in four quick cuts into a wild boar walking on its hind legs.

On the Comet fails to build any great interest in its story but ultimately works as a sort of sketch compilation, somewhat linked by various references to Verne's tale. Viewed as such, it not only provides laughs and some nifty dinosaurs, but also offers the chance to appreciate Karel Zeman's singular flair for the fantastic.

PEOPLE AND PRODUCTION: Karel Zeman, like so many souls with an appreciation of things fantastic, obviously had an affinity for dinosaurs. Besides the features *Cesta do Praveku* (*Journey to the Beginning of Time*) and *On the Comet*, he also created two short films featuring prehistoric creatures. *The Black Diamond* was structured very much like *Journey to the Beginning of Time*, with four youngsters traveling by raft into the prehistoric past. This time, they visit the Carboniferous period and, along with various early animals (including a Dimetrodon very similar to the one in *On the Comet*), witness the birth of coal. *Excursion to the Universe* took its explorers—again, children—on a voyage into space to discover prehistoric life on an imaginary planet.

One Million AC/DC

"Tragedy is happening ... tragedy is done."
1969. USA.
Canyon Films. C, 65m.

CREDITS: *Director* Ed De Priest. *Producer* Ed De Priest. *Written by* Akdon Telmig (Edward D. Wood).
CAST: Gary Kent, Susan Berkely, Sharon Wells, Tod Badker.

Completeness, when applied to a reference book, is good. It does however have a price, and here the price is having to include things like *One Million AC/DC*. The same year that Gary Kent played a sleazy lawyer in *The Mighty Gorga*, he also played a sleazy (and very embarrassed-looking) caveman chief in *AC/DC*, and actually has to say "I'm off to see the lizard." Notable only for the fact that it was apparently written by the notorious Ed Wood, this numbingly boring, "adults-only" fossil features the stuffed deer from *Teenage Caveman* (at least it looks like the same one), a guy in a gorilla suit, a "catfight" intercut with the alligator/lizard battle from *One Million B.C.*, a lot of grapes, false eyelashes so big that eye-blinks produce gusts of wind, a Brontosaurus shot from *Unknown Island*, the incredible Tyrannosaurus puppet from *The Mighty Gorga*, a stiff plastic toy dino, and a bunch of very sad-looking people half-heartedly simulating sexual acts. But take heart: the credits do tell us that "This film meets the requirements set forth in the code of the Adult Film Producers Association."

Despite the short length of the dinosaur sequence, prehistoric animals dominated all advertising for *The Animal World*.

Top: Striking Belgian poster for *Dinosaurus!* gives equal space to the "dinosaur" and "friendly caveman" story elements. *Bottom:* While the United States poster for *Baby* was one of the most boring dinomovie posters ever made, this British version is an eye-catching winner. *Opposite:* The artwork on the beautiful *Unknown Island* poster, especially of the Ceratosaurus, clearly reveals its Charles R. Knight origins.

Above: A sensational British poster for *When Dinosaurs Ruled the Earth,* though it does sport a Styracosaurus and Tyrannosaurus (neither of which are in the film) and a bikinied, redheaded cavegirl who looks nothing like Victoria Vetri! *Opposite top:* Lobby card for *The Beast of Hollow Mountain* offers an unusually clear image of the creature, hand-tinted a reptilian green. *Opposite bottom:* A beautifully lavish and colorful exhibitors' ad seems to be hawking *The Land Unknown* as an escapist, FX-filled "summer movie" nearly 20 years before *Jaws* supposedly originated the concept.

Above: If *The Lost World* (1925) originated the dinomovie genre, the substitution of a carnivorous tyrannosaur type for the actual film's Brontosaurus originated the misleading dinomovie poster. *Opposite top:* Movie posters, like this Belgian example for *The Valley of Gwangi,* are occasionally blessed with truly beautiful art. *Opposite bottom:* Beautiful lobby card from the 1946 rerelease of *King Kong* includes a skillfully hand-tinted still from the Kong-vs.-Tyrannosaurus battle.

G

Opposite top: The fight between knife-wielding Johnny Weissmuller and an Ellis Burman–created man-in-suit dinosaur didn't make it into *Jungle Manhunt* but was all over the film's advertising art. *Opposite bottom:* Like the star dinosaurs of other black-and-white dinomovies, including *The Beast of Hollow Mountain* and *The Beast from 20,000 Fathoms*, the title character of *The Giant Behemoth* was made green on the color-tinted lobby cards. *Above:* Spanish-language "1-sheet" for *The Land That Time Forgot* featured the same basic artwork as the U.S. poster, but with a larger and more colorful presentation.

Above: A gorgeous girl and dinosaurs to boot? What red-blooded American male could resist a movie with a poster like this? *Opposite:* The original poster for *The Land Unknown* is a classic of 1950s "monster movie" poster art.

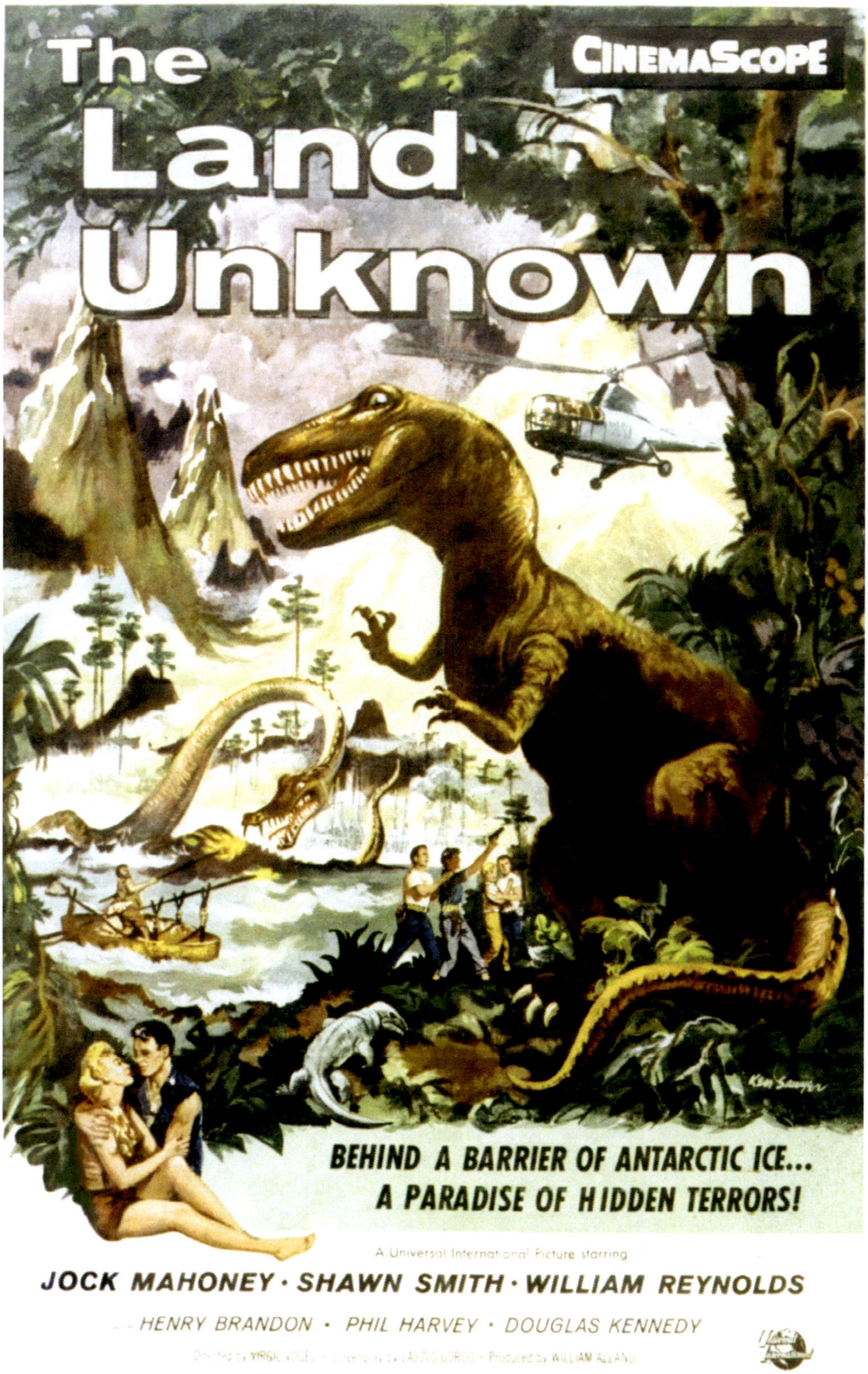
The Land Unknown
CINEMASCOPE
BEHIND A BARRIER OF ANTARCTIC ICE...
A PARADISE OF HIDDEN TERRORS!
A Universal International Picture starring
JOCK MAHONEY · SHAWN SMITH · WILLIAM REYNOLDS
HENRY BRANDON · PHIL HARVEY · DOUGLAS KENNEDY
Produced by WILLIAM ALLAND

K

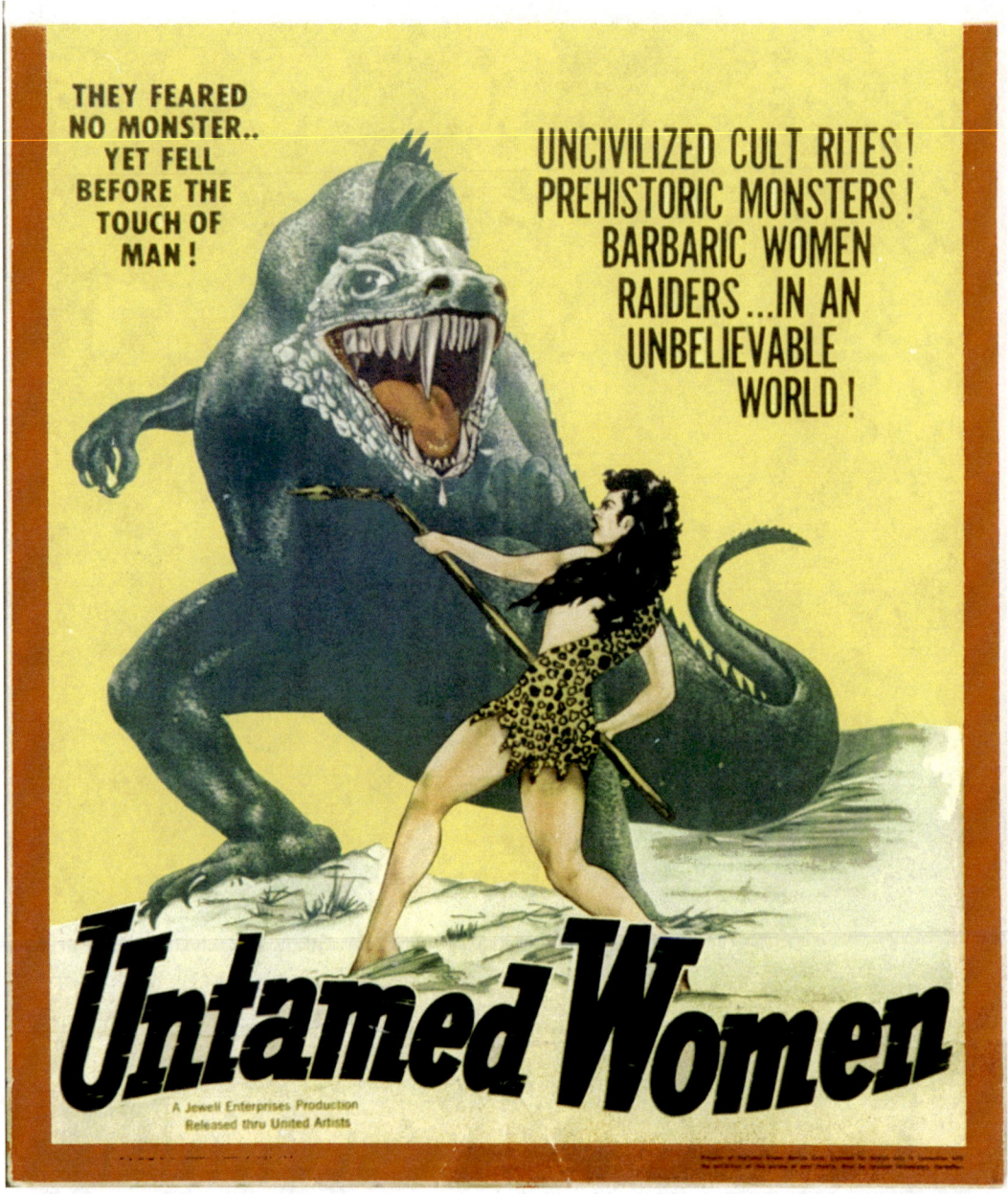

Above: The "dinosaur" on this outrageous *Untamed Women* window card is certainly one of the more, shall we say, *creative* interpretations of a prehistoric beast. *Opposite top:* "You'll be SHOCKED! You'll be STUNNED! You'll be THRILLED!" the ads cried, and though *King Dinosaur* wasn't at all shocking or thrilling, it has been known to stun the unprepared. *Opposite bottom:* Undeniably spectacular images of the "200-foot-tall" creature demolishing some very well-made miniature London landmarks helped rescue *Gorgo* from its unsympathetic characters.

Opposite top: Garish, spectacular, dinosaur-heavy title card for the sometimes garish but decidedly unspectacular *Two Lost Worlds*. *Opposite bottom:* Lobby card "no. 1" of eight from *The Beast from 20,000 Fathoms* set, sought after by collectors as the only one to show the Rhedosaurus. *Above:* Although *The Last Dinosaur* was sent straight to TV in the United States, this poster accompanied a British theatrical release.

Spanish-language poster for *Where Time Began* with nearly every touchstone of the genre: fighting dinosaurs, a volcanic eruption, a gargantuan ape, fleeing humans — all that's missing is a savage beauty in an animal-pelt bikini.

One Million B.C.

(a.k.a. *Man and His Mate* (U. K.), *Cave Man*)

"Not only a meaning, but a complete story as well!"

**½ 1940, USA. United Artists. BW, 80m.

CREDITS: *Directors* Hal Roach, Hal Roach, Jr. *Producer* Hal Roach. *Original Screenplay* Mickell Novak, George Baker, Joseph Frickert. *Descriptive Narration* Grover Jones. *Photographic Effects* Roy Seawright. *Art Direction* Charles D. Hall. *Set Decoration* W. L. Stevens. CAST: *Tumak* Victor Mature. *Loana* Carole Landis. *Akhoba* Lon Chaney, Jr. *Ohtao* John Hubbard. *Peytow* Nigel De Brulier. *Nupondi* Mamo Clark. *Tohana* Inez Palange. *Skakana* Edgar Edwards. *Ataf* Jacqueline Dalya. *Wandi* Mary Gale Fisher. *Archaeologist/Narrator* Conrad Nagel.

AD LINE: "So AMAZING you won't believe your eyes!"

A group of hikers surprised by a sudden cloudburst take shelter in a cave and discover an archaeologist at work inside. He regales them with a story which he has deciphered from the primitive markings and drawings on the cave walls. It is the story of Tumak, a man from the savage Rock tribe, and Loana, a woman from the more advanced Shell tribe, and their adventures one million years ago.

Within the span of a few hours, Tumak's fortunes take some dramatic turns. The young warrior beams with pride when he is given the honor of killing a small horned dinosaur to provide food for the tribe, but things turn sour when he refuses to yield his drumstick to his brutal father and tribal leader, Akhoba. Literally beaten out of the cave, Tumak is injured by a huge mammoth and falls into a river. Carried far downstream, he is found and nursed back to health by the beautiful, blonde Loana of the Shell tribe. As the days pass, Tumak falls in love with Loana and learns the civilized ways of her people. Meanwhile, a savage warrior called Skakana takes over leadership of the Rock tribe after Akhoba is wounded during a hunt. Tumak, having won the respect of the Shell tribe by challenging and killing a marauding Tyrannosaurus, is slowly being assimilated into their community when his old warlike tendencies get the best of him and he injures Loana's friend Ohtao. Tumak is banished (from his second tribe in less than a month), but this time Loana willingly goes with him. The gentle girl is intercepted by the brutish Skakana as she flees from a titanic pair of battling reptiles, but Tumak overcomes the younger man and thus takes over his role as leader of the Rock people. Tumak quickly introduces some civilized Shell tribe practices, but their newfound stability is shattered by a volcanic eruption. Loana and others are trapped in a cave by a massive dinosaur, but the two tribes work together to bury the beast under a man-made rockslide. Tumak and Loana "adopt" a little girl named Wandi who was orphaned by the eruption, and begin their new life as a family.

COMMENTARY: The endless repetition of its dino-lizard scenes has perhaps obscured just how very unusual *One Million B.C.* was back in 1940. No one had seen anything like it. It must also rank as one of the most important dinosaur pictures ever made, if only for the sheer number of other films which, with varying degrees of skill, made use of its special effects sequences.

The picture gets off to an unfortunate start. The present-day prologue with the hikers and the archeologist is so stiff that it's painful to watch. If the dialogue here is any indication, we can be thankful that the rest of the story is virtually a silent film. Not only is the writing laughably stilted, it's long-winded as well; every time the scientist says something, the hiker asks him to repeat it! The archeologist mentions that the cave was home to ancient people, and the hiker says "do you mean a primitive people made this cave their home?" The archeologist states that he has deciphered a story from the wall markings, and the (dim-witted?) hiker says "am I to understand there's a meaning to these marks that you can decipher?" And on

The beauteous Carole Landis, only 21 at the time, clutches Mary Gale Fisher in a *One Million B.C.* publicity shot. Young Miss Fisher seems concerned about the hard, rocky ground below her.

and on. Once the story proper begins, things thankfully get more interesting.

One Million B.C. seems to improve on multiple viewings, as a number of small but skillful flourishes become apparent. There are moments of intentional humor (like when Tumak demonstrates his newfound talent for laughing) but it's never in a tongue-in-cheek manner, and the movie's unswerving resolve to take itself seriously goes far in convincing the viewer to do the same. Whereas the 1966 remake effectively used Mario Nascimbene's music score to contrast the two tribes, the original does it visually. Scenes of the Rock tribe are typified by extremes. They are either very dark (inside the gloomy cave) or searingly bright (out on the dust-choked, rock-bound landscapes), while the Shell tribe sequences are much more moderate-looking. Cinematographer Norbert Brodine makes fine use of the weathered Nevada locations, and the picture never suffers from the "soundstage" feel that plagues many other efforts. Brodine's work, in conjunction with Charles D. Hall's art direction and W. L. Stevens' set decoration, lends the proceedings a convincingly desolate mood.

The greatest strength of *One Million* is its cast and performances. Even sans dialogue, the three leads manage to create surprisingly real characters. Victor Mature effectively conveys Tumak's puzzlement at the strange ways of the Shell people and somehow maintains his dignity even during the film's, shall we say, less plausible moments. Carole Landis skillfully portrays Loana's gentle compassion and wide-eyed naivete (and is every bit as gorgeous as her successor in the role, Raquel Welch). And Lon Chaney, Jr., is a terrific Akhoba. Acting in theatrical style using only his body, and especially his eyes, Chaney somehow generates audience sympathy for a character who, in the early reels, is appallingly brutal. The pantomimed performances are enhanced by Werner R. Heymann's Oscar-nominated score, which is very much in keeping with the film's "silent movie" tenor.

The special effects have been much maligned, mainly because the live lizard technique puts people off on two fronts. Some are upset by the apparent miseries the animals are put through, while others pine for the more dramatic and paleo-accurate results afforded by stop-motion. But leaving these points aside, the film has some striking visuals. However unsavory their tactics, the filmmakers drew some terrific "performances" from their scaly stars, and they look believably massive in most shots. The nonlizard dino scenes, of the baby ceratopsian and the tyrannosaur, are a mixed bag. The little horned dinosaur was played by a pig in costume and looks acceptable, but the man-in-suit tyrannosaur does not. Besides the fact that a human body cannot be reshaped to approximate the physiology of a dinosaur, the costume lacks any subtleties or detail. Ray Harryhausen is dead right when he points out that the beast is carefully obscured behind vegetation throughout most of its rampage.

The photographic effects in *One Million*, especially the traveling mattes, are outstanding. One particular shot of a cavewoman being caught and buried by an onrushing lava floe is still startling today, and the entire eruption is a well-constructed sequence. The FX crew made a concerted effort to deliver the best product they could and pressed into service almost every technique at their disposal, except stop-motion. They used mattes, rear projection, miniatures, trained animals, stunt work, and clever editing, often combining them within a sequence, and their labors were rewarded with a number of effective, even impressive, sequences.

One Million B.C. may generate as wide a variety of opinions from contemporary critics as any film discussed in this book. It's been dismissed as a relic, pigeon-holed as a curio, enjoyed as a "camp" classic, and even hailed as an epic. What cannot be disputed is the fact that it holds a unique place in the

The full gruesomeness of Lon Chaney, Jr.'s, "injury" make-up — including a fractured leg bone protruding from his flesh — was not shown in the film.

genre's history, and remains required viewing for aficionados of dinosaur cinema.

PEOPLE AND PRODUCTION: Just as *One Million B.C.* attempts — in its own skewed, Hollywood way — to show humankind's prehistory, the film itself can tenuously trace its ancestry almost back to cinema prehistory. Early in the 20th century, movie pioneer D. W. Griffith created some of the first filmed portrayals of prehistoric life. *Man's Genesis*, produced in 1912, was a dinosaurless morality play set in caveman times. Griffith upped the ante with *Brute Force* (1913) by including what are likely moviedom's first reptiles as dinosaurs, complete with "prehistoric" make-up additions. An alligator was adorned with multiple accouterments including a pair of protuberances that strangely resemble wings, and a snake (yes, snake) was also given a Mesozoic makeover. *Brute Force* also featured the screen's first full-size mechanical dinosaur — a horned Ceratosaurus that could work its jaws and rock slightly back and forth.

298 • *One Million B.C.*

Moving forward a quarter-century to the late 1930s, Griffith had faded from prominence and his early prehistory films were nearly forgotten, but he got a chance to revisit caveman territory when Hal Roach put him on the *One Million B.C.* payroll. There is no doubt that Griffith was connected to the film (originally titled *Life Begins*), but to what degree and in what capacity may never be positively known. Reports and stories abound, variously claiming that Griffith wrote the screenplay, produced the film, directed parts of it, or supervised the special effects photography. Only the last of these has a flicker of possibility; the rest are surely apocryphal. "Roach wanted to use him only as a consultant and general assistant," biographer Richard Schickel reported in *D. W. Griffith: An American Life*. "Contrary to the impression Griffith gave people at the time, Roach had no firm plan to let Griffith direct the film." Quoted in December 1939 by the *New York Times*, Griffith said, "I am here merely in an advisory capacity. I give what help I can." There are reports that he was to have received an "associate producer" credit before asking to have his name removed. Coincidentally, Roach himself gets that exact credit on American prints of the film's 1966 remake.

Author Stuart Galbraith IV extensively researched *One Million* for his retrospective published in *Filmfax* (no. 48). Digging through the original production files, Galbraith found that Griffith in fact wrote a number of story treatments and a narration, none of which were used. He also directed costume tests featuring several of the principal actors during the summer and fall of 1939, and apparently had legitimate input in casting decisions. Richard Denning was reportedly Hal Roach's first choice for Tumak, but his dinomovie turn would have to wait until *Unknown Island* eight years later. "Most studios had their dashing leading man who was identified with hero parts," Roach explained in *Hollywood Speaks*. "I signed a virile young man named Victor Mature to play those type parts for me." Lovely 21-year-old Carole Landis was selected partially on the basis of her athletic prowess, and proved to be an exceptionally good sport with the studio's photographers—various publicity shots pictured her fearlessly holding a huge, live python, and being held ten feet aloft by the trunk of a mammoth-disguised elephant. Lon Chaney, Jr., soon to gain both fame and critical applause for *Of Mice and Men* and *The Wolf Man*, took the role of Akhoba. He attempted to follow in his father's footsteps by designing his own makeup for Akhoba's gruesome injuries, but was prevented by union regulations from using it. Directorial chores were divided between Hal Roach and his son, with the elder directing most of the live action

In the days before VHS, movie buffs contented themselves with 8mm "digests" of favorite genre films; Castle Films called this *One Million B.C.* excerpt "Battle of the Giants."

and Roach Jr. handling the special effects scenes.

Location filming began in early November 1939 in the "Valley of Fire," near Logandale, Nevada. A 280-person production company toiled for about two weeks at a reported cost of $14,000 per day. Part of the expense was likely due to the effort expended in hoisting cameras and operators to remote vantage points on the surrounding sandstone formations, in order to satisfy the desires of Hal Roach and cinematographer Norbert Brodine for unusual and striking camera angles. Following the strenuous location shoot, filming concluded at the Roach Studios in Culver City, California, and the final cost of *One Million B.C.* was about $570,000. Prerelease industry gossip chastised Roach for tackling such an unconventional story, with words like "silly" and "goofy" frequently heard. Even Roach himself told a reporter "it's a screwy idea." (D. W. Griffith, also present for the interview, dryly commented "I concur in the sentiment.") Yet when the picture opened on March 26, 1940, it was a solid success.

SPECIAL EFFECTS: Except for the obscure British release *Secret of the Loch*, *One Million B.C.* was the first dinosaur-oriented feature film to appear since the *Kong* pictures. Hal Roach apparently never considered using stop-motion animation for his prehistory saga, instead following the example of Griffith's *Brute Force* (and, interestingly, *Secret of the Loch*) by employing present-day reptiles as stand-in dinosaurs. According to Stuart Galbraith, the roster included "tegu lizards and iguanas from South America, monitor lizards and garials from Malaysia, chuckawallas and leopard lizards from Arizona, crocodiles from Cuba." Other animals such as armadillos, elephants, and a coatimundi were procured for the nonreptilian roles.

With Roach Studios effects department head Roy Seawright overseeing the work, a sizable crew set about creating the needed scenes. Fred Knoth, later to revisit the dinosaur genre with *The Land Unknown*, spearheaded the climactic eruption sequence, transformed a live pig into a baby Triceratops, and built the infamous Tyrannosaurus suit using a Charles R. Knight painting as a guide. In his immensely enjoyable *Dinosaur Scrapbook*, author Donald Glut relates a Knoth-told anecdote regarding the costume. It seems that Knoth fashioned a "hastily put-together prototype" suit, intending to replace it with a more polished version for filming. But when Roach saw the suit being worn, he "was so impressed ... that he ordered Knoth to forget the improved version and use the prototype." Portraying the T. rex in the film was veteran stuntman Paul Stader, who twenty years later would supervise the underwater photography for *Dinosaurus!*

Besides Seawright and Knoth, the FX team also included art director Charles D. Hall who supervised construction of the miniatures, and Frank William Young who handled the miniature photography. The animal stars had their own crew. Charles Oelze was the lead "lizard wrangler," while Oscar Weisman had the mammoth job of elephant trainer. The four-legged performers were gathered from various zoos, from the Ringling Bros. circus, and from Lionel Comport, at the time a leading supplier and

The "stego-lizard" was one of many reptile make-up trials and tests which went unused in the released version of *One Million B.C.*

handler of animals for the film industry. The savage sound effects were by Elmer Raguse, head of the Roach Sound Department and a pioneer in cinematic sound recording from the very beginnings of talking pictures. Author J. J. Johnson reported in *Cheap Tricks and Class Acts* that "the sound crew sped up the sounds of lions, dogs, and elephants to denote the roaring bellows of their photographically-enlarged lizards." Seawright and Raguse bagged an Oscar nomination for *One Million B.C.*, back when visual and sound effects were still lumped together in the "Special Effects" category; they lost to Lawrence Butler and Jack Whitney for *The Thief of Bagdad*.

It is ironic that when dinomovie makers chose live reptiles over stop-motion animation, they often claimed that the lizard method was "easier." Unless, that is, you were the person who had to work with the critters. Longtime movie animal trainer Ralph Helfer took two turns as a dino tamer, supervising the reptilian villains for *King Dinosaur* in 1955 and *Island of the Lost* in 1967, and can thus offer some insight into the inherent difficulties. "They're not going to take orders," Helfer told the author. "He's going to do what he does, and then we have to make that work for the scene." For *Island of the Lost*, Helfer had to attach a dorsal fin and neck frill to an 8-foot, 500-pound alligator ... which sounds a little risky. "Well, yes," Helfer admitted. "We sometimes had to bind their jaws a bit, so that we could work up around the face." Charles Oelze personally discovered the perils of directing reptilian actors; John Brosnan reported in *Movie Magic* that Oelze was treated eleven times for lizard bites. The mammals also joined in the mayhem. While doubling for Lon Chaney, Jr., during Akhoba's fight with the prehistoric musk ox (actually an irritable Brahma bull), legendary stuntman Yakima Canutt was injured and very nearly gored.

Perhaps, however, the creatures were simply trying to even up the score. It seems certain that the *One Million* animals—reptiles, especially—were subjected to some inhumane treatment. In *The Dinosaur Scrapbook*, Don Glut relates a disquieting tale personally told to him by Roy Seawright, involving reptiles being deprived of food and given electric shocks to stimulate suitably dramatic and aggressive behavior. First-hand accounts such as this make it difficult to place much stock in the studio's assurances that no cruelty was involved in the filming of the dinosaur sequences, and British officials would not allow the film to be released in England until some of the more savage scenes were cut. Still, as Stuart Galbraith reported, one United Artists exec adamantly maintained that "Hal Roach was in possession of certificates from the American Motion Picture Society for the Prevention of Cruelty to Animals to back up his claim."

The *One Million B.C.* dinosaur and volcano effects had astonishing durability, turning up in a wide variety of B-movies for the next thirty (!) years. A chronology of titles which partook of the film's scenes, test footage, and outtakes reads something like this: *Tarzan's Desert Mystery* (1943), *Two Lost Worlds* (1950), *The Lost Volcano* (1950), (volcano footage only), *Jungle Manhunt* (1951), *Untamed Women* (1952), *Robot Monster* (1953), *King Dinosaur* (1955), *She Demons* (1958), (volcano only), *Teenage Caveman* (1958), *Valley of the Dragons* (1961), *Journey to the Center of Time* (1967), *One Million AC/DC* (1969), and *Horror of the Blood Monsters* (1970). In addition, the clips surfaced in the serial *Superman* (1948), (volcano only), the Three Stooges short *Space Ship Sappy* (1957), and the Mexican productions *Aventura al Centro de la Tierra* and *La Isla de los Dinosaurios*. They even turned up in the bizarre television drama, *Yesterday's World* (1952), and other TV shows. Despite all efforts, this list is surely incomplete.

Far from apologizing for the lack of stop-motion, the film's promotional material actually bragged about it. The studio pressbook promised "no animation whatsoever," and an unknown copywriter came up with what must surely be the amazing ad line of all time: "Actual living animals of a bygone age recreated and filmed by a new secret process!"

One Million Years B.C.

"Man ... superior to the creatures only in his cunning."
*** 1966, U. K. Hammer Films/ 20th Century–Fox. C, 100m.

CREDITS: *Director* Don Chaffey. *Producers* Michael Carreras, Aida Young (associate). *Screenplay* Michael Carreras; based on an original screenplay by Mickell Novak, George Baker, and Joseph Frickert. *Special Visual Effects* Ray Harryhausen. *Special Effects* George Blackwell. *Prologue* Les Bowie.
CAST: *Loana* Raquel Welch. *Tumak* John Richardson. *Sakana* Percy Herbert. *Akhoba* Robert Brown. *Nupondi* Martine Beswick. *Ahot* Jean Wladon. *Sura* Lisa Thomas.

AD LINE: "A time when there was no law and man ... woman ... and beast roamed the earth — untamed!"

On a young planet Earth, scattered tribes of primitive humans scratch out their day-to-day existence. The Rock tribe is led by the brutal Akhoba, father of the young warriors (and rivals) Sakana and Tumak. On their latest hunt, Tumak is given the honor of the kill, but is banished from the tribe for refusing to relinquish his portion to Akhoba. He leaves his mate, Nupondi, and wanders the barren landscape, evading a giant lizard, a clan of savage ape-men, a Brontosaurus, and a giant tarantula along the way. He collapses from exhaustion as he reaches the seashore, and is pulled from the path of a giant sea turtle by the blonde Loana of the benevolent Shell tribe. Meanwhile, the power-hungry Sakana cold-bloodedly pushes Akhoba off a cliff and assumes leadership of the Rock tribe. At the Shell camp, Tumak begins to appreciate the civilized ways of Loana's people even as they learn from him. Tumak proves the value of aggressiveness by boldly saving a little girl from an attacking Allosaurus, but he soon picks a fight with Loana's friend Ahot and is evicted by the appalled tribal chief. So, with Loana now at his side, Tumak again heads into the wilderness.

Out in the wastelands, the couple is separated during a battle between an enormous Triceratops and a bloodthirsty Ceratosaurus. Loana runs right into Sakana's clutches, but Tumak defeats his brother and rightfully becomes the new leader of his original people — the Rock tribe. Tumak's former mate, Nupondi, understandably takes an immediate dislike to the blonde interloper, even as the rest of the Rock women embrace Loana's advanced teachings. One day a great pterodactyl swoops down and carries Loana back to its nest as food for its young (to Nupondi's delight), and only a timely attack by a second pterosaur allows her to survive. Tumak, unaware of Loana's escape, sees the victorious creature feeding on its victim's chicks and mistakenly assumes the worst.

As the treacherous Sakana plots to regain control of the tribe, one independent young man grows tired of Sakana's brutality and defects to Tumak's faction. Loana returns to the Shell village to solicit the help of Ahot and the Shell men, and she and Tumak are reunited just as the young informer arrives with the warning of Sakana's scheme. Tumak and his Shell tribe allies engage Sakana's goons in an all-out battle, but the carnage is interrupted when a nearby volcano erupts! Sakana tries one last time to kidnap Loana amid the confusion, forcing Tumak to finally finish him off. With all quiet at last, the survivors of now-united tribes climb out of the rubble and begin anew.

COMMENTARY: Despite a very shaky track record, the idea of *the remake* must still seem so tempting. Take an old movie that had some sort of proven appeal, get some fresh people together, and make a brand new version of it. But despite the great number of remakes attempted, trying to think of even one which is better than its predecessor can be a real stumper. *One Million Years B.C.* is such a rarity, improving upon its slightly creaky ancestor in *almost* every department. Wilkie Cooper's cinematography, Mario Nascimbene's music score, and most notably Ray Harryhausen's dinosaurs are all superior to their counterparts in the earlier entry, and the result is a delectable treat for any dinosaur fan.

Although the plot of One Million Years B.C. closely follows the 1940 film, the few changes made are decidedly for the better. A great decision right at the start is the elimination of the clunky prologue and flashback device which kicked off Hal Roach's version, substituting Les Bowie's kaleidoscopic "Dawn of Time" sequence which does its job quickly and then lets the picture hit the ground running. Don Chaffey's direction has rarely been praised — or criticized, for that matter — but it's efficient and workmanlike, though perhaps lacking some of the verve which he brought to Jason and the Argonauts. Chaffey never lets the pace drag and never lets a scene go on too long, which is more than can be said of many fantasy film directors. Wilkie Cooper had plenty of experience with FX-heavy projects, having previously shot no fewer than five of Harryhausen's pictures, and he makes excellent use of the beautifully bleak Canary Island locations. Mario Nascimbene's inventive score is another asset, taking an entirely different tack than did Werner Heymann's Oscar-nominated score for the original. The scenes of the Shell tribe are marked by soft woodwinds and gentle melodies, at times enhanced with an ethereal chorus of human voices, while the appearances of Tumak's people are accompanied by severe, rhythmic percussions which connote the hardness of bare rock and bone.

The cast is the one area where the remake takes a back seat to the classic version. John Richardson makes a fine Tumak but Victor Mature was just a bit better, and Carole Landis likewise edges out Raquel Welch as the top Loana. (Some sources assert that Welch's voice was dubbed by actress Nicolette McKenzie, though they don't say why.) The knockout punch is Akhoba — Robert Brown's generic and unremarkable presence cannot hold a cave torch to Lon Chaney, Jr.'s, sympathetic characterization, and the thought of the corpulent Brown besting the athletic 6 ft. 3 in. Richardson in hand-to-hand combat is hard to swallow. Scoring a few points for the new cast is beautiful Martine Beswick, who makes a vivid impression despite little screen time.

Ray Harryhausen once commented: "Some people can't wait until [the animation] is off the screen — they would rather see Raquel Welch's or some other pretty maid's bosom!" Such deviants notwithstanding, for most the commanding reason to watch One Million Years B.C. is the chance to enjoy Ray's magic. The film brims with animated wonders and includes two scenes which are among the maestro's all-time greatest, albeit for different reasons. The giant, prehistoric turtle is arguably Harryhausen's most unimpeachably *convincing* creation, and the attacking Allosaurus is nothing short of a masterpiece. Though the turtle sequence is nowhere near the dramatic success of the allosaur, it is an unmitigated technical achievement. It's one thing to animate a dinosaur, a creature that humans have never seen and thus have no real frame of reference for, and have it look good. It's quite another matter to animate something like a turtle, which everyone is familiar with, and have it move believably. It isn't enough for it just to look good; it has to look like a turtle. Harryhausen's Archelon was sculpted, constructed, and animated so perfectly that many observers have mistaken it for a living creature — incredibly, even the special-effects documentary TV series *Movie Magic* was fooled!

The Allosaurus raid is not just the high point of the film, it is one of the high points in the history of stop-motion. The set-up, pacing, editing, and choreography of the scene, and of course the masterfully integrated animation, are all essentially flawless. It reveals Harryhausen at the very pinnacle of his powers, and often draws rounds of impromptu applause during theater showings; even in this computer-generated age, it has lost none of its ability to enchant. This sequence is also a superb example — maybe *the best* example — of Harryhausen's ingenious talent for integrating animated and

The heroic Tumak (John Richardson) saves a little Shell Tribe girl from Ray Harryhausen's masterfully malevolent Allosaurus in a superlative sequence from *One Million Years B.C.*

live-action elements within a single shot. Unlike lesser artists, he would never stick his humans on one side of the screen and his creature on the other, with a nice straight palm tree conveniently in the center to hide the matte line. Ray's allosaur stalks freely around the frame, as does its human prey, darting left to right, right to left, ripping palm fronds out of the thatched shelter with its teeth and looking for all the world as if it is *really there*. The dinosaurs and people react uncannily to each other's actions, which is a testament not only to the actors but to Ray's on-set direction. Everything clicks — the matching of the miniature terrain to that of the full-size set, the meticulous design of the puppet itself, and the inspired notion to make the creature a "juvenile" that is nearly eye-to-eye with its opponents (an idea revisited with *Jurassic Park*'s raptors). Even the rear-projected elements are impossibly bright and crisp, with no grain or washout to spoil the illusion. Beyond the technical wizardry, the sequence also works beautifully within the film's narrative, rebuking those who bemoan the supposed "episodic" nature of stop-motion fantasy films. The allosaur's defeat brings home the point that aggression is sometimes necessary, and that the "civilized" Shell folks can learn a thing or two from the "primitive" Tumak. After all, only upon witnessing Tumak's daring did the Shell men muster the courage to join in.

There are still more great animation

sequences to come, including two boffo battle scenes, though none can match the brilliance of the allosaur raid. The Ceratosaurus-Triceratops fight is more proof of Harryhausen's innate feel for how animals actually behave — neither creature makes a single move that isn't plausible. But as Neil Pettigrew points out in his *Stop-Motion Filmography*, the scene is a slight let-down coming on the heels of the awesome allosaur episode. The final animation sequence is a another gem, as Loana becomes the prize in a heated contest between two flying reptiles. The pterosaur scenes, which leave Tumak devastated at the sight (he thinks) of his mate being devoured, are successful both technically and dramatically. The two baby 'dactyls are a nifty touch, and the animated biting and swallowing movements as the victor dines on the chicks are totally believable.

There is also, of course, the iguana. It's tough to figure just what to make of this scene. "It was one of my, shall we say, rare miscalculations," Harryhausen told this author, with humor. Time and budget considerations were probable factors, and there are those who interpret the lizard's appearance as a homage to the original's immortal reptilian stars. "Well, they could if they wanted to," Ray said laughingly. "Maybe it was *subconscious*!" The scene actually plays okay, but the best that can be said is that it's as good as a lizard-dino scene can be. The only real glitch in a superlative overall FX effort involves the traveling mattes, which draw a bit too much attention to themselves in certain cuts of the pterodactyl and earthquake sequences. At other times, an obvious matte shot abruptly turns up in the middle of an otherwise shot-on-location sequence, and the effect is disconcerting.

The fundamental premise of the "caveman-and-dinosaurs" movie carries with it unavoidable limitations, yet within these limitations the people behind *One Million Years B.C.* successfully crafted an enjoyable cinematic fantasy. The dinosaurs are wonderful, and the appealing story with its simple message of learning from each other is just engaging enough to keep things going in between the beautiful beasts. Whether enjoyed for Raquel and her fur fashions or Ray and his fantastic fauna, *One Million Years B.C.* is carved in stone on the short list of must-see dinosaur films.

PEOPLE AND PRODUCTION: Having built their reputation and a solid fan following with low-budget, stylish horror movies, England's Hammer Films began in 1966 what would become a short cycle of prehistoric adventures. Producer Michael Carreras based the screenplay for *One Million Years B.C.* directly on Hal Roach's original, and determined from the start that it would be a rather lavish production by Hammer standards. More than anything, he wanted to get the dinosaurs right. "We decided if we're going to make the film at all, we had to have the latest technique of making these things look real," Carreras told author Ted Newsom in *Imagi-Movies*. "It was the company's decision that we wouldn't make the film unless we could get the best." The best, of course, meant Ray Harryhausen, and due to some fortunate timing he was available. A pair of respected British FX men — George Blackwell and Hammer mainstay Les Bowie — were tabbed to handle the physical effects.

With the effects crew set, attention turned to the live action. A bonanza of picturesque filming locations were found on the primitively beautiful islands of Lanzarote and Tenerife, off the west coast of Africa, though they presented challenges for the cast and crew. Some of the harshest weather of the decade hit the Canary Islands chain just as production commenced. "The worst part of making *One Million Years B.C.* was the weather," Raquel Welch said at the time. "The torrential storms — all out of season, of course — were really tornados. And a clear sunny sky would switch to dropping snow with no warning at all." More comfortable were the studio shots, photographed on Stage 2 at Associated British Elstree Studios. The Shell tribe village and other sets were constructed there, adorned with exotic plant life designed by art director Robert Jones and assistant art director Kenneth Tait. Wilkie Cooper, veteran of *The 7th Voyage of Sinbad*, *The Three Worlds of Gulliver*, *Mysterious Island*, *Jason and the Argonauts*, and *The First Men in the Moon*, handled the cinematography. "One of the finest photographers in Great Britain, I think," Harryhausen once said of Cooper. "I've always felt he's done a wonderful job with recording our very exotic locations."

The filmmakers deliberately avoided familiar names when casting the film. According to the movie's production information guide, "Don Chaffey felt that well-known actors would work against a severe handicap if they had been seen often in civilized parts with well-spoken dialogue." (The fact that newcomers also cost so much less just might have entered their minds as well.) Raquel Welch and John Richardson weren't complete unknowns, but their previous pictures had not been of the type to make them into household names. Welch was coming off the lavish 1966 adventure *Fantastic Voyage*, in which all of the actors played second banana to the imaginative visuals, and Richardson had been overshadowed by the imposing presence of horror icons Peter Cushing and Christopher Lee in Hammer's 1965 remake of *She*.

The film was touted as Hammer's 100th production, though in reality it was not. It did turn out to be one of the studio's most financially rewarding efforts, and a good-natured debate regarding the primary reason has continued since its release. Dinosaur and Harryhausen fans insist that credit is due the wonderful prehistoric menagerie, while others cite Miss Welch's physical attributes. Even Hammer realized that the picture had two distinct drawing cards, and actually produced two different television advertising spots. As described in the pressbook, one was "an adult version featuring Raquel Welch," and the other was "a version for children featuring the animals in the picture." There were even rumors of on-set friction between Welch and Harryhausen, but Ray dismisses such stories. "She was very cooperative and very easy to work with," he stated in Marc Shapiro's *When Dinosaurs Ruled the Screen*. "She worked very hard and never complained."

It was commonplace during this era to release different versions of films for European and American audiences, with the stateside viewers always getting the "tamer" of the two. Scenes cut from *One Million Years B.C.* included the grisly outcome of the vicious fight among the "missing links," with the severed head of the slain creature being stuck onto a sharpened stake (accompanied by a gruesomely juicy sound effect), and a sexy ceremonial dance performed by Martine Beswick during her "wedding" to Sakana. Fans of Beswick are probably among the few who remember the next entry in Hammer's prehistory cycle, 1967's *Prehistoric Women*, as it had little to recommend it other than her beauty and commanding presence in the lead role. In fact, that film (a.k.a. *Slave Girls*) might never have been made had it not been for Hammer's desire to wring some more use out of the comparatively expensive sets and costumes created for *One Million*. Hammer's prehistoric tetrad ended with 1971's *Creatures the World Forgot*, which tried to make up for its lack of dinosaurs with flashes of Julie Ege in the altogether.

SPECIAL EFFECTS: After eight consecutive pictures in collaboration with producer Charles Schneer (*The Animal World* notwithstanding), Ray Harryhausen returned to one of his first loves, dinosaurs, when he was "loaned out" from Schneer's Morningside Productions to Hammer Films for its *One Million B.C.* remake. "I hate remakes," Harryhausen told this author, "and the only reason I took it on is I thought we could do better." Do better, indeed — the dinosaurs in *One Million Years* are some of the most zoologically correct ever to appear on-screen. "We wanted the creatures accurate," Harryhausen explained, "so we used Arthur Hayward, a sculptor at the Natural History Museum in London. He sculpted the clay models based on my drawings, and made

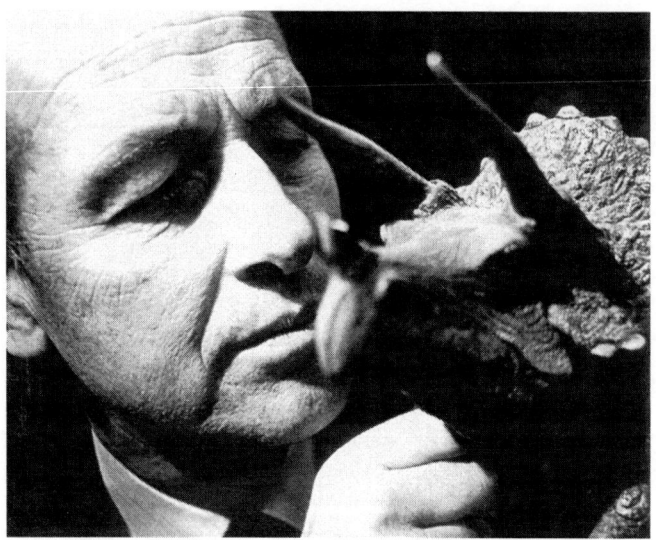

Closeup look at the exquisite *One Million Years B.C.* stop-motion Triceratops and its life-force, Ray Harryhausen.

molds for me, and then I cast and built the animated models. He was a very good artist."

Harryhausen described the film's pre-production in his *Film Fantasy Scrapbook*. "In the early stages of our discussions about the remake, Michael Carreras, Don Chaffey, and I had many meetings as to how we would approach the 1966 version," he recalled. "While Michael reconstructed the screenplay I went back to my drawing board, attempting to devise new animals and different situations involving them." Stop-motion would naturally be the method of choice, but in a throwback to the original, the first "dinosaur" is a live iguana. "Yes, that was a mistake on my part," Harryhausen told me. "I thought by using a live lizard for the first appearance, it would make people believe more in the animated ones, but it did just the opposite." Ray also remembered how difficult the reptilian actors were: "The live lizard did *nothing*. He hardly even blinked his eye. We had three iguanas, and they all kept falling asleep under the hot lights!"

The first stop-motion sequence is the giant sea turtle, which Loana calls an "Archelon." Interestingly, that really is the name of an actual prehistoric turtle, which was huge by today's standards though not as big as portrayed here. "Our intention was to save the more terrifying attackers for the end of the picture," Harryhausen wrote, and his determination to improve on the man-in-suit meat-eater from 1940 resulted in one of the most astonishing stop-motion sequences ever filmed. Though he has been (rightly) reluctant to divulge every last detail and secret of his work, he has revealed that the stunning shot of the squirming allosaur on the end of Tumak's stake involved animated models of both Tumak's arm and the stake, "invisible" suspension wires, and a special air pump and bladder to make the 'saur breathe in stop-motion. Never one to blow his own horn, with a bit of coaxing Ray did admit to the author that "it came out quite impressive," and "worked very well, intimately, with the live action."

The animation of a flying creature presents a whole new set of challenges to the animator. "It takes more time, and one tries to avoid it," Harryhausen said, "but I had two pterodactyls fighting in *One Million*—that was a big problem." In an interview published in *FXRH* (no. 4), he discussed the difficulties involved in "airborne" animation:

> It is, of course, a very long process ... you have to devise a way to suspend the animal on a set of wires that will not pick up photographically. This is done through a travelling matte process sometimes, and at other times you have to paint the wire out of each frame so that it is the exact color of the background—because you are photographing at a very close range when you're photographing a miniature model.

Sharp-eyed amateur paleontologists may notice that the two creatures clearly and deliberately represent two different groups of pterosaurs: a nearly-tailless pterodactyloid and a long-tailed rhamphorhynchoid (the fight's winner). The pterosaur puppets were constructed around the same stop-motion armatures formerly inside the Harpies of *Jason and the Argonauts*, and the 3-inch-high Raquel Welch puppet employed for this sequence was the smallest figure Ray ever animated. "Of course she wasn't able to demonstrate her assets, but she was all there," Harryhausen noted.

Most animation fans are aware of the film's planned but never filmed bronto finale. "The Brontosaurus sequence was going to be the climax, and due to many budget restrictions and various other things, we had to change at the last minute," Harryhausen explained. "We shot a couple of location shots, but that was all." Harryhausen's preproduction drawings for the scene promised some eye-popping visuals, and nothing comparable has ever been included in a dinosaur film before or since. Not quite as well known is another never filmed sequence involving a giant carnivorous bird, described by Wayne Kinsey in his fanzine *The House That Hammer Built*. "One scene was to feature a huge prehistoric bird kept in a pen at the camp of the Shell tribe," Kinsey wrote. "The bird was to have escaped when Loana opened the cage to retrieve one of its eggs and then to be chased through the camp before being snapped up in the hungry jaws of the Allosaurus as it made its dramatic entrance." As Kinsey pointed out, Harryhausen used a similar device three years later for Gwangi's first appearance.

Even without the brontosaur and bird sequences, the painstaking animation still took more than nine months to complete. As famous — or infamous — as the original *One Million B.C.* has become as a source of stock dinosaur footage, it is fitting that the remake's animated beasts would serve as "stock footage" at least once, and they did — in director John Badham's 1983 popcorn-thriller, *Wargames*.

Created publicity shot, featuring the actual stop-motion Brontosaurus puppet, depicts what might have resulted had Ray Harryhausen's planned bronto-versus-cavemen finale been realized.

The People That Time Forgot

"Maybe you weren't meant to make your name in pictures."

** 1977, U. K. Amicus/American International Pictures. C, 90m.

CREDITS: *Director* Kevin Connor. *Producers* John Dark, Max J. Rosenberg, Samuel Z. Arkoff (executive). *Screenplay* Patrick Tilley; based upon "The People That Time Forgot" by Edgar Rice Burroughs. *Special Effects Supervisors* John Richardson (Spain), Ian Wingrove (U.K.).

CAST: *Maj. Ben McBride* Patrick Wayne. *Bowen Tyler* Doug McClure. *Charly* Sarah Douglas. *Ajor* Dana Gillespie. *Dr. Norfolk* Thorley Walters. *Hogan* Shane Rimmer. *Capt. Lawton* Tony Britton. *Sabbala* Milton Reid.

AD LINE: "The 7th Continent (wait a minute, don't we already have seven?) — A lost world shut off by a wall of ice, roamed by beasts unknown to science, ruled by men lost to history, doomed to vanish in a chaos of leaping flames!"

World War I has ended and Major Ben McBride has sailed to the ice-bound, dinosaur-filled continent of Caprona in search of his lifelong friend, Bowen Tyler. On board the *Polar Queen* are McBride, his war buddy Hogan, *London Times* photographer Charlotte "Charly" Cunningham St. Clair, paleontologist Dr. Edwin Norfolk, and an amphibious airplane—the "Amphib," they call it—intended to carry the explorers safely over Caprona's forbidding ice wall. Unfortunately, a giant pterodactyl harasses the Amphib until the poor dumb beast haplessly grinds off its bill in the plane's propeller. McBride manages to land the damaged craft, but when it mires up in a patch of soft ground, it's up to a cooperative Stegosaurus to tow it out. Leaving Hogan behind to repair the plane, the other three set off on foot. They soon meet a young woman named Ajor from the peaceful Galu tribe, and after a brief interruption by a Ceratosaurus they find that she has learned English ... from Bowen Tyler. It seems the Galu befriended Tyler and Lisa Clayton (the only other survivor of Tyler's party) only to see them captured by the dreaded Naga tribe.

While Hogan shoots down pterosaurs and steadily loses his marbles back at camp, McBride tracks Tyler's whereabouts to "the Mountain of Skulls—the city where the Nagas live." McBride and party are intercepted by a deceptively peaceful Naga patrol and brought before the fearsome chief, Sabbala. As the women are prepped for sacrifice, McBride and Norfolk are tossed into a dingy cell only to discover that their next-cell neighbor is Bowen Tyler! The dispirited Tyler tells them of how the Nagas wiped out the Galu race ... and killed his beloved Lisa. The men break free and hurry to the ceremonial chamber, just in time to save Ajor and Charly and make a desperate run for safety. Tyler, spouting Capronan religious dogma, tells McBride that "the land will stop you" and remains behind in a suicidal attempt to impede the Naga pursuers. McBride leads his group—Ajor included—to the Amphib, and pilots the rickety craft safely back to the *Polar Queen*.

COMMENTARY: This sequel to *The Land That Time Forgot* has much in common with its predecessor, yet comes up just short in comparison. The script is not quite as good, the acting is not quite as good, and the dinosaur effects are certainly not as good. *People* does mark something of a recovery from the embarrassment of *At the Earth's Core* but can't measure up to the first film—and one must remember, *Land* itself is no masterpiece.

People generally maintains the serious and straightforward tone of its forerunner, and contains a couple of dinosaur scenes which in a more technically proficient movie could have been classics. The Stegosaurus-as-beast-of-burden sequence and the pterosaur-versus-Amphib dogfight are nifty notions, just outrageous enough to have been a dino buff's delight had they been effectively realized. The dogfight in particular was loaded with possibilities, as evidenced by the fact that a very similar sequence was originally planned for the finale of *The Lost World: Jurassic Park*.

Not only are the *People* dinosaurs less satisfactory than their *Land* counterparts, they're a lot scarcer. The only dinos encountered after the pterodactyl and Stegosaurus are a pair of ceratosaurs that briefly menace Ajor and McBride, and by 27 minutes into the film all of the "real" dinosaurs have come and gone. All we get for the rest of the picture are a few goofy cinemasaurs, including the very same "Giant Saurus" seen fighting Doug McClure in *At the Earth's Core*. (If it could get from Pellucidar to Caprona in one year, perhaps a thorough field study of the species' migratory patterns is in order.)

The best dinosaur effects in *People* are only about equal to the worst effects in *Land*. The Ceratosaurus duo is obscured by smoke and foliage in most shots—a wise decision—and the pterodactyl couldn't look any more starched if it had been plucked from the wall of some intrepid Capronan taxidermist. The Stegosaurus looks marginally passable while standing still, but then it starts to walk away *without moving its legs*! Happily, the miniature and model effects are measurably better than the creatures. The "Amphib" is a neat creation, plausibly designed for a 1920s-vintage aircraft, and the modelwork and photography during its takeoff, flight, and

"A fully grown Stegosaurus!" marvels Dr. Norfolk (Thorley Walters), as Charley (Sarah Douglas) and Ben McBride (Patrick Wayne) look on in *The People That Time Forgot*.

landing are convincing. The climactic volcanic eruption (yes, again) is just as scientifically laughable as the one in *Land*, while being less interesting.

The edge again goes to the earlier film in the casting department. Even when duking it out with dinosaurs, Patrick Wayne can't muster up any more screen presence than he could in the same year's *Sinbad and the Eye of the Tiger*. Sarah Douglas and Thorley Walters do what they can but are stuck with a pair of absolutely by-the-numbers stock characters. Both actors are appealing, but the "emancipated-woman-ahead-of-her-time" and the "upper-crust, slightly-stuffy British scientist" have been pretty much done to death. Shane Rimmer has fun as Hogan, the mechanic who's not quite hitting on all cylinders, and *Star Wars* fans might enjoy seeing David "Darth Vader" Prowse as the Naga executioner. The film's pressbook promised that sexy Dana Gillespie would "fulfill every man's dream of the primitive woman," but her character, Ajor, is no plaything — in one scene, she *breaks off a stalactite* from the cavern ceiling and uses it as a club! The nicest surprise is Doug McClure, who shines in his second, smaller go-round as the ill-fated Tyler. McClure's wounded, weary voice, as a defeated Tyler tells his friend about the tragic fate of his cherished Lisa, carries emotion that is believable and even touching.

People is fairly faithful to Burroughs' story — in spirit if not in the details — but is not as well-paced as the previous film. *Land* nicely uses its pre–Caprona scenes to flesh out its characters, and although something

A bearded Bowen Tyler (Doug McClure) resolutely keeps his eyes on the dinosaurs despite the distractions of Ajor (Dana Gillespie) in *The People That Time Forgot.*

can be said for jumping right into the action, we never learn enough about Charly, Norfolk, or McBride to become interested in them. A number of plot points will have genre fans flashing back to previous dinosaur flicks. We get a tough-guy hero carping about a female being aboard ship until he falls for her (*King Kong*), a woman who's invited only because her newspaper is funding the trip (*The Lost World*—1960 edition), and some nasty polar pack ice that threatens to force the mother ship to abandon the explorers (*The Land Unknown*). There is also a glaring continuity error between the two films. At the end of *Land*, we are told that Tyler and Lisa were "spurned by even the highest—the Galu," but in *People* we learn that the couple "were welcomed by the Galu, and lived with them for more than two years."

Problems and all, *The People That Time Forgot* still has more going for it than many films of its type. The volcanic cavern and "Mountain of Skulls" display some imaginative art direction, Alan Hume's photography of the beautiful Canary Islands locations boosts the realism, and John Scott's rich music score is marvelous—the one element of *People* in which it clearly tops its forbear. But it is quite astounding to compare the special effects in *The People That Time Forgot* to those in *Star Wars*, and then realize that both were released the same year.

PEOPLE AND PRODUCTION: According to a studio promo, *The People That Time Forgot* was "made by the same Amicus team"

A sensational scenario — a giant pterodactyl dogfighting with a vintage airplane — is less than masterfully realized in *The People That Time Forgot*.

that had created *The Land That Time Forgot* two years earlier. This is partially true — a lot of the same personnel did return. Common to both films are director Kevin Connor, producers John Dark and Max J. Rosenberg, cinematographer Alan Hume, production designer Maurice Carter, art director Bert Davey, set dresser Simon Wakefield, and editor John Ireland. Newcomers for *People* include screenwriter Patrick Tilley (replacing James Cawthorn and Michael Moorcock) and special effects creators Ian Wingrove and John Richardson (taking over for Derek Meddings and Roger Dicken). Both Wingrove and Richardson would progress from their unremarkable work in *People* to enjoy prestigious careers in special effects. Wingrove's later projects include *The Dark Crystal* (1982), *Return of the Jedi* (1983), and the underappreciated *Return to Oz* (1985); Richardson worked on such films as *Aliens* (1986), *Willow* (1988), *Starship Troopers* (1998), and a half-dozen entries in the James Bond series.

The Canary Islands have proven a popular filming location for British dinosaur pictures. Hammer Films had exploited the volcanic terrains of Lanzarote and Tenerife for *One Million Years B.C.* and *When Dinosaurs Ruled the Earth*, while Amicus chose the more lush environment of La Palma for *The People That Time Forgot*. With the first two installments of Edgar Rice Burroughs' Caprona (or "Caspak") trilogy in the can, Amicus apparently had plans to complete the cycle. A press release in conjunction with *People* stated: "The third, 'Out of Time's

Abyss,' awaits next to be filmed." But as of 25 years later, it was still waiting.

The Phantom Empire

"This is like a 'Lost World,' y'know, like in the movies!"

*½ 1986, USA. American Independent Productions. C, 83m.

CREDITS: *Director* Fred Olen Ray. *Producers* Fred Olen Ray; Nick Marino, Salvatore Richichi (associate), Tony Brewster (coproducer). *Screenplay* Fred Olen Ray, T. L. Lankford. *Special Make-up Effects* Paul M. Rinehard. *Rotoscope Effects* Bret Mixon. *Special Visual Effects* Mark Wolf, Wizard Works, Cory Kaplan.
CAST: *Cort Eastman* Ross Hagen. *Andrew Paris* Jeffrey Combs. *Eddy Colchilde* Dawn Wildsmith. *Professor Strock* Robert Quarry. *Denea Chambers* Susan Stokey. *Cave Bunny* Michelle Bauer. *Bill* Russ Tamblyn. *The Alien Queen* Sybil Danning.

Professional salvager Cort Eastman spent ten futile years looking for the legendary subterranean civilization of R'lyia, and wants nothing more to do with it. That is, until wealthy and beautiful socialite Denea Chambers makes him an irresistible offer to mount a new search. Cort obtains a rare map from Bill, a rather eccentric survivor of a disastrous former expedition, and sets out with his tough-as-nails female partner Eddy Colchilde, archeology intern Andrew Paris, mineralogist Dr. Artemis "Doc" Strock, and Denea. Deep within the caverns, they meet a gorgeous "cavegirl" who helps them drive off a throng of cannibalistic albino mutants and even assists in retrieving the abducted Denea. They flee the caves and thwart an attack by a laser-equipped robot, but when they emerge onto what they think is the surface it turns out to be R'lyia instead! It is inhabited by a race of marooned alien women, ruled by a statuesque but heartless blonde queen. The explorers are captured, and Paris is brought to the queen's chamber for carnal purposes. But the helpful cavegirl, unofficially named "Cave Bunny," again frees the captives. The group makes a break for the queen's all-terrain rover while constantly dodging the stegosaurs, tyrannosaurs, and other dinosaurs which roam R'lyia. With Cave Bunny accompanying, they almost reach the opening to the surface before the vehicle overheats. They continue on foot, escaping just before the inevitable explosion seals off the entrance to R'lyia, forever.

COMMENTARY: Eight years before *Dinosaur Island*, Fred Olen Ray made *The Phantom Empire*, his first foray into the Lost World genre. In many ways it is typical of his films—woefully underbudgeted and wildly uneven, but not without some redeeming moments.

The problems with this six-day wonder include the goofy-looking mutants, possibly inspired by the "Morlocks" of *The Time Machine* (1960) but looking more like the "sub-terranean mole men" in *Valley of the Dragons*. The big "gore" scene in the prologue is robbed of any shock value by the very fake look of the prop decapitated head, and the picture's midsection is heavily padded with yawn-inducing filler. An opening credit which reads "Special Effects Animation—Bret Mixon" raises hopes of some original stop motion dinosaurs, but no such luck. All the dinos turn out to be *Planet of Dinosaurs* footage, with Mixon's contribution consisting of some rotoscope animation during the robot's laser attack. The few dinosaur shots have little to do with the plot and seem to have been spliced in just to add running time.

On the flip side, *Phantom Empire* does offer some sharp dialogue delivered by marginally interesting characters. Leading the way is Dawn Wildsmith, perfectly cast as the cynical, cheroot-puffing Eddy. "No matter which way ya turn," she philosophizes, "fate always puts a foot out to trip ya." She also provides the most unique Stegosaurus description ever heard: "Just like big puppies, with poker chips on their back." Robert Quarry is fun as the irritable Doc Strock (a nod to director Herbert L. Strock?) and the script is peppered with knowing in-jokes for genre buffs. Eddy quips that "All we need is Gene Autry"—a reference to Autry's 1935 sci-fi/cowboy serial from which this picture lifts its title—and the end credits offer thanks to "the city and county of Caprona" for their cooperation. Stir in a cameo by Robby the Robot, some amusing sight gags (the cannibals turn Denea on a rotisserie), and Sybil Danning setting a new world cleavage record, and there are *almost* enough diversions to counteract all the tedium.

PEOPLE AND PRODUCTION: In the mid-eighties, the indefatigable Fred Olen Ray had an association with Trans World Entertainment, for which he directed *The Tomb*, *Commando Squad* ("it had no commandos and no squad," Ray noted), and *Deep Space*. It was with some of his TWE proceeds that he began production on *The Phantom Empire*. "I loved the old Saturday afternoon serials and wanted to make a *Lost World* type picture," Ray wrote in *The New Poverty Row*. "It was impossible to do a good job with the money we had and the allotted six-day shooting schedule, but I wanted to 'own' my movie so badly that I went ahead and did it anyway. I pulled in a lot of favors, got some great actors, and plunged forward." Several members of Ray's "stock company" are present, including Robert Quarry, Russ Tamblyn, Ross Hagen, Michelle Bauer, and Dawn Wildsmith (Ray's wife at the time). Ray tested the waters and finally accepted a deal with Film Ventures International, but the agreement stipulated that the picture had to run ten minutes longer. "So we went out to Vasquez Rocks County Park and a picture that was supposed to be happening at the center of the earth was now out in the wide open desert!" Unfortunately, the relationship with Film Ventures was not a happy one since, as Ray explained, "the advance money was all we would ever see." Ray sued, and after a year of legal haranguing Film Ventures settled out of court.

The Phantom Empire was the first film released by Ray's new company, American Independent Productions. Yes, in acronym form that's "AIP," in homage to the fondly remembered B-movie outfit of Sam Arkoff and Jim Nicholson. "The company name [was] a bit of a lark, or tribute," Ray stated, "but in its own way it spelled out my philosophy perfectly."

Planet of Dinosaurs

"You could almost like this place."

** 1978, USA. Cinema Dynamics/Filmpartners. C, 84m.

CREDITS: *Director* James K. Shea. *Producers* James K. Shea, James Aupperle (associate), James R. Waite (associate), Stephen Czerkas (executive). *Screenplay* Ralph Lucas. *Story* James Aupperle. *Special Visual Effects* Stephen Czerkas and James Aupperle. *Chief Stop-Motion Animator* Douglas Beswick. *Matte Artist* Jim Danforth. *Spaceship Design* Stephen C. Wathen. *Special Props* Bill Malone.

CAST: *Jim* James Whitworth. *Nyla* Pamela Bottaro. *Capt. Lee Northside* Louie Lawless. *Harvey Baylor* Harvey Shain. *Charlotte* Charlotte Speer. *Chuck* Chuck Pennington. *Derna Lee* Derna Wylde. *Mike* Michael Thayer. *Cindy* Mary Appleseth.

AD LINE: "Trapped in a nightmare world of prehistoric monsters!"

The commercial spaceship *Odyssey* is on a routine mission. The crew includes dedicated but green Capt. Lee Northside, First Officer Nyla, engineer Jim, nurse Charlotte, navigator Chuck (who, when asked about their position helpfully replies "God knows!"), scanner operator Mike, and communications officer Cindy, along with company vice president Harvey Baylor and his secretary, Derna. Their shuttle is auto-jettisoned from the mother ship when the main reactor goes critical, and they barely manage to reach a habitable planet. They ditch the ship in a lake and swim to shore, but Cindy returns to the water to retrieve their transmitter and is killed by an unseen aquatic monster. Lee leads the band to higher ground, constantly fretting over his command abilities. "I'm a technician, not an explorer," he confides to Nyla.

The amazing sight of a giant Brontosaurus and a trio of stegosaurs reveals that the planet is still in its dinosaur age, and before long a hungry Tyrannosaurus also appears. The group tries to move out of the carnivores' reach by climbing a nearby plateau; but Harvey learns that vegetarians can also be dangerous when he steals a ceratopsian's egg and is gored by the protective parent. Possessing different philosophies, Lee favors building a defensive stockade and remaining inconspicuous while Jim insists they must take the initiative and put fear into the beasts. Jim acquiesces, but incidents continue to occur which steadily undermine Lee's assurances of safety. A foot-high spider almost gets Nyla, while Chuck and Charlotte nearly fall victim to an Allosaurus. The band sets out on a dino hunt and succeeds in vanquishing an ostrichlike Struthiomimus, but only when Derna is killed by a huge Tyrannosaurus does Lee grudgingly join in. Debating how best to kill the beast, they decide to try Lee's cautious scheme—poison bait—and fall back on Jim's more "direct approach" only if necessary. They club a small Polacanthus and stuff it with toxic berries, but the T. rex attacks and kills Mike before they can get set up. They next try Jim's idea—planting poison-tipped stakes in the ground—but again the beast appears before they are ready. The formerly timid Lee boldly leads the rex away to buy time for the others to complete the trap, and when the dinosaur returns it runs blindly into their forest of stakes and fatally impales itself. "Maybe now we can make a new world," Jim says.

COMMENTARY: *Planet of Dinosaurs* (not *Planet of the Dinosaurs*, as it is sometimes called) is one of the most dinosaur-rich movies ever made, but sadly the dinosaur scenes are just about all it has to recommend it. In other areas—acting, script, and so on—the movie struggles mightily, leaving only its plentiful and accomplished special effects to carry the load. In a genre where effects often outshine a film's other qualities, *Planet* may have the greatest gap of all.

At its worst, *Planet of Dinosaurs* suffers the ignominy of being unintentionally funny. This is as much due to the dialogue—laced with lines like "this isn't Nebraska!" and "no, no, mythonium tastes terrible"—as to the way it is delivered. Considering some of Lee's comments, it's no wonder that Jim doubts his captain's abilities. When they hear a roar and Harvey asks "what the hell was that?" Lee helpfully replies, "an animal of some sort." Later, Jim is surprised by Lee's choice of a campsite. "Stay here? What for?" Jim asks incredulously. "It's a good spot," answers Lee.

Amazingly, there are a few bright moments. One effective scene shows the group trying to be merry and celebrate their "Happy New World," only to see their facade degenerate into tears as "Auld Lang Syne" plays on the soundtrack in a plaintive, minor key. There are even a few good lines, like when Charlotte and Chuck are stargazing. "You're the navigator, Chuck—which one is Earth?" she asks. "You can't see it from here," he replies, "unless you close your eyes." It seems to be a habit of dinomovies, including *Lost Continent* and *The Beast of Hollow Mountain*, to kill off their comic relief characters, and *Planet* joins in by disposing of the wisecracking Harvey. The basic story premise—whether man must be the aggressor or else see his soul wither and die from playing things too safe—is an interesting idea which could have been the basis for a workable screenplay, and the rare good moments make one wonder why everything else must be so hideously disappointing.

The *Planet* cast was largely made up of nonprofessional performers, and it unfortunately shows. The only player with notable film experience was James Whitworth, so it's not surprising that he turns in the only reasonably professional performance. Pamela Bottaro maintains a natural delivery and manages to give Nyla some personality. As far as everyone else goes, the less said the better. The cast's credibility is not helped by the wardrobe they are given, which recalls the kitschy "futuristic" fashions seen in B-

An uncanny copy of Ray Harryhausen's *Beast from 20,000 Fathoms* "rhedosaurus" is no match for an alien T. rex on the *Planet of Dinosaurs.*

movies and serials of the thirties, forties, and fifties. But credit should be given to the actors, writers, and director for one thing: they never stray into spoofiness. The story is played out — amateurishly and disjointedly, yes — with a straightforward sincerity that makes it at least bearable. Had anyone, anywhere along the line, decided to ham it up, the film would have approached unwatchability. And the photography, done exclusively outdoors, avoids the claustrophobic and fake-looking studio settings often seen.

The special effects in *Planet of Dinosaurs* are every bit as good as the rest of the picture is bad. A very talented team gave life to a variety of prehistoric beasts the like of which has rarely been seen on-screen. Before the film is over we are treated to more than a dozen stop-motion animation sequences, featuring a Brontosaurus, Stegosaurus, Tyrannosaurus rex, Allosaurus, Struthiomimus, Coelophysis, Polacanthus, a "hybrid" ceratopsian, and a deliciously icky spider. And though *Planet* doesn't have that one big signature sequence, like the roping of the allosaur in *The Valley of Gwangi* or the plesiosaur's rampage in *When Dinosaurs Ruled the Earth*, the animation is consistently professional, fluid, and great fun.

The dinosaur puppets are superb, with an attention to detail that withstands the closest of closeups. The live-action and animation composites are skillful and successful, and there's even a bit of Harryhausenstyle interaction when Mike hurls his spear into the T. rex in a single cut. One of the most striking sequences features the giant spider, which unlike its counterparts in other films is not so "giant" as to lose credibility. The spider's appearance is startling and downright creepy, especially when the thing scuttles directly toward the camera with skin-crawling believability. The ceratopsian's gait is less successful—there seems to be something about the heavy-set build of the horned dinosaurs that makes them difficult to animate, and the puppet's tiny 10-inch size undoubtedly compounded the problem. As Neil Pettigrew points out in *The Stop-Motion Filmography*, even the greatest animators have had similar difficulties. Still the sequence works thanks to some neat character animation, as the beast paws at the ground in irritation and seemingly gloats over his victory. Overall the dino action is naturalistic, plausible, and one could almost say, understated. If it lacks the operatic drama of Harryhausen's best or the inspired flourishes of a Jim Danforth masterpiece, it is of inarguably high quality and must be ranked in the upper echelon of dinosaur animation.

Fantasy films, especially those with stop-motion, have often been accused of "wasting" excellent special effects in the service of otherwise dreadful pictures. On this charge, *Planet of Dinosaurs* is grievously guilty. But its dinosaurs are so very *very* good that *Planet* is also a dinosaur fan's ultimate guilty pleasure.

PEOPLE AND PRODUCTION: In the early 1970s, Jim Aupperle and Stephen Czerkas first met while guests at Forry Ackerman's house. "It was an amazing get-together," Czerkas recalled. "Just about everybody was there, from Phil Tippett to Jim Danforth, Dennis Muren and Jon Berg, and of course Ray Harryhausen [who was] the reason we all got together." So began a long-lasting association. "From that point, we started working together a lot," Jim Aupperle told me. "Steve built some models that he let me use in some of my films, and we started to collaborate on a lot of things." A few short years later, Aupperle and Czerkas were introduced to James K. Shea, who was interested in doing a film with animation. Eventually their search for a suitable scenario crossed the path of sci-fi writer David Gerrold. "He had a story called *Deathbeast* that he wanted to do," Aupperle recalled, "and basically we planned to do that as our project." A mutually acceptable agreement could not be reached, however, so an alternative dinosaur story which did not infringe on Gerrold's work had to be found. "We had to somehow come up with futuristic people that were meeting dinosaurs—certain things had been established," Aupperle explained. "That's basically how it ended up in outer space." One early concept even dealt with a race of "intelligent" saurians which would have been in competition with the astronauts, but mindful of the tiny budget things were kept more conventional. (Ironically, this idea was eventually used in *Time Tracers*, one of the films to reuse the *Planet* animation.)

Jim Shea assembled some investors and raised enough funds to begin preproduction. Actors were signed, a cameraman was hired, and shooting venues were chosen. The principal location was north of Los Angeles at Vasquez Rocks, while Hansen Dam in the San Fernando area provided the watery locale for the spaceship-crash sequence. As production geared up, tweaks to the screenplay were proposed and debated. "The one thing I jokingly say we talked Jim Shea out of was ... he wanted to put a bit of nudity in the film," Aupperle explained. "And we were going, 'No! This is going to be like a tribute to Ray Harryhausen, and he wouldn't have nudity in it!'" Stephen Czerkas also remembered the decision to leave out the naughty bits. "What were we thinking?" he said with a smile. "Easily, we could have gotten those kinds of sequences put into it, but we very intentionally wanted it to be a good clean, wholesome, family dinosaur movie that you could bring your kids to."

Live action photography began in the early summer of 1976 and the picture wrapped with the completion of the effects in October 1977, for a total production time of about 18 months. But well before the finish line neared, Shea and company realized that their initial funding was not going to be sufficient. Enter James R. Waite. "It turned out that we hadn't raised enough money," Aupperle

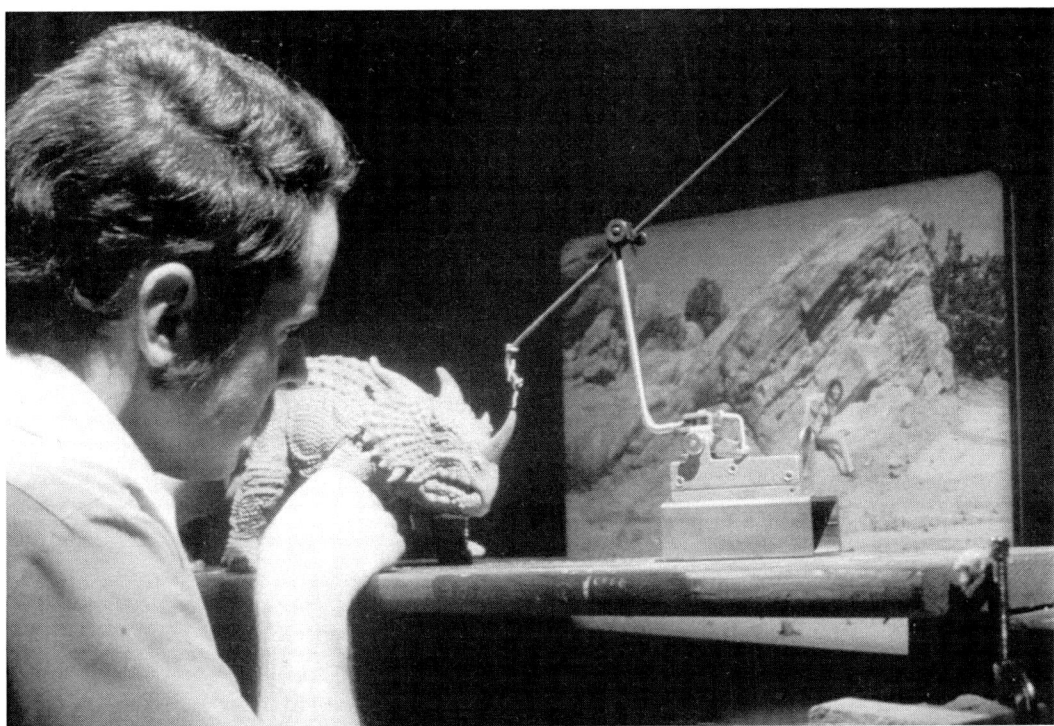

Jim Aupperle animates the Steve Czerkas–created ceratopsian in front of a rear-projection screen for *Planet of Dinosaurs*.

remembered. "Jim Waite was instrumental in raising the money to finish the movie, and also being involved on a day-by-day basis in anything that needed to get done."

With postproduction complete, a big preview screening of *Planet of Dinosaurs* was scheduled. "We had quite a few people — in fact, even Ray Harryhausen came to see it," Aupperle recalled, "so it was like ... everybody we ever wanted to see the film was there." But after months and months of exhausting work, often toiling to midnight or beyond day after day, the flaws hit hard. "After having worked on it so long, I felt sort of in a state of shock," Aupperle admitted. "And it took a long time, but now I'm certainly glad we did it. I don't think somebody realizes how hard it is to do unless they do it themselves. So if nothing else, it gave me a really healthy respect for the people who have pulled it off, and just how hard it is to make a movie." Czerkas likewise seems at peace with their creation. "With all the obstacles that we had, I'm happy with how it turned out," he told me. "Obviously, the shortcomings of the live action ... we don't have to address that *too* much, do we?"

Though seeing its greatest exposure on home video, *Planet of Dinosaurs* did have a brief theatrical release. "I actually remember seeing it in a theater," Czerkas recalled, "where literally, people down in the front would get frustrated, and you would see them get really uncomfortable and finally stand up and start to walk out. Then the dinosaurs would start up again and they would sit back down!" With the passing of time, Czerkas and Aupperle are now able to reflect on the picture more pragmatically. "For both Jim and myself, I think, *Planet of Dinosaurs* was kind of like our college degree in special effects," Czerkas said. "It was such a labor of love — it was certainly not for the money. I mean, there was such a little amount of money involved in that film, if we wanted to make money we should have just had a job at McDonald's or something!" Aupperle concurs with the "on-the-job training" aspects. "Considering what maybe we could have done, the film could have been staged — even in the animation — more imaginatively, but at the time we were kind of learning by doing," Aupperle summed up. "For what we were capable of at the time, it was pretty adventuresome. It's been said — nobody ever sets out to make a bad movie."

SPECIAL EFFECTS: At first, Stephen Czerkas and Jim Aupperle hoped to personally animate all of the dinosaur sequences, "but it [the overall project] just became so much work," Aupperle explained. "You know, we developed even more respect for Ray Harryhausen!" Aupperle, with his background in photography, built the process projectors and designed the lighting and camera setups for the animation, while Czerkas, an accomplished and talented sculptor, made the dinosaur puppets. The armatures were constructed with the help of Victor Niblock, a skilled machinist whose son was friends with Aupperle. Czerkas and Aupperle planned to divide the animation between them, and did, initially. The two worked together animating the Struthiomimus sequence, and Aupperle handled the ceratopsian shots. "But it became apparent that it was just going to be taking up so much time," Aupperle said, "more time than we really could afford." So, they needed a good animator.

Although Doug Beswick had little feature-film experience at the time, he was not unknown within the FX community. "I had known of Doug," Aupperle explained, "primarily through his animation on the Wah Chang dinosaur film [*Dinosaurs ... The Terrible Lizards*], which was very close to what we were doing." Despite the low budget, which naturally limited his pay, Beswick liked the idea and came aboard to assume the animation duties. "There was the stuff Stephen and I had already done, and Stephen animated the Brontosaurus later, and I remember doing a few cuts of the Tyrannosaurus," Aupperle said. "But from that point Doug did most of the animation. I thought he did a tremendous job, and his work really improved the overall quality of the film's effects." Echoing the sentiment, Stephen Czerkas said simply, "we were very, *very* fortunate to have Doug aboard." Soon after *Planet of Dinosaurs*, Beswick would move on to a higher-profile project when he joined the stop-motion team on *The Empire Strikes Back*.

The animation and live-action composites utilized two time-tested methods. Some shots were "Dynamation" style rear-projection setups, while others employed miniature front projection. Besides letting the filmmakers match each shot to the tactic that best suited it, the dual arrangement also allowed two animation setups to be simultaneously maintained so Beswick could animate on one while Aupperle set up the other. "If they were going to be long shots, especially if there was a lot of action, [front projection] gave Doug more room to move the puppets around, and gave us a little more flexibility in how we were going to shoot it," Aupperle pointed out. For simpler shots, "we'd do the split screen with rear projection ... double-exposed in the Ray Harryhausen tradition." Their rear-projection unit utilized an old matte projector originally constructed for the RKO matte department in the 1940s, and Aupperle fashioned their front projector from a secondhand optical printer head. "So we had a rear screen and a front screen going," Aupperle summed up, "and just kind of split up the shots based on what seemed the better approach."

The ceratopsian sequence is a testimony to the good old-fashioned, kitchen-sink inventiveness that has always been the hallmark of intrepid effects artists. To create the illusion of the beast's horn disappearing into poor Harvey's midsection, Jim Aupperle actually trimmed off bits of the horn as he animated. "The horn was cast out of an auto body filler so it was very solid, but I still was able to carve it away with a matte knife as I positioned the head," Aupperle revealed. To make Harvey Shain seem to be raised off his feet without the benefit of any fancy wire

A fundamental stop-motion rear-projection set-up for *Planet of Dinosaurs*. When skillfully photographed, the rear-projected background plate (shot on location) and the miniature dinosaur and wooden stakes will be seamlessly combined with each other.

rigs, he was filmed against a solid blue sky as he pantomimed the action. The cameraman used a quick move to provide the illusion of the actor being lifted out of frame. The dinosaur was then animated against this rear-projected footage, and for a final touch, "I added red paint around the edge of the horn as it went into him," Aupperle said. "It's probably one of my favorite shots from the film." The puppet itself incorporated characteristics of several horned species, and was affectionately dubbed the "Czerkasaurus" by the crew. "It was a make-believe ceratopsian at the time," its maker recalled. "It was just for fun, just trying to make it a little more unique than your standard horned dinosaur." But in the years since, paleontologists have discovered a real species, called Einiosaurus, which remarkably resembles Czerkas' stop-motion creation!

The dinosaur scenes were always intended as an affectionate homage to the great fantasy-film magicians — Ray Harryhausen in particular — who had given so much enjoyment and inspiration to the *Planet* crew. The first nod occurs even before the dinosaurs start to appear. "Where the spaceship crashed, that was very consciously modeled after Ray's, as far as having the ship going down in the water," Aupperle stated, referring of course to *20 Million Miles to Earth*. "I don't think we nearly pulled it off as well as Ray did, but we gave it a try." Later in the film is a cameo appearance by an unmistakable "rhedosaurus" — a remarkable copy of Ray's *Beast from 20,000 Fathoms*. Jim

Aupperle recalled the day Ray himself visited the animation set: "We showed him the dinosaur as it was in progress, so he was even aware of it before we shot it," he said. "He seemed to just be kind of amused that somebody would want to go to that kind of trouble, so I think he took it in the right way."

The villain tyrannosaur's death by impaling also recalls the demise of Harryhausen's Allosaurus in *One Million Years B.C.*, but this scene was less a conscious take-off and more a case of "trying to figure out how to do in a dinosaur," as Aupperle put it. "If the poisoning had worked, I mean, it would have been kind of nicer for the people, but it probably wouldn't have been too visual," he added, with humor. "We could have had the dinosaur wander into the cave, and you just hear a *thump*, and then, 'well, that's it!'"

Not only the star dinosaur, but also the director of *The Beast from 20,000 Fathoms* got into *Planet of Dinosaurs* in a small way. During the sequence where the astronauts place the poison-filled Polacanthus outside the T. rex lair, there are a couple of animation cuts which utilize backgrounds given to Aupperle by none other than Eugène Lourié. They were actually 2¼" slides, shot by Lourié during a visit to Spain. Czerkas and Aupperle had met Lourié years earlier, and even had hopes of doing a film with him. "He had a project called *Dark Wings*, and we did a few little still tests," Aupperle recalled. "That goes way back, but I just remember at the time he had given me these slides. So, for the people who are *very* trivia-minded, Lourié contributed a little bit to our film."

Another well-known genre film figure made a more tangible contribution. "One of the people who helped us out tremendously on the show was Jim Danforth," said Aupperle. "He was very supportive and very encouraging." Though he did no stop-motion, Danforth did create some beautiful matte paintings, one of which serves as the film's final shot. "I'll always be very grateful for Jim's contributions and all of his help," Aupperle stated. "His matte shots helped our production value tremendously." Danforth is equally complimentary of the animation work: "They did a good job; they had fun with it," he said to me. "I like Doug Beswick's work."

In the years since the film's release, the *Planet of Dinosaurs* animation has to some extent become the successor to the infamous *One Million B.C.* lizards, serving as dino stock footage in a number of low and lower budget productions. Various dinosaur scenes from *Planet* have turned up in Fred Olen Ray's *Phantom Empire* and *Demon Sword*, the cheap time-travel adventure *Time Tracers*, the even-cheaper *Galaxy of the Dinosaurs*, the satiric mélange *Pterodactyl Woman from Beverly Hills*, and the sexploitation quickie *Cave Girl Island*. "I suspect that these other films may have made more money off of it than we did!" Jim Aupperle said with a smile. In 1999, the original film was even rereleased with the new title *Monsters of the Lost World*.

Planeta Burg

(a.k.a. *Storm Planet*; *Planet of Storms*)

"Anything's possible on Venus."

*** 1962, USSR. Popular-Science Films Studio. C, 81m.

CREDITS: *Director* Pavel Klushantsev. *Producers* L. Presnyakova, Vladimir Yemelyanov. *Script* A. Kazantsev, P. Klushantsev; after the story *Grandchildren of Mars* by A. Kazantsev. *Sets* M. Tsybasov, V. Alexandrov.

CAST: *Vershinin* Vladimir Yemelyanov. *Bobrov* Georgi Zhzhenov. *Alyosha* Gennadi Vernov. *Shcherba* Yuri Sarantsev. *Masha* Kyunna Ignatova. *Kern* Georgi Teikh.

A three-ship Soviet space mission is approaching Venus when one of the ships, the *Capella*, is destroyed by a meteor. Remaining are the *Sirius*, manned by Alyosha, Bobrov, and mission commander Vershinin, and the *Vega*, carrying Masha, her sweetheart Shcherba, Allan Kern, and Kern's creation, robot John. Shcherba, Kern and John pilot a glider to the surface, but a sudden loss of radio contact prompts Vershinin to take the *Sirius* down to investigate. After landing near a small bay, Alyosha is enchanted by a haunting sound — like a woman's voice — but is jolted back to reality by a narrow escape from a flesh-eating plant. The *Sirius* crew board their hovering "cross-country car" and set out toward Shcherba and Kern on the other side of the bay, unaware that their comrades have ruptured their spacesuits fighting off some dinosaurian lizard-men and have consequently fallen ill with Venusian malaria. The searchers stop to examine a docile Brontosaurus before starting across the bay, but soon must submerge to escape a belligerent Pteradactylus. While on the sea floor, the men discover an encrusted idol — carved by a thinking being — proving that intelligent life has existed on the planet.

Medicated and sheltered by John, Shcherba and Kern regain their strength and become fascinated by an onset of volcanic activity — so fascinated that they linger too long and are forced to have John carry them through the rising lava. John's self-protection directive compels him to dump his load when the temperature nears his tolerance level, but luckily Alyosha makes a timely arrival in the hovercar. The cosmonauts return to base just as the rain-softened ground threatens to topple the *Sirius*, and hastily prepare for liftoff. Trying to set up an automated meteorological station, Alyosha hammers on the jammed cover with a rock he had idly picked up from the sea bottom. The stone breaks to reveal a carving of a female face — beautiful, alien, yet somehow human. "Wait, we can't leave!" he shouts. "They're like us!" His comrades pull the hysterical man into the cabin, and they rocket away to rendezvous with Masha and the *Vega*.

COMMENTARY: Anyone accustomed to campy fare like *Journey to the Seventh Planet* (1962), *Space Monster* (1965), or any of numerous other "space movies" of the 1960s, will find *Planeta Burg* (*Storm Planet*) surprising if not amazing. In an era when American moviemakers were pitting Richard "Jaws" Kiel against 80-year-old Francis X. Bushman in *The Phantom Planet* (1961), Soviet director Pavel Klushantsev was overcoming endless obstacles to create a smart and speculative bit of science fiction.

Planeta Burg may be too deliberately paced for some, but those who stay with it are rewarded with high-quality performances and a multilayered script which combine to create believable characters. Only the first act is a bit *too* slow, with a little too much debate regarding who should go, who shouldn't, and why. More interesting are the later discussions, as the men ponder the relative merits of man versus machine, how an intelligent race could have regressed after colonizing Venus, and other "deep" topics, all without ever sounding pompous. The female of the group doesn't get to land but still has a depth and dimension unheard of in American sci-fi of that day. Then there is robot John, the utterly unexpected comedy relief. No, he doesn't do pratfalls or warn of danger with flailing arms — it's just that his humor gets drier as he gets wetter. Affected by the rain, his too-literal interpretation of Bobrov's radioed questions leads to some amusingly off-the-wall exchanges. "Describe your companions' position," Bobrov says, trying to zero in on their location. "Horizontal position," John replies.

Klushantsev portrays the realities and details of space travel in the manner of *Destination Moon* (1950), but even more successfully. A cosmonaut performs calisthenics against mechanical spring tension; the first man out tests the surface before stepping off; a two-stage lander blasts off for the return trip leaving its lower stage on the surface — all of these would later take place very much as depicted. The film's effects are ahead of their time in many ways — the nifty hovercar predates Luke Skywalker's landspeeder by fifteen years yet was filmed with some of the same trick techniques, and the shots of Masha floating weightless about the cabin are as convincing as any zero–G simulations seen until *Apollo 13* (1995). It's a sure sign of

Robot John, the hovercar, and the dinosaurs are all featured on this Mexican lobby card for *Planeta Burg* (*Storm Planet*).

talent and imagination when a filmmaker can take a seeming liability and turn it into a strength, as Klushantsev does during the glider's flight to the surface. Without the budget to film an extensive miniature sequence of the vehicle's descent, approach, and crash, Klushantsev reveals the events through a radio transmission. In one long cut the *Sirius* crew hang on every word, smiling at hopeful moments, looking down when their comrades seem lost, and before long you realize you're doing the same thing — leaning in toward the screen just as the cosmonauts lean toward their radio.

Finding dinosaurs on Venus may seem just as ridiculous as the monsters discovered in dozens of D-grade space operas, but in 1962 Venus was thought to be quite Earth-like and science had not yet learned of the 800-degree temperatures and sulfuric acid clouds. The Venusian dinos serve a story purpose — setting up the conundrum of how an intelligent race could have existed during the planet's dinosaur age — and are never treated as "movie monsters." The dinosaur simulations are serviceable if not quite up to the level of the overall effects. The Brontosaurus doesn't move too much but looks fine, although the bronto shots early and late in the film seem to be of two different models. The "lizard-men" are designed well enough that, in concert with the quick cuts and obfuscating haze, they also come off satisfactorily. Unfortunately, the pterosaur attack is probably the least effective moment in the film. The beast is puppeteered and photographed well but is let down by its design. Conversely, the flesh-eating plant is outstanding. It is the best-looking, most plausible — really, *only* plausible — carnivorous plant in dinomovie history.

With so much of *Planeta Burg* having been ripped loose and patched together to make *Voyage to the Prehistoric Planet*, *Voyage to the Planet of Prehistoric Women*, and — minus the dinosaurs—*Queen of Blood* (1966), Klushantsev's original film has been unfairly ignored. From its on-target space travel sequences to its intelligent story, from its superior and resourceful special effects to its *really cool* "final shot" (not revealed in the preceding plot summary), *Planeta Burg* is one of the few truly good space-based science fiction films of the 1960s.

PEOPLE AND PRODUCTION: If the remarkable films and visual effects spearheaded by Pavel Klushantsev and his countrymen are finally starting to be noticed by American genre fans, it is entirely due to the efforts of effects artist-historian Robert Skotak. With brother Dennis, Skotak has been responsible for some of the most singularly unforgettable effects sequences of the eighties and nineties, including the Drop Ship crash in *Aliens* (1986) and the nuclear strike nightmare in *Terminator 2: Judgment Day* (1991). Himself a master of miniatures and models, Skotak appreciated and brought to light the earlier work of Klushantsev and other Russian filmmakers in a segment of the *Movie Magic* television series, and then much more comprehensively in his "Red Star Rising" series for *Outré* magazine. The background information in the following paragraphs is but a tiny abstract of Skotak's exhaustive work.

It is difficult to comprehend what conditions were really like in the Soviet Union of the 1960s. In "The Making of *Storm Planet*" (part 11 of "Red Star Rising") Klushantsev spoke of the level of detail his schedules were required to specify — not only descriptions of scenes but exact calendars, estimated costs, and even the amount of film to be exposed on a given day. The groundbreaking nature of Klushantsev's special effects made the monetary predictions all but impossible.

Klushantsev tended to employ the same artists and technicians from film to film and *Planeta Burg* featured several of his regulars, including cinematographer Arkadii Klimov, artist Ivan Ivanovich Yegorov, and effects cameraman Anatoli Lavrentyev. Studio filming took place in Leningrad at the Studio for Popular Science Films. Selected locations included the Crimean city of Yalta, and Vyborg, near Finland's border, for the exteriors of the *Sirius* and its landing area. Primeval-looking prop vegetation was used to dress up the already-striking landscapes. "The whole picture had to be filmed during gloomy weather," Klushantsev told Skotak, "and for Leningrad, that is typical."

SPECIAL EFFECTS: Klushantsev insisted upon the maximum level of reality for the picture's hardware. All of the spaceship interiors and exteriors, space suits, and other props were designed with the cooperation of personnel from the real Soviet space program. The procedural aspects of space flight were also reproduced, or in some cases predicted, based on the latest science. The major props and sets were constructed at plants which actually manufactured analogous items — the hovercar was made by automobile workers, the ships' interiors came from an aeronautical factory, and so on. Robot John was developed with input from many, but principally by artist-designer Alexander Nadyezhin. Inside the fiberglass robot suit was a champion wrestler named Prudkovskii, his great strength making John's on-screen heroics possible.

Several techniques were used for the dinosaur effects. The "Pteradactylus" was designed, built and operated by artists borrowed from the Leningrad Puppet Theater, who also provided the puppet cosmonauts to ride inside the miniature version of the hovercar. For the "lizard-men," young teen boys were dressed in dinosaur outfits meticulously made by a Leningrad theater costumer. "They [the outfits] were assembled out of cast latex rubber scale sections," Skotak wrote, "and glued onto specially sewn body suits." For one brief "atmosphere" shot, live turtles were fitted with dorsal sails, *One Million B.C.* style. The brontosaur's first appearance was realized as a live-action puppet, flawlessly combined with a human actor in a still-impressive "forced perspective" composite. And the meat-eating plant (a "Venus" fly trap?), also the work of Nadyezhin's group, was operated by a combination of coil springs to provide a winding action for the larger tentacles, and an off-camera crew with fishing poles and black wires for the smaller tentacles. *Planeta Burg* was successfully completed under the most difficult conditions, Klushantsev said, because his team was "full of enthusiasm and eager for a monstrously laborious work."

Prehistoric Beast

****   1985, USA. C, 10m.

CREDITS: *A Film by* Phil Tippett. *Editor* Julie Roman. *Music* Mark Adler. *Additional Cinematography* Terry Chostner. *Animation Assistant* Sarah Bruce.

Alberta, Canada — 65 million years ago. It's a moonlit night in the late Cretaceous, and strange animal sounds reverberate through the conifer forests. A cunning, carnivorous Tyrannosaurus rex tears the last shreds from a recent kill, meaning she'll soon have to hunt again. At dawn, a small Monoclonius herd grazes near the edge of the meat-eater's territory, and one incautious member, searching for more of his favorite flowering plant, wanders into the woods. Focused too intently on his treat, he isn't aware that the towering predator is approaching. When he finally senses danger, it's too late. The Monoclonius tries to keep his single horn and protective frill toward his attacker, but the theropod is too agile and determined. Despite a valiant struggle and one on-target thrust by the ceratopsian's horn, the outcome is inevitable.

Unaware of the drama that has claimed one of their own, the rest of the herd munches idly away, while the hunter prepares for the next time …

COMMENTARY: It is very hard to discuss Phil Tippett's *Prehistoric Beast* without getting carried away. It is ten minutes of dinosaur bliss.

Technically speaking, it's virtually flawless; artistically speaking, it's nothing short of *beautiful*. From the incredible skies full of pinks and purples, to the humid richness of the forests, the vignette unfolds in a world that looks utterly real and yet better than real. It's a sort of *enhanced* reality, like a great painter might achieve, and the lighting effects would certainly do a Renaissance master proud. In daytime, the shafts of sunlight filter through the forest canopy and cast dappled patterns on the dinosaurs' skin. At night, cold, silver moonlight reveals their nocturnal activities with an eerie sheen.

The near-perfect music is ominous and anticipatory but never obtrusive, and the camerawork is consistently inventive and full of energy. Dinosaur's-eye point-of-view shots, from both predator and prey, heighten the life-or-death scenario. The hunter's vision is sure and steady, always fixed confidently ahead, while the victim's eyes dart back and forth as he desperately tries to find a way out. During the fight itself, the "cameraman" seems to struggle to keep the thrashing beasts in frame, just as a real wildlife photographer would while shooting a lion subduing a gazelle on the Serengeti.

Then there are the dinosaurs. The animation puppets are amazing, especially the Monoclonius. In its painstaking detail — its wrinkles and scars and warts and patterns — the horned beast can hold its own against anything in *Jurassic Park*. It has to be one of the all-time best stop-motion puppets, and the T. rex is very nearly its match. All of these great qualities would be wasted, though, if the animation was not also of the highest caliber, but of course it is. Tippett's work here is exceptional, full of flourishes and characterization but never straying into implausibility. The rex is simultaneously stealthy and powerful, and the Monoclonius' gait is perhaps the best stop-motion ceratopsian "walk" ever done.

Phil Tippett animates his ill-fated Monoclonius protagonist amid miniature redwood trees salvaged from *Return of the Jedi.*

Prehistoric Beast was a labor of love, and it shows. There can be no argument — it is one of the most successful attempts ever made to convey in the stop-motion medium the grandeur of these animals and their environment. Watching *Prehistoric Beast* emphatically underscores just how fortunate it was for Steven Spielberg, Universal Studios, and dinomovie fans that Phil Tippett stayed aboard on *Jurassic Park.*

PEOPLE AND PRODUCTION: It was the mid–1980s, *Return of the Jedi* was completed, and Phil Tippett decided to take a break from feature work and begin a personal project he had been thinking about. "I had been working pretty intensively [at ILM] for a number of years," Tippett told this author, "and I took about nine months off and made my own project: *Prehistoric Beast.*"

Somewhat like Ray Harryhausen's *Evolution,* the film was originally conceived as a very ambitious effort. "I had been wanting to make a dinosaur feature for quite a while, and this was going to be like an 'episode' from it," Tippett recalled. "Then I culled it down from there for production reasons ... it was turned much more into like a teaser/trailer design." Tippett also thought that the film might find a niche in the educational arena. "Tom Smith was the general manager of Churchill Films at the time, and he was thinking about doing some quasi-educational type things," Tippett recalled. "Not really dry documentaries, but kind of action-oriented tales that would be somewhat representative of the way the creatures actually moved." The idea never panned out, however. "My idea was to educate through entertainment, but nobody quite bought that. At the same time the whole industry was undergoing a huge change as well, from film to tape, and *Prehistoric Beast* never found any kind of a market."

The little film was far from being a

castoff, however. "Ultimately, it paid itself back many many times," Tippett said. "I licensed it to a number of different places." Two of its higher-profile exposures were on Microsoft's *Dinosaurs* CD-ROM (hosted by Don Lessem), and as part of a glossy made-for-television documentary called *Dinosaur!* The TV special, narrated by Christopher Reeve, also featured a great deal of new animation created by Tippett expressly for the program.

Though *Prehistoric Beast* was very much Tippett's project, he did get a little assist from his friends. "Randy Dutra helped me make the molds on some of the puppets—we stayed up all night making molds once," Tippett remembered. "And some of the armatures, Tom St. Amand helped me out on. Randy also helped me out on a couple of shots; it was his first foray into animation." True to the history of intrepid FX artists, Phil made the most of available resources. "*Return of the Jedi* had wrapped up," he noted, "and they had thrown a bunch of the model trees, of the redwood forest from the speeder bike chase, into the trash. So I scavenged those for my forest." Ultimately, Tippett feels the endeavor's greatest value was the opportunity to see a production through from beginning to end. "It was a good project for me, in that I had never before taken a film all the way to completion," he concluded. "So it was an exercise in getting something *finished*."

As a footnote, the film's title was derived from some dialogue in one of Tippett's early inspirations, *King Kong*. Any *Kong* fan will recall Jack Driscoll and Carl Denham walking past the fallen stegosaur. "Dinosaur, eh?" Driscoll asks, and Denham replies, "Yes, Jack ... a prehistoric beast!"

The Prehistoric Man

not viewed 1908, U.K. Urban/Eclipse. BW, Silent.

CREDITS: *Director* Walter R. Booth.

Live action comedy by former stage magician W. R. Booth, whose cinematic endeavors date back as far as the late 19th century. In this short feature, an artist draws a caveman which proceeds to chase the artist. In a stroke of inspiration, the artist draws a dinosaur to eat the caveman.

Prehistoric Peeps

not viewed 1905, U.K. Hepworth Manufacturing Company. BW, Silent.

CREDITS: *Director* Lewin Fitzhamon. *Producer* Cecil Hepworth.
CAST: Sebastian Smith, Hetty Potter, Lottie Martin, Wordsworth Harrison.

The earliest known film to include dinosaurs, based on a successful cartoon series which ran in Britain's *Punch* magazine. The short entry on *Prehistoric Peeps* in the British Film Institute's website archive states that the dinosaurs were "played by actors inside pantomime models." The film also contains appearances by a giant and an ape-man.

Prehistoric Poultry

★★½ 1917, USA. Edison/Conquest Pictures. BW, Silent.

CREDITS: *Director/Animator* Willis O'Brien.

Subtitled "The Dinornis or Great Roaring Whiffenpoof." The prehistoric bird Dinornis, described as "the ancestor of our modern chicken" with "long legs and a kind face," gets falsely blamed when a hunter's catapult-fired rock hits a caveman in the head. The feathered creature takes revenge by loading the hunter into his own catapult and launching him through the air. A domesticated Brontosaurus eats a tree in a brief cameo appearance.

Prehysteria

"They're back, man ... and they're lookin' for trouble."

** 1993, USA. Moonbeam/Paramount. C, 84m.

CREDITS: *Directors* Albert Band, Charles Band. *Producers* Charles Band, Debra Dion (coproducer), Peter Von Sholly (coproducer). *Screenplay* Greg Suddeth and Mark Goldstein; based on an original idea by Peter Von Sholly. *Visual Effects Supervisor* David Allen. *Animation* David Allen, Chris Endicott. *Puppet Effects Supervisor* Mark A. Rappaport. *Dinosaurs Sculpted and Designed by* Andrea Von Sholly.

CAST: *Frank Taylor* Brett Cullen. *Vicki Vandell* Colleen Morris. *Monica Taylor* Samantha Mills. *Jerry Taylor* Austin O'Brien. *Rico Sarno* Stephen Lee. *Louis* Tony Longo. *Ritchie* Stuart Fratkin.

AD LINE: "They're the world's oldest party animals."

Somewhere in the South American rain forest, a native guide leads greedy fossil hunter Rico Sarno to an amazing discovery: five dinosaur eggs preserved in the icy temperatures of a sacred cave. Meanwhile, back in the USA, widower Frank Taylor has his hands full trying to raise his two kids and turn a modest profit from his small raisin farm. Teenage Monica gives him a lot of headaches, but her younger, more level-headed brother, Jerry, actually helps out by gathering and cleaning specimens to sell in the nearby rock shop ... owned by Rico Sarno.

The Taylors visit Sarno's shop frequently, mainly because Frank is steadily falling in love with Sarno's beautiful assistant, Vicki. On the day Sarno returns from his expedition, a mix-up of look-alike picnic coolers transports the dino eggs to the Taylors' basement. Their family dog, Ruby, recently suffered the trauma of having her puppies given away and is only too happy to foster the soon-to-hatch eggs. Jerry and Monica discover the miniature dinosaurs and proceed to name them after pop singers — Hammer the Chasmosaurus, Jagger the Stegosaurus, Paula the Brachiosaurus, Madonna the Pteranodon, and Elvis the Tyrannosaurus rex. Frank is dumbfounded by the minimenagerie but quickly realizes he has bigger problems when a distraught Vicki asks for his help. She tells of how Sarno turned violent, and how she defended herself with a handy chunk of bedrock. "You killed Fred Flintstone?" Frank quips, but when the crazed Sarno shows up with two hired goons the Taylors are forced to relinquish the dinosaurs. Sarno underestimates the cleverness of his adversaries, however, and an embarrassing surprise awaits him during his gala unveiling.

COMMENTARY: The unimaginative "family" entertainment of the eighties and nineties recycled certain plot devices to the point that they became utter clichés, and most of them can be found in *Prehysteria*. First you need a cartoonish villain, accompanied by a couple of even more cartoonish henchmen. The villain's motive must be financial, and often someone who works for him will eventually change sides. You need a well-meaning but clueless and ineffectual set of parents, or more often for some reason, a single parent. You must have a precocious kid or two who are ten times smarter than the parent or the villain, and give them some mildly vulgar "PG-rated" dialogue. Finally, you need a motivation to bring all these clichés together, and in *Prehysteria*, it is a quintet of tiny dinosaurs.

The first 15 minutes demonstrate that *Prehysteria* has many problems. The opening scenes cut repeatedly back and forth between Sarno's South American safari and the Taylors' farm. Might it not have played better to keep the jungle sequence as a self-contained prologue and try to establish a passably mysterious mood? There is a neat moment when the native bearers hear a "taboo" word and scamper ominously into the underbrush, that hints at what could have been. But the choppy intercutting, and the immediate realization that Sarno is going to be a buffoon, pretty much sink the entire first act.

There are attempts to flesh out the Tay-

Jerry (Austin O'Brien) and Monica (Samantha Mills) shmooze with the diminutive dinosaurs of *Prehysteria*.

lors with a backstory and some family stresses, but it's all far too stereotyped. The first time we see teenage Monica, she's talking on the phone, painting her toenails, and chirping dialogue like "IsweartoGod!" It's also puzzling—and vaguely disturbing—that she is dressed in progressively skimpier and sluttier outfits as the movie proceeds. Worse yet is her boyfriend, "Brain-dead Danny," a humorless slacker, surfer-dude type who is almost intolerable.

On a better note, *Prehysteria* is buoyed by one of Richard Band's best scores and some likeable actors who do their darnedest to liven things up. Brett Cullen projects a comfortable, good-guy demeanor and has a nice chemistry with gorgeous Colleen Morris (who uncannily resembles a young Sharon Stone). The kids are fine—Austin O'Brien seems a natural actor, and the fact that Samantha Mills manages to play the bratty Monica without making the viewer throw heavy objects at the screen should probably qualify her for some sort of award. Stephen Lee undoubtedly could have played Sarno as a seething, capable, and at least somewhat threatening villain, but like Wayne Knight in *Jurassic Park* he never gets to do anything but sputter and rant.

The very small dinosaurs are the film's biggest stars. The scarcity of stop-motion is disappointing and the heavy reliance on cable-controlled puppets make the dinos seem awfully placebound, yet they still look surprisingly organic in many shots. Andrea Von Sholly's dino designs are beautiful, the puppets are detailed and well-crafted, and the dinosaurs are more effectively puppeteered than would be the case in either of the *Prehysteria* sequels. Even the most obvious gags, including the inevitable shot of Elvis nipping Monica's tuchis, have a sense of fun. The low budget periodically shows through—the "ancient" Indian cavern looks like it belongs in a *Carol Burnett Show* sketch—but the conscientious efforts of the folks at David Allen Productions keep the dinosaurs looking good.

Prehysteria exemplifies a too-familiar pattern in the movie business. Someone hits upon an inspired concept full of exciting possibilities, and then, as if their work is done at that point, expends little or no effort to do anything memorable with it. The *Toy Story* films had a great idea — toys coming to life when their kids are not around — and ran with it to ingenious and wonderful heights. *Prehysteria* had a great idea — pet-sized dinosaurs — then spent 84 minutes trying to figure what the heck to do with them.

PEOPLE AND PRODUCTION: When direct-to-video mogul Charles Band launched his kid-friendly Moonbeam label, it was no surprise that one of his first projects involved dinosaurs. This was after all 1993, when a half-dozen or more theatrical and videocassette dinomovies were hoping to ride *Jurassic Park* mania to a big payday. In this case, it worked. In video-biz jargon, *Prehysteria* "shipped 70,000 units" and was one of the video hits of the year. It was directed by the father-son team of Albert and Charles Band, but unlike *Doctor Mordrid* which they directed more or less in shifts, this time each Band helmed a separate unit. "It became a practical matter really, because we had to get the schedule done," Albert explained. "Some actors were sitting, not doing anything ... while others were doing something else, so we took advantage."

The *Prehysteria* concept grew out of storyboard artist Peter Von Sholly's "childhood fascination" with dinosaurs and pets. "When I was a little kid, I used to have dreams occasionally of having little pet dinosaurs in terrariums and things," Von Sholly said. "It was just something that stayed with me." He had tried to interest various studios in his "pet" project for some time, without success. "I couldn't understand why nobody wanted to do this picture," he told author Bill Warren. Then, while doing some storyboarding for David Allen, Von Sholly asked Allen to show the script to Charles Band. "Pete came to me with this idea, and I thought it was just great," Band recalled. "I was beginning to work on the whole Moonbeam idea ... and this made perfect sense as a Moonbeam film." Writers Greg Suddeth and Mark Goldstein were brought aboard to rework the screenplay, a potentially costly plot twist involving the dinosaurs growing to full size was eliminated, and *Prehysteria* was a go.

Band had the good fortune, foresight, or both, to cast young Austin O'Brien just before he teamed up with Arnold Schwarzenegger on the heavily hyped misfire, *The Last Action Hero*. Ironically, with *Hero* being devoured whole by Steven Spielberg's dinosaurs, it was Austin's modest "little" dinomovie that was, in its arena, much more successful than his big-screen blockbuster.

SPECIAL EFFECTS: With five prehistoric stars to design and sculpt, Peter Von Sholly knew where to turn. His wife, Andrea, is a talented sculptress and like Peter a big dinosaur enthusiast. "They as a team spearheaded the whole design aspect of the dinosaurs," said Chris Endicott, a mainstay at David Allen Productions and a puppeteer-animator on *Prehysteria*. "They're definitely of the 'Mark Hallett' school, in that kind of direction, if you know your dinosaur illustrators," Endicott asserted. "Peter is a dinosaur illustrator himself, and the designs are definitely to their credit." Peter was on set almost every day and devised many of the dinos' little "bits of business," often right on the spot. "He'd come up with a whole new sequence, and storyboard it over lunch!" Endicott observed.

Like many science-fiction and fantasy films over the years, *Prehysteria* was originally slated to be a more elaborate production. Also as usual, the special effects budget absorbed a big chunk of the cutbacks. Chris Endicott recalled the disappointments. "There were tons of stop-motion shots that had been planned, *tons*, that either got cut out of the picture or turned into RC or cable-controlled puppet shots," he told the author. Only a handful of animation cuts were ultimately filmed, mostly of Madonna the Pteranodon. "A beautiful shot of the Pteranodon

Video poster, featuring Austin O'Brien and a trio of pygmy dinos, simply but successfully tells the prospective movie-renter everything he or she needs to know about *Prehysteria.*

landing on the girl's finger was animated by David," Endicott said. "The hand is a prop, a casting, animated on a little mover, so that's why the puppet and hand match so perfectly." The T. rex and Chasmosaurus were limited to just one animated shot apiece. The shot of the T. Rex walking across the kitchen floor while Austin O'Brien looks through the refrigerator was animated by Chris Endicott in front of a blue screen; David Allen animated the chasmosaur running up and bumping a closed door. "So that's why you build a stop-motion T. rex for only one shot, and why you build a stop-motion chasmosaur for only one shot," Endicott lamented, "because you didn't originally plan them to be one shot."

Most of the dino scenes utilized cable-controlled and rod-puppeted models. "David was there as the director of all the puppeteering," Endicott explained, "and Mark Rappaport was the lead puppeteer." Other members of the puppeteering crew included Stephen R. Barr, Connie Anglund, and Shaun Smith, but as Endicott said, "if there was a vision behind the way that picture looks in terms of the on-set puppeteering, it was David Allen directing the puppeteers." It is probably unfortunate for the quality of the film as a whole that Allen wasn't given more of a say in story matters. "I did come up with some sight gags and editorial suggestions," Allen told Bill Warren. "I did a lot of pseudo-second unit and insert direction on the film, about 20 or so shots, in scenes where the actors were gone and the dinosaurs were on screen by themselves."

The cabled dinosaurs were fairly complex creations. "Jurgen Heimann, under Mark Rappaport, was in charge of the mechanics for the dinosaurs, and they were very sophisticated," Endicott noted. "Especially the Brachiosaurus—the neck movement on that thing was so complicated. In fact it was *so* complicated only *he* could do it, because if you didn't know how to operate the control, you could easily break it." Heimann and the brachiosaur aside, no single puppeteer was really assigned to any one character. "You can't really say who did what, as far as the puppeteering goes," Endicott pointed out, "Because Rappaport liked to make sure everybody got a chance to do everything."

Simultaneously operating five cabled creatures on one small set is inherently troublesome. "You have so many constraints," Mark Rappaport explained. "You have the set constraints, you have multiple puppeteers, sometimes up to 18 puppeteers hidden in different areas ... logistically it's incredible." For scenes requiring Madonna to be operated while perched on Monica's shoulder, "we made a special vest for the actress to wear under her clothing," Rappaport revealed. "It's comfortable, it stretches, and ... all the different servos and motors we have [hidden] in the back." Perhaps "comfortable" is a matter of opinion, however. "It's kind of awkward," Samantha Mills commented, "because it goes out a little more than you're used to and you have to get out of the way of everything. Usually I have Connie [Anglund] with me, because she sort of babysits the pterodactyl while I'm wearing her."

When on-set performance was not an option, the cable-puppet dinos were photographed in front of a blue screen and composited with background plates in postproduction. "With the Madonna character especially, and with some of the walking dinosaurs, there was a lot of blue-screen photography," Endicott recalled. This work was done at David Allen Productions, and as Endicott emphasized, "it was not done with anybody watching a clock. We'd do quite a few takes on that stuff and we were able to rehearse a lot." This extra effort paid off in that the blue screen shots feature some of the film's best puppeteering.

Prehysteria 2

"Stop this ridiculous behavior immediately!"

*½ 1994, USA. Moonbeam/Paramount. C, 81m.

CREDITS: *Director* Albert Band. *Producers* Albert Band, Charles Band (executive), Jerry Goldberg (associate). *Screenplay* Brent Friedman and Michael Davis; based on an original idea by Pete Von Sholly. *Creature Effects Shop Supervisor* Mark Rappaport. *Special Visual Effects* David Allen, Chris Endicott, Brett White. *Stop-Motion Animation* Yan Guo.

CAST: *Brendan* Kevin R. Connors. *Naomi* Jennifer Harte. *Mr. Wellington* Dean Scofield. *Miss Winters* Bettye Ackerman. *Ivan* Greg Lewis. *Mr. Hiro* Michael Hagiwara. *Mr. Cranston* Owen Bush. *Ketchum* Larry Hankin. *Killum* Alan Palo.

AD LINE: "The oldest party animals are back."

When the Taylor family takes a vacation, they leave kindly Mr. Cranston to "dino-sit" their tiny prehistoric pets. However, through an improbable sequence of events, the little stinkers hitch a ride halfway across the country on a freight car. They are jointly discovered by a resourceful tomboy named Naomi, and a classic "poor little rich boy" named Brendan J. Wellington. Terrorized by his lemon-pussed governess, Miss Winters, and starved for attention from his business-obsessed father, Brendan begins to find friendship with Naomi as they haggle over ownership of the dinos. Looking for a place to hide the critters from a pair of overzealous exterminators hired by Miss Winters, Brendan discovers his dad's childhood playroom and decides to renovate the dusty old train set as a birthday surprise. But his father doesn't return from his business trip as promised, and Brendan hurts Naomi's feelings when Miss Winters throws the girl out of the house and he fails to come to her defense. Things turn even worse when Miss Winters confiscates the dinosaurs and locks Brendan in his room. But Naomi, unable to stay mad, springs Brendan from solitary and with the help of Ivan the gardener and Mr. Hiro the chef, the kids spring the dinos. Dad finally gets home, and when he sees his son sleeping in the playroom next to his old train set, he smashes his cell phone, tells Miss Winters off, and sets about making up for lost time.

COMMENTARY: *Prehysteria 2* is an utterly forgettable sequel, failing even more grievously than its predecessor to exploit the possibilities of its premise. Other than the fact that the creatures were dinosaurs in the first film, there's no reason for them to be dinosaurs here. They could be aliens or leprechauns or groundhogs and still serve the humdrum story just as well.

The only slightly noteworthy aspect of *Prehysteria 2* is its willingness to magnify some of its clichés beyond triteness into the realm of the absurd, and it was this factor which led Albert Band to direct the film. "It's very very zany," Band asserted. "We did things in every department that were unrealistic, and yet it worked very well." The scattershot gags register only occasional hits, as when the paramilitary exterminators insist on communicating via walkie-talkie even though they're two feet from each other. Greg Lewis is an enjoyable character actor, and Michael Hagiwara's comic skills make Mr. Hiro's shtick — speaking almost exclusively in pop song titles — almost funny.

As a dinosaur movie, though, *Prehysteria 2* is dreadful. The story is disastrously slow and full of filler, and doesn't seem to end so much as just ... stop. The little dinos are given even sillier antics, like using their tails to pick locks and paint toys, and laughing like cartoon characters at their own shenanigans. Less thought and rehearsal obviously went into the puppet performances, and the Stegosaurus in particular looks to have almost stopped functioning. There are only two eye-opening FX shots: one elegant stop-motion cut of the Pteranodon coming to light, and a nifty composite of the Chasmosaurus ambling all the way across a reflective floor. And look fast for what is (I think) a reference to the T. rex "main road" sequence in *Jurassic Park*.

So great is the appeal of dinosaurs, *Prehysteria 2* was one of the most successful video releases of the year despite its woeful quality. Just think how it might have done had it possessed the slightest bit of imagination.

SPECIAL EFFECTS: By the time *Prehysteria 2* was under way, Mark Rappaport's studio was in charge of all on-set puppet/creature effects for Full Moon, while David Allen and his studio dealt exclusively with the visual effects and stop-motion elements. In fact, several key players from the original film had reduced roles for the sequel. Peter Von Sholly's input diminished significantly, and *Prehysteria* codirector and producer Charles Band took only an executive producer credit.

Prehysteria 2 leans even more heavily than did the original on live-action puppets, photographed on-set, for its dinosaur scenes. With "Elvis" the T. rex still the featured dino, several versions of the puppet were created for specific duties. "There are four different puppets for the T. rex," Mark Rappaport revealed in a "making of" featurette. "There's the [fully] cabled puppet which is very involved, there's the 'biting' head [an insert head and neck for eating and biting close-ups], there's a stop-motion puppet, and the 'stunt' puppet — he's the one who gets beat up." It's doubtful that the stop-motion T. rex received much wear, since it was not used at all.

The stop-motion in *Prehysteria 2* is extremely limited, as Chris Endicott explained. "There are two stop-motion shots. One where Madonna flies in above the other dinosaurs — the stop-motion is just for the Pteranodon; the dinosaurs on the ground were shot on-set and are part of the background plate." The other shot occurs seconds later when Madonna lands on the raisin crate. "This was all animated by Yan Guo," Endicott said. "He's been Paul Jessel's assistant animator on many projects, and is quite an animator in his own right."

The limited involvement of David Allen's studio also included a live-action puppet sequence and one motion control shot. "David supervised one on-set gag," said Endicott, referring to the scene of Miss Winters chasing the dinos down the hall. "The puppeteers were sitting on a dolly and the rods were attached to the dolly ... so the dinosaurs could look like they were really covering ground," Endicott disclosed. "That was the kind of stuff that David would push for, that everybody else would say, 'oh, that's too hard; they'll just have to stand there.'" In another shot, motion control technology was employed to show Hammer running through the mansion's foyer. "That shot was done with the chasmosaur puppeteered in place while the motion control rig moved along the dinosaur, implying movement," Endicott revealed.

Prehysteria 3

"That's maximum whacked."
* ½ 1995, USA. Moonbeam/Paramount. C, 84m.

CREDITS: *Director* Julian Breen (David DeCoteau). *Producers* Karen L. Spencer, Charles Band (executive). *Screenplay* Michael Davis and Neil Ruttenberg; based on original characters by Peter Von Sholly. *Story* Brent Friedman. *Visual Effects* Alchemy FX. *Creature Effects* Mark Rappaport. *Digital Matte Paintings* Randall William Cook.

CAST: *Ella MacGregor* Whitney Anderson. *Thomas MacGregor* Fred Willard. *Uncle Hal* Bruce Weitz. *Michelle MacGregor* Pam Matteson. *Heath MacGregor* Dave Buzzotta. *Needlemeyer* Matt Letscher. *Mr. Yamamoto* John Fujioka. *Mr. Cranston* Owen Bush.

AD LINE: "A comedy that's far above par!"

Hal MacGregor, smarmy resident pro at the King's Road Country Club, has Japanese investor Mr. Yamamoto on the hook to finance his dream resort. But first he must get his hands on the adjoining, run-down miniature golf course owned by his brother Thomas. Hal's niece Ella, who's crazy about anything to do with golf or Scotland, doesn't want her dad to sell, and is more interested in helping him get over the choked putt that has haunted him for 15 years. She gets some unexpected help when five miniature dinosaurs show up, wearing name tags reading Elvis, Hammer, Jagger, Paula, and Madonna. "Too bad none of you crooners are named after Rod Stewart," she laments. The critters

give Thomas a great idea and soon his renovated "Dino-Putt" is buzzing with customers, raising hopes that he will be able to pay off his loan and keep the property. But Hal's scheming once again kills business, and in desperation Ella challenges the gambling-obsessed Hal to a winner-take-all minigolf match. The little dinos and Ella's brother Heath (wearing a Godzilla suit) foil the sabotage efforts of Hal's lackey, Needlemeyer, while Mr. Yamamoto watches and yells "Gojira!" When Thomas finally realizes that his "choke" was really caused by Hal's cheating, he tells his brother off and inspires Ella on to victory.

COMMENTARY: *Prehysteria 3* is not what one would expect from the third installment in the disappointing *Prehysteria* series. Not that it ever resembles a competent movie — it doesn't — but it's so gleefully goofy that it's almost watchable.

Except for the inexplicable idea of putting the "pee-wee dinosaurs" into a golf comedy (?), things start out predictably. Stock characters and plot devices are all in place, including the worn-out "bank note coming due" routine. But the deeper into the movie we go the weirder things get, and by the time it's all over we have witnessed spoofs of or references to *Star Trek*, *Marathon Man*, *Apocalypse Now*, *Caddyshack*, *Godzilla*, the "Zapruder Film," Sean Connery, Grant Woods' painting *American Gothic*, the King Arthur/Excalibur legend, and a "Grey Poupon" commercial. The dinosaurs' antics are even more cartoonish than in *Prehysteria 2*, but puppet sequence director Jesse H. Long offers several extreme closeups which really show off the creatures' impressive detail.

Despite the wildly fluctuating quality of Moonbeam Entertainment's video releases, one constant has been the presence of likable kid actors who don't ham it up on camera, and the youngsters in the *Prehysteria* series — Austin O'Brien, Samantha Mills, Kevin Connors, Jennifer Harte, and here, Whitney Anderson — are all appealing. Fred Willard can be hilarious but has nothing to work with this time, Bruce Weitz is joyously obnoxious, and both of the last two *Prehysteria* entries should have given more screen time to the enjoyable and underused Owen Bush.

The chief aim of the makers of *Prehysteria 3* was obviously to get it done with a minimum of time and money, and there's little evidence that anyone was interested in quality. Its over-the-top outrageousness makes it atypical and occasionally diverting, but never for a moment very *good*.

SPECIAL EFFECTS: As the *Prehysteria* films grew less and less ambitious from an FX standpoint, the perceived need for the input of David Allen Productions decreased. After a minimal contribution to *Prehysteria 2*, Allen's studio had no connection at all to number three, even though Allen and Chris Endicott are in the credits. "Dave DeCoteau and I go back to high school, and for some reason he put David and me in the credits," Endicott told the author. "But we didn't do *anything* on that movie." No blue screen or stop-motion work was done for *Prehysteria 3*, and there are almost no scenes of the dinosaurs performing with the actors. The dino shots were photographed as inserts after principal photography wrapped, and the puppets' delicate mechanisms were plainly showing some wear.

The input of Peter Von Sholly, upon whose concept the series was based, also declined from film to film. On the first film, he had been extremely excited to see his ideas brought to life by David Allen and crew, but from there on things went steadily downhill. Von Sholly storyboarded all three entries, but had little creative say in the last two. "He wasn't very involved and he was very despondent about how badly he felt it was all handled," recalled Endicott, lamenting the haste which dominates most low-budget productions. "On the first film, we did things at David's pace," he said. "We did it until it

Opposite: Ella (Whitney Anderson) and a golf-ball-juggling dinosaur dominate this video store poster for the world's only miniature-dinosaurs miniature-golf comedy, *Prehysteria 3*.

was right, or at least as best we could. David would try to hang on and see if we couldn't get a good take before we had to move on to the next shot."

Pterodactyl Woman from Beverly Hills

"Don't disempower me with infantilisms!"

** 1995, USA. Media Ventures/Troma. C, 99m.

CREDITS: *Director* Philippe Mora. *Producers* Philippe Mora, Bruce Critchley, John F. Remark, Jay Rifkin (executive), Scott Billups (coproducer), Brion James, Beverly D'Angelo, Mark Levy (associate). *Written by* Philippe Mora. *Special Effects Supervisor* Scott Billups.

CAST: *Pixie Chandler* Beverly D'Angelo. *Dick Chandler* Brad Wilson. *Sam/Salvador Dali* Brion James. *Tommy Chandler* Aron Eisenberg. *Jenny Chandler* Sharon Martin. *Dr. Egbert Drum* Stephen McHattie. *Dr. Zavenbrot* Aleks Shaklin. *Susie* Moon Zappa.

While fossil hunting on a sacred Indian burial site, paleontologist Dick Chandler angers the mysterious medicine man who calls himself Salvador Dali, and in so doing brings a curse upon his wife, Pixie. "I've just turned your wife into a pterodactyl," Dali pronounces, and when Dick returns to Beverly Hills he finds Pixie's behavior growing increasingly bizarre. She perches in trees, swallows live fish, and periodically makes complete transformations to go for nocturnal flights over southern California. When she's sighted by the pilot of a stealth fighter, Egbert Drum of the EPSA ("Extraordinary Phenomena Security Agency") investigates. "We've had horny little blue guys from Uranus, Yetis from Tibet, Bigfoot in Louisiana, trolls from Denmark, Brothers from Another Planet," Drum laments, "but this is the first talking pterodactyl from Westwood." While her husband, her teen kids, and her best friend, Susie, try to cope, Pixie seeks help from a strange guru named Sam (also a victim of a Dali curse), and discovers that she's about to lay an egg. Meanwhile, Egbert Drum recruits Sam the guru and Dr. Zavenbrot ("the world's smartest man") to help him get to the bottom of things. When a baby pterodactyl hatches from Pixie's egg, Dick suddenly remembers the whole business with Salvador Dali and his curse. With Egbert and company on their trail, Dick, Pixie, and the kids track down Dali within the "paradigm shift" that he calls home, and after an apology and impassioned plea from Dick, the curse is lifted.

COMMENTARY: Based on its title one might assume *Pterodactyl Woman from Beverly Hills* is an attempt at intentional "bad movie" camp, like the unwatchable *Attack of the Killer Tomatoes*, or some sort of juvenile spoof like *Dinosaur Babes*, but it doesn't fit either category. It's an altogether weird picture, and though it ultimately can't gather itself into a satisfying whole, it does have moments.

First and foremost, *Pterodactyl Woman* is a satire of 1990s America. Various bits make fun of holistic health, $200-an-hour therapists, self-actualization, political correctness, fashionable causes, "Superwoman" syndrome, personal space, and just about every other irritating fad of the decade. Then in the final reel, director Philippe Mora also throws in some dinomovie gags. When we learn that Salvador Dali's time-warped environment is called the "Land of Cheap Special Effects," Pixie's son is ecstatic. "Cool! Stop-motion! Men in suits! Stock footage! Digital animation!" And yes indeed, the dinos we encounter are indeed stop-motion stock footage from — what else? — *Planet of Dinosaurs*. When the *Planet* tyrannosaur shows up, the boy exclaims "Look ... Stopasaurus motionus!" Salvador has a more subdued reaction: "Bruno! Get outta here! Damn stock footage ..." These gags don't really fit with the rest of the movie, but genre fans will enjoy them. The original pterodactyl effects are very limited, consisting of a mediocre hatchling puppet, a few shots of an exceedingly rigid model during the flying scenes, and one computer-generated "morphing" shot.

The loony proceedings are enlivened by some good performances. Beverly D'Angelo is a skilled comedienne and some of her *Pterodactyl Woman* antics—like doing a lovemaking scene while wearing elaborate pterosaur makeup and a pair of prosthetic wings—should probably win her an award for sheer fearlessness. Moon Zappa, playing a talk show host who really wants to run for the Senate, shows a flair for screen comedy, and Brion James is, um, *interesting*, in his dual role as Sam and Salvador. Stephen McHattie as the acerbic, joyless EPSA agent (Sam calls him "morgue features") is given the choicest lines. "I'm the best bull — — detector in the U.S. government," he gravely informs the stealth fighter pilot. "That's why I'm tired all the time." The camerawork by Walter Bal is unusual without being gimmicky, and the catchy, percussion-driven music score by Roy Hay (formerly of the pop group Culture Club) is a nice bonus.

It's tempting to describe *Pterodactyl Woman from Beverly Hills* as "off-the-wall," but it's actually somewhere on the other side of the wall. It's a wildly uneven hodgepodge of sight gags, satire, and silliness, with just enough cleverness and intelligence to avoid laying an egg.

The Puppetoon Movie

*"I think we better give Gumby
a little sample of what I mean!"*

***½ 1987, USA. Leibovit
Productions Ltd. C, 79m.

CREDITS: *Producers* Arnold Leibovit, Fantasy II (associate). *Voice Director and Screenplay (Prologue)* Arnold Leibovit. *Sequence Director (Prologue)* Gene Warren, Jr. *Prologue Animated by* Peter Kleinow. *Artistic Finishing* ("Arnie the Dinosaur") Charlie and Steve Chiodo.
VOICES (prologue/epilogue): Paul Frees, Dallas McKennon, Art Clokey, Dick Beals.

The examples chosen for *The Puppetoon Movie* provide an enjoyable initiation into the singular brand of animation magic that was, and is, George Pal's Puppetoons. This selection of Pal's inventive shorts includes favorites such as *Tubby the Tuba* and *John Henry and the Inky Poo*, musical extravaganzas like *Jasper in a Jam* and *Philips Cavalcade*, out-and-out comedies like *Together in the Weather*, and traditional tales—albeit with a Pal twist—like *The Sleeping Beauty*. *The Little Broadcast*, *The Philips Broadcast of 1938*, *Hoola Boola*, *South Sea Sweethearts*, and *Tulips Shall Grow* complete this sampler.

The classic shorts are bookended by a newly filmed prologue and epilogue, done entirely in stop-motion animation. The new segments feature "Arnie the Dinosaur," (a T. rex type), along with Art Clokey's Gumby and Pokey. The vignette casts Gumby as a film director, Pokey as his assistant, and Arnie as his star villain. It seems Arnie is failing to suitably terrify Barbara the deer, having been mellowed by Pal's gentle and benevolent aura. Gumby can't figure it out until Arnie unspools a collection of Puppetoons for him, and then he finally understands.

COMMENTARY: Arnold Leibovit wanted to do more than splice together a "best of" reel when he decided to make this feature-length anthology. He wanted to make it a film unto itself, and the animated sequences he devised to frame the compilation are appropriate and great fun. The quality of the new animation is a fine match for Pal's lovingly crafted Puppetoons, and there's something very "right" in a group of fantasy characters paying tribute to Pal. "Without George," Arnie the Dinosaur says, "some of us might never have been born." The line was inspired by a comment Art Clokey once made to Leibovit, asserting that he would never have created Gumby had it not been for Pal's influence.

Anyone accustomed to the cheap-jack animation that has predominated since the 1960s will be surprised if not astonished by the opulent staging, meticulous choreography, and intricate detail of Pal's films. Even the simplest of them must have been unbelievably labor-intensive, and they cover a variety of themes. There's humor — and even some double entendres — in *Together in the Weather*, powerful imagery in the Nazi allegory, *Tulips Shall Grow*, and the stunningly realized folk tale of *John Henry and the Inky Poo*, and marvelous music in almost all of them, by such artists as Charlie Barnet and Jack Hylton. Barnet and his orchestra provide a jazz tour de force for *Jasper in a Jam*, a toe-tapping session of cornet-playing totem poles and wah-wah-ing moose heads. The recurring "Jasper" character has brought criticism and charges of racial stereotyping upon the films, but there's clearly no malice involved. Pal himself had fled prewar Europe to *escape* persecution, and anyone who ever met the man knew that he would be the last person to ever create anything deliberately hurtful.

Though *The Puppetoon Movie* is principally a tribute to Pal and the Puppetoons, the presence of Arnie the Dinosaur is what qualifies it for this volume. Arnie's scenes are pure pleasure, proving Pete Kleinow to be a master not only of naturalistic animation but character animation as well. The miniature sets are impeccable with a multitude of details, including a collection of Pal movie posters reproduced in miniature and placed around the walls of Arnie's projection room. The final scene is a stop-motion lover's dream with a veritable swarm of puppets (28, according to Kleinow) from the worlds of television, commercials, and the movies. Look fast and you may see Speedy Alka-Seltzer next to the Pillsbury Dough Boy, or watch one of Joe Dante's *Gremlins* steal a scene from King Kong himself. It's a fittingly fanciful ending for this salute to cinema's gentle giant of fantasy.

PEOPLE AND PRODUCTION: George Pal's studio in the 1940s was a fertile nurturing ground for a number of artists who would have long, even legendary careers. These individuals included Wah Chang and Gene Warren, later to join with Tim Baar to form the special effects house Project Unlimited. In an interview with the author, Chang discussed his days with Pal. "I had polio, and was out for a year. Then I started work at George Pal's studio in the puppet department. I was there for a couple of years." While at Pal's, Chang met a young animator on his first professional job. "Yes, Ray Harryhausen and I got to know each other quite well and through the years have kept in contact," Chang said. "And Willis O'Brien also worked there, but he was there just a very short time." The talents of Chang and Warren, and Harryhausen and O'Brien, and Phil Kellison and Al Hamm and many others, and of course Pal himself, combined to create a group of short films that are still unique today. As Pal told Ed Naha in *Starlog* (no. 10): "The Puppetoons weren't really just for children, you know. They were for everyone."

Very popular in their era, Pal's shorts had fallen into obscurity in recent times until Arnold Leibovit took it upon himself to preserve and revive them. "I felt very strongly that these films represented some of the greatest animation in history," he said, "and yet they were in some ways all but forgotten." While working on his documentary, *The Fantasy Film Worlds of George Pal*, Leibovit screened some 16mm reels at the home of Pal's widow. "I thought to myself, 'somebody has to do something — I have to do something,'" Leibovit continued. "I found the people, I put together some money, and then started the process of transferring the nitrate prints that Mrs. Pal had allowed me to access." The film was released to theaters but has found a larger audience on home video, and as this book goes to press a pristine DVD version — with even more Puppetoons — has just been issued.

SPECIAL EFFECTS: It's natural to wonder why a dinosaur was chosen as the film's "host," given the lack of dinos in Pal's work. "I used a dinosaur because ... well, why not?" Leibovit said. "I mean, what better dimensionally animated character would you do? It just made sense to me that it should be a dinosaur." Arnie's physical features were an amalgam of several influences, starting with the T. rex designed by Jim Danforth for

Caveman. "I talked to Pete about the dinosaurs he animated for Caveman, and I liked the 'fatter' look, so we gave him a little bit more heft," Leibovit pointed out. Venerable voice actor Paul Frees, who voiced Arnie, also had an impact. "After having spent time with Paul, I decided that I would pattern the dinosaur after him," Leibovit said. "Of course, this was the last feature he narrated before his death." And yes, Arnie is named after Leibovit. "Of course, Arnie is me and Barbara [the deer] is my significant other. I did it as kind of a joke ... but it sort of just stuck."

The sequences were created at Fantasy II Film Effects, animated over a two-month period by the prolific Peter Kleinow. "I was one of the owners of Fantasy II," Kleinow told the author. "Gene Warren, Jr., and Leslie Huntley and I started that — we were all three partners." In the mid–1980s Kleinow had elected to leave the pressures of ownership behind, and he did the animation for *The Puppetoon Movie* on a freelance basis. "Gene would oversee the crew getting the sets ready and getting the lighting all set up, so I didn't have to do anything like that," Kleinow said. "Then I'd come in early in the morning and start animating, and go until late in the evening." Although one would never know it from the beautiful results, Kleinow recalled that Arnie was not the easiest puppet to work with. "That armature was very unfriendly and unforgiving — an animator *always* feels he could do better if he had a better armature!"

A fantastic amount of work went into the Arnie sequences. "Pete did a Herculean job of coming in every day and shooting those pieces, and I think it really turned out great," Leibovit emphasized. "It took a lot of work by Pete and Gene Warren and Fantasy II and a lot of the people involved. Gary Campsie put a lot of effort into building miniatures and doing great stuff. There are so many people — John Huneck, Mike Joyce, Charlie and Steve Chiodo — a *lot* of people should be given credit for that sequence." Leibovit gathered an impressive array of stop-motion puppets for the big finale, including the marvelous King Kong replica featured in David Allen's famous Volkswagen TV commercial.

The Puppetoon Movie brought Pete Kleinow's animation career full circle, as his first job in the industry had been with Art Clokey. "I saw an ad in the Pasadena newspaper saying 'animators wanted,' and it happened to be Art Clokey's studio," Kleinow remembered. "I said, 'I saw your ad for animators,' and they said, 'Oh, are you an animator?' and I said, 'Oh, sure!' I had never animated a thing in my *life*." Almost three decades later, with innumerable credits in between, Kleinow was reunited with Clokey's most famous creation. "We really smoothed out Gumby, though," Kleinow pointed out, "and made it a lot more lifelike than it had been back then."

R.F.D. 10,000 B.C.

★★½ 1917, USA. Edison/Conquest Pictures. BW, Silent.

CREDITS: *Director/Animator* Willis O'Brien.

Subtitled "A Mannikin Comedy." Johnny Bearskin is Winnie Warclub's favorite beau, but the unscrupulous mailman ("a fiend in human form!") desires Winnie and secretly swaps Bearskin's romantic valentine for his mean-spirited one. The fair-minded Brontosaurus which pulls the mail cart tears the villain in two (his running legs eventually catch up with and rejoin his top half) and reunites the true lovers, and Johnny even takes over the mail route! Like most of O'Brien's silent shorts, *10,000 B.C.* features simple miniature sets decorated with small stones and real vegetation, and backed by painted landscapes.

Raptor

"She has shut off part of her mind, to avoid thinking about it."

2001, USA. New Concorde. C, 82m.

CREDITS: *Director* Jay Andrews (Jim Wynorski). *Producer* Roger Corman. *Written by* Jay Andrews, Frances Doel, Michael B. Druxman.
CAST: *Sheriff Jim Tanner* Eric Roberts. *Dr. Hyde* Corbin Bernsen. *Barbara Phillips* Melissa Brasselle. *Capt. Connelly* Tim Abell. *Capt. York* William Monroe. *Deputy Ben Glover* Harrison Paige (Page). *Lola Tanner* Lorissa McComas.

Beret-wearing mad scientist Dr. Hyde, trying to clone "a dinosaur with a brain," has a problem in the form of a carnivorous escapee. (Possibly inspired by Fred Flintstone's brontocrane, Hyde envisions his dinosaurs being trained to perform "land clearing and mining.") Macho sheriff Jim Tanner and busty animal control officer Barbara Phillips try to stop Hyde's scheme but the dinos run amok, killing Deputy Ben and sending Jim's busty daughter into "traumatic catalepsia." Hyde captures Jim and Barbara, the dinosaurs wipe out a number of inept special forces personnel (including *Dinosaur Island* alumnus Richard Gabai), and Hyde gets eaten by his own Tyrannosaurus. Finally Jim gets mad, snarls "eat this, Barney," and kills the chief dinosaur.

COMMENTARY: *Raptor* is a fraud—a serving of stale leftovers sliced by Jim Wynorski out of *Carnosaur, Carnosaur II,* and *Carnosaur 3: Primal Species.* Nobody is credited for special effects, because all of the dinosaur sequences are taken from the *Carno*-trilogy. Fashioning a "new" film from scraps of previous ones is old hat for Roger Corman—we all remember his resourceful reworkings of Russian sci-fi pictures in the mid-sixties—but nothing before *Raptor*, not even *Voyage to the Planet of Prehistoric Women*, reeks so rancidly of contemptible, premeditated *ripoff*.

The relatively few original shots in *Raptor*—shot mostly at the Sylmar (California) Department of Water and Power—were fashioned for the sole purpose of setting up the *Carnosaur* clips. Despite eight years of aging having elapsed in the interim, actors Harrison Page and Frank Novak were brought back from the original *Carnosaur* so that their dinosaurian demises—in the town square and the laser corridor, respectively—could be clumsily worked in. Other dino-scenes reused from *Carnosaur* included the three joyriding teens, the poultry truck sequence, and the T. rex head-butting the wall. *Carnosaur II* contributes its control room raptor attack, dino-caused helicopter crash, and woman-in-the-elevator bit. *Carnosaur 3* donates the chewing-through of the elevator cables and the dino-assault on the steel cargo carrier. A plethora of quick, miscellaneous dino shots from all three movies round out the dinosaur content.

The lack of continuity is not merely obvious, but flaunted. Two different helicopter scenes from *Carnosaur II* are placed within moments of each other, turning the sky from bright sunshine to the dead of night in about eight minutes. The shipboard setting of *Carnosaur 3* explains why Hyde's (very landlocked) laboratory has *life preservers* hanging on the walls. Hyde's female flunky Karen (Teresa DePreist) is dressed similarly to Arabella Holzbog in *Carno II* so that her gory death scene can be reused, but nobody bothered to edit out the shots clearly showing Miss Holzbog's face. The finale has Tanner fighting the "alpha T. rex" with a piece of heavy equipment, using a montage of shots from *both* of the first two *Carno* flicks—really, who cares if Tanner's vehicle repeatedly changes from a grey skiploader on uneven dirt to a yellow forklift on smooth pavement?

What to say of the new cast? Corbin Bernsen manages to be simultaneously hammy and bored-looking, and the only way that former Oscar nominee Eric Roberts' career can sink any further would be an infomercial appearance. If *Raptor* does not establish a new low in crass, mercenary attempts to flim-flam gullible video-renters out of their money, it must be mighty close. Compared to this warmed-over *Carnosaur* stew, *Valley of the Dragons* and its recycling of *One Million B.C.* footage is a work of cinematic genius.

Reptilicus

"How long do you expect me to continue this hell?"

* 1962, Denmark/USA. Saga Studio/ AIP. C, 81m.

CREDITS: *Directors* Sidney Pink (U.S.), Poul Bang (Denmark). *Producers* Sidney Pink, Johann Zalabery (executive). *Screenplay* Ib Melchior and Sid Pink. *Original Story* Sid Pink. *Miniatures* Kay Koed.
CAST: *Gen. Mark Grayson* Carl Ottosen. *Lise Martens* Ann Smyrner. *Karen Martens* Mimi Heinrich. *Prof. Martens* Asbjorn Andersen. *Connie Miller* Marla Behrens. *Svend Viltorft* Bent Mejding. *Dr. Dalby* Poul Wildaker. *Mr. Petersen* Dirch Passer. *Capt. Brandt* Ole Wisborg.

AD LINE: "Invincible ... Indestructible! What was the BEAST born fifty million years out of time?"

"Somewhere in the forbidding tundra mountains of Lapland," a mining crew unearths the frozen tail of a prehistoric reptile. Svend, leader of the miners, accompanies the find to the Danmarks Akvarium in Copenhagen. Prof. Otto Martens and Dr. Peter Dalby study the specimen—Martens' two shapely daughters, Lise and Karen, are content to study Svend. One night, Dr. Dalby unwisely sends away the dim-witted but diligent night watchman, Mr. Petersen, and carelessly leaves open the freezing-room door. Instead of decaying, the tail begins to regenerate itself into an entire animal! American General Mark Grayson, in command of the "protective forces," is bored silly until "Reptilicus" suddenly undergoes a growth

Prof. Martens (Asbjorn Andersen), Lise Martens (Ann Smyrner), and Dr. Dalby (Poul Wildaker) examine the defrosted tail of *Reptilicus*.

spurt and breaks out of its tank. "We've got a fight on our hands!" chirps the overjoyed Grayson, enlisting the help of his liaison, Captain Brandt, in drawing up battle plans. When Reptilicus retreats to the sea, Grayson orders a depth charge attack until UNESCO scientist Connie Miller reminds him what will happen if a regenerative creature is blown to bits. Finally, Grayson gets the idea to tranquilize the beast by firing a narcotic-filled bazooka shell into its maw. The plan works, though Brandt is killed in the attempt. Meanwhile, somewhere out on the ocean floor ...

COMMENTARY: *Reptilicus*, history's only Danish giant-monster-on-the-loose picture, has justifiably earned its reputation as one of the most unintentionally funny examples of the genre ever made. Its faults are so numerous and severe as to almost defy analysis.

In the world of low-budget creature features, there is mediocre acting, bad acting, nonacting, and occasionally good acting. Then there is *Reptilicus* acting, best described as "unique." Reportedly caused by the director's insistence that the Danish cast pronounce their lines ve-ry clear-ly, the words come out in a crawling cadence that sounds like a 78 rpm record played at 33⅓. "I have never seen ... bone frag-ments ... like this ... be-fore," Professor Martens says, the syllables oozing like snails from his lips. The draggy delivery is only worsened by the dialogue itself, which runs the gamut from silly (an alarm goes off and Grayson deduces, "Something's happened!") to repetitious ("You'll have to fire *point blank*, at *very close range*!") to downright weird ("He will be *busy* now," Martens smirks leeringly as his own daughters lead Svend away). The cast actually featured some fairly big names—within Denmark, that is. Mimi Heinrich was a rising actress described in the press as "Denmark's answer to Shirley MacLaine," and Dirch Passer, who as "funny Mr. Petersen" provides the wince-inducing comedy relief, was a huge comic star in Denmark. Obviously, none of the charisma these performers surely possessed survived the translation into an English-speaking monster movie.

Appearing as the nightclub chanteuse was popular Danish singer Birthe Wilke. However pleasant is Wilke's voice, the entire "travelogue" interlude that pops up in the middle of the movie is a stunningly abrupt detour. General Grayson, who hasn't a kind word for anyone and hates being in Denmark, inexplicably gets happy feet and goes flitting merrily around Copenhagen spouting historical anecdotes like Tour Guide Barbie. His odyssey takes him to the famous Tivoli Gardens, where Wilke performs the jazzy "Tivoli Nights." Absurdly out of place amidst the giant-monster melodrama, this bizarre montage is nothing short of incomprehensible.

Despite the slo-mo dialogue, excruciating comedy and goofy musical sequence, *Reptilicus* somehow hangs together until we actually see the monster. This wobblin' goblin must surely be the worst prehistoric monster prop ever to appear in a "starring" role. "It seems to be totally unlike any other known dinosaur," Martens says—and boy is he right. Based on the creature's physiology, *Reptilicus* shouldn't even qualify as a "dinosaur movie," but the script insists otherwise. "A giant dinosaur!" Svend marvels, and the beast is later described as "a cross between one of these [indicating an illustration of a sauropod] and an amphibious reptile [impossible, since reptiles by definition are not amphibians]." As realized, it looks more like a cross between a Chinese parade dragon and a novelty shop rubber snake. It has no articulation—its mouth hangs identically agape in every shot—and there is no clue as to how it supposedly propels itself. The "acid slime" eructed by the animal is created through a crude animation effect and looks just as ludicrous as the creature.

Reptilicus has few strengths. The "regeneration" idea is a unique device for reviving a prehistoric beast in modern times, and could probably be made more plausible than the explanations offered in some other films. Rather than rely on miniatures or stock

The spectacle of the snakelike Reptilicus flying on tiny vestigial wings was too far out even for AIP, who cut the airborne scenes prior to the U.S. release.

footage, Sid Pink used his substantial promotional talents to convince the local authorities to provide actual Danish soldiers and weapons for the military scenes. Reportedly, even the shots of the destroyer firing real depth charges were filmed expressly for *Reptilicus*. It's too bad that such an opportunity was squandered on what is otherwise one of the silliest giant monster movies of all time.

PEOPLE AND PRODUCTION: The most telling evidence of this movie's consummate ineptitude is the fact that American International Pictures — the folks who gave the world everything from *Atragon* to *Zontar* — claimed that *Reptilicus* did not meet AIP's standards (!) and refused to release it in its original form. Ib Melchior was brought in to try and salvage the picture, which he attempted to do by redubbing all of the dialogue and removing all of the (apparently hilarious) shots of the stubby-winged serpent in flight.

The whole story of the Danish actors, the accents and slow speech, the dubbing and the laughably inadequate results, is muddled by conflicting information and popular myths. In an interview with Tom Weaver, AIP head Samuel Z. Arkoff told of the first time he saw Sidney Pink's monster epic. "On one of my trips to Europe I made a stop [in Copenhagen] and Sidney, very proud of *Reptilicus*, ran the picture for me," Arkoff recalled. "And I said, 'Sidney — we'll never get by with this!' He had been over there — where everybody talked like that — and he didn't realize that any American audience would have broken up immediately." Melchior, however, recalled things differently, again to Tom Weaver: "Sid knew it was going to be dubbed when it came over [to the States]," Melchior said, "so he told his actors, 'When you speak, be sure to speak distinctly and move your mouths distinctly so that we can dub this.'"

Differing accounts are also told of the film's most (only?) spectacular scene, wherein hundreds of Danes run and bicycle off the Langebro drawbridge. With no stunt performers available, the filmmakers found a local athletic club whose members were willing to take the plunge in exchange for some money and equipment. This major sequence was scheduled to be covered by at least five cameras stationed at various positions around the bridge, but was actually caught by just one. "'Action' was called and the people began running," Melchior reported. "Somebody was supposed to tell all the cameras to start rolling, but nobody did! Luckily, one of the cameramen said, 'Hey, I'm going to shoot anyway,' and that's what they got." But according to Pink, a coincidental barrage of equipment and technical failures—jammed cameras, broken film, and so on—was actually to blame for the lack of coverage.

Some *Reptilicus* lore is absolutely true. The film was shot in two versions—English and Danish—and the paperback tie-in novel did indeed have erotic passages amongst the monster scenes. The bilingual editions were shot simultaneously by having the actors learn their lines in both languages. Pink directed the English takes, after which Poul Bang of Denmark's Saga Studios helmed the

The floppy-scaled *Reptilicus* (sometimes a marionette, sometimes a hand puppet, always ludicrous) flattens a miniature apartment building.

Danish scenes. The *Reptilicus* paperback was the work of Monarch Books, an outfit that turned out a number of sci-fi and fantasy film novelizations in the early sixties. Rather amazingly, considering that the books were based on movies appealing to children, they spiced up the screen stories with flowery but fairly explicit sexual scenes.

SPECIAL EFFECTS: Not much is known about the making of the *Reptilicus* special effects, but Jack Stevenson, a film teacher living in Denmark since 1993, is one of the few authors to have researched Sidney Pink's "Danish" career. In his retrospective "It Came from Beyond Belief: The Incredible B-Movies of Sidney Pink in Denmark," Stevenson reported that Kay Koed—whose on-screen credit simply reads "Miniatures"—designed and constructed an expansive miniature set which reproduced a large section of central Copenhagen in great detail. Stevenson also revealed that artist Orla Høyer created several models of the creature itself, ranging from small puppets to a massive mock-up that could accommodate *two* operators, but it is unclear if any of Høyer's work is actually seen in the film. Some valuable but uncredited assistance was also provided by Bent Barfod, called by Stevenson "Denmark's reclusive stop-motion photography master," even though there is no stop-motion animation in the film.

Return to the Lost World

"This should be delightfully familiar to you!"

* ½   1992, Canada/U.K. Harmony Gold/ Silvio Berlusconi. C, 93m.

CREDITS: *Director* Timothy Bond. *Producers* Frank Agrama, Daniele Lorenzano, Norman Siderow, Harry Alan Towers (executive). *Screenplay* Peter Welbeck (Harry Alan Towers). *Special Effects Created by* Image Quest, Ltd. *Effects Director of Photography/Supervisor* Peter Parks. *Animatronic Supervisor* Richard Gregory.

CAST: *Prof. Challenger* John Rhys-Davies. *Prof. Summerlee* David Warner. *Edward Malone* Eric McCormack. *Malu* Nathania Stanford. *Jim* Darren Peter Mercer. *Jenny Nielson* Tamara Gorski. *Imana* Mary Ann Mandishona.

AD LINE: "Discovering a world beyond belief was only the beginning ..."

The Lost World's newfound peace is threatened when Chief Palala and Imana discover sinister outsiders on the plateau. The party's leader is Dr. Raymonds, an amoral Belgian industrialist prospecting for oil. Imana escapes with a baby Ankylosaurus orphaned by a dynamite blast, but Raymonds captures Palala and casually orders him thrown over the cliff. When Malu luckily finds the still-alive Palala down below, she remembers the vow made by the members of the Challenger expedition. Though professors Challenger and Summerlee are again at odds, all six participants from the first excursion—Malu, Ed Malone, Jenny Nielson, Jim, and the profs—return to the plateau just as the indiscriminate drilling awakens a dormant volcano. Attempting to force Palala's assistance after his "leetle baird" (as he called his airplane) is destroyed, Raymonds briefly kidnaps Imana before being quickly subdued by Challenger's associates. But Malu suddenly realizes that she and her friends have become gods in the tribe's mythology—and are expected to quiet the restless volcano. Challenger luckily brought along a supply of his new explosive, "Challengite," which might be powerful enough to douse the eruptions. Raymonds fakes repentance and volunteers to help Jim fix a broken detonator wire, all the while scheming to abandon the others and save himself. Jim looks Raymonds right in the eye and connects the wire, triggering the blast and apparently sacrificing himself to extinguish both the volcano and Raymonds. The eruptions cease, Ed realizes his true feelings are for Jenny alone, Jim climbs unharmed out of the cave, and Percy the pterodactyl finally makes it home.

COMMENTARY: *The Lost World*, which leads directly into this sequel, somehow found enough good qualities to offset its many flaws and make it entertaining. *Return to the Lost World* is not as fortunate.

Despite numerous remakes, *Return to the Lost World* was the first attempt at a sequel to Conan Doyle's classic story.

wealth. One wonders why he never considered the profit potential of, say, maybe establishing a dinosaur zoo in suburban Brussels? The script also offers two astronomically unlikely survivals—Palala lives through being *thrown off the plateau*, and Jim receives nothing more than ringing ears from a one megaton explosion about ten feet from him. It may sound scientifically outlandish but the idea of blowing out a volcano like a candle has actually been used before ... as the plot of a *Gilligan's Island* episode.

The dinosaurs, somehow, are even scarcer this time. All we get are the same two duckbills behind the same foliage seen in part one, the same T. rex head, and a stiff Ankylosaurus with its baby. There are no attempts to create a feeling of interaction between creature and human, and at no time in either film is any dinosaur, except the rubbery baby ankylosaur, shown full length. *Return to the Lost World* provides a few more chances for John Rhys-Davies to enjoy playing Challenger ("We must not unsheathe the great sword of intellect to cut butter!") but has almost nothing else to recommend it.

The cast, which was the best thing about the first film, is still the best thing about the sequel. But as often happens in sequels, including *The Empire Strikes Back* (1980), the quirks and behaviors which made the characters interesting the first time become overdone and tiresome the second. The professors' constant bickering grows annoying, and the previously resolved Jenny-Malu-Malone love triangle is rekindled—by Nathania Stanford's brief but unexpected nude scene—so it can be resolved all over again. The Raymonds character (incredibly, the actor goes uncredited) is a spewing fountain of overacted bad-guy clichés who sees the petroleum as the plateau's only source of

Robot Monster

"Ro-Man! We can't stand it any longer!"

½ 1953, USA. Three Dimension Pictures. BW, 62m.

CREDITS: *Director* Phil Tucker. *Producers* Phil Tucker, Al Zimbalist (executive), Alan Winston (associate). *Original Screenplay* Wyott Ordung. *Special Photographic Effects* Jack Rabin, David Commons. *Optical Effects* Consolidated Film Industries. *Automatic Billion Bubble Machine* N. A. Fisher Chemical Products.

CAST: *Roy* George Nader. *Alice* Claudia Barrett. *Mother* Selena Royale (Royle). *Father/The Professor* John Mylong. *Johnny* Gregory Moffett. *Carla* Pamela Paulson. *Ro-Man* George Barrows. *Robot Voice* John Brown.

On a picnic with his widowed mother, grown sister Alice and little sister Carla, space-crazy Johnny wakes from a nap and finds everything changed. In a cave where he had earlier visited two kindly archeologists, there now resides the invading alien "Ro-Man" (full title: "Extension Ro-Man XJ2") and his exotic, soap-bubble-emitting equipment. Ro-Man, from the planet Ro-Man, has used the Calcinator death ray to wipe out all life "above Lepidoptera [butterfly] level," but his superior, the Great Guidance, constantly browbeats him over his inability to terminate Johnny's family—the last surviving humans. In Johnny's altered reality, his family now includes a father ("The Professor") and a fiancé for Alice ("Roy")—the same men he previously knew as the kindly archeologists. With an experimental antibiotic having rendered Johnny's clan immune to calcination, Ro-Man resorts to "physical means" to kill Carla and Roy. But when he sees lovely Alice, he decides to bring her back alive. The Professor offers to surrender as part of a ploy to rescue Alice, but Ro-Man is too busy undressing her to be bothered. This is the last straw for the exasperated Great Guidance, who strikes Ro-Man dead and floods the planet with cosmic rays "from which will spring prehistoric reptiles to devour whatever remains of life!" Just as Earth begins to crumble from psychotronic vibrations, Johnny wakes up and finds it was all a dream ... or was it?

COMMENTARY: In an era when hapless, no-budget cinematic relics have gained legions of fans and "so bad it's good" has become a selling point, *Robot Monster* has achieved such notoriety that it is sometimes proposed as the worst film ever made. It is not; nor is George Barrows wearing a gorilla suit topped with a diving helmet the most ludicrous movie monster of the fifties, as anyone who remembers Tabonga, the murderous walking tree in *From Hell It Came*, can attest. *Robot Monster* just may be, however, the most *endearingly* abysmal picture of all time.

Basically, *Robot Monster* is a *King Kong* remake, and Ro-Man's plight is perfectly described by Carl Denham's 1933 summation of his "beauty and the beast" scenario: "The Beast was a tough guy, too. He could lick the world. But when he saw Beauty, she got him. He went soft. He forgot his wisdom and the little fellahs licked him." So, it wasn't the Great Guidance, it was Beauty killed the Beast. *Robot* does have one slightly surprising scene—when Carla is killed and the little girl's "dead" body is lingeringly shown. Such images were strongly discouraged by both the standards of the day and the Motion Picture Production Code.

The film's dinosaur-related elements are as strange as everything else. The dinos are supposedly reanimated by Great Guidance to finish off the human race, but their real purpose is to fill time. The dinosaur scenes are made up of live-lizard stock shots from *One Million B.C.* combined with stop-motion animation from *Lost Continent*. Some prints of *Robot* (possibly from a later television version) also include a meaningless lizard-dino prologue featuring clips from *King Dinosaur*.

More than anything else, the jaw-dropping dialogue is what folks remember about *Robot Monster*. Ro-Man is most often quoted ("I meshed my LPI with the viewscreen auditor, and picked up a count of five") but others have great lines too. There's Roy's romantic banter ("You're so bossy you ought to be *milked* before you come home at night!"), Johnny's insults to Ro-Man ("You look like a pooped-out pinwheel!"), and who can forget Alice, pleading with her dad and beau to let her spend the night with Ro-Man: "You mean there are certain things 'nice girls' don't do? Even if it means that man's millions of years of struggle up from the sea, the slime, the fight to breathe air, to stand erect, to think, to conquer nature—even if all this is stopped cold by a doting father and a jealous suitor?" No spoof or satire could ever

Roy (George Nader) strains to free Alice (Claudia Barrett) from the grip of Ro-Man (George Barrows), but she seems to be enjoying herself.

capture the true qualities of dialogue like this, or recreate the experience of real pictures like *Robot Monster*.

PEOPLE AND PRODUCTION: Phil Tucker's name will forever be joined with *Robot Monster*, his most famous film. Quoted in *The Fifty Worst Films of All Time*, Tucker recalled the genesis of his unique villain. "Well, I originally envisioned the monster as a kind of robot," Tucker said. "I talked to several people that I knew who had robot suits, but it was just out-of-the-way, money wise. I thought, 'I know George [Barrows] will work for me for nothing. I'll get a diving helmet, put it on him, and it'll work!' And that's how it came to be." Fearful that revealing the true cost of the film — about $16,000 — would hurt business, Tucker and the other producers agreed to address budgetary questions with the noncommittal response: "Somewhere under $50,000."

The cast could boast the presence of Selena Royle, a well-respected actress in such films as *The Harvey Girls* and *Courage of Lassie*, as well as solid B-movie veterans George Nader and Claudia Barrett. In a *Filmfax* interview, Barrett reminisced about *Robot*. "The picture was low-low-low budget and my agent at the time was not too pleased [that] I decided to take the part," she said. "But I was an actress and I just wanted to act." Tucker naturally scrimped on set construction wherever possible. "The family home scenes were shot near Dodger Stadium," Barrett revealed. "There was an area that was being renovated for a low-cost housing project. Some walls or dividers remained and were used to separate our living quarters from the outside areas." Barrett fondly remembered her on-screen antagonist. "George Barrows was a Hollywood stuntman who owned his own gorilla costume," she said. "I'm not sure where they came up with the sea diver's helmet. George was big and strong; he was easygoing, and I felt perfectly safe in his arms. Running up and down those hills, George could have dropped me several times. Fortunately, he didn't."

Ein Ruckblic in die Urwelt

not viewed c. 1927. Germany. BW, Silent.

In this obscure and unusual documentary short on prehistoric life, two-dimensional "cut-out" figures, animated frame-by-frame, are skillfully lit and photographed to provide a very naturalistic and atmospheric effect. The title roughly translates as "A Retrospective on Prehistory."

Saurians

"Are you sure someone isn't playing a practical joke on us?"

1994, USA. Polonia Brothers. C, 77m.

The *One Million B.C.* iguanasaurus is one of the disparate images strewn across the *Robot Monster* theatrical poster.

CREDITS: *Director* Mark Alan Polonia. *Producers* Mark Alan Polonia, John Polonia (associate). *Written by* Mark Alan Polonia. *Special Visual Effects* Nightview Productions. *Make-up Effects* John Joseph. *Animation* Annie Dommens and Johnny Suzichi.
CAST: *Alan* Mark Polonia. *Lynette* Maria Davis. *Hunter* Todd Carpenter.

Accomplishing what this author would have thought impossible, *Saurians* manages to prevent *Galaxy of the Dinosaurs* from being the most screamingly amateurish home movie covered in this book. It is so astonishing that it is difficult to know what to say about it.

The tale follows a trio of collegiate fossil hunters, Alan, Lynette, and Charlie, who are on a field trip when an explosion at a construction site frees a Stegosaurus and Tyrannosaurus from hibernation. Alan theorizes that "concentrated rock gas" kept them alive and reports the discovery to his boss, Professor Tanner. Unfortunately, Tanner turns out to be a greedy slimeball who hires a bounty hunter to track down the dinosaurs. The hunter, named "Hunter," forces Alan and Lynette to help him find the dinos, but the tyrannosaur kills the stego and proceeds to do the same to Hunter. Alan blows the T. rex's head off with a stick of TNT and says, "we can be thankful it's all over."

The film was apparently shot silent and then atrociously dubbed. The "acting" is worse than could be done intentionally. The clay figure stop-motion is far more rudimentary than that in Willis O'Brien's earliest experiment, and the live-action puppets are cheap toys. *Saurians* offers no unintentional laughs, no camp value, no shoestring-budget charm; watching the film results only in a sort of bemused torpor, as you uselessly attempt to rationalize how such a thing actually managed to find inclusion in the United States' largest video mail-order catalog.

The Savage

not viewed USA, 1926. First National. BW, Silent.

CREDITS: *Director* Fred Newmeyer.
CAST: Ben Lyon, May McAvoy, Tom Maguire.

This comedic short details the antics of an amiable but pesky Brontosaurus, who follows reporter Lyon from the Mariposa Islands back to New York City. Apparently intended as a spoof, of sorts, of *The Lost World* (also from First National). Sam Hardy, who played Weston, the theatrical agent in *King Kong*, has a small role.

The Secret of the Loch

"If you don't believe in our monster, you better go back the way you came."
*** 1934, U.K. Wyndham Films. BW, 72m.

CREDITS: *Director* Milton Rosmer. *Producer* Bray Wyndham. *Writers* Charles Bennett, Billie Bristow. *Decor and Technical Director* J. [John] Elder Wills.
CAST: *Professor Heggie* Sir Seymour Hicks. *Angus* Gibson Gowland. *Angela* Nancy O'Neil. *Jimmy Anderson* Frederick Peisley. *Maggie* Rosamund John. *Jack Campbell* Eric Hales. *Professor Fothergill* Hubert Harben.

On a dark and misty night in a small pub near Loch Ness, the irascible Professor Heggie and his massive manservant, Angus, swap monster tales with the patrons. Spurred by the frightened locals, Heggie convenes a meeting at the Natural History Museum and offers an astonishing theory: the monster is actually a living Diplodocus! Heggie is promptly tossed out by his incredulous colleagues, but is followed back to Scotland by eager reporter Jimmy Anderson. Several journalists are already gathered at the lochside pub when Jimmy arrives, but only Jimmy is intrepid enough to sneak into Heggie manor through the window of the professor's granddaughter Angela. Heggie vehemently orders Angus to throw the reporter out, but the big Scot notices the tartan of the Macknockie clan on Jimmy's necktie and pronounces him a "brother Macknockie"! After too many whiskies with Angus, Jimmy phones in a fabricated story to his paper which infuriates his editors and Heggie alike. With his news story and his wooing of Angela both floundering, Jimmy is ready to give up until he meets professional diver Jack Campbell, hired by Heggie to explore the "Great Cave." But on Campbell's very first dive, a great shadow falls over him and he never surfaces.

Heggie is brought to trial in connection with Campbell's death. The verdict is "death from misadventure" but Heggie is convinced that the whole mess is Jimmy's fault, and is understandably livid when the newspaperman asks for Angela's hand in marriage! Determined to gain Heggie's favor, Jimmy enlists Angus' help and makes his own dive. He encounters the monster in the inky depths and desperately gives the "raise" signal, unaware that the irrational Heggie has boarded the boat and is holding the crew at gunpoint. Just then Angela and the throng of reporters arrive, distracting Heggie and allowing Angus to grab the gun. Jimmy is winched up just in time, and the monster cooperatively surfaces right next to the camera-toting journalists. Having restored the professor's good name by proving his theory, Jimmy gets a handshake from Heggie, a kiss from Angela, and an eagerly accepted shot of Scotch from big Angus.

COMMENTARY: In these days of Internet movie sites and tell-all coming-attraction trailers (not to mention books like this one!) it's rare to see a movie without already having a fair idea of what to expect. But as I sat down to watch *The Secret of the Loch* I anticipated a typically creaky 1930s-style monster programmer, and was almost dumbstruck by this quirky medley of wit and wordplay, slapstick and spookiness. Though dated and hampered by budgetary blemishes, the presence of unusual talent at several key positions — both in front of and behind the camera — keeps this black-and-white beastie swimming along with its head well above water.

The *Secret of the Loch* begins with back-to-back sequences which illustrate the magnitude of its mood swings. The opening is a truly eerie scene in the picture-perfect little pub, as Heggie delivers an ominous soliloquy about the lore of the legendary monster. Seymour Hicks' riveting presentation, Peter Mendoza's moody score, James Wilson's photography and Milton Rosmer's skilled direction combine to create a passage that positively oozes atmosphere. From this solemn setting we cut to the jaw-dropping scene in the Natural History Museum. Played strictly for laughs and delivering them, it's a comedy sketch that could fit into a Danny Kaye farce or a *Fawlty Towers* episode with equal ease. The humor veers from fairly subtle (the camera pans from a stuffed walrus head on the wall to a dozing, corpulent scientist with a huge, drooping mustache) to broad slapstick (crushed toes, bonked heads, and not one but two sets of loose dentures), mercilessly poking fun at stuffy academia. After this zany segment, the comedy shifts somewhat from visual gags to verbal byplay, as when Jimmy first accosts the professor:

> HEGGIE: "I don't want your filthy publicity!"
> JIMMY: "You're too shy, sir! Everyone wants publicity — where would Greta Garbo be without it?"
> HEGGIE: "Greta Garbo? What group's Greta Garbo? Biological?"
> JIMMY: "No, Swedish."

The reporters-in-the-pub scene is a continuous stream of wordplay so densely packed it takes several viewings to catch everything. The question "monster or professor?" becomes the theme for a running gag. "Crossing the road it was, wi' a lamb in its mouth. Sixty ... seventy feet long," recalls one inebriated Nessie witness. "The lamb or the monster?" asks Jimmy.

The screenplay by Charles Bennett somehow weaves together all the different elements — the comedy, the foreboding feel, and even some Gable/Harlow-type romantic sparring between Jimmy and the sharp-tongued Angela — with surprising success. The script can be faulted only for too closely resembling a certain previous dinosaur tale by Sir Arthur Conan Doyle. Bennett may not have been consciously inspired by *The Lost World*, but he does offer an eager London journalist who begs his editor for an exciting assignment and ends up pursuing a cantankerous, reporter-hating professor, who's ticked off because his colleagues have scoffed at his claims of a living dinosaur.

The monster doesn't show up until the last few minutes and then turns out to be an iguana, but the monster-versus-diver sequence is generally well put together. Light and shadow are deftly used to minimize the inadequacy of the "underwater" sets, and the reptilian actor looms convincingly huge in some shots. Milton Rosmer takes care to show us the 1930s diving technology — massive bolted-on helmets, bulky suits and ballast, a creaking hand-cranked air pump — which was state of the art in 1934 but seems so dangerously primitive now. The thought of descending into the loch's cold, black depths with your life depending on such frail-looking gear generates its own sense of dread, above and beyond the monster factor.

Besides its strange mix of comedy and creepiness, *Secret* has an unusual take on the whole Nessie legend. In the early reels, the monster is perceived as a true "monster." It's "a danger to all of us," to be feared and hopefully exterminated. By film's end, it has metamorphosed into an approximation of its present-day status. Nessie has become a mysterious, magical thing that's a valuable and integral part of Loch Ness, as demonstrated when Heggie emphatically knocks Angus' gun barrel aside.

Ultimately, the picture's technical shortcomings and borrowed plot elements are almost beside the point. *The Secret of the Loch* is a satirical and oddly shaped tale that should be just as satisfying to fans of moody, "Golden Age" monster melodramas as it is to those who appreciate "British humor." This reviewer found it to be a charming picture, but as big Angus reminds us, "Folk have different ideas of charm!"

PEOPLE AND PRODUCTION: Though many people who worked on *The Secret of the Loch* had long and successful cinematic careers, one credit stands out: "Edited by David Lean." The man who would go on to direct some of history's most respected films started out in the cutting room, putting together low-budget "quota quickies" as they were called in England. "I worked on a lot of bad pictures," Lean once recalled, quoted in Kevin Brownlow's *David Lean*. "And bad pictures are very good for one's ego, because the worse they are, the more chance you have of making them better." It was during this time that Lean began to consider other, greater cinematic challenges. "I started to think, as numerous people who work with me think, that I could do better than they could — and that gave me a real urge to do something in the way of direction." Do something, indeed.

To this author's knowledge, the only previously published in-depth examination of *The Secret of the Loch* is found in Bryan Senn's extraordinary *Golden Horrors*, in which Senn emphasizes the value of Milton Rosmer's thespian background. "Rosmer's wealth of acting experience stood him in good stead when he stepped behind the camera," Senn wrote, "and it is no wonder that he was able to coax effective performances from his actors in *The Secret of the Loch*." Rosmer had some actors to work with, too. Seymour Hicks was a hugely respected English stage performer who also enjoyed a prolific film career, and Gibson Gowland's acting résumé reached back through Erich von Stroheim's *Greed* (1925) all the way to D. W. Griffith's *Birth of a Nation* (1915).

Charles Bennett's screenplay for the 1960 remake of *The Lost World* was not his first prehistoric-creature endeavor. "Certainly, *The Secret of the Loch* is one that I thought no one could possibly remember," Bennett told Tom Weaver in *Starlog*. It has always been common for films to parallel the "hot" trends and issues of their day, and *Secret* is an example. "The picture was my idea," Bennett said. "What had happened was, the Loch Ness monster was just starting to hit the London newspapers, and I decided that there *might* be a film in it. This was mid-winter 1933. I got my car out and drove to the Highlands of Scotland."

Bennett based several scenes on his actual experiences. "I didn't find the monster, but I found a pub, and there inside were about ten newspapermen — some from Glasgow, some from Edinburgh and two or three from London," he recalled. "And I found the most beautiful Scotch whisky in the world!" Even though some recent commentators, including Bryan Senn and this author, find much to compliment in Bennett's witty script, Kevin Brownlow reported that "the cutting-room people called Rosmer's film 'killingly funny'" during its production, unfortunately not in the way intended. Bennett didn't like it any better. "It was *terrible*," he claimed. "I was amateurish, a beginner then, but it's *amusing*." Bennett would reuse the title 30 years later for an episode of Irwin Allen's TV series, *Voyage to the Bottom of the Sea*.

The boat crew winches Jimmy Anderson (upper left) to safety as the lizardly Nessie looks on hungrily during the climax of *Secret of the Loch.*

SPECIAL EFFECTS: Six years before *One Million B.C.*, the technicians of *The Secret of the Loch* pressed a humble iguana into duty as the world's most beloved monster. It seems a standard B-movie shortcut, but was there more to it? Peter Costello offers another possibility in his book *In Search of Lake Monsters*. Costello called *Secret* "a pretty bad film," but did point out that "the Monster in it was modeled on Gould's theory of it being a sort of giant newt." Rupert Thomas Gould was an ex-naval officer with an interest in cryptozoology, who published a Loch Ness Monster article in the London *Times* just weeks before *The Secret of the Loch* was announced. As reported by Costello, Gould's writings proposed that "the monster was a hitherto unknown animal along the lines of a vastly enlarged newt." So, Professor Heggie's "Diplodocus" theory notwithstanding, the iguana-as-Nessie ploy may not have been as ludicrous at the time as it seems now.

Unlike some low-budget "live lizard" movies, *Secret* takes the trouble to combine the reptile with a human diver in several shots, mostly using rear projection. John Mitchell, who many years later would do sound recording for David Lean's *The Bridge on the River Kwai* and *A Passage to India*, was a young projectionist back in 1934. His theater was adjacent to Lean's editing room, and he remembered the lizard footage. "In those days, back projection was pretty crude," Mitchell recalled in Brownlow's book. "The screen was always tearing. The iguana ended up as a very blown up image." He also remembered Lean's interest in and talent for all aspects of filmmaking. "David was very much in evidence on the floor. He wasn't just receiving the material in the cutting room but was making comments on the set."

Most of the *Secret* composites use rear projection, but Brownlow reported that a few shots employed an ingenious technique called the Schüfftan process. Invented around 1923 by German film pioneer Eugen Schüfftan, this in-camera process uses a simple mirror to combine a live-action scene with a miniature model, rear-projected image, or painting. As a simplified example, a filmmaker wants to place a live actress into the window of a haunted house that exists only as a scale model. The camera is aimed at the model house, with a glass mirror placed at a 45-degree angle between camera and subject. The actress is positioned to one side, perpendicular to the camera's line of sight, so that the mirror reflects her image into the lens. Much of the mirror's silvering is then meticulously scraped from the glass, allowing the camera to see the model house through the cleared areas. The remaining silvered area still blocks the camera's view of the model's window, replacing it with the woman's reflection. The technique is difficult to master but when skillfully done can produce near-perfect, "live" composites. One can only guess which shots in *The Secret of the Loch* utilize the Schüfftan process; the likeliest candidates are the two composites with the diver in the lower-right corner and the reptile looming in the upper-left.

7 Faces of Dr. Lao

"I ask ... that you believe in me."

*** 1964, USA. MGM. C, 100m.

CREDITS: *Director* George Pal. *Producer* George Pal. *Screen Play* Charles Beaumont; based on the novel *The Circus of Dr. Lao* by Charles G. Finney. *Special Make-up Created by* William Tuttle. *Special Visual Effects* Paul B. Byrd, Wah Chang, Jim Danforth, Ralph Rodine, Robert R. Hoag, A.S.C.

CAST: *Dr. Lao, Apollonius of Tyana, Merlin the Magician, Pan, Medusa, The Abominable Snowman, The Giant Serpent* Tony Randall. *Angela Benedict* Barbara Eden. *Edward Cunningham* John Ericson. *Clinton Stark* Arthur O'Connell.

AD LINE: "What's scary, hairy, spooky, kooky, weird & wonderful? Dr. Lao (that's what!)"

In the early 1900s, a wizened Chinese gentleman rides a yellow jackass into the quiet Arizona town of Abalone, and places an announcement in the local paper for "The Circus of Dr. Lao." The paper's owner, Ed Cunningham, stays busy wooing the beautiful but unreceptive widow Angela, but finds time to write editorials trying to convince Abalone's landowners not to sell out to shifty developer Clint Stark. That night, Dr. Lao's mystical entourage reveals cloaked feelings and hidden truths about the townsfolk — not all of them pleasant. Vain Mrs. Cassan has her eyes opened by the soothsaying Apollonius, Angela's icy demeanor is thawed during a heated interlude with Pan, the God of Joy, and Stark trades barbs with the talking Giant Serpent, soon growing uncomfortable with their cold-blooded similarities. Dr. Lao also presents his "pet," a tiny fish which he says will turn into a gigantic sea-serpent if removed from its bowl.

As night falls again, Dr. Lao presents his grand finale: an allegorical tale of the ancient village of Woldercan, which fell prey to a deceitful outsider and was punished with total oblivion. Afterward, the citizens vote unanimously to turn down Stark's offer. Stark is transformed rather than angered by their act — his long-gone faith in humanity restored. But when his drunken goons free Dr. Lao's pet from its bowl, it grows into a prehistoric-looking monster and promptly chases them away. By next morning, all physical signs of Lao's circus have vanished, but Ed and Angela know that its wonderful effects will last forever.

COMMENTARY: The unique fable called *7 Faces of Dr. Lao* was the fifth and last of fantasy specialist George Pal's turns in the director's chair, and may be the best of the lot. Walking a slippery edge that many fantasies cannot, it is sentimental but not maudlin, gentle but not bland, and clever but not cute. The recurring theme holds that Lao's circus "is like a mirror," and this mirror reflects truths through metaphors—Stark is a "snake," Mrs. Lindquist is "made of stone," Angela is "cold," and so on—and this conceit gets the story's message across without the customary heavy-handedness. *Dr. Lao* is very funny in places and surprisingly grim in others—the scene with Mrs. Cassan and Apollonius is unremittingly dark.

The film's centerpiece is Tony Randall's extraordinary performance. There is a tendency to automatically praise an actor who tackles a multiple role, even if the results are not sparkling. But Randall's transformations, aided by William Tuttle's standout makeups, are truly impressive. Especially enjoyable are moments when Randall breaks into seemingly spontaneous comic riffs, evoking a slightly more sedate version of Robin Williams. He describes his Loch Ness monster in a full-blown Highlands brogue, and shifts into a nasal, public-address monotone as he conducts a tour through his Medusa exhibit — a potentially horrific sequence unexpectedly and successfully played for laughs. An able supporting cast, George Pal's even-handed direction, and Leigh Harline's remarkable "Old-West-meets-Far-East" music score combine to hit all the right notes.

Dr. Lao earns its inclusion in this volume by the obviously plesiosaurian nature of its "Loch Ness monster," whose rampage provides a whimsical and fitting climax. The energetic and expressive stop-motion animation works nicely with the unusual optical and "replacement animation" effects during the growing and shrinking scenes. In a fun bit alluding to the film's title, the creature briefly sprouts six additional heads resembling Dr. Lao, Pan, Merlin, The Abominable Snowman, Medusa, and Apollonius before reverting to its conventional form. The monster is animated to be ferocious without being truly "monstrous," which is just as it should be. There are a few compositing flaws, including some visible matte lines and rather severe color balance discrepancies, but these glitches do little to harm the enjoyment of the sequence or the film as a whole. *7 Faces of Dr. Lao* remains a distinctive and happy entry in the fantasy film fold, and one of George Pal's finest efforts.

SPECIAL EFFECTS: As usual for George Pal's later films, the *Dr. Lao* special effects were handled by Project Unlimited. Wah Chang designed the original conception of the Loch Ness monster, which Jim Danforth then modified somewhat prior to constructing the model. "Wah had done a pastel chalk sketch of the Monster," Danforth recalled, "as sort of a green plesiosaur." Danforth sculpted the main stop-motion puppet based on his own revisions, while Project newcomer Peter Kleinow sculpted the transitional "replacement" figures for the growing and shrinking scenes. The animation itself was the joint effort of both men. "I finished up a bunch of little pieces of things on *The Wonderful World of the Brothers Grimm*, and that's the only thing I did for Project until *7*

Closeup image reveals the artistry of Wah Chang's beautiful Arthur O'Connell/Giant Serpent live-action puppet.

Faces of Dr. Lao," Kleinow told the author. "I did quite a few shots on that, mostly on the Loch Ness monster."

The stop-motion puppet, like so many others, incorporated parts cannibalized from previous armatures. "We used a lot of the *Brothers Grimm* dragon in the Loch Ness monster," revealed Danforth, who had actually conceived his own design for the monster. "Mine was more like a coelacanth that could get up on its lobe fins and run around," he recalled. Gene Warren asked Danforth not to propose the design to George Pal, but when Pal finally saw the sketch years later he professed a preference for Danforth's concept. "He probably just said that to make me feel good," said Jim. As for Kleinow, *Dr. Lao* "was my entrance into the big time. I was really thrilled to be able to do it," he said.

The monster sequence is plagued by some substandard matte work. Danforth wanted to do the compositing with rear projection but couldn't convince the powers that be. While doing rear-projection shots for the earlier *Dinosaurus!*, Project Unlimited ran into trouble caused by the type of film projector used. "It was meant to project into matte paintings," Danforth said of the *Dinosaurus!* equipment. "It had shutters on it, so you wouldn't see the image except when it was being exposed. So, if you've got a matte painting where nothing's moving, that's fine, but for stop-motion animation, you want the picture to be on-screen all the time." Having the picture on-screen meant leaving the shutter open for extended periods, during which the equipment's heat would affect the projected film frame. "The film buckled and warped, and so they had this bad experience with rear projection and didn't want to do it again," Danforth concluded. "So they let MGM put [the composites] together, and I think in some ways they suffered because of it."

Augmenting William Tuttle's splendid make-ups (which netted a special Oscar), Wah Chang created several artistic accessories. "I did the Medusa head—the snakes," Chang recalled, "and the goat legs for Pan." Chang's live-action Arthur O'Connell/snake puppet was used for most of the "Giant Serpent" sequence, save for three brief stop-motion cuts. "Dave Pal did a couple of them, and I did a couple of them," said Danforth, noting that the cigar-swallowing shot was animated by both men. "Dave and I each did the same scene, so it's like, they could pick the one they liked best." So whose shot is in the movie? "I don't to this day know," Danforth replied. The *Dr. Lao* visual effects earned Jim the first of his two Oscar nominations, but the statuette went to Peter Ellenshaw, Hamilton Luske, and Eustace Lycett for Disney's *Mary Poppins*.

64,000,000 Years Ago

★★★½ 1981, Canada. National Film Board of Canada. C, 11m.

CREDITS: *Director* Bill Maylone. *Producers* George Johnson, John Taylor (executive). *Story* Bill Maylone. *Commentary* Robert Duncan, Don White. *Narrator* Sam Payne. *Animation* Bill Maylone. *Backgrounds* Brent Boates. *Scientific Advisor* Loris S. Russel.

It's the very end of the late Cretaceous Period, but dinosaurs still rule the earth. There are mammals scurrying about, but they're nothing but insignificant, sneaky creatures who eke out an existence feeding on dragonflies and other small prey. Many smaller dinosaurs like Ornithomimus must be wary of the huge carnivores such as Tyrannosaurus rex, but some, like the heavily plated Ankylosaurus, have little to fear despite the size difference. The herbivorous, duckbilled Edmontosaurus roams the landscape searching for food, until mating season makes food a secondary concern. But all activities are forgotten when the roar of T. rex is heard. Meanwhile, the little mammal quietly tends to her babies, safe in an underground burrow. On the surface, a female Triceratops prepares a nest and carefully lays her eggs, but while the horned dinosaur is busy driving off the pesky T. rex, the fleet Ornithomimus plunders her clutch. The dinosaurs' time finally ends about 64 million years ago, and "with the death of the huge reptiles, the way was now open for mammals."

COMMENTARY: Some of the most unknown and unseen stop-motion dinosaur animation ever created has been done for short films, and in several cases it is some of the best. To this list, which includes Wah Chang's *Dinosaurs ... The Terrible Lizards* and Phil Tippett's *Prehistoric Beast*, one may add director-writer-animator Bill Maylone's *64,000,000 Years Ago*. This little Mesozoic minimovie is great fun from start to finish, offering a variety of dinosaur species and behaviors and a heroic little mammal as well.

Maylone, who also showcased prehistoric fauna in another short film called *Canada Vignettes: Woolly Mammoth*, packs a lot of personality into his saurian actors. The Ankylosaurus and Triceratops appearances are wondrous, with deft animation and beautifully crafted puppets, and the duckbills are a particularly lively bunch. "They have *better* things to do than fight," the narrator slyly tells us, and they're just about to prove it when their rendezvous is frustratingly interrupted by the arrival of a hungry Tyrannosaurus. The most impressive creature just might be the clever, opossumlike mammal who lives under the dinosaurs' feet. Maylone's animation here is near perfect, whether the creature is pouncing on an insect or tending to her three tiny babies (also animated). The animal's actions, mannerisms, and little quirks are so naturalistic that it's easy to forget you're watching an artificial puppet. Oddly, the film's one slightly weak spot is the T. rex. It's certainly not bad, but in both design and animation it falls just a bit short of the high standard set by the rest of the creatures.

With Maylone's nimble animation, meticulous backgrounds and miniature sets, inventive camera setups, unobtrusive narration, and playful scenarios, *64,000,000 Years Ago* is a delicious eleven minutes for any animation or dinosaur lover.

The Son of Kong

"Here we are, just one big happy family."
**½ 1933, USA. RKO Radio Pictures. BW, 70m.

CREDITS: *Director* Ernest B. Schoedsack. *Producers* Merian C. Cooper (executive), Archie Marshek (associate). *Story* Ruth Rose. *Chief Technician* Willis O'Brien. *Art Technicians* Mario Larrinaga, Byron L. Crabbe. *Technical Staff* E. B. Gibson, Marcel Delgado, Carroll Shepphird, Fred Reese, W. G. White. *Sound Effects* Murray Spivack.

CAST: *Carl Denham* Robert Armstrong. *Hilda Petersen* Helen Mack. *Capt. Englehorn* Frank Reicher. *Capt. Helstrom* John Marston. *Charley* Victor Wong. *Red* Ed Brady.

AD LINE: "A human-lovable laughable beast!"

A month after King Kong's deadly rampage, a contrite and penniless Carl Denham is suffocating under multiple lawsuits. When Charley the cook brings a job offer from Captain Englehorn, Denham is happy to accept. The friends steam off for the Indian Ocean hoping to ferry cargoes among the small islands of the Dutch East Indies, but find business very scarce. At the port of Dakang, Denham befriends Hilda Petersen, a young woman working in a pathetic little circus show, and also renews his acquaintance with Nils Helstrom, the "Norwegian skipper" who gave him the map of Kong's island. Unknown to Denham, Helstrom has killed Hilda's father in a drunken argument and is desperate to leave Dutch territory. He gains passage on the *Venture* by telling a cock-and-bull story about a great treasure on Kong's island, but once at sea both Helstrom and Denham are taken aback to discover the stowaway Hilda also on board.

As the *Venture* reaches its destination, Helstrom gets cold feet listening to tales of the island's awful beasts. He incites a mutiny hoping to take over the ship, only to be promptly tossed into a lifeboat along with Denham, Englehorn, Hilda and Charley. The group is met at the beach by the angry native chief, who blames Denham for Kong's destruction of his village, but they finally find a quiet place to come ashore. Denham and Hilda have just begun to look around when they are astonished to discover a 12-foot, white-furred "Little Kong" mired in a bog, and the remorseful Denham finds himself rescuing the creature and bandaging his injured finger. The ape repays the kindness by becoming guardian of the increasingly romantic couple, saving them from an attacking cave bear and a four-legged reptilian beast, and even revealing that there *really is* a treasure hidden in an ancient Skull Mountain temple. Slowed by a Styracosaurus, Englehorn, Charley and Helstrom finally catch up with Denham and Hilda, but the sight of Little Kong sends Helstrom fleeing in panic. Denham ducks into the temple to get the treasure while Englehorn and the others try to prevent Helstrom from stealing the boat, but a hungry sea monster does that job for them. Suddenly, a great catastrophe of wind and earth tremors starts the entire island sinking beneath the waves, but Little Kong somehow holds Denham above water until the lifeboat arrives. The four survivors are found after days at sea, with enough treasure to make a nice wedding gift for Denham and his bride-to-be.

COMMENTARY: *The Son of Kong* is hard to categorize. In many ways it is unique, and would doubtless be more highly regarded if it didn't have to exist in such an imposing shadow. The film's detractors dwell on what *Son of Kong* is *not*, while its advocates like to point out all the things it *is*; a fair examination requires a look at both.

On the downside, *Son* is totally missing the masterful escalation of mood and tension that permeates the early reels of *King Kong*. The sequel's first half does have drama, including one superbly designed and exciting sequence, but does absolutely nothing to build anticipation for the arrival on the island. Then again, it's not supposed to. The film's light and comedic tenor surely reflects a "we can't top it so let's not try" mindset on the part of its makers. So, they made a comedy/romance/adventure out of it, and *almost* pulled it off wonderfully. A nice balance of humor, villainy, the despair of the Depression era, romance, and the fantastic "monster" elements is sabotaged by a few moments of excess that simply go too far.

The title character of *King Kong* is inarguably the protagonist of that film. This time, Denham is the protagonist and the animated ape is more like a "special guest star." Yet on an utterly different level, Little Kong is an impressive feat of character animation in his own right. The problem is not the inclusion of humorous elements, the problem lies in failing to know where to draw the line. In *Mighty Joe Young* sixteen years later, they came *dangerously* close to making the same mistake again—Joe drums his fingers and spits at his pursuers—but ultimately managed to strike a successful balance. But here, nobody said "whoa, that's far enough" (no one who was listened to, anyway) and so we get several moments that take the character over the top, beyond lightheartedness into goofiness. When Little Kong stares into the camera and shrugs, or spies on Denham and Hilda and covers his snickers, or crosses his eyes after hitting his head—the unavoidable result is to instantaneously yank the viewer out of the story. The crossed-eyes gag unforgivably comes in the middle of the ape's fight with the cave bear, which otherwise is the film's most exciting stop-motion sequence. Having drawn in the audience with the Dakang segment, deftly weaving together affecting images of human desperation and moments of humor, turning Little Kong into a simian Curly Howard is a puzzling, counterproductive decision.

Curiously, it's only with Little Kong that the funny bits go overboard. The picture is full of clever and amusing—but not silly—scenes involving the human actors. The catatonic expressions on the faces of Denham and Englehorn as they watch the "musical monkeys," the knowing winks at the previous film ("did *you* ever catch a monkey?"), even little tossed-off lines like Charley's parting shot to the mutinous crew ("*You* cook now, you die pretty soon!") or Denham's remark as the sputtering Helstrom reaches

Two of the *Son of Kong* creatures were Marcel Delgado originals. His malevolent sea monster is seen here with a puppet version of Nils Helstrom in its maw.

the lifeboat ("Skipper, have we *gotta* save him?") all work within the story flow.

The continuity between *King Kong* and its sequel is carefully maintained, in details if not in mood. None of the returning characters say or do anything that contradicts the events in the first film — even Charley's meat cleaver, held ever at the ready, is a carry-over. Luckily, several *Kong* stars were game for a second hitch. It's painful to imagine *The Son of Kong* without Robert Armstrong, and one of the film's joys is the chance to see more sides of Denham. The crusty, savvy, loyal Captain Englehorn, wonderfully played by Frank Reicher, is Denham's perfect sidekick — one can imagine a viable film series of Denham-Englehorn adventures. Victor Wong invests Charley with sufficient dignity to keep him from becoming an insulting stereotype, and newcomer Helen Mack, barely 20 at the time, easily holds her own among the old pros. Ruth Rose's script is similar to her *Kong* work in its efficiency and tautness, with every piece fitting satisfyingly together. Even the climactic earthquake-hurricane — a phenomenon found in no science book — can be interpreted not as an implausible coincidence of nature but as a mystical, supernatural manifestation wrought by the island's ancient tribal deities, in response to the plundering of the temple.

Besides being an overall disappointment, *Son* is a letdown specifically for dinosaur lovers. After the saurian banquet of *Kong*— Stegosaurus, Tyrannosaurus rex, pterodactyl, Elasmosaurus, Brontosaurus, all featured in fully developed sequences— the dino content of the sequel is minuscule. The only "real" dinosaur is the Styracosaurus which charges Englehorn's group and traps them in the cave, and here the puppet and animation are both superb. The atypical camera angles are effective, including an over-the-shoulder view looking at the trapped humans through the spikes of the creature's frill, and the impact of the massive skull slamming into the cave is palpable. Unfortunately, the sequence seems to merely stop without any sort of conclusion. The other two "dinosaurs" are not meant to represent any known species, detracting from the convincingly prehistoric ambience so carefully developed in *King Kong*. The dragonesque quadruped which invades the temple vaguely resembles a longer-necked, shorter-legged variant of the fictional "Paleosaurus" in *The Giant Behemoth*, and its battle with Little Kong is short but well-animated. The water-borne monster that dispatches Helstrom has a credibly dinosaurian look but comes and goes too quickly. There are only four cuts in all: three of a live-action head and neck and just *one* of the stop-motion version.

The level of detail is not quite up to that of the *Kong* effects, but is still head-and-shoulders above that of most films. With the much shorter schedule, there simply was not time for the effects team to be as ambitious as before. The photographic effects are of high quality, sometimes better than those in *Kong*, and miniature rear projection is again extensively employed. There are fewer of the artistic glass paintings which were such an integral part of the original film, though the ones we do see are effective. The climax showcases not only some expressive animation of Little Kong, but also a stop-motion Carl Denham that's as fine a piece of "human animation" as has ever been done. Ironically, perhaps the most thrilling sequence doesn't involve Little Kong, dinosaurs, or animation. The circus tent fire is a real armrest-grabber, and the uninterrupted tracking shot of petite Helen Mack actually dragging the "unconscious" Clarence Wilson away from the flames, violently kicking obstacles out of her path with no cuts and no stunt doubles, is a small masterpiece by Ernest Schoedsack.

The Son of Kong is in so many ways an enormous comedown from its beloved forefather. Ray Harryhausen is one of countless viewers who find Kong's smaller, sillier progeny to be such a disappointment. At barely 70 minutes, and with its decidedly comedic slant, *Son* is so far from the epic adventure and mythic power of *King Kong* that the two seem to inhabit different worlds. Yet, if Kong's little offspring (the film and the character) can somehow be viewed apart, there is much to enjoy. *The Son of Kong* has truly funny moments, a few touching ones, some unique stop-motion scenes, and one image—Little Kong's hand opening to release Denham just before sliding into the sea, with the remnants of Hilda's petticoat bandage still visible—as memorable as can be found in any genre film of the 1930s.

PEOPLE AND PRODUCTION: Almost concurrently with the release of *King Kong*, production began on the sequel. The RKO executives in New York seemed enthusiastic when Merian Cooper first mentioned it (and why not?), only to shackle it with a $250,000 budget—barely half of that spent on the original. The picture went on the schedule as *Jamboree*, a subterfuge designed "to keep people from visiting the set," as Ernest Schoedsack said. With most of Cooper's time occupied by his studiowide responsibilities, Schoedsack would direct *The Son of Kong* solo.

That so many of the *Kong* crew returned for *Son* is not surprising since so little time elapsed between them. Cooper receives the same "executive producer" credit given David O. Selznick on *Kong*, though Coop made a much greater creative contribution to the sequel than had Selznick to the original. Ruth Rose was again the principal writer and

Denham and Hilda (Robert Armstrong, Helen Mack) look on as Little Kong squares off against a Marcel Delgado–designed "dinosaur."

stated that she followed the time-honored axiom, "If you can't make it bigger, make it funnier." Other returnees included cameramen Eddie Linden, Vern Walker, and J. O. Taylor, sound effects creator Murray Spivack, editor Ted Cheesman, and most of the special effects team (as we'll later see). *King Kong* production assistant Archie Marshek moved up to associate producer, and composer Max Steiner also returned, incorporating much of his *Kong* music into the new score.

Likewise, several cast members reprised their *Kong* roles. Chief among the second-timers was Robert Armstrong, who felt he had a choicer character in the sequel. "For me, personally, the role was better than before," he said in *The Making of King Kong*. "It gave me a great deal more character, swell dialogue and love scenes." Other *Kong* alumni included Frank Reicher, Victor Wong, Noble Johnson, and Steve Clemento, though Johnson and Clemento are seen very briefly. The only dinosaurian holdover was the live-action Brontosaurus, seen rearing up out of the sea in one brief cameo.

With sightseers presumably minimized by the *Jamboree* ruse, filming took place primarily at RKO and on Santa Catalina Island. The dramatic tent fire sequence was shot at the Warner Ranch, and the whole production, including live-action and effects, took less than nine months. The picture turned a solid profit, actually doing better overseas than domestically. Like 1997's *Jurassic Park* sequel, *The Son of Kong* rode the reputation of its predecessor to a big opening, only to fade and never threaten to equal the grosses of the original.

SPECIAL EFFECTS: Only $50,000 of *The Son of Kong*'s modest quarter-million dollar budget was earmarked for special effects, a fact that makes the visuals in the film all the more impressive. The *Kong* FX crew returned practically intact for the follow-up, with Willis O'Brien again "Chief Technician."

It is often reported and widely accepted that O'Brien did only a limited amount of work and little or no animation on *Son of Kong*, though accounts vary regarding the reasons. One popular explanation is that he disliked the lightweight comic tone, but author Paul Jensen points out in *The Men Who Made the Monsters* that O'Brien's early Edison Company shorts "had a broad sense of humor, as did O'Brien himself." Perhaps he felt that the sequel to his greatest creation simply wasn't the place for such tomfoolery. Another slant comes from O'Brien's widow Darlyne. "He felt it was too soon to follow *King Kong* and then there was not going to be enough money to make it good," she stated in a letter published in Steve Archer's *Willis O'Brien: Special Effects Genius*. "He did no animation and was a little unhappy with some of the humor." The budget was certainly a sore point, especially when it dictated the elimination of a dinosaur stampede sequence originally planned for the climax. Still more irritation—though surely unintentional—seems to have come from the codirectors of the original film. "On *King Kong*, Obie and his crew had been left pretty much to themselves—primarily because no one else knew much about effects work—and the filming had gone smoothly," Don Shay wrote in *Cinefex*. "But by the time *Son of Kong* went into production, Cooper and Schoedsack were familiar with the various processes involved and many lengthy debates arose over simple matters which O'Brien felt he could best resolve on his own." Ray Harryhausen corroborated Shay's account. "He was very discouraged about it," Harryhausen told this author. "The producers tried to take over. They thought they knew more of how the picture should be, and Obie never liked to talk about it, even." O'Brien asked to have his name removed from the project, but Cooper refused.

With O'Brien's unofficial abdication,

A dino-battle that never was—the *Son of Kong* styracosaur and *King Kong* tyrannosaur puppets, posed together.

most of the stop-motion was apparently left to E. B. "Buzz" Gibson, Obie's assistant who had done a few bits of animation on *King Kong*. Marcel Delgado fabricated three "Little Kongs," using armatures cannibalized from the *Kong* puppets. The Styracosaurus built and animated for the first film, only to be cut, finally made it to the screen, complemented by a vicious "cave bear" and two "Delgadosauruses"—primordial beasts sprung from the sculptor's imagination. "The big reptile that Little Kong fought in the cave was one I just made up," Delgado recalled in a published letter to George Turner. "Obie told me to just create something new, that nobody had ever seen before, so I did." The malevolent-looking sea serpent is another Delgado original, and an intricate nine-inch puppet duplicate of Robert Armstrong was also made for the cataclysmic finale. The full-scale hand from *Kong* was refurbished and reused, though it's a bit large for an ape "about 12 feet high."

Byron Crabbe and Mario Larrinaga again provided glass paintings, and the islanders' village was also realized only as glass art. The exterior and interior of the temple ruins were detailed miniature sets. According to authors Turner and Goldner, Little Kong's vocalizations were "built upon the chattering of baby gorillas recorded at the San Diego Municipal Zoo," but it's unclear if Murray Spivack was as personally involved with the sound work as he had been on *King Kong*. Happily, none of the animation from either of the *Kong* films ever turned up as stock dinosaur footage for B-movie producers to plunder. Look carefully, though, and you will see one of the beautifully imagined, glass-painted vistas created for *Son of Kong* in Orson Welles' masterpiece, *Citizen Kane*.

Sound of Horror

(a.k.a. *Sound from a Million Years Ago*; *El Sonido de la Muerte*)

"There is nothing there."

1965, Spain. Zurbano Films. BW, 89m.

CREDITS: *Director* José Antonio Nieves Conde. *Producer* Gregorio Sacristan. *Original Story* Sam X. Abarbanel. *Screenplay* Sam X. Abarbanel, Gregg Tallas, José Antonio Nieves Conde, Gregorio Sacristan. *Special Effects* Manuel Baquero.

CAST: *Andre* Antonio Casas. *Pete* Arturo Fernández. *Maria* Soledad Miranda. *Arsilov* James Philbrook. *Dorman* José Bódalo. *Sophia* Ingrid Pitt. *Calliope* Lola Gaos. *Stravos* Francisco Piquer.

Professor Andre, his niece Maria and his assistant, Stravos, are searching for a treasure in the mountains of Greece when they unearth two prehistoric eggs. They take one back to their house but the other lies unnoticed in the cave until it hatches. Before long, Andre's old cronies, Arsilov and Dorman, unexpectedly show up with new info on the treasure hunt, accompanied by their driver, Pete, and Arsilov's girlfriend, Sophia. Later, Stravos enters the cave and is attacked and killed by a noisy, man-sized, *invisible* dinosaur. Calliope the housekeeper believes the cave is cursed and Arsilov agrees, but figures that it surely must have, like, worn off by now. That night, the egg in the house begins to flash and whistle, but Andre comes careening madly into the room and beats the hatchling to a pulp. After Calliope and Andre become the next two victims, the others spread flour on the ground to make the beast's footprints visible and manage to injure it with a couple of well-thrown hatchets. Making a dash for Pete's car (which he has named "Diana"), they fail to realize that the diaphanous dinosaur is on the vehicle's roof. In a final selfless act, Dorman douses the car with gasoline and ignites it, sending the dinosaur, Diana, and himself up in flames and forever (hopefully) ridding the world of the sound of horror.

COMMENTARY: Invisible adversaries have long been a movie mainstay, (dis)appearing in everything from James Whale's classic *The Invisible Man* (1933) and low-budget fare like

Arsilov (James Philbrook) holds the door with all his might while Maria (Soledad Miranda) listens intently for the *Sound of Horror*. That's future horror fave Ingrid Pitt at right.

Phantom from Space (1953), to the high-tech thriller *Hollow Man* (2000). The dinosaur genre, however, would seem to be an unlikely candidate for the invisibility treatment, since a fundamental appeal of such films is the chance to *see dinosaurs*. History has shown that even a poor dinosaur is better than none at all, and *Sound of Horror* is not surprisingly one of the least interesting creature features ever attempted.

Absolutely nothing in *Sound of Horror* works. Director Nieves Conde makes no attempt to exploit the beast's invisibility for suspense or shock effect; nor does he make much use of the unusual landscapes of La Cabrera, Spain, where the exteriors were shot. The acting is amateurish and the script is not only deadly dull but filled with jarring non sequiturs—like when the group is debating what could have torn poor Stravos to shreds and Arsilov suggests, "a heart attack." The female characters are particularly abused, being given nothing to do but cook, act frightened, dance, sunbathe fully clothed, act frightened some more and discuss cosmetics. When an explosion scares Maria, Andre says, "try to be patient with her, Stravos. She's *only* an amateur ... and a *woman*." If someone had uttered such a thing to Beverly Garland in *It Conquered the World*, they'd have probably gotten a fat lip.

With no dinosaur to show (it does become vaguely visible for a couple of seconds as it burns up) the picture has only a few poorly done effects scenes. One optical shot in particular, showing a pair of floating hatchets supposedly embedded in invisible flesh, is quite hilarious. One might expect a film called *Sound of Horror* to at least make an effort with its sound effects, but they're as miserable as everything else. The beast's footsteps sound like the chugs of a steam locomotive, and its alley-cat squalls generate chuckles instead of chills. Battle-hardened bad-movie completists may make it through this dud, but for most the *Sound of Horror* will be an intolerably sour note.

Super Mario Bros.

"Where are we? This is crazy! What IS this place?"

** 1993, USA. Hollywood Pictures. C, 104m.

CREDITS: *Directors* Rocky Morton, Annabel Jankel. *Producers* Jake Eberts, Roland Joffé, Brad Weston (associate), Fred Caruso (coproducer). *Written by* Parker Bennett and Terry Runté, and Ed Solomon. *Visual Effects Design and Supervision* Christopher Francis Woods.
CAST: *Mario Mario* Bob Hoskins. *Luigi Mario* John Leguizamo. *King Koopa* Dennis Hopper. *Daisy* Samantha Mathis. *Iggy* Fisher Stevens. *Spike* Richard Edson. *Lena* Fiona Shaw.

AD LINE: "This ain't no game, it's a live-action thrill ride!"

A pair of blue-collar Brooklyn plumbers, brothers Mario Mario and Luigi Mario, are out on a job when Luigi becomes infatuated with a pretty paleontology student named Daisy. She is actually a princess from a parallel universe of humanoid dinosaurs, created by a meteor impact 65 million years ago. When King Koopa, despotic ruler of "Dinohatten" (get it? MAN-hatten, DINO-hatten …) sends bumbling goons Iggy and Spike to kidnap Daisy, the Marios pursue her into the other dimension. Koopa has risen to power by using his "de-evolution" device to create an army of tiny-brained soldiers called "Goombas," and by turning Daisy's father — Dinohatten's rightful leader — into a fungus. The king yearns to expand his realm, but the two universes can only be merged by inserting the shard of rock mounted in Daisy's necklace back into the meteorite from which it came. Helped by a "baby" T. rex named Yoshi, who was once the king's pet, and a kind-hearted nightclub bouncer named Big Bertha, the Marios manage to spring Daisy from captivity. Koopa's disloyal moll, Lena, gains possession of the shard and begins the merger, but Luigi uses his plumber's tools to remove it in time. The Marios finally subject Koopa to his own de-evolution ray, turning him back into a dinosaur and ultimately into primordial slime. Daisy's father re-evolves into his kingly self, and tranquility returns to Dinohatten.

COMMENTARY: With all the buzz surrounding the upcoming *Jurassic Park* in the early nineties, it's no shock that the makers of *Super Mario Bros.* chose to emphasize the video game's dinosaurian world for the film version. Unfortunately, it turned out much like *Batman and Robin* (1997): great production design and art direction, atmospheric photography, a game cast … and a story so convoluted, uninvolving, and interrupted by pointless action sequences as to defy description.

The writers deserve some credit, I suppose, simply for managing to devise a "real world" backstory by which a pair of Italian-American plumbers from Brooklyn could end up making 30-foot superhero jumps in a world full of mushrooms and Goombas. The "20 years ago" prologue is energetic and intriguing, and bodes well. But it's only a tease, because the entire exposition up until the entry into Dinohatten is leadenly long-winded. Had *King Kong*'s first act been this flabby, we'd have had to sit through a 15-minute scene of Ann Darrow being brought before a judge for swiping that apple.

Not that things get much better inside the reptilian world. Dinohatten, illuminated with garish neon signs and fountains of electrical sparks, *looks* terrific if somewhat reminiscent of previous films. The acting is solid, led by the engaging trio of Bob Hoskins, Samantha Mathis, and John Leguizamo, but not even the indefatigable Hoskins can squeeze any blood out of this celluloid turnip. As others have pointed out, Dennis Hopper's lizardly villain role screamed for an over-the-top performance, yet Hopper,

who can go over the top with the best, inexplicably played it dead straight. There is little to say about Fisher Stevens and Richard Edson or the caricatures they play, and Stevens is no more or less irritating here than usual.

The dinosaur content of *Super Mario Bros.* is fairly meager. The only more or less realistic dinos are the small allosaur-patterned dino vermin which serve as Dinohatten's "rats," one stage of Koopa's de-evolution sequence where he fleetingly resembles a Tyrannosaurus, and Yoshi the little T. rex. Amid the movie's plentiful shortcomings and the *Jurassic Park* phenomenon, not enough has been said about what a splendid bit of mechanical engineering—not to mention puppet performance—Yoshi embodied. Admittedly, the creature was a minor character, didn't weigh thousands of pounds and performed no greatly demanding physical feats, but no animatronic character ever built up until that time, not even Stan Winston's awesome *Jurassic* dinosaurs, demonstrated more organic or fluid movement. The darn thing looks *alive*.

Super Mario Bros. is a textbook example of "all style, no substance." One of the film's tag lines called it a "live-action thrill ride," but there is simply no story, no characters, absolutely nothing to draw you in. No matter how thrilling a roller-coaster is, you have to be on board to get the thrills, and *Mario* leaves its potential riders watching from the ground.

PEOPLE AND PRODUCTION: The job of developing Dinohatten's "look" went to production designer David L. Snyder, veteran of such films as *Brainstorm* (1983), *My Science Project*, and the classic of cinematic design, *Blade Runner* (1982). "What we've done is basically taken all the elements that are in the video game, turned them into a metaphor and combined them with 3-D and real characters," Snyder told Marc Shapiro in *Starlog*. "It's something really strange that's going to surprise audiences." Virtually the whole film was shot in an empty cement plant in North Carolina, turned into a makeshift soundstage. "Man was it hot!" Snyder recalled. "There was a lot of pain and suffering that went into the film, but in the end, it all seemed to work."

Like many such projects, *Super Mario Bros.* endured a number of false starts before finally getting made. The first director announced was Greg Beeman, who was involved back when the film had a radically different concept. Once the husband-wife team of Rocky Morton and Annabel Jankel were installed as the new directors, conceptual artist Patrick Tatopoulos began designing many of Dinohatten's citizens. "I just sit down with a piece of paper and come up with stuff," Tatopoulos said. "I've also been very interested in dinosaurs, anyway. When I was a kid, I always drew them." The artist deliberately tried to stay far away from the dinosaurs featured in the same year's *Jurassic Park*. "They were doing the ultimate real dinosaurs, so I approached this trying to do something funny, cute and cartoony. ... We were attempting a kind of *Blade Runner*-meets-*Beetlejuice* type of movie."

The film's epilogue blatantly sets up a sequel in much the same manner as had *Back to the Future* (1985), but the $40 million *Super Mario* didn't draw the box office necessary to warrant a follow-up.

SPECIAL EFFECTS: The *Mario* creatures were the work of several different effects companies. The microheaded Goombas, created by Makeup & Effects Laboratories (MEL), were men in suits equipped with wearer-operated controls for major head movements and radio controls for more complex facial articulations. MEL also designed and built the dino rats which infest the reptilian city. "They were supposed to be cut from the film," recalled MEL's Allan Apone. "One day when the directors came over to approve some designs, they saw the Allosaurus rat and liked it so much that they put it back in." Koopa's regression through

Opposite: Outlandish Filipino poster for the outlandish yet unsatisfying *Super Mario Bros.*

The amazing "Yoshi"—one of the most sophisticated and lifelike animatronic dinosaurs ever constructed.

Tammy and the T-Rex

"This is not a figment of my imagination!"

1994, USA. Imperial Entertainment. C, 82m.

CREDITS: *Director* Stewart Raffill. *Producers* Diane Raffill, Etka Sarlui (executive), Gary Brockett (associate), Joleen Deatherage (associate), Fernando Celis (coproducer). *Written by* Stewart Raffill and Gary Brockette. *Special Effects Design for T-Rex* Gnome Productions, Bruce Nazarian, Scott Wolf. *T-Rex Provided by* Creative Presentations, Inc. *Make-up Effects* John Carl Buechler.

CAST: *Tammy* Denise Richards. *Michael* Paul Walker. *Byron* Theo Forsett. *Dr. Wachenstein* Terry Kiser. *Helga* Ellen Dubin.

AD LINE: "He's the coolest pet in town!"

Tammy is a perky and curvaceous high school cheerleader in love with clean-cut football jock Michael, but their happiness is threatened by Tammy's psychotically jealous ex-beau, Billy. One night, Billy snaps. He beats the tar out of Michael and dumps him in a wild animal park (called "Wild Animal Park"), and by the time the lions get through with him he's a perfect candidate for crazed scientist Dr. Wachenstein's latest experiment. The doc and his moll, Helga, abduct Michael from intensive care, saw his head open, and transplant his brain into a robotic Tyrannosaurus rex. But the Michael-Tyrannosaurus hybrid is none too happy when he awakens, quickly escaping and taking toothy revenge on Billy and his gang. After the mute creature uses charades to explain things to Tammy, she and her good-natured gay pal, Byron, flee with the fugitive dino as Wachenstein and the local sheriff pursue. Wachenstein becomes the victim of his own creation, but the police destroy the robotic dinosaur in a climactic shootout. Undaunted, Tammy preserves Michael's brain on her bedroom dresser—in a bowlful of booze—while she searches for a new body.

COMMENTARY: *Tammy and the T-Rex* is,

several evolutionary stages in the climax was a combination of make-up work for the first two stages and mechanized puppets for the last two, using prosthetic and mechanical designs by Patrick Tatopoulos, Robert Burman, and Bud McGrew.

The star dinosaur is the lovable pet T. rex, Yoshi, originally designed by Tatopoulos and sculpted by Mark Maitre. "Patrick's design was really something different and not like any dinosaur I had seen before," recalled Maitre, who recommended Dave Nelson to oversee the creature's mechanization. "Dave worked on all the mechanics," Maitre noted, "while I did all the fabrications of the skins, the painting and designs, the teeth, toenails and vacuform pieces that are inside the body, as well as the bladders that allow Yoshi to breathe." The final result was an incredibly complex bit of animatronics, with nearly 200 feet of cable required to articulate the barely three-foot-tall puppet. "To operate Yoshi it takes nine puppeteers," Nelson said on TV's *Movie Magic*. "It's fully cable-controlled, and then the head itself is all radio-controlled. That was pretty difficult to get that synched up—we'd just all coordinate and work together."

Opposite: Video-store proprietors likely scratched their heads trying to choose a category shelf for the inexplicable *Tammy and the T-Rex.*

TERRY KISER DENISE RICHARDS JOHN FRANKLIN

Tammy and the T·REX

He's The Coolest Pet In Town!

I guess, really a love story. But how do you begin to tell the story of how grating a love can be? Other movies have worse production values, more amateurish acting, cheaper dinosaur mock-ups, but there is hardly a film covered in this volume that is so torturously difficult to actually sit through.

It's a mystery what writer-director Stewart "Adventures of the Wilderness Family" Raffill had in mind here. Is it, to use Roger Ebert's term, a "horny teenager" movie? No, there's minimal sexual content. A serious social commentary? Doubtful, with George "Buck" Flower as a good-ol'-boy deputy and a robotic tyrannosaur communicating through charades. It could be a satire, but of what? It was marketed as a zany, family comedy—could that be it? Surely not, with its frequent profanity and sadistic violence. Thank goodness it isn't a musical, since its one song has terrible lyrics. Maybe "black comedy" is the closest—the sequence where Tammy and a grossed-out Byron sort through a morgue's residents in search of a new body for Michael qualifies as such, and it's actually the picture's best scene.

Every character is a cardboard stereotype, from Denise Richards as the cute-as-a-button, sexy/innocent cheerleader (a role she was, admittedly, born to play) and Theo Forsett as Tammy's comedy-relief gay buddy (who talks like Pearl Bailey), to Terry Kiser and Ellen Dubin as the mad scientist and assistant. With their lame, nondescript foreign accents and Dubin towering over the shorter Kiser, they come across as a low-rent Boris and Natasha—minus the wit. The T. rex itself is a marginally impressive, full-scale robot, better than most museum-exhibit creatures but not to be mentioned in the same breath with Stan Winston's work. It has great detail and considerable articulation—as long as it's merely standing still, growling and looking around. Shots of its walking feet and its little front arms doing things (like dialing a telephone!) are human-worn props, and look it.

Denise Richards would go on from *Tammy and the T-Rex* to major roles in such A-list productions as *Starship Troopers* (1997), *Wild Things* (1998) and *The World is not Enough* (1999), but anyone watching *Tammy* hoping for a "before-she-was-a-star" nude scene will be disappointed. But then, anyone who subjects themselves to this vile picture for *any* reason will be disappointed, queasy, and probably in a sour mood for two or three days.

Tarzan's Desert Mystery

"We're gonna have lots of fun traveling across the desert!"

**½ 1943, USA. RKO Radio Pictures. BW, 70m.

CREDITS: *Director* William Thiele. *Producer* Sol Lesser. *Screenplay* Edward T. Lowe. *Story* Carroll Young; based upon characters created by Edgar Rice Burroughs.
CAST: *Tarzan* Johnny Weissmuller. *Connie Bryce* Nancy Kelly. *Boy* Johnny Sheffield. *Hendrix* Otto Kruger. *Karl* Joe Sawyer. *Prince Selim* Robert Lowery. *The Sheik* Lloyd Corrigan.

As World War II drags on, Jane is off in London helping to nurse the wounded. She sends a message to Tarzan, telling of the soldiers returning from Japanese-occupied Burma sick with jungle fever. She urgently needs some of Tarzan's fever medicine "that cured Boy when he was so ill."

As Tarzan, Boy and Cheta trek across the Great Desert to the "fever medicine jungle" (the only place the curative plant grows) they meet Connie Bryce, an American "gal magician" on a USO type of tour. Connie has been recruited to carry a secret message from Sheik Amir of Elecebra (EL-uh-KEE-brah) to his friend Prince Selim of Birherari (BEER-her-AR-ee), warning of a dangerous German agent known as Paul Hendrix. Selim already suspects Hendrix, who has slyly been taking control of Birherari's lucrative trade routes, but can't convince his naive father, the sheik. Connie's successful delivery of the message gives Selim the proof he needs, but Hendrix cold-bloodedly murders the prince and frames Connie for the crime.

Tarzan and Connie Bryce (Johnny Weissmuller, Nancy Kelly) race to free Boy (Johnny Sheffield) from the web of a giant prehistoric spider in *Tarzan's Desert Mystery*.

Tarzan, Boy and Cheta snatch Connie from the gallows and head for the fever medicine jungle, with Hendrix and his aide, Karl, in pursuit.

Tarzan and Cheta leave Connie and Boy at the jungle's edge and go on alone, dodging a variety of giant prehistoric reptiles while gathering the medicinal ingredients. The woman and child try to evade the German agents and get a brief reprieve when a lion kills Karl, but Hendrix finally traps Connie in a cave and it's up to Tarzan to swing in on a vine and kick the Nazi into the web of a gargantuan killer spider. Back in Birherari, the sheik thanks Connie for all her help, she promises to deliver the fever medicine to Jane, and Tarzan, Boy and Cheta head for home.

COMMENTARY: Someone unfamiliar with Edgar Rice Burroughs' body of work may think that mixing Tarzan with prehistoric beasts is an idea that could only be dreamed up by an uninspired B-movie scribe. But Burroughs wrote many such tales, with titles like *Tarzan the Terrible* and *Tarzan at the Earth's Core*, sending his jungle hero into all sorts of lands that time forgot. *Tarzan's Desert Mystery* is the only attempt to bring even a hint of this scenario to the movie screen, though it's much more light caper than grand adventure. The familiar "lost world" touchstones—dinosaurs, giant spider, carnivorous plant—were apparently added just to make the "fever medicine jungle" more mysterious, and really have little to do with the story. Tarzan definitely does not "fight a dinosaur" as some sources claim, though the giant spider does dispatch the villain.

Most of the picture's fun is courtesy of

Tarzan (Johnny Weissmuller), caught by a prehistoric plant in the Fever Medicine Jungle, must have used a particularly loud "Tarzan yell" to summon these Indian, not African, elephants.

Nancy Kelly; just think of Kate Capshaw in *Indiana Jones and the Temple of Doom* (1984) with less whining, more pluck and a better sense of humor. Kelly was a truly talented actress who would later nab a Tony for her role as the mother in the play *The Bad Seed*, a role she reprised in the movie version in 1956, and proves here she could handle glib comedy as well as serious drama. She has some great dialogue — the scene with Connie and her three desert guides is priceless if not (sigh) politically correct — and she turns in an energetic performance about three notches better than a programmer like this has a right to expect. Connie's the kind of big-city gal who tosses off wisecracks like "change here for Schenectady?" in the middle of an African desert, and Kelly looks like she was having a great time. Weissmuller could play Tarzan in his sleep by this point, Sheffield is at his most winning, and Cheta (not "Cheetah") gives one of the funniest performances of her distinguished career — including one sight gag which resurfaced decades later in Steven Spielberg's *E.T. the Extra Terrestrial*! Even the villains, well played by Otto Kruger and Joe Sawyer, show touches of humor. In one scene, Karl sweats and stammers while trying to ad-lib a phony explanation of how one man (Tarzan) managed to defeat his entire party. Hendrix lets him squirm for a few seconds and then dryly smirks, "don't strain yourself, Karl."

By the time RKO took over the Tarzan franchise from MGM, the budgets were skimpier than Weissmuller's loincloth, but

Desert Mystery manages to keep from looking too impoverished. The "Birherari" sets are comparatively opulent, certainly not the tiny 3-sided crackerboxes usually seen in "series" quickies, and Paul Sawtell's music score is happily original. Edward Lowe's screenplay is not only sharp and humorous but employs some downright clever storytelling tactics, like having Boy explain the routes of their upcoming travels to Cheta — and the audience — in a tidy and clear one-minute spiel. Lowe even found a way to make Cheta's shtick into a plausible plot point, a nice change from its customary role as arbitrary "comic relief." Though minor in every way, *Tarzan's Desert Mystery* turns one of the series' most uncharacteristically breezy and lighthearted screenplays into a surprisingly diverting 70 minutes of pleasant nostalgia.

PEOPLE AND PRODUCTION: Producer Sol Lesser's first Tarzan project was *Tarzan the Fearless* (1933) with Buster Crabbe, followed by *Tarzan's Revenge* (1938) with Glenn Morris. His first Tarzan flick with Johnny Weissmuller was *Tarzan Triumphs*, which (not surprisingly in 1943) pitted the jungle man against the Nazi menace. Despite the fact that Jane was nowhere to be seen, *Tarzan Triumphs* made enough money to inspire Lesser to follow it almost immediately with another Janeless, Tarzan-meets-the-Nazis entry, *Tarzan's Desert Mystery*. The screenplay's inclusion of a prehistoric jungle necessitated some dinosaur shots, and stock footage from *One Million B.C.* was pressed into service for the first time. It would not be the last.

During his career Lesser produced more than 15 Tarzan films of one sort or another, but the most potentially intriguing one was never made. Around 1950, right after *Mighty Joe Young*, Lesser and *Joe* producer Merian C. Cooper began planning a combination sequel with the self-explanatory title *Joe Meets Tarzan*. Lex Barker would have played Tarz and one can only assume that Willis O'Brien and Ray Harryhausen would have been involved, but sadly the project never made it past early development.

Teenage Caveman

"I wonder ... how many strange things there are."

**½ 1958, USA. American International Pictures. BW, 65m.

CREDITS: *Director* Roger Corman. *Producers* Roger Corman, James H. Nicholson (executive), Samuel Z. Arkoff (executive). *Screenplay* R. Wright Campbell.
CAST: *The Boy* Robert Vaughn. *The Maiden* Darrah [Darah] Marshall. *The Symbol Maker* Leslie Bradley. *The Villain* Frank De Kova.

AD LINE: "Prehistoric rebels against prehistoric monsters!"

A small Stone Age tribe lives by a strict canon of tribal superstitions and tenets known as the "Law," but one among them, the Boy, is plagued by questions. He wonders why the Law keeps the clan from the lush forests and plentiful game beyond the river. Goaded by a devious rival, the Villain, and despite the warnings of his father, the Symbol Maker, the Boy leads a small party into the forbidden land. The Villain lusts after the comely blonde Maiden who loves the Boy, and so is anxious to see his competition put to death. But the tribal elder decrees a lesser punishment, simply that all "shall keep their voices" from the Boy until he reaches the rite of manhood.

One day, a stranger arrives from the "Burning Plains," a region said by the Law to be lifeless. This contradiction causes some to begin to question the Law but no one is prepared to denounce it, and as the days pass the tension grows between the Boy and the Villain. The Boy still yearns for answers, and despite his love of the Maiden, he departs again. When his father follows, the Villain musters a band of tribesmen and sets out to hunt both of them down. Finally, the group encounters the most feared deity in their mythology: the God That Gives Death with Its Touch. But the "god" turns out to be merely a withered old man, wearing a strange protective suit, and clutching a book filled with images of a history long forgotten.

Dinosaur movies with minimal dinosaurs often focused on other attractions, like pretty Darah Marshall, to draw an audience.

COMMENTARY: *Teenage Caveman* is a hastily filmed, tiny-budgeted, minor B-movie, but within these constraints it's not a bad picture. Despite a title that suggests otherwise, it has a sober script and surprisingly proficient acting, and is not a good choice for someone deliberately looking for bad-movie chuckles. Though not without a few clunker scenes, it never sinks into silliness.

Teenage Caveman stubbornly maintains a measure of dignity. Having English-speaking characters is much less cumbersome than the pseudoarchaic dialects of other "caveman" films, and the womenfolk aren't dressed, or rather undressed, like Spring Break contestants either. R. Wright Campbell's intelligent and measured screenplay is well-handled by a mostly capable cast. Robert Vaughn's performance is thoughtful if a bit too civilized, and he thankfully doesn't overdo the brooding, James Dean/Marlon Brando bit. Leslie Bradley is good as his wise father, Frank De Kova takes only small bites of the scenery during his emotional soliloquies, and Darah Marshall is colorless but attractive as the love interest.

The decidedly skimpy story struggles to fill even its meager 65-minute running time; condensed to 25 minutes, *Teenage Caveman* could have made a swell *Twilight Zone* episode. It's equally skimpy on the dinosaur front, offering only *One Million B.C.* shots (including a number of outtakes) and a single clip of the swamp-bound brontosaurs from *Unknown Island*. The only other "special effect" animal is the valiant Beach Dickerson wearing a budget bear suit.

The "surprise ending" is of course no longer a surprise, but is handled with such grave restraint that it still packs a little punch. The revelation is also neatly foreshadowed by the early scenes of the three tribal elders known as the Keepers of the Gifts. "Why do you build, only to break," the Boy asks one of the Keepers. A really good question, that.

PEOPLE AND PRODUCTION: In 1958, the same year he directed the fairly effective gangster film *Machine Gun Kelly*, Roger Corman also made a little picture called *Prehistoric World* about a restless young man who rebels against the superstitions of his primitive tribe. However, it came out just after American International's box office success *I Was a Teenage Werewolf* (1957), and AIP retitled Corman's entry *Teenage Caveman*. "Aside from its horrible title, *Teenage Caveman* was a pretty good film," said Corman, quoted in Ed Naha's *The Films of Roger Corman*. "I almost died when I saw it emerge with AIP's new title." Corman's reaction is understandable; besides the fact that the silly-sounding name detracts from the film's intended seriousness, Robert Vaughn was actually a mature 25 at the time.

As usual for both AIP and Corman, *Teenage Caveman* had a very low budget. It is padded with stock footage, reuses the monster suit from *Night of the Blood Beast* (1958) as the old man's radiation garb, and even sneaks in a clip of Paul Blaisdell's mon-

"The Beast that Gives Death with its Touch," which turns out to be an old man in an antiradiation suit, approaches the indomitable *Teenage Caveman* (Robert Vaughn).

ster suit from *The She Creature* (1956). "Although we had a strong plot and a very fine young actor, Robert Vaughn, in the lead, we still were hampered by budget limitations," Corman recalled. "The budget showed at times." Like when Vaughn has to carry a supposedly just-killed deer on his back. "Now, deers don't go into a complete state of rigor mortis right after they're killed," Corman said. "I told [the prop man] I didn't want this stiff deer. He told me it was this stuffed deer or no deer." Corman still remembers with a wince a certain preview showing, with the audience really getting into the story until the petrified deer came on-screen.

Someone else who surely remembers *Teenage Caveman* with a wince is Beach Dickerson who plays three parts in the film — and is killed three times. Dickerson is the man who drowns in the "Dirt that Eats Men," a very unpleasant scene to shoot. "I was supposed to fall off a log into this water that was so filthy it almost made me throw up," Dickerson told author Mark Thomas McGee. His second death comes as the "Man from the Burning Plain" who is killed by the superstitious tribesmen. "So I rode into camp wearing this ridiculous beard," Dickerson remembered. "I looked like Ulysses S. Grant in a bearskin." Finally came the time to film the encounter with a vicious bear. "I was waiting for the trainer to show up with the bear," Dickerson said, "when I see this guy coming toward me with a bear suit. 'Oh, my God,' I thought." Dickerson reportedly played a fourth role, as a mourner at the funeral of the drowned boy (yes, his own funeral), but the scene is not present in the commonly available videocassette print of the film.

Teenage Caveman was filmed in only ten days on a budget of less than $100,000. The primary locations included, yes, Bronson Canyon and the equally well-used Iverson Ranch. Some shots, including Beach Dickerson's nausea-inducing drowning scene, were done at the Los Angeles State and County Arboretum in Pasadena. The movie was released on a double bill with *How to Make a Monster*, and received generally favorable reviews.

Theodore Rex

"Whoa-whoa-whoa! What? What?!"
1995, USA. New Line Cinema.
C, 91m.

CREDITS: *Director* Jonathan Betuel. *Producers* Richard G. Abramson, Sue Baden-Powell, Stefano Ferrari (executive), Jonathan Betuel (coexecutive). *Written by* Jonathan Betuel. *Dinosaurs by* John Criswell and Chris Finch. *"Theodore Rex" Suit Performer* Pons Maar.
CAST: *Katie Coltrane* Whoopi Goldberg. *Elizar Kane* Armin Mueller-Stahl. *Dr. Shade* Juliet Landau. *Spinner* Bud Cort. *Edge* Stephen McHattie. *Voice of Theodore Rex* George Newbern. *Voice of Molly Rex* Carol Kane. *Commissioner Lynch* Richard Roundtree.

AD LINE: "The world's toughest cop is getting a brand new partner. He's a real blast from the past. And don't even think of calling him Barney."

In an alternative future, billionaire ecologist Elizar Kane has used genetic technology to bring dinosaurs back to life. But these aren't ordinary dinosaurs — they talk, wear three-toed sneakers, patronize seedy night spots, and the one named Theodore Rex works as a P.R. stooge for the police department. Teddy finally gets his longed-for chance to be a real detective when he is teamed with cybernetically enhanced Katie Coltrane to solve a "dino-cide." Despite interference from Kane's flunky, Edge, and his flunky's flunky, Spinner, the unlikely duo discover the truth: Kane had the saur killed when he threatened to spill the beans regarding the megalomaniac's plan to wipe out the human race and reinvent the earth as his own personal paradise. Teddy has some mixed feelings — Kane is his creator, after all — but he's all cop, and he's determined to rescue his girlfriend, nightclub chanteuse Molly Rex. When Katie is wounded, Teddy must go it alone to put an end to Kane's vile scheme.

COMMENTARY: Writer-director Jonathan Betuel's first dinosaur-related effort, *My Science Project*, was largely a misfire but did show glimmers of promise. *Theodore Rex* shows none. Who could blame Whoopi Goldberg for trying to get out of doing this picture? She looks thoroughly uncomfortable and cannot bring herself to put an ounce of life into her line readings—it's easily the worst performance of her career. *Theodore* is a haphazard pastiche of a "buddy movie," the *Dinosaurs* television show, *Who Framed Roger Rabbit?*, the *Super Mario Bros.* movie, *Adventures in Dinosaur City*, and other influences. The film's big running gag is Teddy's inability to control his tail, which is continually knocking things over, bruising the police commissioner's shins, and thwacking shapely women on the backside. A $35 million budget combined with the fact that an embarrassed New Line Cinema elected not to release *Theodore Rex* theatrically, reportedly made it the most expensive direct-to-video movie to date.

To renege on my earlier statement, *Theodore* does have one tiny flicker of life: the five minute visit to the "Extinct Species Club." Looking like a combination of the "Ink & Paint Club" from *Who Framed Roger Rabbit* and the Mos Eisley cantina from *Star Wars*, the setting has a quirkiness totally absent from the rest of the picture. The room is populated by an impressive variety of humanized dinosaurs, one of which even tries to hit on the Whoopster. Jeff Farley, who sculpted the T. rex for the *Carnosaur* films, also sculpted some supporting characters for this sequence. The dinosaurs' "look"

Whoopi Goldberg looks pained even in the poster for *Theodore Rex*, one of the most astronomically ill-conceived films of all time.

was supposed to be "just sort of more whimsical," Farley told this author. "You know, sort of keeping them somewhat realistic but giving them more a human feeling, obviously, being people in suits." After leaving the club, *Theodore* sinks right back into the doldrums.

The credits contain some familiar FX names—the Chiodo brothers, Gene Warren, Jr., and Fantasy II—but no amount of technical skill could salvage a concept this wretched. The sight of not only Goldberg, but also Bud Cort and Richard Roundtree toiling in a thing like this is exceedingly discouraging. The dinosaur genre has survived *Untamed Women*, *King Dinosaur*, even *Tammy and the T-Rex*, but a couple more wrecks like *Theodore* could threaten it with extinction.

Three Ages

"Through every age there is the faithful worshipper at Beauty's shrine."

***   1923, USA. Metro. BW, 63m, silent.

CREDITS: *Directors* Buster Keaton and Eddie Cline. *Producer* Joseph Schenck. *Story and Titles by* Clyde Bruckman, Joseph Mitchell, Jean Havez. *Art Director* Fred Gabourie.
CAST: *The Young Man* Buster Keaton. *The Girl* Margaret Leahy. *The Rival* Wallace Beery.

Buster Keaton's first feature-length comedy is a still-funny combination of three analogous tales of the male-female relationship, filled with truly clever gags. Set in prehistoric, Roman, and modern times, the scenarios humorously illustrate that the more things change the more they stay the same. (Jim Danforth told me of his feeling that Carl Gottlieb and Rudy de Luca were influenced by the prehistory segment of *The Three Ages* when writing *Caveman*.) At the beginning of the movie are two cuts of a stop-motion animated Brontosaurus, upon which caveman Keaton (also a puppet) rides into the scene. The film's credits contain no mention of animation or special effects, and the identity of the bronto's animator has long been a subject of curiosity within the community of stop-motion practitioners and enthusiasts.

In 1998, effects artist and historian Hal Miles was sorting through old materials in association with the launching of an ambitious stop-motion animation related web site, and rediscovered some tape-recorded interviews he had conducted in the early 1980s. One of his conversations was with stop-motion artist Lou Bunin, best known for the animation in MGM's *Ziegfeld Follies* (1945). Here is what Miles told this author about the Bunin interview:

> I came across one tape where Bunin talks about how he got started in doing dimensional animation, and who actually taught him how to do it. That gentleman's name is Charles Bowers. Bowers, as described in this tape from Lou Bunin, did the effects work on most of Buster Keaton's films, including *Three Ages*. I don't know if he actually built the models and miniatures and things like that, but back then it usually was a one-man operation.

The idea of Charles Bowers creating the *Three Ages* animation seems plausible. Bowers had been involved in cartoon animation and trick films since about 1916, and his talent for photographic illusion was prodigious. All of his films, including *Egged On* (1926), *A Wild Roomer* (1926), *Now You Tell One* (1926), and *It's a Bird* (1930), featured imaginative and innovative special effects and often included stop-motion. About Bowers, *Photoplay* editor James R. Quirk once wrote: "In the world's most individualistic industry, he is Aladdin and the camera is his lamp. He can direct. He can write. He can conceive the most glorious idiocy. He is a *master* of camera wizardry."

By themselves, Bunin's few secondhand comments are not sufficiently conclusive to pronounce the *Three Ages* mystery solved, though it seems perhaps reasonable to consider Bowers the "frontrunner" until displaced by future revelations. Perhaps other researchers will be inspired by this snippet of information to dig deeper into the careers of Bowers and other early effects artists and eventually identify the *Three Ages* animator with absolute certainty, be it Charles Bowers or someone yet unknown.

Time Tracers

"This will fade like a bad dream from your memory."

*   1995, USA. Chase Regency Corporation. C, 101m.

CREDITS: *Director* Bret McCormick. *Producers* Bret McCormick, C. D. Stephens (executive), Tom T. Moore (coexecutive), Christopher Heldman (associate). *Written by* Ted Newsom. *Special Effects Make-up* Joe Riley. *Digital Effects* Light & Shadows Graphix.

CAST: *Dr. Carrington* Jeffrey Combs. *Van* Rocky Patterson. *Casey* Dorenda Moore. *Tom* Tyler Mason. *John Harmon* Christopher Heldman. *Julia Duffy* Barri Kay Murphy. *Rudd* Jim Taylor. *Biff* Mark Nutter. *Ginger* T. J. Myers. *Irina Cho* Veronica Culver.

The brilliant scientist Dr. Carrington, working for the amoral Mr. Rudd and giant Rudd Industries, finally has the top-secret "Kronos" time-travel project ready for testing. An odd collection of people are gathered: Rudd, Carrington, physicist Irina, reporter Tom, security agents Casey and Van, paleontologists John and Julia, bodyguard Biff, and busty starlet–dress designer Ginger (please don't ask). After a brief trial run back to the Civil War, the group — except for Carrington, who remains at Kronos control — swoops back to the Jurassic period. The local dinosaurs almost immediately begin to pick them off one by one, and the survivors are ecstatic when they manage to vanquish their T. rex nemesis. But upon returning to the present they find that their meddling has changed history, and an intelligent saurian-human species called "anthrosaurus" has replaced *Homo sapiens* as the dominant life form. Just when all seems lost, a diminutive alien "from Earth's future" arrives and repairs the corrupted timeline. Just like that.

COMMENTARY: *Time Tracers*, a microbudgeted, barely seen sci-fi entry, recalls in various ways three different films examined in this book. Its stop-motion dinosaurs and spaceship effects are from *Planet of Dinosaurs*, its convoluted time-travel story and penchant for silly technobabble are reminiscent of *Journey to the Center of Time*, and like *Valley of the Dragons* it uses *so much* stock footage that its plot unavoidably begins to parallel that of the original source. In *Dragons*, Cesare Danova and Sean McClory donned animal skins to match those of the *One Million B.C.* cavemen. Here, the timenauts wear special outfits (for "electromagnetic charge protection") which are near-perfect copies of the *Planet of Dinosaurs* uniforms, and actors were selected who physically resembled the *Planet* cast. These tactics allowed the use of clips showing not just the dinos but the people as well, and director Bret McCormick even took the trouble to visually substitute Jim Taylor for Harvey Shain in the ceratopsian goring shot. The only prehistoric creature not from *Planet* is the man-in-a-suit "anthrosaurus," or "Dino-Man" as Tom calls it, but unfortunately the woefully inadequate suit is not even as plausible as the reptilian costume fashioned by Ben Nye for *The Alligator People* (1959).

While enduring the illogical narrative and technical shortcomings, film buffs may find mild relief in the steady stream of obvious but good-natured movie in-jokes. There's a Clint Eastwood soliloquy ("feel lucky? Well do ya, punk?"), a poke at *Jurassic Park* ("you've got some idiotic idea about cloning dinosaurs from DNA?"), and when someone wonders what "Kronos" is, Casey — apparently a Jeff Morrow fan — suggests "some sci-fi flick from the fifties?" Later, the picky paleontologist points out that Brontosaurus should be called Apatosaurus, setting up Rudd for the film's best line: "Yeah, and Tony Curtis' real name is Bernie Schwartz." Even *Planet of Dinosaurs* isn't spared a jab — one character aptly observes that their copycat wardrobe makes them "look like Power Rangers." The cast is lively and the acting is clearly better than that in *Planet of Dinosaurs*, but it's disheartening to see the unique and underused Jeffrey Combs wasted in something this minor.

Blending dinosaurs, comedy, camp, and G-rated cheesecake, *Time Tracers* shows obvious affection for the genre. It's nice that Bret McCormick put forth the effort to use the stock footage creatively, and that he acknowledged *Planet of Dinosaurs* animator Doug Beswick and director Jim Shea in the closing credits. But the movie has far too many problems to be considered more than an amiable curio, and it finally suffers the killing blow of not knowing how — or when — to wrap things up. With each new film to reuse the *Planet of Dinosaurs* animation, the much-abused original seems to look better and better.

T-Rex: Back to the Cretaceous

"*Wow.*"

***½ 1998, USA. Imax Corporation. C, 45m.

CREDITS: *Director* Brett Leonard. *Producers* Antoine Compin, Charis Horton, Michael Lewis (coproducer), Andrew Gellis (executive). *Screenplay* Andrew Gellis, Jeanne Rosenberg. *Story* Andrew Gellis, David Young. *Visual Effects Production* L-Squared Entertainment. *Visual Effects Studio* Blue Sky/VIFX. *Visual Effects Supervisor* Sean Phillips.

CAST: *Ally Hayden* Liz Stauber. *Dr. Donald Hayden* Peter Horton. *Elizabeth Sample* Kari Coleman. *Charles R. Knight* Tuck Milligan. *Barnum Brown* Laurie Murdoch.

AD LINE: "Prepare to go back in time."

Like her father, famous paleontologist Donald Hayden, 16-year-old Ally Hayden loves dinosaurs. She longs to go on a real fossil dig, but must console herself with her summer job as a Natural History Museum tour guide. Ally is thrilled by the museum's latest prize — an oval object found by Dr. Hayden and his assistant, Elizabeth, which just may be a Tyrannosaurus egg. While waiting one evening for her harried, too-busy father, Ally accidentally knocks the egg to the floor and propels herself into an unexplained adventure.

The museum's towering T. rex seems to come alive before her eyes, with flesh and skin forming over the bare skeleton. Ally journeys through time into a Cretaceous forest, and sees a Parasaurolophus family at the

An Ornithomimus on the prowl for eggs instead finds teenage Ally Hayden (Liz Stauber) unwisely reclining in a Tyrannosaurus nest.

edge of a pristine lake. She watches the Deinonychus in a museum painting become real and even meets the artist, the legendary Charles R. Knight. The teenager travels down the Red Deer River, discussing dinosaur theories with famous bone hunter Barnum Brown. And she returns to the Cretaceous to witness a majestic Pteranodon and a fleet-footed Ornithomimus, and comes face to face with a 40-foot-long Tyrannosaurus rex. Finally blasted back to the present by the impact of the dinosaur-killer comet, Ally finds that her dad has the locket she lost during her prehistoric adventure. "Where did you get that?" she asks. "The late Cretaceous," he replies.

COMMENTARY: Living in a comparatively small town is great, but it does have disadvantages. Like when I wanted to see *T-Rex: Back to the Cretaceous* and the nearest IMAX 3-D theater was 200 miles away. Needless to say, after a drive like that I wasn't looking for great or spectacular — I was demanding *awesome*. Happily, *T-Rex* delivered.

Historically, most IMAX films have been pure documentaries or picturesque travelogues. *T-Rex* is one of the first to have a story, with actors saying written dialogue and portraying fictional characters. The screenplay exists only as a vehicle for the visual effects and 3-D imagery but as such it's near perfect, and the characters actually become more believable than those in many conventional films. The story resembles Karel Zeman's *Journey to the Beginning of Time* in several ways. Like the four boys in Zeman's film, Ally is "magically" transported from a Natural History Museum into the dinosaur age, has encounters with the mighty animals, and at the end finds herself back in the museum. Both films even end with the appearance of an artifact which serves as "evidence" that *it really happened*.

The giant IMAX screen demands a naturalistic, understated acting style, and Liz Stauber obviously realized as much. She keeps her actions ever credible and refuses to overplay the "get a grip" moments when she finds herself in the Mesozoic. A young female protagonist is a nice touch in itself, since dinosaur fandom has often been fallaciously considered a "boy thing." Peter Horton, with his measured portrayal, rumpled attire and slightly unkempt beard, looks exactly the part of a paleontologist, and Kari Coleman's energetic portrayal makes an impression even with limited screen time. The Barnum Brown and Charles Knight characters are slightly more exaggerated, but not detrimentally so.

T-Rex was chastised by some critics for shortchanging the audience in the dinosaur department. With all the hoopla, they claimed, the roughly four minutes of dino action just wasn't enough. It's true that the dinosaur sequences are short, and they're so good it's hard not to wish for more, but better to limit the dinos' screen time and get them *right* than to go for too much and compromise the results. Solving the problems of creating computer-generated dinosaurs with the resolution needed for the IMAX process, then adding 3-D to the mix as well, was a massive undertaking. The filmmakers decided to go for quality over quantity, and it was the right choice. My initial fear, that the effects artists would be so concerned with the 3-D considerations that the animation itself would suffer, turned out to be groundless. The animation is masterful, approaching if not equaling ILM's amazing work in *Jurassic Park* and its sequels.

The animators at Blue Sky/VIFX imparted visible, palpable "weight" to the animals, a vital quality missing from less-accomplished digital dinos. The first sight of the bizarrely crested hadrosaurs, the soaring Pteranodon, the Deinonychus emerging from the 2-D painting into 3-D space, and the climactic sequence as Ally gets up close and personal with the Tyrannosaurus, are all eye-popping delights. Another wow is the earlier shot of the museum's T. rex skeleton as it comes crackling eerily to life (recalling David Allen's terrific stop-motion sequence in *Doctor Mordrid*), and then the flesh and skin and teeth magically appear ... it's super stuff.

Making the admittedly long stretches between the dinosaur scenes painless is the enjoyability of the 3-D effects. The film takes the viewer to the Red Deer River and Dinosaur Provincial Park in Alberta, Canada, and truly captures the majestic beauty of these landscapes. The effect of the shots where the airborne camera swoops and dives around and above the craggy cliffs is that the theater itself seems to be soaring through the air. When an assistant on the fossil dig chips a rock with his pick, the audience ducks away from the flying shards. The approach and impact of the dino-killer comet is unlike anything seen before—and is nothing short of spectacular. The modern 3-D technology is so far advanced beyond the primitive attempts of the 1950s that the two are not legitimately comparable. Finally, the towering music score by William Ross is one of the best dinomovie scores ever composed.

The dramatic form as applied by IMAX 3-D technology is still in its infancy, but *T-Rex* is a roaring start. It's a picture you could take your young kids to see ("this is not about dinosaurs being scary or tearing you to pieces," as Brett Leonard said) and have just as big a blast as they would. If the folks young and old in the theater the day I saw *T-Rex* are any indication, it's guaranteed to put a big dopey grin on the kisser of any dinosaur fan.

PEOPLE AND PRODUCTION: *T-Rex* was born in early 1997 as an idea from executive producer and IMAX veteran Andrew Gellis. Convinced that "the idea of putting dinosaurs on the IMAX screen was a natural" as he put it, Gellis brought the concept to director Brett Leonard and his partner Michael Lewis at L-Squared Entertainment. The script was fully storyboarded and a complete timeline designed, from pre- to postproduction. This was translated into an official proposal for IMAX, and in June 1997 *T-Rex* got the go-ahead.

A specialized team was assembled, many with valuable experience in large-format films or computer-generated imagery, or both. Besides Gellis, the group included producers Antoine Compin and Charis Horton who have a long IMAX history, stereographer–camera operator Noel Archambault, who had been involved in most of the large format 3-D films ever made, and director Brett Leonard whose feature film résumé is laden with titles like *The Lawnmower Man*, *Hideaway*, and *Virtuosity*. Philip Currie, curator of dinosaurs at the Royal Tyrell Museum of Paleontology, served as technical advisor.

"IMAX 3-D film presentation has certain requirements that you must be mindful of when you're scouting for locations," producer Charis Horton pointed out in a *T-Rex* press release. "You need to be aware of things stacking up in the foreground of the shots and of the depth of location as well." The camera chosen for *T-Rex*—a 250-pound, "unified" stereoscopic rig with two lenses and two complete film magazines—had to be toted to all of the principal locations. These included Dinosaur Provincial Park and the picturesque Red Deer River in the badlands of Alberta for the scenes where Ally meets Barnum Brown, then on to the Olympia rainforest in northern Washington State for the Cretaceous sequences. "The vegetation and environment is very similar to what scientists believe it was like in the late Cretaceous period," Brett Leonard pointed out. Another key location was the real Royal Tyrell Museum, where scenes were shot in working fossil labs as well as the main exhibit halls.

The even larger than "larger-than-life" effect of the huge IMAX image (individual pores on the skin can be seen during close-ups) had to be kept in mind during casting. "For an actor working in this large-format medium, there's really no place to hide," as Leonard put it. Any overacting or even a bit too much gesticulating could potentially be amplified to the point of absurdity. "If you see someone who is six stories high on the IMAX screen doing crazy stuff and being very big about reactions," Liz Stauber said, "it's probably not going to be as easy for the audience to believe in that character." Peter

Horton did some firsthand research for his role, even accompanying a Royal Tyrell team on a Centrosaurus excavation. "They handed me a tool and I very gently started to pry rock off of this real skull that had been covered for 75 million years," Horton recalled. "And suddenly, I kind of got what the fascination was all about."

Another side effect of IMAX's sheer size is the difficulty of passing off a stunt double as a star. Consequently, Peter Horton and Kari Coleman had to do their own stunts for a harrowing cliff-climbing sequence. "Kari did her stunt six times in a row," Brett Leonard beamed. "We dropped her 35 feet straight down and she was bouncing off of the cliff every time. She was game to go right back up and do it again." For her part, Coleman says she had other concerns besides the danger. "All I could think about when doing that stunt fall was 'boy, people will be sitting in an IMAX theater seeing my rear end six stories high just coming at them in 3-D.'" On a more serious note, Coleman was quick to credit stunt coordinator Michael Weis, "for doing such a great job of training and instilling confidence in my own abilities and my trust in him."

Principal photography started on September 22, 1997, and concluded in mid–November. A massive postproduction effort awaited, during which the film would be edited and its digital stars animated, fine-tuned, and added to the live-action footage.

SPECIAL EFFECTS: To create photorealistic, *stereoscopic* dinosaurs, the folks at

Level-headed Ally Haydn (Liz Stauber) somehow keeps her cool even while confronted by an awesome Tyrannosaurus rex when she goes *Back to the Cretaceous.*

L-Squared Entertainment turned to Blue Sky/VIFX, a visual effects house with credits on such films as *Alien: Resurrection* (1997), *The Relic* (1997), and *Titanic* (1997). "We knew, because of the size and scope of the project, that this wasn't going to be something that we could do in-house," visual-effects producer Jini Dayaneni said in *Cinefex*. The plan called for L-Squared to guide the overall effort, with the actual work being done at Blue Sky/VIFX. Visual-effects supervisor Sean Phillips, having a strong background in both large-format and 3-D films, helmed the job.

Like generations of filmmakers on projects from *King Kong* and *Mighty Joe Young* to *Jurassic Park*, Blue Sky's artists studied real animal movements to enhance their animation. They looked at ostriches and emus, elephants and rhinos, even Komodo dragons. "We wanted to observe how large creatures move, especially how the skin works," explained digital-animation supervisor Michael Necci. Another technique that dates back to the heyday of stop-motion is the use of full-size "stand-in" dinosaurs on the live-action set. "Before we filmed the scenes with the actors in them, we had to decide where the digital dinosaurs would be," Sean Phillips explained. "During the process of blocking the scene, we had full-scale mock-ups of our dinosaurs in the frame, and we used the live-action camera to take a reference clip of film to show us where everything was going to be." Besides being a valuable choreography tool, it gave actress Liz Stauber something to look at so her eye line would be correct in the composite shot.

Meanwhile, *Jurassic Park* alumnus Michael Trcic was hired to sculpt a series of dinosaur maquettes to be scanned into the computer. Working with Trcic and the FX team throughout the creative process were the film's dinosaur consultants, including paleoanatomist Cara Burres and the aforementioned Philip Currie, who was excited by the chance to collaborate on a groundbreaking dinosaur film. "IMAX technology has the potential and reputation for producing images that are so believable that the experience bypasses your brain right into your senses," Currie said.

Unlike the *Jurassic Park* films and TV's *Walking with Dinosaurs* which combined CGI with animatronics, every dinosaur shot in *T-Rex* was computer-generated. The digital dinos were then composited with the stereoscopic backgrounds filmed in the Olympia rainforest. "The dinosaurs in this film exist purely as digital images in the computer," Sean Phillips explained. "The live-action photographic image was digitized and then the synthetically created images were laid on top of the photographed background plates. For the 3-D version of the film, you have a left eye and a right eye dinosaur with slightly different perspectives, shifted in equal amounts to the real backgrounds on which they appear." Meticulous measurements taken on location enabled the artists to perfectly match the angles, distances and perspectives necessary for a wholly convincing final image.

The enormous volume of data (and work) required for *T-Rex* surprised even the filmmakers. Every new FX shot presented a hundred challenges for the small army of artists and technicians, and almost five terabytes — that's five million "meg" — of computer memory were needed by the time everything was done. A long way from the days when Ray Harryhausen would take a steel-and-rubber puppet into a secluded room and work his solitary cinematic alchemy.

Trog

"Poppycock. Insane nonsense."

1970, U.K. Warner Bros. C, 91m.

CREDITS: *Director* Freddie Francis. *Producers* Herman Cohen, Harry Woolveridge (associate). *Screenplay* Aben Kandel. *Original Story* Peter Bryan and John Gilling. *Trog Designed by* Charles Parker.
CAST: *Dr. Brockton* Joan Crawford. *Sam Murdock* Michael Gough. *Inspector Greenham*

Bernard Kay. *Anne Brockton* Kim Braden. *Malcolm Travers* David Griffin. *Magistrate* Thorley Walters. *Trog* Joe Cornelius.

AD LINE: "From a million years back... Horror explodes into today!"

A trio of amateur spelunkers stumble onto a primitive ape-man creature dwelling in an unknown cave in the English countryside. The news reaches the famous anthropologist Dr. Brockton (whose research center is conveniently located about a mile away), and soon the "greatest scientific find of modern civilization" is tranquilized and brought to her lab. The creature, dubbed "Trog" by Dr. Brockton, is to be studied by Brockton, her protégé, Malcolm, and her daughter Anne. They are opposed at every turn by local sourpuss Sam Murdock and police inspector Greenham, who worry that Trog may be dangerous. The scientists show Trog some photos of dinosaur skeletons, inciting him to dream of the days when he shared the earth with live specimens, and even endow him with rudimentary speech skills. But just as Brockton begins making progress, the petulant Murdock sneaks in and releases Trog. Murdock hopes that the savage beast will cause trouble and thus be destroyed, but Trog's first act is to kill his meddling liberator. The frightened creature unfortunately goes on a minor rampage and eventually abducts a little blonde girl (who, in true monster-movie fashion, promptly faints). Dr. Brockton descends alone into Trog's cave and retrieves the child, but is unable to convince the authorities to spare her prize specimen.

COMMENTARY: Like Ray Milland in *The Sea Serpent* (1984), *Trog* is a sad example of an actor from Hollywood's golden age ending a legendary career in a miserable genre film. *Trog* is a dreadful picture, a disaster on every front. It fails as horror, as science fiction, and as drama. It's not campy, and it's not even so bad it's good. It is simply bad — a dismal swan song for Joan Crawford.

Absolutely nothing works in *Trog*. Crawford's stiff and perfunctory performance likely resulted from her lack of interest in the part, and perhaps her effort to deliver lines like "Good boy, Trog!" while keeping a straight face. Michael Gough (rhymes with "off") is at the opposite extreme. His character is overwritten to begin with, and Gough multiplies the problem by spitting out every line as if it were a wedge of lemon. The principal shooting locations — the county of Buckinghamshire and Oakley Court near the Thames river — are as generic-looking as a public golf course, and Trog's too-well-lit cave is not remotely convincing. The film is padded with scene after scene which do nothing but fill time, and worst of all, there is no attempt to address the subject matter with even a shred of conviction.

With one borrowed exception, the fantastical elements are handled no better than anything else. Charles Parker's exaggerated make-up design gives Trog an excessively protruding jaw, though he did provide some fairly intricate mouth articulations. Even the vocalizations and screams tend more toward the comical than the Cro-Magnon. The only bit of *Trog* that shows any creative drive is, yes, the stop-motion dinosaur sequence lifted (without acknowledgment) from *The Animal World*. Even shrunk to three quarters of the screen, edited to four minutes, and with its beautiful Technicolor hues muted and paled, Ray Harryhausen's animation still gives the picture its only flash of life. (The shots of dinosaur skeletons which provoke Trog's dream are also from *Animal World*.) The scenes make little sense in the context of the picture, however, rekindling the familiar complaint about the placing of cavepeople and dinosaurs in the same era. Such anachronisms can be much more easily forgiven in prehistory fantasies like *When Dinosaurs Ruled the Earth* than in a film like *Trog*, which wants its "science" taken seriously.

It is clear that neither Freddie Francis nor Crawford had any emotional investment in *Trog*. According to author Paul M. Jensen in *The Men Who Made the Monsters*, Francis did it primarily for the chance to work with

Three never before published shots, featuring a T. rex–Stegosaurus fight and a Brontosaurus, from the unused stop-motion dinosaur sequence animated by Roger Dicken (top) for *Trog*.

artist and dinosaur enthusiast Roger Dicken was also involved with *Trog*. "I did some [dinosaur] animation for *Trog*," Dicken told the author, "but in the end they used the footage from *Animal World*." Though a skilled sculptor and model maker, Dicken had very little stop-motion experience at the time, and had for that very reason declined Hammer's initial offer to helm *When Dinosaurs Ruled*. "I did have a problem with some of it," he said of the *Trog* animation. "A lamp got knocked off or something, and part of the sky backing on a huge section of it was screwed up." And not even Dicken knows what became of the film. "What happened to that footage, I don't know," he lamented. "It exists somewhere, but who knows where, today. I've got stills from it which I did, but the footage was edited into a reel ... and I never did get a copy."

Two Lost Worlds

"The silent, watching vultures seemed to know."

* 1950, USA. Sterling Productions. BW, 63m.

CREDITS: *Director* Norman Dawn. *Producer* Boris Petroff. *Screenplay* Tom Hubbard. *Story Adaptation* Phyllis Parker and Tom Hubbard. *Sound Effects* John D. Hall. *Special Photographic Effects* Jack R. Glass.

CAST: *Kirk Hamilton* Jim Aurness (James Arness). *Elaine Jeffries* Laura Elliott. *Martin Shannon* William Kennedy. *Janice Jeffries* Gloria Petroff. *Salty* Tim Graham. *Nat Mercer* Fred Kohler, Jr. *John Hartley* Thomas Hubbard. *Captain Tallman* Tom Monroe. *Nancy* Jane Harlan. *Magistrate Jeffries* Pierre Watkins.

AD LINE: "The earth shakes on its axis ... in a land that time forgot! Maddened mastodons wage warfare to the death..."

Crawford, and apparently Crawford did it simply as a job and nothing more. *Trog* is a low ebb in the careers of many people, a dreary and best-forgotten entry in the "missing link" genre.

SPECIAL EFFECTS: Around the same time that he worked with Jim Danforth on *When Dinosaurs Ruled the Earth*, British effects

It is the year 1830. Kirk Hamilton, first mate on the American clipper ship *Hamilton Queen*, is injured in an attack by the notorious pirate ship *Phantom*. Kirk is dropped off at a small Australian settlement for medical treatment, and soon begins to fall in love with the local magistrate's daughter Elaine. This doesn't sit too well with Elaine's fiancé, Martin Shannon, but the two rivals are forced to team up when Elaine and her friend Nancy are abducted by the pirates. Kirk, Martin and some helpful locals set sail in pursuit, and are relieved to find Elaine's 10-year-old sister Janice hiding safely aboard their sloop. Kirk prepares his men with a gung-ho pep talk worthy of Knute Rockne at halftime ("Now men, I don't have to tell you what you're up against!") and a violent sea battle leaves both ships aflame. Kirk, Elaine, Martin, Nancy, Janice, and settler John Hartley escape in a lifeboat, only to come ashore on an island populated with prehistoric reptiles and overlooked by a percolating volcano. Back at the settlement, the *Queen's* skipper learns of the recent events and launches a search mission, even as the island's volcano comes to life. Nancy is killed by flowing lava and a flying volcanic boulder ricochets off of the already-wounded Martin, before the mountain mercifully quiets. With his last breath Martin chivalrously asks Kirk to "take care of Elaine," moments before the *Hamilton Queen* appears triumphantly on the horizon.

COMMENTARY: If there is a reason to sit through *Two Lost Worlds*, a 63-minute festival of stock shots and no more than a tiny footnote in the grand history of dinocinema, it is the chance to watch a very young, pre–*Gunsmoke*, even pre–*Thing from Another World* James Arness—billed as "Jim Aurness"—swaggering across the deck of a 19th-century sailing ship and barking out terrific Hollywood nautical dialogue: "A battery of six pounders mounted on the fo'c's'le and quarterdeck! Lay below and look for damage! Man the pumps!" Even in a picture this cheap, Arness shows the charisma that made him such a popular actor in years to come. The rest of the cast is far less engaging, although young Gloria Petroff handles a tough scene where, quite poignantly, she learns of her father's death.

Two Lost Worlds is a really strange little movie—a standard B-grade swashbuckler until the last 20 minutes when it suddenly turns into a "Lost World" yarn. The pompous, pretentious narration, written by Bill Shaw and read by Don Riss, periodically rears its flowery head to remind viewers that they're watching a potboiler every time the movie threatens to become slightly interesting. The voice-overs repeatedly try to take the art of stilted prose to new levels and often succeed. Here's a sample: "The others flung themselves feverishly down the slope, to quench the agony of parched lips and swollen tongues; threw themselves avidly at the edge of the pool—water! They plunged their burning faces to the wonderful water, and drank with delirious joy." (*Music swells.*) One other baffling point: these people suddenly see *living dinosaurs* right before their eyes, and apparently don't find such a discovery worthy of a single comment. (At the risk of flippancy, I wanted to hear little Janice yell, "Elaine! Come quick! It's those doggone *One Million B.C.* clips again!") Unless you are a maniacal Jim Aurness fan, better to let both of the *Two Lost Worlds* stay that way.

PEOPLE AND PRODUCTION: *Two Lost Worlds* is as negligible a film as one will ever see, yet its director holds a significant place in cinema history. Whatever led Norman Dawn to direct this flimsy patchwork of a film, in an earlier time he was one of the true pioneers of visual effects. His specialty was a time- and money-saving technique called the "glass shot." Instead of constructing an entire three-story building, for instance, one could build just a small section of doorway and then paint the rest of the structure on a pane of glass positioned between the camera and subject. "One of the first film-makers to develop the [glass shot] for professional work was the veteran cameraman-artist-director, Norman Dawn," Raymond Fielding wrote in his essential text, *The Technique of Special Effects Cinematography*. "He became one of the film industry's most frequent and skillful practitioners of the art and introduced it to many other workers in the field."

Two Lost Worlds features scenes cribbed from *Captain Fury* (1939) and *Captain Cau-*

 Gloria Petroff, Tom Hubbard, Laura Elliot, Bill Kennedy, and James Arness face volcanoes, storms, horrendous narration, and stock dino footage in *Two Lost Worlds*.

tion (1940) for much of its seagoing action, in addition to the infamous lizard-alligator "dinosaur" tussle from *One Million B.C.* Hoping nobody would remember the dino effects from Hal Roach's film, the makers of *Two Lost Worlds* not only reused the sequence but made it the focal point of their ad campaign! Blurbs like "reputed to be the most unusual sequence ever filmed" permeate the pressbook, trying pitifully to sound like some kind of inside information leaked ahead of the film's release. Of course, that same pressbook also pointed out that "Gloria Petroff, ten-year-old daughter of producer Boris Petroff, didn't get her important role in this new film because her father was the producer." As if such a thing would ever occur to anyone.

Unknown Island

"Confidentially, I'll be glad when the trip's all over."

** 1948, USA. Film Classics, Inc. C, 76m.

CREDITS: *Director* Jack Bernhard. *Producer* Albert J. Cohen. *Original Story* Robert T. Shannon. *Screenplay* Robert T. Shannon, Jack Harvey. *Art Director* Jerome Pycha, Jr. *Special Effects Photographed and Created by* Howard A. Anderson and Ellis Burman. *Set Decoration* Robert Priestly.

CAST: *Carol Lane* Virginia Grey. *Ted Osborne* Philip Reed. *John Fairbanks* Richard Denning. *Capt. Tarnowski* Barton MacLane. *Sanderson* Richard Wessel. *Edwards* Daniel White. *Golab* Philip Nazir.

AD LINE: "SEE: Prehistoric denizens that defy the imagination! SEE: Man's puny attempt to defeat monstrous beasts!"

In a seedy waterfront dive in Singapore, Ted Osborne and his fiancée, Carol Lane, make a deal with Captain Tarnowski and his first mate, Sanderson, to charter Tarnowski's animal-cage-equipped steamer. The crude and gluttonous Tarnowski is intrigued by Osborne's tales of seeing living prehistoric animals during a wartime flight over an uncharted island — and even more intrigued by the fetching Carol. Tarnowski introduces John Fairbanks, an ex-soldier once shipwrecked on the same island, who has turned to booze to drown the memories of seeing his comrades eaten alive. Fairbanks refuses to go, but Sanderson slips him a sleeping pill and dumps him on board. The ship's superstitious crew of "lascars" (East Indian sailors) attempts a midocean mutiny rather than go to the "taboo island," but their uprising is easily put down.

Sanderson spots a Brontosaurus from offshore and gasps, "Looks like somethin' you'd see during a ten-day binge!" Undaunted, the unlikely group and a handful of disgruntled lascars row to shore. They safely observe a pair of swamp-bound brontosaurs and a sail-backed reptile, but things start going sour when a lascar is caught by a herd of carnivorous "tyrannosaurs," and Carol realizes that Osborne is a selfish milquetoast who only cares about getting enough dino photographs to make him rich and famous. Fairbanks is falling in love with Carol and wants to get her off the island, but Tarnowski is determined to capture "one of those big babies" alive. He forcibly organizes another safari, but the carnivorous dinosaurs attack again and Sanderson is killed by a lascar knife — meant for Tarnowski. Mad with greed, lusting after Carol, feverish with malaria and drunk on whiskey, Tarnowski orders the construction of an oil-soaked barrier around the camp only to accidentally ignite it himself. The group hears a gunshot and hurries to the beach, where they see the lascars' attempt to escape the island ended by the violent undertow. With their lifeboat gone, the camp burned and Osborne getting on everyone's nerves, Fairbanks suggests they make a raft and try to return to the ship. The crazed Tarnowski kidnaps Carol, but she grabs his gun to fend off an attacking Dimetrodon and the pistol's report brings Fairbanks to the rescue. Carol and Fairbanks make a run for the raft, even as a rampaging prehistoric sloth kills Tarnowski and wrestles one of the meat-eating dinosaurs over a cliff. Safely back on the ship, Carol says bye to Osborne and joins Fairbanks at his side.

COMMENTARY: They should have listened to Capt. Tarnowski when he said, "a thing like this takes money... *lots* of money." Because the makers of *Unknown Island* obviously didn't have lots of money. But didn't Ray Harryhausen prove with *The Beast from 20,000 Fathoms* that you *can* do it right, even without lots of money? Well, *Unknown Island* didn't have Ray Harryhausen, either. What they had was a grandiose concept, a special effects crew with plenty of ingenuity but few resources and little applicable experience, a capable and engaging group of actors, and a very familiar storyline spiced with atypical characters and unexpected angles.

Like *The Land That Time Forgot*, a lot of the best parts of *Unknown Island* happen prior to arriving in the lost world. It's a necessary evil in this kind of picture to have an expository sequence near the beginning, to set up the premise. These segments are often dull and talky, but the scenes in the seamy "Port of All Nations Cafe" are well-filmed and effective. The cafe features some meticulous set decoration, and efficiently introduces the quartet of surprisingly developed principal characters. All four are uncommon in one way or another, and the entire first act achieves an almost *Kong*like feel at times.

Virginia Grey's heroine is strikingly self-sufficient for the time, holding her own in verbal exchanges with both Tarnowski and Fairbanks. When the shaky Fairbanks tries to convince her not to go ashore, she quips, "I have nothing to fear — after all,

On its rerelease, *Unknown Island* and its unfortunate latex-suited dinosaurs were paired with none other than *Two Lost Worlds* to create the "All-Time Thrill Show!"

there's some *men* going along." (Ouch!) Philip Reed successfully plays an egotistic pantywaist without straying into caricature, which is not easy. Richard Denning is likable as always, though the script takes him from miserable sot to clean-cut hero with improbable suddenness. The best performance is Barton MacLane's delicious turn as the salty, salacious Tarnowski — there's never been a character quite like him in any dinosaur film. He isn't a "villain" as such, yet he has no redeeming qualities whatsoever. He drinks, fights, abuses his crew and most everyone else, and blatantly lusts after Carol from the first moment he sees her. "I think she's givin' me the once-over right now," he says to Sanderson, well-played by veteran heavy Dick Wessel. Tarnowski even makes a lewd bet with his first mate that within an hour, "she and me'll be ... well, *pals*." He never shows a flash of goodness, remaining a crude, horny, and thoroughly entertaining lout to the end.

Looking back more than five decades, it's hard to guess how the audiences of the day might have received the *Unknown Island* dinosaurs. For some, they were probably sufficient. In a *Filmfax* article, author James C. Reynolds reminisced about sitting in a packed theater and watching the just-released film for the first time. During the meat-eater attack, "the theater audience screamed — delightedly — with fear," Reynolds fondly recalled. Yet it seems unlikely that any adults who remembered *King Kong* or *Fantasia* could have accepted these besuited beasts as credible dinosaurs. The brontos and Dimetrodon are seen so briefly there is little time to pick on them, but the tyranno/ceratosaurs are featured in long,

The principal cast of *Unknown Island*—Barton MacLane, Virginia Grey, Richard Denning, and Philip Reed—are much more believable than the film's imitation jungles.

well-lit scenes that expose every flaw. Even as monster suits go, these are baggy examples that seem to have been fabricated with incredible haste. The dinos do little but walk in place and flap their clumsy jaws, and the bizarrely inadequate sound effects which represent their roars make things even worse.

The "giant sloth" is a puzzling creation, but veteran movie ape-man Ray "Crash" Corrigan somehow breathes some menace into it. The beast's visage is passably ferocious-looking, though it persisted in reminding me of the title creature from *Night of the Demon* (1957). Despite Corrigan's energetic efforts, the climactic fight between the sloth and the carnivorous dinosaur is such a comedown from the similar sequence in *King Kong* that it simply cannot work. It is surprisingly gruesome, though, with plenty of blood in glorious Cinecolor red, and the fate of the sloth's reptilian opponent—falling from a cliff—is an oddly recurring image in dinosaur films. *The Lost World* (1925), *The Animal World*, *Dinosaurus!*, *The Lost World* (1960), *When Dinosaurs Ruled the Earth*, *Caveman*, and *Dinosaur* all include scenes of dinos toppling from various escarpments.

Despite some narrative gaffes (like Fairbanks' instant alcoholism cure), director Jack Bernhard does show a few technical flashes. One effective dolly shot starts out on Fairbanks, Tarnowski, and Carol, tracks over to a group of lascars plotting their escape, then returns to the original conversation all in one cut. But the film's considerable merits cannot fully overcome the multiple liabilities. Compounding the weak dino effects, the studio jungle looks completely artificial and has none of the lurking menace permeating King Kong's habitat. The final blow is the deadly dullness of the finale, as the proceedings slow to a crawl when they should be building to a crescendo. Most of the last reel consists of Tarnowski sleeping, Carol pretending to sleep, and Fairbanks wandering through those darned fake jungles. *Unknown Island* is an interesting curio and its first half-hour is a hoot, but ultimately its droopy dinos and draggy denouement just about sink it.

PEOPLE AND PRODUCTION: *Unknown Island* was one of the most unusual releases from the modest production outfit known as Film Classics. Operating during the latter half of the 1940s, Film Classics specialized in quickly produced mysteries and crime dramas, and with the possible exception of 1950's *The Flying Saucer* (actually more Cold War tale than science fiction), *Unknown Island* was their only sci-fi/fantasy/horror effort. It would also prove to be the only "lost world" entry to appear in all of the 1940s.

According to author James C. Reynolds' full-length *Unknown Island* retrospective in *Filmfax* (no. 63-64), producer Albert J. Cohen commissioned Robert T. Shannon and Jack Harvey to write a screenplay based on Shannon's short story. Hollywood hadn't turned out a true dinosaur movie since *One Million B.C.* eight years earlier, and Cohen surely felt that the public was ready for a new dino adventure. For the first time in movie history—excepting the dinosaur segment of *Fantasia*—the creatures would appear in color.

The decision to use color gives the movie a certain historical significance, though it amounts to little more than providing a good question for a genre-film trivia quiz. It was shot in Cinecolor, an inexpensive process which allowed low-budget studios to make color pictures for very little more than the cost of black-and-white. Cinecolor was a two-color system that produced generally pleasing results using a limited palette, although filmmakers had to choose costume and set colors mindful of these limitations. Having the two separate images located on opposite sides of the film stock also caused unavoidable projection problems, since it was impossible to accurately focus on both elements at once. Although never finding widespread favor, a good number of Cinecolor films were made during the late forties and early fifties including *Flight to Mars* (the first color "space" movie), *Invaders from Mars*, and the camp favorite *Prehistoric Women*. Cinecolor generally did not age well, although as of this writing there has recently appeared a dazzling DVD edition of *Unknown Island* with its humble Cinecolor hues looking beautiful and brand new.

SPECIAL EFFECTS: The dinosaurs of *Unknown Island*—suits and models—were designed and fabricated by Ellis Burman. With his work for films such as *Frankenstein Meets the Wolf Man* (1943), Burman proved himself a skilled and reliable craftsman, and his competency and integrity should not be judged based upon the creaky prehistoric denizens of *Unknown Island*. Burman, who worked more than once with legendary make-up artist Jack "Frankenstein" Pierce, undoubtedly did the best he could with what he had.

Burman chose a good starting place when designing his dinos: the paleo-art of Charles R. Knight. As James Reynolds pointed out in *Filmfax*, a selection of Knight's innovative paintings had been published in *National Geographic* a few years earlier. The basic shapes and structures seen in Knight's work are certainly reflected in Burman's creations, but much was lost in the translation.

The script identifies the featured carnivorous dinos as tyrannosaurs, but Burman actually based them on a Charles Knight painting of a horned Ceratosaurus. The dialogue was never altered, hence the "horned tyrannosaurs" seen in the film. Knight had pictured the ceratosaur in a very upright stance, and unfortunately the necessity of fitting human performers into the suits further amplified this trait. One can assume from Tarnowski's mention of the "giant Brontosaurus" early in the film that the sauropods are meant to represent brontos,

The *Unknown Island* actors spent a lot of time performing in front of ineffectively back-projected creatures; note the edge of the process screen visible at right.

though Burman may actually have based his models on a Charles Knight Diplodocus. The Dimetrodon, or "fin-backed lizard" as Fairbanks calls it, was also inspired by Knight's artwork. The Dimetrodon FX model was about six feet long, and moved along a track hidden by ground cover.

Bob Burns reminisced in *Filmfax* about the time, at age 13, when he got a behind-the-scenes look at *Unknown Island*. Ellis Burman's son was Bob's classmate, providing Bob with the opportunity to visit the *Unknown Island* set *and* see the dinosaur suits in Burman's workshop. "When I saw them hanging from cables in Ellis's studio," Burns recalled, "they were just about the coolest things I had ever laid my eyes on." Three essentially identical suits were made, fabricated of latex-covered canvas. "Inside the suit, a rod came down that enabled the stunt man wearing the costume to wiggle the ceratosaur's head," Burns explained. The mouth worked by a simple wire connected to the jaw, although as Burns correctly pointed out, "the mouth never closed correctly — when the mouth snapped shut, the bottom jaw would be off to the left or right side."

Burns visited the Palmdale, California, shooting location on the day the ceratosaur scenes were filmed, and recalls vividly how the combination of unventilated, rubberized suits and miserably hot weather brutally tested the performers. "Whenever the suited stunt men wanted to rest, they would have to lean against a prop man or another member of the crew," Burns remembered. "The whole thing looked like some sort of weird dinosaur mating ritual." Burns asserts that one shot of a dino actor actually swooning from the heat made it into the finished film. "You can tell from the way that one of the dinosaurs falls over flat — definitely not a planned 'stage fall' — that the poor fellow inside the suit was suffering from heat exhaustion," Burns said.

The movie's improbably vicious "giant sloth" was played by hard-working Ray "Crash" Corrigan. Like other noted gorilla

The battle between a nose-horned Tyrannosaurus and a hairy "giant sloth" (Crash Corrigan) has only a little more energy in the actual film than in this still photograph.

performers Charles Gemora (*Ingagi, Murders in the Rue Morgue*), Emil Van Horn (*Perils of Nyoka, The Ape Man*) George Barrows (*Robot Monster, Gorilla at Large*), and Steve Calvert (*The Road to Bali, Bride of the Gorilla*), Corrigan owned his own ape suit and hired himself out on a day-to-day basis, usually to financially strapped producers lacking the services of a big studio make-up and FX department. To represent the fictional killer sloth — based on a Charles Knight portrait of a Megatherium — Corrigan redressed his gorilla suit with claws, extra fur, and various facial accessories. The 100-degree weather which tortured the dino actors also victimized Corrigan, and he could remain in the suit for only very short stints without rest and refreshment.

Howard A. Anderson and his company, who like Burman could do fine work under the right conditions, handled the film's optical effects. Large-scale rear projection was used to combine the actors with the dinosaurs and other FX elements, but the scenes were hindered by budget and time constraints. Doing rear projection in color was a relatively young science as well, presenting inherent problems that didn't yet have ready solutions. The best part of the Anderson company's work for *Unknown Island* is the skillful use of split screens. Despite there being only three dinosaur suits, Anderson's trickery allows a half-dozen of the beasts to mill about in a single shot. Other notable contributors to *Unknown Island* included make-up artist Harry Ross (*Two Lost Worlds, Lost Continent*), set decorator Robert Priestly (*20 Million Miles to Earth*), and cinematographer Fred Jackman, Jr. (*Earth vs. the Flying Saucers*), who was carrying on a family legacy — his father was a senior member of the FX team on the silent version of *The Lost World*.

However limited the *Unknown Island* dinosaur effects seem, they were good enough to resurface as stock footage in such films as *Teenage Caveman, Horror of the Blood Monsters, Gigantis the Fire Monster* (the first *Godzilla* sequel), and the Mexican production *Aventura al Centro de la Tierra*.

Untamed Women

"Sometimes it confuseth me, too!"
1952, USA. Jewell Enterprises.
BW, 70m.

CREDITS: *Director* W. Merle Connell. *Producers* Richard Kay, Harry L. Rybnick (associate). *Screenplay* George W. Sayre. *Optical Effects* Alfred Schmid. *Special Effects and Art Direction* Paul Sprunck.

CAST: *Steve* Mikel Conrad. *Sandra* Doris Merrick. *Benny* Richard Monahan. *Ed* Mark Lowell. *Andy* Morgan Jones. *Myra* Midge Ware. *Col. Loring* Lyle Talbot.

AD LINE: "Uncivilized cult rites! Prehistoric monsters! Barbaric women raiders ... in an unbelievable world!"

A World War II bomber pilot, known only as Steve, is unable to recall what happened to his crew or his plane. But under the influence of an experimental serum, he begins to remember ...

On a routine mission, Steve's B-17 is shot down into the sea. The copilot is killed but Steve and the rest of the crew — bombardier Benny, navigator Andy, and radioman Ed — manage to reach an uncharted island in a life raft. "I knew just how Columbus must have felt," Steve recalls. The guys are taken prisoner by a tribe of miniskirted beauties ("descendants of the Druids") and brought before Sandra the Priestess. Sandra fears the strangers are like the brutal, murderous "Hairy Men" who came before, but the younger tribeswomen persuade her to spare their lives. In lieu of execution, Sandra leads them into a savage valley full of prehistoric predators, "like a zoo, about a hundred million years ago." The boys are a plucky lot, though, and somehow elude the dinosaurs ("those schmoes" as Benny calls them), mammoths, glyptodonts, and flesh-eating plants.

The strangers' bravery impresses Sandra and she pronounces them friends, but only if they do not "hold speech" with the lovelies. This doesn't sit well with the red-blooded boys, but the bothersome Hairy Men return before they have time to gripe. It takes nearly all of their ammunition to drive the brutes away ("Shoot anything with hair on it that moves!") so Steve sends Sandra and the girls up to their secluded temple for safety — unaware that the temple is built *inside a volcano*! The Hairy Men go on a murderous spree, but Sandra manages to pass the medallion of tribal leadership on to Steve before she expires. He doesn't have long to enjoy it because the volcano erupts a few minutes later, killing pretty much everyone on the island except him. Steve struggles to the life raft and drifts for days until he is finally found, clutching a strange medallion in his hand.

COMMENTARY: With the inordinate attention paid to *Robot Monster* in recent years, one could assume it must certainly be the most unintentionally hilarious film ever to include *One Million B.C.* footage. But the far less notorious *Untamed Women* can give it a run for its funny. *Robot* had the guy in the gorilla suit and diving helmet, but *Untamed* features "primitive" women with mascara, lipstick, and male-fantasy costumes that look like something Betty Rubble might have worn on her wedding night. While the *Robot Monster* pondered aloud the cruelties of fate, Benny the bombardier leers at the "goils" and "dames" one second and quotes the 16th century French writer François Rabelais the next! Curiously, the script actually points out some of the silly aspects of the film. Benny comments on the women's pseudoarchaic dialect, "that 'yea,' 'thou,' 'thine' doubletalk ... sounds like a stock company playin' one-night stands of Shakespeare!" Steve says "everything about them is primitive," but Andy dissents, saying "those women are about the most *unancient* lookin' specimens I ever did see!" Throw in the cheesecaky, poorly rehearsed dance numbers (choreographed by Fawn Pickett, the credits tell us), tired war-movie clichés, and a bomberload of ditzy dialogue, and you're approaching bad-movie Nirvana. It may not be *Mesa of Lost Women* (1953), but it's close.

Untamed Women contains some of the most preposterous movie moments of the fifties, both verbal and visual. A lot of Benny's lines are intended as "comic relief," but are just plain goofy instead. "I always sleep wit' my head t' da north and my feet t' da south," Benny says. "Guess it's my magnetic poysonality!" Later, Andy ogles the priestess and drools, "that Sandra gal has just about as pretty a fuselage as any *four-motor* job I ever did see!" sounding like the evil twin of *Lost Continent*'s Willie Tatlow. (Willie compared planes to women; Andy the reverse.) And forget about sexual equality — lecherous Benny hopes that what "all those broads have is a lotta bounce an' no brains!"

As hapless as the dialogue is, the images are its match. In one scene, Benny tries to explain the concept of airplanes to Sandra by flitting around with his arms extended and going "Bl-b-b-b-b-r-r-r-r-r-r." (His charade does precipitate my favorite line in the film, as a nonplussed Sandra deadpans, "The man has lost his senses.") The Busby Berkeley-on-a-budget dance routines are fairly hilarious, as the glamorized gals go through their cheerleader numbers with toothpaste-commercial smiles. During the volcanic eruption, rocks fall unerringly onto the heads of Steve and Benny with the guided-missile accuracy of coconuts onto Alan Hale, Jr. Then there's the indescribable scene where Andy gives his chosen Druid a lesson in cow-milking using his thumbs as stand-in udders, and the young lass can't figure out why she didn't get any milk.

It is no surprise that *Untamed Women* has a leering, sensationalistic quality. Screenwriter George W. Sayre's résumé is full of exploitation quickies with

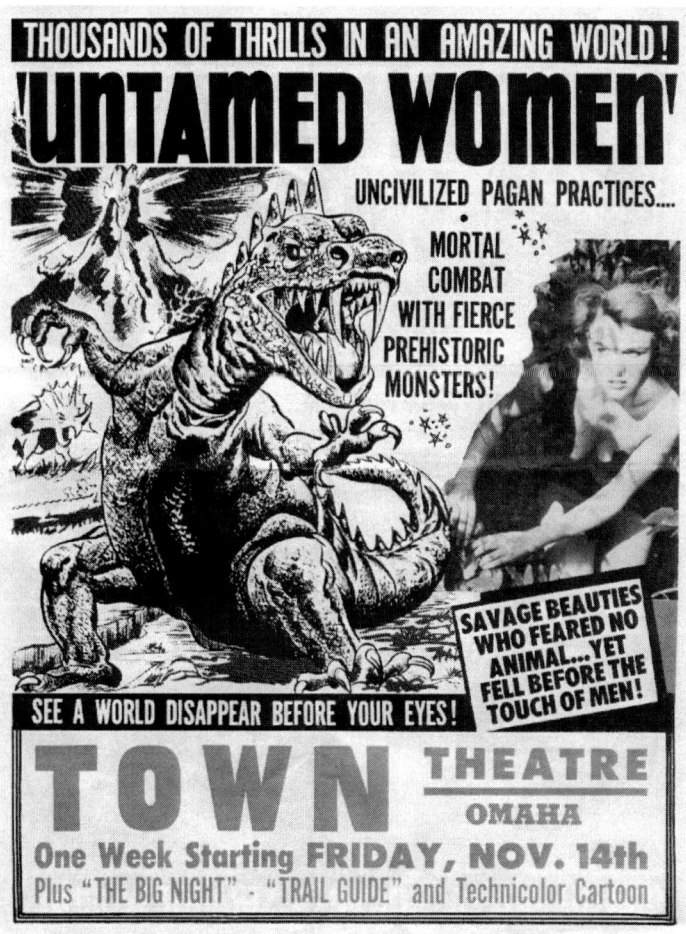

Local theater flyer for *Untamed Women* (showing with the film noir entry *The Big Night*) at Omaha's Town Theater, circa 1952.

lurid titles like *Nearly Eighteen* and *Secrets of a Co-ed*, making it all the more puzzling that *Untamed* hasn't become a favorite of the so-bad-it's-good crowd. Maybe it's the strangely abrupt ending which kills off nearly everybody, or maybe *Untamed* has simply been dismissed as just another flick with *One Million B.C.* clips. But whatever the reason, the film's screaming deficiencies lie hidden like a Lost World, still awaiting discovery.

PEOPLE AND PRODUCTION: Few details survive regarding the making of *Untamed Women*, but there are reports that it was shot in about a week, which is doubtless true. Everything about the film is minor, and almost no one connected with it had a very prolific film career following its release. Stars Mikel Conrad and Doris Merrick had each been in a dozen or so pictures before *Untamed*, but their names virtually disappear from film credits from 1952 on. The producing duo of Richard Kay and Harry Rybnick made a few low-budget programmers in the 1950s, and are actually credited on the American version of *Godzilla, King of the Monsters*. Director W. Merle Connell persisted long enough to shoot *The Cape Canaveral Monsters* for Phil "Robot Monster" Tucker in 1960, focusing his camera on his daughter Linda Connell in her only movie. One exception to this pattern of obscurity was music composer Raoul Kraushaar, who scored dozens of films in a career that lasted from the Great Depression to Watergate. Kraushaar's creepy, almost experimental score for *Invaders from Mars* (1953) is a major part of the movie's success.

Studio campaign manuals, or "press-books," always contained outrageous and impractical publicity schemes, but fittingly those for *Untamed Women* reached new heights (or depths). "Are there any women wrestlers in your town?" the copy asks, going on to suggest that such a lady be placed in the theater lobby with a $100 prize offered to "any other woman who could tangle successfully with her for more than 30 seconds." Other proposed ploys included "improvising a dinosaur on wheels" with an untamed woman riding on its back, and having some "beautiful girls decked out in leopard skin sarongs" confined in a bamboo cage in the lobby!

SPECIAL EFFECTS: The special effects in *Untamed Women* warrant little comment. All of the prehistoric animal shots are clips and outtakes from *One Million B.C.* The airplane crash sequence incorporates both real footage and miniatures, and is actually good enough to raise suspicions that it too might be lifted from another film (though I have been unable to confirm this). Effects men Paul Sprunck and Alfred Schmid seemingly had little to do, and were virtually unheard of before and after. Schmid's optical duties were mostly limited to the combining of the *Untamed* actors with the stock footage. In a postproduction tweak, the shot of the guys scrambling up the cliff face was speeded up to make them appear to climb faster — as if the picture needed help to make it look even sillier!

Paul Sprunck doesn't seem to have had a huge workload either. The physical effects consist of some prop rocks falling around (and on) the actors during the eruption, a few spear hits during the Hairy Men's attack, and the rather unique-looking carnivorous plant. In *Keep Watching the Skies!*, Bill Warren mentions that this leafy menace doesn't seem to appear in any other movie, and may actually have been made expressly for *Untamed Women*.

The Valley of Gwangi

"That's gotta be a humdinger!"

***   1969, USA. Warner Bros./ Seven Arts. C, 96m.

CREDITS: *Director* James O'Connolly. *Producers* Charles H. Schneer, Ray Harryhausen (associate). *Screenplay* William E. Bast; additional material by Julian More. *Creator of Visual Effects* Ray Harryhausen.
CAST: *Tuck Kirby* James Franciscus. *T. J. Breckenridge* Gila Golan. *Champ Connors* Richard Carlson. *Prof. Horace Bromley* Laurence

Naismith. *Carlos Dos Orsos* Gustavo Rojo. *Lopé* Curtis Arden. *Tia Zorina* Freda Jackson. *Rowdy* Dennis Kilbane. *Bean* Mario de Barros. *The Dwarf* Jose Burgos.

AD LINE: "Unbelievable! Creatures of a lost era challenge the best the West has to offer ... Cowboys battle monsters in the strangest roundup of all!"

A man staggers out of the Mexican desert carrying a sack with, it seems, something *alive* inside. He collapses, whispers the strange word "Gwangi," and dies. The man's brother Carlos takes the sack, fatefully ignoring the warnings of the strange blind Gypsy woman at his side.

Not far away, beautiful T. J. Breckenridge and her traveling Wild West Show ride into a small town just as her old flame Tuck Kirby does the same. Tuck enlists a local orphan boy named Lopé as a guide and pays T.J. a visit, over the protests of her surrogate father, Champ. T.J. tries to be angry but her old feelings resurface, and before long she's showing Tuck her soon-to-debut main attraction: a living miniature horse named "El Diablo." Tuck flashes back to his earlier chance meeting with Professor Horace Bromley, a British paleontologist hunting for fossils of the tiny prehistoric horse Eohippus. Tuck shows Bromley the animal — presented to T.J. by the love-struck Carlos — and the ecstatic scientist is eager to learn more. The "blind witch" called Tia Zorina refuses to disclose the location of the "Forbidden Valley," but Bromley slyly reveals the little horse's current whereabouts and follows the gypsies as they attempt to return it.

Tuck, T.J., Carlos and Champ join Bromley and Lopé in trailing the Gypsies to the Forbidden Valley, and soon find themselves in a lost world of prehistoric creatures. A vicious pterodactyl almost gets Lopé, and an ostrichlike Ornithomimus is suddenly caught by the huge Allosaurus known as "Gwangi, the Evil One." A Styracosaurus distracts Gwangi and lets Tuck's party escape, but Gwangi soon finds their campsite. The skillful cowpokes lasso the dinosaur and *almost* gain control before the great animal breaks loose. Gwangi kills Carlos and the Styracosaurus, only to bring a rockslide down upon himself while trying to follow the humans through a narrow passage. Knocked unconscious, Gwangi is captured.

Spectators fill the arena for Gwangi's debut show. Tia Zorina unwisely dispatches her dwarf confidant to free the beast, and the curtain rises to the horrific sight of the small man in Gwangi's jaws. Bromley is crushed by the falling cage door, but the show's outmatched circus elephant confronts Gwangi and buys time for the spectators to escape. Gwangi strides through town, finally cornering Tuck, T.J. and Lopé inside a cavernous cathedral. With the dinosaur momentarily disoriented by a deafening chord from the huge pipe organ, Tuck throws a flaming cresset onto the floor and spirits T.J. and Lopé to freedom. As the townspeople watch the stately cathedral burn, the reptilian screams from inside dwindle and mercifully cease.

COMMENTARY: Released into a film environment embracing *Midnight Cowboy* and *Alice's Restaurant,* critics assailed *The Valley of Gwangi* with the vehemence of the Japanese army bombarding Godzilla. *Gwangi* was treated as an orphan by the studio, did little business in theaters and has failed to equal the popularity of other Harryhausen films on home video. But what happens if you stop dwelling on the old buzz and watch the picture with an open mind? You might enjoy its marvelous music score, notice its skillful cinematography, have fun with some lively supporting performances, and even recognize the touch of Willis O'Brien, who tried to make his original *Gwangi* back before World War II. You will definitely be delighted by the dinosaur action, and you might realize that you had a good time watching a good, entertaining dinosaur fantasy.

Yes, the basic plot is none other than that typical "dinosaur movie" structure, yet the makers of *Gwangi* made a conscious effort to *avoid* clichés in the particulars. For example, the "turn of the century" setting

Only through the movies — and movie magicians — can we marvel at such fantastical images as a circus elephant courageously fighting a prehistoric Allosaurus.

was chosen to avoid the too-familiar spectacle of a prehistoric creature battling modern artillery. (This is a major reason why many movie monsters like Godzilla and Gorgo were portrayed so much larger than actual species—one shot from a howitzer would bring down even the largest real dinosaur.) Yet even conceding the presence of some dino clichés, *Gwangi* still has plenty of surprises up its scaly sleeve.

One thing this sort of picture needs is a great opening to grab the audience right away, and *Gwangi* has it. The precredits prologue, where Carlos finds his mortally wounded brother carrying the squirming sack, and the mystical Tia Zorina utters her fatefully unheeded warning, is one of the great "teasers" in dinomovie history. Then begins the sweeping, spectacular music of Jerome Moross, effectively mixing the big brassy themes of an epic Hollywood western with some ominous fantasy or thriller motifs befitting a good dinosaur tale. Praise for the scores of Harryhausen films is generally reserved for Bernard Herrmann and perhaps Miklos Rozsa, but Moross, whose magnificent score for *The Big Country* (1958) is considered a classic of the western genre, belongs right there with them.

With the rousing music lifting the action, Erwin Hillier's cinematography comes to the forefront. Hillier's work, no doubt with considerable input from Harryhausen, helps the animation sequences to almost seamlessly match the noneffects scenes. In many "stop-motion" films you can actually sense an animated set piece approaching by a jarring, sudden change in camerawork, but in *Gwangi* they didn't lock down the camera every time a dinosaur was about to appear. Even the "money" shot of the pterodactyl sequence, with Lopé snatched right off of his running horse, is a long, continuous pan. Though surely more time-consuming, this approach allows the animation sequences to flow together with the other scenes in a single visual style, as if the whole picture was shot "live" with no special effects necessary.

The sound effects are particularly memorable, especially during the climax when every little sound made by the dinosaur or the humans echoes eerily through the cathedral halls. The efficient screenplay by William Bast keeps the story moving with a happily low quotient of dull patches. Unlike the too-long, museum-bound opening reel of 1960's *The Lost World* or the interminable rock climbing of *Lost Continent*, every scene in *Gwangi* propels the story. Even the characters, like the film itself often described as mere clichés, display unexpected qualities. Carlos, for instance, despite being clearly established as the "bad guy" to Tuck's "good guy," selflessly risks his own life (twice!) to save others.

The performances in *Gwangi* are admittedly not among the picture's strengths, though there are bright spots. Richard Carlson is adequate but probably shouldn't have been third-billed when playing a character who has so little to do with advancing the plot. Gila Golan, whose heavily accented voice reportedly and apparently had to be dubbed, is a liability—albeit a fetching one—as the female lead. On a better note, James Franciscus seems to be enjoying himself, which is the first key to success when portraying a roguish hero. The supporting roles are the most entertaining, including British character player Laurence Naismith as the pompous, unexpectedly self-serving Bromley, and Freda Jackson, who chews the scenery but chews it quite correctly as the blind but all-seeing Tia Zorina.

One is reluctant to dissect Harryhausen's films too surgically—not because they don't possess multiple themes and dimensions, for they often do, but rather because Ray himself has always been wary (rightfully, I think) of the dangers of overanalysis. As he told me, "You can analyze things to death if you try, but it gets a little ludicrous." So, risking ludicrousness, I believe there is an underlying thematic element in *The Valley of Gwangi*, which may or may not have been in the minds of the filmmakers but exists nonetheless. Flowing throughout the film is a current of good versus evil imagery. The dinosaurs' home is "Forbidden Valley," Gwangi is called "the Evil One," the little horse is even named "El Diablo" ("The Devil," in Spanish), and Tia Zorina tries to warn the intruders away with "Defy the law, and perish!" The prehistoric animals are painted as "evil" throughout the movie — Gwangi even burns to death in a hellfirelike inferno inside a cathedral — but the film's final scenes turn the source of the evil inside out. As the people watch the church burn and listen to the dinosaur's fading screams, while a banner reading "Gwangi the Great" hangs ironically in the background, they (and we) realize that the great animal harbored no evil, and the onlookers shed tears as they begin to understand the magnitude of their transgression. There is no "evil" in the animal kingdom, they come to understand; it is only through mankind's weaknesses that evil finds a way to the surface. This time, it was selfishness that killed the beast.

Gwangi is punctuated by visual reminders of humanity's disrespect for the natural world: Horses are used in dangerous circus acts, a bull is kept in captivity to be sacrificed for "sport," and the Eohippus and Allosaurus are captured for material gain. Tuck, T.J. and the show troupe view the dinosaurs as a source of riches ("We are on our way to a fortune," T.J. says), while Bromley, though professing to be concerned for the animals' rights, sees only an avenue to personal glory and a place alongside history's great scientists ("Galileo, Newton, Darwin, Bromley," he muses). It is finally

"The roping of Gwangi"— one of the most remarkable stop-motion sequences ever filmed, in a dinosaur movie or otherwise.

discovered that Tia Zorina's warnings were not quite what they seemed. The "evil" was not the dinosaurs themselves but was rather manifested in the greed and avarice of humankind, flaws which Tia Zorina somehow knew would be revealed by the animals' exploitation. The "Curse of Hell" that the old Gypsy tried to prevent turns out to be merely humanity's own failings, nakedly exposed to the unforgiving light of day. When Gwangi is destroyed, the church—a structure built for the glorification of the Almighty and His kingdom—is destroyed as well. The symbolism of that image seems clear.

Okay, enough of that. The first and best reasons to watch *Gwangi* are Harryhausen's delicious dinosaurs. The fact is, *Gwangi* contains some of Ray's most dynamic, energy-packed animation, resulting in some of the best dinosaur action ever put on film. The work is very nearly flawless—the only glitch is the very stiff stand-in Gwangi glimpsed during the rockslide and in the rolling cage as he's brought to town. This was the last of Harryhausen's dinosaur-themed pictures and he pulled out all the stops, creating visuals that rank as true classics of dino cinema. He also sneaked in a visual homage to Gwangi's original creator, Willis O'Brien, by having the Allosaurus enter the background of a shot and scratch his ear, just as Obie's Tyrannosaurus does in *King Kong*.

The pterodactyl sequence is nothing less than a tour de force—two minutes of stop-motion artistry which serve as a striking demonstration of Ray's uncanny feel for his craft. As the great flier swoops around, spots its prey and zeroes in, its flapping cycle looks exactly "right" for an airborne creature of that size. But then, when it picks up the boy and must bear the added weight, its motions very subtly change. Its wing cycle is altered almost imperceptibly, as it exerts more muscle on the downstrokes to try and lift the extra load. You can *feel* more than see the creature straining ... straining to gain altitude. Oddly, some observers have said that the flap cycle slows down when Lopé is picked up, but it actually speeds up—barely.

It takes frame-by-frame examination to reveal the secret. Without the extra load, the wings' downstrokes and upstrokes occupy about six frames each. With the load, the upstrokes still take about six frames, but the downstrokes are reduced to about five. When I asked Ray about this sequence, he replied with his usual modesty: "Well, that's one of the things you have to do, to make it convincing—those things you inject when you're animating. Everybody looks at things differently, and when you think of picking up the weight of a boy, you feel that the thing must struggle. Some people would overlook that." Many surely would, but even if they attempted it, few if any could realize it with such virtuosity.

As spectacular as the pterosaur is, it's just one of the wondrous animation sequences. The scene of the buckaroos on horseback lassoing the Jurassic predator is jaw-dropping stuff, and is one of two show-stopping visuals (the other being the scene of the young Allosaurus invading the caveman's camp in *One Million Years B.C.*) which serve as perhaps the "trademark" dinosaur scenes of Harryhausen's career. The movements and behavior of the Eohippus—a familiar animal, despite its diminutive size—are never less than completely believable. Ray even had the courage to place his animated "dawn horse" right in the same shot with a live horse, and he pulled it off. There are moments in *Gwangi* when the animator even exceeds himself. The battle between Gwangi and the Styracosaurus is perfectly choreographed, just topping his own terrific Triceratops-Ceratosaurus tussle in *One Million*. Lastly, Gwangi's agonizing demise in the flaming cathedral is one of the most memorable climaxes in creature features, even surpassing the dramatic death throes of Ray's rhedosaurus in *The Beast from 20,000 Fathoms*. Though Harryhausen has often insisted that the original *Gwangi*, if filmed, would have been more spectacular than his version, it cannot be denied that Ray's finale is cinematically and dramatically far better than the allosaur's original fate: being herded over a

The allosaur-styracosaur fight in *The Valley of Gwangi* highlights not only Ray Harryhausen's animation but two superbly crafted stop-motion puppets as well.

cliff by a truck.

Gwangi is not a masterpiece yet it is sprinkled throughout with minimasterpieces, and has a story arc more satisfying than those of many stop-motion fantasies. Valid criticisms can and have been leveled against the film, but what one hopes for in this sort of movie is qualities like atmosphere, and pacing, and other small, thoughtful touches that set it apart and show that its makers were interested in doing quality work, not just getting the film in the can. In *Gwangi*, this effort can clearly be seen. *The Valley of Gwangi* is a fine piece of fantasy filmmaking, and stands among the best all-out "dinosaur movies" ever made.

PEOPLE AND PRODUCTION: The original concept for *Gwangi* was developed by Willis O'Brien and John Speaks back in 1941 for RKO and Speaks' outfit, Colonial Pictures. Extensive preproduction included a script written by Harold Lamb and Emily Barrye and hundreds of drawings done by Obie himself. Actors James Craig and Anne Shirley were selected and Irving Ries was reportedly going to direct. O'Brien, however, so often disappointed in his attempts to bring projects to the screen, again met with bad luck. A shake-up hit the top brass at RKO, and the change in management — along with World War II — resulted in the relatively expensive Technicolor *Gwangi* being shelved. O'Brien used some plot details planned for *Gwangi* in the dinosaurless *Mighty Joe Young*, but Gwangi himself was destined to remain in hibernation, or "suspended animation" if you prefer, for another quarter-century. "You simply cannot account for decisions in the film world," Ray Harryhausen once said, uttering perhaps the most irrefutable statement about Hollywood ever made.

One day while housecleaning, Harryhausen found a copy of the *Gwangi* script and decided to try and resuscitate the project. "It was basically O'Brien's idea," Harryhausen told me. "I hated to think that it would never be made, so when we were looking for a project I found the script that Obie had given me in my garage, and we revamped it a little." Producer Charles Schneer, Harryhausen's longtime collaborator, acquired the story rights, the script was reworked somewhat (with the setting moved from the Grand Canyon to Mexico), and in 1969, the Warner Bros.–Seven Arts production of *The Valley of Gwangi* hit the screens. Despite a lively story and a smorgasbord of stellar dinosaur effects, *Gwangi* was a box-office failure. The lack of response can be partially attributed to the fact that Warner Bros. gave the film virtually no publicity. "My wife's sister lived just around the corner from the theater, and she didn't even know it was playing when it was first released," Harryhausen remembered. "We got caught in the politics of Warner Bros. We started the picture with the Hyman brothers ... and then unfortunately the new management, by the time we finished the picture, didn't appreciate what the previous management had sanctioned." The picture's poor box office is also a function of the time at which it was made. A newly permissive film climate existed during the late '60's, and "a naked dinosaur just wasn't outrageous enough," lamented Ray.

Though set in Mexico, *Gwangi* was filmed on location in Spain in the "Mountains of Tabernas," near the country's southeastern coast. The main bull ring in Almeria was used for the arena scenes, and Cuenca served as the small town. A rather eclectic cast was assembled including former Miss World runner-up Gila Golan, western and creature-movie veteran Richard Carlson, British veteran Laurence Naismith, and Freda Jackson, later to appear in *Clash of the Titans* as, coincidentally, a "blind witch." Director James O'Connolly apparently had a good relationship with his actors, and star James Franciscus felt comfortable enough to make on-set suggestions. "The character I played, for example, I thought lacked humor; he was too straight," Franciscus said in a Ted Newsom *Imagi-Movies* article. "I tried to get a little more charm into him, a little more twinkle."

Ray Harryhausen himself has often lamented that Willis O'Brien's original incarnation of *Gwangi* was never made, and screenwriter William Bast told Ted Newsom that he found inspiration in Obie's visions. "When Ray showed me original O'Brien storyboards, the story just came to life," Bast said. "I wasn't aware there had been a script prepared; we just had the action sequences." Preproduction tasks completed for O'Brien's *Gwangi* were considerable; Marcel Delgado had sculpted the initial design of the title character and Mario Larrinaga had already begun preparing glass paintings. As Harryhausen put it: "If Obie had done it when it was planned ... it would've been magnificent."

SPECIAL EFFECTS: It took Ray Harryhausen almost a year to create the thrilling dinosaur action seen in *The Valley of Gwangi*. Over four months were spent just on the lassoing sequence, a visual effects feast which involved an incredible amount of intricate work. "This one sequence had implanted itself in my mind for years," Harryhausen wrote in his *Film Fantasy Scrapbook*, "since the day in 1942 when I first saw Willis O'Brien's original sketches for the proposed production." In the wonderful *Puppets & People*, author S. S. Wilson discusses this "extremely complex" set piece:

> The ropes, held by the live actors, stretch, without interruptions, from them and their live horses to the puppet Gwangi. In the course of the many composites that make up the sequence, Gwangi snaps some of the ropes with his jaws, actually appears to pull some of the live horses off their feet, and is himself tripped by a rope looped around his foot. Animated ropes on the puppet were lined up with the images of the live ropes on the rear projection screen and moved frame by frame to keep the relative action consistent.

A jeep with a 15-foot-high "monster

Gwangi's grand entrance, where he lunges for and nabs a small ostrichlike dinosaur, was closely echoed by the T. rex–Gallimimus encounter in *Jurassic Park*.

stick" substituted for Gwangi by providing a physical object for the riders to rope. The vehicle was then removed from the frame — by a little "hocus pocus," as Ray said — and the dinosaur substituted. Lest one forget, while attending to all this surgeonlike detail, Harryhausen had to actually animate the character, remaining constantly aware of the dynamics, momentums, and "performance" of the writhing, angry, living creature. No wonder they're called *special* effects.

The pterodactyl sequence is another complex set piece, requiring almost as much painstaking work as did the roping. "The scene ... was very time-consuming inasmuch as each frame of the animated bird had to give the illusion of actual contact with the live boy," Harryhausen explained. A massive crane, kept out of frame, was used to lift Curtis Arden's stunt double from the running horse. The scene's full-size pterodactyl prop was decidedly low-tech — its wings were simply "flopped" by a pair of off-camera assistants — yet it looks surprisingly good. Harryhausen doesn't share this opinion, however. "It was done quickly and I was never happy with it; but when one has a schedule to make you have to sometimes make do," he told me, while also admitting the difficulty of viewing his own work objectively. "You know, when you're close to it, you see it a little differently than an audience."

The Gwangi animation model was one of the most finely crafted stop-motion dinosaurs ever built. "As the title character, it had more to do than an incidental animal," Harryhausen explained, "so I had to make it more detailed and structurally more versatile." Toward this end, Gwangi was considerably larger than the memorable but briefly seen allosaur in *One Million Years B.C.*

"Gwangi had to be able to snarl, bleed, blink and do many more things in front of the cameras because he was seen throughout the film," Ray said, also noting that his vocalizations were created from, among other sounds, "a camel, slobbering." For the Gwangi-versus-elephant sequence, Harryhausen originally planned to feature a live elephant in many shots as in *20 Million Miles to Earth.* A production delay resulted in the loss of the real elephant's services, forcing Harryhausen to accomplish the entire sequence with stop-motion. *Gwangi* holds the record for the most animation cuts in any Harryhausen film: "335 stop-motion cuts," as Neil Pettigrew points out in *The Stop-Motion Filmography.* "Compare this with the 84 that were in *The Beast from 20,000 Fathoms.*" Not every film illusion has to be meticulous or complex, however. To create the appearance of a live "something" inside Miguel's sack during the prologue, "We put a little goat into it," Harryhausen told me with a smile. "I wouldn't want to animate the sack folding!"

With the truly inordinate amount of criticism *Gwangi* has absorbed over the years, it seems only right that a few of the more recent observers, thoughtfully commenting on the movie distanced from the protest-minded era in which it was made, be given their say. "I originally saw this film at a drive-in," James Van Hise wrote in *Hot-Blooded Dinosaur Movies,* "and even that large, the effects work in *Valley of Gwangi* is flawless, and often spectacular." Michael Weldon's *Psychotronic Encyclopedia of Film* calls *Gwangi,* "one of *the best* animated movies ever made … never before or since have animated creatures looked so convincing." In his *Creature Features Movie Guide,* John Stanley ranks it "up there with the best of Harryhausen's work." *The Motion Picture Guide* states that it "contains some of the most breathtaking stop-motion sequences ever put on film." And Neil Pettigrew calls Gwangi's operatic demise "a superb climax to a superb film," and pronounces *The Valley of Gwangi* as "Harryhausen's finest hour."

Valley of the Dragons

(a.k.a. *Prehistoric Valley* [U.K.])

"Not only strange words but strange ideas as well!"

** 1961, USA. Columbia. BW, 79m.

CREDITS: *Director* Edward Bernds. *Producers* Byron Roberts, Alfred Zimbalist (executive). *Screenplay* Edward Bernds. *Story* Donald Zimbalist; based on Jules Verne's *Career of a Comet.* *Special Effects* Dick Albain.

CAST: *Capt. Hector Servadac* Cesare Danova. *Michael Denning* Sean McClory. *Deena* Joan Staley. *Nateeta* Danielle De Metz. *Od-Loo* Gregg Martell. *Tarn* Gil Perkins. *Patoo* I. Stanford Jolley. *Anoka* Michael Lane.

Near Oran, Algeria, in the year 1881, Irish soldier of fortune Michael Denning and French Army captain Hector Servadac prepare to fight a duel over the affections of a woman. Suddenly, a cataclysmic onslaught of wind, earth tremors, and celestial upheavals sweeps away everything and everyone except for the two rivals. "Postponing" the duel, they set out to discover what happened, and over the days to follow encounter a variety of prehistoric reptiles (including "plateosaurs" according to Servadac), mammals, and people. After each man saves the other's life, they forget their quarrel and become friends.

One night, Servadac examines the sky and makes the uncannily accurate deduction that a comet must have hit the earth, broken off a hunk, and joined it with another hunk broken off during prehistoric times. After a woolly mammoth attack separates the two men, each works his way into the good graces of a different tribe of cavepeople. They also find girlfriends— Servadac the blonde Deena, and Denning the brunette Nateeta — and are happy to teach them modern 19th century customs. After Deena is attacked by subterranean mole-men and separated from Servadac, she is captured by a patrol from Nateeta's tribe. But Denning realizes that Deena has learned English from Servadac and sets out to find his friend, unaware that

The delectable Deena (Joan Staley) provides "comet" relief for Hector Servadac (Cesare Danova) in the goofy but good-natured *Valley of the Dragons*.

Servadac is simultaneously setting out to find Deena. Everybody finally finds each other, but just then the volcano erupts and some giant lizards trap Nateeta and friends in a cave. Servadac whips up some homemade gunpowder, and both tribes cooperate to blast a mountain of rocks down onto the beasts. With the tribes now friends, Servadac calculates the comet will return to Earth in seven years. They give their girls a squeeze and agree that seven years isn't long to wait at all!

COMMENTARY: One's credibility can be mortally wounded by saying anything remotely positive about *Valley of the Dragons*, but what the heck. Not one of the movies that reused the *One Million B.C.* dinosaurs could honestly be called a good film, but that doesn't mean they are all devoid of entertainment value, and this is a perfect example. *Dragons* probably uses more *One Million* footage than any other film and thus has numerous story similarities, and the climaxes of the two movies are almost identical. However, this bargain-priced effort parlays an outrageous premise, the sidekicky appeal of its two leads, and hints of spoofiness into a diverting if utterly preposterous prehistory opus.

The basic plot is a tipoff that maybe this thing isn't *meant* to be taken seriously, especially since director Ed Bernds has said, "*ridiculous* is probably not too strong a word." The tongue-in-cheek feel gets stronger as the story proceeds, and although it never becomes an all-out spoof it does seem to be poking fun at the whole cavemen-and-dinos subgenre. Consider the scene

As the "subhuman Neanderthals" victimized the *Valley of the Dragons*, so must the oppressive make-up have victimized the actors.

where the hulking Anoka, explaining to his chief why he dislikes Denning, makes the elder feel the lumps made on his head by the Irishman's fist!

What really saves *Dragons* from fossilization is the byplay between Cesare Danova and Sean McClory, who had mastered the conventions of the "buddy movie" (two guys who hate each other are thrown together, become pals, make wisecracks along the way) when Mel Gibson and Danny Glover were cutting their baby teeth. Danova and McClory play their parts with gusto and a sense of fun, offering a subtle wink that they know the whole thing is absurd and are in on the joke. This approach allows the outlandish tale to work in a weird sort of way, even as a procession of hilariously cheap-looking creatures—subhuman Neanderthals, subterranean mole-men, a giant spider with rigor mortis—are paraded past. Not to overlook the women, Danielle De Metz is a looker, and sexy Joan Staley, in a larger role and with her uninhibited performance, rightfully earns her place alongside fabled cave beauties Carole Landis, Raquel Welch, and Victoria Vetri. *Valley of the Dragons* joins *Teenage Caveman* and *Tarzan's Desert Mystery* as the three most diverting of the many *One Million B.C.* lizard-users, offering an amusing and affable dose of mindless hooey.

PEOPLE AND PRODUCTION: *Valley of the Dragons* followed a strange road to the screen, as director Edward Bernds told Tom Weaver in *Interviews with B Science Fiction & Horror Movie Makers*. Donald Zimbalist, son of *Dragons* executive producer Al Zimbalist, was in England on holiday and happened upon an old edition of Jules Verne's book *Career of a Comet*, initiating the series of events which would culminate in the making of the film. "First, the Jules Verne name meant box-office at that time, the title was unused, unknown, and the work was in the public domain," Bernds explained. "Second, Al had an option to use any or all of the *One Million B.C.* film." The resulting film may not be the only picture in history to have its narrative directly inspired by the content of available stock footage, but it is likely the only instance of someone receiving story credit simply for buying a book. "Al wanted Donald to have a screen credit ... and he finally talked me into it," Bernds explained. Bernds penned a 10-page outline designed to marry Verne's book to the stock footage, Columbia agreed to a minuscule $125,000 budget, and the deal was done.

A decent B-movie cast was assembled, led by smooth Cesare Danova and gregarious Sean McClory. According to a Columbia press release, Danova "came to America to star in the title role of *Ben-Hur* (1959)," but lost the part to Charlton Heston after production was delayed. Ed Bernds cast Danielle De Metz based on his pleasant memories of the actress from the earlier *Return of the Fly* (1959). "I liked her looks and her acting, and I liked *her*," Bernds recalled. And Victoria Vetri of *When Dinosaurs Ruled the Earth* was not the first *Playboy* centerfold to play a glamorous cavegirl—shapely starlet Joan Staley was a sight for 'saur eyes as Miss

November 1958. (Her swimming scene in *Dragons* is almost as revealing—in its own unique way—as her modest centerfold shot.) Gregg Martell's small part as "Od-Loo" came only a year after his hilarious performance as the befuddled Neanderthal in *Dinosaurus!* Despite its shoestring nature, *Valley of the Dragons* "has tremendous vitality on TV," Ed Bernds said. "I get checks that *surprise* me."

SPECIAL EFFECTS: A studio promo for *Valley of the Dragons* claimed that "executive producer Alfred Zimbalist imported assorted reptiles from around the world" to portray the film's dinosaurs, and "through the magic of special effects photography, the reptiles were transformed into pre-historic beasts." Unfortunately, even casual dinomovie fans will know that the only thing actually "imported" was stock footage from other movies. *One Million B.C.* was the major source, but a couple of brief, "un-colorized" clips from Toho's *Rodan* were also borrowed to portray the pterodactyl. *Dragons* also reused one of the prop giant spiders from *World Without End* (1956), another of Edward Bernds' directorial efforts.

Voyage to the Planet of Prehistoric Women

"Though we tried to keep our spirits up, it was still pretty discouraging."

* 1968, USA. Filmgroup/AIP. C, 80m.

CREDITS: *Director* Derek Thomas (Peter Bogdanovich). *Producer* Norman D. Wells. *Screenplay* Henry Ney. *Art Director* Vittorio Ferroini. *Special Effects* Giovanni De Palma, Don Jones, Gary Kent, Walter Robles. *Special Props* Wah Chang.
CAST: *Moana* Mamie Van Doren. *Gill Women* Mary Marr, Paige Lee.

The astronauts of a multiship space mission to Venus find more than they bargained for on the hostile planet. The first two-man crew fights off some five-foot-tall dinosaurs and contracts an infection, and a member of the follow-up crew begins hearing a sound which he insists is the voice of a human girl. His colleagues disagree but it turns out he's right—Venus is home to a race of aquatic, telepathic blondes who worship a pterodactyl god and want nothing more than to expel the offending earthmen. When they find that the intruders have killed their god, the women get really mad and mystically command the volcano to "rain down boiling red-hot earth on the demons." (Venus has earth?) The astronauts survive the eruption but the girls try again, bringing forth rain this time. The water softens the ground and begins to tip over the rocket, but the fellows blast off just in time. The women have lost confidence in their pterodactyl deity, however, and raise the remains of the astronauts' huge robot as their new idol.

COMMENTARY: *Voyage to the Planet of Prehistoric Women* (have to love that title) was Roger Corman's final reworking of the 1962 Russian film *Planeta Burg*. Again a massive chunk of the running time was taken from the Russian footage, though not as much as in the previous *Voyage to the Prehistoric Planet*. The *Planeta Burg* special effects, well-executed and effective in the original film, here serve as meaningless filler. The effects scenes and extensive sequences of the Russian actors spouting rewritten, redubbed dialogue are worked around a few new scenes featuring former sex symbol Mamie Van Doren and several other physically fit young ladies portraying the "Gill Women of Venus," which is actually an alternative title for the picture. That the new plot is not utterly incomprehensible is, I suppose, a testament to the writers and editors. The scenes of the glamorous Gill Women are pure camp, as they wander around the seaside absurdly and revealingly dressed in clingy white slacks and seashell bras. (The credits tell us that the costumes were "executed by Maureen of Hollywood.") Much of the new dialogue is equally laughable, as when one of the less than enthusiastic astronauts wonders why "any people in their right mind" would come to Venus. "Come on Hans," his comrade replies. "We're here, and we're in our 'right minds' ... aren't we?"

PEOPLE AND PRODUCTION: A quick scan of this picture's credits reveals more than one familiar name. Director Derek Thomas is of course actually Peter Bogdanovich, soon to become one of Hollywood's hot young directors with such films as *The Last Picture Show* (1971) and *Paper Moon* (1973). The production coordinator was Polly Platt, who would later amass an impressive list of major credits as a writer, producer, and production designer. Wah Chang is credited with "Special Props." Details of his contributions escaped Chang's memory when speaking with this author thirty years after the fact, but almost certainly his duties involved constructing new props to match those seen in the Russian sequences. These likely included the "dead" pterodactyl and the "remains" of John the robot that the women begin to worship at the end of the film. It is frequently reported that this picture was specifically intended for television, but Fred Olen Ray wrote in *The New Poverty Row* that he distinctly remembers "seeing it in a drive-in theater in Fort Lauderdale in the early 1970s."

Voyage to the Prehistoric Planet

"I'm wondering if we should be here at all."

1965, USA. Filmgroup/AIP.
C, 74m.

CREDITS: *Director* John Sebastian (Curtis Harrington). *Producers* George Edwards, Stephanie Rothman (associate). *Written by* John Sebastian.

CAST: *Professor Hartman* Basil Rathbone. *Marcia Evans* Faith Domergue.

In the year 2020, a mission to land the first humans on Venus is under way. The endeavor is directed via radio by Professor Hartman on Moonbase Lunar 7, and locally monitored by Marcia Evans aboard the orbiting spaceship *Vega*. Commander Lockhart, Doctor Kern, Hans Walters, Andre Ferneau, Allen Sherman, and John the robot descend to the surface. Split into two groups, the explorers contend with a man-eating plant, a pack of diminutive dinosaurs, an alien disease, a torrential rain, an aggressive pterodactyl, a volcanic eruption, and a Brontosaurus, all while trying to decipher the mysteries of the strange artifacts they find. Marcia is tempted to fly down and try to help the poor fellows until Professor Hartman orders her to remain in orbit. A mud slide nearly destroys the astronauts' rocket but they manage to lift off in the nick of time, even as one of their group makes a momentous discovery.

COMMENTARY: *Voyage to the Prehistoric Planet* serves two purposes. One, it proves that English can be dubbed over Russian-speaking lips a bit more successfully — especially if the "new" characters are given similar-sounding names — than it can over Japanese-speaking lips. Two, it makes *Voyage to the Planet of Prehistoric Women*— Roger Corman's other modified reissue of Pavel Klushantsev's *Planeta Burg*—look better by comparison. At least the later entry had a little bit of original storyline, a helping of cheesecake and some camp value, whereas this "version" has nothing — nothing, that is, except a few shots of Basil Rathbone and Faith Domergue both looking so dispirited that it's unpleasant to watch. Rathbone is far removed from his glory days in films like *The Adventures of Robin Hood* (1938) and *The Hound of the Baskervilles* (1939), and Domergue, though never an "A-list" star, had fallen almost as far since her exploits in such genre favorites as *This Island Earth* (1955) and *It Came from Beneath the Sea* (1955). The two have no scenes together in *Prehistoric Planet*, and they are top billed, even though Domergue is on-screen for a total of seven minutes and Rathbone for less than four! Rathbone paces around an ultra-cheap "control room" set saying things like "all we can do now is wait" and "your guess is as good as mine." Domergue is stuck behind a radio desk, speaking almost all her lines into a microphone. The scarcity of new footage means that most of *Planeta Burg* is used, but anyone wanting to see that well-crafted Russian film is strongly advised to seek out the original and stay away from this appalling mutilation.

PEOPLE AND PRODUCTION: It has long been a practice of low-budget filmmakers to hire former and fading stars to try and give their productions a suggestion of "name" value. Such was the case with Basil Rathbone in the mid-sixties. Less than two years before his death, Rathbone signed to appear in two Roger Corman–backed quickies—*Voyage to the Prehistoric Planet* and *Queen of Blood* (1966)—both built around great amounts of footage from Russian sci-fi pictures. In *Faster and Furiouser*, author Mark Thomas McGee reported on Rathbone's experience. "For $3000 he agreed to spend a day and half on one and a half day on the other," McGee wrote. "He ended up working overtime and missed a meal. The Screen Actors Guild demanded overtime pay plus additional monies for the meal violation." According to McGee, producer George Edwards balked at the demands, stating that Rathbone's failure to know his lines had caused the overtime, and that Rathbone himself suggested skipping lunch "to get the thing over with."

In a production having 85 percent of its runtime made up of "borrowed" footage, it's not surprising to find other things borrowed, like composer Ronald Stein's opening title music—any dinomovie fan will instantly recognize it as Stein's theme from *Dinosaurus!*

We're Back! A Dinosaur's Story

"What is wrong with these people?"
** 1993, USA. Universal/Amblin. C, 70m.

CREDITS: *Directors* Dick Zondag, Ralph Zondag, Phil Nibbelink, Simon Wells. *Producers* Stephen Hickner; Steven Spielberg, Frank Marshall, Kathleen Kennedy (executive), Thad Weinlein (coproducer). *Screenplay* John Patrick Shanley; based on the book by Hudson Talbott.

VOICES: *Rex* John Goodman. *Elsa* Felicity Kendal. *Dweeb* Charles Fleischer. *Woog* Rene LeVant. *Louie* Joey Shea. *Cecilia* Yeardley Smith. *Capt. NewEyes* Walter Cronkite. *Prof. ScrewEyes* Kenneth Mars. *Dr. Bleeb* Julia Child. *Stubbs the Clown* Martin Short.

AD LINE: "Wish for a dinosaur and watch all your dreams come true."

A typical day in the Cretaceous Period is interrupted by the arrival of Captain NewEyes, a benevolent inventor from the far future, who flies about in his time-traveling ornithopter granting children's wishes. One really popular wish, to "see real dinosaurs," has prompted the Captain to feed his "Brain Grain" cereal to four local Mesozoic residents—Rex the Tyrannosaurus, Elsa the pterodactyl, Dweeb the Hadrosaurus, and Woog the Triceratops—transforming them into intelligent (if goofy) beings.

NewEyes sends the dinos off to modern-day New York City to seek out the kindly paleontologist Dr. Bleeb, but warns them of his "mad" brother, evil Professor ScrewEyes. In New York the dino-quartet quickly befriends Louie, a prepubescent tough-guy wannabe, and Cecilia, a neglected rich girl, but a riot spawned by the dinosaurs' appearance separates them from their youthful pals. Running away to "join the circus," the children unluckily choose the "Eccentric Circus" of, yes, Professor ScrewEyes, who mesmerizes them into signing a diabolical contract. But the loyal dinos make a bargain with ScrewEyes, agreeing to forfeit their intelligence and become his savage main attractions if he releases the children. When the youngsters (starting to get sweet on each other) realize the sacrifice their prehistoric friends have made, they enlist the help of kindly Stubbs the Clown and set out to return the favor. The disguised kids sneak into the show, where their good-heartedness restores Rex and the others to their brainy, peaceful forms. As ScrewEyes is consumed by his own evil, Captain NewEyes whisks the dinosaurs off to the care of Doctor Bleeb and the adoration of the children at the Natural History Museum.

COMMENTARY: A sign of the mediocrity of *We're Back! A Dinosaur's Story* is the fact that, while other animated features of its era—*Beauty and the Beast* (1991), *Aladdin* (1992), *The Lion King* (1994)—maintain their popularity, this unremarkable effort is nearly forgotten. Not particularly clever, or funny, or pretty to look at, *We're Back!* manages to tell a threadbare story in amazingly convoluted fashion.

Even with its scrawny running time of 70 minutes (five of which are the closing credits), *We're Back!* still resorts to a Keystone Cops–like police chase and other filler bits to pad its length. The originality of the kid characters speaks volumes—a ragamuffin runaway and a poor little rich girl—and the dinosaurs are sketched in similarly superficial terms. The somewhat off-the-wall voice casting helps a little but not enough.

Walter Cronkite essentially plays himself but puts an avuncular charm into his lines (and yes he gets to say, "and that's the way it is"). Julia Child is fun in her few scenes, and Kenneth Mars (Grandpa's voice in the direct-to-video *Land Before Time* sequels) is conventionally menacing as ScrewEyes. John Goodman is adequate as Rex, though he would put much more life into his portrayal of Fred Flintstone the following year.

It's tempting to ponder the significance of NewEyes' "Wish Radio," and the fact that the script has so many kids wishing to see dinosaurs in 1993. Is this a reference to the *Jurassic Park* "too scary" controversy which had some parents saying no to their young children's pleas to see the film? At any rate, *We're Back!* certainly tried to milk some P.R. out of that controversy, being slickly hyped with the line, "Steven Spielberg presents … a dinosaur adventure for the whole family!" One doubts whether many kids found this

The dinosaurian divas of *We're Back!*—Elsa the pterodactyl, Woog the Triceratops, Rex the Tyrannosaurus, and Dweeb the duckbill.

The anything-but-tyrannical Rex croons "Roll Back the Rock (to the Dawn of Time)" during the Macy's Thanksgiving Parade, the only musical number in *We're Back!*

innocuous cartoon to be a satisfactory substitute for the mighty 'saurs of *Jurassic*, especially when a theater marquee reading "Jurassic Park" pops up in *We're Back!* to remind them what they missed. One minute *We're Back!* is shameless schmaltz, like Louie's scenery-chewing, Brandoesque entreaty to Rex: "Don't be just anuddah slob spoilin' da way da world can be!" The next minute it's haunted-house-style chills inside ScrewEyes' dark circus—a setting with a skewed, nightmarish weirdness that could certainly frighten some young kids. The sparse highlights include a few bursts of imaginative animation, one catchy little song, and a couple of amusing bits by Martin Short playing Lou Costello playing Stubbs the Clown.

We're Back! is based on a very popular children's book by Hudson Talbott which, in hindsight, was probably not an ideal choice for a feature-length film. The movie utterly fails to exploit any of the elements which make dinosaurs popular and offers scant entertainment for children or their parents. Even facing such stiff competition as *Carnosaur* and *Super Mario Bros.*, this disappointing effort may turn out to be the least remembered entry in the big dinomovie derby of 1993.

PEOPLE AND PRODUCTION: *We're Back!* was the second release from Amblimation, the all-animation studio launched by Steven Spielberg following the success of *An American Tail* (1986) and *The Land Before Time*. On a project featuring such stylized dinosaurs, it seems odd to find the film's promotional literature strewn with references to "authenticity" and "research," but it's true that in order to stylize or caricature something, one must understand the real something. "A rhino or hippo can give you a good idea of how a Triceratops might have moved," codirector Phil Nibbelink noted, "but what do you base a hadrosaur on?" Or, as codirector Simon Wells asked, "How can you be certain you're creating animation versions of authentic dinosaurs if you've never had the pleasure of meeting one? Practically every child seems to be an expert on dinosaurs these days, so we try to be as scientifically accurate as possible." The dino designers' preparatory work included multiple visits to London's Natural History Museum, but the artists fell back on their own creative instincts to a great degree. "At least when we show a dinosaur dancing on Broadway," Wells pointed out, "nobody can tell us we got it wrong."

When Dinosaurs Ruled the Earth

"Of darkness, of light ... of the Sun, the Earth, the sea ... of Man."

*** 1971, U.K. Hammer Films/ Warner Bros. C, 96m.

CREDITS: *Director* Val Guest. *Producer* Aida Young. *Written for the Screen by* Val Guest; from a treatment by J. B. Ballard. *Special Visual Effects by* Jim Danforth. *Special Effects* Allan Bryce, Roger Dicken, Brian Johncock.
CAST: *Sanna* Victoria Vetri. *Tara* Robin Hawdon. *Kingsor* Patrick Allen. *Khaku* Drewe Henley. *Kane* Sean Caffrey. *Ulido* Magda Konopka. *Ayak* Imogen Hassall. *Ammon* Patrick Holt.

AD LINE: "Enter an age of unknown terrors, pagan worship and virgin sacrifice!"

At the dawn of humankind, fear and superstition rule the scattered tribes. As the powerful chief Kingsor and his Rock tribe prepare to sacrifice three blonde-tressed women to their sun god, a new heavenly body — which will eventually condense to become the moon — violently rips away from the Sun. One of the intended sacrifices, the beauteous Sanna (another heavenly body), escapes in the confusion and falls into the sea. She is rescued by a fisherman named Tara from the neighboring Sand tribe, but Kingsor is convinced that the natural order cannot be put right until Sanna is sacrificed, and prepares to go after her.

Sanna is welcomed by the Sand tribe's wise leader, Ammon, but shunned by others who fear she is responsible for the cosmic upheavals. As the disturbances escalate, compounded by the violent rampage of an escaped Plesiosaurus, the frightened tribespeople are ripe to jump on the bandwagon when Tara's jealous mate, Ayak, casts blame upon the newcomer. Sanna flees into the wilderness one step ahead of Kingsor and his lieutenant, Kane,* but when Tara and his friend Khaku go searching for her they instead find the injured Kane near a Chasmosaurus lair. The horned beast attacks again and kills Khaku, but Kane recovers under the ministrations of Ayak's friend Ulido. Far away, the exhausted Sanna takes refuge inside the shell of a dinosaur egg. Just as a baby emerges from the remaining egg, the mother dinosaur finds Sanna in the nest and accepts the girl as one of her brood!

Days pass. The dejected Tara, mistakenly convinced that Sanna has been killed, is out on patrol when a huge Rhamphorynchus swoops down and carries him to its nest. He defeats the beast, and from his elevated vantage point sees Sanna strolling along with the giant "mother" dinosaur! Unfortunately she is also spotted by one of Kingsor's goons, and the hunt is on again. Kingsor sentences Tara to death for lying to protect Sanna, but nature is on Tara's side. A huge tylosaur attacks the raft upon which Tara has been set adrift, breaking his bonds, and he somehow reaches Sanna's camp before collapsing. After Kingsor's posse tracks down the couple, Sanna is rescued by her dinosaur mother but Tara is scheduled to be burned at the stake. His execution is halted by a sudden swarm of giant crabs and an approaching tidal surge generated by the gravity of the newly formed

---

*The filmmakers began to worry about the unintended biblical connotations of the name "Kane" (sounds like "Cain") and looped it as "KAY-no" in postproduction, hence the variance between the spelling and pronunciation.

moon. Keeping their wits, Tara, Sanna, Kane, and Ulido lash themselves to a sturdy raft to ride out the massive wave, and the two couples face the future together under the moon's gentle glow.

COMMENTARY: Inevitably, *When Dinosaurs Ruled the Earth* is often mentioned in conjunction with Hammer's *One Million Years B.C.*, and is sometimes even called its sequel. It is actually no such thing. Despite multiple similarities between the films, *Dinosaurs* carves out its own niche in the dinos-and-cavepeople genre. The stop-motion creatures are creatively different; the dark, muted cinematography is in contrast to the earlier film's harsh, blazing sunlight; and the woman, not the man, is the protagonist. Despite its dusky illumination, *Dinosaurs* is also more lighthearted than its predecessor, at least during the scenes of Sanna and her saurian family. There is still the anachronistic pairing of humans and dinosaurs in the same era, but I prefer to think of films of this type as "alternative histories" (like Harry Harrison's wonderful novel *West of Eden*), rather than carping about scientific inaccuracy. And once the premise is accepted, *Dinosaurs* is a well-crafted and enjoyable example of its kind.

The plot parallels between *One Million Years* and *When Dinosaurs Ruled* are substantial. A member of one tribe is exiled and finds love in the arms of a member of another tribe. There is a romantic triangle, wherein the male subject has an ex-mate who is jealous of the newcomer (Nupondi in *Years*; Ayak in *Dinosaurs*). And a climactic natural disaster provides somewhat of a deus ex machina resolution — although to its eternal credit *Dinosaurs* chose a nice refreshing tidal wave instead of yet another doggone volcano. The plot of *Dinosaurs* is slightly more involved and thus harder to follow with the limited dialogue, but is energetically played out. In fact, *Dinosaurs'* final act is actually more satisfying than the makeshift ending of the earlier film.

In just about all facets, *When Dinosaurs Ruled* easily holds its own against its predecessor. Admittedly, this sort of movie doesn't severely test its actors, but the cast does a capable job. Victoria Vetri, despite some needlessly unkind comments made by director Val Guest in the years since, delivers a natural and appealing performance. She successfully portrays the simple emotions required, all the while managing not to look too uncomfortable running around in her absurdly tiny cave bikini. Robin Hawdon is fine as Tara, the gentle fisherman who always tries to do the right thing, although one suspects that either Victor Mature or John Richardson could kick Hawdon's skinny tuchis without breaking a sweat. Mario Nascimbene delivers another effective score, in places recalling but never merely rehashing his *One Million Years B.C.* work. The cinematography by Dick Bush exploits the Canary Islands locations to excellent effect, though the film at times does seem somewhat studio-bound. And of course there is the expert stop-motion craftsmanship of Jim Danforth.

The animation in *Dinosaurs* is striking not only for being so skillfully realized, but also due to the atypical dino roster. Instead of the popular but overused Tyrannosaurus, Brontosaurus, Triceratops, and Stegosaurus, we get a more unusual menagerie, and the puppets themselves are beautifully made. The Plesiosaurus sequence early in the film is a rousing start to the dino action, with interaction between the animated and live-action elements that equals Ray Harryhausen's high standards. The creature's rampage is somewhat reminiscent of Danforth's own "Loch Ness monster" sequence from *7 Faces of Dr. Lao*, though much more technically refined. With eerie "firelight" providing most of the illumination, Danforth delivers a bravura set piece which visually resembles no other stop-motion dino sequence on film. The chasmosaur's appearance, excellently animated by David Allen, is also well-conceived, with the creature believably defending its lair rather than simply "happening by" as is so often the case. Sanna's benevolent dino family is a fresh plot twist, leading to some unique and delightful images. The

Posed photographs of sexy Victoria Vetri in her teeny bikini — or fully topless in pictures for the European market — were a big part of Hammer's promotional efforts.

giant crabs may not be as big as Harryhausen's sensational but solitary shellfish in *Mysterious Island* (1961), but they're faster and meaner. And the long-tailed pterosaur, Rhamphorynchus, is brought convincingly to life in a painstaking and marvelously inventive piece of stop-motion magic. Across the board, the plentiful prehistoric stars are dynamically animated and deftly composited with the live-action elements, and the FX work is richly deserving of its Oscar nomination.

Jim Danforth once said that this film is "neither serious enough to be taken seriously, nor is it flamboyant enough to be a grand adventure, nor is it intentionally humorous enough to be a comedy." But what *Dinosaurs* does have is a mythic, "once-upon-a-time" quality that, when coupled with the Romeo and Juliet allusions and the exemplary visual effects, allows the picture to succeed. While it must face the inherent liability of all cavepeople-and-dinosaur pictures (the fact that the whole thing can seem silly if not viewed with the right frame of mind), *Dinosaurs* earns its place in the upper tier of dinomovies, and offers something for everyone. For the dinosaur fan and/or special effects buff, it has some of the best stop-motion dinosaur action ever filmed. For those unenthralled by giant reptiles, it has several really attractive young women, each wearing almost enough cloth to make three tea bags. This picture even had the boldness way back in 1970 to offer a female hero who fends for herself and rescues the *man* from danger. It's a peppy fantasy that takes you back to a vividly imagined dawn of time, when dinosaurs — okay, and bikinis too — ruled the Earth.

PEOPLE AND PRODUCTION: With the 20th Century–Fox and Hammer Film collaboration *One Million Years B.C.* scoring big at the box office, Warner Bros. asked Hammer if it would be interested in making a follow-up. The answer was "yes," but there was one potential problem. Ray Harryhausen was deep into *The Valley of Gwangi* and unavailable to return as dinosaur maestro, so someone else had to be found who could handle such a formidable effects challenge. Warner Bros. turned to their head of postproduction, Rudi Fehr, who in turn contacted special effects legend Linwood Dunn at Film Effects of Hollywood. Dunn immediately recommended a young artist who had worked for him on *It's a Mad, Mad, Mad, Mad World* (1963). The artist was Jim Danforth, and after some delays involving British labor laws, he flew to England. Val Guest was tabbed to direct and write the screenplay, which he loosely based on a treatment by *Empire of the Sun* author J. G. Ballard (billed as J. B. Ballard).

Hammer had sparked the careers of Ursula Andress (in 1965's *She*) and Raquel Welch, and wasted no time "launching" their latest discovery, Victoria Vetri. The promotional featurette *Beauties and Beasts* claimed Vetri was the personal choice of Hammer patriarch Sir James Carreras (though other sources say she was cast by producer Aida Young). "It's very difficult to be precise about what qualities of a girl catch my interest," Carreras stated. "A good face and figure of course, but it's more than that. I can't describe it, but I know it when I see it, and Victoria Vetri has it I'm sure." Vetri had appeared as the September 1967 centerfold in *Playboy* magazine (under the name Angela Dorian), and was understandably selected "Playmate of the Year" in 1968. Such modeling was good preparation for wearing Carl Toms' audaciously skimpy costumes, and occasionally *not* wearing them, too, in revealing scenes snipped from the film's American release. In the G-rated U.S. version, the love scene in Sanna's cave cuts away at the crucial moment; but in the racier European cut, Sanna is seen — from the back, but head to toe — as she is unceremoniously disrobed by Tara and they sink to the ground. The other segment missing from stateside showings occurs moments later — a brief swimming-and-sunning interlude featuring a bare-breasted Miss Vetri. "I don't object to them," Vetri said of her nude scenes, "because I realize that this opportunity to make an impact in films is so important to me that I'm not about to forfeit it out of silly prudery." *When Dinosaurs Ruled the Earth* wasn't a massive hit, but netted a respectable return on its £2.5 million cost.

SPECIAL EFFECTS: Though Jim Danforth was famous as an animator, his contributions to *When Dinosaurs Ruled the Earth* were not limited to stop-motion animation. He directed or codirected all of the effects shots, as well as some second-unit shots unrelated to effects. He was also allowed, as he put it, to "work out the [effects] sequences." As he explained, "Val Guest, the director, wrote the script, but from that point ... unless it was something really specific that Val had in the script, I would say, 'I think this would be better as a long shot,' or 'this would be a medium shot,' 'this would be a closeup,' and that's the way I drew it, and figured out how it would be edited together, and all of that." In a *House of Hammer* article, Val Guest told author John Brosnan about planning the FX sequences. "I said to Jim that I wanted shots of [the dinosaurs] coming towards the camera with the camera also moving," Guest recalled. "I said — do them as if you're doing a dangerous documentary so that when one of these things is coming towards the camera you get the feeling that the cameraman is about to jump into a nearby ditch, which will give it extra reality. So Jim worked on this idea and came up with some fantastic results." Danforth's credit was originally to have read "Special Visual Effects Designed and Directed by," but the contract between the Director's Guild of America and Warner/Seven Arts prohibited use of the term "directed."

The film contains spectacular shots of

An aggressively territorial Chasmosaurus defends its den against trespassing tribesmen in a memorable sequence from *When Dinosaurs Ruled the Earth.*

the Canary Islands landscapes, but other scenes utilized full-size studio interiors. Unfortunately, these sets were constructed too small to accommodate the composition of most shots—in other words, there was no room for the dinosaurs! This situation created the need for a large number of previously unplanned matte paintings. For a variety of reasons, a suitable matte artist could not be found to handle the burgeoning workload, so in addition to his other responsibilities, Danforth was also charged with creating most of the film's matte paintings. In order to hopefully free up some of Danforth's time for the additional matte-painting work, David Allen was brought to England for about seven weeks to assist with the animation.

Danforth and Allen first met in the early 1960s, during a party at the home of Forrest J Ackerman. They later worked together making commercials at Cascade of California. When Cascade was engaged as an effects subcontractor during *Dinosaurs*' production, Danforth arranged for Allen to build the stop-motion crab puppet and do additional armature work. "When I needed animation help, Dave kindly took a leave of absence from Cascade so that he could come to England," Danforth recalled. Allen worked primarily on the Chasmosaurus sequences, animating all but about three shots of that creature. (Danforth animated the falling-off-the-cliff shot, the shot just before the fall, and the shot of the caveman breaking his spear on the chasmosaur's frill.) A few shots of the baby dinosaur's romp with Sanna are also Allen's work.

Although connected to the project from its earliest days, Danforth was not permitted to choose the types of dinosaurs. "I had input into the designs after they were chosen," he said, "but I didn't have much input on what they were." (Nor could he prevent the inclusion of the live-lizard clips from Irwin Allen's remake of *The Lost World*.) The mother dinosaur's design underwent several changes. It was first envisioned as an Acanthopholis—one of the armored ankylosaurs. Unhappy with that look, Danforth considered a design reminiscent of an oversize monitor lizard, but this too was abandoned. The final creature retained attributes of both previous conceptions but had considerably shortened hind legs and was, in Danforth's words, "sort of a made-up thing." It is also Danforth's contribution to that purely cinematic suborder of four-legged carnivorous dinosaurs, which includes Ray Harryhausen's "rhedosaurus" of *The Beast from 20,000 Fathoms* and Willis O'Brien's "paleosaurus" of *The Giant Behemoth*.

The ceratopsian species in *When Dinosaurs Ruled* is unique among stop-motion dinomovies. "They wanted a Triceratops," Jim Danforth recalled, "and I said 'look, you had a Triceratops in *One Million Years B.C.*' and so they said, 'what about a Styracosaurus,' and I said 'Ray's got one of those coming up in *Gwangi*; let's do something different.' So I came up with a Chasmosaurus, not because I have any particular fondness for chasmosaurs, but it was just, you know, sort of what was left."

The pterosaur's appearance, as originally scripted by Val Guest, was a very elaborate sequence of the tribespeople hunting pterosaur eggs for food and encountering not one but two of the winged giants. "It was a great sequence," Danforth told me, "but I just had to say, 'I can't do this for the time and budget that's available—it's just too complicated.'" So he storyboarded the revised, more filmable scenario which appears in the film. Danforth used a variety of ingenious techniques to add a "motion blur" to the pterosaur animation, greatly lessening stop-motion's inherent strobing effect. On some shots he blurred the wings' movement by simply grabbing the puppet (outside the camera's view) and moving it while the shutter was open. On other shots, like when the creature arches its neck and screams, he shot the model through a pane of glass upon which he had applied Vaseline petroleum jelly in the precise areas to soften and "blur" the model's edges.

However, for most shots, Danforth exploited one particular characteristic of the pterosaur puppet. "It was sort of a special-case situation," he explained, "because it tended to fly with its head straight out. It's got that beak, and the tail was kind of out behind and the legs were tucked up, and the way it was hanging on the wires I could just rock it back and forth." The pterosaur lent itself to this strategy because the parts of the creature which would move the *least* during natural flight—beak, body, and tail—all fell along the puppet's axis. Danforth explains his technique:

> I would position it the way I wanted it, and then I'd go in and, with my thumb or finger, just push down on the wing and get it rocking about the amount I wanted to, so it would rock along its own axis. The beak wouldn't really seem to be moving very much, but the wings, which were farther out from the center, would swing through quite an arc. Then I'd watch it and when it was making about the right amount of move each time, I'd step on the foot pedal and the shutter would go over, and it would rock through two or three cycles during the exposure.

Danforth's laborious, meticulous efforts resulted in perhaps the flat-out *smoothest* piece of stop-motion dinosaur action ever put on film, legitimately approaching the fluidity of Industrial Light and Magic's computer-assisted "Go-Motion" animation in 1981's *Dragonslayer*. Danforth himself is proudest of the sequence design—the scene's pacing and editing—but it is also an animation triumph.

Danforth also employed some nifty tricks to combine the animated and live-action elements. In one cut of the giant crab sequence, pools of water in the foreground

Jim Danforth pulled out all the stops for *Dinosaurs*' pterosaur attack. His ingeniously simulated "motion blur" is clearly visible in this frame blowup.

reflect not only the stop-motion crab but the live caveman as well. This was accomplished by placing a piece of glass, at a shallow angle, very close to the animation camera. "You have to have it up close to the camera because otherwise it won't reflect both the [process] screen and the animation model," Danforth explained. An in-camera split screen with a soft-focus edge turned the reflective glass into a "puddle" in the sand, and the combined illusion is very impressive.

Working alongside Danforth was British FX artist Roger Dicken. Like many other special-effects professionals, Dicken was impressed at a young age by the work of those who had gone before. "My early influences were *King Kong* and *Mighty Joe Young*," Dicken affectionately recalled. Growing up in Portsmouth, England, he caught the bug early, often sneaking into a local theater which still ran the old monster films. Then one day Forry Ackerman's *Famous Monsters* magazine appeared on the newsstand, "and that did it for me," Dicken said. "It meant that there were others out there interested in these films. My contemporaries were into sports or model airplanes, and I was making model pterodactyls and things, and experimenting with 8mm animated dinosaur and puppet animation." The clincher was when Ray Harryhausen came to England to make *Mysterious Island*. "I rang him up ... and he invited me and a chum to visit him at Shepperton, and that was it. I was off."

Dicken left Portsmouth and worked his way into the film industry, starting as a prop maker for a London theater. Afterward came a stint with the BBC, some work on the *Thunderbirds* puppet TV series, and other

Jim Danforth's unique, detail-rich Plesiosaurus rampage in *When Dinosaurs Ruled the Earth* is a masterpiece of lighting, mood, and organic animation.

brief engagements. His feature-film career began with Stanley Kubrick's *2001: A Space Odyssey*, for which he helped create the lunar terrains. His first film as effects supervisor was a low-budgeter called *The Blood Beast Terror* (1967), and he kept busy with jobs on *Witchfinder General* (a.k.a. *The Conqueror Worm*, 1968) and other projects until he got a call from Hammer Films regarding their upcoming prehistoric picture. He told Hammer that he didn't have the experience to single-handedly take on such a project, but would certainly be willing to assist. "Jim came over, and we hit it off like wildfire," Dicken said. "We worked together and had a lot of fun, and we had the same humor, and it was terrific."

Though he did no animation, Dicken had a multitude of responsibilities. After setting up the miniature shop at Bray Studios (where the stop-motion work was done) he sculpted several of the creatures, including the Plesiosaurus, Rhamphorynchus, and most of the Chasmosaurus, reproducing the form and skin texture which Danforth had sculpted on one side of the model. He also created the 12-inch stop-motion caveman who gets mauled by a giant crab, and the 18-inch puppets of the four characters who survive the tidal wave. The plan was to feature these puppets in a show-stopping miniature tidal-wave sequence during the climax, but the sequence fell victim to financial belt-tightening. Dicken also constructed a mechanical "hand puppet" version of the tylosaur, although this creation was never used due to still more monetary restrictions (there was no budget for additional electricians to provide the increased illumination necessary for high-speed filming in the Shepperton tank). Dicken ultimately re-created the tylosaur as a stop-motion puppet, using ball-and-socket joints cannibalized from a lamp! "I must say that all of the models were made under Jim's direction," Dicken emphasized. "Jim was the creative chief on the movie, and what he said was what we did, no problem. I was the Delgado and he was the O'Brien."

Yet another planned but unmade sequence involved a swarm of giant ants invading the village. Stop-motion ant armatures were built, and Dicken created a three-foot-long fiberglass ant with posable wire legs and a semi-articulated head for live-action filming. The model was actually shipped to the Canary Islands, and a test shot was filmed with the prop strapped to an actor's back. "A hotel proprietor in the vicinity wanted to buy the ant to display in his bar at the time," Dicken recalled.

As a licensed pyrotechnician, Dicken was also responsible for the postproduction pyro work such as the burning of the plesiosaur. He found through experimentation that rubber paint burned with a "tiny, flickering flame, like miniature fire."

Among many things, Danforth commends Dicken for providing "very necessary comic relief" during the long and pressure-filled shoot. It was due to his extensive contributions (only some of which have been mentioned) that Danforth saw to it that Dicken's name appeared with his own on the Academy Award nomination. As Danforth summed up, "*When Dinosaurs Ruled the Earth* couldn't have been done without Roger Dicken." Over the coming years, Dicken created effects for many films, including *Scars of Dracula* (1971), *The Land That Time Forgot* and *Warlords of Atlantis* (1978), but many of these projects saddled him with grievous limitations in time and resources.

Other effects artists contributing to *When Dinosaurs Ruled* included Allan Bryce and Brian Johncock. Bryce supervised the physical effects, such as smoke pots, weather effects and so on, while Johncock created the "celestial" effects, including the moon's violent separation from the sun. Longtime Hammer trick man Les Bowie also worked on the film, uncredited. Johncock (now known as Brian Johnson) went on to amass quite a résumé, including *The Empire Strikes Back* (1980), *Dragonslayer* (1981), and *The Neverending Story* (1984). Johncock was reunited with Bryce and Dicken on the sci-fi/horror classic *Alien* (1979), for which Dicken created and activated the "Face Hugger" and "Chest Burster" creatures.

When Dinosaurs Ruled the Earth was the first and only stop-motion dinosaur movie ever to be nominated for a visual-effects Academy Award. Remarkably, it lost to Disney's *Bedknobs and Broomsticks* (Alan Maley, Eustace Lycett, Danny Lee). The nomination was the only Oscar nod — of any kind — ever given to a Hammer Films release.

Where Time Began

"There, there, Uncle Otto, none of this is worth arguing about."

** 1978, Spain. Almena Films. C, 86m.

CREDITS: *Director* J. Piquer Simon. *Story by* Charles Puerto, John Piquer, John Melson. *Screenplay by* John Melson; based on *Journey to the Center of the Earth* by Jules Verne. *Special Effects* Frank Prosper, Emilio Ruiz.

CAST: *Prof. Otto Lidenbrock* Kenneth More. *Axel* Pep Munne. *Glauben* Yvonne Sentis. *Hans* Frank Brana. *Olsen* Jack Taylor.

Hamburg, 1898. In a small bookshop, the noted geologist Professor Otto Lidenbrock buys a tattered book titled "The Fantastic Journey of Arne Saknussemm" from a strange old man. When Lidenbrock realizes that the written account is true, he sets out

Opposite: Theatrical poster for *Where Time Began* promised "Jules Verne's Classic Thriller" but the film's new twists bore little resemblance to Verne's original *Journey to the Center of the Earth*.

with his dauntless young niece Glauben and her sweetheart, Axel, to "follow in Saknussemm's footsteps" to the center of the earth. They hire a burly Icelandic shepherd named Hans as a porter, and descend through a cave within isolated Mt. Sneffels. Despite clumsily losing both their water supply and Saknussemm's guidebook, they plod on until they unexpectedly encounter another explorer. The stranger will identify himself only as Olsen, but they graciously allow him to join their party. The intrepid band soon makes their first big discovery: an underground sea. Hans builds a raft and they sail from island to island, catching prehistoric fish, witnessing a battling pair of giant aquatic dinosaurs, and strolling through a dino graveyard. After rescuing Glauben and Axel from a 20-foot ape, Olsen leads them into a mysterious cave and reveals a glimpse of a thriving futuristic society deep inside the Earth. A dinosaur chases them from the cave and they again set sail, but ultimately reach a dead end. Lidenbrock can't accept defeat and goes off his hinges, and a tearful Glauben begs Olsen for help. Moments later, the raft (minus Olsen) begins shooting upward as if by magic. Safely home again, Hans tends his new flock, Axel and Glauben are wed, and Lidenbrock meets an "old" acquaintance in the little bookshop.

COMMENTARY: "Under the earth," Glauben says in *Where Time Began*, "you have to expect the unexpected." True to her words, the movie does provide unexpected developments, especially for anyone anticipating a semi-faithful retelling of Jules Verne's story. Unfortunately, none of the new twists make much sense. The film starts off with perhaps the most bizarre opening theme song in dinomovie history (edging out *The Last Dinosaur* for that honor), a jaunty little singalong ditty called "The Fellow with the Fife." After this curious beginning, the film settles into utter conventionality for most of its length, "building" to the big revelation of the underground, high-tech society. This scene comes out of nowhere, leads to nowhere, and Olsen avoids having to explain it with the cop-out line: "Certain concepts are not yet within the range of human comprehension." (Glauben's response: "I simply can't believe it!") But why do all the inhabitants look like Olsen? How did they get there? Why reveal them to Glauben and Axel at all? What is the point? Who cares?

Compared to the beautiful Carlsbad Caverns locations seen in 1959's *Journey to the Center of the Earth*, the descent scenes are a letdown (no pun intended). While the extreme darkness of the footage is probably more scientifically accurate than the well-lit chambers in the earlier film, it is cinematically dull. Eschewing the live reptiles of the James Mason version, *Where Time Began* uses models and puppets for all of its prehistoric denizens. The giant tortoises are lifeless and pretty awful. The oversized ape is a typical, cheap gorilla suit, but there are some decent attempts to make the creature appear convincingly huge. The battling, seagoing dinos have fair detail but are hindered not only by their generic design (they don't appear to be patterned after any real species) but also by the decision to place them in the water. The scene employs the age-old technique of overcranking the camera to suggest greater size and mass, but splashing water betrays the illusion by the size of the droplets.

Keeping things watchable are the immense likeability of British veteran Kenneth More (here playing a particularly bumbling Lidenbrock), the atypical beauty of Yvonne Sentis, and an overall jovial tone punctuated by some unexpectedly humorous dialogue, like when Glauben announces her desire to join the expedition. "The bowels of the earth," Axel bellows, "is not a fit place for a woman!" J. Piquer Simon, whose other genre credits include *Monster Island* (1981) and *Endless Descent* (1991), directs with an easy hand appropriate to the picture's modest ambitions. Lightweight, lighthearted, and occasionally light-headed, *Where Time Began* is an innocuous, pleasant, and wholly forgettable little adventure.

Women of the Prehistoric Planet

"Lousy— that's what this whole mission is ... lousy!"

½ 1966, USA. Standard Club of California. C, 91m.

CREDITS: *Director* Arthur C. Pierce. *Producer* George Edwards. *Written by* Arthur C. Pierce. *Special Effects* Joseph Zomar. *Special Photographic Effects* Howard A. Anderson Co.

CAST: *Admiral King* Wendell Corey. *Cmdr. Scott* Keith Larsen. *Dr. Farrell* John Agar. *Linda* Irene Tsu. *Tang* Roberto (Robert) Ito. *Mr. Bradley* Paul Gilbert. *The Chief* Stuart Margolin.

Commanded by the legendary Admiral King, the lead vessel of a three-ship space convoy responds to a distress call. One of the other ships, carrying a mixed crew of Centaurans and humans, has crashed on a strange planet inhabited by giant prehistoric reptiles. After King's ship lands, a young woman named Linda wanders off and is found by Tang, the son of a human male and a Centauran female who survived the crash (everyone knows you'll always find Tang in space). Due to the "time paradox," Tang is already 18 years old by the time the rescue ship arrives. Tang and Linda—who, as it turns out, is also half human and half Centauran—fall in love and remain behind on the small blue planet to begin a new civilization.

COMMENTARY: *Women of the Prehistoric Planet* is graphic evidence that space-oriented science fiction films evolved very little

Dr. "Doc" Farrell (a rather hefty John Agar) tries to reason with lovely, lovesick Linda (Irene Tsu) on the decidedly womanless *Prehistoric Planet*.

Mr. Bradley (Paul Gilbert) draws a bead on yet another enlarged iguana in the very minor "dinosaur scene" from *Women of the Prehistoric Planet.*

over the 30-odd years preceding its creation. This relic is on a level with the *Flash Gordon* serials of the 1930s; actually, the old Buster Crabbe yarns are better. Between the plywood sets, the soundstage jungles and the stilted pseudotechnical dialogue, no hallmark of bad sixties sci-fi is missed. The acting is not merely bad but downright anesthetizing. John Agar is at his worst, delivering every line as though a great cosmic truth is flowing from his lips, and Wendell Corey perpetually seems to be in danger of actually dozing off. All the while, Paul Gilbert supplies some of the most unbearable, positively torturous comic "relief" in celluloid history. Despite the utterly misleading title — the planet had no women until the spaceship crash — there are very few "prehistoric" elements, and the film is discussed in this volume only for the sake of completeness. The "dinosaur" scene is just one brief appearance by a particularly docile giant lizard, played in tried-and-true fashion by a pet-shop iguana. On the plus side, there's ... very little. Fans of seventies TV may enjoy seeing Stuart Margolin of *The Rockford Files* and Robert Ito of *Quincy* in early roles. Unfortunately, the big "twist ending" will come as a surprise to nobody. For a real "twist," check out that groovy dance done by the Annette Funicello look-alike who plays the junior communications officer!

SPECIAL EFFECTS: The effects crew for *Women of the Prehistoric Planet* included a pair of surprising names: Jim Danforth and David Allen. Danforth built the FX model of Admiral King's spaceship, the *Cosmos I*, utilizing a process called "electroforming." In this technique, as Danforth explained it to the author, an electrolytic solution is used to deposit copper onto two halves of a silicone mold, after which the two halves are soldered together and then detailed. (If only a similar amount of care had gone into the script.) David Allen oversaw the construction of the scale-model sets. "I was working on a miniature that a rocket crashes into with a number of people, but I was sort of in charge of it, as I recall," Allen told Mark McGee in *Fangoria*. Neither man receives a screen credit.

A few of the props seen in *Prehistoric Planet* have unexpected ties to fantasy-film royalty, as David Allen's longtime associate Chris Endicott revealed. "The film was done at Howard Anderson's which had access to the Paramount lot, and of course Paramount took over RKO which was right next door," Endicott told me. "So David would be allowed to go over to the old RKO prop room and get props." Among these forgotten items were several leftovers from *King Kong*. "He grabbed a bunch of [miniature] trees from *Kong*, and a lot of the set dressing from *Kong* was used in ... [one] sequence."

Later in the film, a large spider kills Stuart Margolin's character. "That's the stop-motion spider from *King Kong*," Endicott disclosed — yes, the animation puppet built for and featured in the unseen but famous "spider-pit sequence." Even though the creature was a bit worse for wear, someone involved with the live-action shooting apparently couldn't resist using it. "It was a seven-legged spider, David said, because one of the legs was broken off of it," Endicott continued. "So the seven-legged spider puppet was used as a prop in *Prehistoric Planet*, and they never returned it to the RKO prop room."

About the lizard shots, it has been reported by some sources that a live iguana was actually set on fire. Director Arthur C. Pierce has denied such an act, and frame-by-frame examination of the sequence supports his claim. It can be seen that the camera was stopped and the reptile removed from the shot just prior to the explosion, and the shots of it "writhing" while ablaze look suspiciously like a rubber model being jiggled by the prop man.

Yor: The Hunter from the Future

(a.k.a. *The World of Yor*)

"I'll show you my past ...
I hope I can figure it out."

*½ 1983, Italy. Columbia. C, 89m.

CREDITS: *Director* Anthony M. Dawson (Antonio Margheriti). *Producers* Michele Marsala, Sedat Akdemir (associate), Ugur Terzioglu (associate). *Screenplay* Robert Bailey and Anthony M. Dawson; based on the novel *Yor* by Juan Zanotto and Ray Collins. *Special Effects* Edward and Tony Margheriti. *Models and Miniatures* Antonella Margheriti.
CAST: *Yor* Reb Brown. *Ka-Laa* Corinne Clery. *Pag* Alan Collins. *Overlord* John Steiner. *Ena* Carole André. *Roa* Ayshe Gul. *Tarita* Marina Rocchi.

AD LINE: "In his quest for his origin, he and the woman he loves must fight hostile tribes. Battle deadly beasts. And try to survive the violent forces of a newly born Earth."

As a peaceful Stone Age tribe prepares a festival, the tribal elder proclaims, "may this day be celebrated with feasting and hunting!" The lovely Ka-Laa and her surrogate father and protector, Pag (realizing that hunting comes *before* feasting), set off to find meat. They pursue a small armored creature, but when a giant Triceratops bursts through the underbrush only the intervention of a stranger called "Yor, the Hunter" prevents tragedy. Yor is on a quest to find his origin, guided only by the medallion around his neck.

The tribe's village is suddenly destroyed by a horde of hairy brutes, and Yor leads Ka-Laa and Pag into the wilderness. Journeying

Yor: The Hunter from the Future

Heroic Yor (Reb Brown) tangles with a blue-skinned, bushy-browed caveman while Ka-Laa (Corinne Clery, center) watches in amazement.

through the domain of the mummy-wrapped desert people, Yor meets the mysterious and beautiful Roa. He notices that her medallion is like his, which is "proof that we represent a race!" Ka-Laa is intensely jealous, but Roa is killed in yet another attack by the hirsute savages. The trio presses onward to the sea, where Yor saves the teenage Tarita from a Dimetrodon and thus earns the hospitality of her seaside tribe. But it seems wherever Yor goes, disaster follows, and just as Tarita's dad tells of the strange "god who fell from the sky," a high-tech laser attack destroys the village. Yor vows to avenge Tarita's people and sails with Pag and Ka-Laa to "the island with a great castle." He is captured by the maniacal dictator, Overlord, who needs Yor's DNA to build a "race of hybrid clones." Pag and Ka-Laa are sequestered by a rebel underground faction, who team up with Yor and his comrades to fight their way out of Overlord's complex just before it blows up. Yor, Ka-Laa, and Pag return to the simple tribes on the mainland, hoping to prevent mankind from tragically repeating history.

COMMENTARY: Somewhere between a bad movie and a "so-bad-it's-good" movie lies *Yor: The Hunter from the Future*. It's loaded with bad elements—acting, dialogue, costumes—but they aren't what make *Yor* so strangely watchable. Rather, it's an over-the-top, swashbuckling spirit that barely saves this low-budget muscleman opus from the scrap heap. The picture has an episodic construction that gives it the feel of a condensed 5-chapter serial, so there's little time to mull over past absurdities before hurtling into the next one.

It's pointless to critique the acting or writing in a movie like this. Reb Brown and Corinne Clery look great in their skimpy togs but are basically as wooden as tree stumps, while John Steiner is all ham as Overlord. Only Alan Collins as the loyal Pag has a moment or two, like when Yor offers him a drink of Triceratops blood as a strength potion and Pag deadpans, "I'd rather stay weak." (Watch Corinne Clery in this shot, as she spontaneously laughs at Collins' line and then tries to quickly compose herself.) The plot is half *Valley of the Dragons*, half *Star Wars*, and all idiocy, but spiced with imaginative moments that are just so *cheeky* they dare you not to enjoy them. When the hero shoots down a huge batlike beast with an arrow, retrieves the carcass, and then uses the dead body as a *hang glider* to rescue Ka-Laa ... I defy the most dedicated curmudgeon to not crack a smile. The final reel is a hoot for any *Star Wars* fan with a sense of humor, as Overlord's stormtroopers aimlessly run around wearing helmets that, literally, seem to be from Darth Vader's rummage sale.

Yor's dinosaurs—all represented by full-scale mechanical puppets—are confined to the story's first half when the action occurs in the "primitive" world. The small, armored Ankylosaurus (or whatever it's supposed to be) doesn't have to do much, but wiggles acceptably. The Triceratops, whose nose horn is so inconspicuous that he's almost a bi-ceratops, is decidedly stiff but maybe a little better than one might expect. The pseudo-Dimetrodon is the most lifeless of the trio, recalling his track-mounted ancestor in 1948's *Unknown Island*.

Yor is an inarguably poor film, enlivened only by its credibility-be-hanged philosophy, some striking Turkish locations, and a music track that recalls Queen's memorably bombastic *Flash Gordon* score. It ultimately can't keep from being bad, but at least it goes down fighting.

APPENDIX A: DINO-CAMEOS AND PALEO-PLOTS

Films with Dinosaurian Themes, Plot Elements, or Isolated Dinosaur Scenes

Amazon Women on the Moon

1987. Directed by Joe Dante, Carl Gottlieb, Peter Horton, John Landis, Robert K. Weiss. Special effects by L. A. Effects Group, Inc. Mechanical effects by Image Engineering. Anthology/sketch film in the mold of (but not as good as) *Kentucky Fried Movie*. Several lizard-osaurs, apparently filmed expressly for this picture, menace the intrepid space crew in a fifties sci-fi spoof. The "Nessie" puppet from *The Loch Ness Horror* also appears ... as Jack the Ripper.

Beneath Loch Ness

2001. Patrick Bergin, Lysette Anthony, Brian Wimmer, Lysa Apostle. Directed by Chuck Comisky. Visual Effects Supervisor: Elliot Worman. Live Action Creature Effects: Alterian Inc. Creature Supervisor: Tony Gardner. Minor but well-intentioned tale, sparked by the scenery-gnawing Bergin as a Scottish version of *Jaws*' shark-hunting Quint, and an admittedly original premise. Here Nessie is merely a supporting monster who actually gets eaten by the real baddie — a 60-foot super-plesiosaur evolved (and noticeably changed) from prehistoric ancestors. Robert Foxworth has an unbilled cameo.

Bringing Up Baby

1938. Katharine Hepburn, Cary Grant. Directed by Howard Hawks. RKO's hilarious romp, about an unusual society lass and a nebbish paleontologist looking for an "intercostal clavicle" to complete his Brontosaurus skeleton, was a major flop when released but is now considered to be the pinnacle of the "screwball" comedy form. The full-size prop skeleton turned up 15 years later in the museum sequence of *The Beast from 20,000 Fathoms*.

Brontosaurus

1979. Directed by Vera Plívová-Simková. English version produced by Faith Frenz-Heckman. A bunch of grade-school kids ditch class to clean up the forest and build a full-size Brontosaurus sculpture out of the rubbish, in this well-meaning but unfortunately dull Czech film with an antipollution message. Award-winning director Plívová-Simková has done much better work.

Clifford

1994. Martin Short, Charles Grodin. Directed by Paul Flaherty. Visual effects by 4-Ward Productions, Inc. Visual Effects Supervisor: Robert Skotak. Visual Effects Director of Photography: Dennis Skotak. Dinosaur Effects Supervisor: Jim Towler. Dinosaur Effects Engineer: F. Lee Stone. Dinosaur Sculptor: Adam Defelice. Excruciating, nearly intolerable comedy casts Short as a 10-year-old (?) monstrosity of a child, who in the climax is almost but not quite (darn it) eaten by an animatronic T. rex in a dinosaur theme park.

The Dinosaur Hunter

1999. Alison Pill, Bill Switzer, Christopher Plummer. Directed by Rick Stevenson. Measured drama of a pair of rural teens having their humdrum lives invigorated by the arrival of a paleontologist who wants to dig for fossils on their farm. Director Stevenson also helmed 1995's *Magic in the Water*. Both Stevenson and young actress Alison Pill nabbed awards at the 2000 Burbank International Children's Film Festival.

Epic: Days of the Dinosaurs

1984. Voices of Ross Higgins, Robyn Moore. Narrated by John Huston. Directed by Yoram Gross. Background Photography: Klaus Jaritz. This oddity from Australian animation specialist Yoram Gross features his trademark — placing cel-animated characters over live-action backgrounds — but is not one of the director's better efforts. Despite the promise of the title, the dinosaurs in this aimless, unsatisfying fable are limited to two short scenes: an attack by a strangely designed tyrannosaur type (whose gait recalls a vaudeville comic doing a broadly exaggerated "sneaking-up-on-you" walk), and a brief appearance by a friendly pterodactyl.

Flash Gordon

1936. Larry "Buster" Crabbe, Jean Rogers, Priscilla Lawson. Directed by Frederick Stephani. Electrical Effects: Norman Dewes. Special Properties: Elmer A. Johnson. Universal's inaugural "Flash Gordon" serial, in 13 parts. Crabbe is energetic, the curvy lines of Rogers and Lawson are displayed in surprisingly unconfining and midriff-baring wardrobes, and the nifty spark-spewing electrical gizmos likely owe much to Kenneth "*Frankenstein*" Strickfadden. The giant reptiles, played by live lizards, are not explicitly called "dinosaurs" (Rogers calls them "ghastly monsters") but they are clearly meant to at least suggest a prehistoric connection — there's even a lizard-versus-lizard fight four years before the more famous one in *One Million B.C.* Bull "*The Lost World*" Montana supposedly plays one of the monkey-men.

The Indian in the Cupboard

1995. Hal Scardino, Litefoot, David Keith. Directed by Frank Oz. Supervisor of Visual Effects: Eric Brevig. Special Visual Effects and Animation: Industrial Light & Magic. The toys brought to life by the magic cupboard include all-too-brief glimpses of Robocop, G.I. Joe, a Cardassian, a Ferengi, and a nifty Tyrannosaurus which is held at bay by Darth Vader and his lightsaber!

Killer Klowns from Outer Space

1987. Grant Cramer, Suzanne Snyder, Royal Dano. Directed by Stephen Chiodo. Special Effects Supervisor: Gene Warren, Jr. Stop-motion Animation: Justin Kohn. In one scene of this bizarre mix of horror and humor, penned by noted stop-motion artists Charles and Stephen Chiodo, one of the murderous alien clowns makes shadow animals with his hands. The fun turns to terror when he generates the shadow of a (cartoon-animated) Tyrannosaurus which proceeds to eat the spectators.

Massacre in Dinosaur Valley

1985. Michael Sopkiw, Susane Carvall. Directed by Michael E. Lemick. There are no dinosaurs in this repellently violent and misogynistic lemon, just a lot of paleontology talk, some *ichnites* (fossilized dinosaur tracks), a dino-worshipping Indian tribe, and a lot of gratuitous female nudity. Sopkiw turns in some of the worst acting in the history of celluloid entertainment.

Metamorphosis

1987. Gene Le Brock, Catherine Baranov. Directed by G. L. Eastman. Special Effects and Make-up by Maurizio Trani. When maverick geneticist Doctor Houseman experiments on himself, he slowly "devolves" into a murderous, perspiring fiend with dark circles under his eyes. In the ostensible climax, he regresses into a six-foot-tall dinosaur and then dissolves.

Naked Gun 33⅓ — The Final Insult

1994. Leslie Nielsen, Priscilla Presley. Directed by Peter Segal. Visual Effects Supervisor: Kimberly K. Nelson. Third installment of the gag-a-second *Naked Gun* film series (inspired by the short-lived TV series, *Police Squad*) features a giddily goofy opening credits sequence, following a police car through a myriad of outrageous settings. The segment's last scene takes the car into a replica of the *Jurassic Park* T. rex paddock, where we see a top-notch stop-motion tyrannosaur built by the Chiodo brothers and animated by Kent Burton.

On the Town

1949. Gene Kelly, Frank Sinatra. Directed by Gene Kelly and Stanley Donen. This knockout, Technicolor MGM musical romps all over New York City, and includes a stop at the Natural History Museum for a number called "Prehistoric Man." A huge dinosaur skeleton crumbles to the ground (recalling *Bringing Up Baby*) in the segment's climax.

One of Our Dinosaurs Is Missing

1975. Peter Ustinov, Helen Hayes. Directed by Robert Stevenson. A British secret agent hides a secret formula on a sauropod skeleton, which subsequently gets towed all over the English countryside by a flock of nannies in this low-energy, laugh-deprived live-action Disney outing.

Pee-Wee's Big Adventure

1985. Paul Reubens, Elizabeth Daily. Directed by Tim Burton. A large, deliberately toy-like stop-motion Tyrannosaurus rex, animated by Rick Heinrichs, wrecks Pee-Wee Herman's beloved bicycle in one of many off-the-wall vignettes.

Robocop

1987. Peter Weller, Nancy Allen, Ronny Cox. Directed by Paul Verhoeven. An excellent stop-motion T. rex, animated by the Chiodo brothers (Edward, Stephen, and Charles), turns up in an ersatz TV commercial for the "6000 SUX" sedan.

Timemaster

1995. Jesse Cameron-Glickenhaus, Pat Morita, Michelle Williams. Directed by James Glickenhaus. Dinosaur effect by Atlantic West Effects, Gabe Bartalos. A rod-puppet tyrannosaur (floating through space inside a bubble?) passes by during a time-travel montage in this nearly unseen — and nearly unwatchable — science-fiction entry.

Toy Story

1995. Voices of Tom Hanks, Tim Allen. Directed by John Lasseter. This the world's first all-computer-animated film is much more than a technical gimmick — it's a witty, funny, exciting movie with a cast of terrific toys, including a green plastic Tyrannosaurus (named Rex, natch) perfectly voiced by Wallace Shawn. "I'm going for fearsome here," he cries, "but I think I'm just coming off as annoying!"

Toy Story 2

1999. Voices of Tom Hanks, Tim Allen. Directed by John Lasseter, codirected by Ash Brannon and Lee Unkrich. Rex the neurotic tyrannosaur is back (again Wallace Shawn) in this superb sequel, which includes among its many pop-culture references a satisfying send-up of a famous *Jurassic Park* scene.

Vulcan

1997. Tom Taus, Jr., Diana Barton, Robert Vaughn. Directed by Cirio H. Santiago. Visual Effects Supervisor: Gerardo Chuidian. Animator Engineer/Stop-Motion Animator: Roderick Banares. Low-budget Philippine production has its heart in the right place, but trying to wrap a feel-good "boy-and-his-monster" fable around the real life 1991 eruption of Mt. Pinatubo (which killed over 300 people) is iffy at best, and not even the *Teenage Caveman* himself, Robert Vaughn, can get this tale of a benevolent, pterodactyl-ish bird god off the ground.

Wargames

1983. Matthew Broderick, Ally Sheedy, Dabney Coleman. Directed by John Badham. Pterosaur Consultant: Bill Watson. The eccentric Professor Falken (John Wood) flies a radio-controlled pterodactyl, and later shows clips of Ray Harryhausen's dinosaurs from *One Million Years B.C.* to Broderick and Sheedy.

APPENDIX B: LOST WORLDS

Dinosaur Films That Might Have Been or Might Yet Be

At the Earth's Core

SEE: *Pellucidar*

Atlantis

TIME FRAME: c. 1927

PREMISE: Epic-scale adventure detailing an unknown society existing in the legendary lost city, lorded over by a dictatorial monarch.

PERSONNEL: Willis O'Brien, Ralph Hammeras, Marcel Delgado, Earl Hudson.

PREHISTORIC CREATURES: Some "prehistoric" mammals and sea creatures were to be featured; whether any true dinosaurs were planned is unknown.

NOTES: O'Brien and Ralph Hammeras planned *Atlantis* as a worthy successor — though not a sequel — to their 1925 triumph, *The Lost World*, but First National Pictures' migration to the west coast along with the studio's financial difficulties contributed to the film's cancellation.

QUOTE: "Obie and Hammeras prepared many idea sketches for *Atlantis* and had numerous plot discussions with [First National exec] Earl Hudson. However, after about three months of intensive work, they began to suspect that the film would never be made in New York." — Don Shay, in *Cinefex* (no. 7, 1982).

Creation

TIME FRAME: 1930–31

PREMISE: An American industrialist, his family and entourage are rescued from a typhoon-stricken yacht by a Chilean submarine, only to be thrust by a seaquake into the water-filled caldera of a gigantic dormant volcano. Amid a lost world of prehistoric life, everyone's true natures are revealed.

PERSONNEL: Willis O'Brien (technical creator, scenario); Marcel Delgado (animation models and miniatures); Mario Larrinaga, Byron Crabbe, Juan Larrinaga, Ernest Smythe (production artists); Harry O. Hoyt (director, scenario); Beulah Marie Dix (script).

PREHISTORIC CREATURES: Triceratops family, Arsinoitherium, Brontosaurus, pterodactyls, Stegosaurus, Tyrannosaurus Rex.

NOTES: Perhaps the most famous dino-movie never made. Bought by RKO's William

LeBaron, *Creation* was subsequently canceled by RKO newcomer Merian C. Cooper. However, Coop's excitement at seeing the amazing visual effects in O'Brien's test reel led directly to Obie's participation in *King Kong*. Film historian George Turner has cited the number of color preproduction drawings as evidence that Technicolor may have been planned for *Creation*.

QUOTES: "Just a lot of animals walking around."—Merian Cooper, on the *Creation* scenario.

"A full year was spent on the extensive preparations required to mount the *Creation* project.... Mario Larrinaga, Byron Crabbe and Ernest Smythe prepared scores of large, detailed renderings.... Marcel Delgado was hard at work on the model dinosaurs, a number of which had never before, nor since, appeared on the screen. Two brief test reels were to be filmed.... One, involving the destruction of the storm-swept yacht ... the second *Creation* test [was] taken from the sequence in which Hallet, portrayed by actor Ralf Harolde, shoots the baby Triceratops and is then pursued by its enraged mother. The test footage ... represented a quantum leap in technique over the comparatively primitive composite work in *The Lost World*."—Don Shay, in *Cinefex* (no. 7, 1982).

SEE ALSO: *King Kong* (Filmography section).

Dark Continent: A Sherlock Holmes Adventure!

TIME FRAME: 1988–

PREMISE: The legendary, fictional sleuth journeys to Africa and encounters Ayesha, "She-Who-Must-Be-Obeyed," from the writings of H. Rider Haggard. Holmes also finds the game's afoot—a dinosaur foot—with a variety of prehistoric beasts also given immortality by the eternal flame.

PERSONNEL: Jim Danforth (story concept, screenplay); Marjorie Vander Hoff, Rick Mitchell (cast, in promotional reel).

PREHISTORIC CREATURES: Spinosaurus, Arsinoitherium, giant snake, others?

NOTES: The second intriguing-sounding entry in Danforth's proposed film series spotlighting Holmes' adventurous side (following *West of Kashmir: A Sherlock Holmes* Adventure!). The Spinosaurus puppet, which can be glimpsed in Don Glut's *Dinosaur Movies* video documentary, utilized the armature made for the vetoed Ceratosaurus of *When Dinosaurs Ruled the Earth*.

QUOTE: "I think as a ten or twelve million dollar picture, somewhere in that range, it's viable. But I don't think a studio would want to make a movie in that range.... There weren't a whole bunch of dinosaurs in that. There's just a *smattering*, let's say, of dinosaurs. I didn't want it to be a dinosaur extravaganza."—Jim Danforth, to the author.

Dinosaur Girl

TIME FRAME: early 1970s

PREMISE: Direct sequel to (or preliminary version of?) *When Dinosaurs Ruled the Earth*.

PERSONNEL: Hammer Films; Victoria Vetri (?).

PREHISTORIC CREATURES: Presumably the baby (at a more developed age) and mother quadruped introduced in *When Dinosaurs Ruled*. Many more species would likely have been featured as well.

NOTES: Unverified. The fanzine *The House That Hammer Built* reported that Hammer Films did indeed have tentative plans for this *When Dinosaurs Ruled* sequel, but Jim Danforth told this author of his vague recollection that *Dinosaur Girl* was "a planned *earlier* version of *When Dinosaurs Ruled the Earth* ... intended to be more of a comedy."

QUOTE: "A projected sequel, *Dinosaur Girl*, planned to continue the adventures of Vetri with her baby dinosaur, was axed."—Wayne Kinsey, in *The House that Hammer Built* (issue six, 1997).

The Dinosaur Kid

TIME FRAME: 1990s–

PREMISE: 10-year-old dinosaur fanatic Sean, his dad, and an adventurous young woman travel into a remote, time-arrested valley. They find not only a plethora of dinosaurs, but also a family of rural bank robbers who stopped aging when they holed up in the valley around 1900. The clan's youngest, Katie, and her ability to communicate with the dinosaurs, may hold the key to Sean's family's escape.

PERSONNEL: Brett Piper (screenplay, visual effects); Kinetic Image Co., Ltd.

PREHISTORIC CREATURES: Centrosaurus, Megalosaurus, Stegosaurus, Mosasaurus, Apatosaurus, Scelidosaurus, Parasaurolophus, Psittacosaurus, Dimetrodon, Triceratops, Pteranodon.

QUOTES: "I've been trying to get [*The Dinosaur Kid*] off the ground since before *Jurassic Park*. Of course, nobody wanted dinosaurs back then."—Brett Piper, in *SPFX* (no. 5, 1997).

"Twenty tons of mind-blowing, bone crunching prehistoric terror ... what more could a boy want?"—tag line for the film (published on the Kinetic Image Co., Ltd. website).

Dinosaurs

TIME FRAME: late 1980s–early 1990s

PREMISE: A visceral and sometimes violent look at the final days of the dinosaurs' reign on earth, told in completely naturalistic fashion.

PERSONNEL: Paul Verhoeven, Phil Tippett (concept, directors); Jon Davison (producer); Walon Green (script); Tom Smith (director); David Allen (director).

PREHISTORIC CREATURES: Styracosaurus (the "hero"), Tyrannosaurus rex (the "villain"), a small mammal named Suri, many more dinosaurs.

NOTES: This project, eventually to be reshaped and reprocessed into Disney's CGI adventure *Dinosaur*, began as an all-stop-motion film with no dialogue, no narration—no words at all. The ill-fated project began when Phil Tippett, during a shooting lull on the set of *Robocop*, said to Jon Davison and Paul Verhoeven, "We should make a dinosaur picture." The all-animated idea later gave way to a stop-motion, rod-puppet mixture, with Suri portrayed by an actor in a suit. The picture was originally to be codirected by Verhoeven and Tippett, then by Tom Smith, and then by David Allen, but this entire incarnation of the film eventually died; only Walon Green's name survives in the *Dinosaur* credits.

QUOTES: "Our pitch to [Jeffrey] Katzenberg was a gritty, true-life adventure where all the storytelling would be carried in action and pantomime.... As a result of Paul's involvement, it was very gritty and had some pretty intense moments ... What we did was construct a neighborhood of characters that inhabited a certain locale and built up a number of scenarios involving them. For the dramatic needs of storytelling, it wasn't possible to be absolutely paleontologically correct."—Phil Tippett, in *Cinefantastique* (vol. 31, nos. 1/2, 1999).

"We wanted to do something meaningful, archetypal, and dimensional instead of straight entertainment, with cute dinosaurs singing.... The reason why I wanted to do it was because it had this cosmic vision about evolution. That sounds a bit over the top but it would have been really good.... There was a gigantic battle at the end as a comet moves closer and closer to Earth. The fight was between the sympathetic styracosaur and the antagonistic Tyrannosaurus rex, and although the good one wins, there's nothing to win any more because the comet hits the Earth.... I think [the film] would have survived for a long time because the concept was so unconventional and daring.... It's a pity that Disney didn't have the vision to go this way."—Paul Verhoeven, in *Cinefantastique* (vol. 31, nos. 1/2, 1999).

SEE ALSO: *Dinosaur* (Filmography section)

Dinosaurs Attack!

TIME FRAME: early to mid–1990s

PREMISE: Film version of Topps' joyously gory bubblegum card set.

PERSONNEL: Gary Gerani (card set creator); Joe Dante, Mike Finnel (producers); Will Vinton (director); Charlie Hass (screenplay).

PREHISTORIC CREATURES: The card set pictured all sorts: meat-eaters, of course, but the herbivores also caused carnage! (Card #10 seems to show the "Paleosaurus" from *The Giant Behemoth* and the "Rhedosaurus" from *The Beast from 20,000 Fathoms*; a Gorgo look-alike is on card #17.)

NOTES: Gerani conceived the cards as a tribute to the fondly remembered *Mars Attacks!* cards from the fifties. After Dante and Finnel optioned *Dinosaurs Attack!* for filming, plans for the project evolved from a "half-serious" treatment with traces of satire to an all-out *Airplane!*-style send-up.

QUOTE: "I have a screenwriting background, so I gave them a treatment, which they very nicely rejected.... Originally, in all fairness to Dante, they did try a version which was pretty close to what I created, in terms of tone ... but then, because *Jurassic Park* reared its big, ugly, Spielbergian head, they became intimidated, because nobody was going to be able to match the magnitude of that."—Gary Gerani, in *Cinefantastique* (vol. 24, no. 2, 1993).

Dino-Warp

TIME FRAME: late 1990s–

PREMISE: A deputy sheriff and a woman lawyer, investigating reports of dinosaurs killing cows, stumble into a top-secret military time travel experiment and soon find themselves battling prehistoric beasts both in the Jurassic and today!

PERSONNEL: Brett Piper (screenplay); Kinetic Image Co., Ltd.; Edgewood.

PREHISTORIC CREATURES: Allosaurus, other dinosaurs and pterosaurs.

NOTES: The published synopsis of *Dino-Warp* has the heroic deputy fighting a dinosaur with a piece of earth-moving equipment, a scenario seen in a great many films through the years. But there *is* a twist here—the deputy *loses* this fight.

QUOTE: "Government scientists release prehistoric monster on a helpless world.... Cool!!"—tag line for the film (published on the Kinetic Image Co., Ltd. website).

The Eighth Wonder

TIME FRAME: c. 1952

PREMISE: To bring the great ape Kong back to the screen via the imposing and sometimes spectacular Cinerama process. Some reports claim that *The Eighth Wonder* was to be a true remake of *Kong*; others say its plot concerned the untold events during Kong's ship voyage to New York.

PERSONNEL: Merian C. Cooper; Willis O'Brien (?).

PREHISTORIC CREATURES: Unknown. Possibly none, had the journey to New York scenario been filmed.

NOTES: Merian Cooper had toyed with the idea of a second sequel to *Kong* immediately after *The Son of Kong*, which would have told the story of Kong's escape, rampage, and recapture in the Malay Archipelago.

QUOTE: "When Cooper was in charge of production for the Cinerama organization, it was rumored that *King Kong* would be re-made in the tri-camera process under its original working title, *The Eighth Wonder*."—Orville Goldner & George E. Turner, in *The Making of King Kong*.

Evolution

TIME FRAME: 1938–39

PREMISE: The history of life on Earth, told entirely in animation.

PERSONNEL: Ray Harryhausen.

PREHISTORIC CREATURES: Dimetrodon, Brontosaurus, Tyrannosaurus Rex, Triceratops, more.

NOTES: Irwin Allen inquired about using Ray's *Evolution* footage for the dinosaur scenes in *The Animal World*, before commissioning Ray and Obie to create a brand new sequence.

QUOTES: "I wanted to show the whole history of the world in stop-motion animation. Of course, my favorite sequence would be the dinosaur sequence, so I started with that particular section of it."—Ray Harryhausen, in *Aliens, Dragons, Monsters and Me.*

"*Evolution* was a 16mm project, very ambitious when I look back at it, but in my naive way I thought I could do it if I took a year, or year and a half.... The picture was never completed because I got discouraged when I saw *Fantasia*. It covered the dinosaur sequence, with Stravinsky's wonderful background music, and I thought, 'Oh, they're covering the same ground, and they did it so beautifully, I might as well abandon it.' But it wasn't for naught— I used all this footage I had experimented with earlier as a sample of what I could do."—Ray Harryhausen, in American Movie Classics' *The Harryhausen Chronicles.*

Farnsworth's Folly

TIME FRAME: c. 1970

PREMISE: Satiric tale of biochemist Franklin Farnsworth, who discovers a way to generate living dinosaurs from DNA.

PERSONNEL: Jim Danforth (original concept, screenplay, visual effects).

PREHISTORIC CREATURE: Monty the Monoclonius.

NOTES: Originally titled *'A' Is for Allosaur*. Monty's name is a tribute to Ernest "Monty" Schoedsack.

QUOTE: "Unlike the scientist in Michael Crichton's *Jurassic Park* (written about fifteen years later) Farnsworth hasn't actually used dinosaur blood; he has 'read' the DNA codes ...

and has reconstructed the entire double helix. For my own amusement, I based portions of *Farnsworth's Folly* on themes and characters from various versions of the classic Faust legend.... I tried to get Ray Bradbury to write the actual screenplay, but he wasn't interested."— Jim Danforth, in *SPFX* (no. 5).

Five Billion B.C.

TIME FRAME: c. 1960 (?)
PREMISE: Prehistory epic briefly planned by writer-director-producer Edgar G. Ulmer.
PERSONNEL: Edgar G. Ulmer; Jim Danforth.
PREHISTORIC CREATURES: Unknown.
NOTES: Ulmer is best known for the atmospheric Bela Lugosi-Boris Karloff pairing *The Black Cat* (1934) and the ultra-low-budget but gripping film noir classic, *Detour* (1945).
QUOTE: "I worked on *Five Billion B.C.*, as far as it got, doing storyboards and stuff. Gene Warren got in on it also, but it never got made."—Jim Danforth, to the author (1998)

Gwangi

TIME FRAME: c. 1941
PREMISE: Dinosaurs and other prehistoric animals are discovered by a traveling "wild west" circus troupe in a hidden region of the Grand Canyon. When the cowboys capture a carnivorous Allosaurus for exhibition, it's an invitation to disaster.
PERSONNEL: John Speaks (coproducer); Willis O'Brien (coproducer, visual effects); Marcel Delgado (animation puppets); Harold Lamb, Emily Barrye (script); Anne Shirley, James Craig (cast).
PREHISTORIC CREATURES: "Gwangi" the Allosaurus, pterodactyl, Triceratops, miniature horses.
NOTES: The reasons for the cancellation of *Gwangi* are vague at best; a reshuffling of the RKO hierarchy and the onset of World War II are the two factors most often cited. The miniature horse, traveling Wild West show, pterosaur attack, roping scene, and interfering ceratopsian in Ray Harryhausen's *The Valley of Gwangi* are all carryovers from Obie's original scenario.
QUOTES: "Preproduction commenced at the old Pathé Studios in Culver City; and once again, Obie developed many ideas and made hundreds of sketches and a few oil paintings. Marcel Delgado, meanwhile, designed the armature and built a prototype model of the Allosaurus featured in the script. He also produced just the head of the Triceratops.... The original agreement with RKO had stipulated that if the studio declined to proceed with the film, Colonial Pictures could pick up all option rights.... Speaks and O'Brien were unable to find alternate financing within the specified time frame."—Don Shay, in *Cinefex* (no. 7, 1982).

"It was ... abandoned after almost a year of preparation of scripts, production sketches, continuity drawings, and about five or six large glass paintings. There also exists, somewhere in Hollywood, three very large oil paintings on hardboard by O'Brien and Jack Shaw.... The disappointment to O'Brien must have been tremendous as this followed closely the disintegration of his *War Eagles* at MGM."—Ray Harryhausen, in his *Film Fantasy Scrapbook*.

SEE ALSO: *The Valley of Gwangi* (Filmography section)

Jongor

TIME FRAME: c. 1983
PREMISE: John Gordon ("Jongor") is an orphan who has grown to adulthood in the Lost Land—a mysterious jungle region in northern Australia—and is forced to fight for existence against ancient and unknown creatures.
PERSONNEL: Jim Danforth (adaptation, screenplay, visual effects).
PREHISTORIC CREATURES: Pteranodon, Arsinoitherium, various dinosaurs.
NOTES: Based on a trilogy of fantasy novellas by author Robert Moore Williams. The project fell through when a noted independent filmmaker refused to pay money owed to Danforth's effects company, rendering Danforth unable to meet the deadline for his final payment on the rights to the Jongor novels.
QUOTE: "There was an underlying intelligence and soul to Robert Moore Williams' work, and I felt that, if carefully adapted, these stories could form the basis of an interesting film—perhaps two films.... As I got more deeply involved in the screenplay, I realized that I had the basis not only of an exciting action film, but of a very poignant human drama as well—this was going to be good."—Jim Danforth, in *SPFX* (no.5, 1997).

Journey to the Center of the Earth

TIME FRAME: mid–1950s

PREMISE: Jules Verne's venerable adventure novel.

PREHISTORIC CREATURES: Unknown.

NOTES: Before becoming a lavish, somewhat idealized fantasy from 20th Century–Fox in 1959, Jules Verne's famous novel was discussed as a possible independent feature to be directed by none other than Eugène Lourié. RKO and Columbia also announced versions of the project within the span of a few months.

QUOTE: "In 1956, Eugène Lourié was scheduled to make the film in Italy as an independent production, and later in the same year, it was announced that Stanley Rubin was scheduled to produce it for RKO ... Columbia announced it as a follow-up to their planned *Mysterious Island*.... Bryan Foy was announced as the producer of the Columbia project.... These various projected versions were dutifully reported in movie trade magazines, but as there was no mention of budgets or scripts, I presume the projects were only tenative."—Bill Warren, in *Keep Watching the Skies!* (*Volume II*)

King Kong

TIME FRAME: mid–1960s.

PREMISE: Merian Cooper's classic tale of beauty and the beast.

PERSONNEL: Michael Carreras (producer); Ray Harryhausen (visual effects); Hammer Films.

PREHISTORIC CREATURES: Unknown.

NOTES: Hammer's Michael Carreras wanted very much to produce a *King Kong* remake, and had Ray Harryhausen unofficially committed to spearhead the special effects. However, RKO would not grant the rights for a remake (sequels yes; remakes no), so Carreras had to settle for a new version of *One Million B.C.* instead.

QUOTE: "Yes, I was a little worried about it, because, how can you top a classic, you know? ... If it *had* to be remade in color, I would remake it with the same story structure."—Ray Harryhausen, to the author (1998).

Land of the Lost

TIME FRAME: 1990s–

PREMISE: The Marshall family falls through a time/space portal while whitewater rafting, emerging in a parallel world of dinosaurs, primitive hominids, and other strange species.

PERSONNEL: Sid and Marty Krofft; Sony Pictures Family Entertainment.

PREHISTORIC CREATURES: Grumpy the T. rex (?), Big Alice the Allosaurus (?), Dopey the baby Brontosaurus (?).

NOTES: A feature film version of the fondly remembered seventies TV series had been tossed around for years, lying motionless at Disney for much of the time. In 1999, Sony Pictures Family Entertainment picked up the project, and preproduction is, supposedly, in the works as this book goes to press.

QUOTES: "The original *Land of the Lost* is the one we're doing the movie of. I think that the adventure that we're doing in this new one is going to attract both our adult audience and automatically attract the kid audience."—Marty Krofft, in David Martindale's *Pufnstuf & Other Stuff* (1998).

"We're going to add characters but of course we're going to have Marshall, Will and Holly and the Sleestaks.... We're going to use some of everything: we're going to combine the low-tech [special effects] with the hi-tech and not lose its sense of humor.... I don't want to make the same mistake as a lot of other pictures that get lost in the effects and forget about the story."—Marty Krofft, in *Cinefantastique* (vol. 31, nos. 1/2, 1999).

Legacy

TIME FRAME: mid–1980s

PREMISE: Husband-and-wife cryptozoology team Rick and Rhonda Taylor race their nemesis, Dr. MacDonald, to find an explanation for a series of dinosaur sightings in present-day New Mexico.

PERSONNEL: Jim Danforth (original concept, screenplay, visual effects).

PREHISTORIC CREATURES: Dinosaurs; species undetermined.

NOTES: Danforth evolved this scenario from a previous screen story he had written called *Trail of the Hell-Beast* which, in one incarnation, also included dinosaurs.

QUOTE: "At that time, I felt there were only three unfilmed ways of bringing dinosaurs logically into the 20th century. One was DNA, which I used for *Farnsworth's Folly*; now I would use one of the other two for *Legacy*. I don't want to reveal this premise.... Although the story is essentially serious, there is much humorous banter between Rick and Rhonda — the similarity to detectives Nick and Nora Charles is intentional." — Jim Danforth, in *SPFX* (no. 5, 1997).

The Legend of King Kong

TIME FRAME: mid–1970s

PREMISE: A new, color version of the classic tale, which would have maintained the Depression era and utilized stop-motion animation for the creature effects.

PERSONNEL: Joseph Sargent (director); Jim Danforth (visual effects); Albert Whitlock (matte painting); Bo Goldman (script); Max Steiner (music, from the 1933 score); Peter Falk, Robert Redford, Susan Blakely (possible cast).

PREHISTORIC CREATURES: Bo Goldman's script included a Parasaurolophus, Triceratops, a flock of Archaeopteryx, giant land crabs and, carried over from the original film, a pterosaur and an Elasmosaurus. Jim Danforth's preproduction notes and drawings included an Arsinoitherium and a gigantic centipedelike insect.

NOTES: Universal and Paramount found themselves both preparing big-budget *King Kong* remakes in the mid–1970s, and unfortunately for Universal (not to mention the world's fantasy film fans) Paramount's was the only one made. Jim Danforth "got the job" on the Universal version with help from Steven Spielberg (who was approached by the studio to direct the picture but declined). The film would possibly have utilized the "Sensurround" process. There was some buzz in the mid–1990s about resuscitating the Universal *Kong*, but nothing came of it.

QUOTE: "If it was going to be done, and if someone was going to do it, I figured I might as well be the one." — Jim Danforth, in *SPFX* (no. 4, 1996).

The Lost Atlantis

TIME FRAME: 1938–1940

PREMISE: The discovery of the mythical sunken city and the huge prehistoric beasts that still live there.

PERSONNEL: Harry O. Hoyt, Fred W. Jackman, Harry Cohn.

PREHISTORIC CREATURES: Unknown.

NOTES: Hoyt and Jackman, both alumni of First National's *The Lost World*, tried in vain to spearhead the making of a dinosaur fantasy with the grandeur and opulence of other late thirties productions such as *The Wizard of Oz* and *Gone with the Wind*. Despite a promising start, the project was doomed to extinction.

QUOTES: "Twenty-five dinosaurs were built at a cost of $600 each, and Jackman shot two reels of stop-motion animation before sponsor Harry Cohn withdrew his support. Two years later it was revived as a Technicolor production with new dinosaurs created by Walter Lantz and Edward Nassour. Columbia again halted production and the film was never completed." — Stephen Jones, in *The Illustrated Dinosaur Movie Guide*.

"The camera's magic brings to vivid, spectacular life the ancient legend of a continent that vanished beneath the waters of the turbulent Atlantic!" — from a promotional poster for *The Lost Atlantis*.

The Lost World

TIME FRAME: mid–1960s

PREMISE: Sir Arthur Conan Doyle's novel.

PERSONNEL: Jim Danforth; Albert Whitlock.

PREHISTORIC CREATURES: Unknown.

NOTES: After completion of *7 Faces of Dr. Lao*, Jim Danforth was briefly employed by Universal while the studio mulled over a project he had pitched called *Species X*. While there he split time between the miniature shop and the matte department, working on films such as *I'd Rather Be Rich* and *Father Goose*, and enjoying the opportunity to work with the legendary Albert Whitlock.

QUOTES: "I was building a one-inch scale Brontosaurus, like 5 feet long. I used to go up and eat with Al because we were buddies.... One day I had the [Brontosaurus] drawing and he said, 'Oh, dinosaurs! I love 'em! I always wanted to do *The Lost World*....' We started this big campaign — *we* used to go around Hollywood visiting producers, and we'd pitch *The Lost World*, but nobody wanted to do it because it hadn't been that long since that terrible Fox remake."—Jim Danforth, to the author (1998)

The Lost World

TIME FRAME: c. 1990
PREMISE: Sir Arthur Conan Doyle's novel.
PERSONNEL: John Landis (director); Richard Matheson (script); Sean Connery (cast, as Prof. Challenger).
PREHISTORIC CREATURES: Unknown.
QUOTE: "We were going to do a very traditional, old-fashioned adaptation.... Unfortunately, it was in development at Universal, and when they bought *Jurassic Park*, they said, 'We don't want to do *The Lost World*.'"—John Landis, in *Cinefantastique* (vol. 24, no. 2, 1993).

Monstrosaurus!

TIME FRAME: 1990s
PREMISE: Two recent geology grads have to contend with their new boss, a pair of uninhibited teen girls, the girls' shotgun-totin' pappy, and a "laminated countertop salesman from Buffalo, N.Y.," as they investigate (and later battle) an electrically-charged, dinosaurish water monster in a dank, dark southern bayou.
PERSONNEL: Brett Piper (screenplay); Kinetic Image Co., Ltd.
PREHISTORIC CREATURE: The titular "Monstrosaurus"—a strange creature resembling a Plesiosaurus, only with heavy-set, sprawling, lizardlike legs in place of its front flippers.

The Natural History Project

TIME FRAME: c. 1983
PREMISE: A youthful duckbilled dinosaur grows to maturity amid a prehistoric world of dreaded predators and loyal friends.
PERSONNEL: Jim Henson, William Stout, Lisa Henson, Warner Bros.
PREHISTORIC CREATURES: Corythosaurus, Tyrannosaurus rex, Alamosaurus, pterodactyl, Triceratops, more.
NOTES: *The Natural History Project* was the film's working title—a final title was never chosen. Reportedly, Jim Henson's daughter Lisa had the initial idea to make the film and started the ball rolling. Noted dinosaur artist Bill Stout penned the screenplay and designed much of the film's "look." The project was aborted when Warner Bros. learned that Don Bluth's *The Land Before Time* was in development, and they didn't want theirs to be perceived as a copycat endeavor.
QUOTE: "We called it *The Natural History Project* because we were afraid somebody else would pick up on the idea before we could get it developed. I created a nice variety of dinosaurs on that film. The way Jim and I were planning to shoot the dinosaurs was with a combination of stop-motion animation and puppetry."—William Stout, in Marc Shapiro's *When Dinosaurs Ruled the Screen*.

Nessie

TIME FRAME: mid–late 1970s
PREMISE: A toxic chemical spill in Loch Ness drives Nessie out of the loch into the sea, while also triggering an amazing growth spurt in the beastie.
PERSONNEL: Michael Carreras, Chris Wicking (screenplay); Bryan Forbes (final shooting script); Hammer Films; Toho Studios; Columbia Pictures.
PREHISTORIC CREATURE: "Nessie," represented as an Elasmosaurus.
NOTES: a.k.a. *Nessie, The Loch Ness Monster*. Seven to $8 million budget. Toho Studios, in collaboration with Hammer, had done a "complete story board" for the film, and had reportedly gone so far as to build a one-fourth scale Nessie model. The project's demise resulted from a combination of several factors, including Hammer's cessation of output (1976's *To the Devil a Daughter* was their last feature release) and a financial scandal involving a Columbia exec.
QUOTES: "I am personally confident that *Nessie* will hit the silver screen at the end of this year, hopefully Christmas 1978.... We've got Sir Peter Scott, the naturalist, involved.... We wanted his approval of the drawings of Nessie and so on."—Michael Carreras, in *The House of Hammer* (no. 17, 1978).

Pellucidar

TIME FRAME: mid–1970s
PREMISE: Edgar Rice Burroughs' *At the Earth's Core*.
PERSONNEL: Jim Danforth (screenplay,

visual effects); Bill Hedge, Jon Berg (consultants).

PREHISTORIC CREATURES: Giant Pteranodons (called Thipdars in Burroughs' novel), other more fanciful beasts.

NOTES: Danforth wrote a script based on E. R. Burroughs' novel which he submitted to Robert M. Hodes (general manager of Edgar Rice Burroughs, Inc.). Hodes in turn presented it to Amicus execs Milton Subotsky and Max Rosenberg. Amicus eschewed Danforth's script and a year and a half later made *At the Earth's Core* with a screenplay by Subotsky.

QUOTES: "I plunged into this screenplay with everything I had ... I set the ending in a location Burroughs had only hinted at: I had the *Mahars* use the *Thipdars* to carry Dian to the one spot in Pellucidar where David [Innes] couldn't save her — the Pendant World. Ingenious Abner Perry ... built a hot-air balloon so Dave could fly to the Pendant World. David rescued Dian and united the tribes of Pellucidar.... Danton Burroughs, ERB's grandson, told me that the first thing he did after seeing the Amicus *At the Earth's Core* was to go to his uncle and say, 'We should have let Danforth or Harryhausen do it.'"— Jim Danforth, in *SPFX* (no. 5, 1997).

The Primevals

TIME FRAME: 1968–present

PREMISE: The story for *Raiders of the Stone Ring* evolved and changed over the years into the final scenario of *The Primevals*, which involves a "Yeti," a university research team, and an incredible, hidden ecosystem with possible alien connections. As David Allen said: "*Raiders of the Stone Ring* was a much more fantasy-oriented story than what we have now.... It was more like a *Star Wars* entertainment experience.... Whereas *The Primevals* is more on the level of *Close Encounters of the Third Kind*. It's more heightened reality than fantasy."

PERSONNEL: David Allen (director, cowriter, visual effects); Charles Band (producer); Randy Cook (cowriter, visual effects); Chris Endicott (visual effects); Kim Blanchette, Kent Burton, Wes Ceafer (animation); Ron Lizzorty ("River Lizard" design and fabrication); David Carson (illustrator); Dave Stipes, Dennis Gordon (miniature makers); Jena Holman (matte painter); Adolfo Bartoli (cameraman); Jeff Farley (make-up); Juliet Mills, Richard Joseph Paul, Robert Cornthwaite, Leon Russom, Tai Thai (cast).

PREHISTORIC CREATURES: "Yeti," the dinosaurish "River Lizard," more.

NOTES: After the Hammer production of *Zeppelin v. Pterodactyls* fell through, the project moved to the proverbial "back burner" for a time. Then in the late 1970s David Allen provided visual effects for Charles Band's sci-fi picture *Laserblast*, beginning a long if mercurial relationship between the two filmmakers. Band committed to the film, now called *The Primevals*, but repeated financial problems caused a series of stops and restarts in the production. When Band's 1980s company, Empire Pictures, was flourishing, *Primevals* was again revived only to halt when Empire folded, and the scenario was more or less repeated with Band's Full Moon company. More financial shortfalls, the difficulties of filming in Romania, and Allen's untimely death in 1999 added to the project's long list of travails.

QUOTES: "I'm not looking for the excellence of *The Primevals* to lay strictly in its visual effects."— David Allen, in *Cinefantastique* (vol. 8, no. 1, 1978).

"It's probably going to show its problems now and then. It's going to be a strange kind of picture. In one way, it's kind of low-budget and you might look at it and say that it has not been adequately produced for the stretch of the theme, and then sometimes it will look pretty extravagant. You may think you know what it's capable of, and then I think it will surprise you."— David Allen, in *Cinefantastique* (vol. 26, no. 4, 1995).

"We are working on it full time. There have been occasional breaks where we did TV commercials, but for the most part Chris Endicott, Wes Ceafer and I are working on *The Primevals*. Also, for the most part, we are just about the only ones working on it, which is making for somewhat slow progress."— David Allen, in *Cinefantastique* (vol. 31, nos. 1/2, 1999).

"As far as I know, *The Primevals* is the only stop-motion creature movie that's being done on the planet Earth, and it deserves better attention."— Jim Danforth, in *Cinefantastique* (vol. 31, nos. 1/2, 1999).

"There have been incredible stories of the

things that have gone wrong — things that were lost, things that were found, people who were owed money, people who were holding negatives — it's just an incredible saga.... Live action has been shot. David was directing the live action in the summer of '94, and we were let go for about a year ... David was brought back in the summer of '95. We started shooting, just David and myself ... or maybe an additional person here or there — at most four people working at one time. So now, five years later, we've got 130 shots done, and that's not halfway in five years plus ... but the picture keeps plugging away. We have a tiny little crew now, three people working counting myself. Kent Burton is a really fine animator that's working on the picture, and Kim Blanchette is doing a shot right now.... Because there was no schedule, and this picture meant so much to David and there were certain shots he really wanted to do, we just did those shots, you know? In retrospect, ... I'm just so glad that we did, and he got to do all the shots that were just burning inside of him — and that, to me, is worth something. David felt this was his best work; he was very proud of it, and so the film definitely *has* to get finished." — Chris Endicott, to the author (September 2000).

SEE ALSO: *Zeppelin v. Pterodactyls*

Raiders of the Stone Ring

SEE: *Zeppelin v. Pterodactyls, The Primevals*

Rulers of the Apocalypse

TIME FRAME: mid–late 1990s

PREMISE: "It contains all of the ingredients of sure fire success — serious social issues such as spousal abuse, dealt with in post-apocalyptic America by a hero who is being targeted for death by his former employer, the FBI. Oh, yes. It also contains dinosaurs ... lots of dinosaurs. Lots and lots of dinosaurs." — Quoted from the Visual Experiences, Inc. website.

PERSONNEL: Warren F. Disbrow; Visual Experiences, inc.

PREHISTORIC CREATURES: Tyrannosaurus Rex, Spinosaurus, Dilophosaurus, Carnotaurus, Baryonyx; (tentative) Tylosaurus. All dinosaurs to be full-size animatronics, cable-controlled and radio-controlled.

NOTES: Roger Corman had discussed the possibility of handling the film's distribution after completion. Beverly Garland was mentioned for a possible role.

QUOTES: "We aren't making a Ray Harryhausen family film. I want to do something violent and dark.... Our dinosaurs look closer to *Jurassic Park* quality than those things in *Carnosaur* and *Dinosaur Island*.... [The dinosaurs] are being made full size, like giant toys. The largest one stands about twelve feet tall and is about twenty feet long.... All of the credit for the mechanics of the dinosaurs and their metal skeletons goes to my father who designed everything and built them." — Warren F. Disbrow, in *Drive-In Cinema* (no. 2, 1997).

Timegate

TIME FRAME: late 1970s

PREMISE: In the near future, the commercial time-travel company Chronex sells "dinosaur safaris" to wealthy adventurers. On one particular excursion to the Cretaceous, one patron's hidden agenda jeopardizes the group's chances to return to the present.

PERSONNEL: Jim Danforth (concept, screenplay, visual effects, director, coproducer); Milton Subotsky (producer); Mel Simon (financier); Bill Taylor (partial story); Randy Cook (storyboards); Phil Tippett, Douglas Beswick, Ken Ralston, Tom St. Amand, Bill Hedge, Nick Seldon, Tom Scherman, Jon Berg (effects crew); Tom Jacobson (production manager); Kenneth Tobey, Jo Morrow, Randy Cook (possible cast members).

PREHISTORIC CREATURES: Pteranodon (built over the Rhamphorynchus armature from *When Dinosaurs Ruled the Earth*), Tyrannosaurus rex, Styracosaurus (adult and baby), Phobosuchus, Monoclonius, Ornithomimus, Hypsilophodont, the fictional "wolf-lizard."

NOTES: Over a year of continuous work went into the project and much live-action footage was shot. Background plates were filmed for various FX sequences involving a miniature avalanche, "rocketmen," and a hovercraft. Then Mel Simon decided the project needed bigger "name" actors than those being considered and bumped the original $1 million budget up to 2 million. "So we had to start all over," Danforth said. "We lost a lot of momentum." Despite all of Danforth's efforts (including talks with Charles Schneer), production never resumed.

QUOTES: "Needless to say, I'm not going to do all the animation myself on this one—never would get it finished."—Jim Danforth, in *Fantasy Film Journal* (no. 2, 1978).

"If we'd just gone ahead and made the one million dollar version, it'd be listed in Leonard Maltin's book now.... I don't know what the rating would've been, but it'd be in there!"—Jim Danforth, to the author (1996).

Trail of the Hell-Beast

SEE: *Legacy*

Valley of the Mist

TIME FRAME: c. 1950

PREMISE: The adventures of a young Mexican boy named Emilio and his efforts to keep his magnificent pet bull from falling into the hands of the mercenary bull trader, Señor Garzon. Trying to help Emilio, a tribe of Indians leads the boy into an unknown valley of prehistoric life, and a mighty battle looms between the gallant bull and a predator from prehistory.

PERSONNEL: Willis O'Brien, Ray Harryhausen, Jesse L. Lasky, Jesse Lasky, Jr.

PREHISTORIC CREATURES: Pterodactyl, Tyrannosaurus rex, Triceratops, more.

NOTES: *Valley of the Mist* was one version of O'Brien's story *Emilio and Guloso*, which went through a great many alterations, name changes, and false starts over the years. As with *Mighty Joe Young*, O'Brien would have supervised the effects for *Mist*, with Ray Harryhausen serving as principal animator. But like so many of Obie's projects, it was not to be. O'Brien and Harryhausen were carried on a meager retainer while preproduction crept forward, but the project collapsed for lack of money. A greatly revised version of the story was finally filmed as the all-puppet film *Emilio and His Magical Bull*.

QUOTES: "[Jesse] Lasky, who had been one of the founders and the first vice president of Paramount Pictures, made arrangements with that company to release the film. Plans were made to shoot in Technicolor on location in Mexico where a good portion of the cast, including the starring role of Emilio, would be recruited from native talent."—Don Shay, in *Cinefex* (no. 7, 1982).

"Jesse Lasky, Sr., was going to produce it [for Paramount], and the screenplay was written by Jesse's son, Jesse Jr. We had a good screenplay, but at that time we couldn't raise the money. I don't know why."—Ray Harryhausen, to the author (1998).

SEE ALSO: *Emilio and his Magical Bull* (Filmography section)

The Volcano Monsters

TIME FRAME: late 1950s

PREMISE: A pair of rival (and abnormally *large*) dinosaurs wake from eons of suspended animation and proceed and lay siege to San Francisco.

PERSONNEL: Ib Melchior, Warner Bros.

PREHISTORIC CREATURES: a paleontologically incorrect Tyrannosaurus and Ankylosaurus—better known as Gigantis (or Godzilla) and Angilas from *Gigantis the Fire Monster*.

QUOTES: "The rights [to *Gigantis*] were sold to Warner Bros. At one point, it was decided to utilize only the monster footage and build an entirely new story around it. The result was *The Volcano Monsters*, written by Ib Melchior.... The new script had Gigantis and Angilas (now simply a Tyrannosaurus and Ankylosaurus) discovered in a state of hibernation in a large cavern or volcano.... Presumably, the monsters would fight in and around Chinatown and Japan Town [in San Francisco], thus explaining the appearance of Japanese characters on billboards, buildings, etc."—Stuart Galbraith IV, in *Japanese Science Fiction, Fantasy and Horror Films*.

War Eagles

TIME FRAME: 1938

PREMISE: An outspoken history teacher and his brash young pilot discover and befriend a colony of Vikings living in a "blind spot" above the Arctic Circle. The Vikings have domesticated the region's giant, white prehistoric "snow eagles" and employ the great birds to ferry foodstuffs from the fertile but dinosaur-filled Valley of the Ancients. When a radio report reveals that America is under attack from an adversarial country, the Vikings mount their war eagles, fly to America with their new friends, and intercept the aggressor's air forces over New York City.

PERSONNEL: Merian C. Cooper (story, producer); Willis O'Brien (visual effects, animation); Marcel Delgado (models and miniatures); Cyril Hume (script); Duncan Gleason (artist); MGM.

PREHISTORIC CREATURES: 15-foot-tall snow eagles, Brontosaurus, Allosaurus, Triceratops, pterodactyls, more.

NOTES: *War Eagles* was intended to be, unlike the hastily filmed *The Son of Kong*, a truly worthy and even more spectacular follow-up to *King Kong* for the Cooper-O'Brien team. Among the visual feasts planned was an all-out aerial battle between the war eagles and a swarm of pterodactyls. Much preliminary work was done by Marcel Delgado, who constructed models of the eagles and an allosaurus, and by Obie, who actually filmed a 400-foot stop-motion test reel. This color footage, sadly, does not survive. After Ray Harryhausen's retirement from filmmaking in the early 1980s, Jim Danforth briefly discussed with Charles Schneer the possibility of rekindling *War Eagles*.

QUOTES: "In September 1939, Hitler and his storm troopers marched into Poland, bringing about the beginning of World War II — and the end of *War Eagles*. Merian C. Cooper reenlisted in the Army Air Corps and ... remained on active duty for the remainder of the war — at which point *War Eagles*, by virtue of its theme which played upon the tensions of impending world hostilities, was then pitifully dated." — Don Shay, in *Cinefex* (no. 7, 1982).

"I first met Willis O'Brien at MGM, when he invited me over to see early drawings of *War Eagles*. I called him by phone at MGM and told him of my interest in prehistoric animals and animation.... Of course I was awed by all of the 200 drawings and oil paintings for *War Eagles*. I remember there was an enormous painting of the Statue of Liberty with eagles perched on the spikes of her helmet, and another painting of the eagles flying around a dirigible.... Obie told me later that MGM was against the picture. They gave O'Brien a place outside in a makeshift tent for his experiments.... I have one of the models of the Viking men used in the animation test reel. It is a small armature which we later used for Jill playing the piano in *Mighty Joe Young*."— Ray Harryhausen, in Steve Archer's *Willis O'Brien: Special Effects Genius*.

Zeppelin v. Pterodactyls

TIME FRAME: c. 1970

PREMISE: A cadre of Allied prisoners escape from a World War I German POW camp in a stolen zeppelin. They drift into a mysterious milieu where their craft is attacked and damaged by a pterodactyl. The airship crash-lands in a time-lost valley of prehistoric creatures and humans (some real; some fictional).

PERSONNEL: David Allen, Jim Danforth, Dennis Muren; Hammer Films.

PREHISTORIC CREATURES: Pterodactyls, giant ground sloth, primitive humans, more.

NOTES: Concept originated when Jim Danforth, Dennis Muren and David Allen teamed up to initiate a fantasy-film project. As development continued, Danforth introduced (to the above premise) the *Sithars*, a race of "intelligent, humanoid mutant lizards" to serve as adversaries. At various points the film was titled *Lost Creations*, *The Glacial Empire*, *Raiders of the Stone Ring*, *The Warriors of Mordium*, and *Primordium: The Arctic World*. During production of *When Dinosaurs Ruled the Earth*, Danforth proposed the project to Hammer Films, but an agreement acceptable to all involved parties was never reached. Hammer designed a poster and announced an upcoming film called *Zeppelin v. Pterodactyls*, even though no contract was ever signed. Coincidental similarities between *Raiders of the Stone Ring* and Disney's *Island at the Top of the World* also caused concerns. Later in the 1970s, David Allen pressed on with a revised version of the project, called *The Primevals*, and the saga continued.

QUOTES: "Early in 1968, Dennis Muren and David Allen asked for my help with a film project on which they were working.... I felt [the presence of the *Sithars*] was necessary in order to have a climax which could top the exciting sequences with which the story began.... The events surrounding the zeppelin were altered and most of my ideas disappeared or were transferred to the sloth, but my essential idea of the mutant-lizard antagonists remained.... I saw the Hammer offer as a wonderful opportunity. Dave saw it differently. He had concerns about the money offered by Hammer, concerns about artistic sovereignty, and concerns about my involvement with the project.... Neither *Raiders of the Stone Ring* nor *Zeppelin v. Pterodactyls* was filmed. Instead, Hammer used the title they had preferred for *Raiders—Creatures the World Forgot*—and made another caveman film."—Jim Danforth, in *SPFX* (no. 5, 1997).

"I had a really nice action sequence plotted out for the zeppelin/pterodactyl dogfight, with the reptiles tearing open the gas-filled envelopes.... [Hammer] had rewritten the story to satisfy their own egos, I suppose, and it was just terrible.... I'm really not in the position to explain exactly why the project eventually died.... Also, I began to see that there might be some problems in developing a working relationship with Jim Danforth and Dennis Muren over a long period of time. I had lived with the project for so long, I was getting sort of set in my ways about how it should be done. There was a bit of squabbling. Nothing serious, just creative overlap."—David Allen, in *Cinefantastique* (vol. 8, no. 1, 1978).

See Also: *The Primevals*

APPENDIX C: IT CAME FROM JAPAN

A Chronology of the Quasi-Dinosaurs from Toho Studios

Gojira

***½ 1954. BW, 98m. *Director* Ishiro Honda. *Producer* Tomoyuki Tanaka. *Screenplay* Takeo Murata, Ishiro Honda. *Special Effects Director* Eiji Tsuburaya. *Monster Cast* Gojira (Godzilla).

DINOSAUR CONTENT: Moderate. Paleontologist Doctor Yamane believes that Godzilla is definitely spawned from dinosaur stock, reanimated by hydrogen-bomb testing.

Gigantis the Fire Monster

a.k.a. *Godzilla's Counterattack*; *Godzilla Raids Again*

** 1955. BW, 82m. *Director* Motoyoshi Oda. *Producer* Tomoyuki Tanaka. *Screenplay* Takeo Murata, Sigeaki Hidaka. *Special Effects Director* Eiji Tsuburaya. *Monster Cast* Gigantis (Godzilla), Angilas (a.k.a. Anguiras). U.S. VERSION: 1959. 78m. *Producers* Paul Schreibman, Harry B. Swerdlon (executive), Edmund Goldman (associate).

DINOSAUR CONTENT: Moderate. Angilas is roughly patterned on—and named after—the armored Ankylosaurus; it is also referred to as an "Angilasaurus." Dr. Yamane (a returning paleontologist from *Gojira*) runs a reel of stock footage from *Unknown Island* and *Gojira* during an orientation lecture. The reel also contains one crude stop-motion shot of two fighting sauropods, the source of which not even Neil Pettigrew—author of the massive *Stop-Motion Filmography*—has been able to sleuth out.

Godzilla, King of the Monsters!

*** 1956. 81m. U.S. version of *Gojira* (1954). *Producers* Richard Kay, Harry Rybnick, Edward B. Barison, Terry Turner (executive), Joseph E. Levine (executive).

Rodan

** 1956. C, 82m. *Director* Ishiro Honda. *Producer* Tomoyuki Tanaka. *Screenplay* Takeshi Kimura, Takeo Murata. *Special Effects Director* Eiji Tsuburaya. *Monster Cast* Two "Rodans," assorted giant insectlike creatures. U.S. VERSION: 1957. 79m. *Producers* Frank King, Maurice King. *English Dialogue* David Duncan.

DINOSAUR CONTENT: Low. The Rodans are based on Pteranodon, but the supersonic flying speed eliminates plausibility. Two clips of Rodan are used to represent a pterosaur in *Valley of the Dragons*.

Varan the Unbelievable

½ 1958. BW, 87m. *Director* Ishiro Honda. *Producer* Tomoyuki Tanaka. *Screenplay* Shinichi Sekizawa. *Original Story* Takeshi Kuronuma. *Special Effects Director* Eiji Tsuburaya. *Monster Cast* Varan. U.S. VERSION: 1962. 70m. *Director* Jerry A. Baerwitz. *Producer* Jerry A. Baerwitz. *Screenplay* Sid Harris.
DINOSAUR CONTENT: None.

King Kong vs. Godzilla

* * ½ 1962. C, 98m. *Director* Ishiro Honda. *Producer* Tomoyuki Tanaka. *Screenplay* Shinichi Sekizawa. *Special Effects Director* Eiji Tsuburaya. *Monster Cast* Godzilla, King Kong. U.S. VERSION: 1963. 91m. *Director* Thomas Montgomery. *Producer* John Beck. *Screenwriters* Paul Mason, Bruce Howard.
DINOSAUR CONTENT: Moderate. Paleontologist Dr. Arnold Johnson, holding a children's dinosaur book, explains that Godzilla is a cross between a Tyrannosaurus and a Stegosaurus!

Godzilla vs. the Thing
a.k.a. *Godzilla vs. Mothra*

* * * ½ 1964. C, 89m. *Director* Ishiro Honda. *Producers* Tomoyuki Tanaka, Sanezumi Fujimoto. *Screenplay* Shinichi Sekizawa. *Special Effects Director* Eiji Tsuburaya. *Monster Cast* Godzilla, Mothra, twin Mothra babies (caterpillar form). U.S. VERSION: 1964. 88m. *Producer*: Titra Productions, Inc.
DINOSAUR CONTENT: None. Though arguably the best "Godzilla movie" ever made, it was the first to completely abandon Godzilla's supposed dinosaurian origins.

Ghidrah: The Three-Headed Monster

* * ½ 1964. C, 92m. *Director* Ishiro Honda. *Producer* Tomoyuki Tanaka (executive). *Screenplay* Shinichi Sekizawa. *Special Effects Director* Eiji Tsuburaya. *Monster Cast* Godzilla, Rodan, Mothra (caterpillar form), Ghidrah (a.k.a. Monster Zero, King Ghidorah). U.S. VERSION: 1965. 81m. *English Dialogue/Dubbing Director* Joseph Bellucci.
DINOSAUR CONTENT: None.

Monster Zero
a.k.a. *Godzilla vs. Monster Zero; Invasion of the Astro Monster*

* ½ 1965. C, 96m. *Director* Ishiro Honda. *Producers* Tomoyuki Tanaka, Henry G. Saperstein (executive), Reuben Bercovitch (executive). *Screenplay* Shinichi Sekizawa. *Special Effects Director* Eiji Tsuburaya. *Monster Cast* Ghidrah (a.k.a. Monster Zero, King Ghidorah), Godzilla, Rodan. U.S. VERSION: 1970. 92m.
DINOSAUR CONTENT: None.

Ebirah, Horror of the Deep
a.k.a. *Godzilla vs. the Sea Monster*

* * 1966. C, 87m. *Director* Jun Fukuda. *Producer* Tomoyuki Tanaka. *Screenplay* Shinichi Sekizawa. *Special Effects Director* Eiji Tsuburaya. *Monster Cast* Godzilla, Ebirah (a giant lobster, a.k.a. "The Sea Monster"), Mothra (adult form), a giant condor. U.S. VERSION: 1968. 82m.
DINOSAUR CONTENT: None.

Son of Godzilla

½ 1967. C, 86m. *Director* Jun Fukuda. *Producer* Tomoyuki Tanaka. *Screenplay* Shinichi Sekizawa, Kazue Shiba. *Special Effects Director* Eiji Tsuburaya. *Monster Cast* Godzilla, Godzilla's son Minira (often called "Minya" in America), the "Gimantises" (oversized mantises, called Kamakiras in Japan), Spiga (a giant spider, called Kumonga in Japan). U.S. VERSION: 1969. 84m.
DINOSAUR CONTENT: None.

Destroy All Monsters

* * * 1968. C, 88m. *Director* Ishiro Honda. *Producer* Tomoyuki Tanaka. *Screenplay* Kaoru Mabuchi, Ishiro Honda. *Special Effects Director* Eiji Tsuburaya. *Monster Cast* Godzilla, Rodan, Mothra (caterpillar form), King Ghidorah, Anguirus, Gorosaurus, Minya, Baragon, Manda, Varan, Spiga. U.S. VERSION: 1969. 86m. Re-

leased by American International Pictures.

DINOSAUR CONTENT: Moderate. Gorosaurus (*King Kong Escapes*) and Anguiras (*Gigantis the Fire Monster*) both return. Baragon is also sometimes considered to be of dinosaurian origin. (And Manda looks strikingly like the title critter of *Reptilicus*!)

Godzilla's Revenge
a.k.a. *All Monsters Attack*

1969. C, 70m. *Director* Ishiro Honda. *Producer* Tomoyuki Tanaka. *Screenplay* Shinichi Sekizawa. *Special Effects Director* Eiji Tsuburaya. *Monster Cast* Godzilla, Minira, Gabarah (other Toho creatures appear courtesy of stock footage). U.S. VERSION: 1971. 69m. *Producer*: Henry G. Saperstein.

DINOSAUR CONTENT: Very Low. Gorosaurus and Anguiras pop up in some brief stock shots.

Godzilla vs. the Smog Monster
a.k.a. *Godzilla vs. Hedorah*

** 1971. C, 85m. *Director* Yoshimitsu Banno. *Producer* Tomoyuki Tanaka (executive). *Screenplay* Yoshimitsu Banno, Kaoru Mabuchi. *Special Effects Director* Teruyoshi Nakano. *Monster Cast* Godzilla, Hedorah (a.k.a. "The Smog Monster"). U.S. VERSION: 1972. 85m. Released by American International Pictures.

DINOSAUR CONTENT: None.

Godzilla on Monster Island
a.k.a. *Godzilla vs. Gigan*

1972. C, 89m. *Director* Jun Fukuda. *Producer* Tomoyuki Tanaka (executive). *Screenplay* Shinichi Sekizawa. *Special Effects Director* Teruyoshi Nakano. *Monster Cast* Godzilla, Anguiras, King Ghidorah, Gigan. U.S. VERSION: 1977. 89m.

DINOSAUR CONTENT: Low. Anguiras, the pseudoankylosaur, guest stars. The film foreshadows Disney's computer-animated *Dinosaur* by having Godzilla and Anguiras actually *speak* in a few scenes! "Hey, Angilas!" "Whatta you want?" "Something funny's going on, you better check!"

Godzilla vs. Megalon

1973. C, 83m. *Director* Jun Fukuda. *Producer* Tomoyuki Tanaka. *Screenplay* Jun Fukuda, Shinichi Sekizawa. *Special Effects Director* Teruyoshi Nakano. *Monster Cast* Godzilla, Megalon, Jet Jaguar, Gigan. U.S. VERSION: 1976. 82m.

DINOSAUR CONTENT: None.

Godzilla vs. the Cosmic Monster
a.k.a. *Godzilla vs. the Bionic Monster*; *Godzilla vs. Mechagodzilla*

*½ 1974. C, 84m. *Director* Jun Fukuda. *Producer* Tomoyuki Tanaka (executive). *Screenplay* Hiroyasu Yamamura, Jun Fukuda; based on an original story by Shinichi Sekizawa and Masami Fukushima. *Special Effects Director* Teruyoshi Nakano. *Monster Cast* Godzilla, Mechagodzilla, Anguiras, King Seesar. U.S. VERSION: 1977. 80m.

DINOSAUR CONTENT: None. Anguiras returns, but by this point his ankylosaur origins are completely abandoned.

Terror of Mechagodzilla

** 1975. C, 83m. *Director* Ishiro Honda. *Producer* Tomoyuki Tanaka (executive). *Screenplay* Yukiko Takayama. *Special Effects Director* Teruyoshi Nakano. *Monster Cast* Godzilla, Mechagodzilla, Titanosaurus. U.S. VERSION: 1978. 89m. *Producer* Henry G. Saperstein (executive).

DINOSAUR CONTENT: Moderate. One Godzilla foe in this entry is "Titanosaurus" (no connection to the actual sauropod dinosaur of the same name), an aquatic but quite dinosaurish beast bearing more than a passing resemblance to the title creature of *Gorgo*. "Headquarters! It looks like a giant fish! No, no … not a fish! A *dinosaur*! A giant dinosaur!"

Godzilla 1985
a.k.a. *Gojira*

**½ 1984. C, 103m. *Director* Koji Hashimoto. *Producers* Tomoyuki Tanaka (executive), Fumio Tanaka (associate). *Screenplay* Shuichi Nagahara; based on the original story "The Resurrection of Godzilla" by Tomoyuki Tanaka. *Special Effects Director* Teruyoshi Nakano. *Monster Cast* Godzilla. U.S. VERSION: 1985. C, 91m. *Director*: R. J. Kizer. *Producer*: Anthony Randel. *Screenplay*: Lisa Tomei. Released by

New World Pictures. Stop-motion animator and effects jack-of-all-trades Ernest D. Farino created the opening titles for the U.S. release, and Raymond Burr reprised his role as reporter Steve Martin from *Godzilla, King of the Monsters!*

DINOSAUR CONTENT: None. Though *Godzilla 1985* is as much a remake of the original *Godzilla* as a sequel to it, the creature's paleontological connections are never even hinted at.

Godzilla vs. Biollante

** 1989. C, 104m. *Director* Kazuki Omori. *Producers* Tomoyuki Tanaka (executive), Shogo Tomiyama (associate). *Screenplay* Kazuki Omori; based on an original story by Shinichiro Kobayashi. *Special Effects Director* Koichi Kawakita. *Monster Cast*: Godzilla, Biollante (a giant rose bush [!] with the soul of a deceased human girl).

DINOSAUR CONTENT: None.

Godzilla vs. King Ghidorah

*** 1991. C, 103m. *Director* Kazuki Omori. *Producers* Shogo Tomiyama, Tomoyuki Tanaka (executive), Tomiya Ban (associate). *Screenplay* Kazuki Omori. *Special Effects Director* Koichi Kawakita. *Monster Cast* Godzilla, King Ghidorah, Mecha-King Ghidorah, "Gojirasaurus."

DINOSAUR CONTENT: High. In one of several plot elements borrowed from *Terminator 2: Judgment Day* (1991), time travelers journey back to the days of WWII to find the plausibly dinosaurish "Gojirasaurus" living on a Lost World–style Pacific island, in an effort to prevent the mutagenic effects of hydrogen-bomb testing from turning the prehistoric creature into "Godzilla" in the year 1954. "That thing may not have been a Tyrannosaurus rex, but I'm almost positive of one thing — what he saw on that island *was* a dinosaur."

Godzilla vs. Mothra

*** 1992. C, 102m. *Director* Takao Okawara. *Producers* Shogo Tomiyama, Tomoyuki Tanaka (executive). *Screenplay* Kazuki Omori. *Special Effects Director* Koichi Kawakita. *Monster Cast* Godzilla, Mothra, Battra (a sort of "anti–Mothra" in the shape of a giant insect).

DINOSAUR CONTENT: None.

Godzilla vs. Mechagodzilla

a.k.a. *Godzilla vs. Super-Mechagodzilla*

*½ 1993. C, 107m. *Director* Takao Okawara. *Producers* Shogo Tomiyama, Tomoyuki Tanaka (executive). *Screenplay* Wataru Mimura. *Special Effects Director* Koichi Kawakita. *Monster Cast* Godzilla, Mechagodzilla, Rodan (who transforms into "Fire Rodan"), Baby Godzilla.

DINOSAUR CONTENT: Moderate. Rodan's pterosaur roots are reintroduced, with the monster's design altered to give a more pterosaurlike appearance. "It's Rodan ... a large form of Pteranodon.... Radiation must have affected him like it did Godzilla."

Godzilla vs. Space Godzilla

** 1994. C, 108m. *Director* Kensho Yamashita. *Producers* Shogo Tomiyama, Tomoyuki Tanaka (executive). *Screenplay* Hiroshi Kashiwabara. *Special Effects Director* Koichi Kawakita. *Monster Cast* Godzilla, Little Godzilla, Space Godzilla.

DINOSAUR CONTENT: None.

Godzilla vs. Destroyer

*** 1995. C, 103m. *Director* Takao Okawara. *Producers* Shogo Tomiyama, Tomoyuki Tanaka (executive). *Screenplay* Kazuki Omori. *Special Effects Director* Koichi Kawakita. *Monster Cast* Godzilla, Godzilla Junior, Destoroyah (an unwelcome by-product of Doctor Serizawa's "oxygen destroyer," used to kill the original Godzilla 41 years earlier).

DINOSAUR CONTENT: None.

Godzilla 2000

**½ 1999. C, 98m. *Director* Takeo Okawara. *Producers* Toshihiro Ogawa, Shogo Tomiyama (executive). *Screenplay* Hiroshi Kashiwabara, Hataru Mimura. *Special Effects Coordinator* Kenji Suzuki. *Monster Cast* Godzilla.

DINOSAUR CONTENT: None.

Godzilla vs. Megaguirus: The G Annihilation Strategy

unavailable for review 2000. C, 105m. *Director* Masaaki Tezuka. *Producer* Shogo Tomiyama (executive). *Screenplay* Hiroshi Kashi-

BIBLIOGRAPHY

Personal Interviews and Correspondence

Aupperle, Jim. Telephone interviews. 6 February 2000, 7 October 2000.
Buechler, John. Telephone interview. 31 July 2000.
Chang, Wah Ming. Telephone interview. 4 May 1997.
Czerkas, Stephen. Telephone interview. 29 October 2000.
Danforth, Jim. Telephone interview. 14 March 1998.
Dicken, Roger. Telephone interview. 23 October 1999.
Endicott, Chris. Telephone interview. 15 September 2000.
Farino, Ernest D. Telephone interview. 12 February 2001.
Farley, Jeff. Telephone interview. 21 June 2000.
Harryhausen, Ray. Telephone interview. 6 June 1998.
Helfer, Ralph. Telephone interview. 27 March 1999.
Kleinow, Peter. Telephone interview. 7 February 2001.
Leibovit, Arnold. Telephone interview. 27 February 2001.
Miles, Hal. Telephone interviews. 6 Nov 1999, 28 June 2000.
Rakoff, Alvin. Letter to the author. 16 March 2000.
Tippett, Phil. Telephone interview. 15 May 2000.
Winston, Stan. Telephone interview. 1 August 2000.

Books

Abbott, L. B. *Special Effects — Wire, Tape and Rubber Band Style*. Hollywood, CA: The ASC Press, 1984.
Annan, David. *Ape: Monster of the Movies*. New York: Bounty Books, 1975.
Archer, Steve. *Willis O'Brien: Special Effects Genius*. Jefferson, NC: McFarland & Co., Inc., 1993.
Bacon, Matt. *No Strings Attached: The Inside Story of Jim Henson's Creature Shop*. New York: Macmillan, 1997.
Behlmer, Rudy, ed. *Memo from David O. Selznick*. New York: Viking Press, 1972.
Brosnan, John. *Movie Magic: The Story of Special Effects in the Cinema*. New York: The New American Library, Inc., 1976.
Brownlow, Kevin. *David Lean*. New York: St. Martin's Press, 1996.
Buchanan, Larry. *It Came from Hunger! Tales of a Cinema Schlockmeister*. Jefferson, NC: McFarland & Co., Inc., 1996.
Burns, Bob, with John Michlig. *It Came from Bob's Basement!* San Francisco: Chronicle Books, 2000.

Costello, Peter. *In Search of Lake Monsters*. New York: Berkley Publishing Corp., 1975.

Culhane, John. *Special Effects in the Movies*. New York: Random House, Inc., 1981.

_____. *Walt Disney's Fantasia*. New York: Abradale Press/Harry N. Abrams, Inc., Publishers, 1987.

Daniel, Dennis, ed. *Famous Monsters Chronicles*. FantaCo Enterprises, Inc., 1991.

Duncan, Jody. *The Flintstones: The Official Movie Book*. New York: Modern Publishing, 1994.

_____. *The Making of The Lost World: Jurassic Park*. New York: Ballantine Books, 1997.

Fielding, Raymond. *The Technique of Special Effects Cinematography*. London: Focal Press, 1965.

Fry, Ron, and Pamela Fourzon. *The Saga of Special Effects*. Englewood Cliffs, NJ: Prentice-Hall, 1977.

Galbraith, Stuart, IV. *Japanese Science Fiction, Fantasy and Horror Films*. Jefferson, NC: McFarland & Co., Inc., 1994.

_____. *Monsters Are Attacking Tokyo!*. Venice, CA: Feral House, 1998.

Glut, Donald F. *The Dinosaur Scrapbook*. Secaucus, NJ: The Citadel Press, 1980.

_____. *Dinosaur Valley Girls: The Book*. Jefferson, NC: McFarland & Co., Inc., 1998.

Goldner, Orville, and George E. Turner. *The Making of King Kong*. Cranbury, NJ: A. S. Barnes and Co., Inc., 1975.

Goodman, Ezra. *The Fifty-Year Decline and Fall of Hollywood*. New York: Simon and Schuster, 1961.

Gottesman, Ronald, and Harry Geduld, eds. *The Girl in the Hairy Paw*. New York: Avon, 1976.

Halliwell, Leslie. *The Filmgoer's Companion*. 6th ed. New York: Hill and Wang, 1977.

Hamilton, Jake. *Special Effects in Film and Television*. New York: DK Publishing, 1998.

Hardy, Phil, ed. *The Overlook Film Encyclopedia: Science Fiction*. Woodstock, NY: Overlook Press, 1994.

Harryhausen, Ray. *Film Fantasy Scrapbook*. 2nd ed. Cranbury, NJ: A. S. Barnes and Co., Inc., 1978.

Helfer, Ralph. *The Beauty of the Beasts: Tales of Hollywood's Wild Animal Stars*. Jeremy P. Tarcher, Inc., 1990.

Holman, L. Bruce. *Puppet Animation in the Cinema: History and Technique*. Cranbury, NJ: A. S. Barnes and Co., Inc., 1975.

Jensen, Paul M. *The Men who Made the Monsters*. New York: Twayne Publishers, 1996.

Johnson, John. *Cheap Tricks and Class Acts: Special Effects, Makeup, and Stunts from the Films of the Fantastic Fifties*. Jefferson, NC: McFarland & Co., Inc., 1996.

Jones, Stephen. *The Illustrated Dinosaur Movie Guide*. London: Titan Books, 1993.

Kinnard, Roy. *Beasts and Behemoths: Prehistoric Creatures in the Movies*. Metuchen, NJ: The Scarecrow Press, Inc., 1988.

_____, ed. *"The Lost World" of Willis O'Brien: The Original Shooting Script of the 1925 Landmark Special Effects Dinosaur Film, with Photographs*. Jefferson, NC: McFarland & Co., Inc., 1993.

Lees, J. D., and Marc Cerasini. *The Official Godzilla Compendium*. New York: Random House, 1998.

Lessem, Don, and Donald F. Glut. *The Dinosaur Society's Dinosaur Encyclopedia*. New York: Random House, 1993.

Lourié, Eugène. *My Work in Films*. San Diego: Harcourt Brace Jovanovich, 1985.

Maltin, Leonard, ed. *Leonard Maltin's Movie & Video Guide 1999*. New York: Penguin Putnam Inc., 1998.

Martindale, David. *Pufnstuf & Other Stuff*. Los Angeles: Renaissance Books, 1998.

Maxford, Howard. *Hammer, House of Horror*. Woodstock, NY: Overlook Press, 1996.

McGee, Mark Thomas. *Beyond Ballyhoo: Motion Picture Promotion and Gimmicks*. Jefferson, NC: McFarland & Co., Inc., 1989.

_____. *Faster and Furiouser: The Revised and Fattened Fable of American International Pictures*. Jefferson, NC: McFarland & Co., Inc., 1996.

Medved, Harry, with Randy Dreyfuss. *The Fifty Worst Films of All Time*. New York: Popular Library, 1978

Millar, Dan. *Special Effects*. London: Quintet Publishing Limited, 1990.

Naha, Ed. *The Films of Roger Corman*. New York: Arco Publishing, Inc., 1982.

Neibaur, James L. *The RKO Features: A Complete Filmography of the Feature Films Released or Produced by RKO Radio Pictures, 1929–1960*. Jefferson, NC: McFarland & Co., Inc., 1994.

Pettigrew, Neil. *The Stop-Motion Filmography: A Critical Guide to 297 Features Using Puppet Animation*. Jefferson, NC: McFarland & Co., Inc., 1999.

Ray, Fred Olen. *The New Poverty Row: Independent Filmmakers as Distributors*. Jefferson, NC: McFarland & Co., Inc., 1991.
Riley, Gail Blasser. *Wah Ming Chang: Artist and Master of Special Effects*. Springfield, NJ: Enslow Publishers, Inc., 1995.
Rovin, Jeff. *The Fabulous Fantasy Films*. Cranbury, NJ: A. S. Barnes and Co., Inc., 1977.
_____. *From the Land Beyond Beyond*. New York: Berkley Publishing Corp., 1977.
Schickel, Richard. *D. W. Griffith: An American Life*. NY: Simon and Schuster, 1984.
Senn, Bryan. *Golden Horrors: An Illustrated Critical Filmography 1931–1939*. Jefferson, NC: McFarland & Co., Inc., 1996.
_____, and John Johnson. *Fantastic Cinema Subject Guide: A Topical Index to 2500 Horror, Science Fiction, and Fantasy Films*. Jefferson, NC: McFarland & Co., Inc., 1992.
Shapiro, Marc. *When Dinosaurs Ruled the Screen*. East Meadow, NY: Image Publishing, 1992.
Shay, Don, and Jody Duncan. *The Making of Jurassic Park*. New York: Ballantine Books, 1993.
Stanley, John. *Creature Features Movie Guide Strikes Again*. Pacifica, CA: Creatures at Large Press, 1994.
_____. *Creature Features: The Science Fiction, Fantasy, and Horror Movie Guide*. New York: Boulevard Books, 1997.
Steen, Mike. *Hollywood Speaks! An Oral History*. NY: G. P. Putnam's Sons, 1974.
Steinbrunner, Chris, and Burt Goldblatt. *Cinema of the Fantastic*. New York: Galahad Books, 1972.
Svehla, Gary J., and Susan Svehla, eds. *Guilty Pleasures of the Horror Film*. Baltimore, MD: Midnight Marquee Press, Inc., 1996.
Tors, Ivan. *My Life in the Wild*. Boston: Houghton Mifflin Co., 1979.
Van Hise, James. *Hot Blooded Dinosaur Movies*. Las Vegas, NV: Pioneer Books, Inc., 1993.
Von Gunden, Kenneth. *Flights of Fancy: The Great Fantasy Films*. Jefferson, NC: McFarland & Co., Inc., 1989.
Warren, Bill. *Keep Watching the Skies! Volume I*. Jefferson, NC: McFarland & Co., Inc., 1982.
_____. *Keep Watching the Skies! Volume II*. Jefferson, NC: McFarland & Co., Inc., 1986.
Weaver, Tom. *Interviews with B Science Fiction and Horror Movie Makers*. Jefferson, NC: McFarland & Co., Inc., 1988.
_____. *Monsters, Mutants and Heavenly Creatures: Confessions of 14 Classic Sci-Fi/ Horrormeisters*. Baltimore, MD: Midnight Marquee Press, Inc., 1996.
_____. *Science Fiction and Fantasy Film Flashbacks: Conversations with 24 Actors, Writers, Producers and Directors from the Golden Age*. Jefferson, NC: McFarland & Co., Inc., 1998.
Weldon, Michael. *The Psychotronic Encyclopedia of Film*. New York: Ballantine Books, 1983.
_____. *The Psychotronic Video Guide*. New York: St. Martin's Press, 1996.
Wilson, S. S. *Puppets & People: Large-Scale Animation in the Cinema*. San Diego, CA: A. S. Barnes and Co., Inc., 1980.
Wray, Fay. *On the Other Hand*. London: George Weidenfeld & Nicolson Ltd., 1990.

Periodicals

Ackerman, Forrest J. "The Prehistoric Story." *Famous Monsters of Filmland* vol. 4 no. 4 September 1962.
_____. "Son of Kong." *Famous Monsters of Filmland* vol. 4 no. 5 November 1962.
_____. "Son of Kong — part 2." *Famous Monsters of Filmland* vol. 4 no. 6 February 1963.
_____. "Son of Kong — part 3." *Famous Monsters of Filmland* vol. 5 no. 2 June 1963.
Altman, Mark A. "The Women of Dinosaur Island." *Femme Fatales* fall 1993.
"The Beast Master." *Famous Monsters of Filmland* no. 212 May/June 1996.
Beeler, Michael. "Jurassic Park in Cartoon Land: The Flintstones." *Cinefantastique* vol. 25 no. 3, June 1994.
Billows, Dennis. "Here There Be Dragons." *Famous Monsters of Filmland* no. 132 March 1977.
Biodrowski, Steve. "Carnosaur!" *Cinefantastique* vol. 24 no. 2, August 1993.
_____. "Dinosaurs Attack!" *Cinefantastique* vol. 24 no. 2, August 1993.
_____. "Jurassic Park: Coordinating the Effects." *Cinefantastique* vol. 24 no. 2, August 1993.
_____. "Jurassic Park: Filming the Dinosaurs." *Cinefantastique* vol. 24 no. 2, August 1993.
_____. "Jurassic Park: Michael Crichton." *Cinefantastique* vol. 24 no. 2, August 1993.

_____. "Stan Winston." *Cinefantastique* vol. 24 no. 2, August 1993.
Biskind, Peter. "A 'World' Apart." *Premiere* May 1997.
Bogle, Charles. "Jim Danforth: A Tale of Cinematic Survival by Stop Motion's Heir Apparent." *Starlog* no. 14, June 1978.
Bohus, Ted A. "An Animated Conversation with Jim Danforth." *SPFX* no. 3 1995.
_____. "An Interview with Effects Wizard Ray Harryhausen." *SPFX* no. 3 1995.
Bonham, Joe. "The Return of Roger Corman." *Starlog* no. 19 February 1979.
Bradbury, Ray. "Hoo-Ray for Harrywood." *Famous Monsters of Filmland* no. 142 April 1978.
Bradley, Matthew R. "Ray Harryhausen: Now and Then." *Filmfax* no. 52 September/October 1995.
"Bringing Dinosaurs to Life." *Jurassic Park Official Souvenir Magazine* 1993.
Brosnan, John. "Lost World Movies." *The House of Hammer* vol. 2 no. 2 1977.
Brunas, Michael. "Son of Kong: Not Just Another Slapdash Sequel." *Midnight Marquee* issue 50 1996.
Burns, Bob. "A Day with the Dinosaurs." *Filmfax* no. 63-64, October/January 1998.
Calandra, Steve. "Warren Disbrow's Low-Budget Dinosaur Thrills." *Drive-In Cinema* no. 2 1997.
Catizone, Rick. "The Fantastic World of Ray Harryhausen." *Drive-in Cinema* no. 2 1997.
Cooper, Warren. "Ray Harryhausen: Master of Fantasy Special Effects." *Science Fiction, Horror & Fantasy* fall 1977.
Counts, Kyle. "Animating Dinosaur: Aladar." *Dinosaur no. 1— The Official Disney's Dinosaur Movie Magazine* 2000.
_____. "Animating Dinosaur: Baylene and Url." *Dinosaur no. 1— The Official Disney's Dinosaur Movie Magazine* 2000.
_____. "Animating Dinosaur: Neera." *Dinosaur no. 1— The Official Disney's Dinosaur Movie Magazine* 2000.
_____. "Chronicling Dinosaur." *Dinosaur no. 1— The Official Disney's Dinosaur Movie Magazine* 2000.
_____. "Modeling Dinosaur." *Dinosaur no. 1— The Official Disney's Dinosaur Movie Magazine* 2000.
_____. "Producing Dinosaur." *Dinosaur no. 1— The Official Disney's Dinosaur Movie Magazine* 2000.
Cox, Vic. "Ray Harryhausen — Acting without the Lumps." *Cinefex* no. 5 July 1981.
Crisafulli, Chuck. "Dinosaurs — Live!" *Fangoria* no. 127 October 1993.
_____. "Prehysteria." *Cinefantastique* vol. 24 no. 2, August 1993.
Danforth, Jim. "Film Concepts, Screenplays & Stories." *SPFX* no. 5 1997.
Danzey, Kevin R. "Amazing Cinema Interview: Bert I. Gordon." *Amazing Cinema* no. 3 July-August 1981.
Del Vecchio, Deborah. "Jim Danforth and the Saga of When Dinosaurs Ruled the Earth." *Chiller Theatre* no. 5, 1996.
Dello Stritto, Frank J. "Monstrous Ambition: The Nightmares of Merian C. Cooper." *Cult Movies* no. 19, 1996.
Delson, James. "'Move that Monster, Mister!' An In-Depth Interview with: Ray Harryhausen." *Fantastic Films* October 1978.
"Dinosaurus! Peril from the Prehistoric." *Famous Monsters of Filmland* no. 119 September 1975.
Dubois, Stephanie. "Man Against Nature: The Challenge of Revisiting Jurassic Park." *The Lost World: Jurassic Park Official Souvenir Magazine* 1997.
Duncan, Jody. "20 Years of Industrial Light & Magic." *Cinefex* no. 65 March 1996.
_____. "The Beauty in the Beasts." *Cinefex* no. 55 August 1993.
_____. "The Making of a Rockbuster." *Cinefex* no. 58 June 1994.
_____. "On the Shoulders of Giants." *Cinefex* no. 70 June 1997.
Dyke, Robert, and Robert Skotak. "Jim Danforth Interview." *Fantascene* vol. 1 no. 2, summer 1976.
"Father of Kong, Farewell." *Famous Monsters of Filmland* no. 110 September 1974.
Fentone, Steve. "Mexi-Monster Meltdown!" *Monster! International* no. 2 October 1992.
Ferrante, Anthony C. "Plumbing the Depths of Super Mario Brothers." *Dinosaur — The Collectible Edition* 1993.
_____. "Sinner and Saint." *Fangoria* no. 205 August 2001.
Fischer, Dennis. "Albert Band." *Cinefantastique* vol. 26 no. 4, June 1995.
_____. "Charles Band: Full Moon Mogul." *Cinefantastique* vol. 26 no. 4, June 1995.
_____. "Creature Creators." *Cinefantastique* vol. 26 no. 4, June 1995.

_____. "Josh Kirby, Time Warrior." *Cinefantastique* vol. 26 no. 4, June 1995.
_____. "The Primevals." *Cinefantastique* vol. 26 no. 4, June 1995.
Fisher, Bob. "When Dinosaurs Rule the Box Office." *American Cinematographer* June 1993.
Fordham, Joe. "T-Rex: Back to the Cretaceous—The Five-Terabyte Solution." *Cinefex* no. 77 April 1999.
Fox, Jordan. "Roy Arbogast." *Cinefex* no. 5 July 1981.
Freer, Ian. "Rumble in the Jungle." *Empire* issue 146 August 2001.
French, Lawrence. "Dennis Muren." *Cinefantastique* vol. 24 no. 2, August 1993.
_____. "Dinosaur Movements." *Cinefantastique* vol. 24 no. 2, August 1993.
_____. "Phil Tippett." *Cinefantastique* vol. 31 nos. 1/2, February 1999.
_____. "Phil Tippett, Dinosaur." *Cinefantastique* vol. 24 no. 2, August 1993.
Galbraith, Stuart, IV. "Long Long Ago Before Jurassic Park: The Making of One Million B. C." *Filmfax* no. 48 January/February 1995.
"The Giant Behemoth." *Mad Monsters* summer 1964.
Gingold, Michael, with Marc Shapiro. "Dinosaur Bytes." *Fangoria* no. 126 September 1993.
Goldman, Steve. "Dinner Is Served." *Empire* issue 146 August 2001.
Goodsell, Greg. "The Weird & Wacky World of Larry Buchanan." *Filmfax* no. 38, April/May 1993.
"Gorgo the Gargantuan." *Famous Monsters of Filmland* no. 50 July 1968.
Green, Howard E. "Bringing Up Baby." *Cinefex* no. 22 June 1985.
Green, Tim. "Ariana Richards: 'I'm Not Scared of Dinosaurs!'" *TV Hits* 1993.
Harris, Ernest. "Retrospective Interview: Ray Harryhausen." *Amazing Cinema* no. 4 September 1981.
Henderson, Jan Alan. "Bob Burns: Fantastic Film Fandom's Goodwill Ambassador." *Filmfax* no. 67 June/July 1998.
Hewitt, Chris. "Bite Back!" *Empire* issue 146 August 2001.
Hoffman, Eric L. "The Beast from 20,000 Fathoms filmbook." *Famous Monsters of Filmland* no. 163 May 1980.
"In Memoriam: The 8th Wonder of the World." *Closeup* no. 3 1977.
"In the Days of the Dinosaurs." *Famous Monsters of Filmland* no. 94 November 1972.
"Is this Caveman Stuff Silly or Sensational?" *Screen Guide* February 1940.
"It's About Time You Met the People That Time Forgot." *Famous Monsters of Filmland* no. 173 May 1981.
Jackson, Wendy. "A Century of Stop-Motion." *Cinefantastique* vol. 31 nos. 1/2, February 1999.
"Jim Danforth: FXJD." *Fantasy Film Journal* vol. 1 no. 2, summer 1978.
Jones, Alan. "In Search of ... Loch Ness." *Cinefantastique* vol. 28 no. 2, September 1996.
_____. "Jurassic Park." *Cinefantastique* vol. 24 no. 2, August 1993.
Kinnard, Roy. "The Lost Worlds of Willis O'Brien (and Beyond)." *Filmfax* no. 16 August 1989.
Kinsey, Wayne. "One Million Years B. C." *The House that Hammer Built* Issue 5.
_____. "When Dinosaurs Ruled the Earth." *The House that Hammer Built* Issue 6.
"Latest Wonder Movie Is Technical Marvel." *Modern Mechanix and Inventions* April 1933.
Lee, Nora. "Creating Dinosaurs for Baby." *American Cinematographer* Mar. 1985.
Leibfred, Philip. "The Cinema Legacy of a Literary Legend: H. Rider Haggard." *Filmfax* no. 30, December/January 1992.
Linaweaver, Brad. "A Trip to Dinosaur Eye-Land." *Famous Monsters of Filmland* no. 202 spring 1994.
"The Lost World: A Fantasticlassic Revisited." *Famous Monsters of Filmland* no. 183 May 1982.
"The Lost World: Trick Photography." *Famous Monsters of Filmland* no. 110 September 1974.
MacQueen, Scott. "Cinematic Archaeology." *Cinefex* no. 55 August 1993.
_____. "Classic Restoration: The Lost World—Found!" *Cinefex* no. 70 June 1997.
Magid, Ron. "Effects Team Brings Dinosaurs Back from Extinction." *American Cinematographer* June 1993.
Mandell, Paul. "Harryhausen's Dinosaurs." *Dinosaur—The Collectible Edition* 1993.
_____. "Of Beasts and Behemoths Part I: The Beast from 20,000 Fathoms." *Fantastic Films* February 1980.
_____. "Of Beasts and Behemoths Part II: The Giant Behemoth." *Fantastic Films* March 1980.

_____. "Of Beasts and Behemoths Part III: Gorgo." *Fantastic Films* May 1980.

_____. "Preproducing The Primevals or: Whatever Happened to Raiders of the Stone Ring." *Cinefantastique* vol. 8 no. 1, 1978.

Mason, Lesley. "The First Lady of the Silver Scream." *Famous Monsters of Filmland* no. 212 May/June 1996.

McGee, Mark. "Jim Danforth & Dave Allen." *Fangoria* no. 8 October 1980.

McGillivray, David. "The Land That Time Forgot." Rev. of *The Land That Time Forgot*, dir. Kevin Connor. *Films and Filming* May 1975.

Meikle, Denis with Christopher Koetting. "The Lost Horrors of Hammer!" *Filmfax* no. 59, February/March 1997.

Meyers, Richard. "Ray Harryhausen: 'I'm Thrilled with the Art of Motion ...'" *Starlog* no. 10 December 1977.

Miller, Ken. "Attack of the Rod Puppet Dinosaurs!" *Film Extremes* no. 2, 1992.

"Monster Invasion 'Jurassic Park.'" *Fangoria* no. 123 June 1993.

"Montana Monster Found in Lost World." *Famous Monsters of Filmland* no. 36 December 1965.

Moriarty, Tim. "Caroline Munro: Beauty Among the Beasts." *Famous Monsters of Filmland* no. 182 April 1982.

Murray, Doug. "A Candid Talk with Special Effects Artist Dave Allen." *Space Trek* vol. 1 no. 1, winter 1978.

_____. "The King Kong You Never Saw!" *SPFX* no. 4, 1996.

Murray, Will. "Ray Bradbury's Dinosaur Chronicles." *Dinosaur — The Collectible Edition* 1993.

Nadler, Harry, and Dave Trengove. "Ray Harryhausen" (interview, part 1) *Castle of Frankenstein* no. 19.

_____, and _____. "Ray Harryhausen" (interview, part II) *Castle of Frankenstein* no. 20.

Naha, Ed. "The Worlds of George Pal." *Starlog* no. 10 December 1977.

"Nat'l Film Theater: Harryhausen & Charles Schneer." *FXRH (Special Visual Effects by Ray Harryhausen)* no. 3 summer 1972.

Newsom, Ted. "A Filmfax Flashback with Veteran Character Actor Ken Tobey." *Filmfax* no. 15, May/June 1989.

_____. "King of Dynamation." *Imagi-Movies* vol. 2 no. 3, spring 1995.

_____. "Ray Harryhausen: Stop-Motion Magician." *Cinefantastique* vol. 31 nos. 1/2, February 1999.

_____. "The Ray Harryhausen Story: Part One — The Early Years." *Cinefantastique* vol. 11 no. 4, December 1981.

Painter, Deborah R. "Tyrannosaurus Wrecks." *Famous Monsters of Filmland* no. 160 January 1980.

Palmer, Randy. "Atomic Atrocities." *Famous Monsters of Filmland* no. 182 April 1982.

_____. "The Master Magician of Monster Movies." *Famous Monsters of Filmland* no. 152 April 1979.

Parla, Paul, and Donna Parla. "Beauty & the Beast from 20,000 Fathoms: An Interview with Paula Raymond." *Filmfax* no. 62 August/September 1997.

_____, and _____. "Ro-Man's Mate: An Interview with Claudia Barrett." *Filmfax* no. 55 March/April 1996.

"Part Two of the Interview: Ray Harryhausen & Charles Schneer at the National Film Theater." *FXRH (Special Visual Effects by Ray Harryhausen)* no. 4 spring 1974.

Pizzello, Stephen. "Chase, Crush, and Devour." *American Cinematographer* June 1997.

Plesset, Ross. "Dinosaur." *Cinefantastique* vol. 31 nos. 1/2, February 1999.

_____. "The Primevals." *Cinefantastique* vol. 31 nos. 1/2, February 1999.

"Ray Harryhausen: FXRH." *Fantasy Film Journal* vol. 1 no. 2 summer 1978.

Rebello, Stephen. "Shooting for an 'A' on 'My Science Project.'" *Cinefex* no. 23 August 1985.

Reynolds, James C. "Unknown Island: Behind-the-Scenes on the 'Other Lost World.'" *Filmfax* no. 63-64, October/January 1998.

Robertson, Barbara. "Raptor Redux." *Computer Graphics World* vol. 24 no. 8, August 2001.

Rosenbaum, Jonathan. "The Land that Time Forgot." Rev. of *The Land that Time Forgot*, dir. Kevin Connor. *Monthly Film Bulletin* February 1975.

Scapperotti, Dan. "The Wonderful Worlds of Jim Danforth." *Cinefantastique* vol. 31 nos. 1/2, February 1999.

Schoell, William. "The Making of Journey to the Center of the Earth." *Filmfax* no. 55 March/April 1996.

"Seven Faces of Dr. Lao." *Famous Monsters of Filmland* no. 65 May 1970.

Shannon, John. "Crash McCreery: Doing Dinosaurs and Such." *Cinefex* no. 69 March 1997.

Shapiro, Marc. "Carnosaur: Roger Corman's Dino-Gore." *Dinosaur— The Collectible Edition* 1993.
_____. "Designer of Tomorrow." *Starlog* no. 193 August 1993.
_____. "In the Shadow of the Dinosaurs." *Fangoria* no. 125 August 1993.
_____. "Park Stranger." *Fangoria* no. 205 August 2001.
_____. "Simon Saurs." *Fangoria* no. 124 July 1993.
_____. "Stalking Through the Pages." *Fangoria* no. 126 September 1993.
_____. "A Terrifying Ticket to Jurassic Park." *Fangoria* no. 124 July 1993.
_____. "A Vacation Back in Time." *Dinosaur— The Collectible Edition* 1993.
Shay, Don. "Dennis Muren— Playing It Unsafe." *Cinefex* no. 65 March 1996.
_____, ed. "Photographs and Memories— Ralph Hammeras." *Cinefex* no. 15 January 1984.
_____. "Willis O'Brien— Creator of the Impossible." *Cinefex* no. 7 January 1982.
Shinnick, Kevin G. "Stop Motion Studio? Yeah ... My Kitchen! Brett Piper." *SPFX* no. 5 1997.
Skinn, Dez, and John Brosnan. "Hammerhead— An Interview with Michael Carreras." *The House of Hammer* no. 17, February 1978.
Skipper, David S. "Fay Wray Remembers." *Monster Times* April 1975.
Skotak, Robert. "David Hewitt: Special Effects Magician." *Filmfax* no. 60 April/May 1997.
_____. "The Fabulous World of Karel Zeman." *Fantascene* no. 3, 1977.
_____. "Famous Fantastic Factoids from Fantasy Films!" *Filmfax* no. 63-64, October/January 1998.
_____. "Red Star Rising— The Lost Years of 'Fantastica' in the Soviet Union: Part Eleven." *Outré* no. 16 1999.
Skotak, Robert, and Dennis Skotak. "Special Effects Designed and Created by: Jack Rabin & Irving Block," *Fantascene* vol. 1 no. 2, summer 1976.
"Son of 1,000,000 B. C." *Famous Monsters of Filmland* no. 39 June 1966.
Spelling, Ian. "Calamity Gal." *Starlog* no. 290 September 2001.
Stanley, John W. "Music to the Max: The Max Steiner Story." *Filmfax* no. 36 December/January 1993.
Stein, Elliott. "The 13 Voyages of Ray Harryhausen." *Film Comment* November-December 1977.
"Suspended Animation: 100 Years of Stop-Motion." *Cinefantastique* vol. 31 nos. 1/2, February 1999.
Svetkey, Benjamin. "The Lizard King." *Entertainment Weekly* no. 380 May 23, 1997.
Tasker, Ann. "Ray Harryhausen Talks about his Cinematic Magic." *American Cinematographer* June 1981.
Taylor, Jeff. "Interview: David Allen." *SPFX* no. 5 1997.
Timpone, Anthony. "Puppet Master Speaks!" *Fangoria* no. 51 January 1986.
Tuchman, Mitch. "Baby: An Interview with John Alcott." *American Cinematographer* Mar. 1985.
Vanderbilt, Scott. "Caveman— the Real Stars." *Cinefex* no. 5 July 1981.
Vaz, Mark Cotta. "Creating the Thrills." *The Lost World: Jurassic Park Official Souvenir Magazine* 1997.
_____. "Engendered Species." *Cinefex* no. 82 July 2000.
_____. "The Motion in Our Minds." *Cinefex* no. 80 January 2000.
Warren, Bill. "Animating Dinosaur: Kron." *Dinosaur no. 1— The Official Disney's Dinosaur Movie Magazine* 2000.
_____. "Developing Dinosaur." *Dinosaur no. 1— The Official Disney's Dinosaur Movie Magazine* 2000.
_____. "Digitalizing Dinosaur." *Dinosaur no. 1— The Official Disney's Dinosaur Movie Magazine* 2000.
_____. "Directing Dinosaur." *Dinosaur no. 1— The Official Disney's Dinosaur Movie Magazine* 2000.
_____. "The Heroes of Jurassic Park." *Starlog* no. 193, August 1993.
_____. "Visualizing Dinosaur." *Dinosaur no. 1— The Official Disney's Dinosaur Movie Magazine* 2000.
_____. "Wild with Prehysteria." *Dinosaur— The Collectible Edition* 1993.
Weaver, Tom. "Cinematosaurs." *Dinosaur— The Collectible Edition* 1993.
_____. "Director of Dinosaurs." *Starlog* no. 193, August 1993.
_____. "His Favorite Things." *Fangoria* no. 124, July 1993.
_____. "The Oldest Working Screenwriter Explains it All." *Starlog* no. 193, August

1993.

_____. "Terror on the Low-Budget Express." *Fangoria* no. 73 May 1988.

Webber, Roy P. "The Career of Ray Harryhausen: A Cause and (Special) Effect." *Horror Biz Magazine* issue 2 fall/winter 1997.

Wilson, S. S. "The Crater Lake Monster." *Cinefantastique* vol. 6 no. 2, fall 1977.

Wolf, Marc. "Stop Frame: The History and Technique of Fantasy Film Animation — part 1." *Cinefantastique* winter 1971.

_____. "Stop Frame: The History and Technique of Fantasy Film Animation — part 2." *Cinefantastique* spring 1972.

Wooley, John. "The Adamson Family." *Fangoria* no. 135 August 1994.

Television

The Fantasy Worlds of Irwin Allen. The Sci-Fi Channel. 3 May 1996.

The Harryhausen Chronicles. Narrated by Leonard Nimoy. American Movie Classics. 27 January 1998.

Hollywood: The Golden Years. "Episode One: Birth of a Titan." BBC and RKO. 1987.

Movie Magic. Prod. GRB Entertainment/Vision Films. Discovery Channel.

Video

Aliens, Dragons, Monsters and Me. Written by Richard Jones. Midwich Entertainment, Inc. 1991.

Dinosaur Movies. Prod. Kevin M. Glover, Donald F. Glut. Simitar Entertainment, Inc., 1993.

Fantastic Dinosaurs of the Movies. Goodtimes Home Video, 1992.

Hollywood Dinosaur Chronicles. Rhino Home Video, 1990.

Hollywood Dinosaurs. Video Treasures, Inc., 1993.

It Was Beauty Killed the Beast: King Kong 60th Anniversary Special — A Behind the Scenes Look. Turner Home Entertainment, 1992.

The Making of Jurassic Park. MCA Universal Home Video, Inc., 1993.

Making The Lost World. Universal Home Video, Inc., 1997.

CD-ROM

Microsoft Cinemania '94. CD-ROM. Microsoft Corporation, 1993.

The Motion Picture Guide 1995 Edition. CD-ROM. CineBooks, 1995.

Online References

"Back to Jurassic Park with Joe Johnston." *IGN FilmForce* 18 July 2001. 23 August 2001 <http://filmforce.ign.com/jp3/articles/301444p1.html>.

"A Brief Biography of Windsor McCay." *Van Eaton Galleries*. 23 February 2002. <http://vegalleries.com/winsorbio.html>.

"A Brief History of Gertie the Dinosaur." *Van Eaton Galleries*. 23 February 2002. <http://vegalleries.com/gerthistory.html>.

"Building a Better Dinosaur with Stan Winston." *IGN FilmForce* 17 July 2001. 23 August 2001 <http://filmforce.ign.com/jp3/articles/301487p1.html>.

Fordham, Joe. "Digitizing with Dinosaurs." *VFXPro* 22 March 2000. 10 March 2002 <http://www.vfxpro.com/article/printerfriendly/0,7226,103899,00.html>.

The Internet Movie Database. <http://www.IMDb.com>.

"Interview with David Shepard." *The Dinosaur Interplanetary Gazette* April 2001. 6 June 2001 <http://www.dinosaur.org/celdinos/cdlwshep01.htm>.

Johns, David. "Walking with Dinosaurs: Computer Graphics." *BBCi*. 9 March 2002 <http://www.bbc.co.uk/dinosaurs/tv_series/graphics.shtml>.

Johns, David. "Walking with Dinosaurs: Production." *BBCi*. 9 March 2002 <http://www.bbc.co.uk/dinosaurs/tv_series/production.shtml>.

"Jurassic Park III." *Canal+ / Cinema* 2001. 23 August 2001 <http://www.canalplus.fr/cinema/speciales/jurassik3/index2.html>.

"Jurassic Park III." Universal Studios official site 2001. 23 August 2001 <http://jp3.jurassicpark.com/macsite/_JURASSIC_PARK_III_.html>.

"The Lost World: The Making of..." *BBCi*. 4 March 2002 <http://www.bbc.co.uk/lost-world/making_of/>.

Stevenson, Jack. "It Came from Beyond Belief—The Incredible B-Movies of Sidney Pink in Denmark." *The Living Color Movie Magazine* 1999. 1 March 2001 <http://hjem.get2net. dk/jack_stevenson/pink.htm>.

Summer, Edward. "Gertie the Dinosaur." *The Dinosaur Interplanetary Gazette*. 23 February 2002. <http://www.dinosaur.org/Gertie.htm>.

Tremont, David. "'The Lost World' TV Series: Building and Puppeteering the T-Rex." 1999. 3 December 2000 <http://www.themodelsmiths.com.au/html/lostworld1.html>.

"Walking with Dinosaurs: The Making of Walking with Dinosaurs." *BBCi*. 9 March 2002 <http://www.bbc.co.uk/dinosaurs/tv_series/making_of.shtml>.

INDEX

Numbers in **bold** *refer to photographs. Letters in* **bold** *refer to the glossy insert.*

Abarbanel, Sam X. 363
Abbott, L. B. 147, 149, 150, 151, 248, 249, 251, 252, 253
Abbott and Costello Meet Captain Kidd 90
Abel, Robert 116
Abell, Tim 340
Abramson, Richard G. 376
The Abyss 51, 80, 166
Ackerman, Bettye 332
Ackerman, Forrest J 82, 184, 186, 195, 316, 418, 420
Acovone, Jay 93
Acquanetta 233, 235
Adam Raises Cain 7
Adam's Rib 7, 103
Adamson, Al 129, 130, 279
Addy, Mark 109, 110, **111**
Adler, Allen 116
Adler, Mark 324
Adventures in Dinosaur City 7–9, **8**, 377
The Adventures of Baron Munchausen 229
The Adventures of Captain Zoom 139
The Adventures of Robin Hood (1938) 410
Adventures of the Wilderness Family 370
Agar, John 61, **425**, 426
The Age of Mammals 9–11, **10**
Agrama, Frank 253, 345
Aguirre, Richard 26
Ainley, Anthony 209, 210
Airplane! 55, 56, 437
Akdemir, Sedat 427

Aladdin 412
Albain, Dick 406
Alchemy FX 137, 138, 333
Alcott, John 22, 23
Alexandrov, V. 320
Algar, James 99
Alice's Restaurant 398
Alien 26, 46, 422
Alien 3 45
Alien: Resurrection 384
The Alien Within 80
Aliens 49, 51, 89, 164, 229, 311, 323
Aliens, Dragons, Monsters and Me (documentary) 438
All Monsters Attack see *Godzilla's Revenge*
Allan Quartermain (novel) 196
Allan Quartermain and the Lost City of Gold 199
Alland, William 214, 216, 217
Allard, Tony 274
Allegro Non Troppo 11
Allen, David 54, 57, 58, 59, 60, 62, 63, 64, 65, 71, 92, 93, 94, 95, 141, 186, 327, 329, 331, 332, 333, 335, 336, 339, 381, 415, 418, 427, 437, 443, 444, 446, 447
Allen, Irwin 12, 14, **15**, 16, 99, 137, 210, 211, 248, 249, 251, 252, 253, 254, 256, 258, 289, 352, 419, 438
Allen, Keith 225
Allen, Nancy 433
Allen, Patrick 414
Allen, Tim 433
The Alligator People 379

Allred, Corbin 137, 138
Along the Moonbeam Trail 11–12, 116
Alterian Inc. 431
Altman, Mark 78
Alves, Joe 57
Amamoto, Eisei 195
Amazing Cinema (magazine) 183
The Amazing Colossal Man 182
Amazon Women on the Moon 137, **232**, 233, 431
American Cinematographer (magazine) 26, 270
An American Tail 202, 413
Ames, Denise 82, 83
Andersen, Asbjorn **341**
Anderson, Howard A. 388, 394, 427
Anderson, Max 27
Anderson, Peter 21, 289
Anderson, Whitney 333, **334**, 335
André, Carole 427
Andress, Ursula 417
Andrews, Jay see Wynorski, Jim
Andrews, Roy Chapman 103
The Andromeda Strain 118
Anglund, Connie 331
The Angry Red Planet 90, 155
The Animal World 12–17, **13**, **15**, **16**, 99, 250, 251, 252, 289, 305, 385, 386, 391, 438, **A**
Ann, Melissa 74, 75
Ann-Margret 110
Annaud, Jean-Jacques 71
Anne of a Thousand Days 211
Anthony, Lysette 431

Antonini, Alfredo *see* Band, Albert
The Ape Man 394
Apocalypse Now 51, 335
Apollo 13 321
Apone, Allan 367
Apostle, Lysa 431
Appleseth, Mary 313
Arachnophobia 132
Arbogast, Roy 54, 58, 60
Archambault, Noel 382
Archer, Steve 186, 362
The Arctic Giant 32
Arden, Curtis 398, 405
Arensma, John Datu 96
Arkoff, Samuel Z. 211, 307, 313, 343, 373
Armstrong, Robert 183, 187, 189, **191**, 357, 359, **361**, 363
Armstrong, Samuel 99
Arness, James 386, 387, **388**
Arnold, Frank 137, 138, 140
Arnold, Jack 216, 217
Assault of the Party Nerds 78
Astley, Edwin 119
At the Earth's Core 17–18, **18**, 209, 211, 213, 308, 443
At the Earth's Core (novel) 442
At the Earth's Core (unmade film) *see Pellucidar*
Atlantic West Effects 433
Atlantis 435
Atragon 343
Attack of the Crab Monsters 198
Attack of the 50 Foot Woman (1958) 29
Attack of the Killer Tomatoes 336
Attenborough, Richard 157, 158, 160, 265, 270
Aupperle, Jim 9, 10, 11, 54, 57, 59, 184, 313, 316, **317**, 318, 319, 320
Aurness, Jim *see* Arness, James
Autry, Gene 313
The Avenger 94
Aventura al Centro de la Tierra 18–20, **19**, 134, 300, 395

Baar, Tim 86, 91, 338
Babe 68, 72, 229
Baby ... Secret of the Lost Legend 20–27, **21**, **24**, **25**, 274, 287, 288, **B**
Bach, Barbara 54, 56
Bach, J. S. 100
Back to the Future 367
Bacon, Matt 108, 229
The Bad Seed (1956) 372
The Bad Seed (play) 372
Baden-Powell, Sue 376
Badham, John 307, 434
Badiyan, Fred 130
Badker, Tod 294
Baerwitz, Jerry A. 450
Bahner, Blake 65
Bailey, Pearl 370

Bailey, Robert 427
Baird, Jason 151
Baker, Diane 147
Baker, George 295, 301
Baker, Rick 286, 288, 289
Baker, Tom 66
Bakker, Robert 160, 164, 247, 248, 267
Bal, Walter 337
Baldwin, Stephen 105, 109, 110, **111**
The Ballad of Big Al (television) 264
Ballard, J. B. *see* Ballard, J. G.
Ballard, J. G. 414, 417
Bambi 103, 200
Ban, Tomiya 452
Banares, Roderick 433
Band, Albert 92, 94, 327, 329, 332
Band, Alexander 94
Band, Charles 54, 92, 93, 94, 95, 137, 138, 327, 329, 332, 333, 443
Band, Richard 94, 139, 328
Bang, Poul 341, 344
Banjo, the Woodpile Cat 202
Banno, Yoshimitsu 451
Baquero, Manuel 363
Baranov, Catherine 433
Barbera, Joseph 104, 106, 109
Barfod, Bent 345
Barison, Edward B. 449
Barker, Lex 373
Barkett, Steve 76
Barnes, George 74
Barnes, Nicky Kentish 225
Barnet, Charlie 338
Barney's Great Adventure 27, 70, 174
Barnholtz, Barry 256
Baron Prasil 292
Baronet, Wili 7
Barr, Stephen R. 331
Barrett, Claudia 347, **348**, 349
Barron, Keith 209, 210
Barrows, George 347, **348**, 348–349, 394
Barry Lyndon 23
Barrye, Emily 403, 439
Barsi, Judith 200
Bartalos, Gabe 433
Bartlett, William 261
Bartoli, Adolfo 443
Barton, Diana 433
Bass, Jules 220
Bast, William E. 397, 400, 404
Batman (television series) 235
Batman and Robin 365
Bats 52
Bauer, Michelle 76, 78, 312, 313
Baum, Thomas 151
Beach Babes 2: Cave Girl Island *see Cave Girl Island*
Beals, Dick 337
The Bear 71

The Beast from Beyond *see Monster*
The Beast from 20,000 Fathoms 28–37, **30**, **31**, **33**, 35, 38, 62, 91, 118, 119, 120, 121, 124, 125, 127, 158, 164, 234, 238, 259, 271, 274, 315, 319, 320, 389, 402, 406, 419, 431, 437, **N**
The Beast from 20,000 Fathoms (short story) 32
The Beast of Hollow Mountain 20, 37–42, **39**, **41**, 89, 98, 135, 145, 314, **E**
Beaumont, Charles 354
Beaumont, Hugh 233, **235**
Beauties and Beasts 417
Beauty and the Beast 412
The Beauty of the Beasts (book) 149
Beck, John 450
Becket 211
Bedknobs and Broomsticks 422
Beebe, Ford 99
Beeman, Greg 367
Beery, Wallace 240, 242, 243, 378
Beethoven 106
Beethoven, Ludwig van 101, 258
Beetlejuice 367
Beginning of the End 182
Behemoth the Sea Monster *see The Giant Behemoth*
Behrens, Marla 341
Bejval, Vladimir 142
Bell, John 170
Bellamy, Ned 44
Belle, Camilla 267
EL Bello Durmiente 20, 42–44
Bellomo, Sarah 54
Dellucci, Joseph 150
Belzberg, Leslie 257
Ben-Hur (1959) 408
Beneath Loch Ness 431
Bennett, Alma 243
Bennett, Charles 248, 251, 350, 351, 352
Bennett, Jeff 203, 204, 205, 206, 207, 208
Bennett, Parker 365
Benson, Jodi 282, 283
Benson, Joey 130
Benson, Martin 124
Bercovitch, Reuben 450
Berg, Jon 62, 63, 64, 65, 131, 133, 288, 316, 443, 444
Bergen, Tushka 151, 152
Bergin, Patrick 256, 257, 431
Berkeley, Busby 396
Berkely, Susan 294
Bernds, Edward 292, 406, 407, 408, 409
Bernhard, Jack 388, 391
Bernier, Sara 96
Bernsen, Corbin 340
Berry, Halle 104
Berwick, Irv 230

Bester, Alfred 89
Beswick, Douglas 9, 11, 84, 85, 86, 95, 186, 287, 288, 289, 313, 318, 320, 379, 444
Beswick, Martine 79, 301, 302, 305
Betral, Victor *see* Bejval, Vladimir
Betuel, Jonathan R. 286, 287, 376, 377
Bevan, Tim 225
Bezanson, Mark 189
Big Bang Animation 256
The Big Country 400
The Big Night 396
Billups, Scott 336
Binger, R. O. 214
Bingham, James R. 32
Bird of Paradise (1932) 190
The Birth of a Flivver 44
Birth of a Nation 352
Bishop, Jennifer 130
Biskind, Peter 271, 273
Bissell, Whit 29, 233, **235**, 236
Black, James 113
Black, Karen 82
The Black Cat (1934) 439
The Black Diamond 294
The Black Scorpion 20, 33, 43, 121, 122, 123
Blackwell, George 301, 304
Blade Runner 367
Blain, Luci 87
Blaisdell, Paul 375
Blakely, Rachel 257
Blakely, Susan 441
Blanchette, Kim 170, 443, 444
The Blob (1958) 53, 90, 92
Block, Irving 117, 122
The Blood Beast Terror 421
Bloodworth, Baker 67
The Blue Gardenia 34
Blue Sky/VIFX 380, 381, 384
Bluth, Don 68, 200, 201, 202, 203, 442
Boates, Brent 356
Bobbitt, Russell 106
Bódalo, José 363
Body Snatchers 80
Bogdanovich, Peter 409, 410
Bond, Timothy 253, 255, 345
Bonomo, Joe 196
The Book of Stars 69
Bookwalter, J. R. 113
Boone, Pat 147, 148, 149, 150
Boone, Richard 220, 221, 222, 267
Booth, Walter R. 326
Borden, Olive 103
Bottaro, Pamela 313, 314
Bottin, Rob 164
Bowers, Charles 378
Bowie, Les 301, 302, 304, 422
Box Office (magazine) 98
Boyes, Christopher 69
Bozzetto, Bruno 11

Brackett, Charles 147, 149
Bradbury, Ray 28, 30, 31, 32, 439
Braden, Kim 385
Bradley, Leslie 373, 374
Brady, Ed 357
Brady, Scott 152, 153, 154, 277, 279
Brainstorm 367
Brana, Frank 422
Brando, Marlon 374
Brandon, Henry 214, 215
Brannon, Ash 433
Brasselle, Melissa 340
Bray, John Randolph (J. R.) 114, 239, 240
Breen, Julian *see* DeCoteau, David
Brennan, Walter 66, 68
Brevig, Eric 131, 133, 432
Brewster, Tony 312
Bricusse, Leslie 205
Bride of the Gorilla 394
The Bridge on the River Kwai 353
Brimble, Nick 225
Bringing Up Baby 31, 34, 431, 433
Brinkley, Ritch 93
Bristow, Billie 350
Britton, Tony 307
Brockett, Gary 368
Broderick, Matthew 434
Brodine, Norbert 296, 299
Bromberg, Serge 245, 247
Brontosaurus 432
Brooke, Hillary 233, 235
Brooks, Oscar J. 42
Brosnan, John 44, 47, 213, 300, 417
Brother Theodore 130
Brourman, Michele 206, 207, 208
Brown, Barnum 103, 116, 381, 382
Brown, Bart 109, 112
Brown, Bryan 151
Brown, Ewing 129
Brown, John 347
Brown, Reb 427, **428**, 429
Brown, Robert 301, 302
Brown, Terry 263
Brown, Thomas 113
Browning, Ricou 135
Brownlow, Kevin 352, 353, 354
Bruce, Carol 204
Bruce, Sarah 324
Bruckman, Clyde 378
Brute Force 44, 137, 297, 299
Bryan, Peter 384
Bryant, Bill 179, **180**, **182**
Bryce, Allan 414, 422
Buchanan, Barry 230, 231, 232
Buchanan, Dee 232
Buchanan, Jane 230, 232
Buchanan, Jeff 232
Buchanan, Larry 227, 230, 231, 232, 233
Buchanan, Randy 232
Buchman, Peter 171, 174

Buck, Frank 195
Budd, George 27
Budrys, Algis 89
Buechler, John Carl 44, 46, 47, 49, 50, 51, 52, 53, 54, 76, 80, 368
Bunin, Lou 378
Bunny, George 241
Burden, Douglas 188
Bureau, Rick 74
Burgos, Jose 398
Burian-Mohr, Christopher 111
Burman, Ellis 157, 388, 392, 393, 394, **H**
Burman, Robert 368
Burnette, Billy 52
Burns, Bob 123, 393
Burns, Jennifer 137, 138
Burr, Raymond 452
Burres, Cara 384
Burroughs, Danton 211, 443
Burroughs, Edgar Rice 17, 209, 210, 211, 213, 258, 307, 309, 311, 370, 371, 442, 443
Burton, Bernard W. 28
Burton, Kent 433, 443, 444
Burton, Tim 25, 161, 433
Bush, Dick 415
Bush, Owen 332, 333, 335
Bushelman, John 178
Bushman, Francis X. 321
Butler, Fred 112
Butler, Lawrence 300
Buttolph, David 34
Buzzotta, Dave 333
Byrd, Paul B. 354
Byrd expedition 215, 217
Byrnes, Burke 200

Cabot, Bruce 183, 187, 189, **191**
Cabot, Ellen *see* DeCoteau, David
Caddyshack 132, 335
Caffrey, Sean 414
Cage, Nicolas 162
Cahiers du Cinéma (French magazine) 89
Cahill, Charles 9, 10
Callisi, Paul 137, 138
Calvert, Steve 394
Calzada, Yancy 95
Cameron, James 51
Cameron, Rod 237
Cameron-Glickenhaus, Jesse 433
Campbell, R. Wright 373, 374
Campsie, Gary 339
Canada Vignettes: Woolly Mammoth 357
Candy, John 76
Canutt, Yakima 300
The Cape Canaveral Monsters 397
Capshaw, Kate 372
Captain Caution 387
Captain Fury 387
Captain Sindbad 238

Cardella, Richard 60, 61, 62
Cardenas, Elsa 133
Cardinal, Ben 275
Career of a Comet (novel) see *Off on a Comet*
Carey, Phil 283, 284
Carlson, Richard 135, 397, 400, 404
Carnosaur 44–50, **47, 48**, 54, 76, 77, 78, 80, 81, 83, 89, 340, 377, 413, 444
Carnosaur II 50–52, 78, 89, 340
Carnosaur 3: Primal Species 52–54, 340
Carpenter, Todd 349
Carradine, David 79, 81
Carradine, John 130, 283, 284
Carreras, James 417
Carreras, Michael 228, 301, 304, 306, 440, 442
Carriles, Lupe 37
Carson, David 443
Carson, Rachel 14
Carter, Ellis W. 215
Carter, Irene 256
Carter, Maurice 210, 211, 311
Carter, Rick 163, 169, 270
Caruso, Fred 365
Carvall, Susane 432
Carvelo, L. B. 239
Casas, Antonio 363
Cascade Pictures of California 62, 80, 418
Casella, Max 67, 69
Casey, Julian 256, 257
Cash, Jim 109
Cassidy, Elaine 261, 262
Castle of Frankenstein (magazine) 36
Cat-Women of the Moon 34
Cave Girl Island 54, 320
Cave Man see *One Million B.C.*
Caveman 9, 43, 54–60, **56, 58**, 59, 68, 77, 78, 82, 92, 112, 133, 139, 339, 378, 391
Cawthorn, James 209, 210, 311
Cayton, William 142, 146
Ceafer, Wes 443
Celis, Fernando 368
Cesta do praveku see *Journey to the Beginning of Time*
Chaffey, Don 301, 302, 305, 306
Chamberlain, Richard 199
Chandler, Chick 233, **235**
Chaney, Lon 216
Chaney, Lon, Jr. 183, 295, 296, **297**, 298, 300, 302
Chang 188
Chang, Martha 27
Chang, Wah Ming 9, 10, 60, 84, 85, **86**, 91, 103, 192, 281, 318, 338, 354, 355, 356, 357, 409, 410
Chaplin, Charlie 190
Cheap Tricks and Class Acts (book) 217, 300

Cheap Tricks Unlimited 290
Cheek, Herb 147, 149, 253
Cheesman, Ted 361
Chesney, Peter 131, 133, 230, 231, 233
Chester, Hal E. 28, 31, 32, 34
Chester, Vanessa Lee 265, 267, 270
Cheza, Fidelis 253
Child, Julia 411, 412
Chiodo, Charles 337, 339, 432, 433
Chiodo, Edward 433
Chiodo, Stephen 337, 339, 432, 433
Chiodo brothers 377, 433
Chopin, Frédéric 259
Chostner, Terry 324
Christian, Paul (Paul Hubschmid) 28, 29, **31**, 34
A Christmas Dream 145
Christopher Strong 190
Chuidian, Gerardo 433
Cimarron (1931) 185
Cincinnati Commercial Tribune 114
Cinecolor 391, 392
Cinefantastique (magazine) 32, 62, 63, 71, 93, 94, 107, 169, 228, 437, 438, 440, 442, 443, 447
Cinefex (magazine) 26, 38, 40, 57, 59, 98, 108, 166, 167, 245, 273, 286, 287, 288, 362, 384, 435, 436, 439, 445, 446
Cinerama 438
Cinesite 112
Cingolani, Luigi 7
The Circus of Dr. Lao (novel) 354
Citizen Kane 363
City Lights 190
Clan of the Cave Bear 4
Clarence the Cross-Eyed Lion 136
Clark, Carroll 183
Clark, Mamo 295
Clash of the Titans 30, 59, 119, 133, 404
Clemento, Steve 183, 361
Clery, Corinne 427, **428**, 429
Clifford 432
Clift, Montgomery 68
Cline, Eddie 378
Clive, Colin 227
Clokey, Art 60, 62, 337, 339
Close Encounters of the Third Kind 26, 60, 130, 162, 443
Closeup (magazine) 189
Clyde, Andy 239
Cobb, Kacey 60, 62
Cochrane, George 289
Cohen, Albert J. 388, 392
Cohen, Bruce 104, 106, 109, 110
Cohen, Herman 384
Cohen, Martin B. 96, 98
Cohn, Harry 441
Coleman, Dabney 434

Coleman, Kari 380, 381, 383
Colicos, John 198, 199
Collins, Alan 427, 429
Collins, Connie 151
Collins, Joan 110
Collins, Ray 427
Combs, Jeffrey 93, 94, 312, 379
Comisky, Chuck 431
Commando Squad 313
Commons, David 346
Compin, Antoine 380, 382
Comport, Lionel 299
Conan Doyle, Arthur 170, 240, 243, 245, 248, 249, 251, 254, 255, 256, 257, 258, 259, 261, 262, 263, 269, 346, 351, 441, 442
Conde, José Antonio Nieves see Nieves Conde, José Antonio
Connell, Linda 397
Connell, W. Merle 395, 397
Connery, Sean 162, 335, 442
Connor, Kevin 17, 208, 211, 307, 311
Connors, Kevin R. 332, 335
The Conqueror Worm see *Witchfinder General*
Conrad, Mikel 395, 397
Consolidated Film Industries 346
Cook, Randall William 54, 56, 57, 59, 60, 62, 63, 64, 92, 95, 137, 138, 333, 443, 444
Cook, Willis 28, 34
Cooper, Gary 190
Cooper, Jack 239
Cooper, Merian C. 183, 185, 186, 187, 188, 189, 190, 191, 192, 195, 357, 360, 362, 373, 436, 438, 440, 446
Cooper, Wilkie 301, 302, 303
Coote, Greg 257
Corbin, Barry 286
Corday, Mara 61
Corey, Wendell 425, 426
Corman, Roger 44, 45, 46, 47, 49, 50, 52, 53, 66, 67, 77, 78, 80, 83, 198, 232, 340, 373, 375, 376, 409, 410, 411, 444
Cornelius, Joe 385
Corniello, Jeff 74
Cornthwaite, Robert 443
Corrigan, Lloyd 370
Corrigan, Ray "Crash" 391, 393, **394**
Cort, Bud 376, 378
Cortez, Stanley 90
Corwin, Linda 290, 291
Cosmic Voyage 256
Costello, Lou 413
Costello, Peter 353
Costner, Kevin 162
Coulouris, Keith 93
Counts, Kyle 73
Courage of Lassie 348
Courtier, Jamie 107, 108, 109
Cowles, Jules 240

Cox, Ronny 433
CPC *see* Cascade Pictures of California
Crabbe, Byron L. 183, 187, 193, 357, 363, 435, 436
Crabbe, Larry "Buster" 373, 426, 432
Craig, James 183, 403, 439
Cramer, Duncan 251
Cramer, Grant 432
Crane, Michael 17
The Crater Lake Monster 60–65, **63, 64**, 89, 231, 239
Cravenna, Alfredo B. 18, 20
Crawford, Joan 384, 385, 386
Crawford, John 44, 49
Crawley Creatures & Associates 264
Creation 188, 190, 191, 192, 435–436
Creative Presentations, Inc. 368
Creature Features Movie Guide (book) 406
The Creature from the Black Lagoon 20, 217, 218
The Creature Shop *see* Jim Henson's Creature Shop
Creatures the World Forgot 4, 305, 447
Creelman, James 183, 190
The Creeping Unknown 237
Crichton, Michael 71, 157, 160, 161, 162, 170, 171, 172, 174, 265, 267, 269, 270, 271, 438
Crist, Paula 26
Criswell, John 7, 376
Critchley, Bruce 336
Cronkite, Walter 411, 412
Crosby, Bing 149
Culhane, John 70, 102, 103
Cullen, Brett 327, 328
Culver, Veronica 379
Cumming, Alan 110
Cundey, Dean 106, 163, 169, 270
Cunningham, Harry 36
Cunningham, Sean S. 131
Curious Pets of Our Ancestors 65
Currie, Philip 382, 384
Curtis, Bonnie 265
Curtis, Tony 379
Curtis, Wanda 179, **180, 182**
Curzon, Aria Noelle 205, 206, 207, 208
Cushing, Peter 17, 18, 305
The Cyclops 183
Czerkas, Stephen 10, 283, 285, 313, 316, 317, 318, 319, 320

Dahl, Arlene 147
Daily, Elizabeth 433
Daktari (television series) 136
Dalya, Jacqueline 295
Damon, Gabriel 200
Dane, David 239
Danforth, Jim 25, 41, 42, 57, 58, 59, 60, 62, 64, 73, 83, 91, 141, 142, 158, 172, 184, 211, 281, 313, 316, 320, 338, 354, 355, 356, 378, 386, 414, 415, 416, 417, 418, 419, 420, 421, 422, 427, 436, 438, 439, 440, 441, 442, 443, 444, 445, 446, 447
D'Angelo, Beverly 336, 337
Dannaldson, Jim 219, 252, 253
Danning, Sybil 312, 313
Dano, Royal 131, 132, 133, 432
Danova, Cesare 379, 406, **407**, 408
Danson, Ted 225, 227, 228
Dante, Joe 77, 161, 338, 431, 437
Danzey, Kevin R. 183
Dark, John 17, 208, 211, 307, 311
Dark Continent: A Sherlock Holmes Adventure! 436
The Dark Crystal 229, 311
Dark Fortress see A Nymphoid Barbarian in Dinosaur Hell
Dark Wings 320
Darrow, Clarence 289
Davey, Bert 311
David, Thayer 147, 148, 149, **150**
David Allen Productions 84, 92, 94, 141, 329, 331, 335; *see also* Allen, David
David Lean (book) 352
Davidson, Jim 81
Davis, Andrew Z. 131
Davis, Andy 152, 153, **154**
Davis, Desmond 119
Davis, Don 174
Davis, Maria 349
Davis, Michael 332, 333
Davis, Ossie 67, 69
Davison, Jon 70, 71, 437
Daw, Joseph 113
Dawley, Herbert M. 11, 104, 116, 243
Dawn, Norman 386, 387
Dawson, Anthony M. *see* Margheriti, Antonio
The Day Time Ended 59
Dayaneni, Jini 384
Dayton, Howard 87, 88
Dean, James 374
Dean, Rick 50, 51, 52, 53
Death Becomes Her 166, 167
Deathbeast (story) 316
Deatherage, Joleen 368
de Barros, Mario 398
De Bont, Jan 267
De Brulier, Nigel 295
Debussy, Claude 11
De Chomon, Segundo 155
DeCoteau, David 54, 113, 335
Deep Impact 174, 233
Deep Space 313
Defelice, Adam 432
de Hoyos, Kitty 18
Dekker, Thomas 206, 207, 208
De Kova, Frank 373, 374

De La Rosa, Myrna 43
De Laurentiis, Dino 215
Delgado, Marcel 41, 90, **91**, 183, 187, 191, 192, 193, 194, 240, 242, 246, 247, 281, 283, 357, 359, 361, 363, 404, 422, 435, 436, 439, 446
Delgado, Victor 91, 281
Deliverance 130
de Luca, Rudy 54, 378
del Valle, Lilia 42
De Metz, Danielle 406, 408
DeMille, Cecil B. 7, 103, 190
DeMita, John 137, 138, **140**
Demon Sword 65–67, 78, 139, 320
Denning, Richard 61, 298, 388, 390, **391**
De Palma, Giovanni 409
De Priest, Ed 294
DePriest, Teresa 340
Dern, Laura 47, 157, 160, 162, 163, 169, 171, 174, 267
DeShazer, Dennis 27
De Souza, Steven E. 104
Destination Moon 160, 321
Destroy All Monsters 195, 450–451
Detour 439
Deutsch, Patti 207
De Vallance, Denis 282
DeVasquez, Devin 131
De Vega, Jose 135
de Vico, Robert 50
de Vry, William 257
Dewes, Norman 432
DeWitt, Jack 37
DeWitt, Louis 37, 40, 42, 117, 122
Dexter, Elliott 7
DeYoung, Cliff 50, 51
Diamond, David 116, 120, 121
Dicken, Roger 60, 184, 199, 209, 210, 211, 212, 213, 311, **386**, 414, 420, 421, 422
Dickens, Thomas R. 81, 82, 83, 84
Dickerson, Charles "Beach" 375, 376
Diehl, John 171
Dietz, Jack 28, 31, 32, 34
Diffring, Anton 210
Diller, Phyllis 278
Dillinger 127
Dino-Warp 438
Dinosaur 2, 67–74, **70, 73**, 84, 102, 112, 255, 391, 437, 451
Dinosaur! (television special) 326
The Dinosaur and the Baboon see The Dinosaur and the Missing Link
The Dinosaur and the Missing Link 44, 74, 240
Dinosaur Babes 74–75, 82, 291, 336
Dinosaur Girl (unmade Hammer film) 436
Dinosaur Girl (unused title for Dinosaur Island) 83

The Dinosaur Hunter 432
Dinosaur Interplanetary Gazette (electronic magazine) 245
Dinosaur Island 75–81, 77, **79**, **80**, 82, 83, 312, 340, 444
The Dinosaur Kid 436–437
Dinosaur Movies (video documentary) 436
Dinosaur ... Secret of the Lost Legend see *Baby ... Secret of the Lost Legend*
The Dinosaur Scrapbook (book) 157, 299, 300
Dinosaur Valley Girls 76, 81–84, 137
Dinosaur Valley Girls: The Book 83
The Dinosaur Zoo 80, 81
Dinosaurs ... The Terrible Lizards 9, 10, 11, 84–86, **85**, **86**, 288, 318, 357
Dinosaurs (early title for *Dinosaur*) 71, 437
Dinosaurs (television series) 9, 377
Dinosaurs Attack! 437–438
Dinosaurus! 16, 62, 78, 86–92, **88**, **90**, **91**, **92**, 124, 158, 164, 172, 239, 250, 255, 271, 356, 391, 409, 411, **B**
Dinotopia (book) 139
Dinotopia (miniseries) 264
Dion, Debra 137, 138, 327
Dippe, Mark 104, 106, 107, 108, 157, 170
Disbrow, Warren F. 444
Discovery Channel 2
Disney, Walt 11, 68, 70, 102, 103, 202
Dix, Beulah Marie 435
Dix, Robert 130
Doctor Mordrid 92–96, 329, 381
Dr. Strange (comic book) 94
Doel, Frances 340
Domergue, Faith 410
Dommens, Annie 349
Donen, Stanley 433
Donner, Richard 161
Dorian, Angela see Vetri, Victoria
Dorian, Antonia 76
Dorn, Ray 152
Doublin, Anthony 50, 52
Doug Beswick Productions, Inc. 286; see also Beswick, Douglas
Douglas, Sarah 307, **309**
Douglas, Shirley 27
Dowlan, William 240
Dowlatabadi, Zahra 203, 204
Dowling, William 243
Doyle, Arthur Conan see Conan Doyle, Arthur
Doyle, Tony 7
Dracula vs. Frankenstein 279
Drago, Harry Sinclair 196

Dragonslayer 4, 166, 288, 419, 422
Dragonworld 73, 124
Drew, Griffen 76, 82
Dreyfuss, Richard 162
Drive-In Cinema (magazine) 444
Druxman, Michael B. 340
Drysdale, George W. 282
Dubin, Ellen 368, 370
Du Chaillu, Paul B. 188
Duel in the Sun 45
Duffy, Thomas F. 265, 267
Dufour, Yvon 198
Duguid, Dale 151
Dukas, Paul 100, 102
Duncan, David 449
Duncan, Jody 106, 269, 270, 272
Duncan, Robert 356
Dunn, Linwood 193, 417
Dunnett, Ninian 274
Dunning process 188, 193
Durning, Charles 204
Dutra, Randal M. 131, 133, 167, 170, 265, 273, 326
Dvořák, Antonín 11
D. W. Griffith: An American Life (book) 298
Dynamation 16, 35, 36, 37, 58, 62, 63, 237, 239, 318
Dynarama 36

Eades, Wilfred 123
Earth vs. the Flying Saucers 36, 395
Eastman, G. L. 433
Eastwood, Clint 286, 379
Ebert, Roger 160, 267, 370
Eberts, Jake 365
Ebirah, Horror of the Deep 450
Eden, Barbara 354
Edeson, Arthur 243
Edson, Richard 365, 367
Edwards, Edgar 295
Edwards, George 410, 411, 425
Edwards, James L. 113
Effa, Karel 292
Effects Associates, Inc. 54, 59
Ege, Julie 305
Egged On 378
The Eighth Wonder 438
Ein Ruckblic in die Urwelt 349
Eisenberg, Aron 336
Eisley, Anthony 152, 153, 154, 277, 278, 279, 281, 283, 284
Ekland, Britt 198, 199
Election 174
Elfman, Danny 56
Elfont, Harry 109
Ellenshaw, Harrison 25
Ellenshaw, Peter 356
Elliott, Laura 386, **388**
Elliott, Mike 44, 46, 50, 76
Elliott, Ross 28
Emerman, Scott 113
Emilio and Guloso (story) 98, 445

Emilio and His Magical Bull 96–98, **97**, 445
Empire (magazine) 176
Empire of the Sun (novel) 417
The Empire Strikes Back 318, 346, 422
Endicott, Chris 71, 92, 94, 95, 137, 138, 141, 142, 327, 329, 331, 332, 333, 335, 427, 443, 444
Endless Descent 424
Enemy from Space 199
Engelberg, Fred 87, 88
Englund, Morgan 52
Enriquez, Thom 67, 73
Epic: Days of the Dinosaurs 432
Epps, Jack, Jr. 109
Ericson, John 354
Ernest, Orien 214, 218
Erwin, Bill 200
Eskuri, Neil 67
Esperon, Manuel 43
E.T. the Extra Terrestrial 26, 166, 275, 372
Evans, Gene 117, 119, 121
Evans, Jimmy 119
The Evil Dead 131
Evolution (1923) 99
Evolution (Harryhausen) 14, 16, 325, 438
The Ewok Adventure 288
Excursion to the Universe 294
Explorations and Adventures in Equatorial Africa (book) 188

Fabregas, Manolo 133
The Fabulous World of Jules Verne 146
Faire, Virginia Brown 243
Fairfax, Marion 240
Falk, Peter 261, 262, 441
Famous Monsters of Filmland (magazine) 17, 78, 420
Fangoria (magazine) 130, 162, 167, 169, 175, 178, 237, 257, 269, 427
Fantamation 63, 64
Fantasia 11, 70, 99–103, **101**, **102**, 200, 202, 282, 289, 390, 392, 438
Fantastic Voyage 305
Fantasy Film Journal (magazine) 445
The Fantasy Film Worlds of George Pal (documentary) 338
Fantasy II Film Effects 274, 277, 337, 339, 377
Farino, Ernest D. 65, 66, 67, 137, 138, 139, **140**, 141, 452
Farley, Jeff 44, 49, 377, 443
Farnsworth's Folly 438–439, 441
Faster and Furiouser (book) 411
Father Goose 441
Fawlty Towers (television series) 351
Fehr, Rudi 417

Fellner, Eric 225
Fellowes, Julian 21, 22
Femme Fatales (magazine) 78
Fentone, Steve 20
Ferguson, Norm 99
Fernández, Arturo 363
Ferrari, Stefano 376
Ferraro, Martin 157
Ferroini, Vittorio 409
Fielding, Raymond 387
The Fifty Worst Films of All Time (book) 348
Fig Leaves 103–104
Filipovsky, Frantisek 292
Film Effects of Hollywood 417
Film Fantasy Scrapbook (book) 306, 404, 439
Filmfax (magazine) 32, 150, 232, 237, 252, 298, 348, 390, 392, 393
The Filmgoer's Companion (book) 157
Films & Filming (magazine) 214
The Films of Roger Corman (book) 375
Finch, Chris 376
Fine, Delia 261
Fine, Larry 278
Finkelstein, Keith 239
Finlayson, James 112
Finnel, Mike 437
Finney, Charles G. 354
The First Circus 7, 104
The First Flyer 114
The First Men in the Moon 305
Fisher, Kenneth J. 283
Fisher, Mary Gale 295, **296**
Fitzgerald, Edward 42, 43
Fitzhamon, Lewin 326
Fitzsimmons, John 113
Five Billion B.C. 439
Flaherty, Paul 432
Flash Gordon (1936 serial) 252, 426, 432
Flash Gordon (1980) 429
Flavin, James 183
Fleischer, Charles 411
Fleischer, Max 32, 99
Fletcher, Joel 73, 74
Flight to Mars 392
The Flintstones 9, 43, 79, 104–109, **105**, **107**, **109**, 110, 112, 167, 229
The Flintstones in Viva Rock Vegas 109–112, **111**
The Flintstones: The Official Movie Book 106
Florea, John 135
Flower, George "Buck" 370
Flying Elephants 112
The Flying Saucer 392
The Flying Serpent 4
Food of the Gods 182
Forbes, Bryan 442
Ford, Harrison 162
Ford, John 158

Fordham, Joe 264
Forsett, Theo 368, 370
Foster, David 54, 57
4-Ward Productions, Inc. 432
Fourzon, Pamela 238
Fox, James 261, 262
Fox, William 103
Foxworth, Robert 431
Foy, Bryan 440
Foyles, Edward J. 99
Fraas, Eberhard 273
Frain, James 225, 227, 228
FrameStore 261, 264
Francis, Freddie 384, 385
Franciscus, James 172, 397, 400, 404
Franco, Larry 171
Franczak, Brian 72
Frankenstein (1931) 243, 392, 432
Frankenstein Meets the Wolf Man 392
Franklin, Richard 257, 259
Fratkin, Stuart 327
Frazetta, Frank 95
Frees, Paul 337, 339
Freiberger, Fred 28, 32
Frenz-Heckman, Faith 432
Freudberg, Judy 200
Frickert, Joseph 295, 301
Friedman, Brent 332, 333
Frizell, Mark 290
From Beyond 94
From Hell It Came 347
Fry, Ron 238
Fuentes, Alma Delia 133
Fujimoto, Sanezumi 450
Fujioka, John 333
Fukuda, Jun 450, 451
Fukushimi, Masami 451
Funicello, Annette 426
Furlong, Edward 51
Fury, Ed 82
Fusco, John 225, 227, 228
FXRH (magazine) 139, 228, 306

Gabai, Richard 76, 77, 78, 340
Gable, Clark 189
Gabourie, Fred 378
Galaxy of the Dinosaurs 54, 113, 179, 320, 349
Galbraith, Stuart, IV 5, 222, 285, 298, 299, 300, 445
Gallagher, Patti 179, **182**
Gamin, Poupee 152
Gamley, Douglas 210
Gampu, Ken 198
The Gangster 127
Gaos, Lola 363
Gappa the Trifibian Monster see *Monster from a Prehistoric Planet*
Garay, Nestor 11
Garbo, Greta 351
Garcia, Juan 42
Gardner, Tony 431

Garland, Beverly 364, 444
Garrison, Richard 60
Gary, Linda 203
Geiss, Tony 200
Gellis, Andrew 380, 382
Gemora, Charles 134, 394
Genius at Work 190
Gentle Ben (television series) 136
George Eastman House 245
Gerani, Gary 437, 438
Gerrold, David 316
Gershenson, Joseph 215
Gertie see *Gertie the Dinosaur*
Gertie on Tour 113
Gertie the Dinosaur (Bray) 114, 240
Gertie the Dinosaur (McCay) 1, 113, 114, 239
Ghidrah: The Three-Headed Monster 450
The Ghost of Slumber Mountain 12, 99, 114–116, **115**, 236, 242, 243, 246, 289
Ghostbusters 45
The Giant Behemoth 62, 116–123, **117**, **121**, **122**, 124, 125, 127, 128, 360, 419, 437, **H**
The Giant Claw 157, 224
Gibson, E. B. 183, 192, 357, 363
Gibson, Mel 408
Gibson, Thomas 110
Gigantis the Fire Monster 395, 445, 449, 451
Gilbert, Paul 425, **426**
Gilford, Jack 54, 56
Gill, Spencer 54, 57
Gillespie, Dana 307, 309, **310**
Gilliam, Terry 293
Gilligan's Island (television series) 92, 346
Gilling, John 384
Giovanni, Marialuisa 11
The Girl in the Hairy Paw (book) 189
Girvin, Terri 26
Gittens, Wyndham 196
The Glacial Empire see *Zeppelin v. Pterodactyls*
Glackens, L. M. 114
Glass, Jack R. 386
Gleason, Duncan 446
Gleason, Jackie 77
Glickenhaus, James 433
Glover, Danny 408
Glover, Kevin M. 81, 83
Glut, Donald F. 44, 81, 82, 83, 84, 112, 157, 299, 300, 436
Gnome Productions 368
Go and Get It 243
Godzilla (character) 4, 5, 30, 125, 195, 196, 220, 221, 335, 398, 400
Godzilla (1998, TriStar) 4, 158
Godzilla 1985 451–452
Godzilla 2000 452

Godzilla, King of the Monsters! 30, 127, 164, 269, 397, 449, 452
Godzilla on Monster Island 451
Godzilla Raids Again see *Gigantis the Fire Monster*
Godzilla vs. Biollante 452
Godzilla vs. Destroyer 452
Godzilla vs. Gigan see *Godzilla on Monster Island*
Godzilla vs. Hedorah see *Godzilla vs. the Smog Monster*
Godzilla vs. King Ghidorah 452
Godzilla vs. Mechagodzilla (1974) see *Godzilla vs. the Cosmic Monster*
Godzilla vs. Mechagodzilla (1993) 452
Godzilla vs. Megaguirus: The G Annihilation Strategy 452
Godzilla vs. Megalon 451
Godzilla vs. Monster Zero see *Monster Zero*
Godzilla vs. Mothra (1964) see *Godzilla vs. the Thing*
Godzilla vs. Mothra (1992) 452
Godzilla vs. Space Godzilla 452
Godzilla vs. Super-Mechagodzilla see *Godzilla vs. Mechagodzilla* (1993)
Godzilla vs. the Bionic Monster see *Godzilla vs. the Cosmic Monster*
Godzilla vs. the Cosmic Monster 451
Godzilla vs. the Sea Monster see *Ebirah, Horror of the Deep*
Godzilla vs. the Smog Monster 451
Godzilla vs. the Thing 450
Godzilla's Counterattack see *Gigantis the Fire Monster*
Godzilla's Revenge 451
Gojira 449
Golan, Gila 397, 400, 404
Golanos, Norita 47
Goldberg, Jerry 332
Goldberg, Whoopi 376, **377**, 378
Goldblum, Jeff 157, 158, 162, 163, 174, 265, 267, 269, 270, 274
Golden, Dan 65, 67
Golden Horrors (book) 352
The Golden Voyage of Sinbad 66
Goldman, Bo 441
Goldman, Edmund 449
Goldman, Gary 200, 202
Goldner, Orville 183, 192, 363, 438
Goldsmith, Charles see Hustak, Zdenek
Goldsmith, Jerry 22
Goldstein, Mark 327, 329
Goliath and the Dragon 281
Golitzen, Alexander 215, 217
Gomer, Steve 27
Gone with the Wind 104, 190, 441
Goodman, John 104, **105**, 106, 132, 411, 412

Gorcey, Leo 62
Gordon, Bert I. 135, 178, 179, 181, 182, 183
Gordon, Dennis 95, 443
Gordon, James B. 147, 248
Gorgo 23, 118, 120, 123–129, **126**, 129, 164, 269, 271, 285, 437, 451, M
Gorilla at Large 394
Gorman, Ned 273
Gorog, Laszlo 214
Gorski, Tamara 253, 345
Gottlieb, Carl 43, 54, 57, 112, 378, 431
Gough, Michael 384, 385
Gould, Rupert Thomas 353
Gowland, Gibson 350, 352
Graham, Kirsty 225, **226**, 227, 228
Graham, Tim 386
Grandchildren of Mars (story) 320
Grant, Cary 34, 189, 216, 431
Grant, Cy 17
Grant, Joe 100
Grass 188
Grasshoff, Alex 220
Graver, Gary 279
Gray-Stanford, Jason 282
Greed 352
Green, Austin 152, 153, **154**
Green, Clifford 21, 23
Green, Ellen 21, 23
Green, Tim 169
Green, Walon 67, 71, 437
Green Acres (television series) 235
Greenberg, Robert H. 209
Greene, Richard 133
Gregory, Richard 253, 261, 264, 345
Gremlins 338
Gresty, Verner 108, 229
Grey, Virginia 388, 389, **391**
Greystoke: The Legend of Tarzan, Lord of the Apes 23
Gries, Tom 178
Griffin, David 385
Griffith, D. W. 44, 137, 297, 298, 299, 352
Grodin, Charles 432
Gross, Arye 131
Gross, Yoram 432
Grossberg, Joseph 84, 95, 137, 138, 141
Grosvenor, Charles 205, 206, 207, 208
Guest, Val 414, 415, 417, 419
Guibord, Sandra 137, 138
Guillaume, Robert 208
Gul, Ayshe 427
Gun Crazy 127
Gunn, Janet 52, 53
The Guns of Navarone 199
Gunsmoke (television series) 387

Guo, Yan 332, 333
Gurney, James 139
Guzzi, Paul 290
Gwangi 41, 70, 398, 402, 403, 404, 439
Gwynne, Fred 201

Hackett, Buddy 57
Hagen, Ross 76, 78, 312, 313
Haggard, H. Rider 196, 198, 436
Hagiwara, Michael 332
Haines, Tim 261, 264
Hale, Alan, Jr. 396
Hales, Eric 350
Hall, Charles D. 295, 296, 299
Hall, Christopher 261, 263
Hall, Huntz 62
Hall, John D. 386
Hall, Kenneth J. 49
Hallenbeck, E. Darrell 286
Hallett, Mark 72, 329
Halliwell, Karen 229
Halliwell, Leslie 157
Halmi, Robert, Jr. 151
Halpin, Luke 135
Halston, Rodger 52
Hama, Mie 195
Hamilton, Randy 282
Hamm, Al 338
Hammeras, Ralph 240, 245, 246, 247, 248, 435
Hamre, Scott 54
Handley, Jim 99
Hankin, Larry 332
Hanks, Tom 433
Hanna, William 104, 106, 109
Hannah, Daryl 162
Hansen, Juliana 204
Hanson, Kristina 86, 88, 90
Hanson, Preston 230
Harben, Hubert 350
Hardwicke, Edward 21
Hardy, Oliver 112
Hardy, Sam 183, 350
Harlan, Jane 386
Harline, Leigh 355
Harlow, Jean 189
Harmon, Mark 275
Harolde, Ralf 436
Harrington, Curtis 410
Harris, Jack H. 86, 87, 88, 89, 90, 91
Harris, Jez 261, 264
Harris, Rob 263
Harris, Sid 450
Harrison, Harry 415
Harrison, John 67
Harrison, Wordsworth 326
Harron, Robert 44
Harryhausen, Fred 36
Harryhausen, Ray 1, 12, 13, 14, **15**, 16, 28, 29, 30, 31, 32, 33, 34, 35, 36, 37, 38, 41, 42, 59, 65, 70, 73, 78, 94, 119, 121, 139, 160, 170, 172, 174, 184, 185, 188, 190, 195,

214, 228, 234, 237, 238, 248, 251, 252, 259, 267, 268, 269, 274, 281, 289, 291, 297, 301, 302, 303, 304, 305, **306**, 307, 315, 316, 317, 318, 319, 320, 325, 338, 360, 362, 373, 384, 385, 389, 397, 398, 400, 402, 403, 404, 405, 406, 415, 416, 417, 419, 420, 434, 438, 439, 440, 443, 444, 445, 446
The Harryhausen Chronicles (television documentary) 438
Harte, Jennifer 332, 335
Hartford, Andrea 283
Hartford, Glen 283
Hartford, Kenneth 283, 285
Harvey, Jack 388, 392
Harvey, Phil 214
The Harvey Girls 348
Harwood, Kate 261
Hashimoto, Keiichi 223
Hashimoto, Koji 451
Hass, Charlie 437
Hassall, Imogen 414
Hatari! 158, 268
Haver, Phyllis 103
Havez, Jean 378
Hawaiian Eye (television series) 154
Hawdon, Robin 414, 415
Hawks, Howard 68, 103, 104, 431
Hay, Roy 337
Hayashi, Shotako 223
Haydn, Richard 248, 249
Hayes, Craig 167
Hayes, Helen 433
Hayes, Jeffrey M. 257, 259
Hayward, Arthur 305, 306
Hayward, Debra 225
Hearn, George 27
Hedge, Bill 443, 444
Hedison, David 248, 249, 251
Hee, T. 99
Heimann, Jurgen 331
Heinrich, Mimi 341, 342
Heinrichs, Rick 25, 433
Heitmeyer, Jayne 256, 257
Heldman, Christopher 379
Helfer, Ralph 135, 136, 137, 149, 178, 179, 181, 182, 183, 300
Henderson, Clark 141
Henderson, Douglas (actor) 179, **182**
Henderson, Douglas (artist) 72, 73
Henderson, John 225, 227, 228
Henderson, Lyn 282
Hendrieth, Yancy 239
Henley, Drewe 414
Henshaw, Jim 257
Henson, Jim 9, 442; *see also* Jim Henson's Creature Shop
Henson, Lisa 442
Hepburn, Katharine 431
Hepworth, Cecil 326

Herbert, Percy 301
Herman, Al 183
Herrman, Peter *see* Herrman, Petr
Herrman, Petr 142
Herrmann, Bernard 148, 400
Hertford, Whitby 204
Hester, Tom 289
Heston, Charlton 408
Hewitt, David L. 130, 152, 153, 154, 155, 277, 278, 279, 280, 281
Hewitt, Jean 277, 279
Heymann, Werner R. 297, 302
Hibshman, Dennis 152
Hickman, Gail Morgan 9, 10, 11
Hickner, Stephen 411
Hickox, Douglas 121
Hicks, Seymour 228, 350, 351, 352
Hidaka, Sigeaki 449
Hideaway 382
The Hideous Sun Demon 152
Higgins, Ross 432
Hill, Robert 37
Hillier, Erwin 400
Hingle, Pat 200, 201
Hinson, Libby 206
The Hitchhiker's Guide to the Galaxy 139
Hoag, Robert R. 354
Hodes, Robert M. 443
Hodges, Adrian 261, 262
Hodges, Ken 119
Hoffman, Roswell A. 214, 217
Hoffman, Shawn 7
Hogan, Heather 203, 204
Holland, Cecil 240, 243
Holland, Crystal 239
Holland, Tom 91
Hollimon, Tina 54
Hollow Man 364
Hollywood Boulevard 77
Hollywood Speaks (book) 298
Holm, Ian 225, 227, 228
Holman, Jena 443
Holmes, John 9
Holt, Patrick 414
Holzbog, Arabella 50, 51, 340
Honda, Ishiro 195, 449, 450, 451
Honey, I Shrunk the Kids 133, 233, 281
Hook 162, 163, 167
Hoola Boola 337
Hoover, Michael 60
Hoover, Tom 113
Hopper, Dennis 286, 365
Horak, Antonín 142
Horner, Jack 72, 164, 175, 176, 272
Horner, James 200
Horror Creatures of the Red Planet see *Horror of the Blood Monsters*
Horror of the Blood Monsters 129–131, 300, 395

Horton, Charis 380, 382
Horton, Peter 380, 381, 383, 431
Horvath, Emil 292
Hoskins, Bob 261, 262, 365
Hot-Blooded Dinosaur Movies (book) 38, 406
The Hound of the Baskervilles (1939) 410
House II: The Second Story 131–133, **132**
The House of Hammer (magazine) 212, 417, 442
The House That Hammer Built (magazine) 307, 436
Houston, Kent 225, 229
How to Make a Monster 376
Howard, Arliss 265
Howard, Bruce 450
Howard, Curly 358
Howard, James Newton 69
Howard, Judy 96
Howard, Tom 123, 128, 129
Howard A. Anderson Co. 179, 425; *see also* Anderson, Howard A.
Howell, Hoke 65, 66
Howie, Jane 264
The Howling 95
Høyer, Orla 345
Hoyt, Arthur 240
Hoyt, Harry O. 240, 243, 435, 441
Hoyt, John 29, 233, **235**, 236, 237
Hubbard, John 295
Hubbard, Thomas 386, **388**
Hubble, Edwin P. 100
Hudson, Earl 240, 245, 435
Hudson, Stephanie 54
The Hudsucker Proxy 233
Huemer, Dick 100
Hughes, Lloyd 240, 242, 254
Hughes, Megan 7
Hulswit, Mart 135
Hume, Alan 56, 210, 310, 311
Hume, Cyril 446
Huneck, John 339
Hunt, Judith 225
Hunter, Neith 50
Hunter, Vic 74
Huntley, Leslie 339
Hustak, Zdenek 142
Huston, John 432
Huston, Paul 21, 23
Hutson, Candace (Candy) 200, 203, 204
Hyatt, Daniel *see* James, Daniel
Hybride Technologies 257, 259
Hyde-White, Wilfrid 198
Hylton, Jack 338
Hyman, Bob 60
Hymes, Gary 273
Hymns, Richard 170

I Was a Teenage Werewolf 235, 375

I'd Rather Be Rich 441
Igami, Masaru 223
Ignatova, Kyunna 320
Iizuka, Masaki 220
I'll Do Anything 228
The Illustrated Dinosaur Movie Guide (book) 441
ILM *see* Industrial Light and Magic
Image Animation 256
Image Engineering 230, 233, 431
Image Quest, Ltd. 253, 255, 256, 345
Imagi-Movies (magazine) 304, 404
IMAX 69, 256, 381, 382, 383, 384
In Prehistoric Days see Brute Force
In Search of Lake Monsters (book) 353
The Incredible Shrinking Man 217
The Indian in the Cupboard 432
Indiana Jones and the Temple of Doom 372
Indiana Jones (trilogy) 174, 254
Industrial Light and Magic 23, 71, 104, 107, 108, 109, 112, 164, 166, 167, 169, 172, 176, 178, 264, 273, 325, 381, 419, 432
Ingagi 394
Ingham, Barrie 137, 138, 139
Ingle, John 203, 204
Inspiration 145
Interviews with B Science Fiction and Horror Movie Makers (book) 89, 91, 154, 408
Invaders from Mars (1953) 235, 392, 397
Invasion of the Astro Monster see *Monster Zero*
The Invisible Man (1933) 243, 363
Ireland, John 311
Irving, Bill 239
La Isla de los Dinosaurios 133–135, **134**, 300
Island at the Top of the World 446
The Island of Dr. Moreau 182
Island of the Lost 135–137, **136**, 300
It Came from Beneath the Sea 410
It Came from Hunger! (book) 232
It Came from Outer Space 217
It Came from the Lake see Monster
It Conquered the World 364
It Was Beauty Killed the Beast 194
Ito, Roberto (Robert) 425, 426
It's a Bird 378
It's a Mad, Mad, Mad, Mad World 417
It's About Time (television series) 42
It's Alive (1968) 232

Jack the Giant Killer 291
Jackman, Fred W. 240, 246, 395, 441
Jackman, Fred, Jr. 395
Jackson, Freda 398, 400, 404
Jackson, Joshua 275
Jackson, Samuel L. 157, 160
Jackson, Wilfred 100
Jacobs, Olu 21
Jacobs, Robert Nelson 67
Jacobson, Tom 444
Jamboree (production title for *The Son of Kong*) 360, 361
James, Brion 336, 337
James, Daniel 120, 123, 127
James, Godfrey 17
Jankel, Annabel 365, 367
Japanese Science Fiction, Fantasy and Horror Films (book) 5, 445
Jaritz, Klaus 432
Jason, Harvey 265
Jason and the Argonauts 291, 302, 305, 307
Jasper in a Jam 337, 338
Jaws 57, 158, 162, 163, 223, 431
Jeffries, Phil 57
Jennewein, Jim 104
Jensen, Paul M. 362, 385
Jersey, Bill 90
Jessel, Paul 333
Jeter, Michael 171, 174
Jim Henson's Creature Shop 104, 107, 108, 109, 112, 164, 225, 229
Jiraskova, Jirina 292
Joe Meets Tarzan 373
Joffé, Roland 365
John, Rosamund 350
John Henry and the Inky Poo 337, 338
Johncock, Brian 414, 422
Johnson, Brian *see* Johncock, Brian
Johnson, Elmer A. 432
Johnson, George 356
Johnson, Ian 151
Johnson, J. J. 217, 300
Johnson, Noble 183, 361
Johnson, Ryan Thomas 50
Johnston, Joe 171, 172, 175, 176, 178
Johnston, Kristen 109, 110, **111**
Jolley, I. Stanford 406
Jones, Dennis E. 109
Jones, Don 409
Jones, F. Richard 112
Jones, Grover 295
Jones, James Earl 162
Jones, Michael F. 44, 49, 83
Jones, Morgan 395
Jones, Robert 305
Jones, Stephen 441
Jones, Trevor 227
Jongor 439
Joseph, John 349

Joseph, Paul 264
Josh Kirby ... Time Warrior: Eggs from 70 Million B.C. 138
Josh Kirby ... Time Warrior: The Human Pets 137–138
Josh Kirby ... Time Warrior: Journey to the Magic Cavern 138
Josh Kirby ... Time Warrior: Last Battle for the Universe 138
Josh Kirby ... Time Warrior: Planet of the Dino-Knights 66, 83, 138–142, **140**
Josh Kirby ... Time Warrior: Trapped on Toyworld 138
Journey to the Beginning of Time 10, 40, 89, 142–147, **143**, **145**, **147**, 294, 381
Journey to the Center of the Earth (1959) 4, 18, 79, 137, 147–151, **150**, 207, 249, 251, 252, 424
Journey to the Center of the Earth (1999) 151–152, 257, 258, 259
Journey to the Center of the Earth (novel) 151, 422
Journey to the Center of the Earth (unmade film) 440
Journey to the Center of Time 130, 152–155, **154**, 300, 379
Journey to the Centre of the Earth (1909) 155
Journey to the Seventh Planet 321
Joyce, Michael 277, 339
Joyner, C. Courtney 92, 94
Joyner, David 27
Judkins, Ron 170
Jumanji 172
The Jungle 4, 237
Jungle Manhunt 155–157, **156**, 300, **H**
Jungle Woman 235
Jurassic Park 2, 45, 46, 47, 51, 69, 71, 72, 76, 82, 87, 102, 106, 107, 108, 110, 157–171, **159**, **161**, **164**, **166**, **168**, 174, 176, 178, 194, 227, 243, 257, 258, 259, 263, 265, 266, 267, 268, 269, 270, 271, 272, 273, 274, 286, 303, 324, 325, 328, 329, 332, 365, 367, 379, 381, 384, 405, 412, 413, 433, 437, 442, 444
Jurassic Park (novel) 161, 269, 438
Jurassic Park III 2, 171–178, **173**, **175**, **177**, 274
Jurassic Punk (song) 82

Kaczmarczyk, Omar 256
Kagel, James 26
Kaminski, Janusz 268, 270
Kandel, Aben 384
Kane, Carol 376
Kaplan, Cory 312
Kaplan, Deborah 109
Karloff, Boris 196, 439
Kasai, Kazuyoshi 220
Kashiwabara, Hiroshi 452

Katsura, Kokan 285
Katt, William 21, 22
Katz, Omri 7
Katzenberg, Jeffrey 437
Katzman, Sam 155
Kaufman, Lloyd 75
Kaufmann, Maurice 117, 124
Kawaji, Tamio 285
Kawakita, Koichi 452
Kay, Bernard 385
Kay, Richard 395, 397, 449
Kaye, Danny 351
Kazantsev, A. 320
Keaton, Buster 378
Keats, Steven 220
Keays-Byrne, Hugh 151
Keen, Bob 256, 257
Keenan, William J. 195, 282
Keep Watching the Skies! (book) 32, 149, 397, 440
Keith, David 432
Kellaway, Cecil 28, 29, **31**, 259
Kellison, Phil 91, 123, 338
Kelly, Gene 433
Kelly, Nancy 156, 370, **371**, 372
Kendal, Felicity 411
Kennedy, Douglas R. 214
Kennedy, Kathleen 104, 105, 157, 160, 162, 165, 171, 176, 200, 265, 269, 411
Kennedy, William 386, **388**
Kent, Gary 277, 294, 409
The Kentucky Fried Movie 431
Kenyon, Sandy 230, 231, 232
Kevan, Jack 214, 218
Kiel, Richard 321
Kikugawa, Chojii 7
Kilbane, Dennis 398
Kiley, Richard 162
Killer Klowns from Outer Space 432
Killough, John 113
Kimball, Bruce 277, 279
Kimble, Bruce *see* Kimball, Bruce
Kimbrough, Charles 207
Kimura, Takeshi 449
King, Frank 123, 127, 129, 449
King, Maurice 123, 127, 129, 449
King Dinosaur 28, 134, 135, 137, 178–183, **180, 182**, 300, 347, 378, **M**
King Dong see *Lost on Adventure Island*
King Kong (1933) 10, 20, 32, 73, 85, 91, 100, 116, 124, 125, 158, 170, 183–195, **187, 191, 193**, 199, 213, 220, 239, 242, 246, 247, 268, 269, 271, 278, 279, 280, 281, 282, 299, 310, 326, 347, 350, 358, 359, 360, 361, 362, 363, 365, 384, 390, 391, 402, 420, 427, 436, 438, 440, 441, 446, **G**
King Kong (1976) 196, 215, 282, 441

King Kong (character) 125, 338, 339, 392, 438
King Kong (television series) 195
King Kong (unmade remake) 440
King Kong Escapes 195–196, 220, 451
King Kong vs. Godzilla 195, 270, 278, 450
The King of Kings 190
King of the Kongo 196
King Solomon's Mines (1937) 198
King Solomon's Mines (1985) 199
King Solomon's Treasure 196–199, **197**
Kinsey, Wayne 307, 436
Kirby, Jack 94
Kirschner, David 104
Kiser, Terry 368, **369**, 370
Kiyoshima, Tomoko 223
Kizer, R. J. 451
Kleihauer, Aylsworth 84
Kleinow, Peter 54, 59, 60, 275, 277, 337, 338, 339, 355, 356
Klimov, Arkadii 323
Klotz, Errol Clyde 275
Klushantsev, Pavel 320, 321, 322, 323, 324, 410
KNB Effects 164
Knep, Brian 167
Knight, Charles R. 15, 247, 299, 381, 392, 393, 394, **C**
Knight, Harry Adam *see* Brosnan, John
Knight, Ted 96
Knight, Wayne 157, 160, 328
Knoth, Fred 214, 217, 219, 299
Kobayashi, Shinichiro 452
Koch, Pete 7
Koed, Kay 341, 345
Koenekamp, Hans 240, 246
Koepp, David 157, 162, 174, 265, 267, 269, 270
Kohler, Fred, Jr. 386
Kohn, Justin 432
Koi, Hideo 285
Konga 278
Konopka, Magda 414
Korman, Harvey 105, 110
Korzen, Benni 220
Kosa, Emil, Jr. 147, 248, 253
Kosloff, Theodore 7
Kotani, Tom 220
Koyanagi, Itoko 285
Kozak, Harley Jane 275
Kraa! The Sea Monster 96
Krakowski, Jane 109, 110, **111**
Kraushaar, Raoul 397
Kremar, Frantisek 146
Krentz, David 72
Krepela, Neil 67, 72, 73
Krieger, Stu 200
Kristofferson, Kris 206
Krofft, Marty 440
Krofft, Sid 440
Kruger, Otto 370, 372

Kubrick, Stanley 421
Kupcik, Arnost 146
Kurata, Junji 223
Kuronuma, Takeshi 450
Kuru Island (story) 127

L. A. Effects Group, Inc. 431
La Isla de los Dinosaurios 133–135, **134**, 300
Labyrinth 229
La Croix, Brandon 205
Ladd, Diane 44, 45, 46, 47
Ladd, Fred 142, 146
Lafleur, Jean 256
Lake, Veronica 216
Lamas, Fernando 248, 249, 251
Lamb, Harold 403, 439
Lambert, Glen 239
Lancaster, Stuart 230
Landers, Lew 155
The Land Before Time 68, 71, 102, 200–203, **201, 202**, 206, 255, 282, 413, 442
The Land Before Time (film series) 78, 412
The Land Before Time II: The Great Valley Adventure 203–204, 205, 207
The Land Before Time III: The Time of the Great Giving 204
The Land Before Time IV: Journey Through the Mists 204–205
The Land Before Time V: The Mysterious Island 205–206, 207
The Land Before Time VI: The Secret of Saurus Rock 206–207
The Land Before Time VII: The Stone of Cold Fire 207
The Land Before Time VIII: The Big Freeze 208
Land of the Lost 440
Land of the Lost (television series, 1970s) 16, 22, 60, 86, 440
Land of the Lost (television series, 1990s) 139
The Land That Time Forgot 17, 56, 208–214, **212, 213**, 308, 309, 310, 311, 389, 422, **I**
The Land Unknown 89, 90, 172, 195, 214–220, **216, 218, 219**, 250, 252, 271, 299, 310, **E, K**
Landau, Juliet 376
Landau, Richard 233, 237
Landis, Carole 270, 295, **296**, 298, 302, 408
Landis, John 257, 431, 442
Lane, Michael 406
Lang, Fritz 34
Lankford, T. L. 312
Lantieri, Michael 104, 106, 108, 157, 162, 163, 164, 167, 169, 170, 171, 176, 178, 265, 272, 286
Lantz, Walter 441
Larrinaga, Juan 435

Larrinaga, Mario 183, 187, 193, 357, 363, 404, 435, 436
Larsen, Keith 425
Laserblast 443
Lasky, Alan 44
Lasky, Jesse L. 445
Lasky, Jesse, Jr. 445
Lasseter, John 433
The Last Action Hero 329
The Last Chapter 211
The Last Dinosaur 18, 195, 220–222, **221, 222**, 258, 267, 424, O
The Last Picture Show 410
The Last Starfighter 287
The Last Voyage 238
Laszlo, Ernest 196
Laurel, Stan 112
Lavagnino, Angelo 125, 126
Lavista, Raul 20, 38
Lavrentyev, Anatoli 323
Lawless, Louie 313
The Lawnmower Man 382
Lawrence of Arabia 139
Laws, Maury 222
Lawson, Priscilla 432
Layton, Eddie 134
Leach, Sheryl 27
Leahy, Margaret 378
Lean, David 352, 353
Leave It to Beaver (television series) 235
LeBaron, William 436
LeBeau, Becky 77
Le Brock, Gene 433
Lee, Christopher 305
Lee, Danny 422
Lee, Paige 409
Lee, Sheldon 277
Lee, Stephen 327, 328
Lees, Nathaniel 261, 262
Legacy 440–441
Legend of Dinosaur and Monster Bird see *The "Legend of Dinosaurs"*
The "Legend of Dinosaurs" 223–224, **224**, 278
The Legend of King Kong 441
Leguizamo, John 365
Leibovit, Arnold 337, 338, 339
Leigh, Vivian 105
Leighton, Eric 67, 71, 72
Lemick, Michael E. 432
Leningrad Puppet Theater 323
Leno, Jay 106
Leonard, Brett 380, 382, 383
Leoni, Téa 171, 174, **175**
Lessem, Donald 1–2, 72, 164, 165, 326
Lesser, Sol 370, 373
Letscher, Matt 333
Levant, Brian 104, **105**, 106, 107, 108, 109, 110, 111, 112
LeVant, Rene 411
Levin, Henry 147, 149

Levine, Joseph E. 449
Levine, Nat 196
Levy, Mark 336
Lewis, Greg 332
Lewis, Jerry 43
Lewis, Michael 380, 382
Lewis, Susan A. 196
Lewis, Suzanne 60
Lifeforce 233
Light & Shadows Graphix 379
Linaweaver, Brad 78
Lincoln, Lar Park 131, 132
Linden, Eddie 361
The Lion 182
The Lion King 70, 201, 412
Lippert, Robert L. 236, 237
Liska, Jindrich 146
Liska, Laine 54
Litefoot 432
The Little Broadcast 337
Little Caesar 190
The Little Mermaid (1989) 283
Little Nemo in Slumberland (comic strip) 114
The Lives of a Bengal Lancer 188
Livingston, Doc 230
Lizzorty, Ron 443
Lloyd, Michael 21
Lloyd, Ted 116
Loch Ness 4, 224–229, **226**
The Loch Ness Horror 227, 228, 230–233, **231, 232**, 431
Logan, Jacqueline 196
Logan, John 9
Lohman, August J. "Augie" 233, 237, 238
London, Jeremy 151
London Times (newspaper) 353
Long, Jesse H. 335
Long, Shelley 54, 56
Longo, Tony 327
Lorenzano, Daniele 253, 345
Loring, John 123
The Lost Atlantis 441
Lost Continent 181, 210, 233–238, **234, 235, 238**, 239, 279, 314, 347, 394, 396, 400
Lost Creations see *Zeppelin v. Pterodactyls*
Lost Horizon 281
Lost in Space (television series) 253
The Lost Island 85
Lost on Adventure Island 239
The Lost Volcano 300
The Lost Whirl 114, 239–240, 247
The Lost World (1925) 36, 90, 146, 164, 191, 193, 240–248, **244, 246**, 252, 254, 259, 262, 269, 279, 293, 350, 391, 395, 432, 435, 436, 441, F
The Lost World (1960) 17, 137, 197, 210, 211, 248–253, **250, 252**, 254, 256, 258, 279, 310, 352, 391, 400, 419

The Lost World (1992) 170, 253–256, **255**, 257, 258, 264, 345
The Lost World (1998) 170, 256–257, 259
The Lost World (1999) 257–261, **260**
The Lost World (2001) 261–264
The Lost World (Conan Doyle novel) 151, 243, 351
The Lost World (Crichton novel) 265, 269, 271
The Lost World (unmade film, 1960s) 441–442
The Lost World (unmade film, c. 1990) 442
The Lost World: Jurassic Park 174, 175, 176, 178, 186, 203, 227, 257, 265–274, **266, 271, 272**, 308, 361
Loubek, Christian 274
Louis-Scott, Karey 230
Lourié, Eugène 23, 28, 29, 30, 32, 34, 35, 91, 93, 116, 118, 119, 120, 121, 122, 123, 124, 125, 127, 128, 129, 164, 285, 320, 440
Love, Bessie 240, 242, 243
Lowe, Edward T. 370, 373
Lowell, Mark 395
Lowery, Dave 270
Lowery, Robert 370
Loy, John 203, 205, 206, 208
L-Squared Entertainment 380, 382, 384
Lucas, George 23, 200, 203
Lucas, James *see* Lukas, Josef
Lucas, Ralph 313
Lucas, Wilfred 44
Ludin, John 203
Lugosi, Bela 119, 130, 207, 439
Lukas, Josef 142
Lukather, Paul 86
Luske, Hamilton 99, 356
Luther, Jeffrey 83
Lycett, Eustace 356, 422
Lynch, Sean 17
Lynn, Kelly 74
Lynne, Iris 74
Lyon, Ben 350
Lyon, Henry 42, 96, 98

Maar, Pons 376
Mabuchi, Kaoru 195, 450, 451
MacDonald, J. R. 84
MacGowran, Jack 117, 119, 121
Machine Gun Kelly 375
Mack, Helen 190, 357, 359, 360, **361**
MacLachlan, Kyle 104, 105
MacLaine, Shirley 342
MacLane, Barton 388, 390, **391**
Macnee, Patrick 198, 199
MacNeille, Tress 204
MacQueen, Scott 245, 247
Macy, William H. 171, 174, **175**
Madison, Guy 37, 38, **41**
Madison, Leigh 117, 119

Magic in the Water 228, 274–277, 276, 432
Magic Island 73
The Magic World of Karel Zeman 145, 147
Magical Media Industries, Inc. 44, 47, 50, 52, 76; *see also* Buechler, John Carl
The Magnificent Ambersons 90
Maguire, Tom 350
Maher, Bill 131, 132
Mahoney, Jock 172, 214, 215, 217, 271
Maine, Robert 137, 138, 141
Maitre, Mark 368
Makeup & Effects Laboratories 367
Make-Up Effects Unlimited 275
Maki, Fuyukichi 223
The Making of Jurassic Park (book) 162
The Making of Jurassic Park (documentary) 162, 164, 170, 257
The Making of King Kong (book) 189, 192, 361, 438
The Making of The Lost World (book) 269, 272
Maley, Alan 422
Malone, Bill 313
Maltin, Leonard 93, 445
Man and His Mate see *One Million B.C.*
Mandell, Paul 14, 121, 123, 125, 127, 128, 129
Mandishona, Mary Ann 345
Mangini, Mark 27
Manning, Virgil 261, 264
Man's Genesis 44, 297
Manuelli, Pasqual 15
Manuli, Guido 11
Marathon Man 335
Marcus, Vitina 248
Marg, Tamia 131, 133
Margheriti, Antonella 427
Margheriti, Antonio (Tony) 427
Margheriti, Edward 427
Margolin, Stuart 125, 126, 127
Margulies, Julianna 67
Marino, Nick 312
Mark Williams Effects 65
Marmo, Malia Scotch 162
Marr, Mary 409
Mars, Kenneth 203, 205, 206, 207, 208, 411, 412
Mars Needs Women 232
Marsala, Michele 427
Marsden, Pam 67, 72, 74
Marsh, Mae 44
Marshall, Darah 373, 374
Marshall, Frank 200, 411
Marshall, William 82
Marshek, Archie 357, 361
Marston, John 357
Martell, Gregg 87, **88**, 89, 406, 409

Martin, Lottie 326
Martin, Sharon 336
Martindale, David 440
Martorana, Marc 7
Marx Brothers 85
Mary Poppins 356
Mason, James 147, 148, **150**, 152, 249, 424
Mason, Paul 450
Mason, Tyler 379
Massacre in Dinosaur Valley 432–433
Massey, Icel Dobell 274
The Master of Adventure 211
Mastrantonio, Mary Elizabeth 51
Masur, Richard 286
Matheson, Richard 442
Mathis, Samantha 365
Mativo, Kyalo 21, 22
Matsumoto, Isao 223
Matteson, Pam 333
Mattson, Robin 135
Mature, Victor 89, 295, 296, 298, 302, 415
Matuszak, John 54, 56
Maureen of Hollywood 409
May, Virginia 285
Maylone, Bill 356, 357
Mazzello, Joseph 157, 160, **161**, 270
McAfee, Anndi 205, 206, 207, 208
McAfee, Scott 203, 204
McAvoy, May 350
McBroom, Amanda 206, 207, 208
McCallum, David 198, 199
McCauley, Peter 257, 259
McCay, John 113
McCay, Winsor 113, 114, 239
McClory, Sean 379, 406, 408
McClure, Doug 17, **18**, 209, 210, 211, **212**, 307, 308, 309, **310**
McComas, Lorissa 340
McCormack, Eric 253, 254, 345
McCormick, Bret 379
McCreery, Mark "Crash" 176, 272
McDonald, Garry 259
McEnery, John 209, 210
McGee, Mark Thomas 376, 411, 427
McGillivray, David 214
McGoohan, Patrick 21, 22
McGrew, Bud 368
McHattie, Stephen 336, 337, 376
McKay, Molly 239
McKennon, Dallas 96, 337
McKenzie, Miki 230, 231, 232
McKenzie, Nicolette 302
McKinney, Austin 281
McManus, George 114
McMullen, Charles 129
McNair, Sue 129
McQueen, Steve 90
McVey, Tony 9, 10
McWade, Margaret 240
Meador, Josh 103

Meador, Philip 21, 286
Meddings, Derek 209, 210, 211, 213, 311
Medina, Patricia 37, 38, 135
Meister, Bob 282
Mejding, Bent 341
MEL *see* Makeup & Effects Laboratories
Melchior, Ib 153, 155, 341, 343, 344, 445
Méliès, Georges 155, 292
Melson, John 422
Melton, Sid 233, **235**
Men in Black 233
The Men Who Made the Monsters (book) 362, 385
Menasco, Milton 240
Mendoza, Peter 351
Mensik, Vladimir 292
Menville, Scott 204
Menzies, William Cameron 104
Mercer, Darren Peter 253, 254, 345
Mercer, Ray 233
Merrick, Doris 395, 397
Mesa of Lost Women 396
Mesce, Bill, Jr. 74
Metamorphosis 433
Metrolight Studios 112
Meyers, Fred 130
Michaels, Julie 93
Michelet, Michel 34
Micheli, Maurizio 11
Michelini, Mark 54
Microsoft Dinosaurs (CD-ROM) 326
Midnight Cowboy 398
Mier, Felipe 42
The Mighty Gorga 258, 277, 281, **278**, **280**, 294
Mighty Joe Young (1949) 15, 29, 34, 36, 60, 80, 98, 122, 124, 194, 195, 238, 281, 358, 373, 384, 403, 420, 445, 446
Mighty Joe Young (1998) 70, 108
The Mighty Kong 281–283, **282**
Miles, Hal 42, 65, 76, 78, **79**, 80, 81, 98, 378
Milestone Productions 76; *see also* Miles, Hal
Milland, Ray 385
Miller, George 151, 152
Miller, Linda 195
Miller, Marvin 179
Miller, Walter 196
Milligan, Tuck 380
Mills, Juliet 443
Mills, Samantha 327, **328**, 331, 335
Milne, Mike 264
Mimura, Wataru 452
Miranda, Soledad 363, **364**
Mission: Impossible (television series) 106
Mission to Mars 233

Mitchell, Jim 171, 176, 178
Mitchell, John 353
Mitchell, Joseph 378
Mitchell, Rick 436
Mitchum, Jim 283
Mixon, Bart J. 275
Mixon, Bret 65, 66, 312
Moby Dick 238
Moccia, Bruce 257
The Model Smiths 257, 259
Modern Film Effects 152, 277
Modern Mechanix and Inventions (magazine) 194
Moffett, Gregory 347
Mohan, Peter 257
The Mole People 217
Molen, Gerald R. 104, 157, 256, 270
Moll, Richard 56
Monahan, Richard 395
Monroe, Tom 386
Monroe, William 349
Monstascope 40
Monster 283–285, **284**
Monster from a Prehistoric Planet 17, 285
The Monster from Beneath the Sea (story) 31, 32
Monster! Illustrated (magazine) 20
Monster Island 424
The Monster That Challenged the World 237, 238
Monster Zero 450
Monsters of the Lost World 320
Monsters of the Past 285–286
Monstroid see *Monster*
Monstrosaurus! 442
El Monstruo de la Montaña Hueca see *The Beast of Hollow Mountain*
Montagna, Luigi see Montana, Bull
Montana, Bull 241, 242, 243, 432
Montgomery, Thomas 450
Monthly Film Bulletin 214
Moorcock, Michael 209, 210, 311
Moore, Connie 283
Moore, Dorenda 379
Moore, Dudley 282, 283
Moore, Julianne 265, 267, 270, **271**, **272**, 274
Moore, Robyn 432
Moore, Tom T. 379
Mora, Philippe 336
Moranis, Rick 104, **105**, 107
More, Julian 397
More, Kenneth 422, 424
Morell, Andre 117, 119, 121
Moreno, Jenaro 133
Moreno, Jose Elias 18
Morgan, Trevor 27, 171, 174
Morheim, Lou 28, 32
Morita, Pat 433
Morneau, Louis 50, 51, 52
Moross, Jerome 38, 400

Morpheus Mike 44
Morris, Colleen 327, 328
Morris, Glenn 373
Morrison, Bill 113
Morrison, Christine 113
Morrow, Jeff 157, 379
Morrow, Jo 444
Morton, Lisa 7
Morton, Rocky 365, 367
Mostel, Zero 68
Mothra 258
Motion Opticals, Inc. 92
The Motion Picture Guide (CD-ROM) 78, 406
Motohashi, Koichi 282
Moussorgsky, Modest 101
Movie Magic (book) 300
Movie Magic (television series) 26, 49, 247, 274, 302, 323, 368
Mrdzek, Ivo 142
Mueller-Stahl, Armin 376
Mulholland, Declan 209, **212**
Mulholland, Tony 261, 262
Mullen, Daniel J. 81
Munne, Pep 422
Muñoz, Antonio 133
Munro, Caroline 17
The Munsters (television series) 218
The Muppets' Christmas Carol 229
Murata, Takeo 449
Murders in the Rue Morgue 394
Murdoch, Laurie 380
Muren, Dennis 157, **164**, 166, 167, 169, 170, 176, 265, 271, 272, 273, 274, 316, 446, 447
Murphy, Barri Kay 379
Murphy, Karen 274
Murphy, Shawn 170
Murray, Bill 56, 76, 132
Murray, Doug 64
My Life in the Wild (book) 228
My Science Project 47, 286–289, **287**, **288**, 367, 377
My Work in Films (book) 29, 32, 120, 127, 128
Myers, T. J. 379
Mylong, John 347
Myron, Ben 27
Mysterious Island 76, 305, 416, 420, 440
Mystery of Life 289–290, **290**

N. A. Fisher Chemical Products 346
Na Kometě see *On the Comet*
Nader, George 347, **348**
Nadyezhin, Alexander 323, 324
Nagahara, Shuichi 451
Nagel, Conrad 295
Naha, Ed 338, 375
Naismith, Laurence 398, 400, 404
Nakaishi, Ryuzo 285
Nakamura, Tetsu 220
Nakano, Teruyoshi 451

Naked Gun 33⅓—The Final Insult 433
The Naked Jungle 154
Naples, Toni 76
Nark-Orn, Willie 275
Nascimbene, Mario 296, 301, 302, 415
Nassour, Edward 37, 40, 42, 96, 98, 441
Nassour, Edward, Jr. 42
Nassour, William 37, 40, 42, 96, 98
National Geographic (magazine) 99, 392
National Lampoon's Vacation 138
The Natural History Project 442
Navarro, Mario 37
Nazarian, Bruce 368
Nazir, Philip 388
Nearly Eighteen 397
Necci, Michael 384
Neill, Sam 157, **159**, 160, **161**, 162, 163, 171, 174
Neill, Steve 60, 62
Nelson, Dave 368
Nelson, Kimberly K. 433
Nerman, David 256, 257
Nessie 228, 442
Neufeld, Sigmund 233
The Neverending Story 422
Nevius, Craig 76
The New Poverty Row (book) 66, 131, 155, 279, 281, 313, 410
New York American (newspaper) 114
New York Herald (newspaper) 114
New York Post (newspaper) 203
New York Telegram (newspaper) 114
New York Times (newspaper) 40, 298
Newbern, George 376
Newfield, Samuel 233, 237
Newman, Laraine 106
Newman, Richard 282
Newman, Samuel 155
Newmeyer, Fred 350
Newsom, Ted 32, 304, 379, 404
Ney, Henry 409
Nibbelink, Phil 411, 413
Niblock, Victor 318
Nichetti, Maurizio 11
Nichols, Dudley 190
Nicholson, James H. 313, 373
Nielsen, Leslie 105, 433
Nieves Conde, José Antonio 363, 364
Night of the Blood Beast 375
Night of the Demon 391
The Night of the Hunter 90
A Night to Remember 199
The Nightmare Before Christmas 73
Nightview Productions 349
Nigro, Carmen 194

Niles, Wendell 96
Nilsson, Anna Q. 7
Nipar, Yvette 93, 94
Nivola, Alessandro 171
No Strings Attached (book) 108, 229
Noah's Ark 246
Noguchi, Haruyasu 285
Nohotu, Tamati Te 261
Noriega, Edward (Eduardo) 37, 38, 39, **41**
Norton, B. W. L. 21, 22, 23, **24**, 27
Norton, Rosanna 106
Nosseck, Martin 96, 98
Nostradamus 140
Nova (television series) 2
Novak, Frank 340
Novak, Mickell 295, 301
Novello, Jay 248
Now You Tell One 378
Nunez, Miguel A., Jr. 50, 51
Nutter, Mark 379
Nye, Ben 379
A Nymphoid Barbarian in Dinosaur Hell 75, 290–291, **291**

O'Brien, Austin 327, **328**, 329, **330**, 331, 335
O'Brien, Darlyne 98, 362
O'Brien, George 103
O'Brien, Willis H. 12, 14, 15, 16, 29, 34, 37, 38, 40, 41, 42, 44, 65, 70, 74, 91, 98, 99, 112, 115, 116, 117, 118, 119, 120, 121, 122, 123, 174, 183, 186, 187, 188, 189, 191, 192, 194, 195, 211, 237, 240, 242, 243, 245, 246, 247, 248, 249, 251, 252, 269, 283, 289, 293, 326, 338, 339, 350, 357, 362, 363, 373, 398, 402, 403, 404, 419, 422, 435, 436, 438, 439, 445, 446
O'Connell, Arthur 354, 355, 356
O'Connolly, James 397, 404
O'Connor, Matthew 274
O'Conor, Joseph 123
Oda, Motoyoshi 449
Odd, David 263
O'Dell, Jennifer 258, **260**
O'Donnell, Rosie 104, 105, 110
Oelze, Charles 299, 300
Of Mice and Men (1939) 298
Off on a Comet (novel) 151, 292, 406, 408
Ogawa, Toshihiro 452
Ohashi, Fuminori 223
Ohkubu, Kinshiro 220
Okawara, Takao 452
The Old Dark House (1932) 243
Olsen, Tracy 152, 153, **154**
Omori, Kazuki 452
On the Comet 292–294, **293**
On the Other Hand (book) 188

On the Town 433
On the Wing 256
Ondrejko, Danny 176
101 Dalmatians (1996) 229
One Million AC/DC 294, 300
One Million B.C. 4, 20, 55, 83, 112, 130, 133, 134, 136, 137, 155, 156, 157, 181, 217, 234, 236, 237, 238, 249, 270, 294, 295–300, **296**, **297**, **298**, **299**, 301, 302, 304, 305, 307, 320, 324, 340, 347, 349, 353, 373, 374, 379, 387, 388, 392, 395, 397, 407, 408, 409, 432, 440
One Million Years B.C. 14, 56, 68, 76, 78, 81, 82, 160, 172, 206, 258, 296, 301–307, **303**, **306**, **307**, 311, 320, 402, 406, 415, 417, 419, 434, J
One of Our Dinosaurs Is Missing 433
O'Neil, Nancy 350
O'Neil, Robert H. 277
Ordung, Wyott 346
Orme, Stuart 261, 263
Orosco, Joey 176
Osborne, Aaron 44
Otsu, Ichiro 223
Ottosen, Carl 341
Out of Time's Abyss (novel) 311
The Outer Limits (television series) 86
Outré (magazine) 323
Overgard, William 220
Oz, Frank 432

Page, Harrison 44, 45, 340
Page, Joanna 261, 262
Paige, Harrison *see* Page, Harrison
Paine, Heidi 65
Painter, Paul 257
Pal, David 91, 356
Pal, George 38, 42, 85, 91, 129, 160, 337, 338, 354, 355, 356
Palange, Inez 295
Palmer, Charles 214
Palmer, Michael 50, 51
Palo, Alan 332
Panettiere, Hayden 67, 69
Panther Girl of the Kongo 238
Panych, Morris 275
Paper Moon 410
Parker, Charles 384, 385
Parker, Phyllis 386
Parker, Tom S. 104
Parks, Peter 253, 255, 256, 345
Parr, Bobby 209
Parrish, Lee 277
A Passage to India 353
Passer, Dirch 341, 342
Pathé Review 285
Patterson, Rocky 379
Paul, Gregory 84, 164
Paul, Richard Joseph 443

Paulsen, Rob 203, 204, 205, 207, 208
Paulson, Pamela 347
Paunescu, Oana 137, 138
Paunescu, Vlad 137, 138
Payeur, Gregorian Minot 256, 257
Payne, Alexander 171, 174
Payne, Sam 356
Peck, Anthony 52
Peck, Bob 157, 160
Pee-Wee's Big Adventure 433
Peerless Camera Company 225, 229
Peisley, Frederick 350
Pellucidar 442–443
Pena, Pascuel Garcia 37
Penhaligon, Susan 209, 210, 211
Pennick, Jack 28, **31**
Pennington, Chuck 313
The People That Time Forgot 17, 18, 56, 199, 209, 211, 307–312, **309**, **310**, **311**
Perils of Nyoka 394
Perkins, Elizabeth 104
Perkins, Gil 406
Perpetual Motion Pictures 112
Perreau, Gigi 152, 153, 154
Perry, Ted 96
Peterson, Pete 117, 119, 120, 121, 122, 123
Pete's Dragon 202
Petroff, Boris 386, 388
Petroff, Gloria 386, 387, **388**
Petru, J. 292
Pettigrew, Neil 3, 94, 131, 132, 186, 291, 304, 316, 406, 449
Peverall, John 209
The Phantom Empire (1935) 313
The Phantom Empire (1986) 66, 78, 312–313, 320
Phantom from Space 364
The Phantom Planet 321
Philbrook, James 363, **364**
The Philips Broadcast of 1938 337
Philips Cavalcade 337
Phillips, Sean 380, 384
Phillips, Zoe 129
Photo Adventures (magazine) 156
Photon VFX (Photon Visual Effects) 151, 257, 259
Photoplay (magazine) 378
Picker, David 151
Pickett, Fawn 396
Pickhart, F. 292
Pickles, Christina 205, 206
Pierce, Arthur C. 425, 427
Pierce, Jack 392
Pill, Alison 432
Pink, Sidney 341, 343, 344, 345
Pinky and the Brain (television series) 203
Pinocchio (1940) 103
Piper, Brett 74, 75, 290, 291, 436, 437, 438, 442

Piquer, Francisco 363
Piquer, John 422
Pirnie, Alex 290
Pitt, Ingrid 363, **364**
Planet of Dinosaurs 10, 54, 61, 66, 78, 113, 285, 289, 312, 313–320, **315**, **317**, **319**, 336, 379, 380
Planet of Storms see *Planeta Burg*
Planet of the Apes (1968) 26, 113
Planet Patrol 95, 96
Planeta Burg 320–324, **322**, 409, 410, 411
Platt, Polly 410
Playboy (magazine) 408, 417
Playboy Channel 83
Plívová-Simková, Vera 432
Ploog, Mike 57
Plowright, Joan 67, 69
Plumb, Edward H. 100
Plummer, Christopher 432
Police Squad (television series) 433
Pollard, Michael J. 88
Polonia, John 349
Polonia, Mark Alan 349
Poltergeist 101
Pomeroy, John 200, 202
Ponchielli, Amilcare 101
Portillo, Rafael 133
Postlethwaite, Pete 265, 267
Poston, Tiffanie 7
Potter, Hetty 326
The Power 60
Powers, Bruce 130
Prancer 275
Pratt, Kyla 27
Prehistoric Beast 165, 324–326, **325**, **357**
The Prehistoric Man 326
Prehistoric Peeps 326
Prehistoric Poultry 326
Prehistoric Valley see *Valley of the Dragons*
Prehistoric Women (1950) 290, 392
Prehistoric Women (1967) 305
Prehistoric World see *Teenage Caveman*
Prehysteria 68, 76, 94, 141, 327–331, **328**, **330**, 333
Prehysteria 2 94, 331–333, 335
Prehysteria 3 54, 333–336, **334**
Premiere (magazine) 271
Prentiss, David 152, 277, 279
Presley, Priscilla 433
Presnyakova, L. 320
Priestly, Robert 388, 394
Primal Species see *Carnosaur 3: Primal Species*
The Primevals 95, 141, 443–444, 446, 447
Primordium: The Arctic World see *Zeppelin v. Pterodactyls*
Prior, Allan 196

The Private Life of Sherlock Holmes 227
Pro FX 257, 259
Prochazka, Jan 292
Project Unlimited 60, 86, 91, 92, 281, 338, 355, 356
Prosper, Frank 422
Prowse, David 309
Prudkovskii 323
Psychotronic Encyclopedia of Film (book) 406
Pterodactyl Woman from Beverly Hills 320, 336–337
Puerto, Charles 422
Pufnstuf & Other Stuff (book) 440
Punch (magazine) 326
The Puppetoon Movie 337–339
Puppetoons 38, 337, 338, 339
Puppets and People (book) 38, 191, 404
Pycha, Jerome, Jr. 388

Q 4, 59
Quaid, Dennis 54, 56
Quarry, Robert 312, 313
Quarshie, Hugh 21
Queen (musical group) 429
Queen of Blood 323, 411
Quentin, John 198
Quest for Fire 4, 71
Quincy (television series) 426
Quirk, James R. 378

Rabelais, François 395
Rabin, Jack 37, 40, 42, 117, 122, 123, 346
Rackley, Luther 220
Rader, Paul 96
Rae, Ted 289
Raffill, Diane 368
Raffill, Stewart 368, 370
Raguse, Elmer 300
Raiders of the Lost Ark 102
Raiders of the Stone Ring see *Zeppelin v. Pterodactyls*
Raimi, Sam 131
Rains, Claude 17, 248, 249
Rakoff, Alvin 196, 199
Ralston, Ken 444
Rambaldi, Carlo 26
Rambling Rose 162
Ramis, Harold 76
Ramsey, Ward 86, 88
Randa, Cestmir 292
Randall, Tony 354, 355
Randas, Lance 113
Randel, Anthony 451
Rankin, Arthur, Jr. 195, 220
Raponi, Isidoro 21, 23, **25**, 26, 27
Rappaport, Mark A. 95, 137, 138, 327, 331, 332, 333
Raptor 339–340
Rathbone, Basil 410, 411
Ratzenberger, John 131, 132
Ravel, Maurice 11

Ravenscroft, Thurl 96
Ray, Fred Olen 54, 65, 66, 67, 76, 78, 79, 80, 83, 131, 155, 279, 281, 312, 313, 320, 410
Ray, Harrison 82
Raymond, Paula 28, 29, **31**, 34
Re-Animator 94
Reason, Rhodes 195
Rebello, Stephen 287
Rector, Jeff 82
Red River 68
Redford, Robert 441
Redgrave, Vanessa 228
Redlin, Bill 153
Reed, Philip 388, 390, **391**
Reese, Della 67, 69
Reese, Fred 183, 193, 357
Reeve, Christopher 326
Regiscope 38, 40, 41
Reichek, Jordan 9
Reicher, Frank 183, 357, 359, 361
Reid, Milton 307
Reiff, Ethan 137, 138
Reisch, Walter 147, 149
Reiser, Paul 51
Reitherman, Wolfgang 70
The Relic 384
Remark, John F. 336
Rendu, Carolyn 108
Rennie, Michael 248, 249
Renoir, Jean 34
Reptilicus 4, 53, 82, 278, 341–345, **341**, **343**, **344**, 451
The Rescuers 202
The Return of Chandu 190
Return of the Fly 408
Return of the Jedi 23, 60, 311, 325, 326
Return to Mayberry 275
Return to Oz 311
Return to The Lost World 255, 345–346, **346**
Reubens, Paul 433
Reynolds, James C. 390, 392
Reynolds, William 214, 215
R.F.D. 10,000 B.C. 339
Rhoades, Arthur 12, 15
Rhodes, Christopher 123
Rhys, Matthew 261, 262
Rhys-Davies, John 253, 254, 255, 345, 346
Rhythm & Hues 109, 112
Rice, Diana 27
Richard, Viola 112
Richards, Ariana 157, **159**, 160, **161**, 163, **166**, 169, 270
Richards, Denise 368, **369**, 370
Richardson, Jay 65
Richardson, Joely 225, 227, 228
Richardson, John (actor) 89, 301, 302, **303**, 305, 415
Richardson, John (special effects) 307, 311
Richichi, Salvatore 312
Riedel, Richard H. 215

Ries, Irving 403
Rifkin, Jay 336
Riley, Joe 379
Rimmer, Shane 307, 309
Rinehard, Paul M. 312
Ring Around Saturn see *Emilio and His Magical Bull*
Riss, Don 387
Rivas, Carlos 37, 38
The River's Edge 45
Roach, Hal 112, 133, 134, 295, 298, 299, 300, 302, 304, 388
Roach, Hal, Jr. 295, 298, 299
The Road to Bali 394
Roberts, Alan 86, **88**, 89
Roberts, Bill 99, 103
Roberts, Byron 406
Roberts, Eric 340
Roberts, Glenn 60
Robinson, Edward G. 190
Robles, Walter 409
Robocop 4, 70, 106, 139, 165, 433, 437
Robot Monster 179, 238, 300, 346–349, **348**, **349**, 394, 395, 397
Robson, William N. 214
Rocchi, Marina 427
Rochfort, Spencer 137, 138, 139
The Rocketeer 172
Rocketship XM 236, 237
The Rockford Files (television series) 426
Rockne, Knute 387
Rodan 409, 449–450
Rodine, Ralph 91, 354
Rodriguez, Ismael 37, 40
Rogell, Sid 251
Rogers, Jean 432
Rojo, Gustavo 398
Roman, Julie 324
Romero, Cesar 233, **235**, 237, 284
Ronson, Peter 147
Roop, J. L. 239, 240, 247
Rose, Lenny 54
Rose, Ruth 183, 187, 190, 357, 359, 360
Rosenbaum, Jonathan 214
Rosenberg, Jeanne 380
Rosenberg, Max J. 208, 211, 307, 311, 443
Rosengrant, John 176, 177
Rosmer, Milton 350, 351, 352
Ross, Dev 203, 204
Ross, Harry 394
Ross, William (composer) 382
Ross, William (writer) 285
Rossner, Danny 256
Rothacker, Watterson R. 240, 243
Rothman, Stephanie 410
Roundtree, Richard 376, 378
Rowley, Jim 27
Royale, Selena *see* Royle, Selena
Royle, Selena 347, 348
Rozkopal, Zdenek 142
Rozsa, Miklos 400

Rubin, Stanley 440
Rubinskis, Wolf 42
Ein Ruckblic in die Urwelt 349
Rudolph the Red-Nosed Reindeer (television) 96
Ruiz, Emilio 422
Rulers of the Apocalypse 444
Runté, Terry 365
Runyon, Jennifer 44, 45, 47
Russel, Loris S. 356
Russell, Jack 30
Russell, Kurt 162
Russom, Leon 443
Ruttenberg, Neil 333
Ryan, Lata 157, 164
Ryan, Sheila 155, **156**
Ryan, Will 200
Rybnick, Harry L. 395, 397, 449
Rydstrom, Gary 170

Sacristan, Gregorio 363
The Saga of Special Effects (book) 238
Sagawa, Kazuo 220
Sage, William, III 282
Sahlin, Don 91
St. Amand, Tom 167, 170, 178, 326, 444
St. John, Jill 248, 249
St. Pierre, Leopold 256
Salazar, Alfredo 133
Salsedo, Frank Sotonoma 275
Sandell, William 106
Sandin, Scott 52
Santiago, Cirio H. 433
Saperstein, Henry G. 450, 451
Sarantsev, Yuri 320
Sarg, Tony 7, 104
Sargent, Joseph 441
Sarlui, Etka 368
Satterfield, Paul 99, 103
Saturday Evening Post (magazine) 28, 31, 32
Saurians 179, 349–350
Savage, John 50, 51
The Savage 350
Savage Harvest 182
Sawa, Nobiko 223
Sawtell, Paul 251, 373
Sawyer, Joe 370, 372
Sayre, George W. 395, 396
Sayre, Rick 167
Sbarge, Raphael 44, 45, 47, 286
Le Scarabée d'or 155
Scardino, Hal 432
Scars of Dracula 422
Scheele, John 25, 26, 286, 288, 289
Scheele, William 25, 26
Schenck, Joseph 378
Scherman, Tom 60, 83, 444
Schickel, Richard 44, 298
Schiff, Richard 265, 267
Schifrin, Lalo 56
Schindler's List 271

Schmid, Alfred 395, 397
Schmidt, Walter Roeber 283
Schneer, Charles H. 228, 305, 397, 404, 445, 446
Schoedsack, Ernest B. 183, 185, 186, 187, 188, 189, 190, 357, 360, 362, 438
Schoell, William 149
Schreiber, Avery 54
Schreibman, Paul 449
Schubert, Franz 101
Schüfftan, Eugen 354
Schüfftan process 354
Schwarzenegger, Arnold 329
Sci-Fi Entertainment Magazine 152
Scofield, Dean 332
Scott, Art 282
Scott, Elliott 126
Scott, Eric 230
Scott, Garland 283
Scott, John 310
Scott, Peter 442
Scourby, Alexander 149
Screamers 141
The Sea Around Us 14
The Sea Serpent 385
Seagal, Steven 125
Seawright, Roy 295, 299, 300
Sebastian, John *see* Harrington, Curtis
The Secret Lab 72
The Secret of Life on Earth 256
The Secret of Nimh 202
The Secret of the Loch 88, 137, 228, 251, 299, 350–354, **353**
Secrets of a Co-Ed 397
Segal, Peter 433
Sekizawa, Shinichi 450, 451
Seldon, Nick 444
Selznick, David O. 105, 183, 188, 360
Semand, Britt 130
Senn, Bryan 352
Senter, Jack 91
Sentis, Yvonne 422, 424
Setena, Bedřich 142
Seton, Bruce 123
7 Faces of Dr. Lao 60, 275, 354–356, **355**, 415, 441
The 7th Voyage of Sinbad 36, 121, 305
Shain, Harvey 313, 318, 379
Shaklin, Aleks 336
Shanley, John Patrick 411
Shannon, Robert T. 388, 392
Shapiro, Marc 46, 63, 162, 175, 305, 367, 442
Sharp, Henry 42, 96, 98
Sharpsteen, Ben 100
Shaver, Helen 200
Shaw, Bill 387
Shaw, Fiona 365
Shaw, Jack 439
Shaw, Sandra 190
Shawn, Wallace 433

Shay, Don 38, 40, 98, 245, 362, 435, 436, 439, 445, 446
She (1935) 198
She (1965) 305, 417
The She Creature 376
She Demons 300
Shea, James K. 313, 316, 379
Shea, Joey 411
Sheedy, Ally 434
Sheen, Darryl 257
Sheffield, Johnny 370, **371**, 372
Shefter, Bert 251
Shell, Tom 76, 77, **80**
Shepard, David 245, 247
Shepphird, Carroll 183, 192, 357
Sheridan, Bob 76, 78
Sherlock Holmes and the Speckled Band (play) 251
Sherman, Richard M. 283
Sherman, Robert B. 283
Sherman, Sam 130
Shiba, Kazue 450
Shields, Malcolm 263, 264
Shinnick, Kevin G. 75, 291
Shirley, Anne 403, 439
Short, Martin 411, 413, 432
Shostak, Murray 256
Shubert, Lynn 230
Sibelius, Jean 11
Sibley, Gretchen 9
Siderow, Norman 253, 345
Siegel, Mark 60, 62
Sills, Milton 7
Silvestre, Armando 133
Simon, Adam 44, 46, 47, 50
Simon, J. Piquer 422, 424
Simon, Mel 444
Simonds, Walter M. 251, 253
Sinatra, Frank 186, 433
Sinbad and the Eye of the Tiger 4, 309
Sinelnikoff, Michael 256, 257, 258, 259
The Sir Arthur Conan Doyle's The Lost World (1998) see Lost World (1998)
The Sir Arthur Conan Doyle's The Lost World (1999) see Lost World (1999)
Siragusa, Peter 67, 69
64,000,000 Years Ago 356–357
Skotak, Dennis 323, 432
Skotak, Robert 237, 238, 323, 432
Slave Girls see Prehistoric Women (1967)
The Sleeping Beauty 337
Smiles, Finch 240
Smith, Douglas Hans 109
Smith, Roy Allen 203, 204
Smith, Sebastian 326
Smith, Shaun 331
Smith, Shawn 214, 215, **216**, 217
Smith, Tom 71, 325, 437
Smith, Yeardley 411
Smyrner, Ann **341**

Smythe, Ernest 435, 436
Snow, William 258, 259
Snow White 202
Snyder, David L. 367
Snyder, Suzanne 432
Sofaer, Abraham 152, 153, 154
Solares, Gilberto Martinez 42
Solares, Raul Martinez 20
Solis, Javier 18
Solomon, Ed 365
Solotoff, Rocky 205
Son of Godzilla 450
The Son of Kong 56, 190, 192, 234, 249, 279, 299, 357–363, **359**, **361**, **362**, 438, 446
El Sonido de la Muerte see Sound of Horror
Sopkiw, Michael 432, 433
Sotomayor, Jaime 18
Sound from a Million Years Ago see Sound of Horror
Sound of Horror 162, 363–365, **364**
South Sea Sweethearts 337
Soylent Green 238
Space Mission to the Lost Planet see Horror of the Blood Monsters
Space Monster 321
Space Ship Sappy 300
Space Trek (magazine) 64
Speaker, Dan 65
Speaks, John 403, 439
Special Effects — Wire, Tape and Rubber Band Style (book) 149, 251
Species X 441
Speer, Charlotte 313
Spellos, Peter 76, 77
Spencer, Karen L. 54, 333
Spevack, Melodee M. 81
SPFX (magazine) 75, 291, 437, 439, 441, 443, 447
The Spider 182
Spielberg, Steven 2, 71, 106, 157, 158, 160, 161, 162, 163, 164, 165, 167, 169, 170, 171, 175, 176, 200, 202, 203, 223, 265, 267, 269, 270, 271, 272, 273, 274, 325, 329, 372, 411, 412, 413, 441
Spiva, Tam 135
Spivack, Murray 170, 183, 187, 194, 357, 361, 363
Spottiswoode, Roger 23
Sprunck, Paul 395, 397
Spry, Robin 257
Stader, Paul 299
Stahl, Jorge 38
Stahl, Rudolf 292
Stairway to Heaven 154
Staley, Joan 406, **407**, 408, 409
Stan Winston Studio 165, 176, 268, 273; see also Winston, Stan
Stanford, Nathania 253, 254, 258, 345, 346

Stanley, John 130, 406
Star Spangled War Stories (comic book) 78
Star Trek (television series) 86, 335
Star Trek IV: The Voyage Home 153
Star Wars 64, 66, 165, 309, 310, 377, 429, 443
Starevitch, Ladislas 34
Stark, Jonathan 131
Starlog (magazine) 34, 46, 72, 251, 283, 338, 352, 367
Starman 60
Starr, Ringo 54, 56–58, 89
Starship Troopers 165, 270, 311, 370
Stauber, Liz **380**, 381, 382, **383**, 384
Steers, Larry 196
Stein, Ronald 411
Steiner, John 427, 429
Steiner, Max 185, 187, 188, 189, 361, 441
Stell, Guillermo Calderon 133
Stephani, Frederick 432
Stephens, C. D. 379
Stephenson, John 104
Stevens, Fisher 286, 365, 367
Stevens, W. L. 295, 296
Stevenson, Jack 345
Stevenson, Rick 274, 275, 432
Stevenson, Robert 433
Stevenson, William 274
Stewart, Rod 333
Stine, Clifford 193, 214, 217
Stipes, David 54, 443
Stockwell, John 286
Stokey, Susan 71
Stokowski, Leopold 100, 102
Stone, F. Lee 432
Stone, Lawrence 259
Stone, Lewis 240, 242
Stone, Sharon 106, 199, 328
A Stone Age Adventure 114
The Stop-Motion Filmography (book) 131, 186, 304, 316, 406, 449
Storm, John 12
Storm Planet see Planeta Burg
Stormare, Peter 265
The Story of a Mosquito 114
Stout, William 72, 442
Stravinsky, Igor 11, 100, 103, 438
Strawberries Need Rain 232
Streep, Meryl 166
Strickfadden, Kenneth 432
Stricklyn, Ray 248
Stripes 76, 77
Strock, Herbert L. 283, 285, 312
Stromberg, William R. 60, 61, 62, 63, 65
Stroud, Don 50
Stuart, Michael 9
Studio Film Services 122

Subotsky, Milton 17, 208, 211, 443, 444
Subspecies 95
Suddeth, Greg 327, 329
Sullivan, Mark 131, 133
A Summer Place 126
Summers, Gary 170
Super-Dynamation 36
Super Mario Bros. 76, 286, 365–368, **366**, **368**, 377, 413
Superman (1948 serial) 300
Superman (1978) 211
Superman (character) 32
Sutherland, John 85
Suzichi, Johnny 349
Suzuki, Kenji 452
Sweeney, D. B. 67, 69
Swerdlow, Harry B. 449
The Swiss Family Robinson 136, 259
Switzer, Bill 432
Sylvester, William 123, 125, 128

Tagoe, Eddie 21
Tait, Kenneth 305
Takarada, Akira 195
Takayama, Yukiko 451
Talbot, Lyle 155, 156, 157, 395
Talbott, Hudson 411, 413
Tallas, Gregg 363
Tamblyn, Russ 65, 312, 313
Tammy and the T-Rex 368–370, **369**, 378
Tanaka, Fumio 451
Tanaka, Tomoyuki 195, 449, 450, 451, 452
Tantin, Roland 21, 27
Taplin, Jonathan T. 21, 23, 25, 286, 287, 288
Tarantula 217
Tarzan and His Mate 194
Tarzan at the Earth's Core (novel) 371
Tarzan the Fearless 373
Tarzan the Terrible (novel) 371
Tarzan Triumphs 373
Tarzan's Desert Mystery 156, 157, 237, 300, 370–373, **371**, **372**, 408
Tarzan's Revenge 373
Tatopoulos, Patrick 367, 368
Taus, Tom, Jr. 433
Taxi Driver 45
Taylor, Bill 444
Taylor, Dan 171, 176, 178
Taylor, Deems 100, 101, 103
Taylor, Elizabeth 104, 105
Taylor, J. O. 361
Taylor, Jack 422
Taylor, Jim (actor) 379
Taylor, Jim (writer) 171, 174
Taylor, John 356
Taylor, Kent 277
Tchaikovsky, Peter Ilyich 100

Technicolor 14, 100, 118, 385, 403, 433, 436, 441, 445
The Technique of Special Effects Cinematography (book) 387
Teegarden, Jim 106
Teenage Caveman 92, 207, 294, 300, 373–376, **374**, **375**, 395, 408, 434
The Teenage Mutant Ninja Turtles 9
Teikh, Georgi 320
Telmig, Akdon 294
The Terminator 60, 164
Terminator 2: Judgment Day 51, 60, 80, 164, 166, 167, 281, 323, 452
Terror of Mechagodzilla 451
Terzioglu, Ugur 427
Testament 45
Tezuka, Masaaki 452
Thai, Tai 443
Thayer, Michael 313
Them! 13
Theodore Rex 376–378, **377**
The Thief of Bagdad (1940) 104, 300
Thiele, William 370
The Thing (1982) 60
The Thing from Another World 32, 387
This Island Earth 217, 410
Thomas, Derek *see* Bogdanovich, Peter
Thomas, Lisa 301
Thompson, Brett 7
Thompson, Brian 93
Thonen, John 93, 94
Thorne, Dianne 74
Thornton, J. Max 152
Thorpe, Jim 190
Thorpe, Richard 196
Three Ages 243, 378
Three Stooges 160, 300
The Three Worlds of Gulliver 305
Threlkeld, William T. 74
Threshold Digital Research Labs 112
Thunderbirds (television series) 420
Tickner, Clive 227
Tierney, Lawrence 65, 66
Tilley, Patrick 307, 311
Time (magazine) 103, 194
Time After Time 153
The Time Machine (1960) 153, 312
Time Tracers 316, 320, 378–380
The Time Travelers 153, 154, 155
The Time Tunnel (television series) 253
Time Warp see Journey to the Center of Time
Timegate 444–445
Timemaster 433
Timothy, Megan 277, 279, 281

Timpone, Anthony 237
Tin-Tan *see* Valdés, Germán
Tippett, Phil 62, 63, 64, 65, 70, 71, 131, 133, 157, 160, 162, 164, 165, 166, 167, **168**, 169, 170, 171, 184, 186, 194, 270, 273, 288, 316, 324, **325**, 326, 357, 437, 444
Titanic (1953) 149
Titanic (1997) 69, 190, 384
Tkach, Cheryl A. 171
To the Devil, a Daughter 442
Tobey, Kenneth 28, 29, 32, 34, 61, 444
Tobyansen, Peter 270
Together in the Weather 337, 338
tom thumb 91, 129
The Tomb 313
Tomei, Lisa 451
Tomiyama, Shogo 452
Toms, Carl 417
The Tonight Show (television) 57
El Toro Estrella see Emilio and His Magical Bull
Tors, Ivan 135, 136, 228
Total Recall 106
Towers, Harry Alan 196, 199, 253, 255, 345
Towler, Jim 432
The Toxic Horror see Monster
The Toxic Monster see Monster
Toy Story 329, 433
Toy Story 2 433
Trail of the Hell-Beast 440
Trani, Maurizio 433
Tranter, Jane 261
Travers, Bill 123, 125, 128
Trcic, Michael 384
Tredway, Wayne 87
Tremont, David 259, 260, 261
T-Rex: Back to the Cretaceous 69, 380–384, **380**, **383**
Trog 17, 43, 384–386, **386**
Troiano, William G. 130
Tron 25
Trotter, Kathi 74, 75
Trousdale, Gary 289
Tsu, Irene 135, **425**
Tsuburaya, Eiji 195, 196, 449, 450, 451
Tsuburaya, Noboru 220
Tsybasov, M. 320
Tubby the Tuba 337
Tucker, Phil 347, 348–349, 397
Tucker, Richard 196
Tulips Shall Grow 337, 338
Turman, Lawrence 54, 57
Turner, Colin 196
Turner, George E. 246, 363, 436, 438
Turner, John 117, 119
Turner, Terry 449
Tuttle, William 354, 355, 356
Twelve Monkeys 229
20 Million Miles to Earth 319, 394, 406

The Twilight Zone (television series) 92, 207, 374
Twins F/X II 256
Twister 267
Two Lost Worlds 300, 386–388, **388**, 390, 394, **N**
2001: A Space Odyssey 421

Uhley, Len 207
Ujlaki, Stephen 225, 228
Ulmer, Edgar G. 439
Under Age 232
Unknown Island 20, 130, 157, 210, 257, 278, 294, 298, 374, 388–395, **390**, **391**, **393**, **394**, 429, 449, **C**
Unkrich, Lee 433
Unsain, Jose Maria Fernandez 18
Untamed Women 76, 179, 300, 378, 395–397, **396**, **L**
Upton, Mike 50
Ustinov, Peter 433

Vail, Justina 52, 53
Valdés, Germán 42, 43, 44
Valdez, Adam 167
Valentine, Scott (actor) 52, 53
Valentine, Scott (writer) 57
Valentine, Tom 230, 231, 233
The Valley of Gwangi 1, 14, 37, 38, 70, 124, 125, 158, 172, 259, 268, 269, 307, 315, 397–406, **399**, **401**, **403**, **405**, 417, 419, 439, **G**
Valley of the Dragons 40, 151, 292, 300, 312, 340, 379, 406–409, **407**, **408**, 429, 450
Valley of the Mist 15, 98, 445
Vallin, Rick 155, **156**
Vampire Men of the Lost Planet see *Horror of the Blood Monsters*
Van Ark, Joan 220, 221
Vander Hoff, Marjorie 436
Vander Pyl, Jean 106
Van Doren, Mamie 409
Van Hise, James 38, 406
Van Horn, Emil 394
Varan the Unbelievable 450
Variety (periodical) 105
Vasaryova, Magda 292
Vasquez, Laura 258
Vaughn, Robert 207, 373, 374, 375, 376, 433, 434
Vaughn, Terri J. 52
Vaughn, Vince 265, 274
Vellacott, Randy 151
Verhoeven, Paul 70, 71, 165, 433, 437
Verne, Jules 147, 148, 149, 151, 155, 292, 294, 406, 408, 422, 424, 440
Vernov, Gennadi 320
Verrall, Paul 261
Verreaux, Ed 176

Vetri, Victoria 56, 408, 414, 415, **416**, 417, 436
Vidon, Henry 117
Vidor, King 190
Village of the Giants 182
Villarreal, Julio 37
Vinton, Will 437
Virgin Islands, U.S.A. 90
Virtuosity 382
VistaVision 72
Vivaldi, Antonio 11
Vogel, Virgil 214, 216, 217, 218, 219, 220
Volante, Vicki 130
The Volcano Monsters 445
von Eltz, Theodore 12
Von Sholly, Andrea 71, 327, 328, 329
Von Sholly, Peter 327, 329, 332, 333, 335
Von Stroheim, Erich 352
Von Zerneck, Danielle 286
Voris, Cyrus 137, 138
Voyage à la Planète Jupiter 155
Voyage to the Bottom of the Sea (television series) 253, 352
Voyage to the Planet of Prehistoric Women 323, 340, 409–410
Voyage to the Prehistoric Planet 323, 409, 410–411
Vulcan 433–434

Waggoner, Lyle 65, 66
Wagner, Richard 51
Waite, James R. 313, 316, 317
Wakefield, Simon 311
Walas, Chris 131, 133
Waldman, Drew 65
Waldman, Grant Austin 65, 66
Walker, H. M. 112
Walker, Ken 81
Walker, Paul 368
Walker, Vernon L. 193, 240, 246, 361
Walking with Dinosaurs (television documentary) 70, 264, 384
Wallace, Edgar 183, 189, 190
Walshaw, Julia 264
Walt Disney's Fantasia (book) 70, 102
Walters, Thorley 307, **309**, 385
War Eagles 439, 445–446
War of the Colossal Beast 182
Ward, Tom 261, 262
Ware, Midge 395
Wargames 307, 434
Warlords of Atlantis 211, 422
Warner, David 253, 254, 345
Warren, Bill 32, 72, 82, 149, 329, 331, 397, 440
Warren, Gene 60, 86, 91, 338, 356, 439
Warren, Gene, Jr. 275, 277, 337, 339, 377, 432

Warrington, Bill 199
The Warriors of Mordium see *Zeppelin v. Pterodactyls*
Watanabe, Akira 285
Watase, Tsunehiko 223
Waterfield, Bob 155, **156**
Watership Down 68
Waterworld 233
Wathen, Stephen C. 313
Watkins, Pierre 386
Watson, Bill 434
Wayne, John 38, 68, 268
Wayne, Patrick 231, 307, **309**
Wayne, Sarah 275, **276**
Weatherup, James 199
Weaver, Judith 108
Weaver, Tom 34, 89, 90, 91, 121, 128, 154, 217, 251, 279, 283, 284, 285, 343, 352, 408
Webster, Derek 137, 138
Weinlein, Thad 411
Weis, Michael 383
Weisburd, Dan E. 86, 89
Weisman, Oscar 299
Weiss, Robert K. 431
Weissmuller, Johnny 155, 156, 157, 370, **371**, **372**, 373
Weitz, Bruce 333, 335
Welbeck, Peter see Towers, Harry Alan
Welch, Raquel 79, 133, 206, 296, 301, 302, 304, 305, 307, 408, 417
Weldon, Michael 406
Weller, Peter 433
Welles, Orson 363
Wells, Norman D. 409
Wells, Sharon 294
Wells, Sheilah 135
Wells, Simon 411, 413, 414
Wells, Tessa 151
Wellsley, Charles 241
Welzer, Irving 203
We're Back! A Dinosaur's Story 71, 76, 411–414, **412**, **413**
Wessel, Richard 388, 390
West, Bob 27
West, Mae 9, 85
West, Mason 264
West of Eden (novel) 415
West of Kashmir: A Sherlock Holmes Adventure! 436
West Side Story 88
Weston, Brad 365
Whale, James 363
What a Whopper! 228
When Dinosaurs Ruled the Earth 55, 60, 63, 172, 211, 239, 253, 258, 268, 311, 315, 385, 386, 391, 408, 414–422, **416**, **418**, **420**, **421**, 436, 444, 446
When Dinosaurs Ruled the Screen (book) 63, 305, 442
When Worlds Collide 235
Where Time Began 18, 422–424, **423**

Whippy, Nicole 261
White, Brett 332
White, Daniel 388
White, Don 356
White, Harry 119
White, Stephen 27
White, W. G. 357
White Pongo 237
Whitehead, Mike 74
Whitlock, Albert 441
Whitman, Stuart 211
Whitney, Jack 300
Whitworth, James 313, 314
Who Framed Roger Rabbit? 126, 163, 377
Wicking, Chris 442
A Wild Roomer 378
Wild Things 370
Wildaker, Poul 341
Wildsmith, Dawn 65, 66, 312, 313
Wiley, Daniel J. 207, 208
Wiley, Ethan 131
Wilhite, Tom 23, 25
Wilke, Birthe 342
Will Vinton Studios 71; *see also* Vinton, Will
Willard, Fred 333, 335
Williams, John 160, 163, 174, 268
Williams, Michelle 433
Williams, Robert Moore 439
Williams, Robin 355
Williams, Steve 167
Williams, Treat 151, 152
Williams process 193
Willis O'Brien: Special Effects Genius (book) 362
Willow 166, 281, 311
Wills, J. Elder 350
Wilson, Brad 336
Wilson, Clarence 360
Wilson, Colin 104, 106, 157, 265, 270
Wilson, Harold 15
Wilson, James 351
Wilson, Nancy 222
Wilson, S. S. 38, 62, 191, 404
Wimmer, Brian 431
Windsor, Marie 237
Winfrey, Jonathan 52, 53
Wingrove, Ian 17, 307, 311
Winston, Alan 346

Winston, Stan 157, 161, 164, 165, 169, 170, 171, 175, 176, 177, 178, 184, 265, 272, 273, 274, 367, 370
Winter, Vincent 123
Wisborg, Ole 341
Witchfinder General 421
The Wizard of Mars 130
The Wizard of Oz 43, 441
Wizard Works 312
Wizards of the Demon Sword see *Demon Sword*
Wizards of the Lost Kingdom II 66
Wladon, Jean 301
Wobber, Herman 74
Wolf, Mark 9, 10, 11, 283, 312
Wolf, Scott 368
The Wolf Man (1941) 298
Wolfe, Ian 248
Womark, David 171
Women of the Prehistoric Planet 4, 135, 153, 425–427, **425, 426**
The Wonderful World of the Brothers Grimm 149, 355, 356
Wong, B. D. 157
Wong, George 95
Wong, Victor 183, 357, 359, 361
Wood, Edward D. 294
Wood, John 434
Woodard, Alfre 67, 69
Wooden, Christopher 76
Woods, Christopher Francis 365
Woods, Grant 335
Woolveridge, Harry 384
The World Is Not Enough 370
The World of Yor see *Yor: The Hunter from the Future*
World Without End 409
Worman, Elliot 431
Wray, Fay 170, 183, 187, 188, 189, 190, 191, 192, 194, 279
Wright, Robin 162
Wright, Samuel E. 67, 69
Wylde, Derna 313
Wyndham, Bray 350
Wynn, Keenan 284
Wynorski, Jim 76, 78, 340

Yagher, Kevin 164
Yamamura, Hiroyasu 451
Yamashita, Kensho 452

Yamazaki, Iwao 285
Yared, Petra 151, 258
Yasbeck, Amy 131, 132
Yeatman, Hoyt 131, 133
Yeaworth, Irvin S., Jr. 86, 89, 90, 91, 92
Yeaworth, Jean 86, 89
Yegorov, Ivan Ivanovich 323
Yemelyanov, Vladimir 320
Yesterday's World (television) 300
Yor (novel) 427
Yor: The Hunter from the Future 427–429, **428**
York, Michael 207
Young, Aida 301, 414, 417
Young, Bruce A. 171
Young, Cannon 205
Young, Carroll 233, 237, 370
Young, David 380
Young, Frank William 299
Young, Fred 128
Young, Sean 21, 22
Young Sherlock Holmes 166
Younger, Jack 87, 88
Yuen, Russell 256
Yulin, Harris 225

Zalabery, Johann 341
Zanotto, Juan 427
Zappa, Moon 336, 337
Zebra in the Kitchen 136
Zecevic, George 7
Zeman, Karel 10, 40, 142, 143, 144, 145, 146, 147, 292, 293, 294, 381
Zemeckis, Robert 163
Zeppelin v. Pterodactyls 443, 444, 446–447
Zhzhenov, Georgi 320
Ziegfeld Follies 378
Zimbalist, Al 178, 179, 346, 406, 408, 409
Zimbalist, Donald 406, 408
Zomar, Joseph 425
Zondag, Dick 411
Zondag, Ralph 67, 71, 72, 411
Zontar the Thing from Venus 232, 343
Zsigmond, Vilmos 129, 130
Zsigmond, William *see* Zsigmond, Vilmos